DATA STRUCTURES

An Object-Oriented Approach

DATA STRUCTURES

An Object-Oriented Approach

William J. Collins
Lafayette College

▲▼
Addison-Wesley Publishing Company
Reading, Massachusetts · Menlo Park, California
New York · Don Mills, Ontario · Wokingham,
England · Amsterdam · Bonn · Sydney · Singapore
Tokyo · Madrid · San Juan · Milan · Paris

The programming assignment problems on pages 209 and 212 are taken from *Pascal Plus* by N. Dale and S. Lilly, copyright © 1985 by D. C. Heath and Company, Lexington, Mass. Reprinted with permission.

Library of Congress Cataloging-in-Publication Data

Collins, William J. (William Joseph)
    Data structures: an object-oriented approach / William J. Collins.
       p.   cm.
    Includes bibliographical references (p.   ) and index.
    ISBN 0-201-56953-1
    1. Data structures (Computer science)   2. Object-oriented programming.
I. Title.
QA76.9.D35C64   1992
005.7'3--dc20   92-3046
                                                                    CIP

2 3 4 5 6 7 8 9 10-HA-95949392

To Karen, Don, and Mark
— with all my love

PREFACE

This book is intended for an introductory course in data structures and analysis of algorithms. The only prerequisite is a course that covers procedures, arrays, and records in Standard Pascal or one of its dialects.

The most distinctive feature of the text is its *object orientation*. One reason for this orientation is that an object can encapsulate the design or implementation of an abstract data type. In addition to data encapsulation, objects also support inheritance. For example, a queue is a list with special restrictions, so the design of the Queue data type can inherit some of the method designs from the List data type.

The development of this book was strongly influenced by the work of the ACM/IEEE-CS Joint Curriculum Task Force. Its final report, "Computing Curricula 1991," contains curricular recommendations for baccalaureate programs in computer science. For example, the report advises that in every subject area of computing, the processes of theory, abstraction, and design should be highlighted. The following paragraphs describe how each of these processes is emphasized in this book.

The *theoretical* aspects of computer science are supported in several ways. First, preconditions, postconditions, and loop invariants are routinely provided. Second, correctness proofs are supplied for nontrivial loops and for recursive subalgorithms. Finally, the time and space requirements for nontrivial subalgorithms are estimated with the help of Big-O notation.

Within the ACM/IEEE-CS report, the term *abstraction* refers to the scientific method: observation, hypothesis, experiment, results. In this book, this can be seen in the run-time analyses of units that implement abstract data types. In each case, an experiment is set up to compare the performance of different implementations. Such empirical studies give students practical insights into several important dichotomies: linked versus contiguous, recursive versus iterative, and dynamic versus static. Laboratory exercises provide additional exposure to the benefits of experimentation.

The process of *design* is introduced in Chapter 3 in the context of software engineering. From that point on, each new abstract data type is defined, designed, and implemented. Within the design stage, each nontrivial subalgorithm is verified and analyzed.

The implementation language is Turbo Pascal, a version of Pascal that includes objects. Turbo Pascal is available on IBM-PCs and compatibles. More importantly, it is easily accessible to anyone who has learned any dialect of Pascal, so an instructor can focus on data structures, not on implementation details.

All of the programs and units described in the book were written in Turbo Pascal 6.0. They were validated and analyzed on an IBM-XT compatible computer, running at a speed of 10 megahertz, with an Intel 8088-1 microprocessor and an Intel 8087 coprocessor.

Organization of the Chapters

Chapter 1 presents those features of Turbo Pascal that are needed in subsequent chapters. The major topics are pointers, units, and objects. Students can understand the rest of the book even if they have not studied this chapter carefully. However, they need to master the details of Turbo Pascal to be able to complete the programming exercises and projects at the end of each chapter.

Chapter 2 contains an introduction to recursion. The goal of this early exposure is to help students understand the recursive subprograms in Chapters 4 through 11, and ultimately to develop their own recursive subprograms. The examples illustrate situations in which recursion is a natural choice for solving the problem. Sometimes (for example, in calculating Fibonacci numbers) an iterative subprogram may be appealing. More often, the difficulty of developing an iterative subprogram leads to an appreciation of the elegance and power of recursion. As an early application of the Principle of Abstraction, the focus in this chapter is on *what* recursion is; the details of *how* recursion is implemented are left to a later chapter.

Chapter 3, Introduction to Software Engineering, outlines the system development life cycle that forms the basis for the treatment of abstract data types in Chapters 4 through 11. For each abstract data type, the formal definition of its operators follows from the data type's responsibilities to its users. The designs of the data type include both the verification of the subalgorithms and an analysis of their time and space requirements. Similarly, the implementations of each data type have both a validation component and an analysis component.

Chapter 4, on the List data type, illustrates the Principle of Abstraction on two levels. First, there is a separation of what the List data type is from how it can be designed (and the linked and contiguous designs are radically different). Second, there is a separation of the linked design from its dynamic and static implementations. In the course of developing the high-precision arithmetic application, we are led to a variation of the linked design, one that *remembers* where the last access to the list occurred.

Chapter 5 explores two list specializations: ordered lists and orderable lists. For both the linked and contiguous designs of the Ordered List data type, six of the nine method designs are inherited from the corresponding designs in the List data type. In the contiguous design, the *binary search* subalgorithm is introduced, verified, and analyzed. The case study, creating and maintaining a class roster, exemplifies the spirit of object-oriented programming: objects communicating with other objects by way of messages. The chief value of orderable lists is that they can be sorted, but a discussion of sort methods is postponed until Chapter 9 so that tree-based sorts can be included.

Stacks and queues are studied in Chapter 6. Since both of these data structures are lists, some of their method designs are inherited from those of the List data type. One stack application reveals how recursion can be implemented by a compiler. Another use of stacks is to convert infix expressions into postfix notation. The queue application is a car wash simulation in which the distribution of arrival times is Poisson. Priority queues are defined, but a worthwhile design is postponed until heaps are presented in Chapter 8.

Chapter 7 introduces the Binary Tree data type. Binary trees are recursive data structures, and most of their properties can be defined recursively. Similarly, most of the nontrivial method-designs are recursive. The multi-linked design of the Binary Tree data type is a straightforward extension of the linked designs from earlier chapters. A threaded multilinked design saves space over the conventional multilinked design. A contiguous design can sometimes be useful but requires that the binary tree be complete.

In Chapter 8, three descendants of the Binary Tree data type are investigated. In a binary search tree, the average time for an insertion, deletion, or search is only $O(\log N)$. A binary search tree is also used in a fast sorting method. Heaps provide an efficient structure for the design of a priority queue and are also the basis for another fast sorting method. Binary expression trees allow us to conveniently evaluate and manipulate binary expressions.

Chapter 9 presents a number of sort methods in the Orderable List data type. The easy-to-design methods, such as SelectionSort and InsertionSort, take $O(N^2)$ time, on average. For the more complex methods (TreeSort, HeapSort, MergeSort, and QuickSort), the average time is only $O(N \log N)$. Several improvements to QuickSort are suggested, and the result is the fastest, empirically, of all the sort methods studied. The chapter concludes with a description of how QuickSort and a merge subalgorithm can be combined to sort a file in only $O(N \log N)$ time, on average.

Search methods are investigated in Chapter 10. Sequential search, binary search, and binary search trees are reviewed. The Table data type is then introduced, along with hashing, the commonly preferred technique for table searching. The times for open-address hashing and chained hashing are analyzed, both mathematically and empirically.

Graphs, trees, and networks are introduced in Chapter 11. After defining, designing, and implementing the Graph data type, we look at some aspects of the Tree and Network data types, such as Kruskal's Algorithm and Dijkstra's Algorithm. Parse trees are presented as one illustration of the importance of trees in computer science.

Chapter 12 introduces Turbo Vision, a hierarchy of objects that can be used to construct a graphical user interface for a program. The properties of a good user interface are discussed, and a program is developed in which Turbo Vision implements the graphical user interface.

Appendixes

Appendix 1 contains the background that will allow students to comprehend the mathematical aspects of the chapters. Functions, summation notation, and the properties of logarithms are covered briefly. The Principle of Mathematical Induction is given the fairly extensive treatment it so richly deserves, but only the material up through the first example is essential. Instructors who want to inject more mathematical rigor into the course should cover the other forms of the principle and the related examples. Of course, the entire appendix can be skipped if the course has discrete structures as a prerequisite.

Appendix 2 supplies a possible coding standard. Instructors may want to modify some (or all) of the conventions. What really matters is that students have the same explicit standard, so they will appreciate the fact that programs also serve as a means of technical communication between humans.

Appendix 3 presents Turbo Pascal's file-handling facilities. Several operators (Assign, Reset, Rewrite, Read, Write, Eof, and Close) are available for any file. Text files must be processed sequentially; however, because they are line-oriented, they have three additional operators (Readln, Writeln, and Eoln). Typed files (also known as *binary* files) permit sequential processing and, with the help of the Seek operator, direct processing.

Strings are the focus of Appendix 4. Because Turbo Pascal supplies a predeclared string data type, we don't take the usual route of defining, designing, and implementing an abstract data type.

Appendix 5 contains additional material about Turbo Pascal types. Specifically, the concept of name equivalence of types leads to discussions of assignment compatibility and parameter correspondence. Finally, typed constants allow programmers to declare constant arrays, constant records, and constant objects.

Appendix 6 introduces virtual methods and polymorphism. Together, they provide objects with a run-time power that extends inheritance. These features are utilized in Turbo Vision as well as many other advanced object-oriented applications.

Additional Materials

An instructor's manual contains teaching suggestions and answers to all of the exercises that are not answered in the back of the book. Enclosed with the instructor's manual is a program disk that includes all of the programs and units referred to in the chapters.

Acknowledgments

Tom McMillan not only wrote the Turbo Vision chapter, he also made numerous contributions to the rest of the book. His assistance is greatly appreciated. The following reviewers gave many valuable suggestions:

Sue B. Pawlan
Allan Hancock College

Joan Krone
Denison University

Charles M. Williams
Georgia State University

Robert G. Strader
Stephen F. Austin State University

Robert Christiansen
University of Iowa

Clark Sexton
Kansas State University

Jack Beidler
University of Scranton

Jeff Parker
Harvard Extension

Keith Pierce
University of Minnesota

Tseliso Mosiuoa and Madoka Kumashiro worked on the preparation of the final draft, ran all of the validation programs, and aided in developing answers to the exercises. Peter Shepard, Andrea Danese, and Lynn Cote of Addison-Wesley offered encouragement and good advice throughout the project. Karen Gerlach and Frances Troup assisted in typing the manuscript. Last, but by no means least, I am grateful to all of the students at Radford University and Lafayette College who helped in the class testing of the book.

Easton, Pennsylvania   **W. J. C.**

CONTENTS

Important Features of Turbo Pascal

CHAPTER 1

This is a book about data structures, not about Turbo Pascal. Turbo Pascal is merely the vehicle for illustrating some implementation details of the data structures. This chapter presents those features, mainly pointers, objects, and units, that are essential to what follows.

Pointers, objects, and units are also available, in a different form, in other modern programming languages such as C^{++}, Eiffel, and Object-Oberon. We will try to separate the underlying concepts from the language details so that you can distinguish the general characteristics from the specifics of Turbo Pascal.

TYPES AND DATA TYPES

One of the critical concepts in a programming language is the data type. Before we can define "data type," we must first define some associated terms. A **type** is a collection of values. For example, the type named *Boolean* has just two values, represented by the constant identifiers False and True. Turbo Pascal's *integer* type consists of all whole numbers between −32768 and 32767, inclusive. For the convenience of programmers Turbo Pascal provides several other types whose values are whole numbers.

type identifier	range
byte	0..255
shortint	−128..127
word	0..65535
longint	−2147483648..2147483647

We loosely refer to any type whose values are whole numbers as an "integer" type. You may be tempted to use *longint* whenever an integer type is needed, but this entails a cost both in terms of memory space and execution time. A variable of type *word* or *integer*, for example, occupies two bytes of memory, whereas a *longint* variable occupies four bytes. Also, on computers that access one or two bytes of memory per fetch, the time to access a *word* or *integer* variable is considerably less than the time to access a *longint* variable.

An **operation** is a process that accomplishes some task. For example, addition is an operation. The execution of

$$3 + 5$$

produces the sum of the integers 3 and 5. Here, + is referred to as the **operator**, 3 and 5 are the **operands**, and 8 is the **result**. For another example, reading from a file is an operation. The execution of

```
Read (ScoreFile, Score)
```

stores a copy of the current component from the file ScoreFile in the variable Score. Here, "Read" is the operator and "ScoreFile" and "Score" are the operands.

A **data type** consists of

1. a type *T*;
2. a collection of operators such that for each operator there is an operand or result whose type is *T*.

For example, in the *integer* data type, the type is *integer* and some of the operators are

```
+, −, *, div, mod, :=, =, and <
```

We do not specify all of the operators in the *integer* data type simply because there are too many of them. In fact, we could declare procedures or functions to define any number of new operators, such as integer exponentiation.

Given a data type whose type is *T*, an ***instance*** of the data type is a variable of type *T*. For example, if we declare

```
var
    MatchFound: boolean;
```

then MatchFound is an instance of the *Boolean* data type. Only Boolean values can be assigned to MatchFound, and only Boolean operations can be applied to MatchFound.

An instance of a data type is also referred to as a ***data structure***. The term "data structure" was once viewed as a central concept in computer science, but in recent years "data type" has become more widely used. "Data structure" has for the most part been relegated to the titles of books and courses in computer science.

Turbo Pascal provides a considerable number of predeclared data types. A ***predeclared*** data type is one that includes implementation details. For example, the *Boolean* data type is predeclared in Turbo Pascal because the reserved words **and**, **or** and **not** are operators in that data type. Starting with Chapter 4, our primary focus will be on ***abstract*** data types—those that are not tied down to any particular implementation. For such data types, we can choose how we want to implement the values and operators.

We can classify Turbo Pascal's predeclared data types as follows:

1. A ***simple*** data type is one whose (type's) values stand alone: they are not composed of other values, nor do they refer to other values. For example, the integer data type is a simple type. Simple data types are further subdivided into the *ordinal* data types, whose values can be ordered from first to last, and the *real* data types.

2. A ***structured*** data type is one whose (type's) values are themselves collections of values from some other type(s). For example, the record type is a structured type because each value is a record—an ordered collection of values from one or more types.

3. A ***pointer*** data type is one in which each value is the machine address of some variable. Pointers are discussed in the next section of this chapter.

Figure 1.1 presents Turbo Pascal's hierarchy of predeclared data types, with some of the associated operators in parentheses.

Some of the operators are "overloaded" that is, their meanings depend on the types that they operate on. For example, the relational operator "<=" means "is less than or equal to" when applied to simple or string types, but means "is a subset of" when applied to sets. Also, the operator "+" can refer to integer addition, real addition, string concatenation, or set union, depending on the types of the operands.

Much of the above chart also applies to Standard Pascal. (We use "Pascal" all by itself for features that apply to both Turbo Pascal and Standard

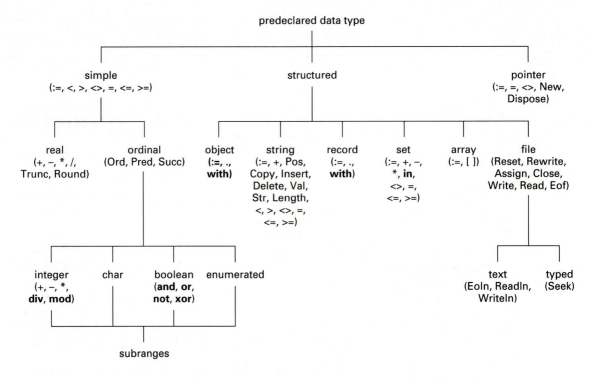

Figure 1.1 Turbo Pascal's hierarchy of predeclared data types (with some operators in parentheses).

Pascal.) But Standard Pascal does not have an object data type. Turbo Pascal objects are introduced later in this chapter. Two other exceptions involve files and strings. Briefly, Standard Pascal has no Seek operator for files, and *string* is not a reserved word. Appendixes 3 and 4 provide detailed information on Turbo Pascal's file data types and string data type, respectively.

Another difference between Standard Pascal and Turbo Pascal is in the order of evaluation of operands for the Boolean operators **and** and **or**. In Standard Pascal, the order of evaluation of operands is *implementation-dependent*: that is, it may differ among processors, and is not necessarily defined for any particular processor. For example, given the expression

A **or** B

most Standard Pascal compilers will generate code to evaluate *A* first and then *B*. But some may generate code so that *B* will not be evaluated if *A* has the value True, because in that case the entire expression must have the value True.

In Turbo Pascal, the latter option, called "short circuiting," is always available. In short circuiting, evaluation of a Boolean expression involving

and or **or** stops as soon as the value of the entire expression has been determined. (Short circuiting is enabled either through the Options submenu of the Main menu or through the compiler directive {$B-}.) Assume, as is the case when Turbo Pascal is installed, that short-circuiting is in effect. Consider the following:

```
if (N > 0) and (Sum / N > 3.0) then
```

If the value of *N* happens to be less than or equal to zero, then the value of the entire Boolean expression must be False, and so the second operand (Sum/*N* > 3.0) is not evaluated. This precludes the possibility of a division-by-zero error at run time.

From now on, in both algorithms and programs, we will assume short circuiting for the Boolean operators **and** and **or**.

POINTERS AND DYNAMIC VARIABLES

Most modern programming languages, including Pascal, allow the programmer to explicitly create and destroy variables during the execution of a program. To help you appreciate the significance of this feature, let's start by classifying the variables you have seen up to now.

A variable that is declared in the declaration part of a program's block is referred to as a *global* variable. A variable that is declared in a subprogram's formal parameter list or block is *local* to that subprogram. Every global or local variable is a *static* variable in the sense that its space is allocated throughout the execution of the block in which the variable is declared.

In Turbo Pascal, the *data segment* is the area of main memory available for all global variables. The maximum size of the data segment is nearly 64K bytes. For all local variables, the memory area is called the *stack segment*, which is discussed in detail in Chapter 6. The size of the stack segment can be set, through the Compiler submenu of the Options menu, to a maximum size of nearly 64K bytes. The default size of the stack segment is approximately 16K bytes.

In some applications, the amount of main memory needed for all global variables (or for all local variables) may exceed 64K bytes for at least some runs. Also, for some applications, it may be preferable to conserve space in main memory by creating variables when they are needed and destroying them when they are no longer needed. In both situations the solution is provided by dynamic variables.

A *dynamic* variable is one that is explicitly created and destroyed by the programmer during the execution of a block. A dynamic variable is not declared in a variable declaration—in fact, it does not even have an identifier. A dynamic variable is always referenced indirectly by means of a **pointer** variable (one whose value is the machine address of a dynamic variable).

The syntax diagram for a pointer type is as follows:

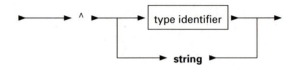

The type identifier (or **string**) that follows the "^" refers to the type of the dynamic variable. This type can be predeclared, as in the following example:

```
type
    IntPtrType = ^integer;
var
    IntPtr: IntPtrType;
```

According to these declarations, IntPtrType is a type identifier for a pointer type: Any variable of type IntPtrType will contain the address of an integer variable. The variable IntPtr is such a (pointer) variable.

Typically, the type of the dynamic variable will not be predeclared but will follow later in that type declaration part. For example,

```
type
    CarPtrType = ^CarType;
    CarType    = record
        Make:  string [10];
        Year:  1900..1999
    end; { CarType }
var
    CarPtr:  CarPtrType;
```

The first type declaration defines CarPtrType as a type identifier for a pointer type: Any variable of type CarPtrType will contain the address of a dynamic variable of type CarType. CarType is then declared as a type identifier for a record type with two fields. Finally, CarPtr is declared to be a variable (identifier) of type CarPtrType. So CarPtr will contain the address of a dynamic record variable with two fields.

Initially, CarPtr will be undefined. To indicate this, we use a question mark as CarPtr's value:

CarPtr

```
?
```

To create a dynamic variable of type CarType, we call the predeclared procedure New. The only actual parameter is the pointer variable, in this case CarPtr, which will contain the address of the dynamic variable. The procedure statement is

```
New (CarPtr)
```

The execution of this procedure statement causes space for a dynamic variable of type CarType to be allocated in a special area of memory known as the **heap**. The address of the dynamic variable is stored in CarPtr. In other words, CarPtr "points to" the dynamic variable. To represent this, we draw an arrow from CarPtr to the dynamic variable:

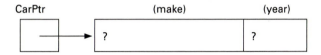

The dynamic variable is referred to as CarPtr^, the variable pointed to by CarPtr.

We can assign or read in values for the fields of CarPtr^. For example,

```
CarPtr^.Make := 'Chevrolet';
CarPtr^.Year := 1957;
```

The first assignment statement can be read as, "Assign to the Make field of the record pointed to by CarPtr the value of 'Chevrolet'". After the two assignment statements are executed, we would have

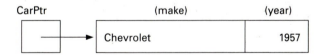

Similarly, we could write

```
with CarPtr^ do
   begin
      Readln (Make, Year);
      if Year < 1950 then
         Writeln ('This is an antique ', Make)
   end; { with CarPtr^ do }
```

Turbo Pascal will allocate to the heap all of main memory beyond what is needed for your program (including the machine−language version of the entire program, the data segment, and the stack segment). Typically, the heap can consume up to 360K bytes. This is a large, but not inexhaustible, amount of space. To destroy a dynamic variable, we call the predeclared procedure Dispose. Just as with the procedure New, the only actual parameter is a pointer variable (*not* a dynamic variable).

For example, the execution of the procedure statement

```
Dispose (CarPtr)
```

deallocates the space that had been allocated to CarPtr^. This space can then be allocated to other dynamic variables.[1] But the execution of the Dispose procedure does not affect CarPtr—it contains the same address as before. To ensure that CarPtr no longer contains a heap address, we assign a special value to CarPtr. The reserved word **nil** denotes a value, in any pointer type, that is not a heap address. The assignment statement

```
CarPtr := nil
```

stores in CarPtr a value that is not a heap address. It then becomes illegal to refer to CarPtr^, as in the following:

```
if CarPtr^.Year < 1950 then
   Writeln (CarPtr^.Make)
```

Whenever you are in doubt as to whether a pointer variable has the *nil* value, you should test its value before trying to reference the corresponding dynamic variable. For example,

```
if (CarPtr <> nil) and (CarPtr^.Year < 1950) then
   Writeln ('This is an antique ', CarPtr^.Make)
```

If CarPtr has the *nil* value, the entire Boolean expression must have the value False, and so, because of short circuiting, the reference to CarPtr^ will not be made.

When a dynamic variable can no longer be referenced, it becomes *garbage*, as in the following program fragment:

```
type
   PtrType = ^integer;
var
   A: PtrType;
begin
   New (A);
   A^ := 8;
   New (A)
```

The dynamic variable that *A* originally pointed to has not been deallocated, but it can no longer be referenced. If you leave too much garbage lying

---

[1]Whenever New is called, a check is made of previously deallocated space to see if there is a large enough contiguous area for the dynamic variable. If so, that area is allocated. If not, new space from the heap is allocated.

around, the heap will overflow and start to overlay the space for other parts of your program; the results are almost always disastrous, often bizarre. The solution to the garbage problem is simple: Recycle your garbage with the Dispose procedure.

Another thing to watch out for is the difference between pointer-variable assignments and dynamic-variable assignments. For example, suppose we start with

```
type
    PtrType =  ^integer;
var
    A,
    B : PtrType;
begin
    New (A);
    A^ := 8;
    New (B);
    B^ := 10;
```

At this point we have

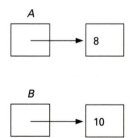

Now suppose we do the following:

```
B^ := A^;
B^ := 2 * B^;
```

These assignments, not surprisingly, will give us

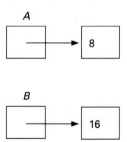

But now suppose that we do the following:

```
B  := A;
B^ := 2 * B^;
```

The first of these assignment statements gives the pointer variable B the same value as the pointer variable A. So the second statement changes the value of A^, as shown in the following picture:

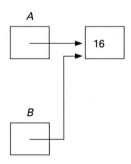

This effect should not be surprising, because the assignment B := A made A^ and B^ different representations of the same variable. However, sometimes the consequences of multiple reference are more subtle. For example, suppose we have the following:

```
type
    PtrType = ^integer;
var
    A: PtrType;
procedure PrintDouble (B: PtrType);
begin
    B^ := 2 * B^;
    Writeln (B: 5)
end; { PrintDouble }
begin
    New (A);
    A^ := 8;
    PrintDouble (A)
```

At first glance you might think that A^ will still have the value 8 after the execution of PrintDouble. After all, B is a *value* formal parameter, and so A's value is unaffected by the execution of the procedure. After the execution of PrintDouble, A will point to the same location it pointed to before the execution of PrintDouble; however, (and this is not obvious), the contents of that location have changed! The underlying situation is the same as in the previous example: A^ changed because B^ changed, and A^ and B^

were the same dynamic variable because B had been assigned the value of A.

If these examples have made you leery of pointers and dynamic variables, you are on the right track. You must be extremely disciplined in using pointers or else your programs will be difficult to understand and maintain. However, don't conclude that working with pointers and dynamic variables is just an error-causing nuisance. They can be a valuable asset to your programming repertoire, as we will see in Chapters 4 through 8. Specifically, in many situations a pointer variable contains the address of a (dynamic) record in which one of the fields is a pointer to another record, which in turn contains a field that is a pointer to still another record, and so on (See Fig. 1.2).

Constructions such as the one in Fig. 1.2 allow us to link together, in the heap, arbitrarily long lists of values. The corresponding type declarations are interesting because they illustrate the only exception to the Pascal rule that an identifier must be declared before it can be used. For example, we could write

```
type
    StudentPtrType =  ^StudentType;
    StudentType     = record
        ID  : word;
        GPA : real;
        Next: StudentPtrType
    end; { StudentType }
```

Note that the identifier StudentType is used—in the declaration of StudentPtrType—before it is declared. If we wanted to use an array instead of dynamic records, the maximum size of the array would have to be declared at compile time and would be limited to the size of the data segment.

A final note (for now) on pointers. Turbo Pascal has a predeclared type, *pointer*, that represents a generic pointer type. A variable of any specific

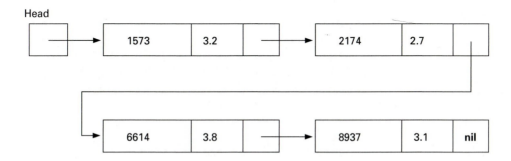

Figure 1.2   **A sequence of dynamic records linked together by pointer fields.**

pointer type is assignment-compatible with any expression of type *pointer*, and vice versa. For example, suppose we declare

```
type
   IPtrType =  ^integer;
   RPtrType =  ^real;
var
   IPtr: IPtrType;
   RPtr: RPtrType;
   XPtr: pointer;
```

Then each of the following assignments is legal:

```
IPtr := XPtr;
XPtr := IPtr;
RPtr := XPtr;
XPtr := RPtr;
```

But *IPtr* cannot be assigned to *RPtr*, and neither can *RPtr* be assigned to *IPtr*.

Variables of type *pointer* cannot be dereferenced: that is, their associated dynamic variables cannot be referenced. For example, *XPtr^* is an illegal reference. But if the associated dynamic variable is of type *integer*, we can first assign

```
IPtr := XPtr;
```

*IPtr^* is now a legal reference to *XPtr*'s dynamic variable.

The type *pointer* is used only infrequently, but as we will see in Chapter 7, it sometimes enables us to avoid a thorny problem.

OBJECTS

Records are valuable structures because they allow us to group together related collections of values. But a record is passive: its fields just lie there waiting to be acted upon. Describing an entity in terms of what it *has* gives only part of the picture. We must also include what the entity *does*. For example, a video cassette recorder (VCR) not only has wires, buttons, and displays, it also plays and records. If you were designing a VCR, you would first focus on what the VCR should *do*, and from that decide what it should *have*.

Turbo Pascal has extended the record concept to objects. An *object* provides an explicit association between a collection of fields and the operations on those fields. An **object** consists of a collection of fields together with a collection of subprograms (called *methods*) that operate on those fields. An object encapsulates the passive components (fields) and active components (methods) into a single entity. This encapsulation increases program modularity: By isolating an object from the rest of the program, we make the program easier to understand and to modify.

But the significance of objects goes far beyond this encapsulation feature, and has led to the development of a powerful approach to problem solving. To oversimplify somewhat, an ***object-oriented*** approach is one in which we try to solve problems by identifying objects associated with the problem and developing them into objects in our program. In Chapter 3 we will explore this approach in depth. For now, let's see how objects are declared and used in Turbo Pascal.

For a simple example of an object, suppose we have developed a data type for students. The type consists of three fields: the student's name, home address, and grade point average (GPA). The only operators are:

To read in a student from the text file StudentFile;

To write out a student;

To see if we have read in the last student; and

To see if the GPA is less than some cutoff value.

In Turbo Pascal, we write the following:

```
type
   AddressType = record
      Street      : string [30];
      CityStateZip: string [20]
   end; { AddressType }
   StudentType = object
      Name        : string [30];
      HomeAddress: AddressType;
      GPA         : real;
      procedure ReadIn;
      procedure WriteOut;
      function Last: boolean;
      function GPALessThan (CutOff: real): boolean;
   end; { StudentType }
```

StudentType has been declared to be an object type (**object** is a reserved word) with three fields and four methods. An object is similar to a record in that each is a grouping; but a record has passive components only, whereas an object has both active and passive components—the methods act on the fields.

To complete the declaration of an object, we must provide declarations for its methods. To distinguish an object's methods from other subprograms, a qualifier is required; the declaration of each method starts with the reserved word **procedure** (or **function**), followed by the object identifier, a period, and the method identifier. Within a method's statement part, the object's fields and methods are referred to without the object identifier. The declarations for StudentType's methods are as follows:

```
procedure StudentType.ReadIn;
begin
   Readln (StudentFile, Name, HomeAddress.Street,
           HomeAddress.CityStateZip, GPA)
end; { ReadIn }
procedure StudentType.WriteOut;
begin
   Writeln (Name);
   Writeln (HomeAddress.Street);
   Writeln (HomeAddress.CityStateZip)
end; { WriteOut }
function StudentType.Last: boolean;
begin
   Last := Eof (StudentFile)
end; { Last }
function StudentType.GPALessThan (CutOff: real): boolean;
begin
   GPALessThan := (GPA < CutOff)
end; { GPALessThan }
```

When an object is created, the resulting variable is an ***instance*** of the object. For example, given the above declaration for StudentType as an object type, we can declare

```
var
   Student: StudentType;
```

The variable Student is an instance of StudentType, and so Student has three fields and four methods. To refer to any field or method of an instance, the instance is followed by a period, followed by the field or method identifier. For example, we can read in the values for Student's fields as follows:

```
Student.ReadIn
```

Later, we might want to write out the values of those fields, provided the value in the GPA field is less than 2.0:

```
if Student.GPALessThan (2.0) then
   Student.WriteOut
```

The value 2.0 is an actual parameter that corresponds to the formal parameter CutOff in the method GPALessThan. But what does the instance Student correspond to? In every method there is a predeclared identifier

Self, which is treated as a variable formal parameter corresponding to the instance that calls the method. Self is an implicit qualifier for each of the objects type fields or methods that are referenced within the declaration of the method. Self can be used explicitly if this will aid clarity. For example, the declaration of GPALessThan could be rewritten as

```
procedure StudentType.GPALessThan (CutOff: real): boolean;
begin
    GPALessThan := (Self.GPA < CutOff)
end; { GPALessThan }
```

For the method call Student.GPALessThan, the instance Student corresponds to Self, and so the effect is to test if Student.GPA is less than 2.0.

Because Self is treated as a *variable* formal parameter, any change to the value of Self's fields is a change to the value of the instance's fields. That is why a call to Student.ReadIn alters the values of Student's fields.

Since an instance is treated as an actual parameter corresponding to Self, you may wonder why an instance is not included in the actual parameter list. The reason is consistency: An instance's fields and methods should be referenced with the same notation. For example,

```
Student.GPA
Student.WriteOut
```

This notation suggests that fields and methods are parts of an instance.

Turbo Pascal's **with** statement has been extended to allow instance references as well as record-variable references. For example, instead of

```
if Student.GPALessThan (2.0) then
    Student.WriteOut
```

we could write

```
with Student do
    if GPALessThan (2.0) then
        WriteOut
```

In object-oriented parlance, a ***message*** is the activation of a method by an instance. For example, in the message

```
Student.GPALessThan (2.0)
```

the instance Student is activating its GPALessThan method. The term "message" is meant to suggest the isolation of the object from the rest of the program.

We noted earlier that the purpose of isolating an object is to promote modularity. For true modularity, this isolation must be physical as well as conceptual. Fortunately, Turbo Pascal provides for the physical separation of program parts with the unit facility.

UNITS

One of the serious drawbacks of Standard Pascal is that only entire programs can be compiled. Any change (no matter how small) to a program
(no matter how large) necessitates that the entire program be recompiled.
As you might suspect, such an environment is hostile to modularity.
Niklaus Wirth, the inventor of Pascal, responded to this deficiency by creating Modula 2, in which program parts, called *modules*, can be separately
compiled. Another descendant of Standard Pascal, the powerful and complex language Ada, allows for the separate compilation of *packages*, which
are similar to modules. In Turbo Pascal, the corresponding entities are
called *units*.

Basically, a **unit** is a separately compiled collection of declarations. The
syntax of a unit is given in the following syntax diagram:

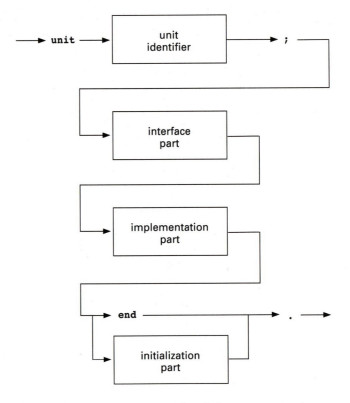

Before we look at these parts in detail, here is a simple example of
a unit:

```
unit Maxima;
interface
```

```
const
   MaxListSize = 1000;
implementation
end. { Maxima }
```

This unit simply provides a value for the constant identifier MaxListSize that will be available for programs and other units.

The Interface Part of a Unit

The interface part of a unit houses the unit's *public* information, that is, the information that is available to any program or other unit that uses the unit. Consequently, the interface part should contain everything a user needs to be able to use the unit (and, ideally, nothing else). Notice that "user" refers to a program or unit, not a person.

For a user of the unit Maxima, the following declaration would be legal:

```
type
   ListRangeType = 1..MaxListSize;
```

In other words, MaxListSize is accessible to users of the unit Maxima. Whether the declaration of MaxListSize is visible to humans depends on whether the unit Maxima is available in source-code form or only in compiled-code form.

A unit's interface part must start with the reserved word **interface**, and can include a **uses** clause, which lists other units used by the unit. The interface part can also contain constant, type, and variable declarations, as well as subprogram headings.

Here are the interface parts from two units. The first declares the object ItemType; the second declares the object ListType.

```
{**************************************************************}
interface
type
   ValueType = record
      Weight: real;
      Cost  : integer
   end; { ValueType }
   ItemType = object
      Value: ValueType;
      procedure SetValue (NewValue: ValueType);
      procedure GetValue (var CurrentValue: ValueType);
      function LessThan (Item: ItemType): boolean;
      function EqualTo (Item: ItemType): boolean;
      function GreaterThan (Item: ItemType): boolean;
   end; { ItemType }
{**************************************************************}
```

```
interface
uses
   ItemInList, { declares the object ItemType }
   Maxima;     { declares MaxListSize }
type
   ProcedureType = procedure (Item: ItemType);
   ListType      = object
      A: array [1..MaxListSize] of ItemType;
      N: 0..MaxListSize;
      procedure Initialize;
      function IsEmpty: boolean;
      function Size: word;
      procedure Retrieve (var Item: ItemType;
                               Position: word);
      procedure Search (var Item: ItemType;
                        var Position: word;
                        var Found  : boolean);
      procedure Insert (Item: ItemType;
                        Position: word);
      procedure Delete (Position: word);
      procedure CopyTo (var NewList: ListType);
      procedure Traverse (Visit: ProcedureType);
   end; { ListType }
{***********************************************************}
```

As illustrated in this last example, the effect of a *uses* clause is the same as if all the declarations in the interface parts of those units had been made at that point. For example, the reference to ItemType in the method heading for Retrieve is legal because ItemType was declared in the interface part of the unit ItemInList.

The Implementation Part of a Unit

Information contained in a unit's implementation part is *private*, that is, not accessible to programs or other units that use the unit. This promotes modularity because changes in implementation details—such as replacing one sort procedure with another—will not affect the users of the unit.

The implementation part must start with the reserved word **implementation**, and consists mainly of a complete subprogram for each subprogram heading contained in the interface part. The implementation part may also include a uses clause and any other declarations that are to be inaccessible to a user.

For the first interface part given above, the implementation part must include complete subprograms for the methods SetValue, GetValue, LessThan, EqualTo, and GreaterThan:

```
implementation
procedure ItemType.SetValue (NewValue: ValueType);
```

```
begin
   Value := NewValue
 end; { SetValue }

procedure ItemType.GetValue (var CurrentValue: ValueType);
begin
   CurrentValue := Value
end; { GetValue }

function ItemType.LessThan (Item: ItemType): boolean;
begin
   LessThan := Value.Cost < Item.Value.Cost
   { This could also be written as follows:            }
   { LessThan := Self.Value.Cost < Item.Value.Cost }
end; { LessThan }

function ItemType.EqualTo (Item: ItemType): boolean;
begin
   EqualTo := Value.Cost = Item.Value.Cost
end; { EqualTo }

function ItemType.GreaterThan (Item: ItemType): boolean;
begin
   GreaterThan := Value.Cost > Item.Value.Cost
end; { GreaterThan }
```

Now that you have seen the methods SetValue, GetValue, and so on, you may wonder why we bothered to declare those methods in the first place. Surely any program or unit that uses the unit ItemInList would have access to the Value field in ItemType and thus could, for example, set an item's value without calling the method SetValue. Typically, however, an object's fields should be referenced only in the object's methods, as we will see in Chapter 3. This enhances modularity because the fields can be changed within the unit without affecting any users of the unit.

Turbo Pascal allows you to enforce this modularity by declaring fields to be private. For example, suppose we declare the following in a unit XManager:

```
type
   XType = object
      A: integer;
      function F (I: integer): integer;
      private
          R: real
   end; { XType }
```

The *R* field can be referenced only in the unit XManager. The field *A* and the method *F* can be referenced within XManager and within any program or unit that uses XManager.

The Initialization Part of a Unit

Ordinarily, a unit's implementation part is immediately followed by the reserved word **end** and a period. Occasionally, however, there may be some initializations that must be done before the unit is first called. For example, a file may need to be reset or rewritten, or an array may need to be zeroed out.

An initialization part consists of a compound statement. For example, we might have

```
begin
   for I := 1 to N do
      A [I] := 0
end.
```

A, *I*, and *N* must be declared earlier, either in the interface part or in the implementation part. Therefore, those variables are global to the unit. The space for all global variables—in the program and in units used directly or indirectly by the program—is allocated from the data segment.

Implementing Objects in a Unit

Units are convenient for implementing objects; the physical encapsulation of a unit complements the logical encapsulation of an object. Specifically, the object is declared in the interface part of the unit and the object's methods are declared in the implementation part. For example, the following unit implements the object StudentType introduced earlier. An initialization part is needed so that StudentFile.dat can be assigned to a file–variable identifier and prepared for reading.

```
unit StudentManager;
{ This unit implements the object StudentType. }
{ Files read: StudentFile.dat                   }
interface
type
   AddressType = record
      Street     : string [30];
      CityStateZip: string [20]
   end; { AddressType }
   StudentType = object
      Name       : string [30];
      HomeAddress: AddressType;
      GPA        : real;
      procedure ReadIn;
      procedure WriteOut;
      function Last: boolean;
      function GPALessThan (CutOff: real): boolean;
   end; { StudentType }
```

```
implementation
var
    StudentFile: text;
procedure StudentType.ReadIn;
begin
    Readln (StudentFile, Name, HomeAddress.Street,
            HomeAddress.CityStateZip, GPA)
end; { ReadIn }

procedure StudentType.WriteOut;
begin
    Writeln (Name);
    Writeln (HomeAddress.Street);
    Writeln (HomeAddress.CityStateZip)
end; { WriteOut }

function StudentType.Last: boolean;
begin
    Last := Eof (StudentFile)
end; { Last }

function StudentType.GPALessThan (CutOff: real): boolean;
begin
    GPALessThan := (GPA < CutOff)
end; { GPALessThan }

begin { Initialization part }
    Assign (StudentFile, 'StudentFile.dat');
    Reset (StudentFile)
end. { StudentManager }
```

The above unit should be stored in the file StudentM.pas, and so the compiled version will be stored in the file StudentM.TPU. "TPU" stands for "Turbo Pascal Unit." A program that uses the unit StudentManager has access to all of the information in the interface part and none of the information in the implementation part. For example, the following program illustrates how units (and objects) can be used. Notice that the program does not directly access any of the fields in StudentType nor the file StudentFile.

```
program StudentStatus;
{ This program sends a brief letter to each student who has}
{ made the Dean's List or has been put on probation.      }
uses
    StudentManager;
const
    DeansListCutOff = 3.2;
    ProbationCutOff = 2.0;
    DeansListMessage =
```

```
                    'Congratulations! You have made the Dean's List.';
            ProbationMessage =
                    'You are now on probation. Shape up or ship out!';
    var
        Student: StudentType;
    begin
        with Student do
            while not Last do
                begin
                    ReadIn;
                    if not GPALessThan (DeansListCutOff) then
                        begin
                            WriteOut;
                            Writeln;
                            Writeln (DeansListMessage)
                        end { on Dean's List }
                    else
                        if GPALessThan (ProbationCutOff) then
                            begin
                                WriteOut;
                                Writeln;
                                Writeln (ProbationMessage)
                            end { on probation }
                end { while }
    end. { StudentStatus }
```

INHERITANCE

We should strive to write program components that are reusable. For example, rather than write a function that calculates the mean of 10 values, we would prefer a function that calculates the mean of any number of values. By writing reusable code, we not only save time, but we also avoid the risk of incorrectly modifying the existing code.

Reusability applies to objects in a special way, known as "inheritance." **Inheritance** is the ability to declare a new object that includes all of the fields and some or all of the methods of an existing object. The previously existing object is called the **ancestor**. The new object, which may declare new fields and methods, is called the **descendant**.

As an example of how inheritance works, let's start with the unit StudentManager, which implements the object StudentType. Suppose that several application programs use StudentManager. A new application involves sending information about dining hall hours during final exam week to each dormitory student. For this application, the dorm student's local address must be available.

We could alter StudentType by adding a local-address field and modifying the ReadIn and WriteOut, and Last methods. However, there are several problems with altering StudentType. First, the unit StudentManager may be available only in compiled form; if this is the case, StudentType cannot be altered. Second, even if the source code for StudentManager is available, it is risky to modify a unit that is being used successfully in existing applications for the sake of a new application.

Instead of rewriting StudentType, we will develop a new object type, DormStudentType, within a new unit:

```
unit DormStudentManager;
{ This unit implements the object DormStudentType as a }
{ descendant of StudentType.                           }
{ Files read: DormStudentFile.dat                      }
interface
uses
   StudentManager;
type
   DormStudentType = object (StudentType)
      LocalAddress: string [30];
      procedure ReadIn;
      procedure WriteOut;
      function Last: boolean;
   end; { StudentInfoType }
implementation
var
   DormStudentFile: text;
procedure DormStudentType.ReadIn;
begin
   Readln (DormStudentFile, Name, LocalAddress)
end; { ReadIn }

procedure DormStudentType.WriteOut;
begin
   Writeln (Name);
   Writeln (LocalAddress)
end; { WriteOut }

function DormStudentType.Last: boolean;
begin
   Last := Eof (DormStudentFile)
end; { Last }

begin
   Assign (DormStudentFile, 'DormStudentFile.dat');
   Reset (DormStudentFile)
end. { DormStudentManager }
```

The object DormStudentType is declared as a descendant of the object StudentType by enclosing StudentType in parentheses after the word *object*.

DormStudentType inherits the three fields of StudentType, and so DormStudentType has four fields. DormStudentType also inherits the GPA-LessThan method from StudentType. But the ReadIn, WriteOut, and Last methods from StudentType have been overridden by new methods with the same identifiers as the old methods. For instances of type DormStudentType, the new methods apply. The old versions apply for instances of type StudentType.

The dining-hall-hours program might be as follows:

```
program Hours;
{ This program notifies dorm students of dining hall }
{ hours during final exam week.              }
uses
    DormStudentManager;
const
    HoursMessage =
'The dining hall will be on normal schedule during finals.';
var
    DormStudent: DormStudentType;
begin
    with DormStudent do
        while not Last do
            begin
                ReadIn;
                WriteOut;
                Writeln;
                Writeln (HoursMessage)
            end { while }
end. { Hours }
```

To the author of the program Hours, all that matters about the object DormStudentType is that it has ReadIn, WriteOut, and Last methods that do what they are supposed to do. It is not necessary for the programmer to know the details of any of those methods, nor whether DormStudentType is a descendant of StudentType; nor does it matter where the information on dorm students is coming from.

In this example there was one ancestor (StudentType) and one descendant (DormStudentType). In some situations there may be an entire hierarchy of object types:

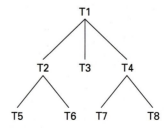

The declaration of T6, for example, would start with

```
type
   T6 = object (T2)
        .

        .

        .

   end; { T6 }
```

The objects T5 and T6 are descendants of T2, and T2 is a descendant of T1. So T5 and T6 are also descendants of T1. To put it mathematically, the relation "is a descendant of" is transitive.

It is possible to have a program that uses both an ancestor and a descendant. For example, we can write

```
program Both;
uses
   StudentManager,
   DormStudentManager;
var
   Student    : StudentType;
   DormStudent: DormStudentType;
```

There would be no confusion as to which version of the method ReadIn (or WriteOut, or Last) applied in any situation. For example,

```
Student.ReadIn
```

refers to the version of ReadIn declared in StudentType, whereas

```
DormStudent.ReadIn
```

refers to the version of ReadIn declared in DormStudentType. The decision as to which version of ReadIn applies is made at compile time, and so ReadIn is called a *static* method. (Appendix 6 describes *virtual* methods, one of the unique and powerful features of object-oriented programming).

A Brief History of Turbo Pascal

In 1983, Borland International produced Turbo Pascal 1.0, one of the first high-speed compilers for microcomputers. For the modest price of $49.95, you got an integrated package: Programs could be edited, compiled, and executed within the same environment.

Turbo Pascal 2.0 (1984) provided support for a math coprocessor, and version 3.0 (1985) supplied graphics tools. The unit facility was added with version 4.0 in 1987—until that time the maximum size of a complete program had been 64K bytes. With version 5.0 (1988), the integrated environ- was expanded to include run-time traces and breakpoints.

Turbo Pascal became object-oriented in 1989, with the somewhat timid version number of 5.5. In 1990, Turbo Pascal 6.0 introduced Turbo Vision, an object-oriented framework for window applications.

The next section introduces two Turbo Pascal subprograms that are useful in comparing the run-time performance of different versions of a subprogram.

RUN-TIME ANALYSIS OF SUBPROGRAMS

Starting with Chapter 4, we will often be developing several alternative subprograms to accomplish a particular task. In comparing subprograms, one important consideration is execution time. For example, if we are comparing two sorting subprograms, we would want to determine how long each one takes to sort a list of values. The time taken may depend heavily on the particular ordering of the list of values chosen. It is not feasible to generate every possible ordering, run the subprogram for each list, and calculate the average time. Instead, we want to generate a sample list that is in no particular order. The statistical concept corresponding to "no particular order" is *randomness*.

To satisfy our needs in the areas of timing and randomness, Turbo Pascal supplies a GetTime procedure and a Random function.

The GetTime Procedure

Turbo Pascal's GetTime procedure calculates the current time. After a call to GetTime, the four actual parameters hold the time in hours, minutes, seconds, and hundredths of a second, respectively. To simplify calculating the current time, we develop a Time function that returns a real value representing the current time in seconds. We embed this function into a unit so that a user is relieved of the responsibility for understanding the details of the GetTime procedure.

```
unit Timer;
{ This unit calculates the current time. The function Time }
{ returns a real value representing the current time in     }
{ seconds.                                                  }
interface
uses
    Dos; { for the GetTime procedure }
function Time: real;
implementation
const
    HundFactor = 100; { hundredths of a second in a second }
    MinFactor  = 60; { seconds in a minute }
    HourFactor = 3600.0; { seconds in an hour. See discussion
                           that follows. }
```

```
function Time: real;
{ This function returns the current time, in seconds. }
var
   Hour,
   Minute,
   Second,
   SecHund: word;
begin
   GetTime (Hour, Minute, Second, SecHund);
   Time := (Hour * HourFactor) + (Minute * MinFactor)
           + Second + (SecHund / HundFactor)
end; { Time }
end. { Timer }
```

To determine how much execution time a task consumes, we calculate the time immediately before and immediately after the code for the task. For example, we often have the following program skeleton:

```
program TestTime;
{ Determine the time a task consumes. We assume that the }
{ execution of the task begins and ends on the same day. }
uses
   Timer; { implements the Time function }
var
   StartTime,
   FinishTime,
   ElapsedTime: real;
begin
   StartTime := Time;
   { Perform the task: }
        .
        .
        .
   FinishTime := Time;
   ElapsedTime := FinishTime - StartTime;
   Writeln ('Elapsed time = ',ElapsedTime: 8: 1, 'seconds.')
end. {TestTime}
```

Suppose that, when Time is first called in the above program, the values returned by GetTime are 18 (hours), 35 (minutes), 12 (seconds), and 14 (hundredths of a second). Then the value assigned to StartTime is $(18 * 3600.0) + (35 * 60) + 12 + (14/100) = 66912.14$ seconds.

Similarly, assume that when Time is called later, the values returned by GetTime are 19, 07, 58, and 71, respectively. Then the value assigned to FinishTime is $(19 * 3600.0) + (07 * 60) + 58 + (71/100) = 68878.71$

seconds. So the time consumed by the task is $68878.71 - 66912.14 = 1966.57$ seconds.

An anomaly in the above calculation is that the constant used to represent the seconds in an hour was real rather than integer. The reason for this is that the variable Hour is of type *word*, and so, if we used the integer 3600 for the seconds in an hour, the product

$$\text{Hour} * 3600$$

would be stored in a word. But if Hour has the value 19, as in the above calculation of FinishTime, then Hour * 3600 = 68400, which is larger than the maximum word value of 65535. This situation is referred to as **over-flow**—the generation of a value too large for its designated location. To get the value into the range of 0..65535, Turbo Pascal calculates the value's remainder when it is divided by 65536. The value stored would be

$$68400 \textbf{ mod } 65536 = 2865$$

No error message would be produced, but the resulting value for Finish-Time would be only 3343.71—that is, 2865 + (7 * 60) + 58 + 0.71. The value for StartTime would be the same as before, namely 66912.14 seconds, since 18 * 3600 = 64800, which is less than 65536. The value of ElapsedTime would then be negative! All of this trouble is avoided by using the real constant 3600.0 because the product Hour * 3600.0 is then stored as 68400.0.

Another potential difficulty with the GetTime procedure is that its accuracy may be off by as much as five hundredths of a second on some (slow) computer systems. In other words, we should not put too much faith in the hundredths digit of ElapsedTime. For that reason, ElapsedTime is printed with only one fractional digit.

The Random Function

Given a collection of numbers, a number is selected **randomly** from the collection if each number has an equal chance of being selected. A number so selected is called a **random number**, and a function that returns a random number is called a **random number generator**. Turbo Pascal's predeclared function Random provides a random number generator.[2] If Random is called without an argument in parentheses, the value returned is a real random number greater than or equal to 0.0 and less than 1.0. For example,

```
X := Random
```

will assign a random value to X so that $0.0 \leq X < 1.0$.

---

[2]Strictly speaking, the Random function is called a *pseudo-random* number generator, since the numbers calculated are not random at all—they are determined by the function. They appear to be random if we do not see how they are calculated.

The Random function can also be called with an argument of type word; the value returned is a random integer greater than or equal to 0 and less than the value of the argument. For example,

```
Random (1000)
```

returns a random integer in the range 0 to 999, inclusive.

The value calculated by the Random function depends on the predeclared longint variable RandSeed. Each time the function Random is called, RandSeed's current value is used in determining RandSeed's next value. This new value for RandSeed, together with the value of the function's argument (if there is one), determines the value returned by the function.

For example, suppose that the statement part of two programs begins with

```
RandSeed := 200;
for I := 1 to 5 do
   Writeln (Random (1000))
```

The output from both programs would be exactly the same:

```
87
247
980
736
281
```

This repeatability can be helpful when we want to compare the behavior of programs, as we will in Chapters 4 through10.

If we do not want repeatability, we start by calling the Randomize procedure. Randomize uses the system clock to provide a random longint value for RandSeed. For example, we can write

```
Randomize;
for I:= 1 to 5 do
   Writeln (Random (1000))
```

Each time the program is run we would get a different sequence of five random integers between 0 and 999, inclusive.[3]

SUMMARY

This chapter introduced several features of Turbo Pascal that you will need in order to understand the material in Chapters 3 through 12.

---

[3]In the unlikely event that, for two executions, Randomize gave RandSeed the same initial value, then the two sequences generated would be the same.

Pointers are powerful (but dangerous) tools. They allow programmers the only access to the *heap*—a potentially large section of main memory. Variables in the heap are called *dynamic* variables because they are explicitly created and destroyed by the programmer at run time. Often, a dynamic variable is a record in which one of the fields contains an item, and another field is a pointer to a dynamic variable of the same record type. Each dynamic record can thus be *linked* to another dynamic record, and the heap can hold a large structure of related items.

An *object* is a collection of fields together with a collection of methods that act on those fields. An *instance* is a variable whose type is an object. A *message* is the invocation of a method by an instance. *Inheritance* is the ability of an object—called a *descendant*—to possess fields and methods declared in another object (an *ancestor*). Once an object is being successfully used in an application, the object should not be modified for the sake of a new application. Instead, the modifications should be incorporated into a descendant. This ensures the integrity of the original object.

Objects are usually declared in units. A *unit* is a separately compiled collection of declarations, together with an optional initialization part. Units can be used by other units and by programs, but only programs can be executed. Declarations and subprogram headings contained in the interface part of a unit are accessible to users of the unit. Any declarations contained in the implementation part are inaccessible to users of the unit. The implementation part of a unit must include a block for each subprogram heading declared in the interface part.

The subprograms GetTime and Random allows programmers to conduct run-time comparisons of alternative versions of a subprogram.

LABORATORY EXERCISES

For each of the following exercises, conjecture what the answer should be. Then enter and run the corresponding program to confirm or reject your conjecture.

1.1   Which of the following type-declaration parts are illegal? Why?

a. **type**
```
   PtrType = real^;
```
b. **type**
```
   PtrType = ^array [1..1000] of boolean;
```
c. **type**
```
   MemoryType = array [1..1000] of boolean;
   PtrType  = ^MemoryType;
```
d. **type**
```
   StringPtrType = ^string [20];
```

e. **type**
```
        StudentType = record
          Name: string [30];
          Next: StudentPtrType
        end; { StudentType }
        StudentPtrType = ^StudentType;
```

f. **type**
```
        StudentPtrType = ^StudentType;
        StudentType = record
          Name: string [30];
          Next: StudentPtrType
        end; { StudentType }
```

1.2   Determine the output from the following program:

```
program Switch;
{ Assignments to pointer variables and dynamic
  variables.}
type
    PtrType = ^integer;
var
    A,
    B: PtrType;
begin
    New (A);
    A^ := 5;
    New (B);
    B^ := 31;
    A^ := B^;
    A^ := A^ - 1;
    Writeln (A^: 4, B^: 4);
    A := B;
    A^ := A^ - 1;
    Writeln (A^: 4, B^: 4)
end. { Switch }
```

1.3   Determine the output from the following program:

```
program Pointers;
{ Carelessness with pointers }
type
    PtrType = ^string;
var
    A,
    B,
    C: PtrType;
```

```
begin
   New (A);
   A^ := 'careful';
   B := A;
   Dispose (A);
   B^ := 'not careful';
   New (C);
   C^ := 'sloppy';
   Writeln (A^: 10, B^: 10, C^: 10)
end. { Pointers }
```

1.4   Suppose that, for a particular application, you need to store 50,000 integers (of type word) in main memory. Furthermore, you want to be able to access any one of those locations without first accessing any of the other locations. Describe how to accomplish this.

1.5   What effect would it have on users of the unit StudentManager if StudentFile were changed to a typed file instead of a text file?

1.6   Declare an object type called InventoryType with the following fields and methods:

PartName—a string of up to 30 characters;

PartNumber,

QuantityOnHand,

ReorderPoint —of type Word;

UnitCost—of type Real;

ReadIn—a procedure that reads in the field values;

WriteOut—a procedure that writes out the field values;

Order (Quantity : word;

```
var Filled : boolean;
var Cost   : real;
var Reorder: boolean)
```

—a procedure that attempts to process an order, as follows:

```
if Quantity > QuantityOnHand then
   Filled gets the value False
otherwise
   Filled gets the value True
   Cost gets the product of Quantity and UnitCost
   QuantityOnHand is decremented by Quantity
   if QuantityOnHand <= ReorderPoint then
      Reorder gets the value True
   otherwise
      Reorder gets the value False
```

1.7 **a.** Develop a unit, ItemInList, that implements the object ItemType (see the **UNITS** section of this chapter).

   b. Develop a program, ItemProg, that uses ItemInList and declares two instances, Item1 and Item2, of the object ItemType.

   c. Send a message with Item1 as the instance, SetValue as the method, and Value1 (whose Weight and Cost fields were earlier assigned values of 10.6 and 50, respectively) as the actual parameter.

   d. Send a message with Item2 as the instance, SetValue as the method, and Value2 (with Weight = 15.0 and Cost = 27) as the actual parameter.

   e. What result will be returned by the following message?

```
Item1.LessThan (Item2)
```

1.8 **a.** Write a program that simulates ten random coin flips. The output from each flip is either "Heads" or "Tails."

   b. Write a program that simulates ten random tosses of two dice. The output from each toss is a pair of integers, each an integer between 1 and 6, inclusive.

1.9 Write a program that calculates the execution time of the following procedure:

```
procedure RandIntDiv;
{ Perform random, integer divisions. }
const
   Seed = 100;
   Count = 10000;
var
   I,
   Quotient: integer;
begin
   RandSeed := Seed;
   for I := 1 to Count do
      Quotient := Random (MaxInt) div (Random (MaxInt)
      + 1)
end; { RandIntDiv }
```

1.10 Write a program to compare the relative speeds of integer division and real division.

   HINT See Exercise 1.9.

1.11 Develop a unit with a Date function. Date returns a longint value representing the number of days elapsed since January 1, 1980.

   HINT Use Turbo Pascal's GetDate function.

1.12 In the program skeleton TestTime, it was assumed that the task started and ended on the same date. Use the unit developed in Exercise 1.11 to remove this assumption.

1.13 (Originally posed by Marilyn Vos Savant)

Welcome to *Let's Make a Deal!* You are given a choice of three doors. Behind one door there is a car; behind each of the other doors there is a skunk. After you make your initial guess, I will peek behind the other two doors and eliminate one of them that does **not** have the car behind it. For example, if your initial guess is door 2 and the car is behind door 3, I will announce "The car is not behind door 1."

After you have made your initial guess and I have eliminated one of the other doors, you must then make your final choice. The question is, "Is it to your advantage to switch, or should you stay with your initial guess?" To help you answer this question, write two programs. In both programs, your choice and the correct choice are generated randomly. The first program plays the game 300 times and always switches. The second program plays the game 300 times and never switches.

Introduction to Recursion

If there is a single skill that distinguishes a novice programmer from an experienced one, it is the understanding of recursion. The goal of this chapter is to give you a feel for situations in which a recursive subprogram is appropriate. Along the way you will start to see the power and elegance of recursion, as well as its potential for misuse.

Recursion plays a key role in Chapters 7 through 9, when we develop algorithms for binary trees and for sorting. But the value of recursion extends far beyond these two topics. For example, recursion simplifies our work on list processing in Chapters 4 and 5. The sooner you are exposed to recursion, the more likely you are to be able to spot situations where it is appropriate and to use it.

Roughly, a subprogram is *recursive* if it contains a call to itself.[1] From this description, you may initially fear that the execution of a recursive subprogram will lead to an infinite sequence of recursive calls. But under normal circumstances, this calamity does not occur, and the sequence of calls eventually stops. To show you how this works, here is the skeleton of the statement part of a typical recursive subprogram:

```
if simplest case then
    solve directly
else
    make a recursive call to a simpler case.
```

---

[1] A formal definition of "recursive" is given later in this chapter (see **indirect recursion**).

This outline suggests that recursion should be considered whenever the problem to be solved has these two characteristics:

1. Complex cases of the problem can be reduced to simpler cases.
2. The simplest case(s) can be solved straightforwardly.

Incidentally, if you are familiar with the Principle of Mathematical Induction (see Appendix 1), you may have observed that these two characteristics correspond to the inductive case and base case, respectively. The relationship between recursion and induction is further explored in Appendix 1.

As we work through the following examples, do not be inhibited by old ways of thinking. As each problem is stated, try to frame a solution in terms of a simpler problem of the same form. Think recursively!

Factorials.   Given a positive integer N, the *factorial* of N, written $N!$, is the product of all integers between N and 1, inclusive. For example,

$$3! = 3 * 2 * 1 = 6$$

and

$$5! = 5 * 4 * 3 * 2 * 1 = 120$$

Another way to calculate 5! is as follows:

$$5! = 5 * 4!$$

This formulation is not helpful unless we know what 4! is. But we can continue to calculate factorials in terms of smaller factorials (At this point you should be saying "Aha"):

$$4! = 4 * 3!$$
$$3! = 3 * 2!$$
$$2! = 2 * 1!$$

Observe that 1! can be calculated directly: its value is 1. Now we work backwards:

$$2! = 2 * 1! = 2 * 1 = 2$$
$$3! = 3 * 2! = 3 * 2 = 6$$
$$4! = 4 * 3! = 4 * 6 = 24$$

Finally, we get

$$5! = 5 * 4! = 5 * 24 = 120$$

For $N > 1$, we reduce the problem of calculating $N!$ to the problem of calculating $(N - 1)!$ We stop reducing when we get to $1!$, which is simply 1. These observations lead to the following Turbo Pascal[2] program:

```
program FactProg;
{ Read in a number and calculate its factorial. }
const
   Prompt = 'Please enter the number whose factorial you
             want: ';
var
   N: integer;
function Factorial (N: integer): longint;
{ Calculate N! recursively. }
begin
   if N = 1 then
      Factorial := 1
   else
      Factorial := N * Factorial (N - 1)
end; { Factorial }
begin
   Write (Prompt);
   Readln (N);
   Writeln (N, ' factorial = ', Factorial (N))
end. { FactProg }
```

In the function Factorial, the function identifier Factorial occurs twice in the assignment statement

```
Factorial := N * Factorial (N - 1)
```

On the left-hand side, the identifier is used to indicate that the expression on the right-hand side has the value calculated by the function. On the

------

[2]With two exceptions, all of the code in this chapter also applies to Standard Pascal, provided that we declare

type
   longint = integer;

The exceptions are:

1. the **unit** Timer;
2. the short-circuit boolean expression in the Count function (see **Counting Clusters in a Table** later in this chapter).

right-hand side, the expression $N *$ Factorial $(N - 1)$ includes a recursive call to the function Factorial.

The following chart traces the execution of the function Factorial with an initial argument of 4:

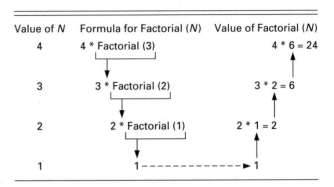

Value of N	Formula for Factorial (N)	Value of Factorial (N)
4	4 * Factorial (3)	4 * 6 = 24
3	3 * Factorial (2)	3 * 2 = 6
2	2 * Factorial (1)	2 * 1 = 2
1	1 ------------→ 1	

As we trace the execution of the function Factorial, we see that the formal parameter N has its value reduced by 1 with each recursive call. But after the final call with $N = 1$, the *previous* values of N are needed for the multiplications. For example, when $N = 4$, the calculation of $N *$ Factorial $(N -- 1)$ is postponed until the call to Factorial $(N - 1)$ is completed. When this finally happens and the value 6 (namely, Factorial (3)) is returned, the value of 4 for N must be available.

Somehow, the value of N must be saved when the call to Factorial $(N - 1)$ is made. That value must be restored after the call to Factorial $(N - 1)$ is completed so that the value of $N *$ Factorial $(N - 1)$ can be calculated. The beauty of recursion is that the programmer need not explicitly handle these savings and restorings; the computer does the work.

Recursion can often make it easier for us to solve problems, but any problem that can be solved recursively can also be solved iteratively. An *iterative* subprogram is one that uses a loop statement. For example, the following program contains an iterative function to calculate factorials.

```
program FactProg2;
{ Read in a number and calculate its factorial. }
const
    Prompt = 'Please enter the number whose factorial you
              want: ';
var
    N: integer;
```

```
function Factorial (N: integer): longint;
{ Calculate N! iteratively. }
var
   Product: longint;
   I      : integer;
begin
   Product := N;
   for I := N - 1 downto 2 do
      Product := Product * I;
   Factorial := Product
end; { Factorial }
begin
   Write (Prompt);
   Readln (N);
   Writeln (N, ' factorial = ', Factorial (N))
end. { FactProg2 }
```

You may well argue that the iterative version follows directly from the definition of factorials, and in that sense it is superior to the recursive version. That is a good point. Furthermore, the recursive version is no more efficient in terms of execution time (and memory utilization) than the iterative version. In fact, both versions take less than one tenth of a second to calculate 12!, the largest factorial less than the largest integer in *longint*. Finally, both subprograms are fairly easy to understand. The iterative version has two more variables, but the recursive version represents your first exposure to a new problem-solving technique, and that takes some extra effort.

In this example, then, the iterative version of the factorial function is slightly preferable to the recursive version. The whole purpose of the example was to provide a simple situation in which recursion was worth considering, even though we ultimately decided that iteration was better. In the next example, an iterative alternative is not as appealing.

Decimal-to-Binary Conversion.   Humans count naturally in base ten because we were born with ten fingers. Computers count naturally in base two because of the binary nature of electronics. One of the tasks a computer performs is to convert from decimal (base ten) to binary (base two). Let us develop a subprogram to solve a simplified version of this problem:

Given a nonnegative integer *N*, write out its binary equivalent.

For example, if *N* is 25, the output is 11001.

There are several approaches to solving this problem. One of them is based on the following observation:

> Since $N = (N \text{ div } 2) * 2 + N \text{ mod } 2$, the rightmost bit has the value of $N \text{ mod } 2$; the other bits are the binary equivalent of $N \text{ div } 2$. (Aha!)

For example, if N is 25, the rightmost bit in the binary equivalent is 25 **mod** 2, namely, 1; the remaining bits are the binary equivalent of 25 **div** 2, namely, 12. We can then obtain all of the bits as follows:

```
25 mod 2 = 1; 25 div 2 = 12
┌─────────────────────────┘
12 mod 2 = 0; 12 div 2 = 6
┌─────────────────────────┘
 6 mod 2 = 0;  6 div 2 = 3
 ┌────────────────────────┘
 3 mod 2 = 1;  3 div 2 = 1
 ┌────────────────────────┘
 1 mod 2 = 1;  1 div 2 = 0
```

We write out these bits from the bottom up, so that the rightmost bit will be written last. The output would then be

   11001

This discussion suggests that we must perform all of the calculations before we do any writing. Speaking recursively, we need to write out the binary equivalent of $N \text{ div } 2$ *before* we write out $N \text{ mod } 2$. In other words, we need to put the recursive call before the Write statement.

We stop when $N \text{ div } 2$ is 0, that is, when N is less than or equal to 1.

The procedure is

```
procedure WriteBinary (N: longint);
{ Write out the binary equivalent of N. }
begin
   if N <= 1 then
      Write (N: 1)
   else
      begin
         WriteBinary (N div 2);
         Write (N mod 2: 1)
      end { else }
end; { WriteBinary }
```

The following table traces the execution of this procedure after an initial call of WriteBinary (20):

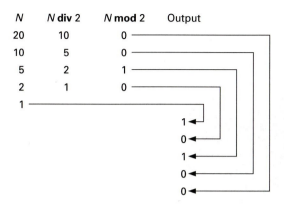

As we noted earlier, the order of the statements in the **else** part of WriteBinary enables us to postpone *any* writing until *all* of the bit values have been calculated. If the order had been reversed, the bits would have printed in reverse order. Recursion is such a powerful tool that the effects of slight changes are magnified.

You are invited to develop an iterative subprogram to solve this problem. (If you would like a hint, see Exercise 2.2.)

After you have completed the iterative subprogram, you will probably agree that it was somewhat harder to develop than the recursive subprogram. This is typical, and probably obvious: Recursive solutions usually flow more easily than iterative solutions to those problems for which recursion is appropriate. Recursion is appropriate when larger instances of the problem can be reduced to smaller instances that have the same form as the larger instances.

For the next problem, an iterative solution may be much harder to develop than a recursive solution.

Towers of Hanoi.   In the Towers of Hanoi game, there are three poles, labelled 'A,' 'B' and 'C,' and several numbered disks of different sizes, each with a hole in the center. Initially, all of the disks are on pole 'A,' with the largest disk on the bottom, then the next largest, and so on. Figure 2.1 shows the initial configuration if we started with four disks, numbered from smallest to largest.

The object of the game is to move all of the disks from pole 'A' to pole 'B'; pole 'C' is used for temporary storage. The rules of the game are:

1.   Only one disk may be moved at a time.

2.   No disk may ever be placed on top of a smaller disk.

3.   Other than the prohibition of rule 2, the top disk on any pole may be moved to either of the other poles.

Figure 2.1

The starting position for the Towers of Hanoi game with four disks.

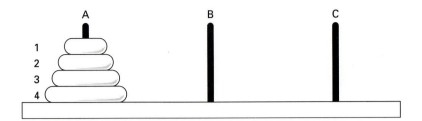

Let's try to play the game with the initial configuration given in Fig. 2.1. We are immediately faced with a dilemma: Do we move disk 1 to pole 'B' or to pole 'C'? If we make the wrong move, we may end up with the four disks on pole 'C' rather than on pole 'B.'

Instead of trying to figure out where disk 1 should be moved initially, we will focus our attention on disk 4, the bottom disk. Of course, we can't move disk 4 right away, but eventually, disk 4 will have to be moved from pole 'A' to pole 'B.' By the rules of the game, the configuration just before moving disk 4 must be as shown in Fig. 2.2.

Does this observation help us to figure out how to move four disks from 'A' to 'B'? Well, sort of. We still need to determine how to move three disks (one at a time) from pole 'A' to pole 'C.' We can then move disk 4 from 'A' to 'B.' Finally, we will need to determine how to move three disks (one at a time) from 'C' to 'B.'

The significance of this strategy is that we have reduced the problem from determining how to move four disks to one of determining how to move three disks. We still need to figure out how to move three disks from one pole to another pole.

But the above strategy can be re-applied. To move three disks from, say, pole 'A' to pole 'C,' we first move two disks (one at a time) from 'A' to 'B,' then we move disk 3 from 'A' to 'C,' and finally, we move two disks from 'B' to 'C.' Continually reducing the problem, eventually we face the trivial task of moving disk 1 from one pole to another.

There is nothing special about the number 4 in the above approach. For any positive integer N, we can describe how to move N disks from

Figure 2.2

The game configuration for the Towers of Hanoi just before moving disk 4 from pole 'A' to pole 'B.'

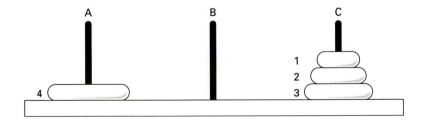

pole 'A' to pole 'B': If $N = 1$, we simply move disk 1 from pole 'A' to pole 'B'. For $N > 1$,

1. First, move $N - 1$ disks from pole 'A' to pole 'C,' using pole 'B' for temporary storage.
2. Next, move disk N from pole 'A' to pole 'B.'
3. Finally, move $N - 1$ disks from pole 'C' to pole 'B,' using pole 'A' for temporary storage.

This does not quite solve the problem because, for example, we have not described how to move $N - 1$ disks from 'A' to 'C'. But our strategy is easily generalized by replacing the constants 'A,' 'B,' and 'C' with variables Origin, Destination, and Temporary. For example, we will initially have

Origin   = 'A'

Destination = 'B'

Temporary = 'C'

Then the general algorithm for moving N disks from Origin to Destination is as follows:

> If $N = 1$, move disk 1 from Origin to Destination.
> Otherwise,
>
> 1. Move $N - 1$ disks (one at a time) from Origin to Temporary.
> 2. Move disk N from Origin to Destination.
> 3. Move $N - 1$ disks (one at a time) from Temporary to Destination.

The following program incorporates this algorithm into a recursive procedure:

```
program Hanoi;
{ Play the Towers of Hanoi game. The initial number of }
{ disks is read in.                                     }
const
   Prompt  = 'Enter the number of disks: ';
   Heading = 'The moves required are as follows:';
type
   PoleType = 'A'..'C';
var
   N: integer; { N holds the number of disks. }
procedure Move (N    : integer;
                Orig,  { Origin }
                Dest,  { Destination }
                Temp   { Temporary }
                   : PoleType);
```

```
{ Write out the steps needed to move N disks from pole Orig }
{ to pole Dest. Pole Temp is used for temporary storage.   }
begin
   if N = 1 then
      Writeln ('Move disk 1 from ', Orig, ' to ', Dest)
   else
      begin
         Move (N - 1, Orig, Temp, Dest);
         Writeln ('Move disk ', N, ' from ', Orig, ' to ',
                  Dest);
         Move (N - 1, Temp, Dest, Orig)
      end { N > 1 }
end; { Move }
begin
   Write (Prompt);
   Readln (N);
   Writeln (Heading);
   Writeln;
   Move (N, 'A', 'B', 'C')
end. { Hanoi }
```

It is difficult to trace the execution of this program because the current values of the formal parameters must be saved when each recursive call is made and restored when the call is completed. So it is not easy to keep track of which disk is currently the origin, which is the destination, and which is the temporary.

A *recursion tree* is a tool that illustrates the execution of a recursive subprogram. The root of the recursion tree is the original call, with branches representing the effects of executing the subprogram, and leaves representing nonrecursive operations. For each call to the recursive subprogram, we list the actual parameters, the values of the actual parameters, and the formal parameters. For example, Fig. 2.3 shows part of the recursion tree for the procedure Move when the actual parameter N has the value 3 in the initial call.

We can now list the sequence of steps needed to move three disks from pole 'A' to pole 'B.' First, we list (from left to right) all of the leaves in the left subtree of Fig. 2.3; then we list the leaf in the middle subtree. Finally, we list all of the leaves in the right subtree, also from left to right. We get:

> Move disk 1 from A to B
> Move disk 2 from A to C
> Move disk 1 from B to C
> Move disk 3 from A to B
> Move disk 1 from C to A
> Move disk 2 from C to B
> Move disk 1 from A to B

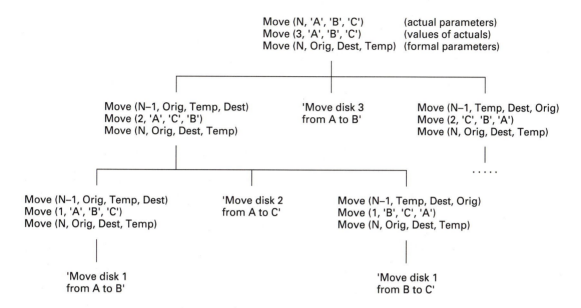

Move (N, 'A', 'B', 'C')   (actual parameters)
Move (3, 'A', 'B', 'C')   (values of actuals)
Move (N, Orig, Dest, Temp)   (formal parameters)

Move (N–1, Orig, Temp, Dest)
Move (2, 'A', 'C', 'B')
Move (N, Orig, Dest, Temp)

'Move disk 3
from A to B'

Move (N–1, Temp, Dest, Orig)
Move (2, 'C', 'B', 'A')
Move (N, Orig, Dest, Temp)

Move (N–1, Orig, Temp, Dest)
Move (1, 'A', 'B', 'C')
Move (N, Orig, Dest, Temp)

'Move disk 2
from A to C'

Move (N–1, Temp, Dest, Orig)
Move (1, 'B', 'C', 'A')
Move (N, Orig, Dest, Temp)

'Move disk 1
from A to B'

'Move disk 1
from B to C'

Figure 2.3   Part of the recursion tree for Move (3, 'A,' 'B,' 'C').

Notice the disparity between the relative ease in developing the recursive subprogram and the relative difficulty in tracing its execution. Imagine what it would be like to trace the execution of Move (15, 'A,' 'B,' 'C')! Fortunately, you need not undergo such torture. Computers handle this type of tedious detail very well. You "merely" provide the program and the computer produces the output.

A recursive subprogram does not explicitly describe the considerable detail involved in its execution. For this reason, recursion is sometimes referred to as "the lazy person's problem-solving tool." If you want to appreciate the value of recursion, try to develop an iterative version of the procedure Move; Exercise 2.5 contains a hint.

Fibonacci Numbers.   The arrangement of scales on pine cones, the florets of daisies, and the family tree of male bees all share a common feature: They exhibit the Fibonacci sequence. This sequence is named after a 13th century Italian mathematician who discovered the sequence: 1, 1, 2, 3, 5, 8, 13, 21, 34, ... Each of the first two terms is 1. After that, each term is the sum of the preceding two terms (for example, 8 = 5 + 3). This definition immediately leads to the recursive function in the following program:

```
program FibRec;
{ Read in N and calculate the Nth Fibonacci number. }
const
    Prompt = 'Enter the number whose Fibonacci number you
               want: ';
```

```
var
    N: integer;
function Fib (N: integer): longint;
{ Calculate the Nth Fibonacci number recursively. }
begin
    if N <= 2 then
        Fib := 1
    else
        Fib := Fib (N - 1) + Fib (N - 2)
end; { Fib }
begin
    Write (Prompt);
    Readln (N);
    Writeln ('The ',N , 'th Fibonacci number is ', Fib (N))
end. { FibRec }
```

Figure 2.4 shows the recursion tree for Fib (6), whose value is 8.

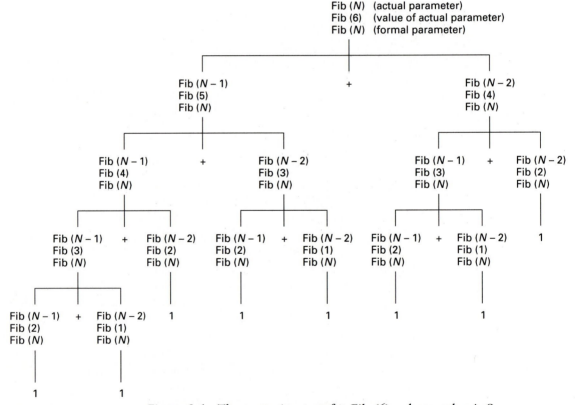

Figure 2.4   The recursion tree for Fib (6), whose value is 8.

Figure 2.4 indicates that the recursive function Fib is horribly ineffi-cient: For example, in calculating Fib (6), Fib (4) must be calculated twice and Fib (3) must be calculated three times. A related inefficiency is that a large number of additions must be performed: In calculating Fib (N), there are Fib (N) ones at the leaves, and so there must be Fib (N) − 1 plusses. In other words, the number of additions required is Fib (N) − 1. For example, seven additions are needed to calculate Fib (6), which has the value 8. For Fib (10), namely 55, the number of additions required is 54.

Let us try to develop an iterative version of Fib that will be more effi-cient than the recursive version. For N > 2, we utilize two variables, Previ-ous and Current, to hold the previous and current Fibonacci numbers, respectively. We initialize both Previous and Current to 1, and then loop as I goes from 3 to N. After each iteration we want Current to hold the Ith Fi-bonacci number and Previous to hold the (I − 1)st Fibonacci number. So within the loop we add Previous to Current and then give Previous the "old" value of Current. The following program implements this design:

```pascal
program FibItr;
{ Read in N and calculate the Nth Fibonacci number. }
const
   Prompt = 'Enter the number whose Fibonacci number you
               want: ';
var
   N: integer;
function Fib (N: integer): longint;
{ Calculate the Nth Fibonacci number iteratively. }
var
   Previous,
   Current,
   Temp      : longint;
   I         : integer;
begin
   if N <= 2 then
      Fib := 1
   else
      begin
         Previous := 1;
         Current  := 1;
         for I := 3 to N do
            begin

               { Make Current hold the Ith Fibonacci }
               { number and Previous hold the (I-1)st }
               { number Fibonacci. }
               Temp      := Current;
```

```
              Current  := Current + Previous;
              Previous := Temp
          end; { for I := 3 to N }
        Fib := Current
      end { N > 2 }
end; { Fib }
begin
   Write (Prompt);
   Readln (N);
   Writeln;
   Writeln ('The ',N , 'th Fibonacci number is ', Fib (N))
end. { FibItr }
```

One immediate observation about the iterative version of Fib is that far fewer additions must be performed than for the recursive version: Iterative Fib (N) requires $N - 2$ additions (for $N \geq 2$), whereas recursive Fib (N) requires Fib$(N) - 1$ additions. For example, to calculate the 30th Fibonacci number (832040) iteratively requires only 28 additions, versus 832039 for the recursive version!

A more accurate comparison of the two versions of Fib can be made by utilizing Turbo Pascal's GetTime procedure. The following program measures the execution time of the iterative version of Fib.

```
program FibTime;
{ Determine the time to calculate the Nth Fibonacci number.}
uses
   Timer; { implements the Time function }
const
   Prompt = 'Enter the number whose Fibonacci number you
             want: ';
var
   N          : integer;
   StartTime,
   FinishTime,
   ElapsedTime: real;
function Fib (N: integer): longint;
      .
      .
      .
end; { Fib }
begin
   Write (Prompt);
   Readln (N);
   Writeln;
   StartTime := Time;
   Writeln ('The ',N , 'th Fibonacci number is ', Fib (N));
```

```
        FinishTime := Time;
        ElapsedTime := FinishTime - StartTime;
        Writeln;
        Writeln ('Elapsed time = ', ElapsedTime: 8: 1, '
                seconds.')
  end. { FibTime }
```

To calculate Fib (30) iteratively on an IBM-PC-XT compatible (10 mega-hertz) took 0.1 seconds. Calculating Fib (30) recursively took 166.0 seconds.

In comparing the recursive and iterative versions of Fib, we note that the iterative version is substantially faster but required slightly more time to develop. This speedup makes the iterative function of Fib preferable. Sometimes, as in the Towers of Hanoi example, a recursive subprogram is preferable to its iterative counterpart because it is substantially easier to develop and is only slightly slower. The point is that neither recursion nor iteration is a panacea—recursive subprograms are often easier to develop, while iterative subprograms usually run faster. In any given application, you will have to choose which is better.

Before we leave this example, let's develop a time-efficient, recursive Fibonacci function by mimicking the iterative version. This function will have three formal parameters: N, Previous, and Current. The corresponding actual parameters for each recursive call are $N - 1$, Current, and Current + Previous. But this gives rise to a technical problem: For the sake of consistency with earlier versions, the function heading for Fib should have only one formal parameter, N. So we will imbed the recursive function, called F, in a function Fib whose heading is the same as for the earlier Fibonacci functions:

```
function Fib (N: integer): longint;
{ Calculate the Nth Fibonacci number recursively. }
   function F (N         : integer;
               Previous,
               Current  : longint): longint;
   begin
     if N <= 2 then
         F := Current
     else
         F := F (N - 1, Current, Current + Previous)
   end; { F }
begin
   Fib := F (N, 1, 1 )
end; { Fib }
```

With this version, only $N - 2$ additions are needed to calculate the Nth Fibonnaci number for $N > 1$. The imbedding of recursion is a common technique. In the next example, the recursive subprogram is imbedded for the sake of efficiency.

Still yet another version of the function Fib is found in Appendix 1; that version is neither recursive nor iterative.

If you think we have beaten to death the topic of Fibonacci numbers, browse through a couple of issues of *Fibonacci Quarterly*, a journal devoted to applications of the Fibonacci sequence.

Counting Clusters in a Table.   This example has several interesting applications. The function developed can be used to estimate the extent of a bacterial infection or to determine landforms in images taken from satellite photographs.

Suppose we are given a table (that is, a two-dimensional array) in which there are only two kinds of entries, called "filled" and "empty." Figure 2.5 shows such a table, with filled entries represented by Xs and empty entries represented by blanks.

All of the filled entries that are connected (horizontally, vertically, or diagonally) constitute a *cluster*. A cluster can represent an infected area in the bacterial application or the landform to be studied in the satellite-imaging application.

Given any entry, we want to count the size of its cluster. For example, for the entry with coordinates (2, 1) in Fig. 2.5, the count is 3 because the filled entries in its cluster are (2, 1), (3, 2) and (4, 2). For the entry with coordinates (5, 7), the count is 6. For any empty entry, the count is 0.

The key observation is this: The count for any filled entry with coordinates (R, C), is one plus the counts of its immediate neighbors. This description is easily translated into recursive function calls:

```
Count := 1 + Count (Table, R - 1, C - 1)
            + Count (Table, R - 1, C)
            + Count (Table, R - 1, C + 1)
            + Count (Table, R, C - 1)
            + Count (Table, R, C + 1)
            + Count (Table, R + 1, C - 1)
            + Count (Table, R + 1, C)
            + Count (Table, R + 1, C + 1)
```

We must make sure that, in counting a cluster, we do not count the same filled entry more than once. For example, in counting the cluster at (7, 8) in Fig. 2.5, the filled entry at (7, 9) is a neighbor of (7, 8) and a neighbor of (6, 9). To avoid counting a filled entry more than once, we make it empty as soon as we encounter it.

Rather than save Table with each recursive call, we will imbed the Count function in a function ClusterCount, with parameters Table, R, and C. ClusterCount simply returns Count (R, C). Because we make each filled entry empty when it is encountered during counting, the parameter Table

Figure 2.5

A table in which each entry is either filled ('X') or empty (' ').

	1	2	3	4	5	6	7	8	9
1									
2	X			X				X	
3		X						X	
4		X				X			
5							X		
6		X	X				X		X
7								X	X

in ClusterCount must be a *value* formal parameter so that the corresponding actual parameter will not be altered.

The function ClusterCount, with appropriate concern for border entries, is shown below.

```
const
    Rows    = 50;
    Columns = 50;
type
    Status    = (Empty, Filled);
    TableType = array [1..Rows, 1..Columns] of Status;
function ClusterCount (Table: TableType;
                       R,
                       C : integer): integer;
{ Counts the number of filled entries in a cluster. }
function Count (R,
                C : integer): integer;
{ Warning: Table is a non-local variable. }
begin
    if not (R in [1..Rows]) or not (C in [1..Columns]) or
            (Table [R, C] = Empty) then
        Count := 0
    else
        begin
            Table [R, C] := Empty;
            Count := 1 + Count (R - 1, C - 1)
                       + Count (R - 1, C)
                       + Count (R - 1, C + 1)
```

```
                        + Count (R, C - 1)
                        + Count (R, C + 1)
                        + Count (R + 1, C - 1)
                        + Count (R + 1, C)
                        + Count (R + 1, C + 1)
        end { filled entry }
end; { Count }
begin
    ClusterCount := Count (R, C)
end; { ClusterCount }
```

This example is similar to the Towers of Hanoi problem in that a recursive design is fairly straightforward, while an iterative design is much harder to develop. This disparity is also illustrated in the next example, from Roberts' delightful book, *Thinking Recursively*. (See Roberts, 1986).

Generating Permutations. A ***permutation*** is an arrangement of items in a linear order. For example, if the items are the letters 'A', 'B', 'C,' and 'D,' we can generate the following 24 permutations:

ABCD	BACD	CABD	DABC
ABDC	BADC	CADB	DACB
ACBD	BCAD	CBAD	DBAC
ACDB	BCDA	CBDA	DBCA
ADBC	BDAC	CDAB	DCAB
ADCB	BDCA	CDBA	DCBA

In general, for N items, there are N choices for the first item in a permutation. After the first item has been chosen, there are $(N - 1)$ choices for the second item. Continuing in this fashion, we see that the total number of permutations of N items is

$$N * (N - 1) * (N - 2) * \ldots * 2 * 1.$$

That is, there are $N!$ different permutations of N items.

We assume, for the sake of simplicity, that N is a constant. (This assumption is removed in Exercise 2.9) We also assume that the string variable S holds N characters, all distinct. We want to develop a procedure to print out all $N!$ permutations of S.

From the above example, where $S = $ 'ABCD', we can print out the permutations of S by printing:

the six permutations that start with 'A';

the six permutations that start with 'B';

the six permutations that start with 'C';

the six permutations that start with 'D'.

How can we print the six permutations that start with 'A'? Look at the list of permutations in the first paragraph of this section and try to figure out how to proceed. (Hint: $6 = 3!$)

The key observation is that, for those six permutations, each one starts with 'A' and is followed by a different permutation of 'BCD.' This suggests a recursive solution. For each of the six permutations of 'BCD,' we write out all of *S*, and so we get the six permutations of 'ABCD' that start with 'A'.

For the next six permutations, we first swap 'A' and 'B,' so that *S* = 'BACD.' We then repeat the above process, this time permuting 'ACD' and printing out all of *S* for each permutation.

For the next six permutations, we start by swapping 'B' and 'C,'—that is, *S* [1] and *S* [3]—so that *S* = 'CABD.' We then permute 'ABD' (that is, *S* [2..4]) and print *S* after each permutation.

For the last six permutations, we start by swapping *S* [1] and *S* [4] (that is, 'C' and 'D') so that *S* = 'DABC,' and then print *S* after each permutation of *S* [2..4] (that is, 'ABC').

The swapping and permuting can be accomplished in a **for** statement. We use *K* rather than 1 as the starting position for the sake of the recursive calls:

```
for I := K to N do
   begin
      Swap (S [I], S [K]);
      Permute (S, K + 1)
   end
```

Notice that when the loop is executed for the first time, *S* [*I*] is swapped with itself. The effect of this is to leave *S* [*I*] fixed during the first iteration. For example, in permuting 'ABCD,' we start by leaving 'A' fixed and permuting 'BCD'.

The stopping condition for the sequence of recursive calls is $K = N$. When this happens, we write out *S*.

The complete procedure is quite brief (we omit the trivial Swap procedure):

```
const
   N = 4;
type
   StringType = string [N];
procedure Permute (S: StringType;
                   K: integer);
{ Write out S for each permutation of S [K..N]. }
var
   I: integer;
begin
   if K = N then
      Writeln (S)
```

```
      else
        for I := K to N do
          begin
            Swap (S [I], S [K]);
            Permute (S, K + 1)
          end { for }
  end; { Permute }
```

The partial recursion tree in Fig. 2.6 illustrates the effect of an initial call of Permute ('ABCD,' 1). For simplicity, and to avoid cluttering up the figure, we show only the values of the actual parameters.

In Exercise 2.6 you are asked to complete this recursion tree. Keep in mind that the value of S is not changed by the recursive calls—S is a value formal parameter—but the value of S *is* changed by the calls to the Swap procedure. For example, when

```
Permute ('BACD', 2)
```

is called, then during the execution of that call, the value of S changes after each call to Swap in the **for** statement. The sequence of values for S is

```
'BACD' { before the first iteration of the for loop }
'BACD' { after Swap (S [2], S [2]) }
'BCAD' { after Swap (S [2], S [3]) }
'BDAC' { after Swap (S [2], S [4]) }
```

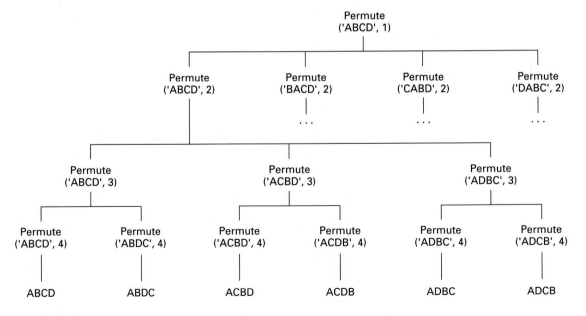

Figure 2.6   A partial recursion tree resulting from an initial call of Permute ('ABCD,' 1).

The development of this recursive procedure was no simple matter; but if you try to develop an iterative version, you may develop a headache instead. Exercise 2.10 contains a vague hint for an iterative subprogram that mimics the recursive version.

Backus Naur Form.   The syntax, or grammatical rules, of a computer language must be defined very carefully so that compilers can be written for those languages. We have already seen one formal method for defining syntax: syntax diagrams (see **UNITS**, Chapter 1). For example, the syntax diagram for "digit" is as follows:

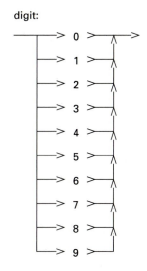

From this we can obtain the syntax diagram for "unsigned integer".

In English, we would say that an unsigned integer consists of any sequence of digits.

Another formal notation for defining syntax is *Backus Naur Form* (BNF). This notation, named after John Backus and Peter Naur, has a recursive flavor. Each BNF definition includes the symbol

: : =

This symbol means "is defined to be" and separates the term being defined from how it is defined. The term being defined is placed inside angle brackets

<   >

The right-hand side of the definition consists of alternate ways to construct the term. A bar

|

separates alternates.

For example, we can define "digit" in BNF as follows:

< digit > ::= 0 | 1 | 2 | 3 | 4 | 5 | 6 | 7 | 8 | 9

This is read "A digit is defined to be either 0 or 1 or 2 or 3 or 4 or 5 or 6 or 7 or 8 or 9." We can use this definition to define "unsigned integer":

< unsigned integer > ::= < digit > | < unsigned integer >
                             < digit >

This says that an unsigned integer can be either a digit all by itself or an unsigned integer followed by a digit. Such a recursive definition is legitimate because one of the alternates does not include the term being defined.

To show how this works, let's use this definition to show that 437 is an unsigned integer. First, note that 4, 3, and 7 are digits according to the definition of digit. Then the alternate

< unsigned integer > ::= < digit >

implies that 4 is an unsigned integer. Since 4 is an unsigned integer and 3 is a digit, the alternate

< unsigned integer > ::= < unsigned integer > < digit >

implies that 43 is an unsigned integer. Finally, since 43 is an unsigned integer and 7 is a digit, the same alternate

< unsigned integer > ::= < unsigned integer > < digit >

implies that 437 is an unsigned integer.

There are many other Turbo Pascal terms that are defined recursively in BNF: identifier, actual parameter list, array type (to allow for multi-dimensional arrays), statement sequence, and so on. For example, an identifier must start with a letter or underscore, and can be followed by any number (including zero) of letters, underscores, and digits. We can define "identifier" in BNF as follows (we skip the simple but tedious definitions of lower-case letter and upper-case letter):

< letter > ::= < lower-case letter > | < upper-case letter >
< identifier > ::= < letter > |_| < identifier > < letter >
                     | < identifier > _ | <identifier> <digit>

From this definiiton, we can verify that each of the following is an identifier:

I
Max_List_Size
Tax1993Return
while

Note that even though "while" satisfies the definition of an identifier, another part of the compiler recognizes "while" as a reserved word.

Indirect Recursion. Turbo Pascal supports indirect recursion. For example, if subprogram *A* calls subprogram *B* and subprogram *B* calls subprogram *A*, then both *A* and *B* are recursive. There is a technical problem here: *An* identifier must be declared before it can be referenced.[3] *B* must be declared before it can be referenced in *A*, and *A* must be declared before it can be referenced in *B*. Turbo Pascal avoids an impasse by means of the "forward directive." A **directive** is a message to the compiler; the *forward directive* informs the compiler that the rest of the current subprogram's declaration does not immediately follow but will be found farther down in the program. For example, we might have

```
procedure A (X: real); forward;
procedure B (N: integer);
  .

  .

  .
begin { the statement part of procedure B }
    .

    .

    .
   A (4.6);
    .

    .

    .
end; { B }
procedure A; { The formal parameter list is omitted. }
  .

  .

  .
begin
    .

    .

    .
   B (3);
    .

    .

    .
end; { A }
```

---

[3]The only exception to this rule is that a dynamic variable's type may be referenced before that type is declared.

Because indirect recursion is legal, we cannot simply define a subprogram to be recursive if it calls itself. To provide a formal definition of "recursive," we first define "active." A subprogram is **active** if it is being executed or has called an active subprogram. For example, consider a chain of subprogram calls

$$A \longrightarrow B \longrightarrow C \longrightarrow D$$

That is, A calls B, B calls C, and C calls D. When D is being executed, the active subprograms are

D, because it is being executed;

C, because it has called D and D is active;

B, because it has called C and C is active;

A, because it has called B and B is active.

We can now define "recursive." A subprogram is **recursive** if it can be called while it is active. For example, suppose we had the following sequence of calls:

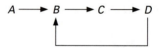

Then B, C, and D are recursive because each can be called while it is active.

The Cost of Recursion. We have seen that a certain amount of information is saved every time a subprogram calls itself. This information is collectively referred to as an ***activation record*** because it pertains to the execution state of the currently (that is, after the call) active subprogram. Each activation record contains:

1. the return address, that is, the address of the statement that will be executed when the call has been completed

2. the value of each value formal parameter (a copy of each actual value parameter is made)

3. the address of each variable formal parameter (two memory accesses are required to access the corresponding actual variable parameter)

4. the values of variables declared in the subprogram's block

5. the address of the value calculated, if the subprogram is a function.

After the call has been completed, the previous activation record's information is restored and the execution of the calling subprogram is resumed. For a long sequence of nested recursive calls, the space requirements for the activation records can be substantial, as is the execution time needed for saving and restoring those records. This is the reason that a recursive subprogram is almost always less efficient, in terms of both execution time and main-memory space, than an iterative subprogram that accomplishes the same task.

For simplicity, an activation record is created whenever any subprogram is called. For nonrecursive calls, the space requirements are often negligible. But a nonrecursive call within a loop can still consume a lot of time in saving and restoring an activation record each time through the loop.

In this chapter we have focused on what recursion is. We postpone to Chapter 6 a discussion of the mechanism, called a "stack," by which the compiler implements the saving and restoring of activation records. Incidentally, as we will see in Chapter 3, the separation of what is done from how it is done is a key principle in problem solving.

SUMMARY

The purpose of this chapter was to familiarize you with the concept of recursion so that you will be able to understand the recursive subprograms in subsequent chapters and to design your own recursive subprograms when the need arises.

A subprogram is **recursive** if it can be called while it is active; an *active* subprogram is one that either is being executed or has called another active subprogram.

Recursion should be considered for any problem that has the following characteristics:

1. Complex cases of the problem can be reduced to simpler cases.

2. The simplest case(s) can be solved straightforwardly.

For such problems, it is often straightforward to develop a recursive subprogram. But it may turn out that an *iterative* subprogram—one that has a loop—may consume less execution time and less memory.

Whenever any subprogram (recursive or not) is called, a new activation record is created to provide a frame of reference for the execution of the subprogram. Each activation record contains

1. the return address, that is, the address of the statement that will be executed when the call has been completed

2. the value of each value formal parameter (a copy of each actual value parameter is made)

3. the address of each variable formal parameter (two memory accesses are required to access the corresponding actual variable parameter)

4. the values of variables declared in the subprogram's block

5. the address of the value calculated, if the subprogram is a function.

Activation records make recursion possible because they hold information that might otherwise be destroyed if the subprogram called itself. When the execution of the current subprogram has been completed, a return is made to the address specified in the current activation record. If that is a subprogram address, the previous activation record is used as the frame of reference for that subprogram's execution.

EXERCISES

2.1 What is wrong with the following function for calculating factorials?

```
function Fact (N: integer): longint;
{ A wrong way to calculate factorials. }
begin
   if N = 1 then
      Fact := 1
   else
      Fact := Fact (N+1) div (N+1)
end; { Fact }
```

2.2 Develop an iterative version of the WriteBinary procedure (see **Decimal-to-Binary Conversion** earlier in this chapter).

*HINT Use a **while** loop to generate the bit values, an array to hold them, and a **for...downto** loop to write them out.*

2.3 Complete the recursion tree in Fig. 2.3.

2.4 Let f be a function that returns the number of moves required to move N disks from one pole to another in the Towers of Hanoi game. Calculate $f(1), f(2), f(3)$, and $f(4)$. Determine the general formula for $f(N)$. You may express it recursively.

2.5 (Warning: This will probably take you at least ten hours of work!) Develop an iterative version of the Move procedure developed for the Towers of Hanoi game.

HINT On odd-numbered moves, the smallest disk is moved clockwise (A ⟶ B ⟶ C) or counterclockwise (A ⟵ B ⟵ C),

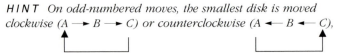

depending on whether the total number of disks is odd or even, respectively. On even-numbered moves, there is only one legal move possible for a non-smallest disk.

2.6   Complete the recursion tree in Fig. 2.6.

2.7   Develop a recursion tree to determine the output from the follow-ing ***incorrect*** version of the Permute procedure after an initial call to

```
Permute ('ABC', 1)
const
   N = 3;
type
   StringType = string [N];
procedure Permute (S: StringType;
                         K: integer);
{ Write out S for each permutation of S [K..N]. }
var
   I: integer;
begin
   if K = N then
      Writeln (S)
   else
      for I := K to N do
         begin
            Permute (S, K + 1);
            Swap (S [I], S [K])
         end { for }
end; { Permute }
```

2.8   Develop a recursion tree to determine the output from the follow-ing ***incorrect*** version of the Permute procedure after an initial call to

```
Permute ('ABC', 1)
const
   N = 3;
type
   StringType = string [N];
procedure Permute (S: StringType;
                         K: integer);
{ Write out S for each permutation of S [K..N]. }
var
   I: integer;
begin
   if K = N then
      Writeln (S)
   else
      for I := K to N - 1 do
```

```
        begin
          Swap (S [I], S [K + 1]);
          Permute (S, K + 1)
        end { for }
  end; { Permute }
```

2.9   Develop a program to write out all permutations of *N* items, where the value of *N* is read in.

HINT The procedure heading for the modified version of Permute should be

```
procedure Permute (A : ArrayType;
                        K,
                        N : integer);
```

The initial arrangement of items is provided by the first actual parameter in the original call to Permute. For example, if we wanted permutations of the first seven letters, we might declare

```
const
   MaxItems = 7;
type
   ItemType = 'A'..'G';
   ArrayType = array [1..MaxItems] of ItemType;
const
   A: ArrayType = ('A', 'B', 'C', 'D', 'E', 'F', 'G');
```

Then, if the value read in for *N* is 5, the call

```
Permute (A, 1, N)
```

will print out all permutations of '*ABCDE.*'
If, instead, we wanted permutations of the first ten positive integers, we could declare

```
const
   MaxItems = 10;
type
   ItemType = 1..MaxItems;
   ArrayType = array [1..MaxItems] of ItemType;
const
   A: ArrayType = (1, 2, 3, 4, 5, 6, 7, 8, 9, 10);
```

Then, if the value read in for *N* is 6, the call to

```
Permute (A, 1, N)
```

will print out all permutations of 1..6.
In all cases, the heading for the Swap procedure is

```
procedure Swap (var First,
                    Second: ItemType);
```

2.10 Try to develop an iterative version of the Permute procedure (see the **Generating Permutations** section of this chapter). Do not assume that N will be 4.

> *HINT In Chapter 6, we present a general method for replacing recursion with iteration. If you come up with a less mechanical way to obtain an iterative procedure after reading that section, please send a copy of your procedure to the author.*

2.11 Given two positive integers I and J, the greatest common divisor of I and J, written

$$GCD\ (I, J),$$

is the largest integer K such that

```
(I mod K = 0) and (J mod K = 0).
```

For example, GCD (35, 21) = 7 and GCD (8, 15) = 1. Develop a Pascal function to calculate GCD.

> *HINT According to Euclid's algorithm, the greatest common divisor of I and J is J if I **mod** J = 0. Otherwise, the greatest common divisor of I and J is the same as the greatest common divisor of J and (I **mod** J).*

2.12 A *palindrome* is a string that is the same from right to left as from left to right. For example, the following are palindromes:

ABADABA
RADAR
OTTO
MADAMIMADAM
EVE

For this exercise, we restrict each string to upper-case letters only. (You are asked to remove this restriction in the next exercise.) Develop a function to test for palindromes. The function heading should be

function Palindrome (S: **string**): boolean;

Palindrome returns True if S is a palindrome and returns False otherwise.

> *HINT A string of 0 or 1 characters is a palindrome. For I < J, S [I..J] is a palindrome if and only if S [I] is equal to S [J] and S [I+1..J−1] is a palindrome. Use this idea to develop an imbedded function*

```
Pal (S, I, J)
```

which tests to see if $S[I..J]$ is a palindrome. Then

```
Palindrome := Pal (S, 1, Length (S))
```

2.13 Extend the function developed in Exercise 2.12 so that, in testing to
see whether S is a palindrome, nonletters are ignored and no dis-
tinction is made between upper-case and lower-case letters. For example, the following are palindromes:

> Madam, I'm Adam.
> Able was I 'ere I saw Elba.
> A man. A plan. A canal. Panama!

2.14 What output is produced by the following program?

```
program Parameters;
var
   N: integer;
procedure Increment (var A,
                          B : integer);
begin
   A := A + 1;
   B := B + 1
end; { Increment }
begin
   N := 3;
   Increment (N, N);
   Write (N)
end. { Parameters }
```

*HINT What is stored in the activation record for a call to
Increment?*

2.15 **a.** Develop a function Power that returns the result of integer exponentiation. The heading is

```
function Power (I: integer;
                    N: word): longint;
{ This function calculates Iᴺ. Overflow is }
{ possible if the result is greater than the }
{ largest value in longint, namely, 2147483647. }
```

     b. If your function in part a is recursive, develop an iterative ver-
sion. If your function in part a is iterative, develop a recursive
version from the observation that for $N > 0$,

$$I^N = I * I^{N-1}$$

    c. Compare the recursive and iterative versions with the help of the unit Timer.

    d. For any positive integer I, we can calculate I^N as

$$\text{Round } (\text{Exp } (N * \text{Ln } (I)))$$

(See Appendix 1 for a mathematical justification of this formula.) Based on this formula, develop a version of the function Power. Compare it with your earlier versions. Incidentally, the machine language versions of Exp and Ln use loops, so this version of Power is implicitly iterative. In fact, as we will see in Chapter 6, even recursion is implemented with loops.

2.16 Give an example of a subprogram for which it cannot be determined until run time whether or not the subprogram is recursive. How can the compiler decide whether to generate code that creates an activation record each time the subprogram is called?

LABORATORY EXERCISE

2.1 Consider the following program:

```
program TestVarVal;
const
    Size = 500;
type
    ArrayType = array [1..Size] of longint;
var
    A: ArrayType;
    I: integer;
procedure Add (var A: ArrayType);
var
    I,
    J,
    K : integer;
begin
    for I := 1 to Size do
        for J := 1 to Size do
            for K := 1 to Size do
                A [I] := A [J] + A [K]
end; { Add }
begin
    for I := 1 to Size do
        A [I] := I;
    Add (A)
end. { TestVarVal }
```

If a value formal parameter replaces the variable formal parameter in the above procedure, will execution time be increased or decreased? Why? Use the Timer unit to test your hypothesis.

If the procedure call is replaced with in-line code, will this produce a minor or substantial decrease in execution time? That is, suppose the statement part of the main program is

```
begin
    for I := 1 to Size do
        A [I] := I;
    for I := 1 to Size do
        for J := 1 to Size do
            for K := 1 to Size do
                A [I] := A [J] + A [K]
end. { TestVarVal }
```

Introduction to Software Engineering

CHAPTER 3

The computers of today are much more powerful than those in use when you were born. In fact, some of the personal computers now available are faster and have more memory than most mainframe computers of 1970. Because of these advances in hardware, it is feasible for computers to solve very complex problems in a relatively short time. The development of the correspondingly large programs requires a systematic approach. Typically, developing a 10,000-line program is much more than twice as difficult as developing a 5,000-line program.

To enable programmers to manage this complexity, the discipline of *software engineering* has emerged. **Software engineering** is the application of principles, techniques, and tools to the production of programs. Most of the relevant concepts will be introduced in this chapter and then illustrated in subsequent chapters. You will be expected to utilize these concepts in several moderately difficult programming assignments.

The focus of this chapter is the *software development life cycle*, a sequence of four stages that comprise a programming project. Some of those stages will have several substages. To give you the big picture, here is a list of those stages in their chronological order:

Problem Analysis—to determine what the program is to do

Program Design—to develop the algorithm and data types to solve the problem

Program Implementation—to develop a validated program to solve the problem

Program Maintenance—for later modifications to the analysis, design, or implementation

Before studying each of these stages in detail, you should note that programming is an iterative process. While working on a later stage, you may find that you need to redo some or all of your work from earlier stages.

I. PROBLEM ANALYSIS

We assume we have been given a description of a problem. This description will probably be brief and may contain ambiguities. But we need to have a clear understanding of the problem before we can build a program to solve the problem. The goal in the problem analysis stage is to develop a clear understanding of *what* is to be done. We intentionally omit any indication of *how* the problem will be solved—for example, the algorithm or data types to be used. In so doing we are practicing the *Principle of Abstraction*:

Principle of Abstraction	When trying to solve a problem, separate what is to be done from how it will be done.

By separating what needs to be done from how it will be done, we avoid getting bogged down in details that should be addressed at later stages.

Most of the work in the problem analysis stage consists in providing *functional specifications*: detailed, unambiguous statements that describe what the program should do in terms of the input and output. The specifications should answer such questions as:

1. What is the format of the input? What are the types and ranges of input values?
2. What is to be the format of the output? What are the types and ranges of output values?
3. Will the program be conversational (that is, will the input be entered in response to the output), or will the input files be created before the program is run? If the program is to be conversational, what will signal the end of the input?

4. How will input errors be handled? (In other words, how much input ed-
    iting is to be performed?) One advantage of conversational programs is
    that when incorrect input is entered, an error message can be printed
    and the user can correct the error immediately.

For example, the following specifications may apply to a year that is to
be input:

> The year should be an integer between 1950 and 1995, inclusive.
> The year should be entered in response to the prompt "Please en-
> ter the year:".
>
> 1. If the value entered is not a four-digit integer, the error mes-
>   sage to be printed is "Error—the year entered is not a four-
>   digit integer."
> 2. If the value entered is a four-digit integer but is not in the
>   range 1950–1995, the error message to be printed is "Error—
>   the year entered is not in the range 1950–1995."
> 3. Each time an incorrect value is entered for the year, the corre-
>   sponding error message and the prompt should be printed.

Should the specifications disallow all input errors? From the point of
view of the developer of the program, the usual answer is "yes." If the program fails, either by terminating abnormally or by producing incorrect output, the programmer will be the prime suspect anyway. Programmers
prefer to construct programs that are *robust*—able to withstand the slings
and arrows of outrageous inputs.

But the final decision on input editing rests with the sponsor, the one
who is paying for the program. The Golden Rule of Programming is "The
one who has the gold makes the rules." In some cases, such as national defense and patient monitoring, the cost of an abnormal termination or incorrect output can be catastrophic. In a business environment, decisions
based on incorrect output can also have disastrous results. Often, however,
some kinds of input errors can safely be ignored. The sponsor may decide,
for example, that it would be too costly, in terms of both programmer time
and execution time, to check the names of each employee's dependents to
make sure those names consist of letters and blanks only.

In accordance with the specifications given, sample input values are
created and the corresponding output is produced (by hand). At this stage,
the sample inputs and sample outputs serve mainly to confirm our understanding of the problem and the input/output formats. Later, after the program has been written, they serve as test cases to increase our confidence
that the program performs according to the specifications. It is preferable
to generate these system tests before rather than after the program has

been written. Otherwise, the way the program is written may (unconsciously) bias how it is tested.

As a simple example, we might have the following system test for a program that calculates the mean of a list of test scores. The sample input is shown in boldface to distinguish the input from the output.

```
System Test:
This program calculates the mean of a list of test scores.
Each score must be an integer between 0 and 100, inclusive.
A value of -1 is used as the sentinel.
Please enter a test score: 80
Please enter a test score: 90
Please enter a test score: 700
    Error: The score must be an integer between 0 and 100,
    inclusive.
Please enter a test score: 70
Please enter a test score: -1
The mean is 80.0.
```

The person who develops the specifications and system tests is a *systems analyst*. A systems analyst has several responsibilities. First, the systems analyst must understand the needs of the users (those who will, ultimately, use the program). Second, the systems analyst and sponsor must agree on the extent of the program. Finally, the systems analyst must be able to describe to the programmers the exact problem to be solved.

All of this communication is greatly facilitated by documentation. Explicit documents such as the functional specifications tend to preclude later disagreements as to what was said and who agreed to what. Documentation provides the only visible evidence of the project other than the program's source code. We will note other kinds of documentation as we discuss later stages in the problem-solving process.

After the specifications and system tests have been provided, the next stage is to develop the algorithm and data types needed to solve the problem.

II. PROGRAM DESIGN

In this stage we design the program that is to solve the given problem. It may be tempting merely to sketch or even ignore the design so you can get on with the "real" work: the Turbo Pascal code. If you yield to this temptation, you will almost inevitably end up with a shoddy program. Imagine a contractor who told the architects just to sketch the blueprints so that the masonry workers, electricians, and plumbers could start working sooner! In Harlan Mills's famous dictum, "Resist the urge to code." The more careful you are in designing the program, the more likely that your program will be correct, efficient, and easy to understand.

There are two components in design: the algorithm and the associated data types. We will discuss data types first to emphasize their independence from the algorithm that uses them. This is in keeping with our object orientation. Meyer (1989) notes that in object-oriented design, we start by asking not what the program does, but what the program does it to!

The emphasis, then, is not so much on designing the program as a whole, but on developing modular program parts. These modules not only make the current program easier to understand and to maintain, but they can be used for other programs as well. A further advantage to this approach is that crucial design decisions need not be made at the outset; first we concentrate on what data types will be needed. And because each data type is isolated from the rest of the program, we can change our minds about a data type later without having to redo the rest of the program.

ABSTRACT DATA TYPES AND OBJECTS

In designing a program to solve the given problem, we start by thinking about what data types will be needed. As we will see in subsequent chapters, we can often get some idea about those data types from the *nouns* in the statement of the problem. For example, the case study problem from Chapter 5 is

> Create and maintain a class roster for a class that holds at most 35 students.

The nouns—class, roster, and students—are all used as data types.

In Chapter 1, we defined a data type as a type together with a collection of operators on that type. All of the types we considered then were predeclared in Turbo Pascal. But in the remaining chapters, the types we will study are not directly available in Turbo Pascal. To avoid any automatic association with Turbo Pascal types, from now on we will use the term *logical domain*, instead of *type*, to refer to the collection of values in a data type.

In order to suggest the interrelationship of a data type's logical domain and operators, we will represent each data type as an object, with methods for the operators.

Once we have chosen a data type, we focus on *using* the logical domain and methods in the data type rather than on how they will be designed or implemented. An ***abstract data type*** (ADT) is a data type that does not have any design or implementation information associated with it.

Abstract data types, unfettered by design constraints and language details, give us maximum flexibility. We concentrate on what the data type does, postponing until later how we will design or implement it. This is a special case of the Principle of Abstraction:

| **Principle of Data Abstraction** | An abstract data type should be used without regard for how its logical domain and methods are designed or implemented. |

For example, suppose that in trying to solve some problem, we decide that we need a data type for dates. Each value in the logical domain of DateType will be a date in some form. What are the *responsibilities* of DateType? That is, what is the data type expected to provide to its users? Perhaps initially the only responsibilities are

1. to determine if a given date is valid;

2. to return the next date after a given date;

3. given a date, to return the previous date;

4. to return the day of the week (such as Tuesday) on which a given date occurs.

These responsibilities are gradually refined into method descriptions. For example, we might have

Valid: A function method that returns the value True if the calling instance is legal; otherwise returns False. For example, any date whose day of month is greater than 31 is an illegal calling instance.

Next: A function method that returns the next date. The value returned is undefined if the calling instance represents an invalid date, such as February 30, 1992.

Previous: A function method that returns the previous date. The value returned is undefined if the calling instance represents an invalid date.

Day: A function method that returns the day of the week (Sunday, Monday, and so on) on which the date occurs. The value returned is undefined if the calling instance represents an invalid date.

Users of the ADT DateType will not care how the logical domain or the methods will be designed. There may be a choice of designs for the values in the logical domain. For example, we may choose any one of the following as the field(s) in the object:

Integers for the month, day and year fields—with values such as 02 for month, 28 for day, and 1993 for year;

An eight-digit integer—with values such as 02281993;

A string of eight characters—with values such as '02281993';

A string of ten characters—with values such as '02-28-1993'.

Similarly, there may be several different ways to design the methods, but such details would be of no help when we are trying to develop a program that uses that data type. Before we even try to design the statements to carry out a method, we should decide exactly what the method is supposed to assume and to accomplish. The formalizations of these concepts—preconditions and postconditions—are introduced later in this chapter.

Another early design decision involves what the method heading should look like. For our method headings, above each formal parameter there will be an arrow to indicate the direction of the flow of information. A downward arrow means that the formal parameter gets its initial value from the corresponding actual parameter, and an upward arrow means that the formal parameter's final value gets sent back to the actual parameter. An arrow over a method name indicates a function method.

For example, we might have

```
Search (Item, Found, Position).
```

Here the formal parameter Item will get its initial value from the corresponding actual parameter and will return its final value to that actual parameter. The formal parameters Found and Position will return their final values to their corresponding actual parameters.

A formal parameter with a downward arrow only is not necessarily implemented in Turbo Pascal as a value formal parameter. For example, a formal parameter with a downward arrow, and whose type is a file type, must be implemented in Turbo Pascal as a variable formal parameter.

Eventually, someone must design and implement the abstract data type. For example, in Chapters 4 through 11 we will design and implement several abstract data types for you to use in programming projects. By working with abstract data types you increase your program's flexibility. The program will not be affected by any decisions regarding the design or implementation of the data type. In particular, even if the design or implementation of the data type is drastically altered, this should not require any change to the program.

The ***design domain***—that is, the design component corresponding to the logical domain—consists of the fields in the object. For example, the design domain for DateType may consist of the following fields:

```
Month,
Day,
Year  : each of type integer;
```

The transition from a logical domain (a type) to a design domain (the fields that represent the type) is a critical step in the program design stage. The decision about which fields to include almost always determines how the methods will be designed (after all, the methods act on the fields).

Items in Abstract Data Types

In Chapters 4 through 11 we will introduce several abstract data types that have wide applicability. In each of those ADTs, each instance of the object type will contain a collection of items. Some of the methods will insert, delete, and retrieve an item into (or from) an instance. The items may be integers in one application that uses the ADT, strings in a second application, and records in a third.

We want to separate the use of these items within an ADT from their declaration in a particular application. We therefore introduce a general-purpose data type, called ItemType. In some applications ItemType may be a predeclared scalar type, such as integer or real, whose operators are also predeclared. In other applications ItemType may be an object: The only field is Value, whose type may vary from one application to the next. The methods will also vary, and may include SetValue, GetValue, and the relational methods LessThan, EqualTo, and GreaterThan.

The Maximum Size Issue

Assume that we have an ADT represented by an object, and each instance of that object contains a collection of items. Should there be a maximum number of items that can be inserted into an instance? In other words, how big can an instance get? If we put no limit on the maximum size of an instance, a correct program could generate an instance that overflows main memory—surely an error. It is better to require a maximum size—either one maximum for all instances or a maximum that depends on the particular application.

Who should provide this maximum value, the developer of the ADT or the user? If the developer determines the maximum, it will have to be "one size fits all" In other words, there would be one maximum size of an instance for all applications. This would be unrealistic. If the maximum size were too small for a given application, the program would fail. If the maximum size were too large, space would be wasted and, again, program failure would result if the application had too many instances of the ADT.

For these reasons, the user should provide the maximum size of an instance of the ADT. In that way, the maximum can vary depending on the application.

We have not yet addressed the issue of how to design the methods in an object. Moreover, we need to determine the overall structure of the design. These concerns lead us to the other major component in program design: the algorithm.

ALGORITHMS

An **algorithm** is a list of explicit statements that provides the solution to a given problem. We will not specify the format of those statements, but we stipulate that each statement be easily translatable into one or more statements in Turbo Pascal.

There are two commonly used approaches to developing an algorithm: top-down design and bottom-up design. We now investigate each of these approaches.

Top-Down Design

To develop an algorithm, we need to transform an initial statement that tells *what* is to be done into statements that describe *how* it will be done. One technique to bring about this transformation is **top-down design**, also known as *stepwise refinement*: The initial statement is refined into more explicit statements, and then each of those statements is refined into still more explicit statements. This process continues until the resulting list of statements constitutes an algorithm.

In a top-down design of an algorithm, we adopt the following conventions:

1. To heighten its visibility, the initial statement is underlined.
2. Every other statement that is to be refined further is enclosed in braces. This is to suggest that such statements are not part of the final algorithm and are not translated into the resulting program.
3. Blank lines and indenting are used to promote readability.

For a simple example, suppose we want to develop an algorithm to solve the following problem: Given the bowling scores in all games in a recent tournament, find the highest score. Each line of input consists of a bowling score, and the output is to be the highest score. The initial statement is

Find the highest score.

After some thought, we decide to refine this statement into three statements:

Find the highest score.
Initialize HighestScore to zero.
Make HighestScore the highest of all the input scores.
Write out HighestScore.

The "Initialize..." and "Write out..." statements can easily be translated into Turbo Pascal, so they are not further refined. After refining "Make HighestScore...," we have the following

Find the highest score.
Initialize HighestScore to zero.

{ Make HighestScore the highest of all the input scores. }
While not End of file do
    Make HighestScore the highest of all scores read in so
    far.

Write out Highest Score.

Since "While not End of file do" can be directly translated into Turbo Pascal, it is not refined. After refining "Make HighestScore the highest of all scores read in so far," we obtain

Find the highest score.
Initialize HighestScore to zero.

{ Make HighestScore the highest of all the input scores. }
While not End of file do

    { Make HighestScore the highest of all scores read in }
    { so far. }
    Read in a score.
    Update HighestScore, if necessary.

Write out HighestScore.

The Read and Update statements can be straightforwardly translated into Turbo Pascal, and so the development of the algorithm is complete.

The *intermediate-level* statements—the statements in braces—are not part of the algorithm, but they are important in several respects. First, because they are at a higher level than Pascal code, they ease the transition from *what* is to be done to *how* it will be done. Second, as we will see later in this chapter, they aid in proving the correctness of the algorithm. Finally, they can serve as comments in the resulting program.

Top-down design has been successfully employed for the last 30 years to develop a wide variety of algorithms. Its best results have occurred when two assumptions have been met:

1. The functional specifications were clearly stated and did not change during design or implementation.

2. The design of the algorithm was isolated from previous or future designs. That is, it was not intended that the components of previous algorithms would be used in the current algorithm, nor that the components of the current algorithm would be used in future algorithms.

Bottom-Up Design

The assumptions that facilitate a top-down design—frozen specifications and limited interest in reusability—are increasingly rare in today's software environment. Instead, programmers recognize the inevitability of change and the importance of reuse.

Rather than attempting to solve each problem from scratch, we seek to *build up* algorithms from what has already been developed. Of course, if nothing that will help is available, we need to work from the bottom up. **Bottom-up design** is the name given to this technique, although *build-up design* is probably more accurate.

In bottom-up design, the algorithm actually becomes secondary to the abstract data types, because these may be reused. With our object-oriented approach, most of our design efforts will be devoted to the development of the objects that represent those abstract data types. Specifically, we will focus on the design domains (that is, the fields) and subalgorithms (for the methods).

As an example of part of a bottom-up design, suppose we are designing the object for the ADT DateType introduced earlier, and we have selected the design domain with month, day, and year fields of type integer. How should we design the subalgorithms themselves? A top-down approach, with details left for other subalgorithms, is appropriate. For example, the design for the Next method may be as follows:

```
Next.
if (Month = 12) and (Day = 31) then
    Set Month and Day to 1, and increment Year
else
    if Day = LastDay (Month, Year) then
        Set Day to 1 and increment Month
    else
        Increment Day
```

The design of the function LastDay—the Year parameter is used in checking for a leap year—is not shown. This is an example of top-down design that does not start with a main algorithm. In fact, once we have designed the objects for solving the problem, the design of the main algorithm usually consists of nothing more than sending a couple of messages.

In order to use a subalgorithm, all we need to know is what the subalgorithm assumes and accomplishes, and the parameter list (including arrows) along with the type of each parameter. This kind of abstraction is usually referred to in terms of subprograms instead of subalgorithms:

Principle of Procedural Abstraction	A subprogram should be called without regard to how it is designed or implemented.

This principle complements the Principle of Data Abstraction by encouraging a modular approach to program design. Each method is designed as a subalgorithm. The user who sends the message that activates the method is blissfully unaware of how the method is designed or implemented.

Algorithm Validation

Before we code our algorithm or subalgorithm into Turbo Pascal, we should convince ourselves that it is both correct and efficient. We deal with correctness first because an incorrect algorithm is useless. Strictly speaking, a *correct* algorithm is one that performs the task that the sponsor intended. During design, it is difficult to fathom what the sponsor really wants, so we assume that the specifications incorporate the sponsor's wishes.

Algorithm validation refers to tools that attempt to establish the correctness of an algorithm, or more often, a subalgorithm. We present three such tools.

1. Testing

The most popular technique for increasing confidence in the correctness of an algorithm is to *test* the algorithm, that is, to trace its execution with a number of sample inputs. We start each test by selecting sample input values from the population of input values for the given problem. We then trace the execution of the algorithm and compare the given output with the output expected according to the problem's specifications.

For example, here is one test of the algorithm developed earlier to find the highest of a list of bowling scores.

Sample Input

135
209
185

Score	HighestScore
135	0
209	135
185	209

Sample Output

209

There are several drawbacks to this method of validating an algorithm. First, it is not feasible to test the algorithm with all possible sample inputs, and so we cannot infer correctness of an algorithm based on testing. As E. W. Dijkstra has put it, testing can reveal the presence of errors but not the absence of errors. Another difficulty is that tracing even one execution of a moderately long algorithm can take quite a bit of time. Finally, there is a danger that, in tracing an execution, we will be influenced by what the algorithm is *supposed* to do rather than what it actually does.

Because of these drawbacks, we will consider testing only for short (but nontrivial) subalgorithms, with sample values chosen for the formal parameters and input variables whose information is needed in the sub-algorithm. The problem of how to select sample inputs is discussed later in this chapter.

2. Algorithm Verification

Another way to increase confidence in the correctness of an algorithm is to *verify* the algorithm, that is, to prove that the algorithm is correct. The concept of algorithm verification is fairly recent in computer science, but it is increasingly recognized as an important tool for developing programs that are clear and error-free. One reason for this is that once you realize that you will be verifying your algorithms, you tend to impose a discipline on your designs so that your algorithms are simple and straightforward.

The fundamental concept in algorithm verification is the assertion. An **assertion** consists of one or more claims about a statement or group of statements. In particular, we can associate with each statement a pair of assertions:

a *precondition*, which refers to the state of the algorithm prior to the execution of the statement;

a *postcondition*, which refers to the state of the algorithm after the execution of the statement.

A *proof of correctness* of a statement S is an informal mathematical proof[1] that if the precondition of S is true and S is executed, then the execution

---

[1]"Informal proof" is not a contradiction in terms. Most proofs are informal—the level of formality depends on the intended audience. In fact, unless you have taken a course in mathematical logic, you have probably not even seen a formal proof.

of *S* eventually terminates and, when it does, the postcondition of *S* is also true.

For a simple example,

```
{ Precondition: N > 0 }
Ratio := NumberRight / N
{ Postcondition: Ratio contains the fraction of questions }
{                answered correctly to total questions.   }
```

Because our approach is informal, we omit from the precondition all irrelevant information (such as whether Ratio had been given a value earlier) and even some relevant information (such as that NumberRight is not undefined). Assertions can be cascaded, that is, the postcondition of one statement can be the precondition of the next statement:

```
{ Assertion: N > 0 }
Ratio := NumberRight / N
{ Assertion: Ratio contains the fraction of questions }
{              answered correctly to total questions.   }
Percent := Round (Ratio * 100)
```

Here, the second assertion is the postcondition of the first statement and the precondition of the second statement. Ultimately, a chain of assertions can prove that an entire algorithm is correct.

Proving the correctness of loop statements is often the most challenging part of verifying an algorithm. That is because there is such a disparity between a loop's static appearance and its dynamic execution. The execution may involve many iterations, that is, executions of the body of the loop.

In order to prove that a loop statement's postcondition is true no matter how many times the body of the loop is executed, we need to focus on those aspects of the loop's body that do not change with each iteration. This observation leads us to the concept of a ***loop invariant***—an assertion that is true before and after each iteration.

For example, let us develop a precondition, postcondition, and loop invariant for the **while** statement in the highest-bowling-score algorithm. The precondition is

```
HighestScore = 0; each score in the input is at least 0.
```

To determine the appropriate postcondition, note that the **while** statement was refined from the following intermediate-level statement:

```
Make HighestScore the highest of all the input scores.
```

If we rewrite this imperative statement as a declarative statement, we obtain an appropriate postcondition:

```
HighestScore contains the highest of all the input scores.
```

Similarly, the body of the loop was refined from the following intermediate-level statement:

`Make HighestScore the highest of all scores read in so far.`

If we rewrite this imperative statement as a declarative statement, we get the following assertion:

`HighestScore contains the highest of all scores read in so far.`

We can prove that this assertion is a loop invariant as follows:

1. The assertion is obviously true prior to the first iteration because at that point no scores have been read in.

2. Assume that, prior to some iteration, HighestScore contains the highest of all scores read in so far. During that iteration a score is read in and, if it is greater than HighestScore, HighestScore gets that score's value. Thus after the iteration, HighestScore still contains the highest of all scores read in so far. We have shown that if the assertion is true prior to an iteration it is also true after the iteration, and therefore true before the next iteration.

Combining this last sentence with the fact that the assertion is true prior to the first iteration, we conclude that the assertion is true before and after each iteration, that is, the loop assertion is a loop invariant.

What is significant here is that we developed the loop statement's precondition, postcondition, and loop invariant, in their imperative forms, even *before* we developed the body of the loop! In effect, we used the postcondition to determine the loop invariant, and then we used the loop invariant to design the loop body. The value of a loop invariant lies more in designing and clarifying the body of the loop than in proving the correctness of the **while** statement.

In general, to prove the correctness of a **while** statement, we assume that the precondition is true, and then

1. Prove that the execution of the **while** statement eventually terminates.

2. Prove that the loop assertion is a loop invariant.

3. Prove that, after the last iteration, the postcondition is true. This usually follows immediately from the truth of the loop invariant. In fact, the loop invariant can be viewed as a progress report on the loop statement's goal of achieving the postcondition.

Proving the correctness of **for** statements is complicated by the fact that the loop control variable changes value *between* iterations. So an assertion that refers to the loop control variable may be true after an iteration but false just before the next iteration. With **for** statements we seek, not a loop invariant, but a loop ***post-invariant***: an assertion that is true after each iteration. For example, suppose we want to add up Salary [1], Salary [2], ..., Salary [N]. The relevant statements and assertions are as follows:

```
Sum := 0

{ Precondition: N >= 0. Sum = 0 }
for I going from 1 to N do
```

$$\{ \text{Loop assertion: Sum} = \sum_{K=1}^{I} \text{Salary [K]} \}$$

```
    Sum := Sum + Salary [I]
```

$$\{ \text{Postcondition: Sum} = \sum_{I=1}^{N} \text{Salary [I]} \}$$

We define an empty sum to be zero.

In general, a correctness proof of a **for** statement proceeds as follows. We assume the precondition and then:

1. We prove that the execution of the **for** statement eventually terminates.

2. Next, we show that the loop assertion is a loop post-invariant.

3. Finally, we prove that after the execution of the **for** statement terminates, the postcondition is true. Typically, we show that the postcondition follows from the precondition if the body of the loop is not executed at all. Otherwise, after the last iteration, the postcondition follows from the loop post-invariant.

A loop post-invariant is also useful with a **repeat** statement because an assertion that is true after each iteration may be false or even undefined prior to the first iteration. This is a common situation in conversational programs.

A detailed proof that a loop assertion is a loop invariant or loop post-invariant often employs the Principle of Mathematical Induction (see Appendix 1). For loop invariants, the base case is implied by the precondition. For loop post-invariants, the base case is implied by the precondition and the action of the loop during the first iteration. For example, we will now outline the correctness proof of the **for** statement in the iterative version of the Fibonacci function. For convenience, we first re-list the Pascal version of the function:

```
function Fib (N: integer): longint;
{**********************************************************}
{                                                        }
{ Description: Calculate the Nth Fibonacci number        }
{ iteratively.                                           }
{                                                        }
{ Precondition (of the function's statement part): N >= 1. }
{ Postcondition : Result is the Nth Fibonacci number.    }
{                                                        }
{**********************************************************}
```

```
var
    Previous,
    Current,
    Temp      : longint;
    I         : integer;
begin
    if N = 2 then
        Fib := 1
    else
        begin
            Previous := 1;
            Current  := 1;

            { Precondition: N >= 3; Previous = 1; Current = 1 }
            for I := 3 to N do

                { Loop assertion: Current holds the Ith     }
                {                 Fibonacci number and Previous}
                {                 holds the (I-1)st Fibonacci }
                {                 number.                     }
                begin
                    Temp      := Current;
                    Current   := Current + Previous;
                    Previous  := Temp
                end; { for I := 3 to N }

            { Postcondition: Current holds Nth Fibonacci   }
            { number.                                       }
            Fib := Current
        end { if N > 2 }
end; { Fib }
```

To prove the correctness of the **for** statement, we start by assuming that its precondition is true, that is, we assume that $N \geq 3$, Previous = 1, and Current = 1. We have three claims to prove:

1. Claim: The loop statement does eventually terminate.

   Proof: Since the loop contains neither an inner loop nor a subprogram call, it is clear that the loop statement terminates after $N - 2$ iterations.

2. Claim: The loop assertion is a loop post-invariant.

   Proof: (See Example 4 in Appendix 1).

3. Claim: After the last iteration of the loop, the post-invariant implies the truth of the postcondition.

   Proof: By Claim 1, the loop will eventually terminate. By Claim 2, after the last iteration of the loop, $I = N$ and Current holds the Nth Fibonacci number. Thus, the postcondition is true.

This example, especially the proof of Claim 2, illustrates a dilemma with correctness proofs: A proof with sufficient detail is often harder to construct than the algorithm itself. A proof without detail is little more than hand waving. Furthermore, even a carefully constructed "proof" may contain errors.

Preconditions, postconditions, and invariants are important abstractions because they deal with the status of variables and what a statement is supposed to accomplish. In that respect they help us to design algorithms, as well as to prove their correctness. In subsequent chapters, we will restrict our correctness proofs to nontrivial loop statements and to recursive subalgorithm calls. The reason for this restriction is that those parts of an algorithm are the hardest to understand, and therefore the most likely to be incorrect.

3. Structured Walkthrough

Another way to increase your confidence in your algorithm is to have others examine your design. They can often uncover flaws that you have missed because, unlike you, they have not had the opportunity to develop an emotional attachment to the algorithm.

One evaluation technique that is widely used in industry is the "structured walkthrough." A structured walkthrough is performed by a team of three or four people. The team members each present their own design; the other members of the team provide constructive criticism of those designs. As a result of the walkthrough, either the current design is approved or a consensus is reached on changes that must be made.

Analysis of Algorithms

According to the Principle of Procedural Abstraction, a subprogram can be called without regard to how it is designed. But the efficiency of a subprogram depends to a great extent on how it is designed. How can efficiency be measured? Specifically, how can we estimate the execution-time and main-memory requirements of a program from an algorithm?

At the program design stage, any measure of the time and space requirements of the program will necessarily be crude because both of these depend on how the algorithm and abstract data types are implemented, as well as on the compiler and computer used. But the value of such estimates can be substantial. If, based on an analysis of the algorithm, we determine that the time or space requirements of the program will be unacceptable, we may decide to redesign the entire algorithm. In such a situation it would be a waste of programmer time and project money to code the original algorithm. If we decide merely to modify the original algorithm, we must take care to preserve correctness as we make those changes.

We take the number of statements executed in a trace of the algorithm as a measure of the execution-time requirements of the corresponding program. Similarly, we take the number of variables in a trace of the algorithm as a measure of the program's main memory requirements. Both of these measures will be represented as functions of the "size" of the problem. For example, the size of a sorting problem is the number of values to be sorted. Typically, a problem with N input records is said to be "of size N."

Given a fixed algorithm (or subalgorithm) for a problem of size N, let Time (N) represent the average (over all possible inputs) number of statements executed in a trace of the algorithm. Similarly, Space (N) represents the average number of variables referenced in a trace of the algorithm. In analyzing the space requirements of a subalgorithm, we will not count any formal parameter that has an upward or two-way arrow. In programming languages, those variables usually occupy the same space as the corresponding actual parameters.

Sometimes we will also be interested in the worst-case or best-case performance of the algorithm. To that end we define WorstTime (N) to be the maximum (over all possible inputs) number of statements executed in a trace of the algorithm. The functions WorstSpace, BestTime, and BestSpace are defined analogously.

We need not calculate these functions exactly, since they are only crude approximations of the time and space requirements of the corresponding program. Instead, we approximate those functions by means of "Big O" notation, which we define in the next paragraph. At the program design stage, this "approximation of an approximation" is quite satisfactory for giving us an idea of how fast or big the program will be.

Definition: Let g be a function with positive-integer arguments. We define $O(g)$, the "order of g," to be the set of functions f such that for some pair of positive constants c and N,

$$|f(n)| \leq c|g(n)| \quad \text{for all } n \geq N.$$

If f is in $O(g)$ we say that f is "of order g" or f is "$O(g)$".

The idea behind Big O notation is that if f is $O(g)$ then eventually f is bounded above by some constant times g, so we can use g as a crude estimate of f. By a standard abuse of notation, we often associate a function with the value it calculates. For example, let g be the function defined by

$$g(n) = n^3, \quad \text{for } n = 1, 2, \ldots$$

Instead of writing $O(g)$, we write $O(n^3)$.

Example 3.1 Let $f(n) = n * (n + 1) + 4$ for $n = 1, 2, \ldots$ Show that f is $O(n^2)$.

Proof: We need to find positive constants c and N such that $f(n) \leq c * n^2$ for all $n \geq N$. Since $n * (n + 1) + 4 = n^2 + n + 4$ for all positive integers n, we know that $f(n) \leq n^2 + n^2 + 4 * n^2$ whenever $n \geq 1$. And so, for $c = 6$ and $N = 1$, $|f(n)| \leq c * n^2$ for all $n \geq N$. Thus f is $O(n^2)$.

In general, if f is a polynomial of the form

$$a_k n^k + a_{k-1} n^{k-1} + \ldots + a_1 n + a_0$$

then we can establish that f is $O(n^k)$ by choosing $N = 1$, $c = |a_k| + |a_{k-1}| + \ldots + |a_1| + |a_0|$ and proceding as in Example 3.1.

The next example shows that we can ignore the base of a logarithm when determining the order of a function.

Example 3.2 Let a and b be positive constants. Show that if f is $O(\log_a n)$ then f is also $O(\log_b n)$.

Proof: Assume that f is $O(\log_a n)$. Therefore there are positive constants c and N such that for all $n \geq N$,

$$|f(n)| \leq c * \log_a n$$

We ignored the absolute value signs since logarithms are always nonnegative. By a fundamental property of logarithms (see Appendix 1),

$$\log_a n = (\log_a b) * (\log_b n) \text{ for any } n > 0.$$

Let

$$c_1 = c * \log_a b$$

Then for all $n \geq N$, we have

$$\begin{aligned} |f(n)| &\leq c * \log_a n \\ &= c * \log_a b * \log_b n \\ &= c_1 * \log_b n, \end{aligned}$$

and so f is $O(\log_b n)$.

One drawback to Big O notation is that it merely gives an upper bound for a function. For example, if f is $O(n^2)$, then f is also $O(n^2 + 5n + 2)$, $O(n^3)$ and $O(n^{10} + 3)$. Whenever possible, we choose the *smallest* element from the following hierarchy of orders:

$$O(1), O(\log n), O(n), O(n \log n), O(n^2), O(n^3), \ldots, O(2^n), \ldots, O(n^n).$$

For example, if $f(n) = n + 7$ for $n = 1, 2, \ldots$, we say that f is $O(n)$. Figure 3.1 shows some more examples of functions and where they fit in the order hierarchy.

Figure 3.1

Some sample functions in the order hierarchy.

Order	Sample Function
$O(1)$	$f(n) = 3$
$O(\log n)$	$f(n) = [n * \log_2(n + 1) + 2] / (n + 1)$
$O(n)$	$f(n) = 5 \log_2 n + n$
$O(n \log n)$	$f(n) = \log_2 n^n$ {see Property 7, Appendix 1}
$O(n^2)$	$f(n) = n * (n + 1)/2$

Another shortcoming of Big O notation is that it approximates the behavior of a function only for arbitrarily large arguments. For example, suppose that the number of statements executed in a trace of algorithm A_1 is given by the following function T_1 in terms of the number of input values n: for $n = 1, 2, \ldots$

$$T_1(n) = 6n\log_2(n + 1) + 15n + 25 \text{ statements executed.}$$

Similarly, for algorithm A_2, suppose that the corresponding function T_2 is given by

$$T_2(n) = n^2/3 - 7n \text{ statements executed.}$$

Then T_1 is $O(n \log n)$ and T_2 is $O(n^2)$, which might lead us to infer that T_1 is "smaller" than T_2. But $T_1(n)$ is *greater* than $T_2(n)$ for $n \leq 200$. In summary, Big O notation can be a helpful tool, but you must exercise caution when using it.

With most subalgorithms (and algorithms) for problems of size n, we can easily determine the smallest functions g_1 and g_2 in the order hierarchy such that Time is $O(g_1)$ and Space is $O(g_2)$. For example, the order of the function Time is affected only by loops and recursive calls.

Let S represent any sequence of statements whose execution includes neither a loop statement (for which the number of iterations depends on n) nor a recursive subalgorithm (for which the number of recursive calls depends on n). The following subalgorithm skeletons provide paradigms for determining the order of the Time function:

1. Time is $O(1)$:

   ```
   S
   ```

2. Time is $O(n)$:

   ```
   S
   for I going from 1 to n do
       S
   S
   ```

3. Time is $O(n^2)$

   a.
   ```
   for I going from 1 to n do
       for J going from 1 to n do
           S
   ```

   The number of times that S is executed is n^2.

   b.
   ```
   for I going from 1 to n do
       for J going from I { not always 1 } to n do
           S
   ```

The number of times that S is executed is

$$n + (n - 1) + (n - 2) + \ldots + 3 + 2 + 1 = \sum_{k=1}^{n} k$$

As shown in Example 1 of Appendix 1, the above sum is equal to $n(n + 1)/2$, which is $O(n^2)$.

4. Time is $O(\log n)$.

```
while n > 1 do
    n := n div 2
    S
```

Let $T(n)$ be the number of times that S is executed. $T(n)$ is equal to the number of times that n can be divided by 2 until $n = 1$. By Example 2 in Appendix 1, $T(n)$ is the largest integer $\leq \log_2 n$. Therefore T is $O(\log n)$ and so Time is also $O(\log n)$.

5. Time is $O(n \log n)$.

```
for I := 1 to n do
    m := n
    while m > 1 do
        m := m div 2
        S
```

The outer loop is executed $O(n)$ times. For each iteration of the outer loop, the inner loop is executed $O(\log n)$ times (see Example 4 above). Therefore, Time is $O(n \log n)$.

Each of the above results has a recursive counterpart. For example, let $P(n, \ldots)$ be the heading of a recursive subalgorithm whose Time we want to find the order of. Then Time is $O(n)$ if P has the form

```
S
if n > 0 then
    P(n-1, ...)
S
```

Similarly, Time is $O(\log n)$ if P has the form

```
S
if n > 1 then
    P(n div 2, ...)
S
```

Design Trade offs

In the previous section we saw how to analyze an algorithm with respect to its time and space requirements. Ideally, we will be able to develop algorithms that are both fast enough *and* small enough. But in the real world, we seldom attain the ideal. More likely, we will encounter one or more of the following obstacles during design:

1. The program's estimated execution time may be longer than that allowed by the *performance specifications,* which state the time and space upper-bounds for all or part of a program.

2. The program's estimated memory requirements may exceed the limit imposed by the performance specifications.

3. The design may require familiarity with a technique about which the designer is only vaguely familiar.

Often, a trade off must be made: A design that reduces one of the three obstacles may intensify the other two. For example, suppose you had to sort a list of up to 10,000 names. One straightforward way to accomplish this would be to read the names into consecutive locations and then sort them with a SelectionSort or other simple sort. Such a subalgorithm would be easy to design and code, but in your program you would need to declare an array big enough to hold 10,000 names, and so a considerable amount of space could be wasted. Furthermore, as we will see in Chapter 9, the execution time of a SelectionSort is much slower than for some other sort subprograms.

You might save space if the design used a linked list instead of an array, but then you would need to be familiar with linked lists (discussed in Chapter 5). And your program would still run slowly. Alternatively, you could design and code a "fast" sort such as Quicksort (discussed in Chapter 9). But what if you are not sure how to design Quicksort? Is it worth learning Quicksort for this one program?

There may be other factors that determine your course of action. If the sort is to be part of a production program—one that is run over and over again—it may well be worth the effort to learn Quicksort. For the sake of reusability, it might be best to develop an orderable-list ADT that incorporates the Quicksort method.

If the program is to be run once on a microcomputer with little memory, learning (or relearning) how to use linked lists might be appropriate. If the program has to be running by midnight, you will probably be grateful that you know how to design and implement *any* sort subalgorithm.

The point is that real-life programming involves making hard decisions. It is not nearly enough that you can design and write programs that run. Adapting to constraints such as those mentioned above will make you a better programmer by increasing your flexibility.

Before we leave the Program Design stage, it is worth emphasizing that all of the work done during this design stage has a documentable component: the description of the ADTs, the algorithm and subalgorithms (including assertions and Big O analysis), the proof of correctness, and the report on the walkthrough. In general, formal documentation at each stage tends to reduce ambiguity and focus responsibility.

III. PROGRAM IMPLEMENTATION

In this stage we code, validate, and analyze the Turbo Pascal program and units that implement the algorithm and abstract data types developed in the previous stage. Our twin goals in coding the design are modularity and clarity. Programs that are modular and clearly written will be easier to validate and to maintain.

The task of achieving program modularity is simplified if our design is modular, which in turn follows from the use of ADTs and from the top-down design of subalgorithms. We will try to achieve program clarity by consistently adopting a set of coding standards, each of which aims at making some feature of a program easy to understand.

Data Encapsulation and Information Hiding

As we implement our ADTs in Turbo Pascal, we will be careful to preserve the modularity we gained through data abstraction. There are two techniques, data encapsulation and information hiding, to help us separate the use of an ADT from its implementation details. The object and unit facilities of Turbo Pascal are fairly well suited to both techniques.

Data encapsulation refers to the isolation of an ADT's implementation from the rest of the program. We will encapsulate, as an object in a unit, the implementation of any ADT. Objects naturally encapsulate an ADT's type and operators. Units contribute to the encapsulation because, as separately compiled entities, they are isolated from the rest of the program.

According to the Principle of Data Abstraction, the users of a data type need not know how that data type is implemented. Modularity is further enhanced if users are prevented from accessing those implementation details. ***Information hiding*** means making the implementation details of an ADT inaccessible to users of that ADT. The purpose of information hiding is protection—of the *users* of the ADT, not of the implementors! The idea is that, with information hiding, programs that use an ADT cannot access its implementation details, and so those programs will be unaffected by any change in those implementation details.

Turbo Pascal supports information hiding in two different ways. First, any information found only in the implementation part of a unit is inaccessible to users of that unit. For example, suppose that in the implementation part of a unit we declare

```
var
    Answer: string [20];
```

Users of that unit can neither access nor modify the value of Answer.

Access to fields (and methods) in an object can also be restricted by making them private. For example, we can declare the ADT DateType as an object in a unit as follows:

```
unit DateUnit;
{ This unit implements the ADT DateType. }
interface
type
    DayOfWeekType = (Sunday, Monday, Tuesday, Wednesday,
                        Thursday, Friday, Saturday);
    DateType = object
        function Valid: boolean;
        procedure GetNext (var Date: DateType);
        procedure GetPrevious (var Date: DateType);
        function DayOfWeek: DayOfWeekType;
    private
        Month,
        Day,
        Year : integer
    end; { DateType }
implementation
    .
    .
    .
end. { DateUnit }
```

DateType's fields cannot be accessed/modified outside of this unit. Unfortunately, this restriction also applies to *descendants* of DateType. For example, if we create another unit, CalendarUnit, that implements CalendarType as a descendant of DateType, then DateType's Month, Day and Year fields cannot be accessed/modified in CalendarUnit.

All of the ADTs we develop in Chapters 5, 6, and 8 will be descendants that access and modify the fields in their ancestors. By enforcing information hiding through private fields, Turbo Pascal has imposed an inheritance tax on descendants! Other object-oriented languages such as C^{++} and Eiffel are superior to Turbo Pascal in this regard. In those languages, implementors of an ADT can allow descendants, but not mere users, to access/modify fields in the object that implements an ADT.

The Sandwich Effect

Assume, as will often be the case, that an ADT of items is implemented as an object in some unit. Specifically, assume the following:

1. the unit XManager implements the object XType;

2. each instance of XType consists of a collection of items;

3. the corresponding object ItemType is implemented in the unit ItemInX.

Then the applications programmer (or team) who develops a program that uses XManager will also be responsible for developing the unit ItemInX. In this way the object XType can be used, for example, in one program in which each item's value is an integer and in another program in which each item's value is a record with several fields. The overall structure is as follows:

```
program Sample;
uses
    ItemInX,
    XManager;
.
.
.
end. { Sample }
```

In a separate file would be:

```
unit XManager;
uses
    ItemInX;
.
.
.
end. { XManager }
```

In a third file, we would have:

```
unit ItemInX;
.
.
.
end. { ItemInX }
```

The unit XManager is "sandwiched" between the program Sample and the unit ItemInX.

Because of the sandwich effect, the unit ItemInX must be compiled before the unit XManager, which in turn must be compiled before the program Sample. After these three modules have been compiled, the machine-language version of the program Sample can be executed.

If a change is later made to the implementation part of the unit ItemInX, then the unit ItemInX must be recompiled. But neither XManager nor Sample need be recompiled because all they rely on is the interface part of ItemInX. However, XManager and Sample must be recompiled if a change is made to ItemInX's interface part. Finally, if a change is made to XManager's interface part, then XManager and Sample, but not ItemInX, must be recompiled.

Traversing an Instance of an Object

For most of the objects we will study, each instance will consist of a collection of items. A ***traversal*** of such an instance is an algorithm that accesses each item in the instance exactly once. The unit that declares the object type will, typically, have a Traverse method, as seen in the following:

```
unit XManager;
interface
uses
   ItemInX; { implements ItemType }
type
   ProcedureType = procedure (Item: ItemType);
   XType = object
      .
      .
      .
      procedure Traverse (Visit: ProcedureType)
   end; { XType }
implementation
   .
   .
   .
end. { XType }
```

ProcedureType is a ***procedural type*** identifier, and Visit is a formal parameter of type ProcedureType. In a call to Traverse, the actual parameter can be any procedure whose type is ProcedureType. In other words, the actual parameter must be a procedure whose only formal parameter is a value formal parameter of type ItemType.

   The unit ItemInX will include procedures that describe what is to be done during a traversal when an item is "visited." For example, suppose we want to write out each item in an instance. Then the interface part of Item-InX would include the heading for a procedure WriteOut that specifies how the item is to be written out:

```
procedure WriteOut (Item: ItemType);
```

Within the implementation part of the unit, the complete declaration of WriteOut is found:

```
procedure WriteOut (Item: ItemType);
{ Postcondition: The value of Item has been written out. }
begin
   Writeln (Item: 7: 2)
end; { WriteOut }
```

A user of the unit XManager would issue the message

```
X.Traverse (WriteOut)
```

to write out each item in the instance *X*.

Coding Conventions

A program serves two purposes: to be compiled and to be read. The compiler's only concern is that the program obey the syntax and semantics[2] of Turbo Pascal. As a document that may be read by you, your instructor (or supervisor), and many others, your program should be clearly written.

In order to promote overall program clarity, we will adopt a comprehensive set of coding conventions, each of which is intended to clarify some aspect of a program. We now present and motivate one of the conventions—the complete list is given in Appendix 2.

Comments

Well-placed, well-written comments can greatly improve the readability of a program. But some comments merely take up space:

```
var
      HighestScore: integer; { the highest score }
```

At the beginning of each program, unit, and subprogram, there should be comments to describe what the module does, the files accessed or modified, and any other information helpful to the reader. Each identifier should be described in a comment unless the comment would be redundant.

Within a statement part, comments to describe what a section of code does—not *how* it is done—should be taken from intermediate-level statements in the design. For example, loop invariants (or post-invariants) should be placed just before the body of the loop that they describe, as in the following:

```
for I := 3 to N do
{ Loop post-invariant: Current holds the Ith Fibonacci }
{                      number and Previous holds the     }
{                      (I-1)st Fibonacci number.         }
begin
   Temp    := Current;
   Current := Current + Previous;
   Previous := Temp
end; { for I := 3 to N }
```

---

[2]*Syntax* refers to the grammatical rules of a language. For example, each constant declaration must be followed by a semicolon. *Semantics* refers to the rules about the meaning of program constructs. For example, it is a semantic error for a program to try to divide by zero because this violates the meaning of the divide operator.

As the primary documentation for the implementation stage, comments should be written carefully and concisely. Commenting should not be viewed as an afterthought, undertaken after the program is working. For a large program, that could take months, and by then you might have forgotten exactly what your own code is supposed to accomplish!

Program Validation

The time-honored method for validating a program is by testing the program. In discussing algorithm testing, we noted three shortcomings:

1. Testing an algorithm can reveal the presence of errors, but not the absence of errors.
2. Applying even one test to a moderately long algorithm can take quite a bit of time.
3. There is a danger that our execution trace will be influenced by what the algorithm is supposed to do, rather than what it actually does.

For program testing, only the first drawback applies: No matter how many times we test a program, we cannot establish its correctness with 100% certainty. But with each successful test, our confidence in the program's correctness increases until, eventually, we are *virtually* certain that the program is correct.

Programmers tend to view their work favorably, even glowingly ("a masterpiece," "a thing of beauty and a joy forever," "the eighth wonder of the world,"...). As such, programmers are ill-suited to test their own programs, because the purpose of testing is to uncover errors in a program. Ideally, the person who constructs test data should hope that the program will fail the test. In a classroom setting, the instructor may appear to satisfy this criterion!

Selecting Test Data

Each test should help to establish that the program satisfies the given specifications. For a simple example, suppose the following specifications are included for a grade report problem:

1. The input should consist of a nonempty list of test scores, each an integer between 0 and 100, inclusive. The output should be the letter grade corresponding to the average score:

    A, if the average score is at least 90.0;
    B, if the average score is at least 80.0 but less than 90.0;
    C, if the average score is at least 70.0 but less than 80.0;
    D, if the average score is at least 60.0 but less than 70.0;
    F, if the average score is less than 60.0.

2. For input values less than 0 or greater than 100, the invalid input value should be printed along with the error message "Score out of range." Such values should be ignored in calculating the average score.

3. If no valid input is provided, the error message to be printed is "Error— no valid input was provided." In this case, no letter grade should be printed.

Special care should be taken to make sure that the program produces the correct grade for "boundary" averages such as 90.0 and 59.9. The program's handling of no input, single inputs, and invalid inputs should be thoroughly tested. Some appropriate tests are

Test 1
90   80   100   90

Test 2
79

Test 3
60   60   60   59   60

Test 4
90   80   101   90

Test 5
(no input)

Test 6
−1   85   930   101

Test 7
101   −100

What about the following test?

Test 8
85   9F   75

Assuming that the specifications did not indicate what was to be done if the input included a noninteger, the program may still be correct even if it crashes with a run-time error message such as "Invalid numeric format." A prudent programmer may design and implement the program to protect against such invalid inputs; however, as we noted earlier, the ultimate responsibility (and authority) lies with the sponsor.

Top-down and Bottom-up Testing

For small programs, it may be convenient to test the program as a whole. For medium-to-large programs, testing should take advantage of the program's modularity—the parts of a program should be tested (component testing) before the whole program is tested (system testing).

Top-down testing is appropriate when the program was designed in a top-down fashion. In top-down design, stepwise refinement is used, first to design the main algorithm, then to design the subalgorithms called by the main algorithm, and so on.

In *top-down testing*, a program's components are coded and tested in the order in which they were designed. The main program is coded and tested first. Once the main program has been validated through testing, the subprograms called by the main program are coded and tested in the order in which they are called. After a given subprogram is coded and tested, all of the subprograms called by that subprogram are coded and tested in the order in which they are called.

Because a main program may have several procedure statements, you may ask how we can test the main program or any of its subprograms before *all* of the subprograms have been coded. The answer lies in the use of *stubs*: dummy subprograms that perform trivial or minimal tasks.

For example, here is a typical stub:

```
procedure WritePostfixorError (Error    : ErrorType;
                                PostfixString: StringType);
{ Postcondition: If there was no error, PostfixString is   }
{                printed. Otherwise, the error message and }
{                its position on the infix line are        }
{                printed.                                   }
const
    WriteStub = 'Postfix or error printed';
begin
    Writeln (WriteStub)
end; { WritePostfixOrError }
```

Each stub is replaced by the actual subprogram code when that subprogram is itself tested.

The major drawback to top-down testing is that it is based on top-down design! In top-down design, crucial design decisions must be made at an early stage. If any of those decisions are flawed, the entire design may be worthless. It is a scant consolation that top-down testing allows us to uncover those flaws early in testing, because testing comes relatively late in the software development life cycle.

Our object-oriented approach is better served by another systematic testing regimen: bottom-up testing.

Bottom-up Testing

In *bottom-up testing*, a program's low-level units—those that are used by, but do not use, other units—are tested and then integrated with higher-level units, which are then tested and integrated with still higher-level units, and so on. Finally, the units are integrated with the program.

To apply bottom-up testing to a unit, we need a ***driver***: a main program whose sole purpose is to allow the unit to be tested. The following driver program illustrates bottom-up testing of a unit that implements an abstract data type. Rather than input the operator identifiers, the operators are encoded as integers. For ease of testing, the input is stored in a file. (For the most part, the details of testing each method have been omitted so you can focus on the overall idea.)

```pascal
program ListDriver;
{ This program tests the units that implement the }
{ ordered-list ADT.                                }
uses
    ItemInList,
    OList1Manager;
const
    MaxOpCode    = 9;
    InitializeOp = 1;
        .
        .
        .
    TraverseOp   = 9;
type
    OpCodeType = 1..MaxOpCode;
var
    Item  : ItemType;
    List  : ListType;
    OpCode: OpCodeType;
procedure ProcessOpCode (OpCode : OpCodeType;
                         var List: ListType);
{ Postcondition: The operation code just read in is }
{ processed.                                        }
{ Called by     : main program                      }
type
    HeadingType = array [OpCodeType] of string [20];
const
    Heading: HeadingType = ('Initialize', ... , 'Traverse');
var
    Item : ItemType;
    Found : boolean;
    Position: word;
    NewList : ListType;
begin
    case OpCode of
        InitializeOp: begin
                          Writeln (Heading [InitializeOp]);
                          List.Initialize;
```

```
                            end; { InitializeOp }

            .

            .

            .

        TraverseOp : begin
                       Writeln (Heading [TraverseOp]);
                       List.Traverse (WriteOut)
                   end; { TraverseOp }
      end { case }
   end; { ProcessOpCode }
   begin { the statement part of ListDriver }
      Assign (Input, 'InFile.dat');
      Assign (Output, 'OutFile.dat');
      Reset (Input);
      Rewrite (Output);
      repeat
         { Loop post-invariant: Each operation code read in   }
         {                      so far has been processed and }
         {                      the resulting list has been   }
         {                      printed.                       }
         Readln (OpCode);
         ProcessOpCode (OpCode, List);
         Writeln;
         List.Traverse (WriteOut);
         Writeln
      until Eof
end. { ListDriver }
```

Because most of our work in subsequent chapters involves the development of objects that implement ADTs, our testing mode will be bottom-up. Top-down testing would be inappropriate because objects have no "tops"!

System Testing

After component testing has been completed, we can test the program as a whole. Inputs for the first few tests are provided as part of the Problem Analysis stage. If the program passes those tests, we conduct additional tests until we are convinced that the program is correct, that is, that it meets the specifications.

---

[3]Grace Hopper, one of the pioneers of computer science, explained how the term came about. In the early 1950s, several programmers at Harvard University could not figure out what was wrong with the program they were working on. Eventually it was discovered that an insect had died inside the computer, and its remains had kept a relay from closing. Once the bug was removed, the program executed correctly.

Errors

If we view testing as an "attack" on the program, the goal of testing is to reveal the program's weaknesses, to show that errors exist. The process of detecting and removing those errors is called "correcting" the program. You may have heard the name "debugging"[3] in reference to this process. But as Dijkstra (1990) has noted, to refer to an error as a "bug" suggests that it is something that happened while the programmer wasn't looking.

As with most other activities, the more you practice error detection and removal, the better you will become at it. However, a programmer's worth depends much more on design skills than correcting skills. An hour of design is worth a day of code-correcting.

Program errors can be classified as follows:

1. *Compile-time errors*. A ***compile-time error*** is one that is detected by the compiler as it attempts to translate your Turbo Pascal program or unit into machine language. A compile-time error such as a missing semicolon or an undeclared identifier is usually easy to fix because of (sometimes in spite of) the associated error message.

2. *Run-time errors*. A ***run-time error*** is one that is detected during the execution of the machine language version of your program. If your program attempted to divide by zero or to access a component beyond the range of an array,[4] an error message would explain what went wrong and where. Run-time errors, like compile-time errors, are usually easy to correct.

3. *Hidden errors*. The true skill of de-erroring lies in the detection of ***hidden errors***: no error messages are given, but the output is incorrect. Some hidden errors result from simple carelessness, such as

```
for I := 1 to N do;
   begin
      ...
   end
```

The semicolon after **do** terminates the **for** statement, and so the body of the loop consists of an empty statement. Many hidden errors are caused by flaws in the program's design. These errors are called *logic errors*. For example, a conversational program might have the following:

```
Readln (Name, GPA);
while (Name <> NameSentinel) and (GPA <> GPASentinel) do
   begin
      .
      .
      .
```

---

[4]The "Range Check" option should be on when you are validating a program or unit.

```
        Readln (Name, GPA)
   end; { while }
```

The intent is to stop looping when both sentinels are reached. Unfortunately, the above loop will continue as long as the Name sentinel has not been read in and the GPA sentinel has not been read in: In other words, the loop will terminate as soon as *either* sentinel is read in! The problem is corrected by replacing **and** with **or** in the loop condition.

Finding logic errors requires detective work. Initially, the only clue is the incorrect output during testing.

The easiest way to find hidden errors in your program is to use the execution-trace facility within Turbo Pascal's Integrated Development Environment (IDE). This enables you to execute your program one line at a time; during execution, you can view the values of expresssions and even modify the values of variables. For complete details, consult the Turbo Pascal User's Guide.

Run-Time Analysis of Programs and Units

We often want to compare the run-time performance of several units that implement an object. To indicate how this might be accomplished, assume that the object type includes methods to initialize an instance and to insert an item into an instance. Also assume that the associated object type for items includes a SetValue method. The program TestTime from Chapter 1 is modified to include storing N (an input variable) random integers into the value fields of an array RandArray of items. An instance is initialized and the start time is calculated. The Insert method is then called N times, after which the finish time is calculated.

Assuming that the instance is declared with the identifier List, the necessary changes to TestTime are as follows:

```
begin
   Write (Prompt);
   Readln (N);
   RandSeed := Seed;
   for I := 1 to N do
      RandArray [I].SetValue (Random (MaxRand));
   List.Initialize;
   StartTime := Time;
   for I := 1 to N do
      List.Insert (RandArray [I]);
   FinishTime := Time;
   .
   .
   .
end. { TestTime }
```

Time testing of subprograms is subject to the same criticism that applies to validation testing: We cannot attain 100% certainty (that one subprogram is faster than another) no matter how many tests are conducted. However, in time testing, statistical techniques allow programmers to measure their confidence objectively. For example, one might say "For sorting 2000 random items, there is at least a 99% probability that procedure P_1 is faster than procedure P_2."

Run-time analysis is especially worthwhile for methods that have wide applicability. Included among these are sorting methods, searching methods, and methods that implement time-critical operators in an abstract data type.

IV. PROGRAM MAINTENANCE

After the Program Implementation stage has been completed, the program is ready for use. Some programs, called "production" programs, are run periodically for several years. As time goes by, it is almost inevitable that such a program will undergo some alterations. **Program maintenance** refers to corrections, enhancements, and other modifications to the specifications, design, and program.

Most program maintenance is directed toward enhancements. Whatever the cause, program maintenance is by no means a minor activity. At many companies, more than 50% of programmer time, on average, is spent on program maintenance. This underscores the need for documentation during all stages of the software development life cycle. Without documentation, maintaining even your own programs is a frustrating and time-consuming task.

SHOULD WE LEARN TO LIVE WITH ERRORS?

As we noted at the start of this chapter, the trend in recent years has been toward increasingly powerful software. (One recent advertisement defined a *large* program as one "with more than one million lines of code.") But there is a continuing shortage of qualified systems analysts and programmers, and management's view of projects has been traditionally characterized by impatience.

As a result, errors are now considered an inevitable feature of "completed" programs. As you might expect, the cost of fixing an error depends on the point at which it is found in the software development life cycle. For example, an error discovered during the maintenance stage is about 100 times more costly to fix than an error detected during the problem-analysis stage (see Boehm, 1981).

What can be done to remedy this unfortunate situation? First—and this is a major change—management must take a long-term view of software. The objects being developed for the current project can be reused forever, so the extra time spent on perfecting those objects is really an investment in the future.

Furthermore, every member of the software team must be obsessed with quality. Systems analysts must work harder to specify exactly what is to be done. Designers and programmers need to intensify their validation efforts. The overall goal should be to create an environment hostile to errors, so that some day software warranties will be as common as hardware warranties.

SUMMARY

This chapter introduced the basic concepts of ***software engineering***: the application of principles, techniques, and tools to the production of programs. The chronology of program production—the software development life cycle—consists of four stages. Each stage has a documentable component, and the entire process is usually iterative, not linear.

In the *Problem Analysis* stage, detailed specifications and systems tests are developed.

During the *Program Design* stage, abstract data types are created and refined into objects. Bottom-up design is used primarily, but the method subalgorithms are designed from the top down. There are substages for the validation and analysis of the objects' methods.

The objects are implemented in a programming language in the *Program Implementation* stage, which also has substages for validation and analysis. The validation of program objects is by bottom-up testing, with drivers.

After the program has been validated, alterations to the analysis, design, and implementation can be made during the *Program Maintenance* stage.

EXERCISES

3.1   Make up your own functional specifications and system tests for each of the following problems:

a.   Given the monthly sales at Old Shucker's Crab House, determine which months had above-average sales.

b.   Given the hours worked and pay rate for a list of employees, determine the gross pay and net pay for each employee.

c.   Given a text file, replace each four-letter word in the file with four asterisks.

3.2   **a.** Develop an abstract data type for checking accounts. Include the logical domain and, for each method, the method heading, precondition, and postcondition.

  b. For the logical design in part a, develop at least two design domains.

3.3   For each loop statement in the following algorithms, develop an appropriate precondition, postcondition, and loop invariant (or loop post-invariant):

a. `{ Make Position the smallest integer in 1..N }`
```
{ such that A [Position] = Item:              }
Position := 1
while A [Position] <> Item do
    Add 1 to Position
```

b. `{ Make A [1..N] Sorted }`
```
for I := 1 to N-1 do

    { Make A [1..I] sorted and <= A [I+1..N]: }

    { Find the position of the smallest of A [I..N]:}
    Position := I
    for J := I+1 to N do

        { Find the position of smallest of A [I..J]: }
        if A [J] < A [Position] then
            Position := J
    Swap A [I] with A [Position]
```

HINT Convert the imperative statements into declarative statements.

3.4   For the While statement in Exercise 3.3.a:

  a. Prove its correctness (you need not use the Principle of Mathematical Induction).

  b. Calculate Time (N).

HINT Assume that each of the N possible final values for Position is equally likely.

  c. Find the smallest function g in the order hierarchy such that Time is $O(g)$.

3.5   Prove the correctness of the inner For statement in Exercise 3.3.b.; then prove the correctness of the outer For statement. You need not use the Principle of Mathematical Induction for either proof.

3.6 **a.** For the inner For statement in Exercise 3.3.b, when $I = 1$, J takes on values from 2 to N; thus there are $N - 1$ iterations of the inner For loop when $I = 1$. How many iterations are there when $I = 2$? When $I = 3$?

      b. Determine, as a function of N, the total number of iterations of the inner for loop as I takes on values from 1 to $N - 1$.

      c. Find the smallest function g in the order hierarchy such that Time (N)—for the outer For statement—is O(g).

3.7 For each of the following functions f, where $n = 1, 2, 3, \ldots$, find the smallest function g in the order hierarchy such that f is O (g):

      a. $f(n) = (2 + n) * (3 + \log(n))$
      b. $f(n) = 11 * \log(n) + n/2 - 3452$
      c. $f(n) = 1 + 2 + 3 + \ldots + n$
      d. $f(n) = n * (3 + n) - 7 * n$
      e. $f(n) = 7 * n + (n - 1) * \log(n - 4)$
      f. $f(n) = \log (n^2) + n$
      g. $f(n) = \dfrac{(n + 1) * \log(n + 1) - (n + 1) + 1}{n}$
      h. $f(n) = n + \frac{1}{2}n + \frac{1}{4}n + \frac{1}{8}n + \frac{1}{16}n + \frac{1}{32}n + \ldots$

3.8 Design the LastDay (Month, Year) subalgorithm referred to earlier in this chapter.

LastDay (Month, Year).

Postcondition: The last day of the Month in the Year is returned.

> *HINT A leap year is one in which February has 29 days. This happens, on average, slightly less than once every four years because the time it takes the earth to revolve around the sun is slightly less than 365.25 days. Specifically, Year is a leap year if Year is divisible by 4 and either Year is not divisible by 100 or Year is divisible by 400. For example, February had 29 days in 1996 and 2000, but only 28 days in 1998 and 2100.*

3.9 **a.** Develop tests for the subalgorithm LastDay (Month, Year) in Exercise 3.8.

      b. Convert LastDay (Month, Year) into a subprogram and develop a driver program to validate that subprogram.

3.10 (This exercise requires familiarity with the Principle of Mathematical Induction). Prove the correctness of the Move statement in the Towers of Hanoi program in Chapter 2.

Precondition: $N > 0$.

Postcondition: N disks have been moved from pole Origin to pole Destination.

The List Data Type

CHAPTER 4

INTRODUCTION

In this chapter we continue our study of abstract data types by introducing the List ADT. After defining, designing, and implementing the List ADT, we present an application of lists: high-precision arithmetic. In the course of developing this application, we improve on one of the designs of the List ADT.

LISTS

In everyday life we construct lists to impose order on reality: grocery lists, sign up sheets, telephone directories, class rosters, TV schedules, and so on. For this reason, problems are often stated in terms of lists:

Given a list of test scores, sort them into increasing order.

Print out a list of all club members whose dues are overdue.

A list has a fairly simple structure, but most programming languages do not have a predefined list type (the language LISP—an acronym for *LISt Processing*—is an exception).

Using the concept of a finite sequence from Appendix 1, we can define what a *list* is:

A list *is a finite sequence of items from the same data type.*

With each of the $N \geq 0$ items in the list, we associate a unique positive integer in $1..N$ called the *position* of the item. For example,

oranges, bananas, pears

is a list of fruits.[1] The item in position 1 is "oranges," the item in position 2 is "bananas," and the item in position 3 is "pears." The commas are not part of the list—they serve merely to separate the items. Duplicate items are allowed:

oranges, bananas, pears, bananas

is a list with "bananas" in positions 2 and 4.

Every list has an ordering in the limited sense that there is an item in position 1, an item in position 2, and so on. But it is more appropriate to say that a list is **ordered** if

1. The item data type includes relational operators for "less than," "equal to," and "greater than."
2. For each value of I between 1 and $N - 1$, the item in position I is less than or equal to the item in position $I + 1$. (The "equal to" allows for duplicate items.)

For example,

ardent, enthusiastic, fervent, fervid, zealous

is an ordered list of five alphabetically-ordered words.

A list is **orderable** if it satisfies property 1 in the definition of *ordered lsit*. The chief use for orderable lists is that they can be sorted into ordered lists. Orderable lists form the basis for all of the sorting methods in Chapter 9.

Chapter 5 will be devoted to ordered lists and orderable lists. Chapter 6 will focus on two other specializations of lists, namely, stacks and queues. In a stack, deletions and insertions can be made only in position 1; in a queue, deletions can be made only in position 1 and insertions can be made only at the end (last position) of the list. This gives us the hierarchy of list data types shown in Fig. 4.1.

---

[1] Ordinarily, we specify only the values from the item data type and ignore the operators unless they are relevant to the discussion.

Figure 4.1

A hierarchy of list
data types, with
chapter references.

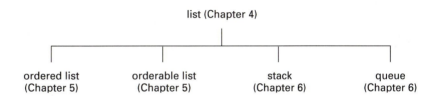

The significance of the hierarchy is this: Our work in Chapters 5 and 6 will be greatly simplified because the designs of those data types will inherit many of the method designs from the List data type.

Defining, Designing, and Implementing an Abstract Data Type

We now introduce a pattern that will be repeated over and over again in subsequent chapters. For each abstract data type we want to study, we start by deciding on the responsibilities of the data type to its users. Specifically, what operations should a user be allowed to perform on any instance of the data type? The data type's responsibilities will be similar for all the data types we will investigate: to make an instance empty, to see if the instance is empty, to insert an item into the instance, and so on.

After we have settled on the responsibilities of the abstract data type, we define the data type by giving its logical domain and method interfaces. Determining the logical domain will be easy: For the abstract data type X, the logical domain is the collection of all Xs. For example, in the ADT List, the logical domain is the collection of all lists; in the ADT Graph, the logical domain is the collection of all graphs. Each method interface (heading, precondition, and postcondition) is refined from one of the responsibilities.

We then present one or more possible design domains, that is, the fields we use to represent each value in the data type. For each design domain, we develop subalgorithms for the methods, along with the validation and analysis of those subalgorithms. Finally, we implement each design in Turbo Pascal, including run-time validation and analysis. The first abstract data type we study, of course, is the List data type.

Responsibilities of the List Data Type

The first step in developing the ADT List is to determine its responsibilities to users. A user of the List ADT should be able to perform operations on the list as a whole:

To create an empty list;

To see if the list is empty;

To obtain the number of items in the list;

To copy the list to another list;

To traverse the list.

Other responsibilities involve individual items in a list:

To retrieve an item, given its position in the list;

To search the list for an item;

To insert an item into a given position;

To delete the item at a given position.

DEFINITION OF THE LIST DATA TYPE

As with any other abstract data type, the List ADT consists of a collection of values (the logical domain) and a collection of methods. In the List ADT, each value is a list (as defined above), and so the logical domain is simply the collection of all lists.

By refining the responsibilities discussed in the previous section, we obtain the method interfaces. Each method interface consists of the method heading, the precondition of a call to the method (unless the precondition is simply True), and the postcondition. In stating the precondition and postcondition of a method, "the list" refers to the instance that called the method.

The collection of methods described in the next section is sufficient for most applications. If some application requires more, we can derive new operators from the given methods—see Exercise 4.8, for example. We say "derive new operators" rather than "derive new methods" for the sake of data abstraction. The design of a method can access/modify the fields in the object, and so any new method designs would be tied to a specific design domain.

We assume that a user of the List ADT will provide:

1. A value for MaxListSize, the maximum list size for the application. The user of the List ADT is required to supply this information, but the developer of the List ADT is *not* required to use MaxListSize. Some designs will use MaxListSize and some will not.

2. An ItemType that either is an object type with an EqualTo method for comparing items, or is a scalar type (so items can be compared with "=").

The user may also supply any number of *visit* subalgorithms that describe what to do with an item during a list traversal.

Methods in the List Data Type

There are nine methods in the List ADT:

1. `Initialize.`

   Postcondition: The list is empty, that is, it does not contain any items.

   Example: Suppose that Lines is an instance of a list. Then sending the message

   `Lines.Initialize`

   makes Lines an empty list.

   Note: An implicit precondition of every other method is that the instance calling the method has already been given a value. An instance can get an initial value in two ways: as the calling instance in Initialize, and as the actual parameter in a call to CopyTo (method number 9).

2. `IsEmpty.`

   Postcondition: True is returned if the list is empty. Otherwise, False is returned.

   Example: Suppose that GroceryList is an instance of a list. If GroceryList consists of the items "oranges" and "tofu," then the message

   `GroceryList.IsEmpty`

   returns the value False.

3. `Size.`

   Postcondition: The number of items in the list has been returned.

   Example: Suppose that GroceryList is an instance of a list. If GroceryList consists of the items "oranges", "tofu," "bread," and "tofu," then the message

   `GroceryList.Size`

   returns the value 4.

   Note a: Strictly speaking, we do not need an IsEmpty method, since we have a Size method—IsEmpty is logically equivalent to (Size = 0). But having an IsEmpty method suggests that there may be a more efficient way to determine if a list is empty than by counting its items.

   Note b: We define a Size method rather than an IsFull method because there may be situations where the actual size of the list is re-

quired. For example, if the size is greater than 200, we may
want to print the items in a single-space rather than double-
space format.

4. **Retrieve (Item, Position).**

    Precondition: $1 \leq$ Position $\leq$ the number of items in the list.

    Postcondition: The item at position Position has been copied into Item.

    Example: Suppose that Petition is an instance of a list. If Petition con-
    sists of the sequence of names Gabe, Tseliso, Ken, and Madoka,
    then sending the message

    `Petition.Retrieve (Name, 4)`

    would give Name the value 'Madoka'.

    Note: The postcondition does not state what might happen if the value
    of Position is less than 1 or greater than the number of items in
    the list. It is the responsibility of the user of the List ADT to en-
    sure that the precondition is true before the method is called.

5. **Search (Item, Found, Position).**

    Postcondition: If there is an item in the list that is EqualTo Item, a copy
    of that item has been stored in Item, Found has been set to
    True, and Position contains the position of that item. Otherwise,
    Item is unchanged and Found has been set to False.

    Example: Suppose that Activity is an instance of a list consisting of the
    following sequence of items:

    concert, play, hockey game, opera

    If Choice contains the value 'play,' then after the message

    `Activity.Search (Choice, Found, Position)`

    Choice will contain the value 'play,' Found will be True, and Po-
    sition will contain the value 2.

    Note: The reason that Item is an output parameter (as well as an input
    parameter) can be seen in the following example. Suppose that
    Club is an instance of a list consisting of members. Each member
    is itself an instance of an object with Name and Address fields,
    and two members are EqualTo each other if they have the same

name. If you knew the name of a member and you wanted the address, you would send the message

`Club.Search (Member, Found, Position)`

After the search (assuming it is successful), Member.Address would contain the address you were looking for.

6. `Insert (Item, Position).`

Precondition: $1 \leq$ Position $\leq 1 +$ the number of items in the list $\leq$ MaxListSize.

Postcondition: A copy of Item is in position Position in the list. For any item x and any position p, if x was in position p just before this call, x is still in position p if $p <$ Position; otherwise x is now in position $p + 1$.

Example: Suppose that Fruits is an instance of a list consisting of the following sequence of items:

oranges, bananas, pears

If the message is

`Fruits.Insert (apples, 3)`

Then after the message is sent, the list will be

oranges, bananas, apples, pears

7. `Delete (Position).`

Precondition: $1 \leq$ Position $\leq$ the number of items in the list.

Postcondition: The item that was in position Position just before this call has been deleted from the list. For any other item x and any position p, if x was in position p just before this call, x is still in position p if $p <$ Position; otherwise, x is in position $p - 1$.

Example: Suppose that GoodWords is an instance consisting of the following sequence of items:

generous, benevolent, greedy, altruistic, eleemosynary

If the message is

`GoodWords.Delete (3)`

Then after the message is sent, the list will be

generous, benevolent, altruistic, eleemosynary

↑

8. `CopyTo (NewList).`

    Postcondition: NewList has been given a distinct copy of the list.

    Example: Suppose that Petition is an instance of a list consisting of the
    following sequence of items:

    Jon, Jean, Sarah, Madoka, Bob

    Then the message

    `Petition.CopyTo (NewPetition)`

    would make NewPetition a list consisting of the following se-
    quence of items:

    Jon, Jean, Sarah, Madoka, Bob

    Note: The phrase "distinct copy" in the postcondition implies that sub-
    sequent changes to NewList will not affect the list, and vice
    versa. For this reason, the CopyTo method should be considered
    the *assignment statement* for lists.

↓

9. `Traverse (Visit).`

    Postcondition: Each item in the list has been accessed according to its
    position: The item in position 1 was accessed first, then the item
    in postion 2, and so on. The action taken during each access is
    prescribed by the subalgorithm Visit (supplied by the user),
    whose only formal parameter is Item.

    Example: Suppose that Temperatures is an instance of a list consisting
    of the following sequence of items:

    85, −32, 71, 0, 51, −3

    If the PrintNegative subalgorithm prints out an item if it is less
    than 0, then the message

    `Temperatures.Traverse (PrintNegative)`

    would produce the following output

    −32
    −3

DESIGNS OF THE LIST DATA TYPE

Now that we have fixed on the methods in the ADT List, we need to decide on the design domain, that is, on the fields to represent a list. Based on that decision, we then design the object's methods.

In the next two sections we present two fundamentally different design domains for the List ADT. In the **linked** design domain, with each item in the list we associate the address of the next item in the list; the only field in the object contains the address of the first item.

In the **contiguous** design domain, the items are stored consecutively, according to their positions; that is, the second item is stored immediately after the first, the third item is stored immediately after the second, and so on. In this design domain, there are two fields in the object: an array to hold the items and an integer to hold the size of the list.

As we will see in this and subsequent chapters, once we have settled on a design domain, the method designs will often follow easily. For this reason, the determination of the design domain is critical in the design of an ADT.

The term "design," rather than "implementation," is appropriate here because the subalgorithms are written in pseudocode rather than Turbo Pascal. Furthermore, as we will see later in this chapter, the linked design can be implemented in at least two different ways: dynamically (with pointers) or statically (with array indexes). By abstracting the design from the implementation, we preserve flexibility and avoid premature involvement with the technicalities of Turbo Pascal.

Linked Design of the List Data Type

For this design, the items in the list are stored in records called *nodes*, where each node is referenced by its address. Each node has an Item field and a Next field. The Next field contains the address of the node with the next item in the list. The design domain consists of a single field, named Head, which contains either a null address or the address of the node with the first item.

We use the term "linked" to describe this representation because each item is linked by an address to the next item in the list. A list with a linked representation is called a "linked list." For example, an instance *L* of a linked list of integers might have addresses and items arranged as follows:

L. Head

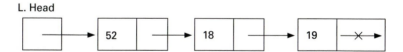

A null address is represented by an arrow with an 'X' through it. The variable at the base of an arrow contains the address of the node at the head of the arrow. We say that the variable "points to" the node. For example, L.Head points to a node. The two fields in that node may be referred to as "L.Head's node's Item" and "L.Head's node's Next." For the sake of simplicity, we shorten these references to "L.Head's Item" and "L.Head's Next."

The notation "L.Head's Item" is an abstraction for an address reference. Don't assume that Head will be a pointer and that L.Head's Item is just an alias for L.Head^.Item. We will get to the implementation details in due time, and there is another implementation of addresses (namely, array indexes) that is, in some respects, better than a pointer implementation.

The designs of subalgorithms for the nine methods now follow without much difficulty.

1. **`Initialize.`**

    A. Subalgorithm

    `Head := null`

    B. Verification

    We do not verify a subalgorithm unless it is recursive or contains a nontrivial loop statement.

    C. Analysis

    The Time (that is, the average number of statements executed in a trace of the subalgorithm) and Space (that is, memory locations needed) are both O(1).

2. **`IsEmpty.`**

    A. Subalgorithm

    `Return the value of (Head = null)`

    B. Verification

    No verification is needed.

    C. Analysis

    Time and Space are O(1).

3. **`Size.`**

    A. Subalgorithm

    To count the number of items in the list, we start at the head of the list with Count equal to zero. To avoid destroying the list as we advance through it, we use TempHead instead of Head. During each iteration, we want Count to be equal to the number of items we have accessed so far. That is, Count should equal the number of items in the whole list minus the number of items in the sublist starting at TempHead. So in the loop, we add one to Count and advance TempHead.

The complete subalgorithm is

$\uparrow$

<u>Size.</u>

```
Count      := 0
TempHead := Head
while TempHead <> null do
    { Make Count equal to the size of the list minus }
    { the size of the sublist starting at TempHead.   }
    Add 1 to Count
    TempHead := TempHead's Next
Return the value of Count
```

B. Verification

We prove the correctness of the While statement. Although it may well be argued that this statement is trivial and thus not deserving of verification, this is a good opportunity to see a simple example of a correctness proof.

Precondition: Count = 0; TempHead = Head.

Postcondition: Count = size of list.

Loop assertion: Count = size of list − size of sublist starting at TempHead.

We start the proof of correctness by assuming that the precondition is true (this is obvious, anyway).

Claim 1: The execution of the While statement eventually terminates.
Proof: Let the nonnegative integer N represent the number of items in the list. Then the execution of the While statement will terminate in exactly N iterations.

Claim 2: The loop assertion is a loop invariant.
Proof : Prior to the first iteration, TempHead points to the first item in the list, and so the size of the list is the size of the list starting at TempHead. Since Count = 0, the loop assertion is true prior to the

first iteration. Assume that the assertion is true prior to some iteration; then, during that iteration, Count is incremented and the size of the sublist starting at TempHead is decremented. Thus, the assertion is true after that iteration, and is therefore true prior to the next iteration.

We conclude that the loop assertion is true before and after each iteration; that is, the loop assertion is a loop invariant.

Claim 3: After the last iteration, the postcondition is true.
Proof: After the last iteration, TempHead is null, and so the size of the sublist starting at TempHead is 0. Therefore, according to the loop invariant, Count equals the size of the list.

C.   Analysis

The body of the loop is executed exactly N times, and so Time (N) is O(N). Space (N) is O(1).

4.   <u>Retrieve (Item, Position)</u>.

A.   Subalgorithm

Because we are starting at the first item, we loop Position − 1 times:

```
TempHead := Head
for I := 1 to Position - 1 do
    TempHead := TempHead's Next
Item := TempHead's Item
```

B.   Verification

No verification is needed.

C.   Analysis

Space is O(1) because the only additional variables needed for the execution of this algorithm are Position, TempHead, and I. The variable Position can take on any value between 1 and N, and we assume that each of these occurrences is equally likely. The For loop will be executed Position − 1 times, and so it will be executed $0, 1, 2, \ldots,$ or $N − 1$ times. The average of these values is

$$\frac{0 + 1 + 2 + \ldots + (N − 1)}{N}$$

Since the numerator is equal to $N * (N − 1)/2$, the average number of iterations of the For loop is $(N − 1)/2$, which is O(N). And so Time is O(N).

5. <u>Search (Item, Found, Position).</u>

A. Subalgorithm

We start TempHead at the head of the list, with Found = False and Position = 1. We keep bumping TempHead and incrementing Position until either TempHead is null (indicating we are at the end of the list) or TempHead's Item is EqualTo Item.

The complete subalgorithm is

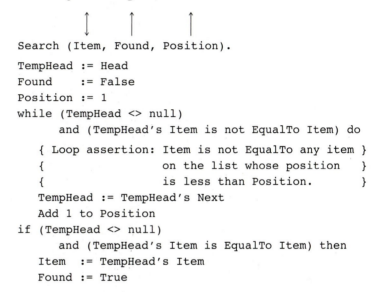

```
Search (Item, Found, Position).

TempHead := Head
Found    := False
Position := 1
while (TempHead <> null)
      and (TempHead's Item is not EqualTo Item) do

    { Loop assertion: Item is not EqualTo any item }
    {                    on the list whose position }
    {                    is less than Position.      }
    TempHead := TempHead's Next
    Add 1 to Position
if (TempHead <> null)
      and (TempHead's Item is EqualTo Item) then
    Item  := TempHead's Item
    Found := True
```

B. Verification

The proof of correctness of the While statement is left as an exercise. The postcondition is "Either Position is greater than the size of the list, or TempHead's Item, whose position is Position, is EqualTo Item."

C. Analysis

For a successful search (one in which a match for Item is found), the number of iterations can vary from 1 to N, and so the average number of iterations is

$$\frac{1 + 2 + \ldots + N}{N}$$

which is $(N + 1)/2$. Therefore, Time is $O(N)$ for a successful search. For an unsuccessful search, N iterations are required, and so Time is also $O(N)$. For both successful and unsuccessful searches, Space is $O(1)$.

6. Insert (Item, Position).

   A. Subalgorithm

       If Position = 1, we want to insert Item at the head of the list. Other-
       wise, we want to insert Item in front of the item in position Posi-
       tion; part of this involves changing the address of the item in
       position Position − 1. Therefore, we start TempHead at Head and
       loop until TempHead points to the item in position Position − 1.
       We then insert Item at the head of the list pointed to by Temp-
       Head's Next field.

       Since TempHead initially points to the first item, we need to loop
       Position − 2 times. The subalgorithm so far is

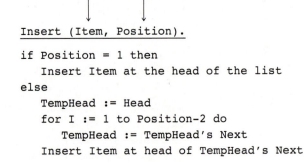

```
Insert (Item, Position).

if Position = 1 then
    Insert Item at the head of the list
else
    TempHead := Head
    for I := 1 to Position-2 do
        TempHead := TempHead's Next
    Insert Item at head of TempHead's Next
```

       Rather than duplicate the statements to insert Item, we will develop
       a subalgorithm InsertAtHead, and so the complete subalgorithm
       for Insert is as follows:

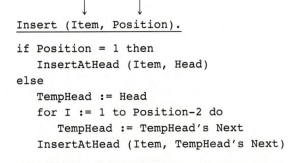

```
Insert (Item, Position).

if Position = 1 then
    InsertAtHead (Item, Head)
else
    TempHead := Head
    for I := 1 to Position-2 do
        TempHead := TempHead's Next
    InsertAtHead (Item, TempHead's Next)
```

       The subalgorithm InsertAtHead will have Item and Link as pa-
       rameters. (The identifier Link is generic: it could refer to Head or
       to TempHead's Next.) In order to insert Item at the head of the list,

we first need to allocate space for a new node. Since a node can be referenced only by an address, we let NewLink be the variable that contains the address of this new node. For example, suppose Link and Item are as follows:

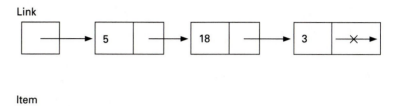

After allocating space for a new node pointed to by NewLink, we have

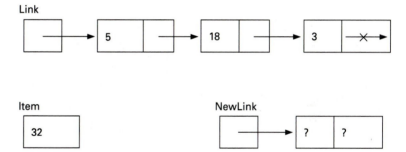

We now copy Item and Link into NewLink's fields, giving us

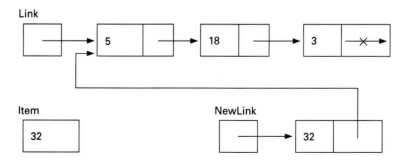

Finally, we copy NewLink into Link, and so we have

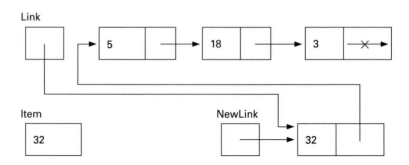

The subalgorithm InsertAtHead is

InsertAtHead (Item, Link).

```
Allocate space for a new node pointed to by NewLink.
NewLink's Item := Item
NewLink's Next := Link
Link           := NewLink
```

The most significant feature of inserting in a linked list is this: *A new item is inserted without moving any of the items already in the list*! For example, suppose that Letter is an instance of a list with the items *S, C, R, A,* and *M*:

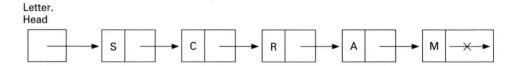

Then sending the message

```
Letter.Insert (E, 4)
```

would have the following effect on the list (for the sake of clarity, we also show the value of TempHead):

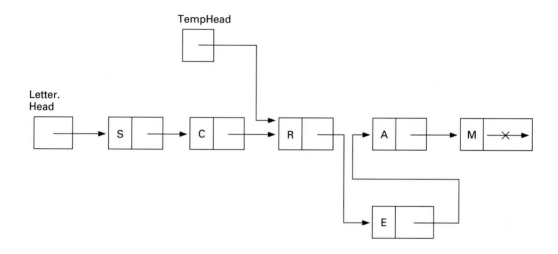

B. Verification

No verification is needed.

C. Analysis

By an analysis that is almost identical to that of Retrieve, we see that Time is $O(N)$ and Space is $O(1)$.

7. `Delete (Position).`

A. Subalgorithm

This subalgorithm is similar to Insert, except that InsertAtHead is replaced with DeleteFromHead.

```
Delete (Position).
if Position = 1 then
    DeleteFromHead (Head)
else
    TempHead := Head
    for I := 1 to Position-2 do
        TempHead := TempHead's Next
    DeleteFromHead (TempHead's Next)
```

In DeleteFromHead, with Link as the only parameter, we want to replace Link with Link's Next. But we also want to deallocate the space previously pointed to by Link so that space can be allocated later. We introduce OldLink to save Link's original value, and so we get the complete subalgorithm for DeleteFromHead:

```
DeleteFromHead (Link).

OldLink := Link
Link    := Link's Next
Deallocate the space pointed to by OldLink
```

Just as with insertions, deletions from a linked list are accomplished without any movement of items. For example, suppose that Letter is an instance of a list with the items *S*, *C*, *R*, *A*, and *M*:

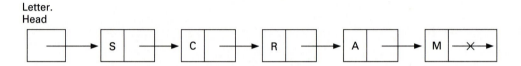

Then sending the message

```
Letter.Delete (3)
```

would have the following effect on the list (for the sake of clarity, we also show the value of TempHead):

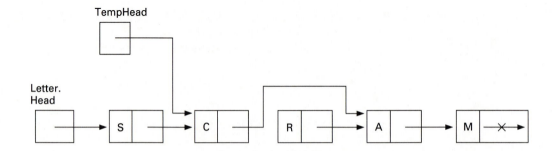

The node whose item is R is no longer part of the list, even though that node's address field points to the node on the list whose item is A. The space for *R*'s node has been deallocated, so that space could be allocated in a subsequent call to Insert.

B. Verification

No verification is needed.

C. Analysis

Time is O(N) and Space is O(1).

8. <u>CopyTo (NewList).</u>

A. Subalgorithm

We start with the simple case—here, an empty list. If Head contains a null address, we set NewList's Head to a null address so that NewList will also be empty. Otherwise, we have two subtasks to perform:

  i. Insert Head's Item at the beginning of NewList.

  ii. Copy the sublist starting at Head's Next onto the end of NewList.

There are two problems with this. First, the second subtask suggests a recursive call, but Head's Next is not an object. The solution is to have CopyTo call a recursive subalgorithm in which Head's Next can be an actual parameter. This subalgorithm, CopyItems, will have Head as the formal parameter. NewList will be a nonlocal instance. The subalgorithm for CopyTo is simply

<u>CopyTo (NewList).</u>

CopyItems (Head)

The second problem is that if the original list is not empty, we cannot insert anything into NewList until NewList has been initialized. So we must make sure that we have reached the end of the original list, and set NewList's Head to null, *before* we start inserting the list's items into NewList. To put it another way, we must complete the last recursive call, in which the rest of the list is an empty list, before we start inserting items onto NewList. To do this, we perform subtask ii before subtask i. Each insertion is then made at the head of NewList.

By utilizing the InsertAtHead subalgorithm described earlier, we obtain the complete subalgorithm for CopyItems:

<u>CopyItems (Head).</u>

```
If Head = null then
   NewList.Head := null
else
   CopyItems (Head's Next)
   InsertAtHead (Head's Item, NewList.Head)
```

An execution trace will help you to see how this subalgorithm works. Initially, assume we have

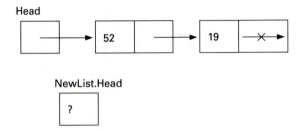

Since Head is not null, a recursive call to CopyItems is made. At the start of the execution of this first recursive call, we have:

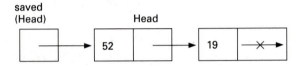

Since Head is not null, a second recursive call is made.
At the start of execution of the second recursive call to CopyItems, we have

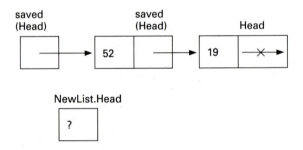

During the execution of that second recursive call, Head is null, and so NewList.Head is assigned the value null:

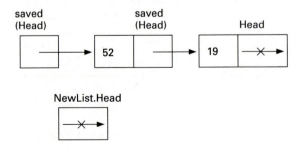

That completes the execution of the second recursive call, so the execution of the first recursive call is resumed with the execution of InsertAtHead. Just prior to the execution of that subalgorithm, we have

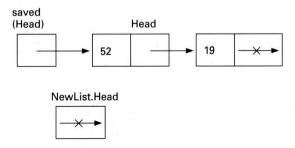

Head's Item has the value 19. After that item has been inserted at the head of NewList, we have

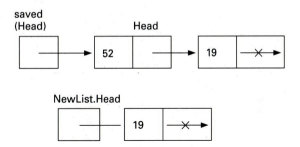

That completes the execution of the first recursive call to CopyItems, so the execution of the original call is resumed with the execution of InsertAtHead. Just prior to that execution, we have

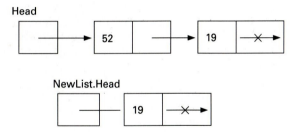

After the insertion of Head's Item at the head of NewList, we have

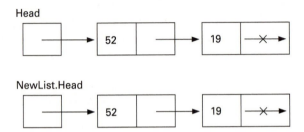

That completes the execution trace, and NewList has a copy of the original list.

B.   Verification

How can we prove the correctness of the recursive subalgorithm CopyItems? Because of the close connection between recursion and induction (see Appendix 1), we use the Principle of Mathematical Induction. The basic idea behind the proof is this: For any non-negative integer N, if we want to copy a list with $N + 1$ items to NewList, we first copy the last N items (all but Head's Item) to NewList, and then we copy Head's Item.

For $N = 0, 1, 2, \ldots$, let S_N be the statement: If the original list contains N items and CopyItems (Head) is called, NewList gets a distinct copy of the original list.

i.   Base case ($N = 0$): Since $N = 0$, the original list must be empty. When CopyItems (Head) is executed, NewList.Head gets the value null. Thus, S_0 is true.

ii. Inductive case: Let N be any nonnegative integer and assume that S_N is true. We need to show that S_{N+1} is true. Therefore, assume that the original list contains $N + 1$ items and that CopyItems (Head) is called. Since Head is not null, a call to CopyItems (Head's Next) is made. Since the sublist starting at Head's Next has only N items, the induction hypothesis (namely, that S_N is true) applies. Thus, the execution of CopyItems (Head's Next) gives NewList a distinct copy of the N items in the rest of the original list. Head's Item is then inserted at the head of NewList, and so NewList has a distinct copy of all $N + 1$ items in the original list. Thus, S_{N+1} is true.

Therefore, by the Principle of Mathematical Induction, S_N is true for any nonnegative integer N. This completes the proof of correctness of the subalgorithm CopyItems.

C. Analysis

There are N calls to CopyItems in which an insertion is made. During the execution of each of those calls, an item is inserted at the head of NewList, so each call takes only O(1) time. Thus, for CopyItems, the Time is O(N) statements. Due to the N recursive calls, Space is O(N) locations.

D. Notes

An iterative design of CopyTo can easily be developed, but its Time is O(N^2). An iterative version of CopyTo with Time in O(N) is somewhat harder to come by (see Exercise 4.10).

Can you see why CopyTo, rather than ":=", should be used for assigning one list to another? The reason is this: Since the only field in the linked design of a list is Head, the statement

```
NewList := OldList
```

merely gives NewList.Head the value of OldList.Head. Subsequent changes to OldList would be reflected in NewList, and vice versa.

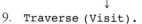

9. **Traverse (Visit).**

A. Subalgorithm

An iterative design is easy to develop (as is a recursive design):

```
TempHead := Head
while TempHead <> null do
    Visit (TempHead's Item)
    TempHead := TempHead's Next
```

B. Verification

No verification is needed.

C. Analysis

Time is O(N) and Space is O(1).

Contiguous Design of the List Data Type

Contiguous means "adjoining." In a contiguous design, items are stored one after the other, and so there is no need for a pointer to indicate where the next item is. For the contiguous design of the ordered list data type, the object type will have two fields:

A: whose type is array [1..MaxListSize] of ItemType;

N: whose type is 0..MaxListSize.

The items are stored in A, and N contains the number of items in the list. For any value of I between 1 and N, the item whose position on the list is I is stored at index I in the array A. For example, if the instance contains the items with values 52, 18, and 19, the representation of the instance is

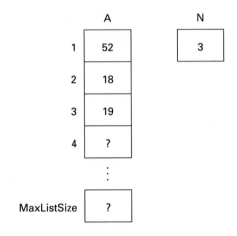

With this representation of a list, all of the method designs are straightforward.

1. <u>Initialize.</u>

    A. Subalgorithm

        ```
        N := 0
        ```

    B. Verification
        No verification is necessary.

    C. Analysis
        Time and Space are O(1).

2. <u>IsEmpty.</u>

    A. Subalgorithm

        ```
        Return the value of (N = 0)
        ```

    B. Verification
        No verification is necessary.

    C. Analysis
        Time and Space are O(1).

3. `Size.`

   A. Subalgorithm

     Return the value of N

   B. Verification

     No verification is necessary.

   C. Analysis

     Time and Space are O(1). Recall that for the linked design, Time was O(N).

4. `Retrieve (Item, Position).`

   A. Subalgorithm

```
Item := A [Position]
```

   B. Verification

     No verification is necessary.

   C. Analysis

     Time and Space are O(1). Recall that the Time for the linked design of Retrieve was O(N).

5. `Search (Item, Found, Position).`

   A. Subalgorithm

     The design is similar to the linked design of Search. The subalgorithm is

```
Found    := False
Position := 1

while (Position <= N)
      and (A [Position] is not EqualTo Item) do
   Add 1 to Position

if (Position <= N)
      and (A [Position] is EqualTo Item) then
   Item  := A [Position]
   Found := True
```

   B. Verification

     No verification is needed.

C. Analysis

The analysis is similar to that of the linked Search.
Time is O(N) and Space is O(1) for both successful and unsuccessful searches.

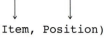

6. `Insert (Item, Position).`

A. Subalgorithm

We first move the items in *A* [Position..*N*] down one slot in the array, starting at *A* [*N*] so we do not destroy an item before moving
it. We then insert Item and adjust *N*. The complete subalgorithm is

```
Insert (Item, Position).

{ Move remaining items down one slot: }
for I := N downto Position do
   A [I+1] := A[I]

A [Position] := Item
Add 1 to N
```

B. Verification

No verification is needed.

C. Analysis

Position can take on any value between 1 and *N* + 1 (we assume
that each of these is equally likely), so the number of iterations of
the For loop can be any value between *N* and 0. The average of
these values is

$$\frac{0 + 1 + 2 + \ldots + N}{N + 1}$$

Since the numerator has the value $N * (N + 1)/2$, the average number of iterations of the For loop is $N/2$, and so Time is O(N). Space
is O(1).

7. `Delete (Position).`

The design and analysis of the Delete subalgorithm closely follow those
of Insert, except that the space at *A* [Position] must be closed instead of
opened. We present the complete subalgorithm only:

A. Subalgorithm

```
for I := Position to N-1 do
   A [I] := A [I+1]

Subtract 1 from N
```

B. Verification

No verification is needed.

C. Analysis

Time is $(N-1)/2$, which is $O(N)$. Space is $O(1)$.

8. `CopyTo (NewList).`

A. Subalgorithm

```
for I := 1 to N do
    NewList.A [I] := A [I]
NewList.N := N
```

B. Verification

No verification is needed.

C. Analysis

Time is $O(N)$. Space is only $O(1)$, since the space for NewList was allocated in the calling algorithm.

9. `Traverse (Visit).`

A. Subalgorithm

```
for I := 1 to N do
    Visit (A [I])
```

B. Verification

No verification is needed.

C. Analysis

Time is $O(N)$ and Space is $O(1)$.

IMPLEMENTATIONS OF THE LIST DATA TYPE

In this section we develop several units to implement the ordered list data type. Each implementation corresponds to either the linked or contiguous design developed in the two preceding sections.

We can implement the linked design's addresses in at least two ways: by pointers or by array indexes. The first implementation is **dynamic** because the nodes are dynamic variables whose space is allocated from the heap. The second implementation is **static** because the nodes are indexed variables in an array whose size is unchanged—that is, static—during the execution of the program or unit in which the instance is declared.

In addition to the implementations of the linked design, there will also be an implementation of the contiguous design.

All of the units were validated with the help of a driver program. For purposes of comparison, all of the run-time analyses are discussed in one section.

Dynamic Implementation of the Linked Design

One way to implement the addresses in the linked design is with Turbo Pascal pointers. In this implementation, called a *dynamic* implementation, each node is a dynamic variable whose space is allocated from the heap. The relevant declarations are

```
type
   AddressType = ^Nodetype;
   ListType = object
      Head: AddressType;
      procedure Initialize;

         .

         .

         .

   end; { ListType }
   Nodetype = record
      Item: ItemType;
      Next: AddressType
   end; { NodeType }
```

To translate the method subalgorithms into Turbo Pascal code, we utilize the correspondence shown in Table 4.1.

Table 4.1 The correspondence between linked-design terminology and dynamic-implementation terminology for lists.

Design	Dynamic Implementation
null	**nil**
Head's Item	Head^.Item
Head's Next	Head^.Next
Allocate space . . . pointed to by NewLink	New (NewLink)
Deallocate space pointed to by OldLink	Dispose (OldLink)

For example, here is the dynamic implementation of the linked design of the Search method:

```
procedure ListType.Search (var Item : ItemType;
                           var Found : boolean;
                           var Position: word);
{ Postcondition: If there is an item on the list that }
{ is EqualTo Item, a copy of that item has been       }
{ stored in Item, Found has been set to True and      }
{ Position contains the position of that item.         }
{ Otherwise, Item is unchanged and Found has been set }
{ to False .                                          }
var
    TempHead: AddressType;
begin
    Found    := False;
    Position := 1;
    TempHead := Head;
    while (TempHead <> nil)
          and not (Item.EqualTo (TempHead^.Item)) do
        { Loop invariant: Item is not EqualTo any item on the}
        {                 list whose position is less than   }
        {                 Position.                          }
        begin
            TempHead := TempHead^.Next;
            Inc (Position)
        end; { while }
    if (TempHead <> nil) and (Item.EqualTo (TempHead^.Item))
        then
        begin
            Item  := TempHead^.Item;
            Found := True
        end { if }
end; { Search }
```

In the above method, it was only for aesthetics that we used

```
Item.EqualTo (TempHead^.Item)
```

instead of

```
TempHead^.Item.EqualTo (Item)
```

The latter is a direct translation of the pseudocode:

```
TempHead's Item is EqualTo Item
```

The complete unit, List1Manager, is on disk. There is another unit, SList1Manager, in which it is assumed that the items are scalar. SList1Manager differs from List1Manager only in the Search method. Instead of

```
Item.EqualTo (TempHead^,Item)
```

we would have

```
Item = TempHead^.Item
```

Static Implementation of the Linked Design

For the dynamic implementation of the preceding section, the space for nodes was allocated from the heap. The size of the heap can be adjusted through a compiler directive in the main program or through a compiler option in the Compiler menu. The default size, 640K bytes, would allow the heap to consume most of main memory on some systems. Because of the heap's large potential size, pointer variables—the variables that contain heap addresses—are four bytes in length. Another aspect of the heap's flexibility, besides size, is that it can store dynamic variables of many types within the same program.

As often happens, there is a trade off here between flexibility and efficiency. We now introduce a storage facility that is, under some circumstances, more efficient (in terms of access time) than the heap. This facility is an array, and it is dedicated to a single purpose: storing the nodes in all lists for a given application. As we noted earlier, the space for an array is allocated statically, that is, for the remainder of the block in which the list instances are declared. The major restriction of this static implementation is that the size of an array is much smaller than the maximum size of the heap.

For this implementation, we assume that all list instances in the application will occupy a maximum of 20000 bytes, so that other data may also be stored in the data segment. We refer to this array as Pile to suggest its similarity to the heap. Addresses are implemented as array indexes, with 0 the implementation of a null address. The size of each node is equal to the size of an item plus two bytes (for the size of an index); that is, we can declare

```
const
    NodeSize = SizeOf (ItemType) + 2;
```

If we allow 20000 bytes for Pile, then the index type is 1..PileLast, where PileLast = 20000 div NodeSize.

For programs that access the heap, the "heap manager" keeps track of available locations so that New and Dispose will work properly. With Pile, the unit ListManager must include code to create and maintain the list of available locations, known as the *free list*. The indexes on the free list are stored in one of two places. The "head" of the free list is stored in the variable Free. The other indexes are stored in the Next fields of nodes in Pile.

Figure 4.2

The initial configuration of Pile and Free.

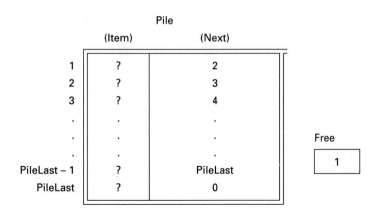

Initially, all of Pile is available, so Free will be set to 1, Pile [1].Next to 2, Pile [2].Next to 3, and so on. After these initializations, Pile and Free will be as shown in Fig. 4.2.

Space for a node is allocated at the index stored in Free, which is then adjusted to contain the "next" free index. For example, suppose that the items' values are pets represented as strings. To make this example easier to follow, we will insert items in such a way as to preserve an alphabetical ordering. If Pets is initialized (that is, Pets.Head is set to 0) and then we call

```
Pets.Insert ('dog', 1)
```

we would have the picture shown in Fig. 4.3.

In Fig. 4.3, Pets.Head contains 1, and so the head item in the pet list is stored in the node at index 1 in the array Pile. That item, 'dog', has no successor, so the Next field in that node contains 0. The free list starts at index 2 in Pile—that is why Free contains the value 2.

Suppose we now insert the following items into Pets: 'snake' into position 2, 'cat' into position 1 (because 'cat' comes before 'dog'), 'fish' into po-

Figure 4.3

The configuration of Pile, Free, and Pets of Fig. 4.2 after 'dog' has been inserted in Pets.

	Pile (Item)	Pile (Next)
1	dog	0
2	?	3
3	?	4
.	.	.
.	.	.
.	.	.
PileLast − 1	?	PileLast
PileLast	?	0

Free: 2   Pets.Head: 1

Figure 4.4

The configuration of Pile, Free, and Pets of Figure 4.3 after 'snake', 'cat', 'fish', and 'gerbil' have been inserted into Pets in positions 2, 1, 3, and 4, respectively.

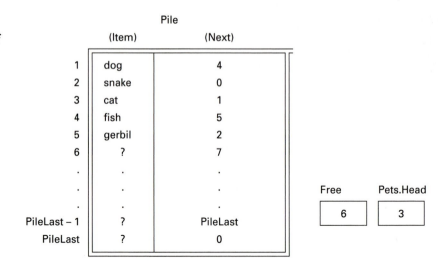

sition 3, and 'gerbil' into position 4. Then we will get the picture shown in Fig. 4.4.

Notice that the Pets.Head and the Next fields, not the array indexes, determine the positions of the items. For example, 'cat' is at the head of the list, that is, in position 1, even though it is stored at index 3 in Pile. The Next field at index 3 is 1, which indicates that the item in position 2, namely 'dog', is stored at index 1.

When space for a node is deallocated, the index of that now free location is stored in Free. But before that is done, the previous value of Free is stored in the location's Next field; in that way the rest of the free list is not lost. For example, if we now delete the item in position 5, namely 'snake', Pets would be as shown in Fig. 4.5.

Figure 4.5

The configuration of Pile, Free, and Pets of Figure 4.4 after the item in position 5 ('snake') is deleted from Pets.

	Pile (Item)	(Next)
1	dog	4
2	snake	6
3	cat	1
4	fish	5
5	gerbil	0
6	?	7
.	.	.
.	.	.
.	.	.
PileLast − 1	?	PileLast
PileLast	?	0

Free

| 2 |

Pets.Head

| 3 |

Figure 4.6

The configuration of Pile, Free, and Pets of Figure 4.5 after the item in position 3 ('fish') has been deleted from Pets.

Pile

	(Item)	(Next)
1	dog	5
2	snake	6
3	cat	1
4	fish	2
5	gerbil	0
6	?	7
·	·	·
·	·	·
·	·	·
PileLast − 1	?	PileLast
PileLast	?	0

Free

4

Pets.Head

3

Notice that the item 'snake' is not physically removed from Pile; it is simply no longer linked to the items in Pets. If we now delete the item in position 3, namely 'fish', Pets would be as shown in Fig. 4.6.

The indexes in a free list need not be increasingly ordered. For example, in Fig. 4.6, Free contains 4 and Pile [4].Next contains 2.

The techniques described here also apply to other lists. For example, if we start with the configuration in Fig. 4.6, initialize Pets2, and then insert 'ferret', 'rabbit', and 'canary' into positions 1, 2, and 1, respectively, in Pets2, we would get the configuration shown in Fig. 4.7.

Pile

	(Item)	(Next)
1	dog	5
2	rabbit	0
3	cat	1
4	ferret	2
5	gerbil	0
6	canary	4
7	?	8
·	·	·
·	·	·
·	·	·
PileLast − 1	?	PileLast
PileLast	?	0

Free

7

Pets.Head

3

Pets2.Head

6

Figure 4.7 The configuration of Pile, Free, Pets, and Pets2 after 'ferret', 'rabbit', and 'canary' are inserted into an initially empty Pets2.

Here are the necessary type, constant, and variable declarations for the static implementation of the linked design of the List ADT:

```
type
    AddressType = word;
    ListType = object
        Head: AddressType;
        procedure Initialize;
        .
        .
        .
    end; { ListType }
    NodeType = record
        Item: ItemType;
        Next: AddressType
    end; { NodeType }
const
    PileBytes = 20000; { The array Pile is allocated
                              up to 20000 bytes. }
    PileLast = PileBytes div SizeOf (NodeType);
    PileType = array [1..PileLast] of NodeType;
var
    Pile : PileType;
    Free,
    I    : AddressType;
```

All of the above declarations are in the interface part so that descendants of the object ListType can use them.

The initialization part is

```
begin { unit initialization }
    for I := 1 to PileLast - 1 do
        Pile [I].Next := I + 1;
    Pile [PileLast].Next := 0;
    Free                 := 1
end. { ListManager }
```

To translate the linked design of the list ADT into a static implementation, we utilize the correspondence shown in Table 4.2.

For example, here is the static implementation of the linked design of the Search method:

```
procedure ListType.Search (var Item : ItemType;
                               var Found : boolean;
                               var Position: word);
```

---

*Table 4.2 The correspondence between
linked-design terminology and static-
implementation terminology for lists.*

Linked Design	Static Implementation
null address	0
Head's Item	Pile [Head].Item
Head's Next	Pile [Head].Next
Allocate space…pointed to by NewLink	NewLink := Free; Free := Pile [Free].Next
Deallocate the space pointed to by OldLink	Pile [OldLink].Next := Free Free := OldLink

---

```
{ Postcondition: If there is an item on the list that }
{ is EqualTo Item, a copy of that item has been        }
{ stored in Item, Found has been set to True and       }
{ Position contains the position of that item.         }
{ Otherwise, Item is unchanged and Found has been set }
{ to False .                                           }
var
    TempHead: AddressType;
begin
    Found    := False;
    Position := 1;
    TempHead := Head;
    while (TempHead <> 0)
        and not (Item.EqualTo (Pile [TempHead].Item)) do
        { Loop invariant: Item is not EqualTo any item on }
        {                 the list whose position is less }
        {                 than Position.                  }
        begin
            Inc (Position);
            TempHead := Pile [TempHead].Next
        end; { while }
    if (TempHead <> 0)
        and (Pile [TempHead].Item.EqualTo (Item)) then
        begin
            Item  := Pile [TempHead].Item;
            Found := True
        end { if }
end; { Search }
```

Implementation of the Contiguous Design

The implementation of the methods in the contiguous design is straightforward. Here are the highlights from the interface part:

```
interface
uses
   ItemInList, { implements ItemType }
   Maxima;  { declares MaxListSize }
type
   ProcedureType = procedure (Item: ItemType);{see Traverse}
   ListType = object
      A: array [1..MaxListSize] of ItemType;
      N: word;
      procedure Initialize;
      ...
   end; { ListType }
```

The validation of all the list implementations used the program List-Driver outlined in Chapter 3 and on disk in the Ch4 directory.

Run-Time Analysis of List Implementations

To decide which list implementation(s) should be made available to users, we need to compare their performances at execution time. The program TestTime described in Chapter 2 was run in the following experiment: For each unit, we determined the time to insert items into 1000 randomly selected positions in an initially empty list. The items are objects; the values of the items are irrelevant because the position parameter determines where an item is placed. For simplicity, a constant item (with value 'serene') was inserted 1000 times in the experiment.

To illustrate the effect of randomly selecting the positions, let's start with an empty list. The first item is inserted into position 1. The second insertion can be into either position 1 or 2, selected randomly. In general, for any nonnegative integer I, if there are I items already in the list, the next position for an insertion is randomly chosen from $1, 2, \ldots, I + 1$.

The experiment was then repeated for 2000 randomly selected positions. The results are shown in Table 4.3.

The actual times obtained in the experiment depend on the computer used as well as the program. Those values would change substantially on a faster or slower computer, so we should view the results relatively rather than absolutely. The results shown in Table 4.3 are noteworthy is several respects:

1. The contiguous implementation of Insert is much slower than either of the linked implementations. Why is this so? Let's look at what happens when an item is inserted.

Table 4.3 The time, in seconds, to insert N
six-byte items into randomly selected
positions with each of the list
implementations.

Implementation	N = 1000	N = 2000
linked, dynamic	6.4	24.1
linked, static	8.6	32.8
contiguous	23.5	96.1

Suppose the list currently has 500 items and we want to insert an item into position 250. Both linked and contiguous implementations will loop approximately 250 times. However, while the loop in the linked versions merely bumps the link (from TempHead to TempHead's Next), the contiguous version must *move* an item from one position to the next higher position in the array. Thus, the bigger the item, the longer the insertion takes.

To corroborate the contiguous implementation's sensitivity to the size of the items, another experiment was conducted. This experiment was the same as the preceding one except that the item inserted had a one-byte value instead of a six-byte value. The results of this second experiment are shown in Table 4.4.

2. The dynamic implementation of the linked design of Insert was faster than the corresponding static version. This is mildly surprising because the address of a node in the dynamic implementation is a four-byte pointer; in the static implementation the address of a node is a two-byte index.

Table 4.4 The time, in seconds, to insert N
one-byte items into randomly selected
positions in an initially empty list under each
list implementation.

Implementation	N = 1000	N = 2000
linked, dynamic	6.3	23.8
linked, static	5.3	20.1
contiguous	7.4	29.9

The only statement executed often enough to account for the time difference is the link-bumping statement that constitutes the loop body in Insert:

```
TempHead := TempHead^.Next          { DYNAMIC }
TempHead := Pile [TempHead].Next { STATIC }
```

One hypothesis that would explain the slowness of this static version is that when an array component is referenced, the entire component is retrieved from memory. That means that the record Pile [TempHead] would be retrieved from memory, and then the assignment of the Next field of that record to TempHead would be made. A compiler might generate code to retrieve the entire record as an optimization on the grounds that other fields in the record might be needed shortly. Retrieving an entire dynamic record might not save any time in many cases, because often (as here) only the Next field is accessed.

This hypothesis is supported by the results in Table 4.4: When one-byte items are inserted, the static implementation is *faster* than the dynamic.

3. In comparing the times to insert items within each implementation, we see an increase of about a factor of four from the time to insert 1000 items to the time to insert 2000 items. This reflects the fact that inserting N items into randomly selected positions in an initially empty list takes $O(N^2)$ time.
Specifically, for $I = 1, 2, \ldots, N$, inserting an item into position

```
Random (I) + 1
```

requires $0, 1, 2, \ldots, I - 1$ loop iterations, depending on the value returned by the function Random. (For the linked versions, the number of loop iterations is actually in $0 .. I - 2$.) Assuming that each of these I events is equally likely, the average number of loop iterations to insert the item is

$$\frac{\sum_{k=0}^{I-1} k}{I} = \frac{(I-1) * I}{2 * I} = \frac{I - 1}{2}$$

The average number of loop iterations to insert all N items is then

$$\sum_{I=1}^{N} (I - 1)/2 = N * (N - 1)/4 = N^2/4 - N/4$$

which is $O(N^2)$.
Since Time $(N) \approx N^2/4 - N/4$, we have

$$\begin{aligned} \text{Time } (2N) &\approx (2N)^2/4 - (2N)/4 \\ &= 4 * N^2/4 - 2 * N/4 \\ &\approx 4 * \text{Time } (N) \end{aligned}$$

This experiment was modified to insert one-byte items instead of six-byte items. The results are shown in Table 4.4.

Comparing Tables 4.3 and 4.4, we observe that the dynamic implementation of the linked design is the fastest of all three implementations unless the item size is very small. For large items, the dynamic implementation is a compelling choice because of its insensitivity to item size. Furthermore, the dynamic implementation stores the items in the heap (up to 360K bytes), which is different from the space allocated for the data segment (about 64K bytes in Turbo Pascal). Both the static and contiguous implementations compete with the user's program for space in the data segment.

A LIST APPLICATION: HIGH-PRECISION ARITHMETIC

Turbo Pascal's longint type allows up to ten digits of precision, and this is sufficient for most applications. But sometimes we may need many more digits of precision. For example, certain applications in public-key cryptography involve numbers with hundreds of digits. The reason for generating such large numbers is that, unless you are given their factors beforehand, it is very difficult to obtain those factors in a reasonable amount of time. So the factors can be used to encode and, later, decode information.

Let's try to solve the following related problem:

Read in two very long integers and print out their sum.

For this problem, the maximum size (MaxSize) of a very long integer will be 1000 digits. We assume that each input value consists of a string of ASCII characters representing a positive integer, with no leading zeros, that has MaxSize digits at most. We will allow each input value to be spread over several lines and terminate with the letter 'X'. If the sum has more than MaxSize digits, then an overflow message is printed instead of the sum.

For example, if the input is

1234X
56789X

then the output would be

58023

In true object-oriented fashion, we start by looking for abstract data types to work with. One ADT is immediately visible: VeryLongInt. Notice that this corresonds to the main noun phrase in the statement of the problem. The logical domain of this ADT is, of course, the collection of very long integers. The only methods pertinent to the current problem are:

1. `ReadIn`

   Precondition: Each input value consists of a string of ASCII characters
   representing a positive integer, with no leading zeros, whose

length is less than or equal to MaxSize. Each input value is terminated with the letter 'X'.

Postcondition: The very long integer (that is, the calling instance) has been constructed from the input.

$$\downarrow \quad \downarrow \qquad \uparrow$$

2. <u>Add (A, B, Overflow).</u>

Precondition: *A* and *B* are very long integers of, at most, 1000 digits each.

Postcondition: If the sum of *A* and *B* has at most 1000 digits, that sum has been stored in the calling instance and Overflow has been set to False. Otherwise, Overflow has been set to True.

3. <u>Print.</u>

Postcondition: The very long integer (that is, the calling instance) has been written out.

In Programming Project 4.2 you are asked to define, design, and implement other operators.

The algorithm to solve the problem is then fairly simple. In fact, because it calls only these operators, the algorithm practically writes itself.

We will focus our attention on the design of the object VeryLongInt. First, and most important, we must decide on the design domain. What fields should be used to represent the logical domain? Since each instance will consist of up to 1000 digits, a list comes to mind as a good choice (especially in view of the heading of this section!).

So each instance of a very long integer will have a Number field of type ListType and methods ReadIn, Add, and Print. Each instance of Number will consist of a list of digits, that is, each item will be a digit.

In designing the methods in VeryLongInt, we will observe the Principle of Data Abstraction with respect to the List ADT: Instances of a list will not reference the list's fields directly. At this point we do not know what those fields are, because we do not know (or care) whether the list's design is contiguous or linked.

In arithmetic, addition is performed from right to left. For example, suppose we want to add

$$\begin{array}{r} 1234 \\ + \; 56789 \\ \hline \end{array}$$

The two rightmost digits (4 and 9) are added first. We will store the digits in a number in reverse order so that the least significant digits will be conveniently available in position 1 of their respective lists. (In Exercises 4.13 and 4.14, you are asked to store each number in its normal order: most significant digit in position 1, and so on.)

Now that we have decided that the Number field should contain the number in reverse order, the design of ReadIn becomes clear: Each character read in that is between '0' and '9' (to ignore blanks and end-of-line markers) is converted to the corresponding digit and inserted into position 1 of Number. The complete design is

<u>ReadIn.</u>

```
Number.Initialize
repeat
    Read in CurrentChar
    if CurrentChar is in ['0'..'9'] then
        Digit := Ord (CurrentChar) - Ord ('0')
        Number.Insert (Digit, 1)
until CurrentChar = 'X'
```

Before we try to design the Add method, let's look at the steps involved in adding two numbers represented as digit sequences in reverse order. Suppose the two numbers to be added are 1234 and 56789. The digit sequences would be

and

The sum, in reverse order, is stored in positions $1, 2, \ldots$ of Number. Since each item holds only one digit, a carry must be generated if the sum of two digits is greater than or equal to 10. For example, when 4 and 9 are added, the digit 3 is stored in position 1 of Number and a carry of 1 is generated. Then, 3 plus 8 plus that carry equals 12, so the digit 2 is stored in position 2 of Number, and another carry of 1 is generated. The number of times the loop is executed is the larger of the sizes of the numbers to be added. After the last iteration, if the carry is 1 and Larger is equal to Max-Size, Overflow has occurred.

The design of Add is as follows:

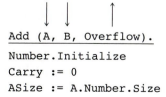

<u>Add (A, B, Overflow).</u>

```
Number.Initialize
Carry := 0
ASize := A.Number.Size
```

```
BSize := B.Number.Size
if ASize > BSize then
   LargerSize := ASize
else
   LargerSize := BSize
for I := 1 to LargerSize do
   { Loop assertion: the I least-significant digits in the }
   {                      sum have been stored in positions 1   }
   {                      through I of Number.                   }
   if I <= ASize then
      A.Number.Retrieve (ADigit, I)
   else
      ADigit := 0
   if I <= BSize then
      B.Number.Retrieve (BDigit, I)
   else
      BDigit := 0
   Digit := ADigit + BDigit + Carry
   if Digit >= 10 then
      Digit := Digit - 10
      Carry := 1
   else
      Carry := 0
   Number.Insert (Digit, I)
if (Carry = 1) and (LargerSize = MaxSize) then
   Overflow := True
else
   Overflow := False
   if Carry = 1 then
      Number.Insert (Carry, LargerSize + 1)
```

The proof that the loop assertion is a loop post-invariant is left as an exercise. The Big-O analysis is postponed until after we complete the design of the Print method.

The design of the Print method is somewhat easier. Since Number has the digits in reverse order, we will print out those digits in reverse order so that the output will be in the correct order. One way to accomplish this is to retrieve the digit in position 1, print out the rest of the digits in reverse order, and then print out the digit in position 1. This suggests an embedded recursive subalgorithm PrintReverse. The number of recursive calls is Number.Size. The design of Print is simply

Print.

```
SizeOfNumber := Number.Size
PrintReverse (1)
```

The design of PrintReverse, with SizeOfNumber as a non-local variable (for efficiency), is

```
PrintReverse (I).

if I <= SizeOfNumber then
    Number.Retrieve (Digit, I)
    PrintReverse (I + 1)
    WriteOut (Digit)
```

The WriteOut subalgorithm is supplied by the developer of the Item data type. The verification of PrintReverse is left as an exercise, as is the development of an iterative version of Print.

Up to this point everything we have done is independent of how the List ADT was designed. But the analysis of the ReadIn, Add, and Print methods cannot be performed unless we know which design of the List ADT is being used. For example, in ReadIn there is a call

```
Number.Insert (Digit, 1)
```

If N represents the number of digits, then the loop that contains the call takes $O(N)$ time in the linked version of Insert, but $O(N^2)$ time in the contiguous version. The contiguous version takes longer because inserting a new item in position 1 of an array requires that all other items be moved first.

So let us assume, for the sake of discussion, that the linked design of the list ADT has been chosen. Then, if I takes on values between 1 and N, Retrieve (Item, I) and Insert (Item, I) will take $O(N)$ time. As a result, both Add and Print will take $O(N^2)$ time.

It seems that we should be able to do better. We would expect that we could read in two numbers of size N and print out their sum in $O(N)$ time. The trouble with the linked versions of Retrieve and Insert is that they always start back at the beginning of the list. This reflects the fact that the only field in a linked-list object is Head.

AN IMPROVED LINKED DESIGN OF THE LIST DATA TYPE

In the application just discussed (and in many others), it would help if we could keep track of the current position and the current item in a linked list. This leads us to a new version of the linked design domain of the list ADT. In addition to the Head field, there will be two other fields:

Current: contains the address of the item that was most recently retrieved or inserted or that preceded the item most recently deleted.

CurrentPos: the position of the item pointed to by Current.

When a list is initialized, Current is set to a null address and CurrentPos is set to zero. Whenever the first item in a list is deleted, then there are two cases:

1. If the list is now empty, Current is set to a null address and CurrentPos is set to zero.
2. Otherwise, Current points to the first item on the list and CurrentPos is set to 1.

The following sequence of calls illustrates the effect on Current and CurrentPos of Retrieve, Insert, and Delete.

1. `Initialize`

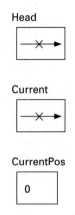

2. `Insert ('q', 1)`

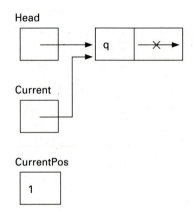

3. Insert ('t', 2)

Head

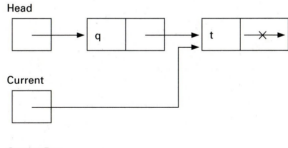

Current

CurrentPos

4. Insert ('d', 3)

Head

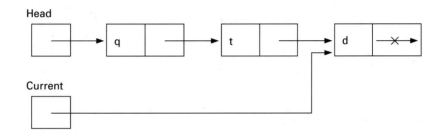

Current

CurrentPos

5. Delete (2)

Head

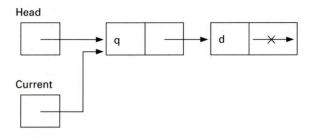

Current

CurrentPos

6. Retrieve (Item, 2)

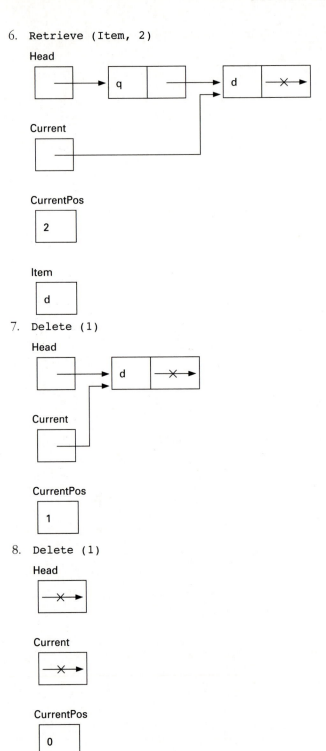

7. Delete (1)

8. Delete (1)

How does the addition of these two fields affect the list ADT? From the user's perspective, nothing has changed (except, possibly, run-time efficiency). But we need to alter the designs of Initialize and several other methods—Retrieve, Search, Insert, Delete, and CopyTo. Mainly, we must decide whether to start at position 1 or at CurrentPos, and we must update Current and CurrentPos.

Maintaining Current and CurrentPos will slightly increase the work to be done in many of the method designs. Is it worth it? The advantage of this new design is that fewer loop iterations are required for retrieving, searching, inserting, or deleting whenever the value of the Position parameter is greater than or equal to CurrentPos.[2] The extent of the speed up can be seen below in the time analysis of Retrieve.

We now present the design for the new version of Retrieve. The designs of Search, Insert, Delete, and CopyTo are similar and are left as exercises. The essential change from the original version of Retrieve presented earlier in this chapter is that, if Position is greater than or equal to CurrentPos, TempHead should start at Current and the loop should start at CurrentPos.

The complete subalgorithm is as follows:

```
Retrieve (Item, Position).

if Position >= CurrentPos then
    TempHead := Current
    Start    := CurrentPos
else
    TempHead := Head
    Start    := 1
for I := Start to Position - 1 do
    TempHead := TempHead's Next
Item         := TempHead's Item
Current      := TempHead
CurrentPos   := Position
```

It might seem that there is no need to worry about verifying this subalgorithm since the loop statement is trivial. But the correctness of this subalgorithm depends on *and ensures* the following assertion:

Invariant	If Head is null, Current is null and CurrentPos = 0. Otherwise, Current's Item is at position CurrentPos.

[2]Special case: If Position is 1 and CurrentPos is 0, then no loop iterations are required for an insertion, as before.

We refer to this assertion as an "invariant" because it is true before and after each call to Retrieve (and to Search, Insert, and Delete). In other words, it becomes part of the precondition and postcondition of these methods.

To prove that this assertion is an invariant of each of these methods, we first show that the method preserves the assertion. That is, we show that if an instance satisfies the assertion prior to a call to the method, the instance also satisfies the assertion after the call. Then we observe that the assertion is established for any instance when it is given an initial value. Finally, we note that an implicit precondition of each method is that the calling instance has already been given an initial value.

After all this buildup, the proof that Retrieve satisfies the invariant is easy, and the rest of the proof of Retrieve's correctness is even easier.

The time analysis of Retrieve is not so easy. Let P and C stand for Position and CurrentPos, respectively, and let N represent the size of the list. We want to determine the average number of iterations of the loop. This average is taken over all N^2 possible values of P and C; both P and C can take on any value between 1 and N. If $P \geq C$, then $P - C$ iterations are required; otherwise, $P - 1$ iterations are required.

In the original version of Retrieve, $P - 1$ iterations were required for each value of P. So the new version of Retrieve has fewer iterations whenever $P \geq C$. How many fewer? For example, if P is 5 and $P \geq C$, C can take on any value between 1 and 5. The number of iterations for each of those values is 4, 3, 2, 1, and 0, respectively. The savings over the original version of Retrieve are 0, 1, 2, 3, and 4 iterations, respectively. In general, for each value of P between 1 and N, there is a savings of $1 + 2 + \ldots + P - 1$ iterations over the original version of Retrieve. The average saving in iterations is therefore

$$\frac{\sum_{P=1}^{N} \sum_{I=1}^{P-1} I}{N^2} = \frac{\sum_{P=1}^{N} \frac{P(P-1)}{2}}{N^2}$$

The value of this expression is, approximately, $N/6$; see Exercise 4.19. Since the average number of iterations in the original version of Retrieve is $(N - 1)/2$, the average number of iterations in the new version is, approximately, $N/3$.

On average, then, the new version of the linked design requires only about two-thirds as many loop iterations as the original version. The situation is even better for the Add and Print methods in the high-precision application. Each retrieval or insertion is at position CurrentPos + 1, and so each retrieval or insertion takes only 1 iteration! Thus, both of those methods take only $O(N)$ time. This confirms our belief that it should take only $O(N)$ time to read in and print out the sum of two N-digit numbers.

We are now ready to translate our method designs into Turbo Pascal. We choose a dynamic implementation; but it is inappropriate to modify the unit, List1Manager, that implements the original linked design, for two reasons:

1. Perhaps only the compiled version is available.
2. Some descendants of List1Manager might not want the extra baggage of the Current and CurrentPos fields.

In general, it is best not to alter a completed unit unless it is found to be incorrect. Instead of changing List1Manager, we will define a descendant of it named List1aManager.

The interface part of this new unit is as follows (the complete unit is on disk in directory Ch4):

```
interface
uses
    ItemInList,
    List1Manager;
type
    ListType = object (List1Manager.ListType)
        Current   : AddressType;
        CurrentPos: word;
        procedure Initialize;
        procedure Retrieve (var Item: ItemType;
                                Position: word);
        procedure Search (var Item    : ItemType;
                          var Found    : boolean;
                          var Position: word);
        procedure Insert (Item    : ItemType;
                          Position: word);
        procedure Delete (Position: word);
        procedure CopyTo (var NewList: ListType);
    end; { ListType }
```

This unit was validated with the same ListDriver program used to validate List1Manager.

In the preceding section of this chapter we described an experiment to test the run-time performance of the three implementations of the list ADT that had been developed at that time. The same experiment was performed on List1aManager. Table 4.5 shows how well this implementation compared with the other three implementations.

As expected, the new version of the dynamic-linked implementation took only about two-thirds as long as the original dynamic-linked implementation. The unit List1aManager is the clear choice for inserting items into randomly selected positions. Furthermore, as the high-precision application indicated, the unit is excellent for consecutive retrievals, insertions, and deletions. The line editor programming assignment is just such an application.

Table 4.5 The time, in seconds, to insert N six-byte items into randomly selected positions with each of the list implementations.

Implementation	N = 1000	N = 2000
linked, dynamic (original)	6.4	24.1
linked, dynamic (improved)	**4.5**	**16.5**
linked, static	8.6	32.8
contiguous	23.5	96.1

This new design and implementation took some extra work, but it was worth it. From now on, this is the version we will be referring to when we say "the improved linked design."

SUMMARY

In this chapter we defined, designed, and implemented the List ADT. In the linked design, each item is stored as a field in a record called a *node*. Each node also contains a Next field, which contains the address of the node with the next item in the list. An instance of a list has a single field, Head, that contains the address of the first node. For this linked design, we investigated both dynamic (address = pointer) and static (address = array index) implementations.

We also studied a contiguous design, in which items were stored in an array A [1..MaxListSize]. The fields in the design domain were the array A and N, an integer variable that holds the current size of the list. This design was easily translated into a Turbo Pascal implementation.

Finally, to remedy the poor performance of the linked design for consecutive retrievals, insertions, and deletions, we extended the linked design by adding Current and CurrentPos fields. As Table 4.5 indicates, the dynamic implementation of this improved linked design is superior to the other implementations of the List ADT for performing random insertions in a list.

EXERCISES

4.1   **a.**   Suppose that Letters is an instance of a list. Show the sequence of letters in the list after each of the following messages is sent:

```
Letters.Initialize
Letters.Insert ('f',1)
```

```
Letters.Insert ('i',2)
Letters.Insert ('e',1)
Letters.Insert ('r',2)
Letters.Insert ('c',4)
Letters.Insert ('e',4)
Letters.Delete (1)
Letters.Insert ('p',1)
Letters.Insert ('e',2)
Letters.Insert ('t',8)
Letters.Delete (7)
```

b. Develop a unit, SItemInList, in which ItemType is declared to be of type char. Include a WriteOut procedure that writes out the item. Also, develop a unit, Maxima, in which MaxListSize is a constant identifier with a value of 100.

c. Incorporate the messages in part a into a program that uses the units SItemInList and Maxima from part b. The program will also use SList1Manager, an implementation of the List ADT in which it is assumed that the items are scalar.

d. Add a Traverse message to the program so that the final version of the list is printed out.

4.2 Redo Exercise 4.1 for EmployeeList, another instance of a list. Each item in EmployeeList is of type EmployeeType, also called ItemType and declared in the unit ItemInList. ItemType is an object in which ValueType is a record with Name and Address fields. Employee is an instance of EmployeeType. The sequence of (assignments and) messages is as follows:

```
EmployeeList.Initialize
Value.Name := 'Martens'
Value.Address := 'Easton'
Employee.SetValue (Value)
EmployeeList.Insert (Employee,1)
Value.Name := 'Wassmer'
Value.Address := 'Allentown'
Employee.SetValue (Value)
EmployeeList.Insert (Employee,2)
Value.Name := 'Plottner'
Value.Address := 'Bethlehem'
Employee.SetValue (Value)
EmployeeList.Insert (Employee,2)
Value.Name := 'Lyttle'
Value.Address := 'Bethlehem'
Employee.SetValue (Value)
EmployeeList.Insert (Employee,1)
```

The unit ItemInList is on disk as Ch4\Exer\ItemInList.pas.

4.3   Trace the execution of the methods in Exercise 4.1.a for the linked, contiguous, and improved linked designs.

4.4   Trace the execution of the methods in Exercise 4.1.a for the dynamic and static implementations of the linked design.

4.5   For seven of the nine methods in the List ADT, the Big-O Time is the same for both the linked and contiguous designs. For example, CopyTo takes $O(N)$ Time in both the linked and contiguous designs. Which two methods have different Big-O Times for the linked and contiguous designs?

4.6   Suppose that Petition is an instance of a list that has already been given an initial value (either as the calling instance to Initialize or as the actual parameter to CopyTo). As a user of the List ADT, develop pseudocode to ensure that the precondition of the Insert method is satisfied before the message Petition.Insert (Name, Position) is sent. (Note: The precondition of the Insert method is as follows: $1 \leq$ Position $\leq 1 +$ number of items in the list $\leq$ MaxListSize.)

4.7   Part of the precondition for the Insert method asserts that the number of items already in the list is less than MaxListSize. This assertion puts on the user the burden of avoiding overflow. Suppose we modify the precondition and postcondition for Insert to put the burden of avoiding overflow on the developer of the List ADT:

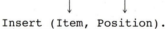

Insert (Item, Position).

Precondition: $1 \leq$ Position $\leq 1 +$ the number of items in the list.

Postcondition: If, before this call was made, the number of items in the list was less than MaxListSize, then
1. A copy of Item is in position Position in the list.
2. For any item x and any position p, if x was in position p just before this call, x is still in position p if $p <$ Position; otherwise x is now in position $p + 1$.

Redesign the linked and contiguous designs of the Insert method to reflect the new precondition and postcondition.

4.8   As a *user* of the list ADT, develop each of the following subalgorithms from the given nine methods. DO NOT USE ANY OF THE FIELDS IN THE LINKED OR CONTIGUOUS DESIGNS!

a. DeleteItem (Item, List).

Precondition: There is an item in List that is EqualTo Item.

Postcondition: An item that is EqualTo Item has been deleted from List.

b. `Merge (List1, List2).`

Postcondition: List1 contains all of the items that were in List1 together with all of the items that were in List2. (If an item appeared once in List1 and once in List2, that item would appear twice in the merged list.)

c. `UniqueCount (List).`

Postcondition: The value returned is the number of unique items in List. (An item is *unique* if it does not appear more than once in the list.)

d. `Equals (List1, List2).`

Postcondition: True has been returned if and only if each item in List1 is EqualTo an item in List2 and each item in List2 is EqualTo an item in List1.

4.9 What is the Big-O time of the following version of the linked CopyTo method?

```
CopyTo (NewList).
NewList.Head := null
for I := 1 to Size do
    Retrieve (Item, I)
    NewList.Insert (Item, I)
```

4.10 Develop an iterative version, with Time in O(*N*), of the linked CopyTo subalgorithm.

H I N T   Set up and maintain a variable Tail, which contains the address of the last item in NewList.

4.11 Remove the assumptions of no-leading-zeros and no-overflow-during-input in the addition problem for very long integers.

4.12 Modify the design of the VeryLongInt object as follows: Each item consists of a five-digit integer. What effect will this have on run-time efficiency?

4.13 Develop a design for the Add method in the VeryLongInt data type that takes only O(*N*) time if the contiguous version of the list ADT is used.

H I N T   Store the digits in Number in their normal order, with the most significant digit in position 1, and so on.

4.14 Develop a design for the Add method in the VeryLongInt data type that takes only O(N) time if the original linked version of the list ADT is used.

   HINT   Save A and B and then use a destructive loop to add them. In that loop, store each sum digit in position 1 of Number. Reverse Number after the loop.

4.15 What is the advantage of using the variables ASize and BSize, instead of A.Size and B.Size, in the design of the Add method?

4.16 Prove that the loop assertion in the design of the Add method is a loop post-invariant.

4.17 Prove the correctness of the PrintReverse subalgorithm.

   HINT   Use the Principle of Mathematical Induction.

4.18 **a.** Develop an iterative version of the Print method in the Very-LongInt ADT.

   HINT   Use a temporary list of digits, PrintList. After initializing PrintList, traverse Number; the visit subalgorithm inserts each digit into position 1 of PrintList. Then traverse PrintList to print out each digit.

   b. Determine the time and space requirements for the Print subalgorithm developed in part a for the original linked, improved linked, and contiguous designs of the List ADT.

4.19 Prove that, for any positive integer N,

$$1^2 + 2^2 + 3^2 + \ldots + N^2 = N\,(N + 1)\,(2N + 1)/6$$

   HINT   Use the Principle of Mathematical Induction.

4.20 Use the result from Exercise 4.19 to show that

$$\frac{\displaystyle\sum_{P=1}^{N} \frac{P(P-1)}{2}}{N^2} = \frac{N}{6} * \left(1 - \frac{1}{N^2}\right)$$

4.21 Exercise 4.8 indicates that the given collection of methods in the list ADT is not as large as it could be. In this exercise you will prove that the collection is not as small as it could be. Specifically, show that Initialize, IsEmpty, Retrieve, Insert, and Delete form a fundamental collection in the sense that the other four methods could be derived as operators from those five.

For example, show that a user of the list ADT can derive

$$\downarrow \qquad \uparrow$$

`CopyTo (List, NewList).`

from Initialize, IsEmpty, Retrieve, Insert, and Delete.

HINT   Start by making a reverse copy of List while destroying it:

```
TempList.Initialize
while not List.IsEmpty do
   List.Retrieve (Item, 1)
   List.Delete (1)
   TempList.Insert (Item, 1)
```

Now make two reverse copies (List and NewList) of TempList while destroying it.

4.22   Determine the (sometimes pitiful!) time and space requirements for the derivations of CopyTo, Size, Search, and Traverse in Exercise 4.21. For this exercise, you may take into account the original linked, improved linked, and contiguous designs of Initialize, IsEmpty, Retrieve, Insert, and Delete.

4.23   In both the dynamic and static implementations of the linked design of the List ADT, we declared AddressType first, then ListType, and finally NodeType. We could also have declared AddressType first, then NodeType, and finally ListType. Explain why any other order of declarations would be illegal.

4.24   **a.** As a *user* of the List ADT, develop a subalgorithm for the following operator:

$$\downarrow$$

`TraverseBackwards (Visit).`

Postcondition: Each item in the list, starting with the last item and proceeding to the first, has been accessed. The action performed on each accessed item is determined by the subalgorithm Visit, whose only parameter is an item.

b. Assuming the contiguous design of the List ADT, calculate the time and space requirements for your TraverseBackwards subalgorithm.

c. Assuming the improved-linked design of the List ADT, calculate the time and space requirements for your TraverseBackwards subalgorithm.

d. Suppose we discover that many applications of the List ADT involve backwards traversals. We therefore decide to modify the definition of the List ADT to include TraverseBackwards as a **method**. With the contiguous design of the List ADT, develop a subalgorithm for TraverseBackwards that requires $O(N)$ time and $O(1)$ space. With the linked (or improved linked) design of the List ADT, develop a TraverseBackwards subalgorithm that requires $O(N^2)$ time and $O(1)$ space, and another TraverseBackwards subalgorithm that requires $O(N)$ time and $O(N)$ space.

e. A *doubly-linked* design of the List ADT allows us to easily develop a subalgorithm for the TraverseBackwards method that requires only $O(N)$ time and $O(1)$ space. In a doubly-linked design, the design domain consists of Head and Tail fields. In a nonempty list, the Tail field contains the address of the node in the last position in the list. Each node contains a Previous field as well as the usual Item and Next fields. The Previous field contains the address of the previous node in the list. Pictorially,

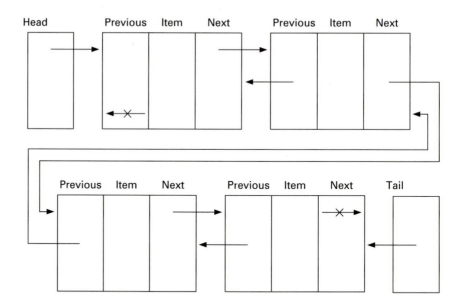

For simplicity, we define a list to be empty if its Head field contains a null address, so the Tail field is undefined in an empty list.

With this doubly-linked design, develop subalgorithms for the TraverseBackwards, Insert, and Delete methods.

LABORATORY EXERCISES

4.1 Conjecture the run-time effect—for the dynamic-linked, static-linked, and contiguous implementations—of each of the following errors in a call to Insert:

a. The list had not been given an initial value (through Initialize or CopyTo);

b. Position $> 1 +$ the number of items in the list;

c. The number of items already in the list is equal to MaxListSize.

Create short programs to test your conjectures.

4.2 The intent of the following user-defined procedure is to delete all of the items in a list. Determine what is wrong with this procedure.

```
procedure DeleteAll (var List: ListType);
var
    I: integer;
begin
    for I := 1 to List.Size do
        List.Delete (I)
end; { DeleteAll }
```

Fix the procedure so that it works as intended.

PROGRAMMING ASSIGNMENTS

Programming Assignment 1

PROBLEM   Develop a small line editor.

ANALYSIS:

Specifications: A line editor is a program that manipulates text line by line. We assume that each line is no more than 80 characters long. Each editing command begins with a dollar sign (and no other line begins with a dollar sign). There will be no more than 55 lines of text. Before each error message is printed, a bell should sound. There are seven editing commands:

1. $Insert

Each subsequent line (up to the next editing command) will be inserted in the text after the current line. The "current line" becomes the last line inserted. For example, if the text is (">" indicates the current line),

```
 Now is the
>time for
```

```
citizens to come to
the
aid of the party.
```

then the sequence

```
$Insert
all
good
```

will cause the text to become

```
Now is the
time for
all
>good
citizens to come to
the
aid of the party.
```

Note: If the text is full, an attempted insertion should be rejected and the error message "***Error: Insertion rejected: text already full." should be printed. For example, if the text contained 54 lines, we could have the following (with output boldfaced):

```
$Insert
Time for
All
*** Error: Insertion rejected: text already full.
```

The error message refers to the attempt to insert the line containing "All" into a text that already contains the maximum 55 lines.

2. $Delete m,n

Each line in the text between lines m and n, inclusive, will be deleted. If the current line had been in this range, the new current line will be line $m - 1$ (this may be line 0).

For example, if the text is

```
Now is the
time for
all
>good
citizens to come to
the
aid of the party.
```

then the command

```
$Delete 3,5
```

will cause the text to become

```
 Now is the
>time for
 the
 aid of the party.
```

The following error messages should be printed when appropriate:

```
*** Error: A line number (or the comma) has been omitted.
*** Error: The first line number is greater than the
           second.
*** Error: The first line number is less than 1.
*** Error: The second line number is greater than the
           number of lines in the text.
```

3. `$Line m`

   Line m becomes the current line. For example, if the text is

   ```
    Mairzy doats
    an dozy doats
   >an liddle lamsy divy.
   ```

   then the command

   ```
   $Line 1
   ```

   will make line 1 the current line:

   ```
   >Mairzy doats
    and dozy doats
    and liddle lamsy divy.
   ```

   The command

   ```
   $Line 0
   ```

   followed by an insert command, is used to insert lines at the beginning of the text.

   An error message should be printed if *m* is either less than zero or greater than the last line number in the text. See command 2 above.

4. `$Change %x%y%`

   In the current line, each occurrence of the string given by *x* will be replaced by the string given by *y*. For example, suppose the current line is

   ```
   aid of the party.
   ```

Then the command

```
$Change %a%vo%
```

will cause the current line to become

```
void of the pvorty.
```

If we then issue the command

```
$Change %pvo%a%
```

we would get

```
void of the arty.
```

Notes:

(a)   If either *x* or *y* contains a percent sign, another delimiter should be used in the command. For example,

```
$Change #0.16#16%#
```

(b)   The string given by y may be the null string. For example, if current line is

```
aid of the party.
then the command
$Change %of %%
```

will change the current line to

```
aid the party.
```

(c)   An error message should be printed if the delimiter occurs fewer than three times.

5.   `$Last`

The line number of the last line in the text will be printed. For example, if the text is

```
 I heard a bird sing
>in the dark of December.
 A magical thing
 and a joy to remember.
```

then

```
$Last
```

will cause **4** to be printed. The text (and current line marker) will be unchanged.

6. `$Print m,n`

   Each line (and line number) in the text, from lines *m* through *n*, inclusive, will be printed. For example, if the text is

   ```
    Winston Churchill once said that
   >democracy is the worst
    form of government
    except for all the others.
   ```

   then the command

   ```
   $Print 1,3
   ```

   will cause the following to be printed:

   1 Winston Churchill once said that
   2 democracy is the worst
   3 form of government

   The text (and current line marker) are unchanged. An error message should be printed if
   (a) a line number (or the comma) is omitted from the command;
   (b) *m* is greater than *n*;
   (c) *m* is less than 1 or *n* is greater than the last line number in the text.

7. `$Done`

   This terminates the execution of the text editor.

   An error message should be printed for any illegal command (such as "$End" or "?Insert").

System Test 1 *(sample output is boldfaced)*:

```
$Insert
You can fool
some of the people
some of the times,
but you can't foul
all of the peeple
all of the time.
$Line 3
$Print 3
```
*** Error: A line number (or the comma) has been omitted.
```
$Print 3,3
```
3 some of the times,
```
$Change %s%%
$Print 3,3
```

```
3 ome of the time,
$Change %o%so
*** Error: Delimiter % occurs only twice. Please try again.
$Change %o%so%
$Print 3,3
3 some sof the time,
Change %sof%of%
*** Error: Command must begin with $. Please try again.
$Change %sof%of%
$Print 3,3
3 some of the time,
$Line 0
$Insert
Lincoln once said that
you can fool
some of the people
all the time and
all of the time and
$Last
11
$Print 1,11
1 Lincoln once said that
2 you can fool
3 some of the people
4 all the time and
5 all of the time and
6 You can fool
7 some of the people
8 some of the time,
9 but you can't foul
10 all of the peeple
11 all of the time.
$Line 6
$Change %Y%y%
$Print 6,6
6 you can fool
$Line 7
$Change %some%all%
$Print 7,7
7 all of the people
$Line 9
$Change %ul%ol%
$Print 9,9
9 but you can't fool
$Line 10
$Change %ee%eo%
```

```
$Print 10,10
```
10 all of the people
```
$Delete 4,4
$Print 1,11
```
*** Error: The second line number is greater than the number
**   of lines in the text.**
```
$Print 1,10
```
1 Lincoln once said that
2 you can fool
3 some of the people
4 all of the time and
5 you can fool
6 all of the people
7 some of the time,
8 but you can't fool
9 all of the people
10 all of the time.
```
$Done
```

System Test 2

```
$Insert
Life is full of
successes and lessons.
$Delete 2,2
$Insert
wondrous oppurtunities disguised as
hopeless situations.
$Last
3
$Print 1,3
```
1 Life is full of
2 wondrous oppurtunities disguised as
3 hopeless situations.
```
$Line 2
$Change %ur%or%
$Print 1,3
```
1 Life is full of
2 wondrous opportunities disguised as
3 hopeless situations.
```
$Done
```

> *H I N T   Because of the possibility of a missing line number or*
> *comma in several commands, each command line should be*
> *read in as a character string. Use the string data type*
> *described in Appendix 4.*

Programming Assignment 2

Define, design, and implement the following operators in the VeryLongInt
data type:

```
Subtract
Multiply
Divide { include both quotient and remainder }
EqualTo
LessThan
```

The unit VeryLong.pas includes the ReadIn, Add, and Print methods.

Ordered and Orderable Lists

CHAPTER 5

INTRODUCTION

In this chapter we continue our study of lists with two specializations of lists: ordered lists and orderable lists. Strictly speaking, an ordered list is itself a specialization of an orderable list, but we will look at ordered lists first because they have fewer methods. The definition, designs, and implementations of the ordered and orderable list data types are simplified because most of the method designs are inherited from the improved-linked and contiguous designs of the List data type.

In an ordered list, insertions, deletions, and searches are made by comparing the item to be inserted, deleted, or sought with other items already in the list. By exploiting the ordering of items, we obtain a design of the Search method that takes only O(log N) Time. This design, the *binary search algorithm*, is perhaps the best known algorithm in computer science.

An **orderable list** is one that can be sorted into an ordered list. In fact, the chief attraction of orderable lists is that they have given rise to a wide variety of sorting algorithms. However, we will postpone a discussion of sorting until Chapter 9, because two of the most important sort methods—TreeSort and HeapSort—are based on concepts introduced in Chapter 8.

The case study in this chapter, "Updating a Class Roster," is an application of ordered lists. It illustrates bottom-up design and other aspects of an object-oriented approach to the software development life cycle.

ORDERED LISTS

We begin by recalling the definition of "ordered list" from Chapter 4. A list of N items is said to be ***ordered*** if

1. The item data type includes relational operators for "less than," "equal to," and "greater than."
2. For each value of I between 1 and $N - 1$, the item in position I is less than or equal to the item in position $I + 1$. (The "equal to" allows for duplicate items.)

For example,

> canary, cat, dog, gerbil

is an ordered list of four pets; the ordering is alphabetical. As noted in the definition, duplicates are allowed in ordered lists. For example,

> 52, 53, 57, 57, 81, 102

is an ordered list of six integers.

The ordering in an ordered list imposes a restriction on users. As we will see in the next section, the user of an ordered list cannot specify where a given item is to be inserted. This prevents the user from destroying the ordering. In return for accepting this restriction, the user is assured that the list will always remain ordered. Beyond that restriction, the user's rights—that is, the data type's responsibilities—are the same as for the List ADT.

Definition of the Ordered List Data Type

We now define the Ordered List ADT. The logical domain is the set of all ordered lists; this is, of course, a subset of the set of all lists. Of the nine methods defined in the next section, six are unchanged from the List ADT. Even the designs—improved-linked and contiguous—are inherited intact from those of the List ADT. The Search, Insert, and Delete methods have new interfaces and new designs to reflect the fact that the list is ordered.

We assume that a user of this data type will provide the Item data type, which, unless the items are scalar, is an object type that includes the relational methods LessThan, EqualTo, and GreaterThan. These relational methods are provided for the sake of generality, so that the items need not be scalar. The user must also provide MaxListSize, the maximum allowable size of an ordered list for the particular application. Finally, the user may provide any number of subalgorithms that describe what actions are to be taken for each item during a list traversal.

Methods in the Ordered List Abstract Data Type

There are nine methods in the Ordered List ADT. Of these, six have the same *method interface*—heading, precondition, and postcondition—as methods in the List ADT. The Search, Insert, and Delete interfaces are different from those of the List ADT. Here are all nine method interfaces:

1. <u>Initialize.</u>

   Postcondition: The list is empty.

2. <u>IsEmpty.</u>

   Postcondition: True is returned if the list is empty. Otherwise, False is returned.

3. <u>Size.</u>

   Postcondition: The number of items in the list has been returned.

4. <u>Retrieve (Item, Position).</u>

   Precondition: $1 \leq$ Position $\leq$ the number of items in the list.

   Postcondition: The item at position Position has been copied into Item.

5. <u>Search (Item, Found, Position).</u>

   Postcondition: If the list is empty, or if there is no item on the list that is EqualTo Item, then Item is unchanged, Found = False, and Position contains the position at which Item could be inserted without disordering the list. Otherwise, an item EqualTo Item has been copied into Item, Found = True, and Position contains the position of that item.

   Note a: For example, if we have the following list of alphabetically ordered item values:

   concert, hockey game, opera, play

   then a search for the item with value 'movie' would leave Item unchanged, Found = False, and Position = 3. Notice that the item with value 'movie' belongs in position 3.

   Note b: For another example, suppose that the items' values are names and we want to retrieve each item whose name starts in the last half of the alphabet ('M'..'Z'). We would Search for the Position of the first name GreaterThan 'M' and then Retrieve each item from position Position to position Size.

Note c: The reason that Item is an output (as well as an input) parameter is the same as for the Search method in the List ADT. For example, suppose that the items in the list have Name and Address fields, and that two items are EqualTo each other if they have the same name. If you knew the name of an item in the list and you wanted the address, you could call Search.

6. **Insert (Item).**

    Precondition: The number of items in the list is less than MaxListSize.

    Postcondition: Item has been inserted in the list in such a way that the list remains an ordered list.

    Note a: The reason that the position where Item should be inserted is not a parameter is that the position of an item in a list is determined by the ordering, *not* by the user.

7. **Delete (Item).**

    Precondition: There is an item in the list that is EqualTo Item.

    Postcondition: An item that is EqualTo Item has been deleted from the list.

    Note: It is the user's responsibility, before Delete is called, to ensure that there is an item in the list that is EqualTo Item. A user can do this by means of the Search method. Of course, there may be many situations where the user is certain, even without calling Search, that the precondition of Delete is satisfied.

8. **CopyTo (NewList).**

    Postcondition: NewList has a distinct copy of the list.

9. **Traverse (Visit).**

    Postcondition: Each item in the list has been visited according to its position: The item in position 1 has been visited first, then the item in postion 2, and so on. The action taken for each item is determined by the actual procedural parameter corresponding to the formal parameter Visit.

Linked Design of the Ordered List Data Type

We will adopt the improved-linked and contiguous design domains from the previous chapter. In the linked design domain, the ordered list object will have three fields: Head, Current, and CurrentPos. The only method designs we need to provide are those for Search, Insert, and Delete. All of the other designs are inherited intact from the improved-linked design.

The linked designs for Search, Insert, and Delete are as follows:

5. <u>Search (Item, Found, Position).</u>

    A. Subalgorithm

        This version of Search is an improvement over the design of Search in the List ADT because we can take advantage of the fact that the calling instance is ordered. In particular, we can start TempHead at Current as long as Current's Item is less than or equal to Item. Also, we stop looping as soon as TempHead's Item is greater than or equal to Item, and so we need not go through the entire list if Item is not there.

        The complete subalgorithm is:

<u>Search (Item, Found, Position).</u>

```
Found := False
if (Current <> null)
      and (Current's Item not GreaterThan Item) then
   TempHead := Current
   Position := CurrentPos
else
   TempHead := Head
   Position := 1

{ Make Position greater than the position of any }
{ item on the list that is LessThan Item:        }
while (TempHead <> null) and
      (TempHead's Item is LessThan Item) do

   { Make Position greater than the position of any }
   { item that is LessThan TempHead's Item:         }
   TempHead := TempHead's Next
   Add 1 to Position

if (TempHead <> null) and
      (TempHead's Item is EqualTo Item) then
```

```
Item          := TempHead's Item
Found         := True
Current       := TempHead
CurrentPos := Position
```

B. Verification of the while statement

Precondition: Found = False; Position is greater than the position of any item that is LessThan TempHead's Item. (If TempHead is null, we interpret this assertion to mean that Position is greater than the position of any item on the list.)

Postcondition: Position is greater than the position of any item on the list that is LessThan Item.

Loop assertion: Position is greater than the position of any item that is LessThan TempHead's Item.

To prove the correctness of the loop statement, we start by assuming that the precondition is true.

Claim 1: The execution of the while statement eventually terminates.

Proof: Let N represent the size of the list. Since TempHead is bumped to point to the next node during each iteration, the execution of the loop terminates after no more than N iterations.

Claim 2: The loop assertion is a loop invariant.

Proof: Prior to the first iteration, there are no items on the list that are LessThan TempHead's Item. Thus, the assertion is true prior to the first iteration. Now, assume that the assertion is true prior to some iteration. By the action of the loop, TempHead points to the next item (or TempHead is null) and Position is incremented. This implies that the assertion is true after that iteration and thus is true prior to the next iteration. Therefore, the assertion is true before and after each iteration—in other words, the assertion is a loop invariant.

Claim 3: After the last iteration, the postcondition is true.

Proof: If TempHead is null after the last iteration, then—by the loop invariant—Position is greater than the position of any item on the list. Thus, the postcondition is true. On the other hand, if Temp-Head is not null, then the loop must have terminated, because TempHead's Item was GreaterThan or EqualTo Item. By the loop invariant, Position is greater than the position of any item that is LessThan TempHead's Item. Therefore, Position is greater than the position of any item that is LessThan Item—that is, the postcondition is true in this case also.

Note: The Search method preserves the following invariant: If Current is not null, then Current's Item is at position CurrentPos. For if Item is not found, then Current and CurrentPos are not modified; and if Item is found on the list, TempHead's Item at position Position is retrieved. The last two assignment statements in the subalgorithm then guarantee that Current's Item is at position CurrentPos.

C. Analysis

Because the execution of the loop terminates as soon as TempHead's Item is greater than or equal to Item, the average number of iterations in both the successful and unsuccessful cases is about the same. The only difference is that, for a successful search, the number of iterations ranges from 1 to N, whereas for an unsuccessful search, the number of iterations ranges from 0 to N.

The analysis in both cases is similar to that of Retrieve from the preceding chapter. The average number of iterations is approximately $N/3$, and so Time is $O(N)$. Space is $O(1)$.

6. <u>**Insert (Item).**</u>

A. Subalgorithm

The following design is similar to that of CopyTo from Chapter 4. Insert will call an embedded recursive subalgorithm, InsertItem. The only actual parameter will be either Current or Head, depending on whether or not Item is greater than Current's Item.

The subalgorithm Insert is simply

<u>Insert (Item).</u>

```
if (Current <> null)
      and (Item is GreaterThan Current's Item) then
   InsertItem (Current)
else
   CurrentPos := 1
   InsertItem (Head)
```

InsertItem has TempHead as a formal parameter and TempHead's Next as the corresponding actual parameter for each recursive call. The complete subalgorithm for InsertItem is

<u>InsertItem (TempHead).</u>

```
if (TempHead = null)
      or (Item is not GreaterThan TempHead's Item) then
```

```
     { Insert Item at the head of TempHead's list: }
     Allocate space for a new node pointed to by NewHead
     Copy Item and TempHead into NewHead's Item
          and Next fields, respectively
     TempHead := NewHead
     Current := NewHead
  else
     Add 1 to CurrentPos
     InsertItem (TempHead's Next)
```

B. Verification

An inductive proof of correctness, similar to that of CopyTo in Chapter 4, is left as an exercise.

C. Analysis

The number of recursive calls is the same as the number of loop iterations in an unsuccessful search of the list. As we saw in the analysis of the Search subalgorithm, the average number of loop iterations is approximately $N/3$. Since the average number of recursive calls is approximately $N/3$, Time and Space are both $O(N)$.

An iterative version of Insert is somewhat harder to develop than the recursive version. The reason is that once we have located the node that Item should be inserted in front of, we have overshot the node whose Next field should be altered to effect the insertion. One solution, reminiscent of the iterative design of the Fibonacci function from Chapter 2, is to include another address variable, Previous. Current is advanced to where the insertion should be made and Previous points to the node before Current's node. After the insertion, Current is adjusted so that it points to the newly inserted item. The details (except for the InsertAtHead subalgorithm) are as follows:

```
Insert (Item).

if (Head = null)
      or (Item is LessThan or EqualTo Head's Item) then
     CurrentPos := 1
     InsertAtHead (Item, Head, Current)
  else
     if Item is LessThan Current's Item then
        CurrentPos := 1
        Current    := Head
     Previous := Current
     Current  := Current^.Next
     Add 1 to CurrentPos
```

```
      while (Current <> nil)
            and (Item is GreaterThan Current's Item) do
         Previous := Current
         Current  := Current's Next
         Add 1 to CurrentPos
      InsertAtHead (Item, Previous's Next, Current)
```

The verification and analysis of this design are left as exercises.

7. <u>Delete (Item).</u>

   A. Subalgorithm

We develop a recursive version of Delete similar to the recursive design of Insert. The only complication is that Current must be adjusted to point to the item *before* the deleted item. As long as there is at least one recursive call to DeleteItem, all we need to do is set Current to TempHead (and increment CurrentPos) just before that call. To take care of the other case, namely that the item to be deleted is Head's Item, we set Current to Head (and CurrentPos to 1) before the original call to DeleteItem.

The Delete and DeleteItem subalgorithms are as follows:

<u>Delete (Item).</u>

```
if Item is GreaterThan Current's Item then
   DeleteItem (Current)
else
   Current    := Head
   CurrentPos := 1
   DeleteItem (Head)
```

<u>DeleteItem (TempHead).</u>

```
if Item is EqualTo TempHead's Item then

   { Delete Item from the head of TempHead's list: }
   OldHead  := TempHead
   TempHead := TempHead's Next
   Deallocate the space for OldHead's node.
   if IsEmpty or (CurrentPos > 1) then
      Subtract 1 from CurrentPos
   else
   Current := Head
```

```
    else
       Current := TempHead
       Add 1 to CurrentPos
       DeleteItem (TempHead's Next)
```

B. Verification

Assume the precondition that Item is on the list. We must first show that the execution of the DeleteItem subalgorithm eventually terminates. There will be, at most, N calls to DeleteItem, and so its execution will eventually terminate. At the start of the final execution of the DeleteItem subalgorithm, we will have Item EqualTo TempHead's Item, and so Item will be deleted from (the head of) some sublist of the original list. This proves that the postcondition (Item is deleted from the list) is true when the execution of the subalgorithm terminates.

The proof that the invariant (relating Current to CurrentPos) is preserved is easily obtained by induction on the number of recursive calls.

C. Analysis

Just as for the Insert subalgorithm, Time is $O(N)$ and Space is $O(N)$.

Contiguous Design of the Ordered List Data Type

For a contiguous design of the Ordered List ADT, we can utilize the contiguous design of the List ADT from Chapter 4. The design domain, as before, consists of two fields:

A: whose type is array [1 .. MaxListSize] of ItemType;

N: whose type is 0 .. MaxListSize.

The designs of Initialize, IsEmpty, Size, Retrieve, CopyTo, and Traverse are inherited intact from the contiguous design of the List ADT. The designs of Insert and Delete are simple once we have found (via the Search method) where the item should be inserted or deleted.

The design of the Search method is interesting because it exploits the "direct access" property of arrays. By "direct access" we mean that the item at any position can be accessed without first accessing other items. With a linked design, only sequential access is possible; for example, if we are at position 5 and we want to access an item at position 12, we must first access all items at positions between 5 and 12.

The designs of Search, Insert, and Delete are as follows:

5. Search (Item, Found, Position).

A. Subalgorithm

The hardest part of designing the Search subalgorithm is to find the position where Item is or belongs. To find that position, we need not start at position 1 and search sequentially. Instead, we perform a *binary search*, so called because the segment of the list being searched is successively divided in two until the search is complete.

Here is the general form of a binary search. At any time, the segment of the list being searched is from position First to position Last, where these are initially 1 and N, respectively. We can think of the list as consisting of three regions:

1. 1.. First − 1. All items in this region are LessThan Item.

2. First.. Last. This is the region currently being searched.

3. Last + 1.. N. All items in this region are GreaterThan Item.

See Fig. 5.1.

We then calculate the middle position, (First + Last) div 2, and compare A [Middle] to Item. If A [Middle] is EqualTo Item, we have found a match, and we should stop searching because Middle is an appropriate value for Position. If A [Middle] is LessThan Item, we reset First to Middle + 1 and continue searching. Finally, if A [Middle] is Greater than Item, we reset Last to Middle − 1 and continue searching. The search continues as long as we have not found a match and First ≤ Last.

For example, suppose that MaxListSize is 15, Item's value is 'Sam,' and the instance's fields are as shown in Fig. 5.2.

Figure 5.1

The three regions in a list at any stage in a binary search.

(items)	LessThan Item	?	GreaterThan Item
(positions)	1 ... First − 1	First ... Last	Last + 1 ... N

Initially, we have

First	Last	Middle
1	12	6

A [First]	A [Last]	A [Middle]	Item
Ben	Zhengmao	Keith	Sam

Figure 5.2

The fields in the
contiguous design of
an ordered list.

Since 'Keith' is LessThan 'Sam,' First is changed to Middle + 1.
During the next stage of the search, we have

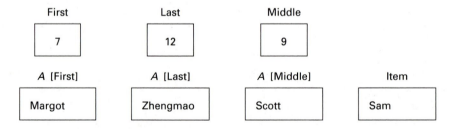

Since 'Scott' is GreaterThan 'Sam', Last is changed to Middle − 1,
and so for the next stage we have

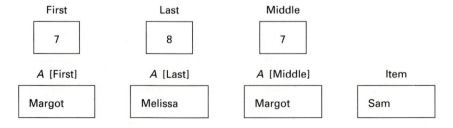

'Margo' is LessThan 'Sam', and so First is changed to Middle + 1. At the beginning of the next stage we have

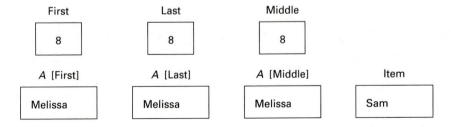

First	Last	Middle
8	8	8

A [First]	A [Last]	A [Middle]	Item
Melissa	Melissa	Melissa	Sam

Because 'Melissa' is LessThan 'Sam', we change First to Middle + 1, that is, 9. First is now greater than Last, and so the search stops. The design so far is as follows:

```
Initialize First to 1, Last to N and Found to False

{ Find where Item is or belongs in the list: }
while (not Found) and (First <= Last) do

    { Loop assertion: For all I in [1..N]:       }
    {    if I < First, A[I] is LessThan Item;    }
    {    if I > Last, A[I] is GreaterThan Item. }
    Middle := (First + Last) div 2
    if A [Middle] is EqualTo Item then
        Item     := A [Middle]
        Found    := True
        Position := Middle
    else
        if A [Middle] is LessThan Item then
            First := Middle + 1
        else
            Last := Middle - 1
```

Our only remaining task is to calculate Position when Item is not on the list. At the beginning of any stage in the search, we must have First ≤ Last, and so the value given to Middle must be such that First ≤ Middle ≤ Last. Then, whether we change First to Middle + 1 or Last to Middle − 1, we have First ≤ Last + 1. If Item is not EqualTo any item on the list, the search must have ended with First > Last. Thus, we must have First = Last + 1, and so there are three possibilities:

1. Last = 0, First = 1. In this case, Item is LessThan any item on the list, and so the appropriate value for Position is 1, that is, First.

2. Last = N, First = $N + 1$. In this case, Item is GreaterThan any item on the list, and so the appropriate value for Position is $N + 1$, that is, First.

3. $1 \leq$ Last $<$ First $\leq N$. In this case, A [Last] LessThan Item and A [First] GreaterThan Item, and so the appropriate value for Position is First.

In all three cases, Position gets the value of First.

The complete subalgorithm is as follows:

```
Search (Item, Found, Position). {Binary Search}

Initialize First to 1, Last to N and Found to False


{ Find where Item is or belongs in the list: }
while (not Found) and (First <= Last) do

   { Loop assertion: For all I in [1..N]:    }
   {    if I < First, A[I] is LessThan Item; }
   {    if I > Last, A[I] is GreaterThan Item. }
   Middle := (First + Last) div 2
   if A [Middle] is EqualTo Item then
      Item   := A [Middle]
      Found  := True
      Position := Middle
   else
      if A [Middle] is LessThan Item then
         First := Middle + 1
      else
         Last := Middle - 1
if not Found then
   Position := First
```

B. Verification

We prove the correctness of the loop statement.

Precondition: First = 1, Last = N, Found = False.

Postcondition: The position where Item is or belongs has been found.

Loop assertion: For all I in $[1..N]$,

   (if $I <$ First, A [I] is LessThan Item) and
   (if $I >$ Last, A [I] is GreaterThan Item).

Claim 1: The execution of the loop statement eventually terminates.

Proof: During each iteration, either Found is set to True, First is incremented, or Last is decremented. Therefore, the loop condition (not Found and First $\leq$ Last) will eventually become False and the execution of the loop statement will terminate.

Claim 2: The loop assertion is a loop invariant.

Proof: See Example 2 in Appendix 1 for a proof that uses the Principle of Mathematical Induction.

Claim 3: After the last iteration, the postcondition is true.

Proof: After the last iteration, we must have either Found = True or First > Last. If Found = True, then A [Middle] is EqualTo Item, and so the postcondition is true. As we noted earlier, if First > Last, then First = Last + 1. Therefore, by the loop invariant, Item should be inserted at position First. Thus, in either case, the postcondition is true.

C. Analysis

We first note that the space requirements are always $O(1)$. For the time requirements, we will provide the analysis for a successful search. (See Exercise 5.16 for the analysis in the case of an unsuccessful search.) The best case occurs when the middle item is the item sought. In this case, the loop is executed only once, and so BestTime (N) is $O(1)$.

In the worst case, the search continues until First = Last. The following chart will help us to estimate the number of iterations in this case.

N	Number of Iterations
1	1
2	2
3	2
4	3
5	3
6	3
7	3
8	4
9	4
10	4
11	4
12	4
13	4
14	4
15	4
16	5
17	5

For the values of N in this chart, we see that when N is a power of 2, the number of iterations is $(\log_2 N) + 1$; otherwise, the number of iterations is between $\log_2 N$ and $(\log_2 N) + 1$. We therefore conjecture that for all N,

the number of iterations $=$ Trunc $(\log_2 N) + 1$

This claim can be proved by induction (see Exercise 5.14). We conclude that WorstTime is $O(\log N)$.

The average number of iterations is also $O(\log N)$ (see Exercise 5.15). In other words, Time is $O(\log N)$.

A recursive version of the Search subalgorithm is considered in Exercise 5.7.

$\downarrow$

6. <u>Insert (Item)</u>.

   A. Subalgorithm

   We first call Search to find the position where Item belongs. After that, the design is exactly the same as the contiguous design of Insert in the List ADT.

   The complete subalgorithm is

   $\downarrow$

   <u>Insert (Item)</u>.

```
Search (Item, Found, Position)

{ Move remaining items down one slot: }
for I := N downto Position do
    A [I+1] := A[I]
A [Position] := Item
Add 1 to N
```

   B. Verification

   No verification is needed.

   C. Analysis

   The call to Search takes $O(\log N)$ time, but the "for" statement is executed, on average, approximately $N/2$ times, and so Time (N) is $O(N)$. Space (N) is $O(1)$.

   $\downarrow$

7. <u>Delete (Item)</u>.

   The design and analysis of the Delete subalgorithm are similar to that of Insert. We present only the complete subalgorithm:

A. Subalgorithm.

```
Search (Item, Found, Position)

{ Close up the space: }
for I := Position to N-1 do
   A [I] := A [I+1]
Subtract 1 from N
```

Implementations of the Ordered List Data Type

Based on the designs we have just discussed, a dynamic-linked recursive and a contiguous implementation were developed. The development, validation, and analysis of a static linked implementation is left as an exercise. Instead, we will also consider a dynamic linked implementation with iterative procedures for Insert and Delete. The details of these implementations contain no surprises, so we do not list them here. They are on disk as OList1Manager.pas, OList2Manager.pas, and OList3Manager.pas. Each implementation was validated with the help of a driver program—OList-Driver.pas—similar to the one used to validate implementations of the List ADT.

Run-Time Analysis of the Ordered List Implementations

We will compare the run-time performance of each implementation. First, we make some general observations. For N consecutive insertions or deletions, the linked implementations will take only $O(N)$ time, versus $O(N^2)$ time for the contiguous implementation. But the contiguous implementation is better for random searches: $O(\log N)$ time versus $O(N)$ time for the linked implementations.

The program TestTime described in Chapter 3 was run in the following experiment: For each unit, we determine the time to insert 1000 items into an initially empty list. ItemType is an object whose Value field contains a random six-byte string. The experiment was then repeated with 2000 items. The results are shown in Table 5.1.

Table 5.1. The time, in seconds, to insert N items into an initially empty list with each of the ordered-list implementations. ItemType is an object whose Value field contains a random six-byte string.

Implementation	$N = 1000$	$N = 2000$
linked, dynamic, recursive	36.5	147.7
linked, dynamic, iterative	33.8	137.0
contiguous	28.2	105.6

Some of the results in Table 5.1 are as expected. For example, when N is doubled, the time is multiplied by four. That is because the average time to make N insertions in an ordered list is $O(N^2)$.

We might also have predicted that the iterative version of the linked dynamic implementation would be faster than the recursive version. The main reason for this is that recursive subprograms save values that seldom change, such as return addresses. But don't forget that the iterative design was more complicated than the recursive design.

Table 5.1 does contain at least one possible surprise. The linked-dynamic implementations of the Ordered List ADT are much slower than the linked-dynamic implementation of the List ADT (see Table 4.3). Can you think of an explanation for this?

Basically, the difference is due to the fact that insertions in an ordered list require comparisons between items. The larger the items, the longer the comparisons take. More important, when the items are objects, the comparisons are implemented as function calls (to LessThan, EqualTo, and GreaterThan). Any subprogram call, even if it is not recursive, involves saving and restoring an activation record.

The time for the linked dynamic insertions should decrease substantially if we replace the function calls with in-line comparisons <, =, and >). This change requires that the items be scalar items instead of objects. The results of conducting the above experiment on scalar items are shown in Table 5.2.

By using scalar items instead of object items, we were able to eliminate the function calls (to LessThan and so on) in the dynamic-linked implementations. This reduced the time for random insertions by about half.

But what about the contiguous implementation? Why did the time for random insertions remain about the same when we switched from function calls to in-line comparisons? The reason is that the comparisons take place in the Search subprogram, and each binary search makes, on average, only $O(\log N)$ comparisons. This is negligible when compared with the $O(N)$ time for the real work in a contiguous insertion—moving items to make room for the item to be inserted.

Table 5.2. The time, in seconds, to insert N items into an initially empty list with each of the ordered-list implementations. ItemType is **string** *[6], and each item is a random six-byte string.*

Implementation	$N = 1000$	$N = 2000$
linked, dynamic, recursive	19.8	79.8
linked, dynamic, iterative	17.2	69.3
contiguous	27.8	106.7

A hidden disadvantage of the contiguous implementation is that the space for a list is allocated from the Data Segment, which is the space for all global variables in a program. Because the size of the Data Segment is only about 64K bytes, for some applications a user might not want some of this space allocated for lists. In such cases, a dynamic implementation (using the heap) is a compelling choice.

In summary, the contiguous implementation is better if the user is willing to have list space allocated from the Data Segment, and if either of the following is true:

1. The items are objects and the application requires many random insertions and deletions.

2. The application is oriented more toward random searching than random inserting/deleting.

In conclusion, a user should be supplied with a total of four implementations: the contiguous and linked-dynamic iterative implementations for both object items and for scalar items.

For each of these four implementations, there should be sufficient information to allow users to make the appropriate selection. For example, some of the information for the contiguous implementation for scalar items is as follows:

Unit Name: SOList3Manager

Purpose: To implement the Ordered List ADT. It is assumed that the items are of a scalar type.

Object Type: ListType

Special Features

1. This unit uses the units SList3Manager, SItemInList, and Maxima.

2. Space for instances is allocated from the Data Segment.

Methods

1. `procedure ListType.Initialize;`
   `{ Postcondition: The list is empty.  }`
   `{ Time (N) is O(1). Space (N) is O(1). }`

2. `function ListType.IsEmpty: boolean;`
   `{ Postcondition: Returns true if and only if the list }`
   `{                is empty.                            }`
   .
   .
   .

Here is the interface part of that unit:

```
interface
uses
    SItemInList, { implements ItemType for scalar items }
    Maxima,  { for MaxListSize }
    SList3Manager; { implements the List ADT for scalar }
                        { items                          }
type
    ListType = object (SList3Manager.ListType)
        procedure Search (var Item : ItemType;
                              var Found : boolean;
                              var Position: word);
        procedure Insert (Item: ItemType);
        procedure Delete (Item: ItemType)
end; { ListType }
```

CASE STUDY

The following case study illustrates several of the software engineering features introduced in Chapter 3: the role of input editing in programming projects, the Principle of Data Abstraction, bottom-up design, and the modularity induced by an object-oriented approach. Because the case study is little more than an application of ordered lists, the design is fairly straightforward.

CASE STUDY 5.1: UPDATING A CLASS ROSTER

Problem: Create and maintain a class roster for a class that holds a maximum of 35 students.

I.   Problem Analysis

Specifications

1. The input (from the keyboard) and output (to the screen) from one execution of the program should correspond to one conversational session: Each input value should be entered, left justified, in response to a prompt. Each prompt ends with a colon followed by two blank spaces. Incorrect input values should generate an error message and a reprompt. It is assumed that the user will eventually enter a correct value.

2. The first prompt should be:

    `Would you like to see the instructions? (Y/N):`

    If the input is or begins with the character 'Y,' the instructions given in Specification 4 are printed. If the input is or begins with the character 'N,' those instructions are not printed. If the input starts with neither 'Y' nor 'N,' the error message is

    `Illegal answer. Must be Y or N.`

3. The rest of the input consists of a sequence of requests. Each part of a request should be entered in response to a prompt. The prompts are

    ```
    Please enter the request:
    Please enter the student's name:
    Please enter the student's ID:
    Please enter the student's class code:
    ```

4. The request can be either Add, Drop, Find, Print, or End; trailing blanks and any extra characters (beyond the fifth character) are ignored. The student's name consists of a maximum of 30 characters in last-first-middle form; any characters beyond the first 30 are ignored. The ID consists of six digits; any characters beyond the first six are ignored. The student's class code consists of two letters and indicates whether the student is a freshman (FR), sophomore (SO), junior (JR), senior (SR), special (SP), or audit (AU); any characters beyond these two are ignored.

5. If the request is Add, then the request should also include the student's name, ID, and class code. For Drop and Find, only the name and ID should be included. For Print and End, nothing else should be included. Any superfluous information is ignored.

6. It is an error if the request is neither Add, Drop, Find, Print, nor End. For example, ADD, FindIt, and Quit are illegal. For an illegal request, the error message is

    `Illegal request. Must be Add, Drop, Find, Print or End.`

7. It is illegal if any of the (first) six characters in the ID are not digits. If this occurs, the error message is

    `Illegal ID. Must consist of six digits.`

8. It is an error if the class code is not one of the six legal codes given in (4). If this occurs, the error message is

    `Illegal class code. Must be FR, SO, JR, SR, SP, AU.`

9. It is an error if the request is Add and the roster is already full. If this occurs, the student is not inserted in the roster and the error message is

    `Student not added—class already full.`

10. It is an error if the request is Add and the given student has the name
     and ID of a student already on the roster. If this occurs, the request is
     not carried out and the error message is

     ```
     Student not added—already on roster.
     ```

11. It is an error if the request is Drop and there is no student on the ros-
     ter with the name and ID of the given student. If this occurs, the re-
     quest is not carried out and the error message is

     ```
     Student not dropped—not on roster.
     ```

12. If the request is Add and there are no errors, the student should be
     inserted in the class roster.

13. If the request is Drop and there are no errors, the student should be
     deleted from the class roster.

14. If the request is Find, the output should be either

     ```
     Yes, the student is in the class.
     ```

     or

     ```
     No, the student is not in the class.
     ```

     depending on whether the student is in the class roster.

15. If the request is Print, the roster should be printed in alphabetical
     order by students' names. If two students happen to have the same
     name, the one with the lower ID is printed first.

16. If the request is End, that is a sentinel to signal the end of the input.

System Test 1 (input values always follow a prompt):

```
Create and maintain a class roster.
The maximum number of students allowed in the class is 35.
Would you like to see the instructions? (Y/N): N
-------------------------------------------------------------
Please enter the request: Add
Please enter the student's name: Carter Anthony James
Please enter the student's ID: 402107
Please enter the student's class code: JR
-------------------------------------------------------------
Please enter the request: Delete
Illegal request. Must be Add, Drop, Find, Print or End.
Please enter the request: DROP
Illegal request. Must be Add, Drop, Find, Print or End.
Please enter the request: Drop
Please enter the student's name: Cohn Maxwell Paul
Please enter the student's ID: 315555
Student not dropped—not on roster.
-------------------------------------------------------------
```

```
Please enter the request: Add
Please enter the student's name: Baten Melinda Jane
Please enter the student's ID: 628962
Please enter the student's class code: FR
------------------------------------------------------------
Please enter the request: Find
Please enter the student's name: Peary Michael John
Please enter the student's ID: 48316
Illegal ID. Must consist of six digits.
Please enter the student's ID: 483316
No, the student is not in the class.
------------------------------------------------------------
Please enter the request: Add
Please enter the student's name: Mendez Mark Andrew
Please enter the student's ID: 530372
Please enter the student's class code: SR
------------------------------------------------------------
Please enter the request: Add
Please enter the student's name: Chao Jing-Wen
Please enter the student's ID: 834547
Please enter the student's class code: FR
------------------------------------------------------------
Please enter the request: Drop
Please enter the student's name: Carter Anthony James
Please enter the student's ID: 402107
------------------------------------------------------------
Please enter the request: Print
Name                 ID        Class code
Baten Melinda Jane   628962    FR
Chao Jing-Wen        834547    FR
Mendez Mark Andrew   530372    SR
------------------------------------------------------------
Please enter the request: Add
Please enter the student's name: Chao Jing-Wen
Please enter the student's ID: 834547
Please enter the student's class code: SR
Student not added—already on roster.
------------------------------------------------------------
Please enter the request: End
```

System Test 2:

```
Create and maintain a class roster.
The maximum number of students allowed in the class is 35.

Would you like to see the instructions? (Y/N): Yes

The request can be either Add, Drop, Find, Print or End;
trailing blanks are ignored and any extra characters beyond
```

```
the fifth character are ignored. The student's name consists
of at most 30 characters in the form: last first middle;
any extra characters beyond the first 30 are ignored. The
ID  consists of six digits; any extra characters beyond
the first six are ignored. The student's class code consists
of two letters and indicates whether the student is a
freshman (FR), sophomore (SO), junior (JR), senior (SR),
special (SP) or audit (AU); any extra characters beyond
these two are ignored.
------------------------------------------------------------
Please enter the request: Add
Please enter the student's name: A1
Please enter the student's ID: 000001
Please enter the student's class code: SO
------------------------------------------------------------
Please enter the request: Add
Please enter the student's name: A2
Please enter the student's ID: 000002
Please enter the student's class code: SO
------------------------------------------------------------
   .
   .
   .
------------------------------------------------------------
Please enter the request: Add
Please enter the student's name: A35
Please enter the student's ID: 000035
Please enter the student's class code: SO
------------------------------------------------------------
Please enter the request: Add
Please enter the student's name: A36
Please enter the student's ID: 000036
Please enter the student's class code: SO
Student not added—class already full.
------------------------------------------------------------
Please enter the request: End
```

II.   Program Design

We start by looking for objects, and we don't have far to look. Of the three nouns in the statement of the problem ("class", "roster," and "students"), "class" is the most inclusive; so we will make ClassType an object with the following methods:

1. `Initialize.`

    Postcondition: The class is empty.

Note: An implicit precondition of every other method is that the instance calling the method has already called Initialize.

2. `ProcessRequests.`

   Postcondition: Each request has been read in and processed.

3. `ProcessAdd.`

   Postcondition: The student's name, ID, and class code have been read in. If the class is already full, the overflow error is printed. Otherwise, if there is already a student in the class with the same name and ID of the student just read in, the duplicate error is printed. Otherwise, the student is added to the class.

4. `ProcessDrop.`

   Postcondition: The student's name and ID have been read in. If there is no student in the class with the name and ID of the student just read in, the missing-student error is printed. Otherwise, the student is dropped from the class.

5. `ProcessFind.`

   Postcondition: The student's name and ID have been read in. If there is a student in the class with the same name and ID as the student just read in, the "in class" message is printed. Otherwise, the "not in class" message is printed.

6. `ProcessPrint.`

   Postcondition: The students in the class have been printed alphabetically by students' names, with the ID (in increasing order) as secondary key.

The fundamental design decision regarding the object ClassType is the design domain, that is, the number and types of the fields. Referring back to the statement of the problem, "roster" is the only relevant property of a class, and so we select Roster as the only field in the object ClassType. To facilitate the printing of the students in the class, Roster will be an ordered list. The ordering will be alphabetical by name; for identical names, the ordering will be by increasing IDs.

We do not try to design the methods in ClassType just yet. Because an object-oriented approach is bottom-up, we will first get to the bottom and then work our way up.

Since the ordered list ADT has already been defined (and developed), we can immediately turn our attention to the lowest level: the items in the ordered list. The only remaining noun in the statement of the problem is "students," and so we decide that each item will be an object representing a student. The methods LessThan, EqualTo, and GreaterThan will be in

StudentType, because Roster is an ordered list. The only other methods needed are to read in the name, ID, and class code. The six methods are:

1. **LessThan (Student).**

    Postcondition: True has been returned if the calling instance comes
              before Student in the ordering. Otherwise, False has been
              returned.

2. **EqualTo (Student).**

    Postcondition: True has been returned if the calling instance has the
              same name and ID as Student. Otherwise, False has been
              returned.

3. **GreaterThan (Student).**

    Postcondition: True has been returned if the calling instance comes
              after Student in the ordering. Otherwise, False has been
              returned.

4. **GetName.**

    Postcondition: The student's name has been read in.

5. **GetID.**

    Postcondition: The student's six-digit ID has been read in.

6. **GetClassCode.**

    Postcondition: The student's class code has been read in.

We now design the object StudentType. The fields will be Name, ID, and ClassCode. The GetName method simply writes out the name prompt and reads in the student's Name. By setting the maximum length of Name, ID, and ClassCode to 30, 6, and 2 characters, respectively, we avoid having to worry about extra characters.

GetID consists of a loop that continues until a legal ID has been obtained. Because testing for a legal ID is not easily done in a Boolean expression, we introduce a Boolean variable, IDIsOK, which is initialized to False before the loop statement is executed. Within the loop, the ID prompt is printed, an ID is read, and the ID error is printed if the ID's length is less than six or if the ID contains nondigit characters. The test for nondigit characters proceeds as follows: A counter, I, is initialized to 1 and then incremented as long as $I \leq 6$ and ID $[I]$ is a digit character. After the execution of this inner-loop statement is completed, I should have the value 7.

The complete method is

```
GetID.
Initialize IDIsOK to False
repeat
   Writeout IDPrompt
   Read in ID
   if Length (ID) < 6 then
      Write out IDError
   else

      { Check for non-digit characters: }
      I := 1
      while (I <= 6) and (ID [I] in ['0'..'9']) do
         Increment I
      if I <= 6 then
         Writeout IDError
      else
         IDIsOK := True
   until IDIsOK
```

The GetClassCode method is similar to but simpler than GetID, and so its design is left as an exercise, as are the designs of the relational methods LessThan, EqualTo, and GreaterThan.

We now turn to the design of ClassType's methods. The Initialize method merely calls Roster.Initialize. Note that Class.Initialize is a call to the Initialize method in ClassType, whereas Roster.Initialize is a call to the Initialize method in OListType. There is no conflict even though the methods have the same name.

The method ProcessRequests has a loop that continues until the request is 'End'. Each time through the loop, the request prompt is written and a request is read in and processed. The processing of requests (except 'End,' which does nothing) is taken care of in separate methods, and so the complete subalgorithm for ProcessRequests is:

```
ProcessRequests.

repeat
Write out PromptRequest
Read in Request
if Request = 'Add' then
   ProcessAdd
else
   if Request = 'Drop' then
      ProcessDrop
   else
      if Request = 'Find' then
         ProcessFind
```

```
          else
             if Request = 'Print' then
                ProcessPrint
             else
                if Request <> 'End' then
                   Writeout ErrorRequest
until Request = 'End'
```

The ProcessAdd subalgorithm starts by reading in a student's name, ID, and class codes. Error messages are printed if the roster is already full or if the student has the same name and ID of a student already on the roster; otherwise, the student is inserted in Roster.

<u>ProcessAdd.</u>

```
with Student do
   GetName
   GetID
   GetClassCode
with Roster do
   if Size = MaxListSize then
      Write out ErrorFull
   else
      Search (Student, Found, Position)
      if Found then
         Write out ErrorDuplicate
      else
         Insert (Student)
```

We omit the design of ProcessDrop because of its similarity to the design of ProcessAdd. Finally, we omit the designs of ProcessFind and ProcessPrint because each of the subalgorithms consists of little more than a call to the Search or Traverse method.

    Finally, we design the main algorithm. We need to print instructions if asked, initialize the class, and then process the requests. By relegating the task of printing instructions to a subalgorithm, we have completed the design of the main algorithm:

<u>ClassRoster (InstructionsFile).</u>

```
PrintInstructions (InstructionsFile)
Class.Initialize
Class.ProcessRequests
```

The subalgorithm PrintInstructions consists of a loop that continues until the user answers 'Y' or 'N' to the prompt ('Do you want the instructions printed? (Y/N):   '). The complete subalgorithm is

```
PrintInstructions (InstructionsFile).
repeat
    Write out InstructionsPrompt
    Read in Answer
    if Answer = 'Y' then

        { Print the instructions: }
        Reset (InstructionsFile)
        while not Eof (InstructionsFile) do
            Read from InstructionsFile into InstructionLine
            Write out InstructionLine
    else
        if Answer <> 'N' then
            Write out ErrorAnswer
until (Answer = 'Y') or (Answer = 'N')
```

Algorithm Validation

We first validate the methods in StudentType. The only loop statement worthy of verification is the while statement in GetID. The postcondition is "I = 7 or ID [I] is not in ['0'..'9']." The truth of this assertion follows immediately from the loop condition and the fact that the execution of the loop eventually terminates.

In the method ProcessRequests (as well as in the subalgorithm PrintInstructions), the repeat statement is fairly straightforward: During each iteration, either an error message is printed or the correct input has been entered. Eventually, according to the assumption in Specification 1, the correct input will be entered. A proof of correctness would be inappropriate because there is no progression in the loops: Each iteration is independent of previous iterations.

Algorithm Analysis

The Time and Space requirements for PrintInstructions are $O(1)$ because this subalgorithm is independent of N (that is, Roster.Size). All of the other subalgorithms call, either directly or indirectly, methods from the ordered-list ADT. The time and space estimates for a method can be provided to a user without violating the Principle of Data Abstraction. Therefore, we will utilize those estimates (specifically, the estimates given in the user information at the end of the preceding section). The Time and Space requirements for the other subalgorithms, except ProcessRequests, are as follows:

1. ProcessAdd: Time (N) is $O(N)$; Space (N) is $O(1)$.
2. ProcessDrop: Time (N) is $O(N)$; Space (N) is $O(1)$.

3. ProcessFind: Time (N) is $O(\log N)$; Space (N) is $O(1)$.

4. ProcessPrint: Time (N) is $O(N)$; Space (N) is $O(1)$.

The analysis of ProcessRequests is complicated by the fact that the specifications did not indicate any relationship between the number of requests and the size of the roster. We can state that Time (N) must be at least $O(N)$ because ProcessRequests calls ProcessAdd, whose Time is $O(N)$. Also, Space (N) must be $O(N)$ because all of the space for the roster is allocated during the execution of ProcessRequests.

Finally, the time and space requirements for the item methods are $O(1)$ because these are independent of the size of the roster.

III. Program Implementation

The unit ItemInList was coded and validated first. The only implementation details worth noting are the field-width specifications in the WriteOut procedure. These were set to obtain the output format shown in System Test 1.

This unit, and the other parts of the case study code, are in the directory Ch5\CaseStud on disk.

To validate the unit ItemInList, an ItemDriver program was used. All tests were passed, and so our confidence in the unit ItemInList was increased.

The unit ClassManager was implemented and validated next. In validating ClassManager, we included tests for overflow, duplicate students, and missing students.

Finally, the program was coded and validated. The validation included the two system tests given in the Problem Analysis stage. The program itself, as usually happens in object-oriented programming, is fairly small. Here is the entire program (except for the PrintInstructions procedure):

```
program ClassRoster;
{***********************************************************}
{                                                         }
{ Programmer   : Bill Collins                             }
{                                                         }
{ Description  : Create and maintain a class roster.      }
{                                                         }
{ Calls        : PrintInstructions, ProcessRequests       }
{                                                         }
{ Files Read   : Instruct.dat                             }
{                                                         }
{ Precondition : See Specifications.                      }
{                                                         }
{ Postcondition: See Specifications.                      }
{                                                         }
{***********************************************************}
```

```
uses
   Maxima,  { declares MaxListSize }
   ItemInList, { implements StudentType }
   ClassManager; { implements ClassType }
const
   Heading1 = 'Create and maintain a class roster.';
   Heading2 =
   'The maximum number of students allowed in the class is ';
   Period = '.';
var
   Class         : ClassType;
   InstructionsFile: Text;

begin { the statement part of the main program }
   { Print headings: }
   Writeln (Heading1);
   Writeln (Heading2, MaxListSize: 1, Period);

   Assign (InstructionsFile, 'Instruct.dat');
   PrintInstructions (InstructionsFile);
   Class.Initialize;
   Class.ProcessRequests
end. { ClassRoster }
```

Now that we have completed the case study, you may ask, "Is that all there is?" Neither the design nor the implementation required a major effort. By focusing on the objects involved, we kept reducing the complexity of the problems. When you look at the program and units, it is a good sign if you think that everything is obvious.

ORDERABLE LISTS

Another specialization of a list is an orderable list. In an **orderable** list, the items can be compared, but the list is not necessarily in order. The Orderable List ADT inherits all nine of the method designs from the improved-linked and contiguous designs of the List ADT, and also has the following five methods:

1. <u>Sort.</u>

   Postcondition: The list is ordered.

   ↑

2. <u>IsInOrder.</u>

   Postcondition: True has been returned if the list is in order. Otherwise, False has been returned.

3. SearchInOrder (Item, Found, Position).

Precondition: The list is ordered.

Postcondition: The list is ordered. If the list is empty, or if there is no item on the list that is EqualTo Item, then Item is unchanged, Found = False, and Position contains the posiiton at which Item could be inserted without disordering the list. Otherwise, an item EqualTo Item has been copied into Item, Found = True, and Position contains the position of that item.

We could not use Search as the name for this method because the unordered Search was already inherited from the List ADT.

4. InsertInOrder (Item).

Precondition: The list is ordered; the number of items in the list is less than MaxListSize.

Postcondition: Item has been inserted into the list. The list is ordered.

5. DeleteInOrder (Item).

Precondition: The list is ordered. There is an item in the list EqualTo Item.

Postcondition: An item EqualTo Item has been deleted from the list. The list is ordered.

The most important of these methods is the Sort method. We will devote all of Chapter 9 to the study of different designs of this method.

The Orderable List ADT presents the user with maximum freedom. A given instance can be unordered at the beginning of the program, and methods appropriate to an unordered list (such as inserting by position) may be utilized. The instance can then be sorted and thereafter treated as an ordered list.

But with this freedom comes danger. For example, after an instance has been sorted, there is nothing to stop the user from inserting by position, which may disorder the list. If there is any doubt as to whether a list is in order, the user should call IsInOrder before attempting the SearchInOrder, InsertInOrder, and DeleteInOrder methods.

SUMMARY

The focus of this chapter was the Ordered List ADT. Most of the method interfaces and designs were unchanged from those of the List ADT. One notable exception was the Search method. By utilizing the direct access feature of arrays, we were able to develop a binary search subalgorithm in the contiguous design. With a binary search, we can conduct searches in $O(\log N)$ time, on average.

The case study, creating and maintaining a class roster, served mainly to illustrate the object-oriented approach to program development.

The Orderable List ADT was introduced, but we postpone until Chapter 9 the designs of its essential method, the Sort method. The reason for this is that several valuable sort techniques are related to binary trees, the subject of Chapters 7 and 8.

EXERCISES

5.1 **a.** Suppose that Animals is an instance of an ordered list. Show the sequence of animals in the list after each of the following messages is sent:

```
Animals.Initialize
Animals.Insert ('dog')
Animals.Insert ('cow')
Animals.Insert ('pig')
Animals.Insert ('goat')
Animals.Insert ('cat')
Animals.Insert ('sheep')
Animals.Insert ('horse')
Animals.Insert ('chicken')
```

   b. Develop a unit, SItemInList, in which ItemType is declared to be of type **string** [15]. Include a WriteOut procedure that writes out the item. Also, develop a unit, Maxima, in which MaxListSize is a constant identifier with a value of 100.
   c. Incorporate the messages in part a into a program that uses the units ItemInList and Maxima from part b. The program will also use SOList1Manager, an implementation of the Ordered List ADT in which it is assumed that the items are scalar.
   d. Add a Traverse message to the program so that the final version of the list is printed out.

5.2 Trace the execution of the messages in Exercise 5.1 for both the improved-linked and contiguous designs.

5.3 Given the ordered list created in Exercise 5.1, trace the execution of the following messages for the contiguous design:

    a. Item := 'goat'
         Animals.Search (Item, Found, Position)
    b. Item := 'bull'
         Animals.Search (Item, Found, Position)

5.4 Of the nine methods in the Ordered List ADT, which three methods have different Big-O times for the improved-linked and contiguous designs?

5.5 **a.** In the binary search subalgorithm described in this chapter, for most iterations there will be two comparisons between A [Middle] and Item because, usually, they will not be equal. Rearrange the comparisons between A [Middle] and Item in the subalgorithm so that, for most iterations, there will be only 1.5 comparisons (on average) between those items.
    b. What effect will the change suggested in part a have on the Big-O time for the subalgorithm? What about run-time performance?

5.6 Exercise 5.5 suggested how to change the binary search subalgorithm so that, on average, only about 1.5 comparisons between items were made during each iteration. The following version is even better: Only one comparison between items is made per iteration. This is sometimes called the "forgetful" version because the loop does not stop even if A [Middle] is EqualTo Item.

```
Search (Item, Found, Position).

Initialize First to 1, Last to N and Found to False

{ Find where Item is or belongs in the list: }
while First < Last do
   Middle := (First + Last) div 2
   if A [Middle] is LessThan Item then
      First := Middle + 1
   else
        Last := Middle
if (N = 0) or (A [First] is GreaterThan Item) then
   Position := First
else
   if A [First] is LessThan Item then
      Position := N + 1
```

```
else
    Item     := A [First]
    Found    := True
    Position := First
```

a. Determine an appropriate loop assertion for the while loop.

b. How does the Big-O time for this subalgorithm compare with that of the original version? What about run-time performance?

5.7 Develop a recursive version of the binary search subalgorithm.

> *HINT Develop a recursive subalgorithm SearchItem, with formal parameters First and Last. Search calls SearchItem. Item, Found, and Position are nonlocal variables within SearchItem.*

5.8 The following is an *incorrect* version of the binary search subalgorithm. Give an example of an ordered list that reveals the error.

```
Search (Item, Found, Position).
Initialize First to 1, Last to N and Found to False.

{ Find where Item is or belongs in the list: }
repeat

    { Loop assertion:  For all I in [1..N]:    }
    {                      if I < First, A[I] is LessThan }
    {                      Item;                          }
    {                      if I > Last, A[I] is           }
    {                      GreaterThan Item.              }
    Middle := (First + Last) div 2
    if A [Middle] is EqualTo Item then
        Item     := A [Middle]
        Found    := True
        Position := Middle
    else
        if A [Middle] is LessThan Item then
            First := Middle + 1
        else
            Last := Middle - 1
until Found or (First > Last)
if not Found then
    Position := First
```

> *HINT This subalgorithm is the same as the correct version, except that we have replaced the while statement with a repeat*

statement. Such a replacement is illegal if the condition in the while statement is initially false. What must the list look like if the following condition is false right after we initialize Found to False, First to 1, and Last to N?

```
(not Found) and (First <= Last)
```

5.9   The direct access facility of arrays makes a binary search an appropriate technique for a contiguous design of the Ordered List ADT. A binary search can also be used with a linked design. To give you an idea of how this might work, suppose we are searching for an item on the list. We can obtain the middle item as follows:

```
Middle := (First + Size) div 2
TempHead := Head
for I := First to Middle - 1 do
   TempHead := TempHead's Next
```

   a.   Develop a binary search subalgorithm for the linked design.
   b.   Determine the Big-O time of this subalgorithm.

5.10   The implementation of the contiguous design of the Ordered List ADT was, of course, static. In a dynamic contiguous implementation, the items would still be in an array, but the array would be in the heap. Part of the declaration of ListType is as follows:

```
type
   ArrayType = array [1..MaxListSize] of ItemType;
   ListType  = object
      APtr:  ^ArrayType;
      N    : integer;
      procedure Initialize;
         .
         .
         .
   end; { ListType }
```

(None of the method implementations would be inherited from the List ADT implementations.)

Can you think of an application in which a dynamic contiguous implementation would be preferred over both the dynamic-linked and static-contiguous implementations?

5.11   As a *user* of the ordered-list ADT, develop each of the following subalgorithms from the given nine methods. *Do not use any of the fields in the linked or contiguous designs!*

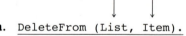

   a.   DeleteFrom (List, Item).

       Postcondition: All items in List that are GreaterThan or EqualTo Item have been deleted from List.

b. `Merge (List1, List2).`

Postcondition: List1 contains all of the items that were in List1 together with all of the items that were in List2. (If an item appeared once in List1 and once in List2, that item would appear twice in the merged list.)

c. `UniqueCount (List).`

Postcondition: The value returned is the number of unique items in List. (An item is *unique* if it does not appear more than once in the list.)

d. `Equals (List1, List2).`

Postcondition: True has been returned if and only if each item in List1 is EqualTo an item in List2, and each item in List2 is EqualTo an item in List1.

5.12 Develop an iterative version of the linked Delete subalgorithm.

5.13 Use the Principle of Mathematical Induction to prove that for $K = 1, 2, 3, \ldots$,

$$\sum_{i=1}^{k} (i * 2^{i-1}) = (K - 1) * 2^k + 1$$

5.14 Prove that, in the worst case for a successful binary search, the number of loop iterations is

$$\text{Trunc } (\log_2 N) + 1$$

HINT Use the "strong" form of the Principle of Mathematical Induction, as in Example 3 of Appendix 1.

5.15 Show that, on average, the binary search subalgorithm makes $O(\log N)$ iterations for successful searches.

HINT Because the average number of iterations is a non-decreasing function of N, it is sufficient to prove the claim for values that are one less than a power of 2. So assume that $N = 2^K - 1$ for some positive integer K.

In a successful search, one iteration is needed if the item sought is at position $(N + 1)/2$. Two iterations are needed for the item sought if it is at position

$$(N+1)/4 \quad \text{or} \quad 3(N + 1)/4$$

Three iterations are needed if the item sought is in any one of the four positions:

$$(N + 1)/8, 3\ (N + 1)/8, 5\ (N + 1)/8, 7\ (N + 1)/8.$$

Continuing in this fashion, we see that the total number of iterations required for all successful searches is

$$(1 * 1) + (2 * 2) + (3 * 4) + (4 * 8) + (5 * 16)$$
$$+ \ldots + K * 2^{K-1}$$

The average number of iterations is this sum divided by N. Now use the result from Exercise 5.13 and the relation

$$K = \log_2(N + 1)$$

5.16 Show that, for unsuccessful searches, the binary search subalgorithm makes $O(\log N)$ iterations.

5.17 Suppose that Scores is an instance of an *orderable* list. Each item is an integer betweeen 5 and 62, inclusive, and the items are to be in increasing order. Describe the effect on the list of the following messages:

```
Scores.Initialize
Scores.Insert (12, 1)    { insert 12 in position 1 }
Scores.InsertInOrder (8) { insert 8 where it belongs }
Scores.InsertInOrder (19)
Scores.Insert (57, 2)
```

LABORATORY EXERCISES

5.1 On your computer, run the experiment summarized in Table 5.2 of this chapter. Estimate how long it would take to insert 4000 random, six-byte strings into an initially empty ordered list. Find out how close your estimate was to the actual time.

5.2 Modify the Case Study program/units to accommodate the following specification changes:

a. The class limit is to be read in, and should be an integer between 1 and 500, inclusive. The prompt is

```
Please enter the class limit:
```

If the response is not an integer in the allowed range—for example, if the response is 600 or 3G2—the error message is

```
Error: the class limit must be an integer between 1
and 500, inclusive.
```

A reprompt is then given.

b. At the beginning of the program, the user inputs the file name that contains the class roster (or will contain the roster if the roster does not exist). The class roster is then read from the file (or initialized) and updated. At the end of the program, store the class roster in the file.

PROGRAMMING ASSIGNMENTS

Programming Assignment 1

Problem: To develop a small system for local libraries. The system keeps track of the fiction books available at each of several branches. Each branch keeps its books in a list arranged in alphabetical order by the author's name. Books by the same author are arranged alphabetically by title. There may be several copies of the same book in a branch. Patrons can ask the library to find the number of copies of a book currently available at a particular branch.

Specifications

1. Every input string for 〈title〉, 〈author〉, and 〈branch〉 is a maximum of 10 alphabetic characters, left justified.

2. All input should be in response to a prompt. Incorrect input values should generate an error message and a reprompt. Unless otherwise specified below, the error message should be "Error: Incorrect response." It is assumed that the user will input a correct response eventually.

3. To set up the first branch of the library:

    `Please enter the name of the branch:`

    Then, or to set up each other branch of the library:

    `Please enter Book, Branch, or EndBranch:`

    If the word "Book" is entered, this means that the following book is available at that branch. The next prompt is

    `Please enter the author's name:`

    and the next prompt is

    `Please enter the title:`

    After that, the Book-Branch-EndBranch prompt is repeated.

    If the word "Branch" is entered, then prompt for the name of the branch and give the Book-Branch-EndBranch prompt.

    There will be, at most, 10 branches and 20 books at each branch. It is assumed that the response "EndBranch" will be entered eventually. This separates the branch initializations from the requests.

4. A customer can make one of the following requests:

    ```
    Checkout <author> <title> <branch>
    Return <author> <title> <branch>
    Number <author> <title> <branch>
    ```

    These requests, each with four prompts, can come in any order and are terminated by an EndRequest response. The initial prompt for a customer request is:

    ```
    Please enter Checkout, Return, Number, or EndRequest:
    ```

5. For Checkout, if there is no copy of the book at that branch, print the message "Sorry, ⟨title⟩ by ⟨author⟩ is not in stock at branch ⟨branch⟩." Otherwise, delete one copy of the book from that branch and print "The book ⟨title⟩ has been taken out by you."

6. For Return, accept the book and print "Book ⟨title⟩ by ⟨author⟩ has been returned to branch ⟨branch⟩."

7. For Number, find the number of books at the branch and print "Branch ⟨branch⟩ has ⟨number⟩ copies of ⟨title⟩ by ⟨author⟩."

8. For EndRequest, print out the books, arranged in alphabetical order by author, for each branch. For each author, print out the titles, alphabetically ordered, and the number of books of each title by that author.

9. See the system tests for the output formats.

System Test 1:

```
Please enter the name of the branch: Blacksburg
Please enter Book, Branch or EndBranch: Book
Please enter the author's name: Adams
Please enter the title: Life
Please enter Book, Branch or EndBranch: Book
Please enter the author's name: Adams
Please enter the title: Life
Please enter Book, Branch or EndBranch: Book
Please enter the author's name: Adams
Please enter the title: Works
Please enter Book, Branch or EndBranch: Branch
Please enter the name of the branch: Shawsville
Please enter Book, Branch or EndBranch: Burns Error:
Incorrect response.
Please enter Book, Branch or EndBranch: Book
Please enter the author's name: Burns
Please enter the title: Poems
Please enter Book, Branch or EndBranch: Book
Please enter the author's name: Wirth
Please enter the title: Programs
```

```
Please enter Book, Branch or EndBranch: Book
Please enter the author's name: Flon
Please enter the title: Structures
Please enter Book, Branch or EndBranch: Radford Error:
Incorrect response.
Please enter Book, Branch or EndBranch: Branch
Please enter the name of the branch: Radford
Please enter Book, Branch or EndBranch: Book
Please enter the author's name: Aho
Please enter the title: Algorithms
Please enter Book, Branch or EndBranch: Book
Please enter the author's name: Knuth
Please enter the title: Algorithms
Please enter Book, Branch or EndBranch: EndBranch
Please enter Checkout, Return, Number, or EndRequest: Return
Please enter the author's name: Evans
Please enter the title: Dances
Please enter the name of the branch: Shawsville
Book 'Dances' by Evans has been returned to branch
Shawsville.
Please enter Checkout, Return, Number, or EndRequest:
Checkout
Please enter the author's name: Knuth
Please enter the title: Algorithms
Please enter the name of the branch: Radford
The book 'Algorithms' has been taken out by you.
Please enter Checkout, Return, Number, or EndRequest:
Checkout
Please enter the author's name: Knuth
Please enter the title: Algorithms
Please enter the name of the branch: Radford
Sorry, 'Algorithms' by Knuth is not in stock at branch
Radford.
Please enter Checkout, Return, Number, or EndRequest: Number
Please enter the author's name: Knuth
Please enter the title: Algorithms
Please enter the name of the branch: Radford
Branch Radford has 0 copies of 'Algorithms' by Knuth.
Please enter Checkout, Return, Number, or EndRequest: Number
Please enter the author's name: Evans
Please enter the title: Dances
Please enter the name of the branch: Shawsville
Branch Shawsville has 1 copy of 'Dances' by Evans.
Please enter Checkout, Return, Number, or EndRequest:
EndRequest
```

The books in each of the branches are:

Branch	Author	Title	Number of Copies
Blacksburg	Adams	Life	2
		Work	1
Radford	Aho	Algorithms	1
Shawsville	Burns	Poems	1
	Evans	Dances	1
	Flon	Structures	1
	Wirth	Programs	1

System Test 2:

```
Please enter the name of the branch: Riner
Please enter Book, Branch, or EndBranch: Book
Please enter the author's name: Reagan
Please enter the title: My Turn
Please enter Book, Branch, or EndBranch: Book
Please enter the author's name: Reagan
Please enter the title: My Turn
Please enter Book, Branch, or EndBranch: Book
Please enter the author's name: Reagan
Please enter the title: My Turn
Please enter Book, Branch, or EndBranch: EndBranch
Please enter Checkout, Return, Number, or EndRequest:
Checkout
Please enter the author's name: Reagan
Please enter the title: My Fern
Please enter the name of the branch: Riner
Sorry, 'My Fern' by Reagan is not in stock at branch Riner.
Please enter Checkout, Return, Number, or EndRequest:
EndRequest
```

The books in each of the branches are:

Branch	Author	Title	Number of Copies
Riner	Reagan	My Turn	3

> *H I N T   Use three ListManager units—one for branches, one for authors, and one for titles. Each item in BranchList has a branch-name field and an author-list field. Each item in Author-List has an author-name field and a title-list field. Each item in TitleList has a title-name field and a number-of-copies field.*

Programming Assignment 2

Problem: To keep track of the lists of members in a set of clubs as members join, quit, and change clubs, as given by the input. Periodically, the input will ask you to print all the members in a given club or to find all the clubs to which a given person belongs.

Specifications

The input will consist of a list of up to 20 clubs, one per line, followed by the word End, followed by a list of commands (see next section), followed by the word End. There can be no more than five members in each club. Each club, person, and command will take up ten spaces, left justified. Input values will be entered in response to a prompt. Each input error will result in an error message and a reprompt. It is assumed that eventually the correct input will be entered.

The following errors should be detected:

1. If no input is given, an error message should be printed.

2. If more than 20 clubs are given, an error message should be printed, and only the first 20 clubs should be counted.

3. If an attempt is made to insert more than five members into a club, an error message should be printed and the additional members (beyond five) are not admitted.

4. If an illegal command, person, or club is given, an error message should be printed.

Commands and Output

The six possible commands are listed below, together with their semantics, associated input, and output. Each command is entered in response to the prompt

`Please enter a command:`

For a person, the prompt is

`Please enter a person's name:`

For a club, the prompt is

`Please enter a club's name:`

1. `Join <person> <club>`

   Add the given person to the given club. If the person is already in the club, the error message is "Error — ⟨person⟩ is already in ⟨club⟩." But no reprompt is given and ⟨person⟩ is not added again to ⟨club⟩. If the club is not one of the clubs listed originally, the error message is "Error — ⟨club⟩ is an illegal club name."

2. `Quit <person> <club>`

   Delete person from club. If the person is not in the club, the error message is "Error — ⟨person⟩ is not in ⟨club⟩."

3. `Change <person> <club1> <club2>`

   Delete person from club1, then add person to club2.

4. `Print <club>`

Print all the members in the club.

Output: "The members in ⟨club⟩ are:", followed by the list of members in alphabetical order, one per line.

5. `Find <person>`

Find and print all the clubs to which the person belongs.

Output: "⟨person⟩ belongs to the following club[s]:" followed by the list of clubs, in any order, one per line.

6. `Merge <club1> <club2>`

Merge the list of members for the two clubs. If a person is in both clubs, the name should occur only once in the merged list. From now on, the merged clubs can be referred to by either club name.

System Test 1:

```
Please enter a club's name or End: Kiwanis
Please enter a club's name or End: Lions
Please enter a club's name or End: Elks
Please enter a club's name or End: YMCA
Please enter a club's name or End: End
Please enter a command or End: Join
Please enter a person's name: Smith
Please enter a club's name: YMCA
Please enter a command or End: Join
Please enter a person's name: Fixx
Please enter a club's name: Eagles
Error - Eagles is an illegal club name.
Please enter a club's name: YMCA
Please enter a command or End: Join
Please enter a person's name: Smith
Please enter a club name: Lions
Please enter a command or End: Switch
Error - illegal command.
Please enter a command or End: Change
Please enter a person's name: Smith
Please enter a club's name: YMCA
Please enter a club's name: Elks
Please enter a command or End: Join
Please enter a person's name: Peters
Please enter a club's name: YMCA
Please enter a command or End: Join
Please enter a person's name: Jones
Please enter a club's name: Lions
Please enter a command or End: Print
```

```
Please enter a club's name: YMCA
The members in YMCA are:
Fixx
Peters
Please enter a command or End: Find
Please enter a person's name: Smith
Smith belongs to the following club[s]:
Lions
Elks
Please enter a command or End: Merge
Please enter a club's name: Elks
Please enter a club's name: YMCA
Please enter a command or End: Join
Please enter a person's name: Sullivan
Please enter a club's name: Elks
Please enter a command or End: Print
Please enter a club's name: Elks
The members in Elks are:
Fixx
Peters
Smith
Sullivan
Please enter a command or End: Quit
Please enter a person's name: Fixx
Please enter a club's name: Elks
Please enter a command or End: Type
Error - illegal command.
Please enter a command or End: Print
Please enter a club's name: YMCA
The members of YMCA are:
Peters
Smith
Sullivan
Please enter a command or End: Merge
Please enter a club's name: Elks
Please enter a club's name: Lions
Please enter a command or End: Quit
Please enter a person's name: Sullivan
Please enter a club's name: Elks
Please enter a command or End: Print
Please enter a club's name: YMCA
The members of YMCA are:
Jones
Peters
Smith
Please enter a command or End: End
```

System Test 2:

```
Please enter a club's name or End: Red Sox
Please enter a club's name or End: Padres
Please enter a club's name or End: Yankees
Please enter a club's name or End: End
Please enter a command or End: Join
Please enter a person's name: Ruth
Please enter a club's name: Red Sox
Please enter a command or End: Change
Please enter a person's name: Hurst
Please enter a club's name: Red Sox
Please enter a club's name: Padres
Error - Hurst is not in Red Sox.
Please enter a command or End: Join
Please enter a person's name: Ruth
Please enter a club's name: Red Sox
Error - Ruth is already in Red Sox.
Please enter a command or End: Change
Please enter a person's name: Ruth
Please enter a club's name: Red Sox
Please enter a club's name: Tigers
Error - Tigers is an illegal club name.
Please enter a club's name: Yankees
Please enter a command or End: Print
Please enter a club's name: Red Sox
The members of Red Sox are:
Please enter a command or End: Print
Please enter a club's name: Yankees
The members of Yankees are:
Ruth
Please enter a command or End: End
```

HINT Use a club list instead of setting up an array of clubs. Each item in ClubList will have a club-name-list field and a member-list field. ClubNameList will contain the names by which the club is known.

Stacks and Queues

CHAPTER 6

In this chapter we introduce two abstract data types: the Stack data type and the Queue data type. Their values—stacks and queues—can be accessed or modified only in a very limited way, so we are able to design and implement both data types quite easily. In fact, many of the designs are inherited from the linked or contiguous designs of the List ADT. Best of all, both stacks and queues have a wide variety of applications.

STACKS

A **stack** is a list in which insertions, deletions, and retrievals can be made only at the first position of the list. The first item is referred to as the "top" item on the stack.

To illustrate this, think of a tray holder in a cafeteria. Insertions and deletions are made only at the top. To put it another way, the tray that was most recently put on the holder will be the next one to be removed. This defining property of stacks is sometimes abbreviated "Last In, First Out," or LIFO. In keeping with this view, an insertion is referred to as a "push," and a deletion as a "pop."

Figure 6.1(a) shows a stack with three items; Figures 6.1b, c, and d show the effect of two pops and a push.

At first you might wonder how a structure as simple as a stack can be useful. But it is precisely the simplicity of a stack that makes it so easy to

Figure 6.1

A stack through
several stages of
pops and pushes:
17 and 13 are
popped, then 21
is pushed.

```
Top Item → 17
           13        13
           28        28         28          28
           (a)       (b) Pop 17 (c) Pop 13  (d) Push 21
                                            21
```

use. To give you some idea of the importance of stacks, let's look at a
couple of stack applications before we get into the nitty-gritty of defining,
designing, and implementing the Stack data type.

Stack Machines.   Some computers, such as the Burroughs Corporation B-
5000, are known as *stack machines* because a stack in the arithmetic logic
unit provides the operands for most arithmetic instructions. For example,
suppose that the variables B, C, and D contain the values 37, 5, and 10, respectively. For a Pascal assignment such as

```
A := B + C * D
```

a stack machine would execute the sequence of instructions shown in
Fig. 6.2.
     A Load instruction retrieves the contents of its operand from memory
and pushes that value onto the stack. The Multiply instruction retrieves the
top item on the stack, pops the stack, retrieves the top item, pops the
stack, multiplies the values of those two items, and pushes the product
onto the stack. The Add instruction is similar to Multiply, and Store retrieves the top item on the stack and stores that item in the given operand.
     Figure 6.3 shows the effect on the stack of executing the sequence of
instructions in Fig. 6.2.

Figure 6.2

A sequence of
instructions for a
stack machine.

Load B
Load C
Load D
Mult
Add
Store A

Figure 6.3

The effect on the
stack of executing
the sequence of
instructions in
Fig. 6.2. Note
that the Store
instruction does not
affect the stack.

```
                            10
                5           5           50
     37         37          37          37          87
  (Load B)   (Load C)    (Load D)   (Multiply)    (Add)
```

As Figure 6.3 indicates, intermediate results are stored on the stack, not in main memory. As a result, fewer memory accesses are required, and time is saved.

Predeclared stacks. The programming languages PL/I[1] and FORTH have a built-in stack. In PL/I, the ALLOCATE statement reserves space at the top of the stack and specifies a variable to refer to the top item. The FREE statement pops the stack. For example, we can write

```
ALLOCATE N;
N := 5;
ALLOCATE N;
N := 12;
PUT DATA (N);
FREE N;
PUT DATA (N);
```

The first PUT DATA statement would output the value 12 and the second would output the value 5.

In FORTH, we can define new functions to operate on the predeclared stack. For example, we can define a function that pushes onto the stack the average of the top two values on the stack:

```
:AVERAGE + 2 /
```

If the top item was 25 and the second item was 7, the effect of calling AVERAGE would be as follows:

1. Retrieve 25; pop; retrieve 7; pop; add 7 and 25; push 32 onto the stack.
2. Push 2 onto the stack.
3. Retrieve 2; pop; retrieve 32; pop; divide 32 by 2; push 16 onto the stack.

Now that we have whetted your interest in stacks, we will get to the technicalities of the Stack data type. Then we will come back to study two other applications. The first of these, and probably the best reason for having stacks, is the implementation of recursion by a compiler. The second relates to the translation of arithmetic expressions into machine language.

Responsibilities of the Stack Data Type

From our experience with the List data type and from the definition of a stack, we can easily determine what the Stack data type is responsible for

---

[1] Pronounced "P L One." The "I" is a Roman numeral, not a letter, but we will probably never see PL/II.

providing its users. We have some responsibilities that apply to the stack as a whole:

to make the stack empty;

to see if the stack is empty;

to determine the size of the stack;

to copy the stack to a new stack.

We don't need to be able to search or traverse a stack: the only item we can access is the top item. The other responsibilities pertain only to the top item in the stack:

to retrieve the top item on the stack;

to push an item onto the top of the stack;

to pop the top item from the stack.

Some authors combine retrieving and popping into a single responsibility that pops the top item and retrieves it. Also, calculating a stack's size and copying a stack can be handled in terms of the other responsibilities (see Exercise 6.5).

In the next section, we refine the seven responsibilities listed here into method interfaces as part of the definition of the Stack data type.

Definition of the Stack Data Type

We now define the Stack ADT. The logical domain is the collection of all stacks. The seven methods in the Stack ADT are given below. Since every stack is a list, we require each user of the Stack ADT to provide, as MaxList-Size, the maximum size that the stack can attain. Users must also supply the Item data type, but as there is no traversal method for a stack, no additional operators need be supplied.

Here are the seven methods:

1. `Initialize.`

   Postcondition: The stack (the instance that called this method) is empty.

   Note: An implicit precondition of every other method is that the calling instance is not undefined. That is, the calling instance must have appeared earlier, either as the calling instance to Initialize or as the actual parameter to CopyTo.

2. `IsEmpty.`

   Postcondition: True is returned if the stack is empty. Otherwise, False is returned.

3. `Size.`

   Postcondition: The number of items in the stack has been returned.

4. `RetrieveTop (Item).`

   Precondition : The stack is not empty.

   Postcondition: Item contains a copy of the top item on the stack.

   Note a: This method is equivalent to Retrieve (Item, 1), where Retrieve is from the List ADT. Retrieve is not a method in the Stack ADT because users are not allowed to access an item in an arbitrary position.

   Note b: It is the user's responsibility to make sure that the stack is not empty before RetrieveTop is called. Otherwise, the developer of the Stack ADT accepts no responsibility for what might happen: incorrect answers, program files destroyed, thermonuclear war, or worse!

5. `Push (Item).`

   Precondition: The number of items in the stack is less than MaxListSize.

   Postcondition: Item has been inserted at the top of the stack.

   Note a: This method is equivalent to Insert (Item, 1), where Insert is from the List ADT.

   Note b: It is the user's responsibility to make sure that the stack is not full before Push is called.

6. `Pop.`

   Precondition: The stack is not empty.

   Postcondition: The item that was on top of the stack (just before this operator was applied) has been deleted from the stack.

   Note a: This method is equivalent to Delete (1), where Delete is from the List ADT.

   Note b: It is the user's responsibility to make sure that the stack is not empty before Pop is called.

7. `CopyTo (NewStack).`

   Postcondition: NewStack contains a distinct copy of the stack.

   Note: Just as in the List ADT, the CopyTo method should be considered the *assignment operator* for stacks. See Laboratory Exercise 6.1.

Designs of the Stack Data Type

Since a stack is a list, we can develop linked and contiguous designs of the Stack ADT based on the linked and contiguous designs of the List ADT in Chapter 4. For either the linked or contiguous design domains, the uninherited method designs are quite simple.

A Linked Design of the Stack Data Type

For a linked design domain, we take a lazy approach by borrowing from the original linked design of the List ADT. The only field in the design domain is Head (the Current and CurrentPos fields from the improved linked design would be of no help here.) The designs for the stack methods Initialize, IsEmpty, Size, and CopyTo are inherited from their list ancestor. The designs of RetrieveItem, Push, and Pop use the Retrieve, Insert, and Delete methods from the List ADT:

↑

4. RetrieveTop (Item).

    Retrieve (Item, 1)

↓

5. Push (Item).

    Insert (Item, 1)

6. Pop.

    Delete (1)

None of these subalgorithms requires verification. What about Time and Space? In a linked design, operations at the head of the list take $O(1)$ Time, and so the above three subalgorithms take $O(1)$ Time. Each of the three subalgorithms takes $O(1)$ Space.

A Contiguous Design of the Stack Data Type

As with the linked design of the Stack ADT, we start with the contiguous design of the list ADT from Chapter 4. The design domain has two fields:

1. A: array [1..MaxListSize] of ItemType;

2. N: 0..MaxListSize

The designs of the Initialize, IsEmpty, Size, and CopyTo methods are inherited. Based on our experience with the linked design of the Stack ADT, you might be tempted to design RetrieveTop, Push, and Pop as a retrieval, insertion, and deletion, respectively, from A [1]. This approach works well for RetrieveTop, but recall that an insertion in position 1 of a contiguous list requires N iterations to make room for the new item. Similarly, a deletion from position 1 requires $N - 1$ iterations.

However, can achieve O(1) time for pushes and pops by a slight change in perspective: Instead of thinking of A [1] as the top item on the stack, think of A [N] as the top item! Then, RetrieveTop, Push, and Pop all operate at A [N], and so no additional movement of items is needed.

For example, if we pushed 28, 13, and 17 onto an initially empty stack, the contiguous representation would be as follows:

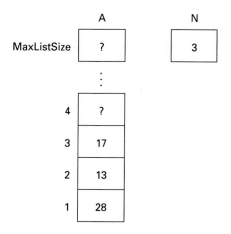

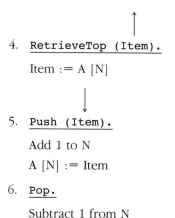

The array index 1 is shown at the bottom to suggest that the item in that position is at the bottom of the stack.

The designs for the uninherited methods now flow smoothly:

↑

4. **RetrieveTop (Item).**

    Item := A [N]

↓

5. **Push (Item).**

    Add 1 to N

    A [N] := Item

6. **Pop.**

    Subtract 1 from N

Just as with the linked design, these subalgorithms have Time and Space in O(1).

Implementations of the Stack Data Type

As you would expect, the dynamic linked, static linked, and contiguous implementations follow easily from the designs just described. For example, here is the interface part from the dynamic-linked implementation:

```
unit Stack1Manager;
{ This unit presents a dynamic-linked implementation of }
{ the stack ADT as a descendant of the list ADT.        }
interface
uses
   ItemInList,
   List1Manager;
type
   StackType = object (List1Manager.ListType)
      procedure RetrieveTop (var Item: ItemType);
      procedure Push (Item: ItemType);
      procedure Pop
   end; { StackType }
```

Validation of the Stack Implementations

Each of the three implementations—dynamic linked, static linked, and contiguous—was validated with the help of a driver program similar to the List-Driver program of Chapter 4.

Run-Time Analysis of the Stack Implementations

To test the run-time behavior of each of the three implementations, the program TestTime from Chapter 3 was modified as follows: The integers 1 through N were pushed onto an initially empty stack; a sequence of N random pushes and pops was then performed. The results of this experiment are shown in Table 6.1.

The results in Table 6.1 suggest that all of the implementations are very fast, with the contiguous implementation the fastest of the three.

Table 6.1 The time in seconds to push N integers onto an initially empty stack, followed by N random pushes or pops.

N	Dynamic Linked	Static Linked	Contiguous
1000	0.44	0.32	0.22
2000	0.99	0.61	0.49

Now that you have seen how easy it is to design and implement the Stack ADT, let's look at a couple of important applications.

Stack Application 1: How Compilers Implement Recursion

You have already seen several examples of recursive subprograms in Chapters 2, 4, and 5. In obedience to the Principle of Abstraction, we focused on what recursion did and ignored the question of how recursion is implemented by the compiler. We now outline how a stack is utilized in implementing recursion, and the time-space implications for subprograms (especially recursive subprograms) in that utilization.

Each time a subprogram call occurs, whether it is a recursive subprogram or not, the return address in the calling program is saved. This way, the computer will know where to resume execution in the calling program after the execution of the subprogram has been completed. Also, a substantial amount of information about the subprogram's local variables must be saved. This is done to prevent the destruction of that information in case the subprogram is (directly or indirectly) recursive. As we noted in Chapter 2, the compiler saves this subprogram information for all subprograms, not just the recursive ones. This information is collectively referred to as an "activation record" or "stack frame."

Each activation record includes:

1. A variable that contains the return address in the calling program.

2. A variable that contains the address of a location that will hold the value calculated, if the subprogram is a function.

3. For each variable formal parameter, a variable that contains the *address* of the corresponding actual parameter.

4. For each value formal parameter, a variable that initially contains a *copy* of the value of the corresponding actual parameter.

5. Each variable declared in the subprogram's block.

Part of main memory—up to about 64K bytes—is allocated for a run-time stack onto which an activation record is pushed when a subprogram is called, and from which an activation record is popped when the execution of the subprogram has been completed. During the execution of that subprogram, the top activation record contains the current state of the subprogram.

For a simple example, let us trace the execution of a program that includes the WriteBinary procedure from Chapter 2. The return addresses have been commented as RA1 and RA2.

```
program DecToBin;
{ This program reads in a nonnegative decimal integer and }
{ outputs its binary equivalent.                          }
procedure WriteBinary (N: longint);
{ Write out the binary equivalent of N. }
```

```
begin
   if N <= 1 then
      Write (N: 1)
   else
      begin
         WriteBinary (N div 2);
         Write (N mod 2: 1)       { RA2 }
      end { else }
end; { WriteBinary }
const
   Prompt =
'Enter a nonnegative integer whose binary value you want: ';
   Error = 'Error--you entered a negative integer.';
var
   N: longint;
begin
   Write (Prompt);
   Readln (N);
   if N < 0 then
      Writeln (Error)
   else
      WriteBinary (N)
end. { RA1 }
```

The procedure WriteBinary has the value formal parameter N as its only local variable, and so each activation record will have two fields:

1. One for the return address.

2. One for the value of the value formal parameter N.

Assume that the value read in is 6. When WriteBinary is called from the main program, an activation record is created and pushed onto the stack, as shown in Fig. 6.4.

Since $N > 1$, WriteBinary is called recursively with 3 (that is, 6 **div** 2) as the value of the actual parameter. A second activation record is created and pushed onto the stack (see Fig. 6.5).

Since N is still greater than 1, WriteBinary is called again, this time with 1 (that is, 3 **div** 2) as the value of the actual parameter. A third activation record is created and pushed (see Fig. 6.6).

Figure 6.4

The activation stack just prior to WriteBinary's first activation. RA1 is the return address.

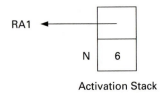

Activation Stack

Figure 6.5

The activation stack
just prior to the
second activation of
WriteBinary.

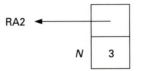

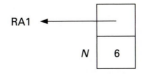

Activation Stack
(two records)

Figure 6.6

The activation stack
just prior to the
third activation of
WriteBinary.

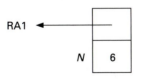

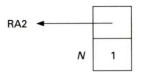

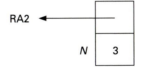

Activation Stack
(three records)

Since $N \leqq 1$, the value of N is written. The output is

1

This completes the third activation of WriteBinary, and so the stack is popped and a return is made to the address RA2. The resulting stack is shown in Fig 6.7.

The Write at RA2 in WriteBinary is executed, and the value output is 3 **mod** 2, namely

1

Figure 6.7

The activation stack
just after the
completion of the
third activation of
WriteBinary.

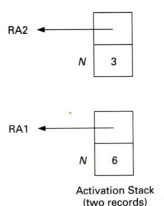

Activation Stack
(two records)

The stack is popped again and another return to RA2 is made, as shown in Fig. 6.8.

The output from the Write statement at RA2 is the value of 6 **mod** 2, namely

0

That completes the original activation of WriteBinary. The stack is popped once more, leaving it empty, and a return to RA1—at the end of the program—is made. The entire output is

110

which is the binary equivalent of 6, the value input.

The preceding discussion should give you a general idea of how recursion is implemented by the compiler. We have ignored the fact that the size of each activation record must be saved as part of the activation record so that the correct number of bytes can be popped.

The compiler must generate code for the creation and maintenance, at run time, of the activation stack. Each time a call is made, the entire local environment must be saved. This can be somewhat inefficient, in terms of both time and space, if a large array is passed to a value formal parameter. In that case, a copy of the entire array must be stacked whenever a call is made.

Figure 6.8

The activation stack
just after the
completion of the
second activation of
WriteBinary.

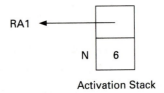

Activation Stack

If you have designed a recursive subalgorithm, you should assess the potential impact of recursion's time-space overhead on your program. If you decide that the overhead is excessive, you will need to convert the recursive subalgorithm to an iterative one. This can always be done, but the iterative subalgorithm may need to create and maintain its own stack of information to be saved.

The time required to make the conversion should also be considered. Some recursive subalgorithms, such as the Factorial and Fibonacci functions, can easily be converted to iterative subalgorithms; but sometimes the conversion is nontrivial, such as for the Towers of Hanoi, ClusterCount, and Permute procedures of Chapter 2, and most of the recursive subalgorithms in Chapters 4, 5, 7, 8, and 9. Furthermore, the iterative version may well lack the simple elegance of the recursive version, and this may complicate verification and maintenance.

You should by all means continue to design recursive subalgorithms whenever the conditions are appropriate. The preceding discussion on the activation stack was intended to help you to make better–informed trade-off decisions.

Stack Application 2: Converting from Infix to Postfix

In the previous section we saw how a compiler or interpreter could implement recursion. In this section we present another "internal" application: the translation of arithmetic expressions from infix notation into postfix notation. This can be one of the key tasks performed by a compiler (as it creates machine-level code) or an interpreter (as it prepares to evaluate an arithmetic expression).

In infix notation, a binary operator is placed between its operands. For example, Fig. 6.9 shows several arithmetic expressions in infix notation.

For the sake of simplicity, we initially restrict our attention to expressions with single-letter identifiers, parentheses, and the binary operators $+$, $-$, $*$, and $/$.
The usual rules of arithmetic apply:

1. Operations are normally carried out from left to right. For example, if we have

    $$A + B - C$$

Figure 6.9

Several arithmetic expressions in infix notation.

$A + B$
$B - C * D$
$(B - C) * C$
$A - C - H/B * C$
$A - (C - H)/(B * C)$

then the addition will be performed first.

2. If the current operator is + or − and the next operator is * or /, then the next operator is (normally) applied before the current operator. For example, if we have

$$B + C * D$$

then the multiplication will be carried out before the addition. For

$$A - B + C * D$$

the subtraction is performed first, then the multiplication and, finally, the addition.

We can interpret this rule as saying that multiplication and division have "higher precedence" than addition and subtraction.

3. Parentheses may be used to alter the order indicated by rules 1 and 2. For example, if we have

$$A - (B + C)$$

then the addition is performed first. Similarly, with

$$(A - B) * C$$

the subtraction is performed first.

Figure 6.10 shows the order of evaluation for the last two expressions in Fig. 6.9.

The first widely used programming language was FORTRAN (from FORmula TRANslator), so named because its compiler could translate arithmetic formulas into machine-level code. In early (pre-1960) compilers, the translation was performed directly—an awkward process, because the machine-level code for an operator cannot be generated until both of its operands are known. This problem is exacerbated by the need to handle parenthesized subexpressions.

Modern compilers do not translate arithmetic expressions directly into machine-level code. Instead, they can utilize an intermediate form known

Figure 6.10

The order of evaluation for the last two expressions in Fig. 6.9.

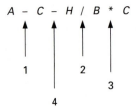

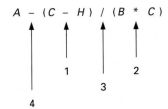

as *postfix* notation.[2] In postfix notation, an operator is placed immediately after its operands. For example, given the infix expression $A + B$, the postfix form is $A \, B \, +$. For $A + B * C$, the postfix form is $A \, B \, C \, * \, +$ because the operands for $+$ are A and the product of B and C. For $(A + B) * C$, the postfix form is $A \, B \, + \, C \, *$. Since an operator immediately follows its operands in postfix notation, parentheses are unnecessary and therefore not used. Fig. 6.11 shows several arithmetic expressions in both infix and postfix notation.

How can we convert an arithmetic expression from infix notation into postfix notation? Let's view the infix notation as a string of characters and try to produce the corresponding postfix string. The identifiers in the postfix string will be in the same order as they are in the infix string, so each identifier can be appended to the postfix string as soon as it is encountered. But in postfix notation, operators must be placed after their operands. So when an operator is encountered in the infix string, it must be saved somewhere temporarily.

For example, suppose we want to translate the infix string

$$A - B + C * D$$

into postfix notation. (The blanks are for readability only—they are not considered part of the infix expression.) We would go through the following steps:

'A' is moved to postfix

'−' is stored temporarily

'B' is appended to postfix, which is now 'AB'

When '+' is encountered, we note that since it has the same "precedence" as '−', the subtraction should be performed first by the left-to-right rule. So the '−' is appended to the postfix string—which is now 'AB−'—and '+' is saved temporarily

'C' is appended to postfix, which now is 'AB−C'

Multiplication has higher precedence than addition, so '*' should be moved to postfix before '+'. But '*' must also be stored somewhere tem-

Figure 6.11

Several arithmetic expressions in both infix and postfix notation.

Infix	Postfix
$A - B + C * D$	$A \, B \, - \, C \, D \, * \, +$
$A + C - H/B * C$	$A \, C \, + \, H \, B/C \, * \, -$
$A + (C - H)/(B * C)$	$A \, C \, H \, - \, B \, C \, */+$

---

[2]Postfix notation was invented by Jan Lucasiewicz, a Polish logician. It is sometimes referred to as Polish notation.

porarily because one of its operands (namely, 'D') has not yet been appended to postfix

When 'D' is appended to postfix, the postfix string is 'AB−CD'

'*' is appended, making the postfix string 'AB−CD*'

Finally '+' is appended, and the final value of postfix is 'AB−CD*+'

The temporary storage facility referred to in the previous paragraph is handled conveniently with a stack. The rules governing the operator stack are:

R1.   Initially, the stack is empty.

R2.   For each operator in the infix string,

```
Loop until the operator has been pushed onto the
operator stack:
    If the stack is empty or the operator has
    higher precedence than the operator on the top
    of the stack then
        Push the operator onto the stack
    else
        Pop the operator on top of the stack
        and append that popped operator to the
        postfix string.
```

R3.   Once the end of the input string is encountered,

```
Loop until the operator stack is empty:
    Pop the operator on top of the stack and append
    that popped operator to the postfix string.
```

For example, Fig. 6.12 shows the history of the operator stack during the conversion of

$$A + C - H/B * C$$

to its postfix equivalent.

How are parentheses handled? When a left parenthesis is encountered in the infix string, it is immediately pushed onto the operator stack, but its precedence is defined to be *lower* than any of the binary operators. When a right parenthesis is encountered in the infix string, the stack is repeatedly popped, and each popped item appended to the postfix string, until the "operator" on the top of the stack is a left parenthesis. Then that left parenthesis is popped but not appended to postfix, and the scan of the infix string is resumed.

For example, when we translate $A * (B + C)$ in postfix, the items *, (, and + would be pushed and then all would be popped when the right parenthesis is encountered. The postfix form is

$$A B C + *$$

Figure 6.12

The conversion of $A + C - H/B * C$ to postfix notation. At each stage, the top of the stack is shown as the leftmost item.

Infix Expression: $A + C - H/B * C$

Infix Character	Operator Stack	Postfix String
A	(Empty)	A
+	+	A
C	+	AC
–	–	AC+
H	–	AC + H
/	/–	AC + H
B	/–	AC + HB
*	*–	AC + HB/
C	*–	AC + HB/C
	–	AC + HB/C*
	(Empty)	AC+HB/C*–

For a more complex example, Fig. 6.13 illustrates the conversion of

$$X - (Y * A/B - (Z + D * E) + C)/F$$

to its postfix form.

At each step in the conversion process, we know what action to take as long as we know the current character in the infix string and the top character on the operator stack. We can therefore create a table to summarize the conversion. The row indexes represent the possible values of the current infix character. The column indexes represent the possible values of the top character on the operator stack. The table entries represent the action to be taken. Such a table is called a "transition table" because it directs the transition of information from one form to another. Figure 6.14 shows the transition table for converting a simple expression from infix notation to postfix notation.

The graphical nature of the transition table in Figure 6.14 enables us to see at a glance how to convert simple expressions from infix to postfix. We could now design and implement a program to do just that (see Programming Assignment 6.1 at the end of this chapter). The program may well incorporate the transition table in Figure 6.14 for the sake of extensibility; more complex expressions can be accommodated by expanding the table.

Tokens

A program that utilized Figure 6.14 would probably not work with the characters themselves because there are too many possible (legal) values for each character. For example, a transition table that used a row for each legal infix character would need at least 33 rows. If we changed the specifications to allow multicharacter identifiers, we would need millions of rows!

Figure 6.13

The conversion of $X - (Y * A/B - (Z + D * E) + C)/F$ from infix to postfix. At each stage, the top of the stack is shown as the leftmost item.

Infix Expression: $X - (Y * A/B - (Z + D * E) + C)/F$

Infix Character	Operator Stack	Postfix String
X	(Empty)	X
$-$	$-$	X
$($	$(-$	X
Y	$(-$	XY
$*$	$*(-$	XY
A	$*(-$	XYA
$/$	$/(-$	$XYA*$
B	$/(-$	$XYA * B$
$-$	$-(-$	$XYA * B/$
$($	$(-(-$	$XYA * B/$
Z	$(-(-$	$XYA * B/Z$
$+$	$+(-(-$	$XYA * B/Z$
D	$+(-(-$	$XYA * B/ZD$
$*$	$*+(-(-$	$XYA * B/ZD$
E	$*+(-(-$	$XYA * B/ZDE$
$)$	$+(-(-$	$XYA * B/ZDE*$
	$(-(-$	$XYA * B/ZDE*+$
	$-(-$	$XYA * B/ZDE*+$
$+$	$+(-$	$XYA * B/ZDE*+-$
C	$+(-$	$XYA * B/ZDE*+-C$
$)$	$(-$	$XYA * B/ZDE*+-C+$
	$-$	$XYA * B/ZDE*+-C+$
$/$	$/-$	$XYA * B/ZDE*+-C+$
F	$/-$	$XYA * B/ZDE*+-C + F$
	$-$	$XYA * B/ZDE*+-C + F/$
	(Empty)	$XYA * B/ZDE*+-C + F/-$

Postfix Expression: $X \ Y \ A * B/Z \ D \ E * + - C + F/-$

Instead, the legal characters would usually be grouped together into "tokens." A **token** is the smallest meaningful unit in a program. Each token has two parts: a generic part that holds its class and a specific part that enables us to recapture the character(s) tokenized. For converting simple infix expressions to postfix, the token classes would be Identifier, RightPar, LeftPar, AddOp (for + and −), MultOp (for * and /), and Empty (for a dummy value). The specific part would contain the position, in the infix string, of the character tokenized. For example, given the infix string

$$A + B * C$$

to tokenize 'B,' we would set its class to Identifier and its position to 3.

In Turbo Pascal there are five token classes:

1. identifier

2. unsigned number

Figure 6.14

The transition table
for converting simple
expressions from
infix notation to
postfix notation.

	Top character on operator stack			
Current infix character	(	+, −	*, /	empty stack
	Action taken			
Identifier	Append to postfix	Append to postfix	Append to postfix	Append to postfix
)	Pop; pitch "("	Pop to postfix	Pop to postfix	Error
(	Push	Push	Push	Push
+, −	Push	Pop to postfix	Pop to postfix	Push
*, /	Push	Push	Pop to postfix	Push
end of expression	Error	Pop to postfix	Pop to postfix	Done

3. label
4. character string
5. special symbol

The class "special symbol" includes reserved words (also called "word symbols"), parentheses, operator symbols, brackets, and delimiters (commas, semicolons, colons, periods, and double periods).

The structure of tokens varies widely among compilers. For example, the specific part of a variable identifier's token might contain an address into a table, called a *symbol* table. At that address would be stored the identifier, an indication that it is a variable identifier, its type, initial value, the block it is declared in, and other information helpful to the compiler. For a label, the specific part might contain the positive integer that is the label's value. Because the specific part depends on the class of the token, tokens can be thought of as variant records in which the class is the tag field.

Extending the Infix-to-Postfix Conversion Algorithm

We can extend the infix-to-postfix conversion algorithm in several ways. For example, suppose we want to allow multicharacter identifiers with digits as well as lowercase and uppercase letters. Each identifier must start with a letter. To facilitate the recovery of the identifier from its token, the specific part of each token would consist of a start position and an end position.

In a compiler, there is no postfix string. Instead, the tokens themselves, in postfix, are made available to the section of the compiler (the Semantic Analyzer) that determines the machine-language meaning of each token.

We can also extend the infix-to-postfix conversion algorithm by allowing additional operators. This entails little more than expanding the transition table. We illustrate with two examples.

The assignment operator is represented in Pascal, Eiffel, and Ada by ":=", in C^{++}, COBOL, and FORTRAN by "=", and in APL by "←". Since the processing involves tokens only, the program representation is irrelevant for our purposes, except that ":=" is interesting to consider because it suggests the possibility of writing a Turbo Pascal compiler in Turbo Pascal!

It would make no sense to try to write a Turbo Pascal program to compile any Turbo Pascal program into machine-level code because the compiler itself would first have to be compiled into machine−level code. But it is possible, and even plausible, to write a "bootstrap" compiler—a compiler for a subset of a language which is then used to develop a compiler for the full language.

We would start with a subset of Turbo Pascal from which we could define every feature not in the subset. For example, the subset would include the **repeat** and **if** statements but not the **for**, **while**, or **case** statements, because these can be defined in terms of **repeat** and **if**. Next, we would develop a compiler for the mini-version of Turbo Pascal. This compiler could be written in assembly language, C, or a high-level language such as SNOBOL. Naturally, a compiler for mini-Turbo Pascal would be somewhat simpler to develop than a compiler for all of Turbo Pascal. Finally, we would develop, in mini-Turbo Pascal, a compiler for Turbo Pascal. Our task would then be complete, as the following diagram shows:

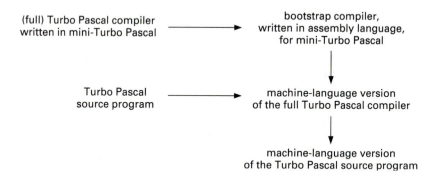

We now resume our discussion on how to treat assignment operators. When the assignment-operator token is encountered as the infix token, an error has occurred unless the operator stack is empty. For an empty stack, a Push is prescribed. Since assignment should be the last operation performed in an assignment statement, the assignment-operator token is not popped and appended to postfix until the end of the statement is reached. To accomplish this, the assignment operator will be given lower precedence than the other operators. Because we are now converting assignment statements, not arithmetic expressions, only an identifier, an assignment operator, and a statement terminator (that is, Empty) are legal infix tokens when the stack is empty.

Exponentiation, usually represented by ** or ^, has a higher precedence than multiplication and division. We must also decide the order in which exponentiations are to be performed. In arithmetic, exponentiations are performed from right to left. For example,

$$2^{2^4} = 2^{(2^4)} = 2^{16} = 65536 \text{ (whereas } (2^2)^4 = 4^4 = 256).$$

We will use the order dictated by arithmetic. If the exponentiation token appears as both the infix token and the stack token, a Push should be applied so that the latter exponentiation will be performed before the earlier one.

Figure 6.15 shows the transition table augmented to include the assignment and exponentiation operators. For the sake of simplicity, we do not provide detailed error information.

Prefix Notation

In the previous section we described how to convert an infix expression into postfix notation. Another possibility is to convert from infix into *prefix* notation, in which each operator immediately precedes its operands.

Figure 6.15

The transition table for converting simple assignment statements, including exponentiations, into postfix notation.

	Stack Token					
INFIX TOKEN	(	Add Op	Mult Op	Expon Op	Assign Op	Empty
	Action taken					
Identifier	Append to postfix	Append to postfix	Append to postfix	Append to postfix	Append to postfix	Append to postfix
)	Pop & pitch	Pop to postfix	Pop to postfix	Pop to postfix	Error	Error
(	Push	Push	Push	Push	Push	Error
Add op	Push	Pop to postfix	Pop to postfix	Pop to postfix	Pusyh	Error
Mult op	Push	Push	Pop to postfix	Pop to postfix	Push	Error
Expon op	Push	Push	Push	Push	Push	Error
Assign op	Error	Error	Error	Error	Error	Push
Empty	Error	Pop to postfix	Pop to postfix	Pop to postfix	Pop to postfix	Done

Figure 6.16	Infix	Prefix
Several arithmetic	$A - B$	$- A \; B$
expressions in both	$A - B * C$	$- A * B \; C$
infix and prefix	$(A - B) * C$	$* - A \; B \; C$
notation.	$A - B + C * D$	$+ - A \; B * C \; D$
	$A + C - H/B * D$	$- + A \; C */H \; B \; D$
	$A + (C - H)/(B * D)$	$+A/- C \; H * B \; D$

We will see one justification for doing this in Chapter 8, where one of the methods in the Expression tree ADT has a prefix expression as a formal parameter.

Figure 6.16 shows several expressions in both infix and prefix notation.

How can we convert a simple arithmetic expression from infix to prefix? As in infix-to-postfix, we will need to save each operator until both of its operands have been obtained, but we cannot simply move each identifier to the prefix string as soon as it is encountered. Instead, we will need to save each identifier—in fact, each operand—until its operator has been obtained.

The saving of operands and operators is easily accomplished with the help of two stacks, OperandStack and OperatorStack. Initially, both stacks are empty. When an identifier is encountered in the infix string, that identifier is pushed onto OperandStack. When an operator is encountered, it is pushed onto OperatorStack if that stack is empty. Otherwise, one of the following cases applies:

1. If the operator is a left parenthesis, push it onto OperatorStack (but left parenthesis has lowest priority).

2. If the operator has higher priority than the top operator on OperatorStack, push the operator onto OperatorStack.

3. If the operator's priority is equal to or lower than the priority of the top operator on OperatorStack, pop (after retrieving) the top operator, Opt1, from OperatorStack and pop the top two operands, Opnd1 and Opnd2, from OperandStack. Concatenate Opt1, Opnd2, and Opnd1 together and push the result onto OperandStack.

4. If the operator is a right parenthesis, treat it as having lower priority than +, −, *, and /. Case 3 will be applied until a left parenthesis is the top operator on OperatorStack, then pop that left parenthesis.

The above process continues until we reach the end of the infix expression. We then repeat the following actions from case 3 (above) until OperatorStack is empty:

```
Pop Opt1 from OperatorStack.
Pop Opnd1 and Opnd2 from OperandStack.
Concatenate Opt1, Opnd2 and Opnd1 together and push the
result onto OperandStack.
```

When OperatorStack is finally empty, the top (and only) operand on OperandStack will be the prefix string corresponding to the original infix expression.

For example, if we start with

A + B * C

then the history of the two stacks would be as follows:

	Infix Character	OperandStack	OperatorStack
a.	A	A	
b.	+	A	+
c.	B	B A	* +
d.	*	B A	* +
e.	C	C B A	* +
f.		*BC A	+
g.		+ A * BC	

The prefix string corresponding to the original string is

+ A * B C

For a more complex example, suppose the infix string is

A + (C - H) / (B * D)

Then the items on the two stacks during the processing of the first right parenthesis would be as follows:

	Infix Character	OperandStack	OperatorStack
a.	)	H C A	(+

	-CH	(
b.	A	+
	OperandStack	OperatorStack
	-CH	
c.	A	+
	OperandStack	OperatorStack

During the processing of the second right parenthesis in the infix string, we would have

		D	*
		B	(
		-CH	/
a.	)	A	+
	Infix Character	OperandStack	OperatorStack
		*BD	(
		-CH	/
b.		A	+
		OperandStack	OperatorStack
		*BD	
		-CH	/
c.		A	+
		OperandStack	OperatorStack
		/ - CH * BD	
d.		A	+
		OperandStack	OperatorStack
e.		+ A/ - CH * BD	(empty)
		OperandStack	OperatorStack

The prefix string is

+ A / - C H * B D

QUEUES

A *queue* is a list in which items are deleted or retrieved from position 1 and inserted at the last position. The item at position 1 is called the *head* (or *front*) item and the item at the last position is called the *tail* (or *rear*) item.

The first item inserted (at the tail) will eventually be the first item to be deleted or retrieved (from the head). The second item inserted will be the second item to be deleted or retrieved, and so on. This defining property of queues is sometimes referred to as "First Come, First Served," "First In, First Out," or simply FIFO.

A queue is unordered in the sense that the head item is not necessarily LessThan or EqualTo the item in position 2 of the queue. But a queue possesses a certain kind of ordering: Items are deleted or retrieved in the same order in which they were inserted. There is an inherent fairness in this chronological ordering, even though waiting in a queue can be a very frustrating experience. (Waiting in a stack would be even worse—unless you are a procrastinator!)

The examples of queues are numerous and widespread:

cars in line at a drive-up window

fans waiting to buy tickets to a ball game

customers in a checkout line at a supermarket

airplanes waiting to take off from an airport

We could continue listing queue examples almost indefinitely. Later in this chapter we will present a major application of queues in the field of computer simulation.

Figure 6.17 shows a queue through several stages of insertions and deletions.

Figure 6.17

A queue through an insertion and a deletion.

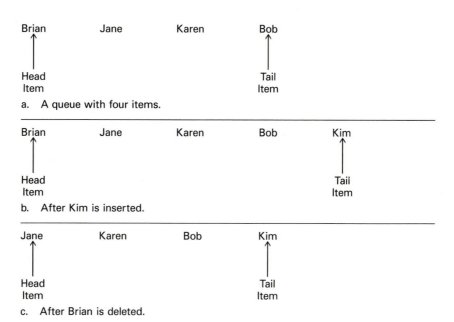

a. A queue with four items.

b. After Kim is inserted.

c. After Brian is deleted.

The responsibilities of the Queue data type are just what you would probably expect:

to make the queue empty;

to see if the queue is empty;

to determine the size of the queue;

to copy the queue to another queue;

to retrieve the item at the head of the queue;

to insert an item at the tail of the queue;

to delete the item at the head of the queue.

In the next section we easily refine these responsibilities into method interfaces.

Definition of the Queue Data Type

In the Queue ADT, the logical domain is the set of all queues, which is a subset of the set of all lists. Several of the method interfaces are the same as for the List ADT. There are seven methods in all:

1. `Initialize.`

    Postcondition: The queue is empty.

2. `IsEmpty.`

    Postcondition: True has been returned if the queue is empty. Otherwise, False has been returned.

3. `Size.`

    Postcondition: The number of items in the queue has been returned.

4. `RetrieveHead (Item).`

    Precondition: The queue is not empty.
    Postcondition: The head item of the queue has been copied into Item.

5. `InsertTail (Item).`

    Precondition: The number of items in the queue is less than MaxListSize.
    Postcondition: A copy of Item is the tail item of the queue.
    Note: This method is sometimes referred to as Enqueue instead of InsertTail.

6. `DeleteHead.`

Precondition: The queue is not empty.

Postcondition: The item that was the head item of the queue (just before this method was called) has been deleted from the queue.

Note: This method is sometimes referred to as Dequeue instead of DeleteHead.

↑

7. `CopyTo (NewQueue).`

Postcondition: NewQueue contains a distinct copy of the queue.

A Linked Design of the Queue Data Type

Because a queue is a list, we will expand on either the linked or contiguous design domain of the list ADT. In the linked design domain, we include a Tail field as well as the inherited Head field:

Head contains a null address (for an empty queue) or the address of the head item;

Tail, in a nonempty queue, contains the address of the tail item.

Notice that the meanings of Head and Tail imply that a queue is considered empty if Head contains a null address. In an empty queue, the value in Tail is undefined (that is, meaningless).

The designs of Initialize, IsEmpty, and Size are inherited intact from the linked design of the List ADT. The designs of the uninherited methods are as follows:

↑

4. `RetrieveHead (Item).`

`Retrieve (Item, 1)`

↓

5. `InsertTail (Item).`

The only technicality here is that an insertion in an empty queue requires that both Head and Tail point to the inserted item:

```
Allocate space for a node pointed to by NewTail
NewTail's Item := Item
NewTail's Next := null
if Head = null then
    Tail := NewTail
    Head := Tail
else
    Tail's Next := NewTail
    Tail        := NewTail
```

6. DeleteHead.

```
Delete (1)
```

For each of these subalgorithms, Time and Space are O(1).

7. CopyTo (NewQueue).

The reason that we cannot simply inherit ListType's version of CopyTo is that NewQueue.Tail is not affected in that version. Therefore, we will treat the calling instance as a list instance, OldList, by setting OldList.Head equal to Head. (Recall that a descendant has access to its ancestor's design domain.) We then copy OldList to NewQueue and set NewQueue.Tail to point to the last item in NewQueue.

The complete subalgorithm is as follows:

```
CopyTo (NewQueue).

OldList.Head := Head
OldList.CopyTo (NewQueue)
with NewQueue do
    if Head <> null then
        Tail := Head
        while Tail's Next <> null do
            Tail := Tail's Next
```

Time and Space are O(N), just as they were for the linked design of CopyTo in the List ADT.

A Contiguous Design of the Queue Data Type

For the contiguous design of the Queue ADT, the design domain includes Head and Tail fields as well as the fields in the contiguous design domain of the List ADT, giving us a total of four fields:

1. `A: array [1..MaxListSize] of ItemType;`

2. `N: the size of the queue;`

3. `Head, the index of the head item` (this field has an undefined value for an empty queue);

4. `Tail, the index of the tail item` (this field has an undefined value for an empty queue).

In this design, an empty queue is characterized by the value of N only.

The method designs for Initialize, IsEmpty, and Size are inherited from the contiguous design of the List ADT. The designs of the remaining meth-

ods turn out to be somewhat more involved than you might have anticipated. We start with the easy one, RetrieveHead:

$\uparrow$

4. `RetrieveHead (Item).`

   `Item := A [Head]`

We now develop the preliminary designs for both InsertTail and Delete-
Head. The reason we do this simultaneously is that both methods can affect the utilization of the array A. Roughly, insertions are handled as
follows:

```
To insert Item at the tail of the queue, add 1 to Tail, make
Item equal to A [Tail] and add 1 to N.
```

What about deletions? Suppose we want to delete the head item from the
queue of six items shown in Fig. 6.18.

One way to delete the head item (Rieman) is to move the other five
items up one slot in the array, as shown in Fig. 6.19.

However, if deleting the head requires moving the remaining $N - 1$
items, the time for that deletion will be O(N). Can you think of a faster way?
How about this: To delete the head item, simply add 1 to Head (and decrement N). The effect of this on the queue of Fig. 6.18 is shown in Fig. 6.20.

There is a hangup with this approach to insertions and deletions: Head
gets incremented for deletions and Tail gets incremented for insertions, but
neither is ever decremented. We could eventually have a situation like the
one shown for a five-item queue in Fig. 6.21.

Figure 6.18

**A queue with
six items.**

	A
1	Rieman
2	Paige
3	Malte
4	Stephanie
5	Peter
6	Hartono
7	?
8	?
9	?
10	?
11	?
12	?
13	?
14	?
15	?

N	Head	Tail
6	1	6

Figure 6.19

Deleting the head
item from the queue
in Fig. 6.18 by
moving the
remaining items.
Note that the item in
A [6] is not part of
the queue because
Tail = 5.

	A
1	Paige
2	Malte
3	Stephanie
4	Peter
5	Hartono
6	Hartono
7	?
8	?
9	?
10	?
11	?
12	?
13	?
14	?
15	?

N	Head	Tail
5	1	5

Figure 6.20

Deleting the head
item from the queue
in Fig. 6.18 by
adjusting Head.

	A
1	Rieman
2	Paige
3	Malte
4	Stephanie
5	Peter
6	Hartono
7	?
8	?
9	?
10	?
11	?
12	?
13	?
14	?
15	?

N	Head	Tail
5	2	6

Because the size of the queue (5) is less than MaxListSize (15), the queue can absorb more insertions. But where can "Kurt," for example, be inserted? A [1] is a good choice. The fact that "Rieman" is already there is irrelevant because "Rieman" is no longer one of the queue's items. Figure 6.22 shows how the resulting six-item queue would be represented.

The array A is being treated as a *circular* array: Index 1 is considered the successor of index 15. This view of a queue affects the designs of both the InsertTail and DeleteHead subalgorithms, which we now provide.

5. InsertTail (Item).

Figure 6.21

A queue with five items: Janet, Khurram, Troy, Kayvan, and Dave.

A	
1	Rieman
2	Paige
3	Malte
4	Stephanie
5	Peter
6	Hartono
7	Ed
8	James
9	Joey
10	Kush
11	Janet
12	Khurram
13	Troy
14	Kayvan
15	Dave

N	Head	Tail
5	11	15

Figure 6.22

A queue with six items: Janet, Khurram, Troy, Kayvan, Dave, and Kurt.

A	
1	Kurt
2	Paige
3	Malte
4	Stephanie
5	Peter
6	Hartono
7	Ed
8	James
9	Joey
10	Kush
11	Janet
12	Khurram
13	Troy
14	Kayvan
15	Dave

N	Head	Tail
6	11	1

To insert in an empty queue, both Head and Tail must be adjusted to 1. Also, if Tail = MaxListSize, then Tail must be set to 1. We need not concern ourselves with detecting a full queue because the precondition of this sub-algorithm is that the queue is not full.

```
if N = 0 then
   Tail := 1
   Head := 1
else
   if Tail = MaxListSize then
      Tail := 1
   else
      Add 1 to Tail
```

```
A [Tail] := Item
Add 1 to N
```

Note: The inner if statement could be replaced with

```
Tail := (Tail mod MaxListSize) + 1
```

6. **DeleteHead.**

```
if Head = MaxListSize then
    Head := 1
else
    Add 1 to Head
Subtract 1 from N
```

Note: The if statement could be replaced with

```
Head := (Head mod MaxListSize) + 1
```

The Time and Space for each of the above methods is O(1).

Finally, we tackle the design of the CopyTo method. We start by copying N, Head, and Tail to the corresponding fields in NewQueue. (At this point, we could simply copy A to NewQueue.A and be done. But if MaxListSize is much larger than N, we would be doing a *lot* of extra work.)

If N is 0, there are no items to copy. Otherwise, if Head is less than or equal to Tail, we simply copy to NewQueue.A the items from indexes Head to Tail. If Head is greater than Tail, we first copy the items at the front of the queue (from indexes Head to MaxListSize) and then copy the items at the back of the queue (from indexes 1 to Tail).

The complete subalgorithm is

7. **CopyTo (NewQueue).**

```
NewQueue.N := N
NewQueue.Head := Head
NewQueue.Tail := Tail
if N <> 0 then
    if Head <= Tail then

        { Copy A [Head..Tail] to NewQueue.A: }
        for I := Head to Tail do
            NewQueue.A [I] := A [I]
    else

        { Copy A [Head..MaxListSize] to NewQueue.A: }
        for I := Head to MaxListSize do
            NewQueue.A [I] := A.[I]

        { Copy A [1..Tail] to NewQueue.A: }
        for I := 1 to Tail do
            NewQueue.A [I] := A [I]
```

Time is O(N) because N items are moved. Space is only O(1) because the space for NewQueue will already have been allocated prior to the call to CopyTo.

Implementations of the Queue Data Type

The two preceding sections suggest four implementations:

1. Linked dynamic;
2. Linked static;
3. Contiguous, with an "if" statement to implement circularity;
4. Contiguous, with modular arithmetic to implement circularity.

All of the translations are straightforward. For example, here is the heading and interface part of a contiguous implementation:

```
unit Queue1Manager;
{ This unit provides a contiguous implementation of the  }
{ queue ADT. An if statement is used to implement        }
{ circularity.                                           }
interface
uses
    Maxima,
    ItemInList;
    List3Manager;
type
    QueueType = object (ListType)
       Head,
       Tail : word;
       procedure RetrieveHead (var Item: ItemType);
       procedure InsertTail (Item: ItemType);
       procedure DeleteHead;
       procedure CopyTo (var NewQueue: QueueType)
    end; { QueueType }
```

Each of the four implementations of the Queue data type was validated with a program, QueueDriver, that is similar to ListDriver in Chapter 4. All of the implementations passed all of the tests.

Run-Time Analysis of the Queue Implementations

QueueTimer, a program similar to StackTimer, was constructed to test the run-time behavior of each of the four implementations. In QueueTimer, the items 1 through N (input) are inserted into an initially empty queue. Another loop is then executed in which, as I goes from 1 to N, a random sequence of insertions (of I) and deletions is made. The results for each of the four implementations are shown in Table 6.2.

Table 6.2 The time (in seconds) to insert the first N integers into an initially empty queue and then, as I goes from 1 to N, randomly insert I or delete from the queue.

		Implementation			
		Dynamic Linked	Static Linked	Contiguous with "if"	Contiguous modular
N	1000	0.55	0.28	0.28	0.32
	2000	1.10	0.66	0.60	0.66

Table 6.2 suggests that none of the implementations took very long in this experiment. The dynamic linked implementation was the slowest, possibly because of the overhead of using four-byte pointers for addresses. The other three implementations used two-byte addresses. The dynamic linked implementation has an advantage in that space for the queue is allocated from the heap rather than from the data segment. For applications in which global variables take up a lot of space, the dynamic linked implementation may be the only possibility.

Computer Simulation

A *system* is a collection of interacting parts. We are often interested in studying the behavior of a system—an economic system, a political system, an ecological system, or a computer system. Because systems are usually complicated, we may utilize a model to make our task manageable. A *model*—a simplification of a system—is designed so that we may study the behavior of the system.

A physical model is similar to the system it represents, except in scale or intensity. For example, we might create a physical model of tidal movements in the Chesapeake Bay or of a proposed shopping center. War games, spring training, and scrimmages are also examples of physical models. Unfortunately, some systems cannot be modelled physically with currently available technology—there is, as yet, no physical substance that could be expected to behave like the weather, for example. Often, as with pilot training, a physical model may be too expensive, too dangerous, or simply inconvenient.

Sometimes we may be able to represent the system with a mathematical model: a set of assumptions, variables, constants, and equations. A mathematical model is certainly more tractable than a physical model. In many cases, such as Distance = Rate * Time and the Pythagorean Theorem, the mathematical model can be solved analytically in a reasonable amount of time. Many mathematical models, however, do not have such a handy solution. For example, most differential equations cannot be solved analytically, and an economic model with thousands of equations cannot be solved by hand in a reasonable period of time.

In such cases the mathematical model is usually solved on a computer. Computer models are essential in complex systems such as weather forecasting, space flight, and urban planning. The use of computer models is called "computer simulation." There are several advantages to working with a computer model rather than the original system:

1. *Safety*. Flight simulators can assail pilot trainees with a welter of dangerous situations such as hurricanes and hijackings, and no one gets hurt.[3]

2. *Economy*. Simulation games in business-policy courses enable students to run a hypothetical company in competition with other students. If the company goes "belly up," the only recrimination is a lower grade for the student.

3. *Speed*. The computer makes predictions soon enough for you to act on them. This feature is essential in almost every simulation, from the stock market to national defense.

4. *Flexibility*. If the results you get do not conform to the system you are studying, all you have to do is change your model. This feedback[4] feature is shown in Fig. 6.23.

These benefits are so compelling that computer simulation has become the accepted method for studying complex systems. This is not to say that computer simulation is a panacea for all systems problems. A model is a simplified representation of an actual system, and simplification necessarily introduces disparities between the model and the system. For example, suppose you had developed a computer simulation of the earth's ecosystem

Figure 6.23

Feedback in computer simulation.

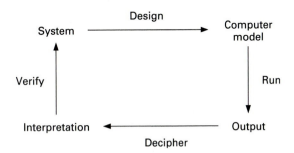

---

[3]Except once, when a trainee panicked because one of his engines failed during a simulated blizzard. He "bailed out" of his simulated cockpit and broke his ankle when he hit the unsimulated floor.

[4]*Feedback* **is a process in which the factors that produce a result are themselves affected by that result.**

30 years ago. You probably would have disregarded the effects of aerosol sprays. Many scientists now suspect that these have a significant impact on the ozone layer and thus on all land organisms.

Another disadvantage of computer simulation is that its results are often interpreted as predictions, and prediction is always a risky business. For this reason, a disclaimer such as the following usually precedes the results of a computer simulation: "If the relationships among the variables are as described and if the initial conditions are as described, then the consequences will probably be as follows . . . ."

A Queue Application: A Simulated Car Wash

Queues are employed in many simulations. The items on a queue may be cars waiting at the entrance to a tunnel, customers in a checkout line at a supermarket, airplanes in a holding pattern, and so on. For example, we now illustrate the use of a queue in simulating traffic flow at Speedo's Car Wash.

We assume that there is one station in the car wash, that is, there is one "server." Each car takes exactly ten minutes to get washed. At any time there can be at most five cars waiting on a queue to be washed. If an arrival occurs when there is a car being washed and there are five cars on the queue, that arrival is turned away as an "overflow" and not counted as a customer.

The problem we want to solve is this:

> Given a list of arrival times at the car wash, calculate the average waiting time per customer.

The average waiting time is determined by adding up the waiting times for each customer and dividing by the number of customers. Here are some of the details regarding arrivals and departures:

1. If an arrival and departure occur during the same minute, the departure is processed first.
2. If a customer arrives when the queue is empty and no cars are being washed, the car starts getting washed immediately; it is not put on the queue.
3. A customer leaves the queue, and stops waiting, once the car starts through the ten-minute wash cycle.

The following is a sample list of arrival times:

5 5 7 12 12 13 14 18 19 25 999 (a sentinel)

From the nouns in the statement of the problem, we choose CarWash and Customer as the objects we will work with. For CarWash, the key methods will involve processing arrivals and departures; that is, the simulation will be "event driven." For now, four methods can be identified:

```
Initialize
ProcessArrival
ProcessDeparture
AverageWaitingTime { a function }
```

For Customer, we need two methods (for now, at least):

```
Arrive
Depart
```

Because Customer is at a lower level than CarWash, we will start its design first. What will the design domain consist of? (That is, what fields will each customer have?) One of the fields will be the arrival time of the customer. (This is sometimes referred to as a *time stamp*.) We also need to keep track of the customer's waiting time and, to see if it is time for a departure, the minutes the customer has left in the wash. The fields in Customer are:

```
ArrivalTime
WaitingTime
MinutesLeft
```

The rest of the design of Customer is left as an exercise. What about the design domain of CarWash? Several fields come immediately to mind: NumberOfCustomers, NumberOfOverflows, and SumOfWaitingTimes. We will also need a queue to hold the customers waiting to be washed. NextArrivalTime will help us keep track of whether the next event will be an arrival or a departure. Finally, CurrentTime enables us to calculate a customer's waiting time when that customer finally leaves the queue and starts into the wash station.

Rather than designing CarWash's methods, we will simply show how the simulation progresses. After initializing CarWash, we start processing the arrival times. The first customer, at time 5 (minutes), is put in the wash station immediately. The current state of the simulation—the values of the revelant fields in CarWash and Customer—is shown in Fig. 6.24.

Figure 6.24

The state of the simulation after the arrival of the first customer at time 5 (minutes).

CarWash:

Queue	NumberOfCustomers	CurrentTime
(empty)	1	5

NextArrivalTime	SumOfWaitingTimes
5	0

Customer:

ArrivalTime	WaitingTime	MinutesLeft
5	0	10

Figure 6.25

The state of the simulation after the arrival of the sixth customer at time 13 (minutes).

CarWash:

Queue	NumberOfCustomers	CurrentTime
5, 7, 12, 12, 13	6	13

NextArrivalTime	SumOfWaitingTimes	
14	0	

Customer:

ArrivalTime	WaitingTime	MinutesLeft
5	0	2

the queue). After the sixth customer arrives at time 13, the state of the simulation is as shown in Fig. 6.25. In that figure, the Queue field of Car-Wash shows only the arrival times of the customers.

The arrival at time 14 is an overflow because the queue is already full. At time 15, MinutesLeft becomes 0, and so the first customer departs from the car wash. The customer at the head of the queue, whose ArrivalTime is 5, is deleted from the queue. The waiting time for that customer is Current-Time $-5 = 15 - 5 = 10$ (minutes).

After the arrival at time 18, the state of the simulation is as shown in Fig. 6.26.

The arrival at time 19 is an overflow. At time 25, there is a departure and an arrival. The state of the simulation after that arrival is shown in Fig. 6.27.

The customer being washed departs at time 35. The customers on the queue depart at times 45, 55, 65, 75, and 85. Their waiting times are

$$35 - 12 = 23,$$
$$45 - 12 = 33,$$
$$55 - 13 = 42,$$
$$65 - 18 = 47,$$
$$75 - 25 = 50$$

The sum of all the waiting times is 223 (minutes) and so the average waiting time is $223/8 = 27.875$ minutes per customer.

Figure 6.26

The state of the simulation after the arrival at time 18.

CarWash:

Queue	NumberOfCustomers	CurrentTime
7, 12, 12, 13, 18	7	18

NextArrivalTime	SumOfWaitingTimes	
19	10	

Customer:

ArrivalTime	WaitingTime	MinutesLeft
5	10	7

Figure 6.27

The state of the simulation after the arrival at time 25.

CarWash:

Queue	NumberOfCustomers	CurrentTime
12, 12, 13, 18, 25	8	25

NextArrivalTime	SumOfWaitingTimes
999	28

Customer:

ArrivalTime	WaitingTime	MinutesLeft
7	18	10

Randomizing the Arrival Times

It is not necessary that the arrival times be read in. They can be generated by your simulation program, provided the input includes the *mean arrival time*—the average time between arrivals for the population. In order to generate the list of arrival times from the mean arrival time, we need to know the distribution of arrival times. We now define a function that calculates the distribution, known as the *Poisson distribution*, of times between arrivals. The mathematical justification for the following discussion is beyond the scope of this book; the interested reader may consult Hogg (1983, pages 162ff).

Let X be any time between arrivals. Then $F(X)$, the probability that the time until the next arrival will be at least X minutes from now, is given by

$$F(X) = \text{Exp} \ (-X/\text{MeanArrivalTime})$$

For example, $F(0) = \text{Exp} \ (0) = 1$; that is, it is certain that the next arrival will occur at least 0 minutes from now. Similarly, F (MeanArrivalTime) = Exp $(-1) \approx 0.4$. F (10000 * MeanArrivalTime) is approximately 0. The graph of the function F is shown in Fig. 6.28.

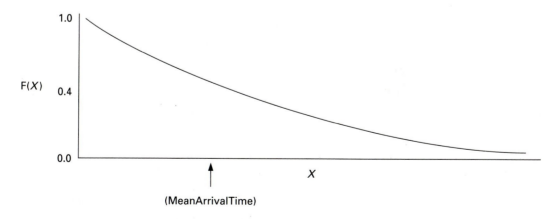

Figure 6.28 Graph of the Poisson distribution of interarrival times.

To generate the arrival times randomly, we introduce an integer variable called TimeTillNext, which will contain the number of minutes from the current time until the next arrival. We determine the value for TimeTill-Next as follows. According to the distribution function F given above, the probability that the next arrival will take at least TimeTillNext minutes is given by

$$\text{Exp } (-\text{TimeTillNext} / \text{MeanArrivalTime})$$

This expression represents a probability: specifically, a real number that is greater than 0 and less than or equal to 1. To randomize this probability, we associate the expression with a random value in the same range. Recall that the function Random, when called with no actual parameter, returns a real value that is greater than or equal to 0 and less than 1. Thus the value of 1−Random is greater than 0 and less than or equal to 1. So we equate

$$1 - \text{Random} = \text{Exp } (-\text{TimeTileNext}/\text{MeanArrivalTime})$$

The appropriate value for TimeTillNext is found by solving this equation for TimeTillNext:

$$\text{TimeTillNext} := \text{Round } (-\text{MeanArrivalTime} * \text{Ln } (1 - \text{Random}))$$

We rounded the result so that TimeTillNext will be an integer.

To illustrate how the values would be calculated, suppose that the mean arrival time is six minutes and the list of values of $1 - \text{Random}$ starts with 0.448024, 0.930171, and 0.664904. Then the first three values of TimeTill-Next will be

5, that is, Round (−6 * Ln (0.448024)),
0, that is, Round (−6 * Ln (0.930171)), and
2, that is, Round (−6 * Ln (0.664904)).

Thus, the first customer will arrive 5 minutes after the car wash opens and the second customer also will arrive at time 5. The third customer will arrive 2 minutes later, at time 7.

PRIORITY QUEUES

A variation of the queue, the *priority queue*, is a commonplace data structure. The basic idea is that we have items waiting in line for service. Selection is not strictly on a first-come-first-served basis. For example, patients in an emergency room are treated based on the severity of their injuries, not on when they arrived. But if two patients have the same injury, the one who arrives first is treated first.

A ***priority queue*** is a list in which:

1. Each item is an object with a Priority method that returns a positive integer, with 0 representing the lowest possible priority.

2. Each insertion is made after (that is, farther from position 1 than) any item already on the priority queue that has equal or higher priority.

3. Retrieval and deletion are of the item with highest priority. If two or more items have the highest priority, the one closest to position 1 is chosen.

Priority queues combine ordering characteristics of queues (that are ordered chronologically) and ordered lists (that are ordered by priorities). Depending on which kind of ordering we want to highlight, we can visualize a priority queue in either of two ways. Viewed as a queue, items are inserted at the tail; for retrievals and deletions, a search is conducted starting at position 1 to find the item with highest priority. Figure 6.29 shows such a priority queue through a sequence of insertions and deletions. Each item has name and priority fields.

We can also visualize a priority queue as an ordered list: Each item is inserted after items with equal or higher priority and before items with lower priority. Retrievals and deletions take place at position 1. Figure 6.30 shows the same sequence of insertions and deletions as in Fig. 6.29 under this representation.

Figure 6.29

A priority queue through this sequence of insertions and deletions: Insert Kim, Insert Joe, Insert Mark, Insert Jen, Delete Highest, Delete Highest, Delete Highest. This representation emphasizes the chronological ordering of a queue.

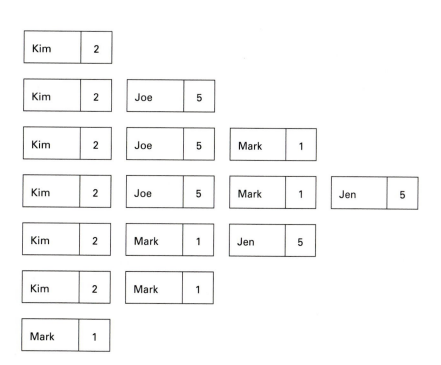

Figure 6.30

A priority queue through a sequence of insertions and deletions. This representation suggests that a priority queue is an ordered list of items.

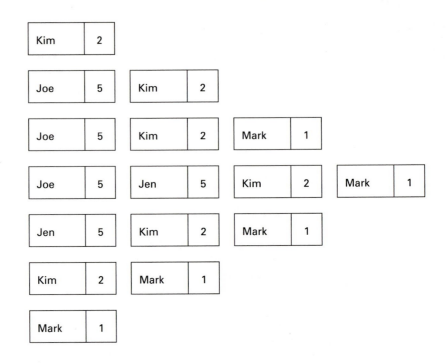

Either representation satisfies the definition of a priority queue. A user can visualize the priority queue in the way that makes the most sense for the given application. The developer of the Priority Queue ADT may choose a different representation, but the results will be the same.

Priority queues occur in a variety of situations. For example, jobs waiting to use the central processing unit on a mainframe computer are normally prioritized, with terminal jobs getting higher priority than batch jobs and, within either of those categories, faculty jobs getting higher priority than student jobs. For a lively discussion of some other priority-queue applications, see Dale, 1990.

The methods in the Priority Queue ADT are the same as those in the Queue ADT, except that RetrieveHead, InsertTail, and DeleteHead are replaced with the following:

↑

4. `RetrieveHighest (Item).`

    Postcondition: The item with highest priority has been copied into Item. If more than one item has the highest priority, the one closest to position 1 has been copied into Item.

↓

5. `Insert (Item).`

Precondition: The number of items in the priority queue is less than MaxListSize.

Postcondition: Item has been inserted into the priority queue after any item with the same or higher priority.

6. `DeleteHighest`.

Precondition: The priority queue is not empty.

Postcondition: The item on the priority queue that had—before this call—the highest priority has been deleted. If more than one item has the highest priority, the one closest to position 1 has been deleted.

Designs of the Priority Queue Data Type

Our first attempt at designing the Priority Queue ADT is to inherit from the linked or contiguous design of the Queue ADT. However, if we inherit the design of InsertTail, as in the first representation (Fig. 6.29) both retrievals and deletions will take $O(N)$ time. On the other hand, if we use the second representation (Fig. 6.30) and inherit the designs of RetrieveHead and DeleteHead, then insertions will take $O(N)$ time. We therefore abandon our hope of simply using one of the queue designs from before.

If the number of different priorities is not very large, we can represent a priority queue as a contiguous list of queues, where each queue contains all the items of a given priority. For example, Fig. 6.31 shows the multiqueue representation of the priority queue from Figs. 6.29 and 6.30 right after the insertion of Jen.

In a multiqueue representation of a priority queue, the priority field wastes space, but it is a field in each item, and so it is the user's responsibility. With this representation, the design of a priority queue data type is straightforward. A suitable implementation might have an array of queues, each implemented dynamically (with Head and Tail fields). For a priority queue with N items and M possible priorities, we would need space for the N items, N pointers, and $2M$ queue fields. The time requirements for priority queue operations are the same as for the corresponding queue opera-

Figure 6.31

A multiqueue representation of the priority queue from Figs. 6.29 and 6.30 after the insertion of Jen.

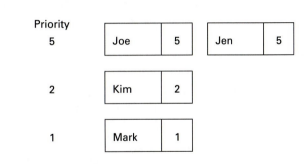

tions, namely, O(1), except that retrievals and deletions from the head require a search to find the highest-priority nonempty queue.

The major drawback to such a multiqueue implementation is that if the number of priorities is high—say, *M* greater than 1000—the overhead of 2*M* queue fields is considerable. In Chapter 8 we introduce a different design and implementation that eliminates this overhead at a cost of increased, but still less than O(*N*), time.

SUMMARY

A *stack* is a list in which retrievals, insertions, and deletions can take place only at position 1. This *last-in-first-out* restriction simplifies the design of the corresponding methods for both the linked and contiguous design domains. Compilers implement recursion by generating code for creating and maintaining an *activation stack*: a run-time stack that holds the state of each active subprogram. Another stack application occurs in the translation of infix expressions into machine code. With the help of an operator stack, an infix expression can easily be converted into a postfix expression, which is an intermediate form between infix and machine language.

A *queue* is a list in which retrievals and deletions can take place only at position 1 (the head), and insertions can place only at the last position (the tail). A linked design of the Queue ADT is fairly straightforward. For an efficient contiguous design, the values in the Head and Tail fields are incremented with each deletion and insertion, respectively. For this to work, the array is treated as a *circular* array; that is, after the component at index MaxListSize, the next component is at index 1. The inherent fairness of the *first-come-first-served* restriction has made the queue a part of many systems. The Queue ADT plays a key role in the development of mathematical models to study the behavior of those systems.

In a *priority queue*, each item has a priority. When an item is enqueued, its position in the priority queue is greater than (that is, farther from position 1) the position of any item on the priority queue with equal or higher priority. Retrieval and deletion are of the item with highest priority; if two or more items are tied for highest priority, the first one of them enqueued is chosen.

EXERCISES

6.1 Suppose that LetterStack is an instance of a stack. Each item is a single letter. Show what this stack will look like after each of the following messages is sent:

a. LetterStack.Initialize

b. LetterStack.Push ('a')

    c. LetterStack.Push ('b')

    d. LetterStack.Push ('c')

    e. LetterStack.Pop

    f. LetterStack.Pop

    g. LetterStack.Push ('d')

    h. LetterStack.Push ('e')

    i. LetterStack.Pop

6.2 Trace the execution of the messages in Exercise 6.1 for both the linked and contiguous designs of the Stack ADT.

6.3 Use a stack of activation records to trace the execution of the recursive Factorial function after an initial call of Factorial (4).

6.4 As a *user* of the Stack ADT, design an operator to print out the items in a stack, from top to bottom. The heading is

```
Print (Stack).
```

> **HINT** *Don't assume that, because Stack is an input parameter, Pop will not affect the calling instance (see Laboratory Exercise 6.1).*

6.5 Show that the Size and CopyTo methods in the Stack ADT can be developed from the other five methods by a *user* of the Stack ADT.

6.6 Translate the following expressions into postfix notation:

    a. $X + Y * Z$

    b. $(X + Y) * Z$

    c. $X - Y - Z * (A + B)$

    d. $(A + B) * C - (D + E * F/((G/H + I - J) * K))/L$

    e. $A + B * C \char94 D/E - F$

    f. $A + B * C \char94 D \char94 (E - F)/G$

(In parts e and f, ^ represents exponentiation. In part f, assume that exponentiations are to be performed from right to left.)

6.7 Translate each of the expressions in Exercise 6.6 into prefix notation.

6.8 An expression in postfix notation can be evaluated at run time by means of a stack. For simplicity, assume that the postfix expression consists of integer values and operators only. For example, we might have the following postfix expression:

$$8\ 5\ 4\ +\ *\ 7\ -$$

The evaluation proceeds as follows: When a value is encountered, it is pushed onto the stack. When an operator is encountered, the first and second items on the stack are retrieved and popped, the operator is applied (the second item is the left operand, the first item is the right operand) and the result is pushed onto the stack. When the postfix expression has been processed, the value of that expresson is the top (and only) item on the stack.

For example, for the above expression, the contents of the stack would be as follows:

			4
		5	5
___ →	8	8	8
9		7	
8	72	72	65

Convert the following expression into postfix notation and then use a stack to evaluate the expression:

$$5 + 2 * (30 - 10/5)$$

6.9   Develop a subalgorithm to evaluate an infix arithmetic expression consisting of integer values, integer operators $(+, -, *, /)$, and parentheses.

6.10 Develop a subalgorithm to evaluate a Boolean expression consisting of Boolean values, Boolean operators (**and**, **or**, **not**), and parentheses. For example, the value of

```
True and (False or not True)
```

is False.

HINT   See Exercises 6.8 and 6.9.

6.11 Suppose that items A, B, C, D, E are pushed, in that order, onto an initially empty stack instance Stack, that Stack is then popped four times, and that as each item is popped off Stack, it is inserted into an initially empty queue instance Queue. If one item is then deleted from Queue, what is the NEXT item to be deleted?

6.12 The free list was introduced in the static implementation of the linked design of the list data type. For which data type is it *most* appropriate to say that the free list is an instance of that type?

   a.   the Stack ADT
   b.   the Queue ADT
   c.   the Ordered List ADT
   d.   the Priority Queue ADT

6.13 Suppose that Flights is an instance of a queue. Each item is an integer between 1000 and 9999, inclusive. Show what the queue will look like after each of the following messages is sent:

    a. `Flights.Initialize`
    b. `Flights.InsertTail (1215)`
    c. `Flights.InsertTail (1035)`
    d. `Flights.InsertTail (2117)`
    e. `Flights.DeleteHead`
    f. `Flights.InsertTail (1999)`
    g. `Flights.DeleteHead`

6.14 Trace the execution, for both the linked and contiguous designs of the Queue ADT, of the messages in Exercise 6.12.

6.15 As a *user* of the Queue ADT, design an operator to Print out the items in a queue from the head item to the tail item. The heading is

$$\downarrow$$

`Print (Queue).`

H I N T Start by calling the CopyTo method (see Laboratory Exercise 6.1).

6.16 Trace the car wash simulation if the maximum arrival time is 25, the mean arrival time is 6 minutes, and the arrival times are generated from the sequence of values of $1 -$ Random given in System Test 2 for Programming Assignment 2, using the formula

```
TimeTillNext := Round (- MeanArrivalTime * Ln (1 -
                Random))
```

6.17 Suppose that Jobs is an instance of a priority queue. For simplicity, assume that each item consists only of a priority, between 0 and 127, inclusive. Show what the priority queue will look like—for both representations (namely, a queue and an ordered list)—after each of the following messages is sent:

    a. `Jobs.Initialize`
    b. `Jobs.Insert (3)`
    c. `Jobs.Insert (12)`
    d. `Jobs.Insert (3)`
    e. `Jobs.Insert (22)`
    f. `Jobs.Insert (5)`
    g. `Jobs.Insert (12)`
    h. `Jobs.DeleteHighest`
    i. `Jobs.DeleteHighest`

6.18 Show that, in the linked or contiguous design of the Priority Queue ADT, if the Insert subalgorithm simply calls InsertTail, then both retrievals and deletions will take O(N) time. Also, show that if the DeleteHighest subalgorithm simply calls DeleteHead, then insertions will take O(N) time.

6.19 As a *user* of the Priority Queue ADT, design a Print operator to print out the priority queue from head to tail. The heading is

$$\downarrow$$

Print (PQueue).

LABORATORY EXERCISE

6.1 Suppose that we use a dynamic linked implementation of the Stack ADT. If ItemType = char, conjecture what the effect of executing the following program will be:

```
program WhatThe;
uses
    ItemInList,
    Stack1Manager;
var
    Stack1,
    Stack2 : StackType;
    Letter : char;
begin
    Stack1.Initialize;
    Stack2.Initialize;
    Stack1.Push ('X');
    Stack2 := Stack1;
    Stack1.Pop;
    with Stack2 do
       begin
          Push ('Y'); { allocates the space deallocated}
                      { by previous pop                 }
          while not IsEmpty do
             begin
                RetrieveTop (Letter);
                Writeln (Letter);
                Pop
             end { while }
       end { with }
end. { WhatThe }
```

Run the program to test your conjecture. Find and correct the error in the program.

HINT *":=" is not a method in the Stack ADT.*

PROGRAMMING ASSIGNMENTS

Programming Assignment 1

Problem: Given a list of arithmetic expressions in infix notation, convert each legal expression to postfix notation.

Specifications

1. The program is to be conversational: Each input line is entered, left justified, on the line after the prompt "Please enter an infix expression or press 'Enter':". It is assumed that an empty line (from pressing the "Enter" key) will eventually be entered.

2. Each input line should contain 0 to 40 characters in infix notation. An empty line (from pressing the "Enter" key) signals the end of the input. Each character should be one of the following:
   a. a singleletter, uppercase identifier;
   b. a left or right parenthesis;
   c. a binary operator: +, −, *, /.
   No blanks are allowed.

3. The following heading is to be printed: "Program to convert simple arithmetic expressions from infix notation to postfix notation." Specification 2 is then to be printed, preceded by a blank line.

4. If the line contains more than 40 characters, it is not processed and the error message printed is "Error—line contains more characters than allowed."

5. Every other error is to be treated in the following way: Under the character that generated the error, there should be a caret (^). The next line has the form "Error in position" followed by the position of the erroneous character and one of the following messages:

   ```
   : Illegal character
   : First character an operator
   : Last character an operator
   : Identifier followed by an identifier
   : Right parenthesis followed by an identifier
   : Operator followed by an operator
   : Left parenthesis followed by an operator
   : Identifier followed by a left parenthesis
   ```

: Right parenthesis followed by a left parenthesis
: Operator followed by a right parenthesis
: Left parenthesis followed by a right parenthesis
: Unmatched left parenthesis
: Unmatched right parenthesis

For example

A+B*(+C)
         ∧

Error in position 6: Left parenthesis followed by an operator

Note: Only the first such error in a line need be detected.

6. If the input line does not contain any errors, then the next output line will be blank and on the next line are printed "Postfix:" and the expression in postfix notation. For example,

A*(B+C-D)
Postfix: ABC+D-*

7. There will always be two consecutive blank lines printed before the prompt is printed.

System testing should cover not only all possible errors (see Specifications 4 and 5) but also entries in the transition table (see Fig. 6.14). The first two inputs in System Test 1 check that the program properly handles the non-error entries in the transition table. The next 14 inputs check that the program properly handles the errors in Specifications 4 and 5. System Test 2 checks some simple cases and boundary conditions.

System Test 1

Program to convert simple arithmetic expressions from infix notation into postfix notation.
Each input line should contain 0 to 40 characters in infix notation. An empty line (from pressing the "Enter" key) signals the end of the input. Each character should be one of the following:
    1. a single-letter, upper-case identifier;
    2. a left or right parenthesis;
    3. a binary operator: +, -, *, /.
No blanks are allowed.

Please enter an infix expression or press 'Enter':
(A+B)*C-(D+E*F/((G/H+I-J)*K))/L
Postfix: AB+C*DEF*GH/I+J-K*/+L/-

Please enter an infix expression or press 'Enter':
A+(B)*(C-D/(E+F*G-H)*J+K)-L
Postfix: ABCDEFG*+HI/=/J*-K+*+L-

Please enter an infix expression or press 'Enter':

```
A+B+C+D+E+F+G+H+I+J+K+L+M+N+O+P+Q+R+S+T+U
```

Error - line contains more characters than allowed.

Please enter an infix expression or press 'Enter':
```
X-Y;
   ^
```

Error in position 4: Illegal character

Please enter an infix expression or press 'Enter':
```
/B*C
^
```

Error in position 1: First character an operator

Please enter an infix expression or press 'Enter':
```
T/U-
   ^
```

Error in position 4: Last character an operator

Please enter an infix expression or press 'Enter':
```
A-B/(CD+E)
      ^
```

Error in position 7: Identifier followed by an identifier

Please enter an infix expression or press 'Enter':
```
A+(C)E-F
     ^
```

Error in position 6: Right parenthesis followed by an
identifier

Please enter an infix expression or press 'Enter':
```
X*/Y
  ^
```

Error in position 3: Operator followed by an operator

Please enter an infix expression or press 'Enter':
```
(/P*Q)
 ^
```

Error in position 2: Left parenthesis followed by an
operator

Please enter an infix expression or press 'Enter':
```
W(S+T)
 ^
```

Error in position 2: Identifier followed by a left
parenthesis

Please enter an infix expression or press 'Enter':
```
X-(Y*Z)(A+B)
       ^
```

Error in position 8: Right parenthesis followed by a left
parenthesis

Please enter an infix expression or press 'Enter':
```
D*(V*)
     ^
```

```
Error in position 6: Operator followed by a right
parenthesis
Please enter an infix expression or press 'Enter':
A*B*()-G
       ^

Error in position 6: Left parenthesis followed by a right
parenthesis
Please enter an infix expression or press 'Enter':
A+(B-(C+(D/E))*F
   ^

Error in position 3: Unmatched left parenthesis
Please enter an infix expression or press "Enter":
A*(B-(C+(D/E))))*F
              ^

Error in position 16: Unmatched right parenthesis
Please enter an infix expression or press 'Enter':
```

System Test 2

```
Program to convert simple arithmetic expressions from infix
notation into postfix notation.
Each input line should contain 0 to 40 characters in infix
notation. An empty line (from pressing the "Enter" key)
signals the end of the input. Each character should be one
of the following:
    1. a single-letter, upper-case identifier;
    2. a left or right parenthesis;
    3. a binary operator: +, -, *, /.
No blanks are allowed.
Please enter an infix expression or press 'Enter':
X-Y+Z
Postfix: XY-Z+
Please enter an infix expression or press 'Enter':
X-(Y+Z)
Postfix: XYZ+-
Please enter an infix expression or press 'Enter':
X-Y*Z
Postfix: XYZ*-
Please enter an infix expression or press 'Enter':
X*Y-Z
Postfix: XY*Z-
Please enter an infix expression or press 'Enter':
X*(Y-Z)
Postfix: XYZ-*
Please enter an infix expression or press 'Enter':
(((((((((((A)))))))))))
Postfix: A
```

```
Please enter an infix expression or press 'Enter':
A/B/C/D/E/F/G/H/I-J-K-L+M+N*O*P*Q*R
Postfix: AB/C/D/E/F/G/H/I/J-K-L-M+NO*P*Q*R*+
Please enter an infix expression or press 'Enter':
```

Programming Assignment 2

Problem: Simulate the traffic at Barfin' Bob's checkout counter.

Specifications

1. Assume that the Poisson distribution (see Fig. 6.28) applies to both the arrival times and the service times.

2. At any time, no more than five customers can be waiting in line in addition to the customer already being served. If an arrival occurs when a customer is being served and there are five customers waiting in line, that arrival is turned away as an overflow and not counted as a customer.

3. If an arrival and a departure occur during the same minute, the departure is processed.

4. If a customer arrives when there is no one being served and no one in line, that customer is served immediately.

5. A customer leaves the waiting line once that customer starts getting served.

6. The *mean service time* is the average time, out of the whole population of customers, for customers to get served.

7. The *average queue length* is the average number of customers waiting in line during each minute of the simulation. The average queue length can be calculated as the sum of the waiting times divided by the number of minutes of the simulation.

8. The input consists of three integers (each preceded by a prompt):
   a. the maximum number of minutes during which arrivals can occur;
   b. the mean arrival time (for the population);
   c. the mean service time (for the population).
   If any of these values is outside of 1..999, the error message to be printed is

   ```
   Error--value must be an integer in 1..999.
   ```

   A reprompt (see the system tests for prompt formats) is then given. It is assumed that a correct value will be entered eventually.

   EXTRA CREDIT: Print the error message and reprompt if the input contains a nondigit character. For example,

   3x

9. The output should start with the following:

    ```
    Simulation of traffic at Barfin' Bob's checkout counter.
    Enter the number of minutes during which arrivals can
    occur:
    Enter the average number of minutes between arrivals:
    Enter the average number of minutes for service:
    ```

10. The next part of the output consists of three columns of information about arrivals and departures. The column headings are:

    ```
    Time    Event    Elapsed Time
    ```

    Each event is either an arrival or a departure. For an arrival, the output should be the time of the arrival and the words "Arrival" or "Arrival—Overflow". For a departure, the output should be the time of the departure, the word "Departure," and the elapsed time from when the customer arrived.

11. The final part of the output consists of the summary statistics: the (sample) average queue length per minute of the simulation, the (sample) average waiting time per customer, the (sample) average service time per customer, and the number of overflows. The first three of these values should be rounded to the first fractional digit.

System Test 1

```
Simulation of traffic at Barfin' Bob's checkout counter.
Enter the number of minutes during which arrivals can occur:
20
Enter the average number of minutes between arrivals: 3
Enter the average number of minutes for service: 7
Time    Event                      Elapsed Time
  2     Arrival
  3     Departure                      1
  3     Arrival
  3     Arrival
  4     Arrival
  4     Arrival
  6     Arrival
  6     Arrival
  8     Departure                      5
  9     Arrival
 13     Arrival - Overflow
 14     Arrival - Overflow
 17     Departure                     14
 18     Arrival
 19     Arrival - Overflow
 19     Arrival - Overflow
 21     Departure                     17
 34     Departure                     30
 40     Departure                     34
```

```
40        Departure              34
51        Departure              42
67        Departure              49
```

The Average Queue Length was 2.4 customers.
The Average Waiting Time was 17.9 minutes.
The Average Service Time was 7.2 minutes.
There were 4 overflows.

System Test 2

Simulation of traffic at Barfin' Bob's checkout counter.
Enter the number of minutes during which arrivals can occur:
25
Enter the average number of minutes between arrivals: 0
Error--value must be an integer in 1..999.
Enter the average number of minutes between arrivals: 7
Enter the average number of minutes for service: 3

Time	Event	Elapsed Time
6	Arrival	
6	Departure	0
9	Arrival	
9	Arrival	
10	Arrival	
11	Departure	2
11	Arrival	
12	Arrival	
13	Departure	4
17	Departure	7
19	Arrival	
21	Departure	10
21	Arrival	
25	Departure	13
25	Arrival	
26	Departure	7
28	Departure	7
34	Departure	9

The Average Queue Length was 1.0 customers.
The Average Waiting Time was 3.8 minutes.
The Average Service Time was 2.8 minutes.
There were 0 overflows.

Note: The (pseudo-)random numbers on which these simulations
were based were obtained by using a seed of 200 and the
following sequence of values of 1 - Random:

0.448024
0.930171
0.664904

```
0.458717
0.960897
0.841950
0.879060
0.499252
0.881360
0.386704
0.276786
0.259694
0.744819
0.229629
0.548383
0.818152
0.916723
0.439180
0.146415
0.444374
0.993748
0.213097
0.100655
0.007101
0.073493
0.268595
0.185316
0.897585
0.007420
0.652793
0.930979
0.641599
0.067654
0.241785
0.028155
0.619841
0.148263
0.512121
0.137341
0.655674
0.261319
0.208420
0.348849
0.453187
0.871667
0.950900
0.979189
0.233732
0.411714
0.176550
```

The Binary Tree Data Type

In this chapter we introduce the Binary Tree ADT. Binary trees are important mathematical constructs, and we will devote the first part of this chapter to their properties. Like a horse raised for breeding rather than for racing, the Binary Tree ADT is useful mainly for its descendants. From an owner's perspective, breeding is less fun than racing, and this chapter will be less exciting than Chapter 8, where we study the descendants.

One of the descendants of the Binary Tree ADT, the Binary Search Tree ADT, allows items to be inserted or deleted in O(log N) time, on average. This compares very favorably with the O(N) time required for inserting or deleting in an ordered list. TreeSort, one of the fast sorting algorithms of Chapter 9, utilizes a binary search tree.

Another descendant of the Binary Tree ADT is the Heap[1] ADT. One of the defining properties of a heap makes a contiguous design and implementation convenient. For this reason, the priority queue ADT is often designed and implemented with a heap. A heap is also the basis for HeapSort, another of the fast sorting algorithms developed in Chapter 9.

The third descendant we will consider later is the Expression Tree ADT. Expression trees allow for simple algorithms to evaluate the original expression and to perform symbolic differentiation and integration on the expression.

---

[1]This is unrelated to the heap that is used for dynamic variables.

DEFINITION AND PROPERTIES

The following definition sets the tone for the whole chapter:

> *A **binary tree** T is either empty or consists of an item, called the **root item**, and two disjoint binary trees, called the **left subtree** and **right subtree** of T.*

We denote those subtrees as Left (T) and Right (T), respectively. Note that this definition of a binary tree is recursive, and almost every nontrivial binary tree method has a straightforward recursive design.

In depicting a binary tree, the root item is shown at the top, by convention. To suggest the association between the root item and the left and right subtrees, we draw a southwesterly line from the root item to the left subtree and a southeasterly line from the root item to the right subtree. Fig. 7.1 shows several binary trees.

Figure 7.1

Several binary trees.

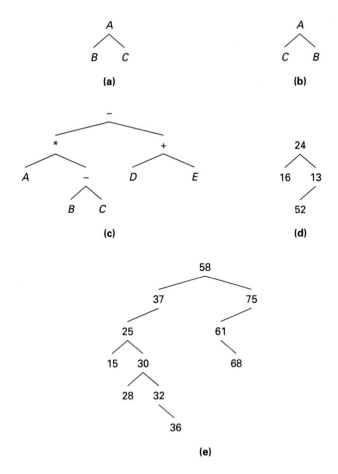

The binary tree in Fig. 7.1(a) is different from the binary tree in Fig. 7.1(b) because B is in the left subtree of Figure 7.1(a), but not in the left subtree of Fig. 7.1(b). A subtree of a binary tree is itself a binary tree, so Fig. 7.1(a) has seven binary trees: the whole binary tree, the binary tree whose root item is B, the binary tree whose root item is C, and four empty binary trees.

The line from a root item to a subtree is called a **branch**. An item whose associated left and right subtrees are both empty is called a **leaf**. A leaf has no branches going down from it. In the binary tree shown in Fig. 7.1(e), there are four leaves: 15, 28, 36, and 68.

Each item in a binary tree is uniquely determined by its location in the tree. For example, let T be the binary tree shown in Fig. 7.1(c). There are two items in T with value "−". We can distinguish between them by referring to one of them as "the item whose value is '−' and whose location is the root of T" and the other one as "the item whose value is '−' and whose location is the root of the right subtree of the left subtree of T." We loosely refer to "an item" in a binary tree when, strictly speaking, we should specify both the item and its location.

Let T be the following binary tree:

We say that x is the **parent** of y and that y is the **left child** of x. Similarly, we say that x is the **parent** of z and that z is the **right child** of x. In a binary tree, each item has zero, one, or two children. For example, in Fig. 7.1(d), 24 has two children, 16 and 13; 13 has 52 as its only child; and 16 and 52 are childless (they are leaves).

In a binary tree, the root item does not have a parent, and every other item has exactly one parent. Continuing with the terminology of a family tree, we could define sibling, grandparent, grandchild, first cousin, ancestor, and descendant. For example, an item A is an **ancestor** of an item B if B is an item in the tree whose root item is A. To put it recursively, A is an ancestor of B if A is the parent of B, or if one of A's children is an ancestor of B.

Roughly, the height of a binary tree is the number of branches between the root and the "farthest" leaf (the leaf with the most ancestors). The following recursive definition allows us to distinguish between the height of an empty binary tree and the height of a single-item binary tree.

Let T be a binary tree. We define H(T), the **height** of T, as follows:

if T is empty,
    $H(T) = -1$
else
    $H(T) = 1 +$ the maximum of $\{ H(\text{Left}(T)), H(\text{Right}(T)) \}$

For example, the height of the binary tree in Fig. 7.1(a) is 1, and the height of the binary tree in Fig. 7.1(e) is 5.

Height is a property of an entire binary tree. For each item in a binary tree, we can define a similar concept: the level of the item. Let T be a nonempty binary tree. For any item x in T, we define Level (x), the **level** of item x, as follows:

> if x is the root item,
>> Level $(x) = 0$
> else
>> Level $(x) = 1 +$ Level $(x$'s parent)

For example, in Fig. 7.1(e), the level of 30 is 3 and the level of 36 is 5. An item's level is also referred to as that item's **depth**. The height of a binary tree is equal to the level of the farthest leaf.

A **two-tree** (sometimes called a *strictly binary tree*) is a nonempty binary tree in which either both subtrees are empty or both subtrees are two trees. (In other words, in a two-tree, each item has either zero or two branches going down from it.) For example, the binary trees in Figs. 7.1(a), (b), and (c) are two-trees, but the trees in Figs. 7.1(d) and (e) are not two-trees.

A nonempty binary tree is **perfectly balanced** if its left and right subtrees have the same height and both are either empty or perfectly balanced. For example, the binary trees in Figs. 7.1(a) and (b) are perfectly balanced. The binary tree in Fig. 7.1(c) is not perfectly balanced because its left subtree has a height of 3 and its right subtree has a height of only 2.

Each perfectly balanced binary tree is a two-tree (see Exercise 7.4.i), but the converse is not necessarily true. For example, the tree in Fig. 7.1(c) is a two-tree but is not perfectly balanced. For perfectly balanced binary trees, there is a relationship between the height and number of items in the tree. For example, if the tree has a height of 2, there must be exactly 7 items:

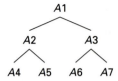

What if the tree has a height of 3? Of 4? For a perfectly balanced binary tree T, can you conjecture the formula for the number of items in T as a function of $H(T)$?

A somewhat weaker notion is that of a complete binary tree. A binary tree T is *complete* if:

1. T is perfectly balanced (except possibly at the lowest level), and
2. all of the leaves at the lowest level are as far to the left as possible.

(By "lowest level," we mean the level farthest from the root.)

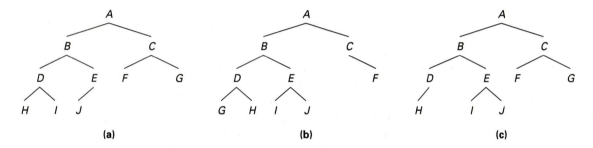

Figure 7.2 Three binary trees, of which only (a) is complete.

For example, any perfectly balanced binary tree is complete. Also, the tree of Fig. 7.2(a) is a complete binary tree. The tree in Fig. 7.2(b) is not complete because it does not satisfy property 1 above, and the tree in Fig. 7.2(c) is not complete because it does not satisfy property 2 above.

In a complete binary tree, we can associate a "position" with each item. The root item is assigned a position of 1. For any item at position i, the position of its left child is $2i$ and the position of its right child is $2i + 1$. For example, the positions of the ten items in the complete binary tree of Fig. 7.2(a) are as follows:

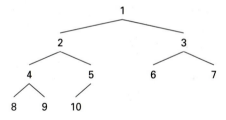

For the sake of generality, we will define the position of an item in an arbitrary binary tree to be the position the item would have if the tree were extended to form a complete binary tree. For example, in the following binary tree, each item is a letter, and the position of each item is given as a superscript:

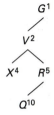

As we will see later, the position of an item is important in the contiguous representation of a binary tree.

For any binary tree T, we denote the number of items in T by $N(T)$ and the number of leaves in T by $L(T)$. By using functional notation, we can easily denote the number of items and leaves in the left and right subtrees of T. For example, the number of leaves in the right subtree of T is $L(\text{Right}(T))$.

Obviously, $L(T) \le N(T)$, and $L(T) = N(T)$ if and only if T consists of at most one item. The following theorem characterizes the relationships between $L(T)$, $N(T)$, and $H(T)$.

Theorem 7.1.   For any nonempty binary tree T,

$$L(T) \le \frac{N(T) + 1}{2} \le 2^{H(T)}.$$

Furthermore, $L(T) = \dfrac{N(T) + 1}{2}$ if and only if T is a two-tree. Also, $\dfrac{N(T) + 1}{2} = 2^{H(T)}$ if and only if T is perfectly balanced.

All of the parts of this theorem can be proved by induction on the height of T. Some of the details are given in Example 7 of Appendix 1. As it turns out, most theorems about binary trees can be proved by induction on the height of the tree, because if T is a binary tree of height $H(T)$, then $\text{Left}(T)$ and $\text{Right}(T)$ each have height less than $H(T)$. Therefore, the Strong Form of the Principle of Mathematical Induction applies.

Traversals of a Binary Tree

Recall, from Chapter 3, that for an instance that consists of items, a ***traversal*** of that instance is an algorithm that accesses each item in the instance exactly once. Let T be any instance of a binary tree. We identify four different traversals of T:

1. Inorder traversal (Left-Root-Right). If T is not empty, first perform an inorder traversal of $\text{Left}(T)$, then access the root item of T, and finally, perform an inorder traversal of $\text{Right}(T)$.

    We now use this recursive description to list the items in an inorder traversal of the following binary tree:

    We start by performing an inorder traversal of $\text{Left}(T)$:

25

This becomes the current version of *T*. Since Left (*T*) is empty, we access the root item of *T*, namely 25. That completes the traversal of this version of *T*, since Right (*T*) is empty. At this point, *T* refers to the original tree. We next access *T*'s root item:

$$31$$

After that, we perform an inorder traversal of Right (*T*):

This becomes the current version of *T*. We start by performing an inorder traversal of Left (*T*):

$$42$$

Since its left subtree is empty, we access the root item, 42. The right subtree of this subtree is empty. We next access the root item of *T*:

$$47$$

Finally, we perform an inorder traversal of Right (*T*):

$$50$$

Since its left subtree is empty, we access the root item, namely 50. We are now finished since its right subtree is also empty.

The complete listing is:

$$25 \quad 31 \quad 42 \quad 47 \quad 50$$

It is no accident that the items are listed in (increasing) order—in fact, this is how the inorder traversal got its name. We will devote part of Chapter 8 to the study of those binary trees for which an inorder traversal accesses the items in increasing order.

2. Postorder Traversal (Left-Right-Root). If *T* is not empty, first perform a postorder traversal of Left(*T*), then perform a postorder traversal of Right(*T*), and finally, access the root item of *T*.

    For example, a postorder traversal of:

accesses the items in the following order:

A B C + ∗

We can view the above binary tree as an "expression tree": Each nonleaf is a binary operator whose operands are the associated left and right subtrees. With this interpretation, a postorder traversal produces postfix notation.

3. Preorder Traversal (Root-Left-Right). If T is not empty, first access the root item of T, then perform a preorder traversal of Left(T), and finally, perform a preorder traversal of Right(T).

For example, a preorder traversal of:

accesses the items in the following order:

   $* A + B C$

If we view the tree as an expression tree, a preorder traversal produces prefix notation.

A search that employs a preorder traversal is called a **_depth-first search_** because the search goes to the left as deeply as possible before searching to the right. For example, suppose we make a depth-first search of:

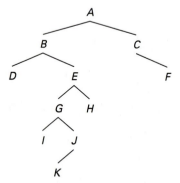

Then the order in which the items will be accessed is

   $A B D E G I J K H C F$

Depth-first searches facilitate *backtracking* algorithms. The general idea with such an algorithm is that a sequence of choices is made, perhaps randomly, to try to obtain a solution to a problem. At some point, it may be discovered that the solution is unattainable with the current choices. The last choice for which an alternative has not been tried in the current sequence is then undone and another choice made. It may be necessary to backtrack through several levels, but if there is some sequence of choices that will lead to a solution, that sequence will eventually be found. In Chapter 11, we will study depth-first searches for a generalization of binary trees known as *graphs*.

4. Breadth-First Traversal (Level-By-Level). First access the item at level 0, then the items at level 1 from left to right, then the items at level 2 from left to right, and so on. Finally, the items at level $H(T)$ are accessed from left to right. In short, items are accessed in the numerical order of their positions.

For example, suppose we perform a breadth-first traversal of the following binary tree, with the position numbers as superscripts:

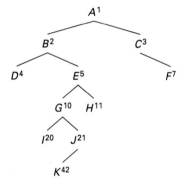

The order in which items would be accessed is:

$$A \, B \, C \, D \, E \, F \, G \, H \, I \, J \, K$$

As we will see later in this chapter, designing a breadth-first traversal can be simplified with the help of the Queue ADT. The other traversals are naturally recursive, so their designs are based ultimately on the Stack ADT.

From the properties we have seen so far, we will now determine the responsibilities of the Binary Tree ADT.

RESPONSIBILITIES OF THE BINARY TREE DATA TYPE

Just as with all the other abstract data types we have studied, the responsibilities of the Binary Tree ADT to its users fall into two categories: those that apply to a binary tree as a whole and those that apply to individual items in a binary tree. Let's start with the global responsibilities.

The first few responsibilities are standard. A user should be able:

to make the binary tree empty;

to see if the binary tree is empty;

to calculate the current size of the binary tree.

In some situations, a binary tree's height may be even more important than its size; therefore, a user should be able:

to calculate the current height of the binary tree.

Users may also want to make a copy of the entire binary tree, or of its left or right subtree. This suggests three more responsibilities:

to copy the binary tree to another binary tree;

to copy the left subtree to another binary tree;

to copy the right subtree to another binary tree.

The binary tree is responsible for allowing traversals in any of the four ways we described in the preceding section. Specifically, a user should be able:

to perform inorder, postorder, preorder, and breadth-first traversals of a binary tree.

The remaining responsibilities relate to individual items: to search for, retrieve, insert, and delete an item in a binary tree. This leads to an interesting problem. How can we place the items in an arbitrary binary tree?

One possibility is to store each item in some kind of order according to the value of the item. This idea is attractive if the items are ordered. In fact, in the next chapter we will see two different ways to store ordered items. In general, however, the items may not be ordered, so storing items according to their values will not work.

Another way to store an item is by specifying its position in the tree. For example, suppose we start with the following binary tree (position numbers are superscripts):

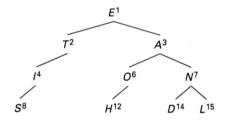

We can insert R in position 13, to give us

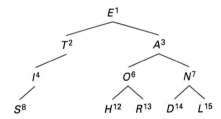

For a positional insertion to make sense, the parent's position must already be occupied. Note, for example, that in this binary tree, we could not insert an item into position 10 because there is no item in position 5. Checking for an occupied parent may be either easy or difficult, depending on the kind of binary tree we are working with.

A further complication arises with deletions. If the item at a nonleaf position is deleted, how should the tree be restructured? For example, suppose we delete the item in position 1 from the following tree:

We cannot decide which item should become the root unless we know more about the relationship between the items and the tree's structure. This information is available to the descendants of the Binary Tree ADT, but not available to the Binary Tree ADT itself.

Maybe that's it! The best solution to the problem of determining item-related responsibilities is simply to *ignore* them. Since the sole purpose of the Binary Tree ADT is to be the ancestor of some important data types, we will let those descendants determine their own item-related responsibilities. This decision ensures that we will not waste a lot of time on difficult designs of methods when those designs would be of no value to a descendant.

Now that we have settled on the responsibilities for the Binary Tree ADT, we can proceed to define, design, and implement that data type.

DEFINITION OF THE BINARY TREE DATA TYPE

In this section we will define the Binary Tree ADT. The logical domain is the set of all binary trees. We assume that a user will supply:

MaxTreeSize, the maximum size of a binary tree for the given application;

Any number of subalgorithms for visiting each item during a traversal.

There are eleven methods in the Binary Tree ADT:

1. **Initialize.**

    Postcondition: The binary tree is empty.

    Note: An implicit precondition of every other method is that the calling instance has already been given an initial value. An instance can be given an initial value either as the calling instance to Initialize or as the actual parameter in a call to CopyTo (the fifth method).

2. **IsEmpty.**

    Postcondition: True has been returned if the binary tree is empty. Otherwise, False has been returned.

3. **Size.**

    Postcondition: The number of items in the binary tree has been returned.

4. **Height.**

    Postcondition: The height of the binary tree has been returned.

5. **CopyTo (NewTree).**

    Postcondition: NewTree has a distinct copy of the binary tree.

    Note: This method, as well as the next two, is often given as a function that returns the distinct copy.

6. **RetrieveLeft (Tree).**

    Precondition: The binary tree is not empty.

Postcondition: Tree contains a distinct copy of the left subtree of the binary tree.

7. `RetrieveRight (Tree).`

Precondition: The binary tree is not empty.

Postcondition: Tree contains a distinct copy of the right subtree of the binary tree.

8. `TraverseInOrder (Visit).`

Postcondition: An inorder traversal of the tree has been performed. The action taken when an item was accessed is given by the subalgorithm Visit.

9. `TraversePostOrder (Visit).`

Postcondition: A postorder traversal of the tree has been performed. The action taken when an item was accessed is given by the subalgorithm Visit.

10. `TraversePreOrder (Visit).`

Postcondition: A preorder traversal of the tree has been performed. The action taken when an item was accessed is given by the subalgorithm Visit.

11. `TraverseBreadthFirst (Visit).`

Postcondition: A breadth-first traversal of the tree has been performed. The action taken when an item was accessed is given by the subalgorithm Visit.

DESIGNS OF THE BINARY TREE DATA TYPE

We present three designs of the Binary Tree ADT. As usual, these designs are characterized by the design domains (that is, the fields in each binary tree object). In the first two designs, the items are linked by addresses, so the only field is an address field. In the third design, an array holds the items.

A Multilinked Design of the Binary Tree Data Type

The first design of the Binary Tree ADT is similar to the linked design of the List ADT in Chapter 4. The design domain consists of only one field, Root, which contains the address of a node. Each node has Item, Left, and Right fields. For the sake of simplicity, we often refer to those fields as Root's Item, Root's Left, and Root's Right (rather than Root's node's Item and so on).

The Left and Right fields will contain *binary trees,* **not** addresses. This makes it easier for us to exploit the recursive nature of binary trees. And as it turns out, of the eleven designs, seven are recursive. The other four are one-liners.

This design is referred to as *multilinked* because each node has, loosely speaking, two link fields. (Technically, each node has two object fields, each of which contains a link field.)

The method designs are as follows:

1. <u>Initialize.</u>

   ```
   Root := null
   ```

   ↑

2. <u>IsEmpty.</u>

   Return the value of (Root = null)

   ↑

3. <u>Size.</u>

   ```
   if Root = null then
       Return the value 0
   else
       with Root's node do
           Return the value of 1 + Left.Size + Right.Size
   ```

The details of a correctness proof, by induction (strong form) on the height of the tree, are left as an exercise.

There is one activation of Size for each subtree of the tree. For a tree of N items, there are $2N + 1$ subtrees (including the tree itself)—see Exercise 7.10. We conclude that Time, BestTime, and WorstTime are all $O(N)$.

The space requirements depend on the longest sequence of nested recursive calls, and this depends on the height of the tree. In the worst case, the tree is a chain—for example, either

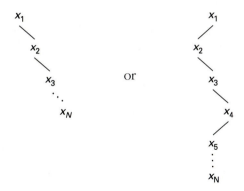

In the worst case, a sequence of N nested recursive calls will occur. With each call, some constant amount of information is saved, and so WorstSpace is O(N).

The best case occurs when the tree has minimal height—that is, when the tree is perfectly balanced at least through level H(T) − 1. Then the tree must have height Trunc ($\log_2(N)$)—see Exercise 7.2.e. In this case, the longest chain of nested recursive calls is only Trunc ($\log_2(N)$), and so BestSpace is O(log N).

For the average case of a binary tree with N items, we must consider all N! binary trees that can be generated with N items. The average height of a binary tree is O($N^{\frac{1}{2}}$) (see Knuth, 1973), so the (average) Space is O($N^{\frac{1}{2}}$). For large values of N, the value of $N^{\frac{1}{2}}$—that is, Sqrt(N)—is much smaller than N but larger than $\log_2 N$. For example, when N is one million, Sqrt(N) is one thousand and $\log_2 N$ is less than 20.

4. **Height.**

The subalgorithm follows from the definition of Height given earlier in this chapter:

```
if Root = null then
    Return the value -1
else
    with Root's node do
        LeftHeight  := Left.Height
        RightHeight := Right.Height
    if LeftHeight > RightHeight then
        Return 1 + LeftHeight
    else
        Return 1 + RightHeight
```

The temporary variables LeftHeight and RightHeight allow us to avoid recalculating Left.Height or Right.Height. The correctness of the subalgorithm is obvious because the subalgorithm was derived from the definition.

The time and space analysis is similar to that of the Size method. WorstTime, BestTime, and Time are $O(N)$ because there are $2N - 1$ recursive calls. WorstSpace is $O(N)$, BestSpace is $O(\log N)$, and Space is $O(N^{\frac{1}{2}})$ because these orders represent the worst, best, and average heights (and nested recursive call chains) of a binary tree.

$\uparrow$

5. `CopyTo (NewTree).`

By mimicking the linked design of the List ADT's CopyTo method, we arrive at the following subalgorithm:

```
if Root = null then
   NewTree.Root := null
else
   with Root's node do
         { Insert Item at NewTree's root: }
         Allocate space for a node pointed to by NewTree.Root
         NewTree.Root's Item := Item
         Initialize NewTree.Root's Left and Right subtrees
         Left.CopyTo (NewTree.Root's Left)
         Right.CopyTo (NewTree.Root's Right)
```

The correctness of CopyTo can be proved by induction (strong form) on the height of the tree. Time and Space are $O(N)$.

$\uparrow$

6. <u>`RetrieveLeft (Tree).`</u>

Root's Left is a binary tree, so it can call CopyTo. The subalgorithm is

`Root's Left.CopyTo (Tree)`

Time and Space are $O(N)$.

$\uparrow$

7. <u>`RetrieveRight (Tree).`</u>

`Root's Right.CopyTo (Tree)`

Time and Space are $O(N)$.

$\downarrow$

8. <u>`TraverseInOrder (Visit).`</u>

```
if Root <> null then
    with Root's node do
        Left.TraverseInOrder (Visit)
        Visit (Item)
        Right.TraverseInOrder (Visit)
```

As you might expect by now, correctness can be proved by induction (strong form) on the height of the tree. The analysis of the time and space requirements are the same as for Size. WorstTime, BestTime, and Time are O(N). WorstSpace is O(N), BestSpace is O($\log N$), and Space is O($N^{1/2}$).

The designs of TraversePostOrder and TraversePreOrder are almost identical to that of TraverseInOrder, and so those designs are left as exercises.

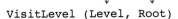

11. **TraverseBreadthFirst (Visit).**

At each level, we need to visit each item. With the help of a subalgorithm to visit all the items at a given level, the TraverseBreadthFirst subalgorithm is simply:

```
for Level := 0 to Height do
    VisitLevel (Level, Root)
```

The design of VisitLevel proceeds as follows: For a nonempty tree, if Level is 0, we simply visit the item; otherwise, we recursively visit the items in the left subtree at level Level-1 and the items in the right subtree at level Level-1. The subalgorithm is:

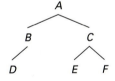

VisitLevel (Level, Root)

```
if Root <> null then
    with Root's node do
    if Level = 0 then
        Visit (Item)
    else
        VisitLevel (Level-1, Left.Root)
        VisitLevel (Level-1, Right.Root)
```

To illustrate, suppose the binary tree is:

During the first iteration of the For loop in TraverseBreadthFirst, Level = 0. In VisitLevel, since Level = 0, we simply visit A.

During the second iteration of the For loop, Level = 1. With Level = 1 in VisitLevel, we first visit all the items at level 0 in the left subtree:

As a result, we visit *B*.

We then visit each item at level 0 in the right subtree:

As a result, we visit *C*.

Finally, Level = 2. In VisitLevel, we first visit each item at level 1 in the left subtree:

As a result, we visit each item at level 0 in its left subtree, so *D* is visited. Since the right subtree of this tree is empty, we return to Visit-Level to visit each item at level 1 in the original tree's right subtree:

As a result, we visit each item at level 0 in its left and right subtrees, so *E* and *F* are visited.

The correctness of VisitLevel can be obtained by induction on the height of the tree.

The major shortcoming of the VisitLevel subalgorithm is that, for any value of Level, we always start back at the root of the original tree. From this, you would expect that its performance will be worse than $O(N)$.

The worst case occurs when the tree is a chain, in which case the number of nested recursive calls is $1 + 2 + 3 + \ldots + N - 1 = N *$

$(N - 1)/2$; thus WorstTime is $O(N^2)$. The longest sequence of nested recursive calls is $N - 1$ (for traversing the lowest level), so WorstSpace is $O(N)$.

In the best case, when the tree is perfectly balanced, no recursive calls are needed to visit the item at level 0. The two items at level 1 each require one recursive call, and the four items at level 2 each require two recursive calls. The total number of recursive calls is $2 * 1 + 4 * 2 + 8 * 3 + ... + (N + 1)/2 * \log_2[(N + 1)/2]$. It can be shown by induction that, for any positive integer K,

$$\sum_{i=1}^{k} (2^i * i) = (k - 1) * 2^{K+1} + 2$$

When we substitute $\log_2[(N + 1)/2]$ for K in this sum, we conclude that the number of recursive calls is $(N + 1) \log_2(N + 1) - 2N$, which is $O(N \log N)$. Thus BestTime is $O(N \log N)$. The longest sequence of Nested recursive calls is approximately $\log_2 N$, so BestSpace is $O(\log N)$.

Since the average height of a binary tree is $O(N^{\frac{1}{2}})$, on average, the longest sequence of Nested recursive calls is $O(N^{\frac{1}{2}})$; thus the average Space is $O(N^{\frac{1}{2}})$. On average, visiting one of the N items will require about half that many recursive calls, so the average Time is $O(N^{\frac{3}{2}})$.

Can we improve on this design? It seems that we should be able to traverse level by level in $O(N)$ time. One way to accomplish this is to start at the root of the tree and generate, level by level, a list of roots of nonempty subtrees. We need to retrieve these roots in the same order as they were generated so that the items can be visited level by level. What kind of list allows items to be retrieved in the same order as they were inserted? A *queue*!

This improved version of TraverseBreadthFirst is as follows:

```
TraverseBreadthFirst (Visit) { IMPROVED }

RootQueue.Initialize
if Root <> null then
   with RootQueue do
      InsertTail (Root)
      while not IsEmpty do
         RetrieveHead (TempRoot)
         DeleteHead
         with TempRoot's node do
            Visit (Item)
            if not Left.IsEmpty then
               InsertTail (Left.Root)
            if not Right.IsEmpty then
               InsertTail (Right.Root)
```

For example, suppose we start with

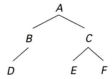

The values enqueued are roots, that is, (addresses). Prior to the first iteration of the While loop, the address of the tree in which *A* is the root item is enqueued, so we illustrate the queue's contents as

During the first iteration, that address is dequeued, *A* is visited, and the roots of *A*'s left and right subtrees are enqueued. At the end of that iteration, the queue contains two addresses:

———▶ B

and

———▶ C

During the next iteration, the address at the head of the queue is dequeued, *B* is visited, and the root of *B*'s left subtree is enqueued. The contents of the queue after that iteration are:

———▶ C

and

———▶ D

During the next iteration, *C* is visited and the roots of its left and right subtrees are enqueued. At the end of that iteration, the queue contains:

———▶ D

———▶ E

———▶ F

During the next three iterations, these addresses are dequeued in turn and the corresponding items visited.

A suitable loop assertion is, "For all the roots that have been deleted from RootQueue so far, the items in their nodes have been visited in breadth-first order." The proof of correctness is left as an exercise.

During each iteration of the While loop, one root is deleted from RootQueue. The total number of roots inserted in RootQueue is the same as the number of items in the tree, namely, N. Thus, since each of the queue methods takes only $O(1)$ time (for either the linked or contiguous design), the Time for the improved TraverseBreadthFirst is $O(N)$.

The space analysis depends on the size of RootQueue. In the best case, when the tree is a chain, RootQueue's size never exceeds 1. If the tree is perfectly balanced, RootQueue's size grows to $(N - 1)/2$ just before the $(N - 1)/2$ items at the lowest level are visited. The average case is similar to the worst case. We conclude that BestSpace is $O(1)$, and WorstSpace and Space are $O(N)$.

Here is one last observation about the traversal designs: The inorder, pre-order, and postorder traversals used recursion (and therefore stacks), whereas the improved breadth-first traversal used a queue.

A Threaded Design of the Binary Tree Data Type

In the preceding section we saw that the WorstSpace performance of several subalgorithms was $O(N)$ because we had a chain of $O(N)$ Nested recursive calls. To gauge the actual cost of this, suppose that we are using a dynamic implementation of the Binary Tree ADT. The inorder, preorder, and postorder traversals require, in the worst case, that N activation records be on the run-time stack at one time. The size of each activation record is at least 14 bytes (four for Root, four for a pointer to the Visit procedure, four for the return address, and two for the size of the activation record). Therefore, the run-time stack must have a capacity of at least $14 * N$ bytes.

In applications that consume a lot of main memory, it may be advisable to keep the size of the stack segment low, say 16K bytes, rather than allow the maximum of about 64K bytes. In such circumstances, recursive traversals should be avoided. Of course, an iterative traversal that creates and maintains its own stack is not much better.

We would like to be able to perform inorder traversals in $O(1)$ space even in the worst case. The situation for preorder traversals is similar and is left as an exercise. We will discuss postorder traversals at the end of this section.

In the recursive version of an inorder traversal described in the preceding section, we needed to save the parent of a node when we called:

```
Left.TraverseInorder (Visit).
```

We had to save the parent so that we could later visit the parent's item.

Another way to accomplish the same objective is the following: For any empty right subtree, make Right.Root point to the successor, in an inorder traversal, of the current node. Such a link is called a *thread*. For example, the following binary tree has threads pointing to the successors of nodes whose right subtrees are empty:

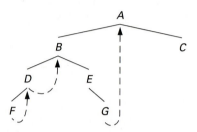

F has a thread pointing back to D, because D will be visited right after F; similarly, D has a thread back to B, and G has a thread back to A. C has an empty right subtree, but no thread, because C is the last node visited in an inorder traversal.

Once the threads are in place, the basic idea behind an iterative, inorder traversal is this: Start at the root; continue until each item has been visited; and, during each iteration, go left as far as possible, visit the item, then follow the threads back until a nonempty right subtree is found.

The complete subalgorithm is as follows:

```
TraverseInOrder (Visit)

If Root <> null then
    Done      := False
    TempRoot := Root
    while not Done do

        { Move left as far as possible: }
        while TempRoot's Left not empty do
            TempRoot := TempRoot's Left.Root
        Visit (TempRoot's Item)

        { Search for a non-empty right subtree: }
        while (TempRoot's Right is empty) and not Done do
            if TempRoot's Right.Root is a thread then
                TempRoot := TempRoot's Right.Root
                Visit (TempRoot's Item)
            else
                Done := True
        if TempRoot's Right is not empty then
            TempRoot := TempRoot's Right.Root
```

Let's trace the execution of this subalgorithm for the threaded tree given above. Initially, TempRoot points to the root item, A, so we have:

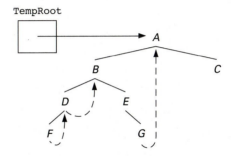

We then start into the outer loop and immediately move left as far as possible. After leaving the first inner loop, TempRoot is pointing to *F*:

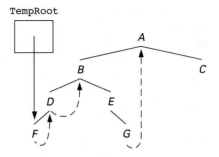

We now visit TempRoot's Item, namely *F*, and then search for a nonempty right subtree. Within that loop, since TempRoot's right root is a thread, we adjust TempRoot to point to *D* and visit *D*:

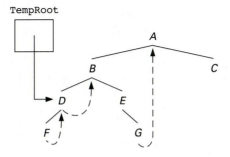

Again, TempRoot's right root is a thread, and so we adjust TempRoot to point to *B* and visit *B*:

TempRoot

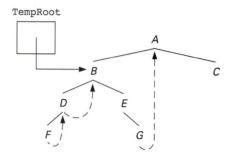

B's right subtree is not empty, so we break out of the search loop and adjust TempRoot to point to *E*, which ends the first iteration of the outer loop:

TempRoot

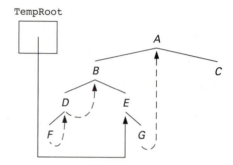

We leave the rest of the trace as an exercise.

A suitable loop assertion for the outer While statement is, "All the items that precede (in an inorder traversal) TempRoot's Item have been visited in order." The proof of correctness is left as an exercise.

The root of each subtree is accessed no more than twice (once in reaching it, and possibly once more from a thread). This implies that Time is $O(N)$. WorstSpace (and thus BestSpace and Space) is $O(1)$ because the subalgorithm allocates space for only two variables: TempRoot and Done.

The almost identical details of a preorder traversal are left as an exercise. Finally, a postorder traversal may be handled recursively as in the multilinked design, with the warning that WorstSpace is $O(N)$. For a design of TraversePostOrder whose WorstSpace is only $O(1)$, we must add a left thread (pointing to the predecessor in an inorder traversal) as well as a right thread. The details are given in Kruse (Kruse, 1987, pages 543–546).

We have not yet discussed how to distinguish a thread from an ordinary link; however, because this is an implementation issue, we will ignore it for now.

Figure 7.3

A contiguous
representation of the
complete binary tree
in Fig. 7.2(a).

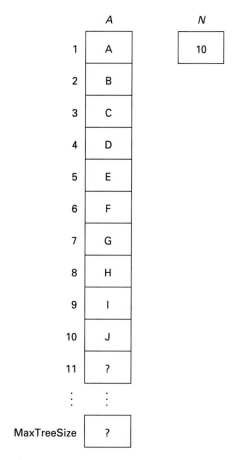

A Contiguous Design of the Binary Tree Data Type

The details for a contiguous design of the binary tree ADT seem obvious, but we will soon encounter a difficulty. The design domain consists of two fields:

A: array [1..MaxTreeSize] of ItemType

N: 0..MaxTreeSize

In other words, *A* will hold the items and *N* will contain the number of items currently in the tree. For example, given the complete binary tree in Fig. 7.2(a), the contiguous representation is as shown in Fig. 7.3.

A contiguous representation of an incomplete binary tree will have gaps. For example, Fig. 7.4 shows a contiguous representation of the following incomplete binary tree:

Figure 7.4

An incomplete
binary tree and a
contiguous
representation of it.

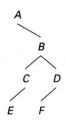

	A
1	A
2	?
3	B
4	?
5	?
6	C
7	D
8	?
9	?
10	?
11	?
12	E
13	?
14	F
.	.
.	.
.	.

N

6

There is no way to determine from this representation what is in the tree and what is not in the tree. For example, if the undefined values in the array *A* happen to be letters, the item in position 2 would seem to be as much a part of the tree as the item in position 3. To avoid this problem, we restrict the contiguous design to *complete* binary trees only.

The contiguous designs for the binary tree methods are as follows:

1. `Initialize.`

   ```
   N := 0
   ```

2. `IsEmpty.`

   ```
   Return the value of (N = 0)
   ```

3. `Size.`

   ```
   Return the value of N
   ```

4. `Height.`

   The height of a nonempty complete binary tree is Trunc ($\log_2 N$) (see Exercise 7.2.e.). The subalgorithm is simply

   ```
   if N = 0
       Return the value -1
   else
       Return the value of Trunc (log₂N)
   ```

5. `CopyTo (NewTree).`

   ```
   NewTree.N := N
   for I := 1 to N do
       NewTree.A [I] := A [I]
   ```

6. `RetrieveLeft (Tree).`

   This would be easy if we had the linked version's Left and Right fields. We don't, so we'll just have to grind out the subalgorithm. We must copy each item in the tree's left subtree into the appropriate position in Tree. We let *I* represent a position in the original TreeArray and *J* represent a position in Tree.A. Initially, *I* will be 2 and *J* will be 1, and we will keep copying as long as *J* is less than or equal to *N*. The correspondence of positions is as follows:

I	J
2	1
4	2
5	3
8	4
9	5
10	6
11	7
16	8
17	9
18	10
.	.
.	.
.	.

For each value of *J* that is a power of 2, we go through an inner loop *J* times to copy those items in *A* that are in positions $2J$, $2J + 1$, $2J + 2$, ... into positions J, $J + 1$, $J + 2$, ... of Tree.A.

The complete subalgorithm is:

```
RetrieveLeft (Tree).

I := 2 {Index in A }
J := 1 {Index in Tree.A }
while I <= N do
    { Copy the left subtree at level log₂I of A }
    { into Tree.A:                            }
    for K := 1 to J do
        if I <= N then
            Tree.A [J] := A [I]
            J := J + 1
            I := I + 1
        I := 2 * J
Tree.N := J - 1
```

A suitable loop assertion for the While statement is, "All items in the left subtree of *A* whose level is less than $\log_2 I$ and whose position is at most *N* have been copied to Tree.A."

For the For statement, a suitable loop assertion is, "The first *K* items in the left subtree of TreeArray whose level is $\log_2 I$ and whose position is at most *N* have been copied to Tree.A."

The proofs of correctness for both loop statements are left as exercises.

The number of items copied is approximately $N/2$, so Time is $O(N)$. Space is $O(1)$; note that the space for Tree.A was allocated in the calling algorithm.

7. `RetrieveRight (Tree).`

The development of the subalgorithm is similar to that of RetrieveLeft, and so it is left as an exercise.

8. `TraverseInOrder (Visit).`

The idea is the same as for the linked design: First, we traverse the left subtree, then visit the item, and finally, traverse the right subtree. We don't have the Left and Right fields that we had in the linked version, but we can get along without them. If we want to traverse the subtree starting in position I, its left subtree starts in position $2 * I$ and its right subtree starts in position $2 * I + 1$. I will be the parameter in an embedded subalgorithm InOrderTraverse.

The subalgorithm TraverseInOrder is simply:

```
TraverseInOrder (Visit)

if N > 0 then
   InOrderTraverse (1)
```

The InOrderTraverse subalgorithm is not much harder:

```
InOrderTraverse (I)

if I <= N then
   InOrderTraverse (2 * I)
   Visit (A [I])
   InOrderTraverse (2 * I + 1)
```

Once again, the proof of correctness follows by induction (strong form) on the height of the tree.

Time is $O(N)$ because there are $O(N)$ recursive calls. Space is $O(\log N)$ because, in a complete tree, the longest sequence of nested recursive calls is equal to the height of the tree (i.e., Trunc $(\log_2 N)$).

The designs, verifications, and analyses of TraversePostOrder and Traverse-PreOrder are almost identical to TraverseInOrder's, so these are left as exercises.

$\downarrow$

11. `TraverseBreadthFirst (Visit).`

The design of TraverseBreadthFirst is simple:

```
for I := 1 to N do
    Visit (A [I])
```

IMPLEMENTATIONS OF THE BINARY TREE DATA TYPE

The three designs we have discussed lead us to several implementations of the Binary Tree ADT. The multi-linked design can be implemented dynamically (with pointer variables) or statically (with indexes into a predeclared array). The threaded design can also be implemented dynamically or statically; the major implementation issue is how to represent the threads. The implementation of the contiguous design is straightforward.

Before proceeding, we should address a key issue: How we can validate any implementation if we do not have an Insert method? All we can get from the given methods is an empty binary tree, and we cannot test much with an empty tree.

As we noted earlier, the descendants of the Binary Tree ADT will supply the additional methods—Insert, Delete, and so on. So we will postpone, until the next chapter, the validation of each implementation.

A Dynamic Implementation of the Multilinked Design

With one exception, which we will discuss, the multi-linked design easily lends itself to a dynamic implementation. The correspondence between linked-design and dynamic-implementation terminology is the same as in Chapter 4. The unit heading and interface part are as follows:

```
unit BinTree1Manager;
{ This unit implements the multi-linked design of the }
{ Binary Tree data type dynamically.                   }
interface
uses
    ItemInBinTree;
type
    AddressType = ^NodeType;
    ProcedureType procedure (Item: ItemType);
BinTreeType = object
    Root: AddressType;
    procedure Initialize;
```

```
   function IsEmpty: boolean;
   function Size: word;
   function Height: integer; { Height may be -1 }
   procedure CopyTo (var NewTree: BinTreeType);
   procedure RetrieveLeft (var Tree: BinTreeType);
   procedure RetrieveRight (var Tree: BinTreeType);
   procedure TraverseInOrder (Visit: ProcedureType);
   procedure TraversePostOrder (Visit: ProcedureType);
   procedure TraversePreOrder (Visit: ProcedureType);
   procedure TraverseBreadthFirst (Visit: ProcedureType);
end; { BinTreeType }
NodeType    = record
   Item : ItemType;
   Left,
   Right: BinTreeType
end; { NodeType }
```

Notice that in NodeType, Left and Right are binary trees, not addresses. Also, BinTreeType is a recursive type because in the definition of BinTreeType, several parameters are of type BinTreeType.

The difficulty with this unit comes when we try to implement the queue-based version of TraverseBreadthFirst. Because this information is not needed by the user, the following **uses** clause is put in the implementation part:

```
uses
   Queue1Manager;
```

Queue1Manager uses ItemInList. What are the items that are enqueued and dequeued? They are addresses (i.e., pointers to NodeType). However, the declaration of AddressType is given in the interface part of BinTree1-Manager. Can ItemInList use BinTree1Manager? No, because this would lead to a vicious circle: BinTree1Manager cannot be compiled until Queue1 Manager is compiled, Queue1Manager cannot be compiled until ItemInList is compiled, and ItemInList cannot be compiled until BinTree1Manager is compiled!

One way around this impasse is for ItemInList to be the following unit:

```
unit ItemInList;
{ This unit implements ItemType for the list ADT. }
interface
type
   ItemType = pointer;
implementation
end. { ItemInList }
```

From our discussion in Chapter 1 of Turbo Pascal's predeclared type *pointer*, we know that any variable of type AddressType is assignment-compatible with this ItemType. Therefore, we need not use BinTree1 Manager in ItemInList. This almost gets us out of the woods. The one remaining problem is that the queue method RetrieveHead has a variable formal parameter of type ItemType. The method call:

```
RetrieveHead (TempRoot)
```

would generate a compile-time error message to the effect that the types of the actual and formal parameters are not name-equivalent. They are assignment-compatible, but this is not good enough for a variable formal parameter.

The solution is to declare a temporary pointer, TempPtr, of type *pointer*. TempPtr is used as the actual parameter in the call to RetrieveHead, and is then assigned to TempRoot.

The code for TraverseBreadthFirst is as follows:

```
procedure BinTreeType.TraverseBreadthFirst
   (Visit:ProcedureType);
{ Postcondition: A breadth-first traversal of the tree has }
{                been performed. The action taken when an  }
{                item was accessed is given by the         }
{                subalgorithm Visit.                       }
var
   RootQueue: QueueType;
   TempRoot : AddressType;
   TempPtr  : Pointer;
begin
   RootQueue.Initialize;
   if Root <> nil then
   with RootQueue do
      begin
         InsertTail (Root);
         while not IsEmpty do
            begin
               RetrieveHead (TempPtr);
               TempRoot := TempPtr;
               DeleteHead;
               with TempRoot^ do
                  begin
                     Visit (Item);
                     if not Left.IsEmpty then
                        InsertTail (Left.Root);
                     if not Right.IsEmpty then
                        InsertTail (Right.Root)
                  end { with TempRoot^ do }
            end { while }
      end { with RootQueue do }
end; { TraverseBreadthFirst }
```

A static implementation of the multi-linked design can be developed on its own, but it is probably easier to derive it from the dynamic implementation. Essentially, a statement such as:

```
TempRoot := TempRoot^.Left.Root
```

is translated into:

```
TempRoot := Pile [TempRoot].Left.Root
```

The array Pile would have nodes as components, where each node has Item, Left, and Right fields. The translation of New and Dispose follows the same pattern as in Chapter 4, except that the Left fields (rather than the Next fields, as with lists) hold the indexes in the free list.

Dynamic and Static Implementations of the Threaded Design

Almost all of the details of implementations of the threaded design are the same as for implementations of the multi-linked design. The major difference is that we must now implement the threads.

In a dynamic implementation, we add a Boolean field, RootIsAThread, to the object BinTreeType:

```
type
   BinTreeType = object
      Root         : AddressType;
      RootIsAThread: boolean;
         .
         .
         .
```

The implementation of most of the details of the threaded design is slightly complicated by the addition of the RootIsAThread field. For example, to Initialize, we must do two things:

```
Root           := nil;
RootIsAThread := False
```

To give you more of the flavor of this implementation, here are the ugly details of the TraverseInOrder method:

```
procedure BinTreeType.TraverseInOrder (Visit:
         ProcedureType);
{ Postcondition: An inorder traversal of the tree has been }
{                performed. The action taken when an item   }
{                was accessed is given by the subalgorithm  }
{                Visit.                                      }
var
   Done    : boolean;
   TempRoot: PtrOrThreadType;
```

```
begin
   if not IsEmpty then
      begin
         Done      := False;
         TempRoot := Root;
         while not Done do
            begin
                { Move left as far as possible: }
                while not TempRoot.Address^.Left.IsEmpty do
                    TempRoot := TempRoot.Address^.Left.Root;
                Visit (TempRoot.Address^.Item);

                { Search for a non-empty right subtree: }
                while (TempRoot.Address^.Right.IsEmpty)
                        and (not Done) do
                    if TempRoot.Address^.Right.RootIsAThread
                    then
                        begin
                            TempRoot := TempRoot.Address^
                                        .Right.Root;
                            Visit (TempRoot.Address^.Item)
                        end { using thread to retreat. }
                    else
                        Done := True;
                    if not TempRoot.Address^.Right.IsEmpty then
                        TempRoot := TempRoot.Address^.Right.Root
            end { while not Done }
      end { if Root <> nil do }
end; { TraverseInOrder }
```

The situation is somewhat simpler with a static implementation of the
threaded design, because no additional field is needed. The reason is that
normal array indexes are always greater than zero. Thus, we can treat a
positive array index as a normal link, a zero index as a null address, and a
negative index as a thread.

For the sake of descendants, Pile and Free are included in the interface
part. Here are some of the details of this implementation:

```
unit BinTree4Manager;
{ This unit implements the multi-linked design of the }
{ binary-tree data type statically, with threads.     }
interface
uses
   ItemInBinTree;
```

```
type
   AddressType = integer; { to allow for negative values }
   .

   .

   .
const
   PileBytes = 20000;
   PileLast = PileBytes div SizeOf (NodeType);
type
   PileType = array [1..PileLast] of NodeType;
var
   Pile : PileType;
   Free : AddressType;
implementation
uses
   Queue1Manager; { implements QueueType }
var
   I : AddressType;
procedure BinTreeType.Initialize;
{ Postcondition: The binary tree is empty. }
begin
   Root := 0
end; { Initialize }
function BinTreeType.IsEmpty: boolean;
{ Postcondition: True has been returned if the binary tree }
{                is empty. Otherwise, False has been       }
{                returned.                                 }
begin
   IsEmpty := (Root <= 0) { Note <= }
end; { IsEmpty }
function BinTreeType.Size: word;
{ Postcondition: The number of items in the binary tree }
{                has been returned.                     }
begin
   if IsEmpty then
      Size := 0
   else
      with Pile [Root] do
         Size := 1 + Left.Size + Right.Size
end; { Size }
procedure BinTreeType.TraverseInOrder(Visit: ProcedureType);
{ Postcondition: An inorder traversal of the tree has been }
{                performed. The action taken when an item  }
{                was accessed is given by the subalgorithm }
{                Visit.                                     }
```

```
          .
          .
          .
          { Search for a non-empty right subtree: }
          while (Pile [TempRoot].Right.IsEmpty)
                  and (not Done) do
              if Pile [TempRoot].Right.Root <= 0 then { Note }
                begin
                    TempRoot := -Pile [TempRoot].Right.Root; {Note}
                    Visit (Pile [TempRoot].Item)
                end { using thread to retreat. }
          .
          .
          .
end; { TraverseInOrder }
```

The only detail worth dwelling on in the contiguous implementation is the translation into Pascal of Trunc ($\log_2 N$) in the design of Height. From the discussion of logarithms in Appendix 1, we see that:

$$\log_2 N = \log_e N / \log_e 2$$

This gives us the statement:

```
Height := Trunc (Ln (N) / Ln (2))
```

We mentioned at the beginning of this chapter that the Binary Tree ADT was valued more for its descendants than for itself. In the next chapter, we will study these powerful descendants and, in passing, validate the five implementations of the Binary Tree ADT.

SUMMARY

A *binary tree* is either empty or consists of an item, called the *root item*, and two binary trees, called the *left subtree* and *right subtree* of the root. As this definition suggests, recursion plays a large role in the study of binary trees: Most properties of binary trees can be defined recursively.

In trying to determine the responsibilities of the Binary Tree ADT, we decided to omit all responsibilities related to inserting or deleting individual items, because it is difficult to frame these responsibilities in a way that would be suitable for descendants of the Binary Tree ADT. Those descendants will supply their own item-related responsibilities.

We developed a multi-linked design for the eleven methods in the Binary Tree ADT. Four of those method designs consisted of a single line, and the other seven were recursive, with correctness proofs by induction on the height of the tree. For the BreadthFirstTraversal method, we ultimately rejected the recursive version with its $O(N^{\frac{3}{2}})$ Time and $O(N^{\frac{1}{2}})$ Space. Instead, we chose a queue-based subalgorithm that took only $O(N)$ Time but $O(N)$ Space.

For the other traversal methods, the space requirements can be reduced to $O(1)$ by replacing null addresses with *threads*: the addresses of successors/predecessors under inorder traversal. The Time requirements were unchanged when threads were used.

The contiguous design went smoothly, but we had to assume that the binary tree was complete.

The implementations—dynamic and static for both the multilinked and threaded designs, contiguous for the contiguous design—were straightforward. But we had to postpone validation until the next chapter because the Binary Tree ADT did not have an Insert method.

EXERCISES

7.1 Answer the questions below about the following binary tree:

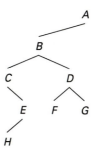

  a. What is the root item?
  b. How many items are in the tree?
  c. How many leaves are in the tree?
  d. What is the height of the tree?
  e. What is the height of the left subtree?
  f. What is the height of the right subtree?
  g. What is the level of *F*?
  h. What is the depth of *C*?
  i. How many children does *C* have?
  j. What is the parent of *F*?
  k. What are the descendants of *B*?
  l. What are the ancestors of *F*?
  m. What would the output be if the items were written out during an inorder traversal?

    n. What would the output be if the items were written out during a postorder traversal?

    o. What would the output be if the items were written out during a preorder traversal?

    p. What would the output be if the items were written out during a breadth-first traversal?

7.2 **a.** Construct a binary tree of height 3 that has eight items.

    b. Can you construct a binary tree of height 2 that has eight items?

    c. For N going from 1 to 20, determine the minimum height possible for a binary tree with N items.

    d. Based on your calculations in part c, try to develop a formula for the minimum height possible for a binary tree with N items, where N can be any positive integer.

    e. Let N be any positive integer. Use induction on N to show that for binary trees with N items, the minimum height possible is Trunc $(\log_2 N)$.

7.3 **a.** What is the maximum number of leaves possible in a binary tree with 10 items? Construct such a tree.

    b. What is the minimum number of leaves possible in a binary tree with 10 items? Construct such a tree.

7.4 **a.** Construct a two-tree that is not complete.

    b. Construct a complete tree that is not a two-tree.

    c. Construct a complete two-tree that is not perfectly balanced.

    d. How many leaves are there in a two-tree with 17 items?

    e. How many leaves are there in a two-tree with 731 items?

    f. A two-tree must always have an odd number of items. Why?

HINT   Use Theorem 7.1 and the fact that the number of leaves must be an integer.

    g. How many items are there in a perfectly balanced binary tree of height 4?

    h. How many items are there in a perfectly balanced binary tree of height 12?

    i. Use induction on the height of the tree to show that any perfectly balanced binary tree is a two-tree.

    j. Use the results from part i and Theorem 7.1 to determine the number of leaves in a perfectly balanced binary tree with 63 items.

7.5 As a *user* of the Binary Tree ADT, develop a subalgorithm to count the number of leaves in a binary tree. The subalgorithm interface is

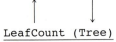

LeafCount (Tree)

Postcondition: The number of leaves in Tree has been returned.

7.6 Suppose that Scores is an instance of a binary tree and Scores contains:

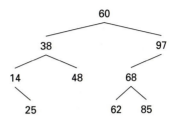

Trace the execution of:

`Scores.TraverseBreadthFirst (WriteOut)`

in the queue-based design of TraverseBreadthFirst described in this chapter. Assume that the WriteOut subalgorithm writes out the visited item.

7.7 Complete the trace of the threaded inorder traversal described in this chapter.

7.8 Show that the multi-linked design of the Size method described in this chapter is correct.

7.9 Show that a binary tree with N items has $2N + 1$ subtrees (including the entire tree). How many of these subtrees are empty?

7.10 Develop subalgorithms for postorder and preorder traversals in the multi-linked design of the Binary Tree ADT.

7.11 Prove the correctness of the While statement in the improved version of TraverseBreadthFirst in the multi-linked design of the Binary Tree ADT.

7.12 Develop a threaded design of the TraversePreOrder method.

7.13 Develop the TraversePostOrder and TraversePreOrder subalgorithms in the contiguous design of the binary tree ADT.

7.14 Modify the threaded design of TraverseInOrder to calculate Size in only O(1) Space.

7.15 Modify the threaded design of TraverseInOrder to calculate Height in only O(1) Space.

Descendants of the Binary Tree Data Type

In this chapter we study three descendants of the Binary Tree ADT. Binary search trees are ordered in such a way that the average time for an insertion, deletion, retrieval, or search is only $O(\log N)$. They are widely used in situations where there are a lot of random insertions and deletions. Heaps also have a special ordering, one that is suitable for worst-case sorting and for designing and implementing priority queues. Expression trees provide a simple way of visualizing an arithmetic expression in which the operators have two operands. We can then easily perform some mathematical operations on the expression, such as symbolic differentiation or integration.

BINARY SEARCH TREES

We start with a recursive definition of a binary search tree:

> A **binary search tree** T is a binary tree such that either T is empty or
>
> 1. Each item in Left(T) is LessThan the root item of T;
> 2. Each item in Right(T) is GreaterThan the root item of T;
> 3. Left(T) and Right(T) are binary search trees.

Duplicate items are not allowed in a binary search tree. Figure 8.1 shows an example of a binary search tree.

Figure 8.1

A binary search tree.

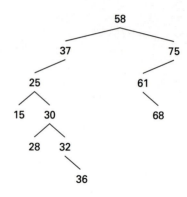

An inorder traversal of a binary search tree accesses the items in increasing order. For example, with the binary search tree in Fig. 8.1, an inorder traversal accesses, in order,

15 25 28 30 32 36 37 58 61 68 75

A binary search tree is so called because of the situation that can occur when the tree is perfectly balanced. For example, suppose we have:

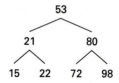

A search for a given item accesses the same items as a binary search would in the contiguous design of the Ordered List ADT. The root item in a tree (or subtree) corresponds to the middle item in a list (or sublist).

Binary search trees serve the same purpose as ordered lists: to provide a structure for storing items in order. As we will see shortly, a binary search tree is usually more efficient than an ordered list when it comes to inserting and deleting items. In fact, binary search trees are unsurpassed for maintaining order throughout a sequence of insertions and/or deletions.

Based on what we have seen already about binary search trees, let's try to formulate the responsibilities of the Binary Search Tree ADT.

Responsibilities of the Binary Search Tree Data Type

What responsibilities does the Binary Search Tree ADT have to its users? The global responsibilities (those associated with an instance as a whole, rather than with individual items) are the same as in the Binary Tree ADT, except that the only traversal provided is an inorder traversal. This makes sense in light of the fact that the purpose of a binary search tree is to maintain items in order.

The local responsibilities, those related to individual items, are typical: searching for, inserting, deleting, and retrieving an item. Searches, insertions, and deletions will be based on the ordering of the items, not on their positions in the tree. The only retrieval provided is for the root item.

From this description of responsibilities, we now proceed to the definition, design, and implementations of the Binary Search Tree ADT.

Definition of the Binary Search Tree Data Type

In defining the Binary Search Tree ADT, we assume that each user will supply an ItemType in which either the items are scalar or there are methods (LessThan, EqualTo, and GreaterThan) for comparing items. The user will also supply any number of visit subalgorithms that describe the action to take as each item is accessed during a traversal. Finally, the user is responsible for defining MaxTreeSize, the maximum size of a binary search tree for the application.

The logical domain is the collection of all binary search trees, a subset of the collection of all binary trees. There are twelve methods, eight of which have the same interfaces as methods in the Binary Tree ADT. Of course, a user can derive new operators, as needed, from the given methods.

The binary search tree methods are as follows:

1. **`Initialize.`**

   Postcondition: The binary search tree is empty.

2. **`IsEmpty.`**

   Postcondition: True has been returned if the tree is empty. Otherwise, False has been returned.

3. **`Size.`**

   Postcondition: The number of items in the tree has been returned.

4. **`RetrieveRoot (Item).`**

   Precondition: The tree is not empty.
   Postcondition: The root item has been copied into Item.

5. **`RetrieveLeft (Tree).`**

   Precondition: The tree is not empty.

Postcondition: The left subtree has been copied into Tree.

6. **RetrieveRight (Tree).**

Precondition: The tree is not empty.

Postcondition: The right subtree has been copied into Tree.

7. **Search (Item, Found).**

Postcondition: If there is an item in the binary search tree that is EqualTo Item, that item has been copied into Item and Found has the value True. Otherwise, Found has the value False and Item is unchanged.

8. **Insert (Item).**

Precondition: The number of items in the binary search tree is less than MaxTreeSize; there is no item in the tree that is EqualTo Item.

Postcondition: Item has been inserted into the tree (which remains a binary search tree).

9. **Delete (Item).**

Precondition: There is an item in the binary search tree that is EqualTo Item.

Postcondition: The item EqualTo Item has been deleted from the tree (which remains a binary search tree).

10. **Height.**

Postcondition: The height of the tree has been returned.

11. **CopyTo (NewTree).**

Postcondition: NewTree contains a distinct copy of the tree.

12. **TraverseInOrder (Visit).**

Postcondition: The items in the tree have been visited in order.

Designs of the Binary Search Tree Data Type

We will base our designs of the Binary Search Tree ADT on the multi-linked and multi-linked threaded designs of the Binary Tree ADT. The contiguous design of the Binary Tree ADT assumes that the tree is complete, so it is inappropriate for binary search trees.

There is a difficulty in applying the multi-linked design of the Binary Tree ADT to the Binary Search Tree ADT. The Root field will be inherited, and Root contains the address of a node, so the type of each node will also be inherited. But in the Binary Tree ADT (and therefore in the Binary Search Tree), the Left and Right fields in each node will contain instances of the Binary Tree ADT, *not* instances of the Binary Search Tree ADT.

As a result, we cannot make recursive calls such as:

```
Root's Left.Insert (Item)
```

since Insert is not a method in the Binary Tree ADT. (Even if there were an Insert method in the Binary Tree ADT, it would not be the Insert method we wanted). We can get around this inconvenience with imbedded recursion: Insert, with Item as its formal parameter, simply calls InsertItem, with Root as its formal parameter. Within InsertItem, we can make recursive calls such as:

```
InsertItem (Root's Left.Root)
```

This scheme has the added benefit of saving space because Item will be a nonlocal variable in InsertItem.

A Multilinked Design of the Binary Search Tree Data Type

We will utilize the same design domain as we did for a binary tree; that is, the binary search tree object will have a single field, Root, that contains either a null address or the address of a node with Item, Left, and Right fields. Those fields are referred to as Root's Item, Root's Left, and Root's Right. As we noted above, the Left and Right fields contain instances of the Binary Tree ADT, not of the Binary Search Tree ADT.

We inherit the designs of the following methods from the multi-linked design of the Binary Tree ADT:

Initialize

IsEmpty

Size

RetrieveLeft

RetrieveRight

Height

CopyTo

TraverseInOrder

All we have to do now is to develop designs for the four uninherited methods. RetrieveRoot's design is trivial and the other three designs are naturally recursive. The design of the Delete method is complicated by the fact that deletion of an item that has two children requires restructuring the tree.

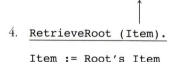

4. `RetrieveRoot (Item).`

    `Item := Root's Item`

We must design the Insert and Delete methods before the design of Search because the way items are inserted and deleted determines how long it will take to search for them. We could (but of course we won't) carelessly ignore the binary nature of binary search trees and make insertions and deletions in a chain. For example, after inserting 28 into:

we could end up with:

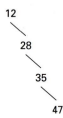

Searches would then take $O(N)$ time.

8. `Insert (Item).`

    As suggested in the preceding section, we will call an imbedded recursive subalgorithm:

    `InsertItem (Root)`

The design of InsertItem proceeds as follows: If the tree is empty, Item is inserted at the root; otherwise, Item is inserted in either the left or right subtree, depending on whether Item is LessThan or GreaterThan the root item (EqualTo is not possible).

The subalgorithm InsertItem is:

```
InsertItem (Root)

if Root = null then
    InsertAtRoot (Root, Item)
else
    if Item is LessThan Root's Item then
        InsertItem (Root's Left.Root)
    else
        InsertItem (Root's Right.Root)
```

The design of InsertAtRoot is simply:

```
InsertAtRoot (Root, Item)

Allocate space for a new node pointed to by Root
Root's Item := Item
Initialize Root's Left and Right subtrees
```

For example, suppose that Tree is an instance of a binary search tree, and Tree contains:

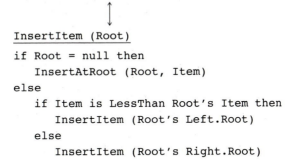

After the message Tree.Insert (28) is sent, Tree would contain:

We leave the correctness proof of Insert as an exercise (by strong induction on the height of the tree).

In a time and space analysis of InsertItem, the worst case occurs when the tree is a chain. This happens when, for example, the items inserted into the tree happen to be in increasing order, such as,

In this case the average number of recursive calls for an insertion is $(0 + 1 + 2 + \ldots + N - 1)/N$ (i.e., $(N - 1)/2$), and so WorstTime is O(N). WorstSpace is also O(N).

The best case occurs when the tree is perfectly balanced on every level, except (possibly) the level farthest from the root. In this case, the average number of recursive calls for an insertion is proportional to the height of the tree. We saw in Chapter 7 that the height of such a tree is O(log N) (see Exercise 7.2.e), so BestTime and BestSpace are both O(log N).

The average height of a binary search tree is only O(log N) (see Aho, Hopcroft and Ullman, 1983, pages 160–162). It follows that Time and Space are O(log N).

Recall, from Chapter 7, that the average height of a binary tree is O($N^{\frac{1}{2}}$). Does it seem plausible to you that the average height of a binary tree is greater than the average height of a binary search tree? To get an idea of what is going on, look at all of the binary trees and binary search trees that can be constructed from the letters a, b, and c.

For arbitrary binary trees, the order is irrelevant; so, for each of the three possible root items, we can have zero, one or two children in the left subtree. If there are two children in the left subtree, there are two possibilities for the root of the left subtree, and for each of those possibilities, the remaining item can be in either the left or right subtree of that left subtree. The total number of binary trees from a, b, and c is 30, and all of them are equally likely. Figure 8.2 shows the ten binary trees with a at the root. Since each of the letters a, b, or c is equally likely as the root item, the average height of the thirty binary trees is the same as the average height of the ten trees in Fig. 8.2. There are eight trees of height 2 and two trees of height 1. Since each of these trees is equally likely, the average height is $(8 * 2 + 2 * 1)/10$, which is 1.8.

Figure 8.2

The ten binary trees, with *a* at the root, that can be constructed from *a*, *b*, and *c*.

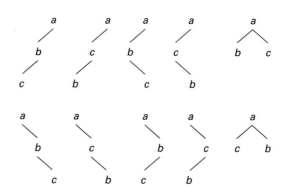

Only five binary search trees can be constructed from the letters *a*, *b*, and *c*; see Fig. 8.3. Each of the first four of the binary search trees in Fig. 8.3 is generated by exactly one sequence of insertions. For example, the only sequence of insertions that will generate the first search tree is: Insert *c*; Insert *b*; Insert *a*. The rightmost binary search tree in Fig. 8.3, the one with *b* at its root, is twice as likely as the other four search trees. That is because there are two sequences of insertions that will generate the tree with *b* at its root:

1. Insert *b*; Insert *a*; Insert *c*.
2. Insert *b*; Insert *c*; Insert *a*.

The average height is therefore $(4 * 2 + 2 * 1)/6$, which is 1.67.

The design of an iterative subalgorithm for Insert is similar to the linked design of the iterative subalgorithm for an insertion in an ordered list (see Chapter 4). The terms *Parent* and *Child* better reflect a tree's hierarchical structure than do *Previous* and *Current*. Because the inserted item becomes a leaf in the tree, the loop continues until Child is empty. A suitable loop assertion is "Item belongs in Child's subtree of Parent." The insertion is then made in Parent's left or right subtree. The complete, iterative subalgorithm for Insert is as follows:

```
Insert (Item) { Iterative Insert }
if Root = null then
    InsertAtRoot (Root, Item)
```

Figure 8.3

The five binary search trees that can be constructed from the letters *a*, *b*, and *c*.

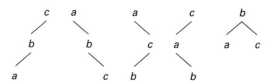

```
else
   Child.Root := Root
   repeat
      Parent := Child
      if Item is LessThan Child.Root's Item then
         Child.Root := Child.Root's Left.Root
      else
         Child.Root := Child.Root's Right.Root
   until Child.IsEmpty

   with Parent do
      if Item is LessThan Root's Item then
         InsertAtRoot (Root's Left.Root, Item)
      else
         InsertAtRoot (Root's Right.Root, Item)
```

(The design of InsertAtRoot was given earlier.) The time analysis for iterative Insert is the same, up to order, as that for recursive Insert-Item. The space requirements are $O(1)$ in the best, worst, and average cases.

9. **Delete (Item).**

The subalgorithm is simply:

`DeleteItem (Root)`

We now design DeleteItem. To delete Item from the tree, we must first find where Item is in the tree; that is, we must find the subtree in which Item is the root item. We then delete that root. By postponing the hard work (deleting the root), we easily obtain a recursive version of the DeleteItem subalgorithm:

DeleteItem(Root).

```
RootItem := Root's Item
if Item Equals RootItem then
   DeleteRoot (Root)
else
   if Item is LessThan RootItem then
      DeleteItem (Root's Left.Root)
   else
      DeleteItem (Root's Right.Root)
```

An iterative version of Delete is similar to the iterative version of Insert. The details are left as an exercise.

We now design the DeleteRoot subalgorithm. If either the left or right subtree is empty, we simply prune the root; that is, we replace the root with the root of the right subtree (if the left subtree is empty) or with the root of the left subtree, and then deallocate the space allocated to the root's former node. Figure 8.4 shows a "before and after" example in this case.

Otherwise, both subtrees are nonempty. To get an idea of how to proceed in this case, suppose we want to delete the root of the tree in Fig. 8.5.

Before 28 can be removed from the tree in Fig. 8.5, we must find an item to substitute for 28. The only items suitable in this regard are the immediate predecessor, 26, and the immediate successor, 37. For example, if we substitute 37 for 28 in Fig. 8.5, then delete the root from the tree whose root item is the "old" 37, we would get the tree shown in Fig. 8.6.

Because a root item's immediate successor is the leftmost item in the right subtree, that Leftmost item has no left child. Deleting that item is covered by the first case above.

Figure 8.4

(Top) A binary search tree from which the root is to be deleted and in which the left subtree is empty; (bottom) The same binary search tree after the root has been deleted.

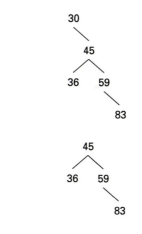

Figure 8.5

A binary search tree from which the root item is to be deleted.

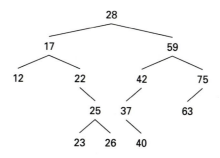

Figure 8.6

The binary search tree obtained from the binary search tree in Fig. 8.5 when 28 is deleted by substituting its immediate successor, 37, for 28 and then deleting the "old" 37.

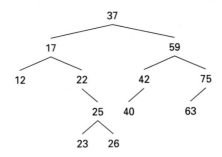

The DeleteRoot subalgorithm is shown below. The Prune subalgorithm simply replaces the root with the root of the left or right subtree, whichever is appropriate. The hard work, finding and deleting the successor, is postponed.

DeleteRoot (Root)

```
with Root's node do
    if Left.IsEmpty or Right.IsEmpty then
        Prune (Root)
    else
        DeleteSuccessor (Right, Successor)
        Item := Successor
```

The Prune subalgorithm is easy:

Prune (Root)

```
OldRoot := Root
if Root's Right.IsEmpty then
    Root := Root's Left.Root
else
    Root := Root's Right.Root
Deallocate the space pointed to by OldRoot
```

Finally, we develop the DeleteSuccessor subalgorithm, with the formal parameter Tree. If Tree's left subtree is empty, then Tree's Root item is the Successor of the item to be deleted; we then prune that root from the tree. Otherwise, we delete the successor from Tree's left subtree. The subalgorithm is not so difficult after all, and this is one of the nice features of top-down design of a subalgorithm: If you postpone the hard work long enough, it becomes easy!

```
DeleteSuccessor (Tree, Successor)

with Tree.Root's node do
    if Left.IsEmpty then
        Successor := Item
        Prune (Tree.Root)
    else
        DeleteSuccessor (Left, Successor)
```

The correctness proofs of DeleteItem and DeleteSuccessor are left as exercises. The times, up to order, are the same as for the recursive InsertItem. Note that the farther down the tree we go to find the item to be deleted, the less distance we need to travel to find its successor.

Now that we have seen how insertions and deletions are performed, we can get to the design of the Search subalgorithm.

7. <u>Search (Item, Found).</u>

   SearchItem (Root)

   In designing SearchItem, we first look at the simple case: If the tree is empty, Found gets the value False. Otherwise, the Item is compared with the root item: if EqualTo, Found gets the value True and the root item is copied into Item; if LessThan, the left subtree is searched; or, if GreaterThan, the right subtree is searched.

   The complete subalgorithm is:

   ```
   SearchItem(Root)

   if Root = null then
       Found := False
   else
       RootItem := Root's Item
       if Item is EqualTo RootItem then
           Found := True
           Item := RootItem
       else
           if Item is LessThan RootItem then
               SearchItem (Root's Left.Root)
           else
               SearchItem (Root's Right.Root)
   ```

The correctness of SearchItem is easily established by induction on the height of the tree.

The number of recursive calls in a successful search for an item is exactly the same as the number of recursive calls to insert the item, so we can simply transport the results on recursive insertions: WorstTime and WorstSpace are both $O(N)$. BestTime, BestSpace, and (average) Time and Space are all $O(\log N)$. These results hold for unsuccessful searches as well as for successful searches. Since unsuccessful searches always terminate with an empty subtree, the time and space requirements depend solely on the height of the binary search tree.

An iterative subalgorithm can be designed without much difficulty. (As a general guide, iteration has about the same design complexity as recursion when the tree need not be altered or traversed; however, searching is one of the few situations where these two conditions hold.) We use a temporary tree, TempTree, to avoid altering the binary search tree itself. During each iteration in which Item is not found, TempTree is replaced by its left or right subtree. A suitable loop invariant is: Item is in the tree if and only if Item is in the subtree TempTree. The subalgorithm is:

<u>Search (Item, Found)</u> {Iterative search}

```
TempTree.Root := Root
Found := False
while not TempTree.IsEmpty and not Found do
   RootItem := TempTree.Root's Item
   if Item is EqualTo RootItem then
      Found := True
      Item := RootItem
   else
      if Item is LessThan RootItem then
         TempTree.Root := TempTree.Root's Left.Root
      else
         TempTree.Root := TempTree.Root's Right.Root
```

The correctness proof is left as an exercise.

The time analysis is the same, up to order, as for the recursive version. The space requirements are $O(1)$ in all cases.

Implementations of the Multilinked Design

We can implement the multi-linked design of a binary search tree either dynamically or statically. For each of these two choices, we can implement the recursive or iterative designs of several of the methods. This gives us a total of four implementations. The interface part of the dynamic implementations is as follows:

```
interface
uses
    ItemInBinTree,
    BinTree1Manager;
type
    BSTType = object (BinTreeType)
        procedure RetrieveRoot (var Item: ItemType);
        procedure Search (var Item : ItemType;
                                var Found: boolean);
        procedure Insert (Item: ItemType);
        procedure Delete (Item: ItemType)
    end; { BSTType }
```

Each implementation was validated with the help of a driver program that tested all twelve methods. To complete the validation of the corresponding implementations of the Binary Tree ADT, we also tested TraversePreOrder, TraversePostOrder, and TraverseBreadthFirst.

Run-Time Analysis of the Implementations

We now compare the implementations of the binary search tree data type with respect to their execution times. The program TestTime from Chapter 3 was modified to test the time to insert random integers in an initially empty binary search tree. The results are shown in Table 8.1.

There are several noteworthy aspects of Table 8.1:

1. For each of the two values for N, there is not much difference among the four implementations.

2. For each implementation, the difference in execution times for $N = 1000$ versus $N = 2000$ illustrates that inserting N items into an initially empty binary search tree is an $O(N \log N)$ operation. See Exercise 8.17 for more details on this.

3. In comparing the results in Table 8.1 with the analogous results for ordered lists in Chapter 5, we see that random insertions in a binary search tree take much less time than random insertions in an ordered

Table 8.1. The time, in seconds, to insert N random integers into an initially empty binary search tree.

N	dynamic recursive	dynamic iterative	static recursive	static iterative
1000	1.33	1.61	1.17	1.38
2000	2.98	3.57	2.70	3.12

list. To relate this observation to Note 2, O(*N* log *N*) time is much less than O(*N²*) time.

4. The recursive implementations are slightly faster than the corresponding iterative implementations. This attests to the efficiency of a recursive approach to binary search trees.

A Threaded Design?

Recall, from Chapter 7, that a *right thread* is a special pointer to the inorder successor of an item. Right threads enable inorder and preorder traversals of a binary tree in O(1) space even in the worst case. Threaded design allowed us to reduce the WorstSpace for Search, Size, and Height to O(1).

The Binary Search Tree ADT inherited the TraverseInOrder, Size, and Height methods from the binary tree ADT. Therefore, it is reasonable to develop a threaded design for the Binary Search Tree ADT as a descendant of the threaded design of the Binary Tree ADT.

A threaded design will not help, however, with what is often a far more serious problem than O(*N*) WorstSpace—namely, O(*N*) WorstTime. O(N) WorstTime occurs with the multi-linked designs of Size, Retrieve, Search, Insert, Delete, Height, and TraverseInOrder. We would like to avoid O(*N*) WorstTime for these methods. The key is to keep the height of the binary search tree in O(log *N*) in all cases.

How can we maintain a height of only O(log *N*) in a binary search tree? One possibility is to restructure the tree after each insertion and deletion to make it complete. For example, suppose we start with the following (complete) binary search tree:

After inserting 25 and then restructuring, we would have:

Note that if we had simply inserted 25 by the Insert subalgorithm described earlier in this chapter, it would have been in the right subtree of 12. Restructurability is a property of binary search trees, not of binary trees in general. However, the restructuring into a complete binary search tree would itself take O(*N*) time, so we would still have O(*N*) WorstTime!

In the next section, we describe how to achieve O(log *N*) height in all cases without all the work of maintaining a complete tree. This restricted form of a binary search tree is called an AVL tree. AVL trees enable us to achieve O(log *N*) WorstTime and O(log *N*) WorstSpace in the designs of Insert, Delete, Search, Size, Height and TraverseInOrder. The time and space estimates of the other designs are unchanged from before.

AVL Trees

An **AVL** tree is a binary search tree that either is empty, or in which:

1. the heights of the left and right subtrees differ by at most 1, and

2. the left and right subtrees are AVL trees.

AVL trees are named after the two Russian mathematicians, Adelson-Velskii and Landis, who invented them in 1962. Figure 8.7 shows several AVL trees, and Fig. 8.8 shows several binary search trees that are not AVL trees.

In Fig. 8.8, the first binary search tree fails to satisfy part 1 in the definition of AVL tree, the second fails to satisfy part 2, and the third fails to satisfy both parts.

Figure 8.7

Three AVL trees.

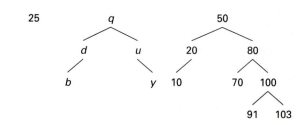

Figure 8.8

Three binary search trees that are not AVL trees.

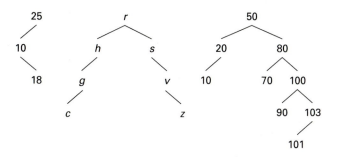

The AVL Tree ADT is a descendant of the Binary Search Tree ADT. There will be no new methods, but the multi-linked design domain contains another field, BalanceFactor, that takes on a value of "L," "=," or "R". When an AVL tree or subtree has a BalanceFactor of "L," its left subtree has height that is one greater than the height of the instance's right subtree. A BalanceFactor of "=" means that the tree is empty or both left and right subtrees have the same height. Finally, a BalanceFactor of "R" means that the height of the right subtree is one greater than the height of the left subtree.

For example, Fig. 8.9 shows the AVL trees in Fig. 8.7 redrawn to include balance factors, in bold, below the root item in each tree and subtree.

The introduction of balance factors raises a question: How is the "AVL-ness" of the tree (as reflected in the balance factors) maintained? Let us start with the easy case. A tree is assigned a balance factor of "=" when it is Initialized.

The balance factors are adjusted, if necessary, during each insertion and deletion. For any insertion or deletion that makes the height of either the left or right subtree more than one greater than the other subtree's height, the tree is rebalanced. The detailed designs of rebalancing are part of Programming Assignment 8.1, but we now sketch and exemplify the main ideas.

A recursive subalgorithm of the Insert method is similar to the recursive subalgorithm of Insert for binary search trees, except that we must now take care of the balance factors and the balance of the tree. For an insertion at the root of a tree, the tree's balance factor remains at "=". That is why, in Fig. 8.9, each tree whose root item is a leaf has a balance factor of "=".

For an insertion in a left or right subtree, we may need to adjust the balance factor and (possibly) rebalance the tree. For a simple example of rebalancing, suppose we insert, in sequence, the items with values 90, 95, 155. The construction of the tree, with balance factors in bold, would be as follows:

Figure 8.9

The AVL trees of Fig. 8.7 redrawn to include balance factors.

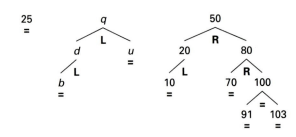

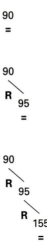

Since this last tree no longer is an AVL tree, some rebalancing is appropriate. The rebalancing performed in this case is called a "left rotation." With a left rotation, we make the root of the right subtree the root of the entire tree, giving us:

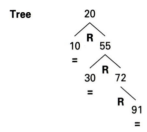

We now give a slightly more complicated left rotation. Note, however, that for most insertions the adjustment of balance factors is easy to figure out and no rebalancing is necessary. Suppose that 91 has just been inserted into the following tree:

Some rebalancing is needed because the height of the right subtree is 2 and the height of the left subtree is 0. We want a left rotation so that the root of the right subtree becomes the root of the entire tree. The left rotation is accomplished in four stages (we temporarily omit the balance factors because they may be inaccurate during the rotation):

1. Save the right subtree (of the tree to be rebalanced):

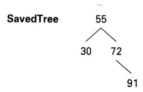

2. Replace the right subtree of Tree with the left subtree of SavedTree. In this example, the subtree whose root item is 30 becomes the right subtree of the tree whose root item is 20. We now have:

3. Replace the left subtree of SavedTree with Tree:

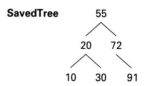

4. Finally, SavedTree replaces Tree. The entire tree, with balance factors in bold, is

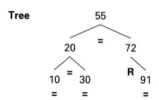

For a final example of a left rotation, consider the following tree in which 103 was the last item inserted:

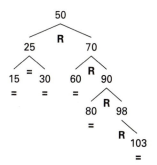

Again, some rebalancing is required. But where? The entire tree needs rebalancing, so you might think that the root would be recognized first as being in need of rebalancing. Actually, this is not so. Recall that in an insertion, the recursive calls work down the tree. After the insertion is made at a leaf, the returns from the recursive calls are made back up the tree. Thus, the first tree seen to need rebalancing is the one whose root item is 70. Its left subtree has a height of 0 and its right subtree has a height of 2.

The left rotation of that tree uses the same four steps as in the first example, and 90 becomes the root of the rebalanced tree. The tree rooted at 50 is unchanged except that its right subtree becomes rooted at 90 instead of at 70. The entire tree, now an AVL tree, is:

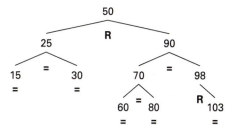

To summarize, a left rotation is performed on a tree when:

1. the tree's balance factor had been "R";

2. the insertion increased the height of the right subtree;

3. after the insertion, the right subtree's balance factor became "R".

The actions taken for a "right rotation" are symmetric to the actions taken for a left rotation. For example, suppose we have just inserted 5 into the following tree:

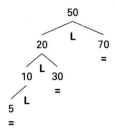

With a right rotation, the root of the left subtree becomes the root of the tree to be rebalanced. Again, the four steps given in the first example apply, except that the words "left" and "right" are swapped. For example, step 2 becomes:

2. Replace the left subtree of Tree with the right subtree of SavedTree.

A right rotation of the tree just given produces the following AVL tree:

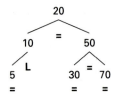

A right rotation is performed on a tree when:

1. the tree's balance factor had been "L";

2. the insertion increased the height of the left subtree;

3. after the insertion, the left subtree's balance factor became "L".

Can you think of any other situations in which rebalancing is needed? What about the following?

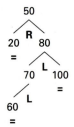

Rebalancing is necessary because the height of the left subtree is 0 and the height of the right subtree is 2. A left rotation will still leave the tree badly unbalanced. What we will do, in two steps, is to make 70 the root of the entire tree. First, we perform a right rotation on the right subtree, giving us:

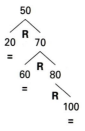

Then, we perform a left rotation on the entire tree. The resulting AVL tree is:

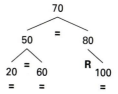

This "double rotation" (a right rotation on the right subtree, followed by a left rotation on the entire tree to be rebalanced) is performed when:

1. the tree's balance factor had been "R";
2. the insertion increased the height of the right subtree;
3. after the insertion, the right subtree's balance factor became "L".

The final rebalancing technique is another kind of double rotation. A left rotation is performed on the left subtree, followed by a right rotation on the entire tree to be rebalanced. For example, suppose that 30 has just been inserted into the following tree:

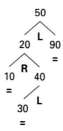

We start by performing a left rotation on the left subtree, and then perform a right rotation on the entire tree to be rebalanced. The resulting AVL tree is:

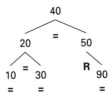

This kind of "double rotation" (a left rotation on the left subtree, followed by a right rotation on the entire tree to be rebalanced) is performed when:

1. the tree's balance factor had been "L";

2. the insertion increased the height of the left subtree;

3. after the insertion, the left subtree's balance factor became "R".

If an insertion or deletion destroys the "AVL-ness" of a binary search tree, only one rotation (a single or a double) will restore the balance. This implies that the rebalancing itself is not costly in terms of time. We have not yet established that AVL trees avoid the $O(N)$ WorstTime of binary search trees for insertions and deletions. That is shown in the next section.

The Height of an AVL Tree

We conclude our discussion of AVL trees by showing, as promised, that the height of an AVL tree is always $O(\log N)$. If the tree is perfectly balanced, its height is $\log_2((N + 1)/2)$. Thus, the height of an AVL tree is $O(\log N)$ in the best case; so all we need to show is that, in the worst case, the height of an AVL tree is also $O(\log N)$.

When does the worst case occur? In other words, for a given value of N, how high can an AVL tree of N items be? As Kruse (see Kruse, 1987) suggests, rephrasing this question helps us to answer it. Given a height, what is the minimum number of items in any AVL tree of that height?

For $h = 0, 1, 2, \ldots$, let N_h be the minimum number of items in an AVL tree of height h. Clearly, $N_0 = 1$ and $N_1 = 2$. The values of N_2 and N_3 can be seen from the following AVL trees:

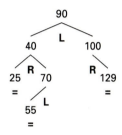

Suppose that T is an AVL tree with height h and with N_h items, for some value of h > 1. Either Left(T) or Right(T) must then have height h − 1, and the other one must have height h − 1 or h − 2. In fact, the subtree heights must be h − 1 and h − 2 because T has the minimal number of items for an AVL tree of height h. For this same reason, Left(T) and Right(T) must also have a minimum number of items. Thus, one of Left(T) and Right(T) must have height h − 1 and N_{h-1} items, and the other must have height h − 2 and have N_{h-2} items. A tree always has one more item than the number of the items in its subtrees; that is,

$$N_h = N_{h-1} + N_{h-2} + 1$$

for any value of h > 1.

This last equation looks a lot like the formula for generating Fibonacci numbers. In fact, AVL trees that are as sparse as possible are called "Fibonacci trees." From this equation and the values of N_0 and N_1, we can show (by induction, of course) that:

$$N_h = \text{Fib } (h + 3) - 1,$$

for all values of h ≥ 0.

We can show by induction on h (see Exercise 8.12) that:

$$\text{Fib } (h + 3) - 1 \geq \left(\tfrac{3}{2}\right)^h, \text{ for } h = 0, 1, 2, \ldots .$$

Therefore, $N_h \geq \left(\tfrac{3}{2}\right)^h$, for h = 0, 1, 2, ... Taking logs (in any base) of both sides of this inequality, we get:

$$\log N_h \geq h * \log \left(\tfrac{3}{2}\right).$$

Rewriting this in a form suitable for a Big O claim,

$$h \leq c * \log N_h, \text{ where } c = \frac{1}{\log \left(\tfrac{3}{2}\right)}.$$

In other words, an AVL tree with N items has O(log N) height even in the worst case.

In the next section, we explore another kind of binary tree whose height is always O(log N): the heap.

THE HEAP DATA TYPE

A **heap** T is a complete binary tree in which either T is empty, or:

1. Each item in Left (T) is LessThan or EqualTo the root item of T.
2. Each item in Right(T) is also LessThan or EqualTo the root item of T.
3. Left (T) and Right (T) are heaps.

Figure 8.10 shows a heap with ten integer items.

The ordering in a heap is top-down, but not left to right: Each root item is greater than or equal to each of its children, but some left siblings may be greater than their right siblings and some may be less. In Fig. 8.10, for example, 85 is greater than its right sibling (36), but 29 is less than its right sibling (55).

A heap is a curious structure, but it is useful in a variety of applications. We will present two such uses: for the design and implementation of priority queues (Chapter 6) and for the HeapSort sorting algorithm (Chapter 9).

This leads us to a discussion of the responsibilities of the Heap ADT.

Responsibilities of the Heap Data Type

Most of the global responsibilities of the Binary Tree ADT also apply to the Heap ADT; however, in the Heap ADT there is no need to copy the left or right subtree, and the only suitable traversal is breadth-first.

The local (i.e., item-related) responsibilities are position-oriented, since position is a significant feature of a complete binary tree. To make sure we always have a complete binary tree, insertions and deletions are allowed only in the last position. In other words, each inserted item becomes the rightmost leaf at the lowest level of the tree, and the only item that can be deleted is the rightmost leaf at the lowest level. Any item can be retrieved by its position.

Finally, we add two new kinds of responsibilities, one local and one global. For the sake of sorting, the items in any two positions can be swapped. Such swaps can temporarily produce a complete binary tree that violates the definition of a heap; thus there is a responsibility to restore the heap property to a complete binary tree.

Figure 8.10

A heap with ten integer items.

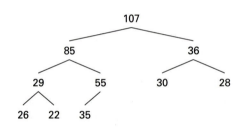

Definition of the Heap Data Type

We will now define, design, and implement the Heap ADT. We assume that the user will supply an ItemType in which items can be compared, Max-TreeSize, and any number of subalgorithms to specify what to do with a visited item during a traversal.

The logical domain, of course, is the collection of all heaps, which is a subset of the collection of all binary trees.

> *An implicit precondition and postcondition of each of the following heap methods is that the calling instance is a complete binary tree, but not necessarily a heap.*

Most of the method interfaces (headings, preconditions, and postconditions) are the same as those from the Binary Tree ADT. There are eleven heap methods:

1. `Initialize.`

   Postcondition: The calling instance is empty.

2. `IsEmpty.`

   Postcondition: True has been returned if the calling instance is empty. Otherwise, False has been returned.

3. `Size.`

   Postcondition: The number of items in the calling instance has been returned.

4. `Retrieve (Item, Position).`

   Precondition: $1 \leq$ Position $\leq$ the number of items in the calling instance $\leq$ MaxTreeSize.

   Postcondition: The item at position Position has been copied into Item.

5. `InsertLast (Item).`

   Precondition: The number of items in the calling instance is less than MaxTreeSize.

   Postcondition: Item has been inserted as a new leaf at the end of the calling instance.

6. **`DeleteLast.`**

   Precondition: The calling instance is not empty.

   Postcondition: The item that was in the last position in the calling instance prior to this call has been deleted.

7. **`Swap (I, J).`**

   Precondition : $1 \le I$; $2 * I \le J \le$ the number of items in the calling instance; the subtree rooted at position I (and including position J) is a heap, except (possibly) in position I.

   Postcondition: The items in positions I and J have been swapped in the calling instance; the subtree rooted at position J is a heap except (possibly) in position J.

   Example: Suppose that we start with the following complete binary tree:

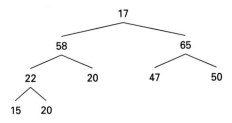

   If the method call is Swap (1, 3), the precondition is satisfied because the (sub)tree rooted at position 1 is a heap except at position 1. After swapping, we have:

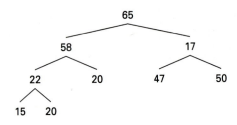

   The postcondition is satisfied because the subtree rooted at position 3 is a heap except at position 3.

   The Swap method is used in conjunction with the ReHeap method, defined next.

8. `ReHeap (I, J).`

Precondition : $1 \leq I \leq J \leq$ the number of items in the calling instance, which is a complete binary tree; the subtree rooted at position I (and whose last item is in a position $\leq J$) is a heap, except (possibly) in position I.

Postcondition: The subtree rooted at position I (and whose last item is in a position $\leq J$) is a heap.

Example: Suppose we start with the following complete binary tree (a heap, except for positions 1 and 10):

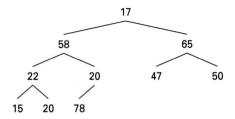

If the method call is ReHeap (1,9), the precondition is satisfied because, except for the root item, the tree in positions 1 through 9 is a heap. The postcondition can be achieved in many ways. One arrangement that satisfies it is:

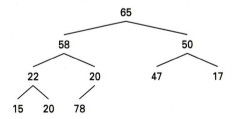

Reheaping is essential in the HeapSort algorithm that we will present in Chapter 9. You might be able to get an idea of how that algorithm works from the following example. If we start with a ten-item heap, and call:

```
Swap (1,10)
ReHeap (1,9)
```

then the largest item will be in position 10, and the items in positions 1 through 9 form a heap. If we now call:

```
Swap (1,9)
ReHeap (1,8)
```

then the largest item will be in position 10, the second largest in position 9, and the items in positions 1 through 8 form a heap.

9. `Height.`

Postcondition: The height of the calling instance has been returned.

10. `CopyTo (NewHeap).`

Postcondition: NewHeap contains a distinct copy of the calling instance.

11. `TraverseBreadthFirst (Visit).`

Postcondition: The items in the heap have been visited by position, starting with the item in position 1.

Design of the Heap Methods

Our design of the Heap ADT will utilize the contiguous design domain of the binary tree ADT. Therefore, each heap object will have two fields:

A: array [1..MaxTreeSize] of ItemType;
N: 0..MaxTreeSize

The designs of the following methods are inherited from the contiguous design of the Binary Tree ADT:

Initialize

IsEmpty

Size

Height

CopyTo

TraverseBreadthFirst

Except for ReHeap, the designs of the uninherited methods are simple:

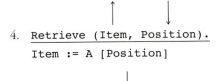

4. `Retrieve (Item, Position).`
    `Item := A [Position]`

5. `InsertLast (Item).`
    `Increment N`
    `A [N] := Item`

6. `DeleteLast.`

   `Decrement N`

   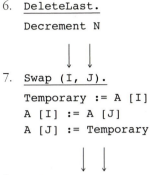

7. `Swap (I, J).`

   ```
   Temporary := A [I]
   A [I] := A [J]
   A [J] := Temporary
   ```

8. `ReHeap (I, J).`

   According to the precondition, the subtree rooted at position I is a heap, except (possibly) in position I. We make that subtree a heap as follows: If $A [I]$ is LessThan its larger child, we swap the two, then reheap the subtree rooted at the position the larger child held before the swap.

   The complete subalgorithm is:

   ```
   ReHeap (I, J)
   if 2 * I <= J then { A [I] has at least one child }
      if 2 * I = J then { only one child}
         PositionOfLarger := J
      else
         if A [2 * I] is GreaterThan A [2 * I + 1] then
            PositionOfLarger := 2 * I
         else
            PositionOfLarger := 2 * I + 1
      if A [I] is LessThan A [PositionOfLarger] then
         Swap [I, PositionOfLarger]
         if 2 * PositionOfLarger <= J then
            ReHeap (PositionOfLarger, J)
   ```

A proof of correctness can be obtained by induction on the height of the subtree rooted at I. The details are left as an exercise.

In the worst case, when $I = 1$ and $J = N$, the number of calls to ReHeap is the number of times that N can be divided in two until $N = 1$; that is, WorstTime is Trunc ($\log_2 N$), which is O($\log N$). For the average time, we let I vary between 1 and N, with an average value of N **div** 2. This position is only one level away from a leaf, so Time is O(1).

An iterative subalgorithm for ReHeap is not hard to develop. The basic idea is that we sift the item in position I down the tree until we have a heap. During each iteration, the item in position I is compared to its larger child. If the heap property is violated, a swap is made and *I* is given the position of that larger child.

The subalgorithm is as follows:

```
ReHeap (I, J) { Iterative version }
IsAHeap := False
while not IsAHeap and (2 * I <= J) do
    { Find the position of the larger child: }
    if 2 * I = J then { only one child }
       PositionOfLarger := J
    else
       if A [2 * I] is GreaterThan A [2 * I + 1] then
          PositionOfLarger := 2 * I
       else
          PositionOfLarger := 2 * I + 1
    if A [I] is LessThan A [PositionOfLarger] then
       Swap [I, PositionOfLarger]
       I := PositionOfLarger
    else
       IsAHeap := True
```

We will prove the correctness of the While statement. Its precondition is the precondition of the subalgorithm, together with the statement that IsAHeap is False. The postcondition of the While statement is the postcondition of the subalgorithm.

Loop assertion: The subtree rooted at position *I* and including position *J* is a heap, except (possibly) at position *I*.

Assume that the precondition is true.

Claim 1: The execution of the While statement eventually terminates.

Proof: During each iteration, either *I* is increased or IsAHeap is given the value True. Therefore, the loop condition must eventually become false.

Claim 2: The loop assertion is a loop invariant.

Proof: The loop assertion, as part of the precondition, is true prior to the first iteration.

Assume that the loop assertion is true prior to some iteration. The subtree of the larger child must then be a heap. If no swap is made during the iteration, the subtree with items in [*I*..*J*] must be a heap, so the heap assertion is true at the end of that iteration. Otherwise, the item in position *I* is swapped with its larger child and *I* gets the position of that larger child. Since that subtree (rooted at the new value of *I*) was a heap prior to the iteration, it will still be a heap, except (possibly) at position *I*. Thus, the loop assertion is true at the end of that iteration.

Since the value of the loop assertion does not change between iterations, if the assertion is true at the end of an iteration it must be true prior to the next iteration. We conclude that the loop assertion is true before and after each iteration. That is, the loop assertion is a loop invariant.

A Heap-Based Design of the Priority Queue Data Type

A priority queue can be represented as a descendant of a heap. The ordering is by priorities; the item with highest priority will be at the root. For items with equal priorities, the ordering is chronological—first-in, first-out. For the sake of simplicity, we will temporarily ignore this requirement. The designs of all of the priority queue methods are inherited from the contiguous design of the heap ADT (except for RetrieveHighest, Insert, and DeleteHighest).

After we present each of those designs in terms of the heap methods, we will reinstate the requirement of a chronological ordering for items of equal priority.

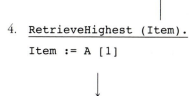

4. `RetrieveHighest (Item).`

    `Item := A [1]`

5. `Insert (Item).`

    It is easy enough to insert Item at the end of the priority queue, but we must then restore the heap property of the calling instance. For example, suppose the items consist of priorities only, and the priority queue is:

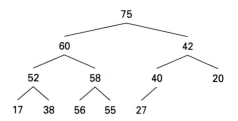

If the call is:

`Insert (45)`

we start by inserting 45 at position 13:

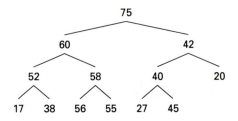

We now need to "sift up" 45 to its proper position among its ancestors. To accomplish this, we first apply ReHeap to:

to get:

We then apply ReHeap to the tree of which this is the left subtree, namely:

This call to ReHeap gives us:

Finally, we apply ReHeap to the entire tree:

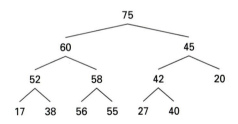

No swaps are made, and the tree is now a heap. The roots at which Re-Heap is applied are at positions Size **div** 2, Size **div** 4, Size **div** 8, and so on.

The complete subalgorithm is:

```
Insert (Item)

Add 1 to N
A [N] := Item
Root := N div 2
while Root >= 1 do
    ReHeap (Root, N)
    Root := Root div 2
```

A suitable loop assertion of the While statement is: "The calling instance is a heap except (possibly) for the subtree whose root item is in position Root." When Root $= 0$, we interpret the assertion as saying that the calling instance is a heap.

The correctness proof of the While statement is left as an exercise.

The number of iterations of the While statement is Trunc $(\log_2 N)$. Each ReHeap takes only O(1) time because, at worst, a parent and child are swapped. Thus, for Insert, Time is O($\log N$). Space is O(1).

6. `DeleteHighest.`

   The item to be deleted must be in position 1, so we swap that item with the item in the last position, then decrement N. Finally, we restore the heap property to the tree.

   The complete subalgorithm is

```
DeleteHighest

Swap (1, N)
Decrement N
ReHeap (1, N)
```

The call to ReHeap takes O(log N) time, and so Time is O(log N). Space is O(1).

Finally, we must address the problem of equal priorities. Why do these pose a problem? Consider the following heap:

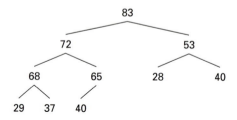

According to the chronological ordering, the item with priority 40 in position 7 should be retrieved or deleted before the item with priority 40 in position 10. However, after DeleteHighest removes 83, the resulting heap is:

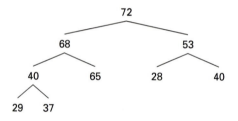

The item with priority 40 that had been in position 10 is now in position 4, so it will be retrieved or deleted *before* the item with priority 40 in position 7.

We can avoid this problem by associating with each item not only a priority, but also its chronological order. For example, we can initialize a variable Count to zero and add 1 to Count whenever an insertion is made. Instead of inserting an item, we insert a node with an Item field and a Count field. We define Node1 to be LessThan Node2 if the priority of Node1's Item is less than the priority of Node2's Item, or if the items have equal priority and Node1's Count is greater than Node2's Count.

In the heap shown here, the items (priorities) 72, 68, 65, and 53 will be deleted in order. At that point, the item with priority 40 and Count of 10 (that is, the item inserted last) will be LessThan the item with priority 40 and Count of 7. So whichever of these two items was inserted earlier will be lifted into position 1, from where it will be deleted next.

The implementation and validation of the contiguous design were straightforward, and the validation of the contiguous implementation of the Binary Tree ADT followed easily.

BINARY EXPRESSION TREES

A ***binary expression tree*** is a binary tree in which each nonleaf represents a binary operator and each leaf represents a simple operand (an identifier or value). Figure 8.11 shows several expression trees.

Suppose we wanted to evaluate the expression represented by the first expression tree in Fig. 8.11. The addition cannot be performed until its two operands have been evaluated. Since one of its operands is the product of A and 2, the multiplication must be performed before the addition.

In general, the farther an operator is from the root of the expression tree, the sooner it will be evaluated. For operators at the same level, the order of evaluation is irrelevant. For example, in the evaluation of the expression depicted by the second expression tree in Figure 8.11, the subtraction could be performed before the multiplication, or vice versa.

The two preceding paragraphs suggest that one of the responsibilities of the Binary Expression Tree ADT is to evaluate the tree. This leads us to an even more important responsibility: building a binary expression tree. How can this be done? As we indicated in Chapter 6, we can build an expression tree from an expression in prefix notation. Before we get into the details of how this is done, it is time that we defined the Binary Expression Tree ADT.

Definition of the Binary Expression Tree Data Type

We assume that the user of the Binary Expression Tree ADT will provide one or more "Visit" subalgorithms and an Item data type which includes IsAnOperator and StringValue methods. The IsAnOperator method returns True if the item is an operator, and False if the item is an operand. The StringValue method returns a string: either the operator ("+," "−," "*," or "/") or the value of the item in string form, such as "124.75." In practice, the items will often be tokens.

In the Binary Expression Tree ADT, the logical domain is, of course, the collection of all binary expression trees. Seven of the ten methods' inter-

Figure 8.11

Several binary expression trees.

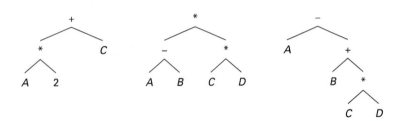

faces are the same as those from the Binary Tree ADT. RetrieveRoot, BuildTree, and Evaluate are new methods.

1. **`Initialize.`**

   Postcondition: The binary expression tree is empty.

2. **`IsEmpty.`**

   Postcondition: True has been returned if the tree is empty. Otherwise, False has been returned.

3. **`Size.`**

   Postcondition: The number of items in the tree has been returned.

4. **`RetrieveRoot (Item).`**

   Precondition: The tree is not empty.

   Postcondition: The root item has been copied into Item.

5. **`RetrieveLeft (Tree).`**

   Precondition: The tree is not empty.

   Postcondition: The left subtree has been copied into Tree.

6. **`RetrieveRight (Tree).`**

   Precondition: The tree is not empty.

   Postcondition: The right subtree has been copied into Tree.

7. **`BuildTree (Prefix).`**

   Precondition: Prefix contains a list of items representing an expression in prefix notation.

   Postcondition: The calling instance contains the binary expression tree corresponding to the prefix expression.

   Example: Suppose that Prefix contains:

   + 5.0 * 2.0 4.0

After the method call, the calling instance will be

8. **Evaluate.**

Postcondition: The real value of the calling instance has been returned.

Example: If the calling instance is:

the value returned will be 13.0.

9. **CopyTo (NewTree).**

Postcondition: NewTree contains a distinct copy of the tree.

10. **TraversePostOrder (Visit).**

Postcondition: Each item in the tree has been visited, in postorder.

We do not include a preorder traversal because the prefix form of the expression is already available to a user (see the parameter for BuildTree). We do not include an inorder traversal because it will not necessarily correspond to the correct order of evaluation of operands. For example, the inorder traversal of the second tree in Fig. 8.11 is:

$$A - B + C * D$$

But the infix expression corresponding to that tree is

$$(A - B) + C * D$$

Design of the Binary Expression Tree Data Type

The design domain will be the multi-linked design domain inherited from the design of the binary tree ADT: Each binary expression tree will be an object with a single field, Root. Root contains either a null address or the address of a node with three fields: Item, Left, and Right. As we noted earlier in the context of binary search trees, Left and Right are instances of the Binary Tree ADT, not of the Binary Expression Tree ADT.

Here are the designs of the uninherited methods:

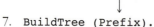

7.   `BuildTree (Prefix).`

If Prefix is not empty, we retrieve its first item and insert that item at the root of the tree. If that item is an operator, we then recursively build the left and right subtrees from the rest of Prefix (that is, excluding the first item).

The only problem is a technical one: With each call to BuildTree, we need to delete the first item from Prefix. However, if the list implementation uses addresses, the actual parameter corresponding to Prefix will be destroyed even though Prefix is a value formal parameter. We avoid this problem with an embedded recursive subalgorithm, Build.

BuildTree simply makes a distinct copy of Prefix and calls Build.

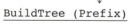

`BuildTree (Prefix)`

```
Prefix.CopyTo (NewPrefix)
Build (Root, NewPrefix)
```

Build does the real work:

`Build (Root, Prefix)`

```
if not Prefix.IsEmpty then
   Prefix.Retrieve (Item, 1)
   Prefix.Delete (1)
   Allocate space for a new node pointed to by Root
   Copy Item into Root's Item field, and Initialize
   Root's Left and Right subtrees
   if Item.IsAnOperator then
      with Root's node do
         Build (Left.Root, Prefix)
         Build (Right.Root, Prefix)
```

A correctness proof can easily be obtained by induction on the number of subexpressions in Prefix. The induction is not on the height of the tree, because that would beg the question of whether the tree had been correctly constructed.

N refers to the number of items in Prefix. The time and space requirements are O(N) in all cases because a distinct copy of Prefix is made. Also, there is one call to Build for each item in Prefix.

8. `Evaluate.`

Evaluate simply calls EvaluateItem:

`Return the value of EvaluateItem (Root)`

The design of EvaluateItem will be recursive. If the tree is not empty, we retrieve the root item. If that item is an operator, we evaluate the left and right subtrees, then add, subtract, multiply, or divide (depending on the operator). Otherwise, we convert the string value to a real value and return that value.

The subalgorithm is:

```
EvaluateItem (Root)

if Root <> null then
   RetrieveRoot (Item)
   if Item.IsAnOperator then
      LeftValue := EvaluateItem (Root's Left.Root)
      RightValue := EvaluateItem (Root's Right.Root)
      case Item.StringValue of
         '+': Return LeftValue + RightValue
         '-': Return LeftValue - RightValue
         '*': Return LeftValue * RightValue
         '/': Return LeftValue / RightValue
   else
      Convert StringValue to RealValue
      Return RealValue
```

Correctness can be proved by induction on the height of the tree.

Time is O(N) because there is one call to EvaluateItem for each item in the tree. The space requirements depend on the number of nested recursive calls, which in turn depends on the height of the tree. Worst-Space is O(N), and this occurs when the tree is chainlike: In each subtree, either the left subtree or right subtree is a simple operand. Space is O(log N) on average.

Implementations of the Binary Expression Tree Data Type

We can develop a dynamic or static implementation of the Binary Expression Tree ADT. The only details worth mentioning are related to the Evaluate method.

In Pascal, the case expression (between the reserved words **case** and **of**) must be of an ordinal type. The predeclared type *char* is ordinal, but StringValue must be able to accommodate more than a single character in case the item is a simple operand. One way to solve this problem is to introduce a new variable Operator, of type *char*, which gets StringValue if the item is an operator. A better solution is to replace the case statement with nested **if** statements. This is not quite as elegant as the case construction, but it has the clear virtue that multi-character operators (such as ":=" and "**") would be allowed.

The other problem involves the conversion of StringValue into RealValue. Turbo Pascal's Val procedure (see Appendix 4) converts a string representing an integer or real value into its numeric equivalent.

The EvaluateItem function, in a dynamic implementation, is:

```
function EvaluateItem (Root: AddressType): real;
{ Postcondition: The real value of the calling instance has}
{               been returned.                            }
var
    Item       : ItemType;
    LeftValue,
    RightValue: real;
    Code       : integer; { 0 if the first actual parameter }
                          { to Val is a number in string    }
                          { form.                           }
begin
    if Root <=> nil then
        begin
            RetrieveRoot (Item);
            if Item.IsAnOperator then
                begin
                    LeftValue := EvaluateItem (Root^.Left.Root);
                    RightValue := EvaluateItem (Root^.Right.Root);
                    if StringValue = '+' then
                        EvaluateItem := LeftValue + RightValue
                    else
                        if StringValue = '-' then
                            EvaluateItem := LeftValue - RightValue
                        else
                            if StringValue = '*' then
                                EvaluateItem := LeftValue*RightValue
```

```
                                      else
                                        if StringValue = '/' then
                                           EvaluateItem := LeftValue /
                                                                   RightValue
                        end { item is an operator }
                      else
                        begin
                          Val (StringValue, RealValue, Code);
                          EvaluateItem := RealValue
                        end { item is a simple operand }
                  end; { EvaluateItem }
```

In Chapter 11, we will encounter an extension of binary expression trees, namely *parse trees*. Parse trees are used by a compiler in determining the structure of an entire program, not merely a binary expression.

SUMMARY

This chapter introduced three specializations of binary trees: binary search trees, heaps, and binary expression trees. For each of the corresponding ADTs, most of the method designs were inherited from either the multi-linked or contiguous designs of the Binary Tree ADT.

A *binary search tree T* is a binary tree in which either *T* is empty, or:

1. Each item in Left (T) is less than *T*'s root item;

2. Each item in Right (T) is greater than *T*'s root item;

3. Left (T) and Right (T) are binary search trees.

This recursive definition was mimicked in the designs of the Search, Insert, and Delete methods. The design of the Delete method needed special care since deletion of an item with two children requires restructuring the tree. On average, searches, insertions, and deletions take only $O(\log N)$ Time, so binary search trees are ideal for situations where there are a lot of insertions and deletions; but the items must be available, in order, at any time.

If the items to be inserted are already in order or in reverse order, the resulting tree will be a chain, with $O(N)$ Time for inserting, deleting, or searching. This unfortunate circumstance can be avoided with a special kind of binary search tree called an *AVL tree*. In an AVL Tree, the left and right subtrees are of approximately equal height, so the average time for insertions, deletions, and searches is always $O(\log N)$.

A *heap* is a complete binary tree which either is empty, or in which the items in the left and right subtrees are less than or equal to the root item; those subtrees are also heaps. The key method in the Heap ADT is ReHeap, which restores the heap property to a complete binary tree. Because a heap is a complete binary tree, its height is always O(log N), so heaps are useful whenever there is a need for a semiordered, compact structure. One such situation is in the design of the Priority Queue ADT.

In a *binary expression tree*, each nonleaf is a binary operator, and each leaf is a simple operand. Binary expression trees can be created from a prefix expression, then operated on mathematically (evaluated, integrated, differentiated, and so on).

EXERCISES

8.1   **a.** Show the effect of making the following insertions into an initially empty binary search tree:

30, 40, 20, 90, 10, 50, 70, 60, 80

b. Find a different ordering of these items whose insertions would generate the same binary search tree as in part a.

8.2   Describe in English how to delete each of the following from a binary search tree:

a. an item with no children
b. an item with one child
c. an item with two child

8.3   Suppose that Scores is an instance of a binary *search* tree. Each item is an integer between 0 and 100, inclusive. Show what Scores will look like after each of the following messages is sent:

a.   Scores.Initialize
b.   Scores.Insert (50)
c.   Scores.Insert (80)
d.   Scores.Insert (92)
e.   Scores.Insert (75)
f.   Scores.Insert (77)
g.   Scores.Insert (61)
h.   Scores.Insert (23)
i.   Scores.Insert (70)
j.   Scores.Insert (65)
k.   Scores.Insert (72)
l.   Scores.Insert (40)
m. Scores.Insert (30)
n.   Scores.Delete (23)
o.   Scores.Insert (23)
p.   Scores.Delete (50)
q.   Scores.Insert (90)

       r.   Scores.Insert (91)

       s.   Scores.Delete (80)

       t.   Scores.Delete (61)

8.4   Trace the execution of Scores.Insert (77) (part f of Exercise 8.3) with the recursive and iterative designs of the Insert method.

8.5   Trace the execution of Scores.Delete (50) (part p of Exercise 8.3) with the recursive design of the Delete method.

8.6   Show the effect of making the following insertions in an initially empty AVL tree:

10, 20, 30, 40, 50, 60, 70, 80, 90

8.7   **a.**   Show the effect of the method call Reheap (1, 9) on the following complete binary tree:

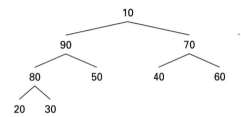

       b.   Trace the execution of the above method call for both the recursive and iterative Reheap subalgorithms.

8.8   Give an example of a complete binary tree with ten items in which the call:

```
ReHeap (3, 10)
```

would be legal. Notice that the item in position 10 will not be in the subtree rooted at position 3.

8.9   Suppose that Jobs is an instance of a priority queue designed as a heap. Each item consists of a priority only. Show what Jobs will look like after each of the following messages is sent:

       a.   Jobs.Initialize

       b.   Jobs.Insert (37)

       c.   Jobs.Insert (28)

       d.   Jobs.Insert (55)

       e.   Jobs.Insert (77)

       f.   Jobs.Insert (72)

       g.   Jobs.Insert (81)

       h.   Jobs.Insert (26)

i.   Jobs.Insert (58)
j.   Jobs.Insert (63)
k.   Jobs.Insert (20)
l.   Jobs.DeleteHighest
m. Jobs.DeleteHighest
n.   Jobs.DeleteHighest
o.   Jobs.DeleteHighest

8.10 The following example shows the unfairness of using priorities only in a priority queue. Suppose that Patients is an instance of a priority queue. Trace the execution, in the heap-based design, of the execution of the following messages:

a.   Patients.Initialize
b.   Patients.Insert (40)
c.   Patients.Insert (35)
d.   Patients.Insert (40)
e.   Patients.Insert (83)
f.   Patients.DeleteHighest
g.   Patients.DeleteHighest

In this example, the 40 inserted in part d would be deleted before the 40 inserted in part b. Modify the heap design to keep track of the chronological order of insertions (for example, using a Count variable).

8.11 In the multi-linked design of the binary search tree ADT, prove the correctness of each of the following:

a.   the recursive Insert subalgorithm
b.   the iterative Insert subalgorithm
c.   the iterative Search subalgorithm
d.   the recursive Delete subalgorithm
e.   the recursive DeleteSuccessor subalgorithm

8.12 Develop and validate iterative subalgorithms for Delete and Delete-Successor in the multi-linked design of the Binary Search Tree ADT.

8.13 Show that, for $h = 0, 1, 2, \ldots,$

$$\text{Fib } (h + 3) - 1 \geq \left(\tfrac{3}{2}\right)^h.$$

HINT For $h > 1,$

$$\left(\tfrac{3}{2}\right)^{h-1} + \left(\tfrac{3}{2}\right)^{h-2} = \left(\tfrac{3}{2}\right)^{h-2} * \left(\tfrac{3}{2} + 1\right) > \left(\tfrac{3}{2}\right)^{h-2} * \left(\tfrac{9}{4}\right)$$

8.14 Prove the correctness of the recursive and iterative designs of Re-Heap in the heap ADT.

8.15 Build a binary expression tree from the following prefix expression:

$$- + A / * B C D E$$

8.16 Start with the following infix expression:

$$10 * (2 + 8 - 4) / 12$$

   a. Convert the expression to prefix notation.
   b. Build the expression tree.
   c. Evaluate the expression tree.

8.17 In the multi-linked design of the Binary Expression Tree ADT, show how BuildTree could be designed if the formal parameter were in postfix notation instead of in prefix notation.

   HINT Start at the end of the expression.

8.18 For inserting N items in an initially empty binary search tree, we have

$$\text{Time } (N) \approx kN \log_2 N \text{ seconds}$$

   Given that, for $N = 1000$, Time $(N) \approx 1.37$ seconds, estimate Time (2000).

   HINT $1.37 \approx k (1000) \log_2 1000$

8.19 Let T be a perfectly balanced binary search tree. Then the number of items, N, in T must be one less than a power of 2. Show that the total number of recursive calls for an insertion is $(N + 1)/N * \log_2(N + 1) - 2$.

   HINT Zero recursive calls are required to insert the root item, one recursive call to insert the root's two children, two recursive calls to insert the root's four grandchildren, and so on. Since there are $(N+1)/2$ leaves, the average number of recursive calls is

$$0*1 + 1*2 + 2*4 + 3*8 + \ldots + \log_2[(N+1)/2]* (N+1)/2$$

   We can rewrite this as

$$\sum_{i=1}^{k} (i * 2^i)$$

   where $k = \log_2((N + 1)/2)$.
   It can be shown by mathematical induction that for any positive integer k,

$$\sum_{i=1}^{k} (i * 2^i) = (k - 1) * 2^{k+1} + 2$$

PROGRAMMING ASSIGNMENT

Design and implement (including validation and run-time analysis) the AVL Tree ADT.

Sorting Methods

CHAPTER 9

INTRODUCTION

One of the most common computer operations is ***sorting***, that is, putting a list of items in order. From simple, one-time sorts for small lists to highly efficient sorts for frequently used mailing lists and dictionaries, the ability to design and implement sort methods is an important skill in every programmer's repertoire.

When we defined the Orderable List ADT in Chapter 5, we noted that sorting was the main reason that there was such a data type. We have postponed a detailed investigation of sort methods in that data type until now so that we could take advantage of some of the tree-related techniques introduced in Chapter 8.

Following convention, we will assume that the items to be sorted are scalar. The difference in speed between scalar and nonscalar sorting is substantial (chiefly because nonscalar comparisons require calls to LessThan, EqualTo, and GreaterThan), and execution-time speed is the essential criterion by which a sort method is judged. Of course, a simple change (of LessThan for <, and so on) is all that would be needed to sort nonscalar items.

There are two further restrictions we will impose on the sort methods we will investigate. First, we will assume that the items are to be sorted into increasing order, although decreasing order can be obtained with a minor change. Second, we will consider comparison-based sorts only; that is, the sorting entails comparing items to other items. Comparisons are not necessary if we know, in advance, the final position of each item. For example, if we start with an unsorted list of 100 distinct integers in the range 1..100, we know without any comparisons that the integer 1 must end up in position 1, and so on.

For orderable lists, there are at least two design domains we can employ: the contiguous design domain and the linked design domain. For the sake of simplicity, we will design all of the sort methods based on the contiguous design domain. The object type of the calling instance will be an orderable list with two fields:

> *A*: array [1..MaxListSize] of ItemType;
> *N*: 0..MaxListSize.

In a programming assignment at the end of the chapter, you are invited to try designing and implementing the sort methods with the linked design domain.

We will illustrate the effect of each sort method on the following list of ten integers:

> 59 46 32 80 46 55 87 43 70 81

In analyzing a sorting subalgorithm, our primary concern will be time, particularly Time(N) and WorstTime(N). In some applications, such as national defense and life support systems, the worst-case performance can be critical. We will see several sort methods that provide a kind of insurance policy against unacceptably bad worst-case performance.

For each sort subprogram, validation will take the form of a driver that calls the subprogram to sort 50 random integers. The run-time analysis of each sort method will employ a TestTime program.

SOME SIMPLE SORTS

In this section we present some easily developed sorting subalgorithms.

1. SelectionSort

Subalgorithm. The general idea is this: Get the smallest item into position 1, then the second smallest into position 2, and so on. In other words, for each value of I between 1 and $N - 1$, make A [1..I] sorted and $\leq$ A [$I + 1$..N]. The subalgorithm is as follows:

```
SelectionSort

for I := 1 to N-1 do
```

```
{ Make A [1..I] sorted and <= A [I+1..N]: }
{ Find the position of the smallest of A [I..N]: }
Position := I
for J := I+1 to N do

    { Find the position of smallest of A [I..J]: }
    if A [J] < A [Position] then
        Position := J

Swap A [I] with A [Position]
```

Example. Let $N = 10$ and let the values in $A [1..10]$ be the ones given in the preceding section. Here is the execution trace through the first three swaps:

A [1..10]	I	J	Position
59 46 32 80 46 55 87 43 70 81	1		1
		2	2
		3	3
		4	
		5	
		6	
		7	
		8	
		9	
		10	
(Swap A [1] with A [3])			
32 46 59 80 46 55 87 43 70 81	2		2
		3	
		4	
		5	
		6	
		7	
		8	8
		9	
		10	
(Swap A [2] with A [8])			
32 43 59 80 46 55 87 46 70 81	3		3
		4	
		5	5
		6	
		7	
		8	
		9	
		10	
(Swap A [3] with A [5])			
32 43 46 80 59 55 87 46 70 81			

Verification.

Inner For statement:

Precondition: Position $= I$.

Postcondition: A [Position] $\leq A$ $[I..N]$.

Loop assertion: A [Position] $\leq A$ $[I..J]$.

Assume that the precondition is true.

1. Claim: The execution of the inner For statement eventually terminates.

    Proof: The number of iterations is exactly $N - I$.

2. Claim: The loop assertion is a loop post-invariant.

    Proof: At the end of the first iteration, we have A [Position] $\leq$ A $[I..I + 1]$. At the start of any subsequent iteration, A [Position] $\leq A$ $[I..J - 1]$, so after that iteration, A [Position] $\leq$ A $[I..J]$.

3. Claim: After the last iteration, the postcondition is true.

    Proof: At the end of the last iteration, $J = N$; so, by the loop post-invariant, the postcondition must be true.

Outer For statement:

Postcondition: A $[1..N]$ sorted.

Loop assertion: A $[1..I]$ sorted and $\leq A$ $[I + 1..N]$.

1. Claim: The execution of the outer For statement eventually terminates.

    Proof: The number of iterations is exactly $N - 1$.

4. Claim: The loop assertion is a loop post-invariant.

    Proof: After the first iteration, A $[1] \leq A$ $[2..N]$. At the start of any iteration after the first, we have A $[1..I - 1]$ sorted and $\leq$ A $[I..N]$, but after that iteration we have A $[I] \leq A$ $[I + 1..N]$. Therefore, we have A $[1..I]$ sorted and $\leq A$ $[I + 1..N]$.

3. Claim: After the last iteration, the postcondition is true.

    Proof: At the end of the last iteration, we have A $[1..N - 1]$ sorted and $\leq A$ $[N..N]$. Therefore, A $[1..N]$ must be sorted.

Analysis.   The Time for SelectionSort is determined by the number of iterations of the innermost loop:

$$(N - 1) + (N - 2) + (N - 3) + \ldots + 1$$

$$\sum_{i=1}^{N-1} i = \frac{(N - 1)N}{2}$$

which is $O(N^2)$.

The number of iterations is independent of the initial arrangement of the items, so BestTime, WorstTime, and Time are all the same, and so all are $O(N^2)$. For future reference, note that only $N - 1$ swaps are made.

Space (N) is $O(1)$ because all we need are a couple of loop control variables and a temporary.

2.   BubbleSort (For Bubbleheads Only?)

This is a commonly used, but uncommonly bad, sorting technique. We study it here so you will know why it should be avoided.

Subalgorithm.   To BubbleSort a list, start at the beginning of the list and compare each item with the next item; swap if necessary. Then start back at the beginning, comparing and swapping. Continue until A $[1..N]$ is sorted. To avoid needless comparisons, each pass[1] goes only as far as the last interchange from the preceding pass. The subalgorithm is:

```
BubbleSort

FinalSwapPos := N
repeat

    { Make A [FinalSwapPos+1..N] sorted }
    { and >= A [1..FinalSwapPos]: }
    SwapPos := 1
    for I := 1 to FinalSwapPos - 1 do

        { Make A [I+1] >= A [1..I]: }
        if A [I] > A [I+1] then
            Swap A [I] with A [I+1]
            SwapPos := I
    FinalSwapPos := SwapPos
until FinalSwapPos = 1
```

Example.   Here is what happens during the first three passes, with the list shown each time a pair is swapped and the just-swapped items underlined:

A [1..10]	FinalSwapPos	SwapPos	I
59 46 32 80 46 55 87 43 70 81	10	1	1
46 59 32 80 46 55 87 43 70 81			
			2
46 32 59 80 46 55 87 43 70 81		2	
			3
			4

---

[1]A **pass** is a loop that accesses some subsequence of a list.

A [1..10]	FinalSwapPos	SwapPos	I
46 32 59 46 80 55 87 43 70 81		4	
			5
46 32 59 46 55 80 87 43 70 81		5	
			6
			7
46 32 59 46 55 80 43 87 70 81		7	
			8
46 32 59 46 55 80 43 70 87 81		8	
			9
46 32 59 46 55 80 43 70 81 87	9	9	
		1	1
32 46 59 46 55 80 43 70 81 87			
			2
			3
32 46 46 59 55 80 43 70 81 87		3	
			4
32 46 46 55 59 80 43 70 81 87		4	
			5
			6
32 46 46 55 59 43 80 70 81 87		6	
			7
32 46 46 55 59 43 70 80 81 87		7	
			8
	7	1	1
			2
			3
			4
			5
32 46 46 55 43 59 70 80 81 87	5	5	

Verification.   The verification of BubbleSort is left as an exercise. A suitable loop assertion for the repeat statement is:

   A [FinalSwapPos + 1..N] is sorted and $\geq A$ [1.. FinalSwapPos].

For the For statement, a suitable loop assertion is:

   A [$I + 1$] $\geq A$ [1..I].

Analysis.   If the list is already in increasing order (of course, the sub-algorithm does not "know" this), the Repeat loop is executed just once, and the For loop is executed $N - 1$ times. Thus, the total number of loop iterations is $N - 1$, and BestTime (N) is O(N).

   If the list happens to be in decreasing order, FinalSwapPos will be decremented by one after each iteration of the Repeat loop. Thus, the Repeat loop will be executed $N - 1$ times. During each iteration of the Repeat loop, the For loop will be executed FinalSwapPos $- 1$ times. The total number of For loop iterations is:

$$N - 1 + N - 2 + N - 3 + \ldots + 2 + 1$$

Thus, WorstTime (N) is $O(N^2)$.

Calculation of Time (N) is beyond the scope of this book (see Knuth, 1975). Even the formula for the average number of inner-loop iterations is weird:

$$\frac{(N^2 - N)}{2} - \frac{(N + 1) \ln(N + 1)}{2}$$

$$+ \left(\frac{N + 1}{2}\right)\left(\ln 2 + \lim_{k \to \infty}\left[\sum_{i=1}^{k} \frac{1}{i} - \ln k\right]\right)$$

$$+ \frac{2}{3}\sqrt{2\pi(N + 1)} + \frac{31}{36} + \text{some terms in } O(N^{-\frac{1}{2}})$$

Thus, Time is $O(N^2)$.

Note the large number of swaps: approximately $N^2/8$, versus $N - 1$ for Selection Sort. The reason that BubbleSort requires so many swaps is that the distance moved during each swap is exactly one position. The heavy swapping does not directly affect the time estimates but will seriously affect the run-time performance.

Space is merely $O(1)$.

BubbleSort is better than SelectionSort only when the items are in order or nearly in order. As Knuth (1975) says, "In short, the bubble sort seems to have nothing going for it, except a catchy name and the fact that it leads to some interesting theoretical problems."

3. InsertionSort

Subalgorithm. For each value of I between 2 and N, we start with $A[1..I - 1]$ already sorted, and we "sift" $A[I]$ down into its proper position, thus leaving $A[1..I]$ sorted. The sifting is accomplished in a right-to-left scan starting at position I. The subalgorithm is:

InsertionSort

```
for I := 2 to N do

    { Make A [1..I] sorted: }
    J := I

    { Move A [J] into its proper position in A [1..I]: }
    while (J > 1) and (A [J-1] > A [J]) do

        { Make A [1..J-1] sorted and A [J..I] sorted: }
        Swap A [J] with A [J-1]
        Decrement J
```

In this subalgorithm, whenever a swap takes place, the temporary variable always gets the same value: $A[I]$. For example, when $I = 5$ in the following list, the temporary gets the value 21 three times!

18 22 29 34 21

By moving the assignments to and from the temporary outside of the inner loop, we obtain an improved version of InsertionSort:

<u>InsertionSort</u> {IMPROVED}

```
for I := 2 to N do

    { Make A [1..I] sorted: }
    J           := I
    Temporary := A [J]

    { Open the correct place for Temporary in A [1..I]: }
    while (J > 1) and (A [J-1] > Temporary) do

        { Make A[1..J-1] sorted; Temporary <= A[J..I] sorted:}
        A [J] := A [J-1]
        Decrement J

    A [J] := Temporary
```

Example. The trace of the first five passes, with $A[1..I]$ underlined after each pass, is as follows:

A [1..10]										I	J	Temporary
59	46	32	80	46	55	87	43	70	81	2	2	46
59	59	32	80	46	55	87	43	70	81		1	
<u>46</u>	<u>59</u>	32	80	46	55	87	43	70	81			
										3	3	32
46	59	59	80	46	55	87	43	70	81		2	
46	46	59	80	46	55	87	43	70	81		1	
<u>32</u>	<u>46</u>	<u>59</u>	80	46	55	87	43	70	81			
										4	4	80
<u>32</u>	<u>46</u>	<u>59</u>	<u>80</u>	46	55	87	43	70	81			
										5	5	46
32	46	59	80	80	55	87	43	70	81		4	
32	46	59	59	80	55	87	43	70	81		3	
<u>32</u>	<u>46</u>	<u>46</u>	<u>59</u>	<u>80</u>	55	87	43	70	81			
										6	6	55
32	46	46	59	80	80	87	43	70	81		5	
32	46	46	59	59	80	87	43	70	81		4	
<u>32</u>	<u>46</u>	<u>46</u>	<u>55</u>	<u>59</u>	<u>80</u>	87	43	70	81			

Verification. The verification of improved InsertionSort is left as an exercise. Suitable loop assertions can be gleaned from the intermediate-level statements at the beginning of each loop body in the subalgorithm.

Analysis. The For loop will always be executed $N - 1$ times. If the list starts out in increasing order, the number of iterations of the While loop will be zero, so the total number of iterations will be $N - 1$. Thus, BestTime (N) is $O(N)$.

If the list starts out in decreasing order, the number of iterations of the While loop will be:

$$1 + 2 + 3 + \ldots + N - 2 + N - 1$$

Thus, WorstTime (N) is $O(N^2)$.

In the average case (see Exercise 9.10), there will be approximately $N^2/4$ iterations of the While loop, so Time (N) is $O(N^2)$.

Space (N) is simply $O(1)$.

As we will see later in this chapter, the run-time performance of the improved version of InsertionSort is much faster than that of BubbleSort in both the average and worst cases.

By "sifting down" from $A[I]$ rather than sifting up from $A[1]$, we obtain the best time when the list is already in order, and very good time when the list is almost in order. We will take advantage of this behavior later in the chapter.

HOW FAST CAN WE SORT?

For each of the sort methods of the preceding section, Time was $O(N^2)$. Before we look at some faster sorts, let's spend a few moments to see how much of an improvement is possible. It can be shown (see Knuth, 1975) that for comparison-based sorts, any sort method must make, on average, at least $\log_2(N!)$ comparisons, so Time$(N) \geq \log_2(N!)$ for any such sort method. By applying Stirling's Approximation to $N!$, we conclude (see Exercise 9.11) that any comparison-based sort method requires at least $O(N \log N)$ Time. So a *fast* sort is one whose Time is $O(N \log N)$.

FAST SORTS

In this section, each sort method's Time is only $O(N \log N)$. For some, the WorstTime is also $O(N \log N)$, while for others the WorstTime is $O(N^2)$. Later in this chapter, when we look at the run times of all the sort methods discussed, we will see how huge the difference is between an $O(N \log N)$ algorithm and an $O(N^2)$ algorithm.

4. TreeSort

Subalgorithm.   The items on the list are inserted, one by one, into a binary sort tree. A **binary sort tree** is the same as a binary search tree, except that duplicates are allowed. According to the Insert subalgorithm for binary search trees, an item EqualTo the root item would be inserted into the right subtree. After constructing the binary sort tree, we retrieve the items back into *A* with an inorder traversal. The BackToA subalgorithm has *A* and *I* as nonlocal variables.

<u>TreeSort</u>

```
Tree.Initialize
for I := 1 to N do
    Tree.Insert (A[I])
I := 0
Tree.TraverseInOrder (BackToA)
```

$$\downarrow$$

<u>BackToA (Item)</u>

```
Add 1 to I
A [I] := Item
```

Example.   We show the initial value of *A*, then the binary sort tree Tree, and the final value of *A*.

<u>A [1..10] { initially }</u>

59 46 32 80 46 55 87 43 70 81

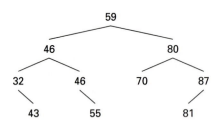

<u>A [1..10] { finally }</u>

32 43 46 46 55 59 70 80 81 87

Verification.   No verification is needed. Recall that Insert was verified in Chapter 8, and the same algorithm for binary search trees also works for binary sort trees.

Analysis.   Assume, for the sake of simplicity, that all of the items on the list are distinct. If the items on the list are in increasing order or in decreasing order, for example, the tree will be a chain. The number of nested recursive calls (or, in an iterative Insert, loop iterations) will be $1 + 2 + \ldots + N - 1 = N * (N - 1)/2$; that is, WorstTime is $O(N^2)$. We can reduce the WorstTime to $O(N \log N)$ by using an AVL tree rather than a binary sort tree.

In the best case, the initial arrangement of items on the list is such that the tree ends up to be perfectly balanced, except (possibly) on the level farthest from the root. We saw in Chapter 8 that the average number of nested recursive calls to insert N items is $O(\log N)$, so the total number of nested recursive calls to insert N items is $O(N \log N)$. In other words, Best-Time (N) is $O(N \log N)$.

The average (over all $N!$ initial arrangements of items) number of iterations or nested recursive calls is approximately N times the average height of a binary sort tree. The average height of a binary sort tree is $O(\log N)$, just as for a binary search tree. Thus, Time is $O(N \log N)$.

5.   MergeSort

Subalgorithm.   A top-down, recursive approach, reminiscent of the binary search subalgorithm from Chapter 5, keeps splitting the list in two until the list size is one, and then merges the two halves. The first and last indexes in A of the sublists will vary, so MergeSort simply calls an embedded (for efficiency) recursive subalgorithm:

<u>MergeSort</u>

```
SplitAndMerge (1, N).
```

By postponing the work of merging two sublists, we easily obtain the Split-AndMerge subalgorithm:

<u>SplitAndMerge (First, Last)</u>

```
if First < Last then
    Middle := (First + Last) div 2
    SplitAndMerge (First, Middle)
    SplitAndMerge (Middle+1, Last)
    Merge (First, Middle, Middle+1, Last)
```

The Merge subalgorithm merges two sorted sublists into one sorted sublist. The items are moved, one by one, into a temporary array and then copied back into A. The subalgorithm is:

<u>Merge (LeftFirst, LeftLast, RightFirst, RightLast)</u>

```
{ Precondition: A [LeftFirst..LeftLast] sorted;          }
{               A [RightFirst..RightLast] sorted;        }
```

```
{                          LeftFirst <= LeftLast = RightFirst - 1; }
{                          RightFirst <= RightLast.                 }
{ Postcondition: A [LeftFirst..RightLast] sorted.                  }
I := LeftFirst
J := RightFirst
K := 1
while (I <= LeftLast) and (J <= RightLast) do

    { Move the smallest K items from              }
    { A [LeftFirst..RightLast] into Temp [1..K]:  }
    if A [I] <= A [J] then
        Temp [K] := A [I]
        Increment I
        Increment K
    else
        Temp [K] := A [J]
        Increment J
        Increment K

{ Move the rest (if any) of A [LeftFirst..LeftLast] }
{ to Temp:                                          }
while I <= LeftLast do
    Temp [K] := A [I]
    Increment I
    Increment K

{ Move the rest (if any) of A [RightFirst..RightLast] }
{ to Temp: }
while J <= RightLast do
    Temp [K] := A [J]
    Increment J
    Increment K

{ Move Temp [1..K - 1] to A [LeftFirst..RightLast]: }
for I := 1 to K - 1 do
    A [I - 1 + LeftFirst] := Temp [I]
```

Example. A recursion tree is a handy tool for illustrating the effect of recursive calls. The actual parameters to SplitAndMerge (abbreviated to
Split) and the original values in *A* are shown as we move down the tree.
The calls to Merge and their effects on *A* are shown below the following
(partial) recursion tree:

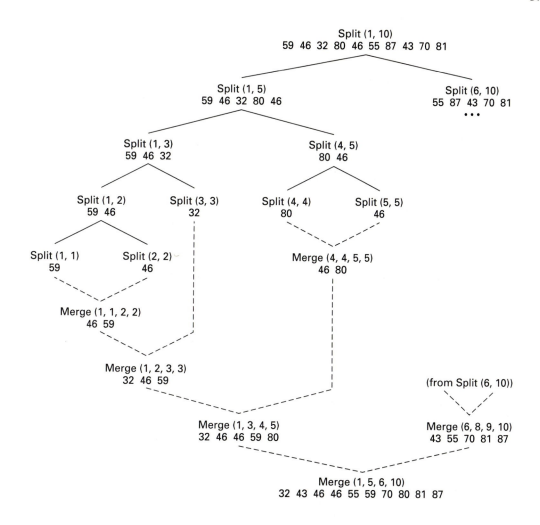

Verification.   The verifications of SplitAndMerge and the first loop statement in Merge are left as exercises.

Analysis.   The number of statements executed is, approximately, the number of levels in the recursion tree times the number of statements executed at each level. The number of levels in the recursion tree is the number of times that N can be halved until we get to 1 (that is, about $\log_2 N$ times). At each level, the total number of statements executed is, approximately, the total number of iterations of the four loops in Merge. At each level (except, possibly, the lowest), N items in ordered sublists are merged into larger sublists. To merge N items, the total number of iterations of the first three loops is always N, and the total number of iterations of the fourth loop is also N.

Thus, WorstTime (N), BestTime (N), and Time (N) are proportional to $\log_2 N * (2 * N)$, so all of those are $O(N \log N)$. Not only is MergeSort fast in the average case, its worst-case behavior is as good as possible (up to order).

In all cases, the space requirements are $O(N)$ because of the temporary array. In a linked design, no arrays are needed, but finding the midpoint of a linked list takes $O(N)$ time (versus $O(1)$ time in the contiguous design).

We can develop an iterative version of MergeSort by taking a bottom-up approach: On the first pass, merge consecutive pairs of singletons into (sorted) doubletons. On the second pass, merge consecutive pairs of (sorted) doubletons into (sorted) quadrupletons. On the third pass, merge consecutive pairs of (sorted) quadrupletons into (sorted) octupletons. Continue in this manner until $A [1..N]$ is sorted. The subalgorithm is:

```
MergeSort { Iterative }

Size := 1
while Size < N do

    { Loop invariant: A [1..Size], A [Size+1..2*Size], }
    {                 ... are all sorted.               }
    LeftFirst := 1
    while LeftFirst + Size <= N do

        { Loop invariant: All consecutive pairs of sub- }
        {                 lists in A [1..LeftFirst] of  }
        {                 size 2*Size have been sorted. }
        { Calculate sublist bounds: }
        LeftLast := LeftFirst + Size - 1
        RightFirst := LeftLast + 1
        if RightFirst + Size - 1 > N then
            RightLast := N
        else
            RightLast := RightFirst + Size - 1

        Merge (LeftFirst, LeftLast, RightFirst, RightLast).
        LeftFirst := RightLast + 1
        Size := Size * 2
```

Example. We show the effect on $A [1..10]$ of each iteration of the outer loop:

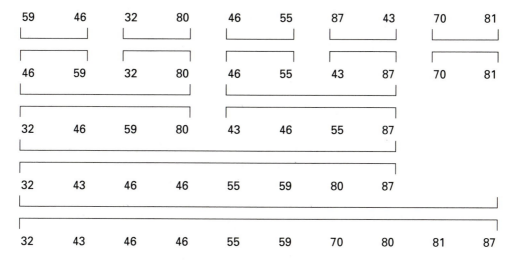

Verification.   The verification of this version of MergeSort is left as an exercise.

Analysis.   By an analysis similar to that of the recursive version, we see that Time, BestTime, and WorstTime are O(*N* log *N*), and Space is O(*N*).

6. HeapSort

The HeapSort method was invented by J.W.J. Williams (1964). It is based on the Heap data type from Chapter 8 (actually, the Heap ADT was invented because of HeapSort). HeapSort works as follows: Given an orderable list of *N* items in *A*, we first insert them into a complete binary tree and make it a heap. Next, we swap the first and last items, thereby putting the largest item into position *N*, where it belongs. We then reheap the tree in positions 1 through *N* − 1. We repeat this swap-and-reheap process until the items in positions 1 through *N* of the tree are sorted. Finally, we retrieve the items back into *A*.

   The Insert, Swap, ReHeap, and Retrieve methods were developed in Chapter 8, so all that remains is to make a heap from a complete binary tree. Suppose we have the following complete binary tree of ten items:

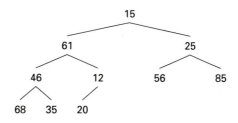

Recall that the ReHeap method can be applied to any subtree that is already a heap, except (possibly) at its root. The leaves, in positions 6 through 10, are automatically heaps; so the subtrees rooted at positions 5, 4, and 3 are heaps, except (possibly) at their roots. After reheaping these subtrees, we get:

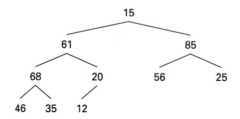

Because the subtrees rooted at positions 4 and 5 are heaps, the subtree rooted at 2 is a heap, except (possibly) at its root. After reheaping that subtree, we get:

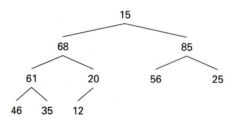

The subtrees rooted at 2 and 3 are now heaps, so we can reheap the entire tree:

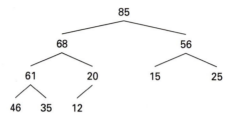

In the general case, a complete binary tree of N items, the largest nonleaf position is N **div** 2. To make the entire tree a heap, we successively reheap the subtrees rooted at N **div** 2, N **div** 2 $-$ 1, ..., 1.

The complete HeapSort subalgorithm is

<u>HeapSort</u>

```
with Heap do

    { Insert A [1..N] into a complete binary tree: }
    Initialize
    for I := 1 to N do
        InsertLast (A [I])

    { Heapify the tree: }
    for I := N div 2 downto 1 do
        ReHeap (I, N)

    { Put the items, from largest to smallest, into }
    { positions N, N-1, ..., 1 in the tree: }
    for I := N downto 2 do
        Swap (1, I)
        ReHeap (1, I-1)

    { Copy the items from the tree back into A: }
    for I := 1 to N do
        Retrieve (A [I], I)
```

Example. If we start with our usual sample list of items, after the execution of the first For statement we will have the following complete binary tree (not a heap):

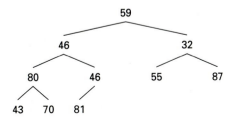

When we reheap the subtree rooted at position 5, we change:

to:

Reheaping the subtree rooted at position 4 causes no swaps since the root item, 80, is greater than or equal to each of its children. Reheaping the subtrees in positions 3, 2, and 1 requires only one swap each, so we get the following heap:

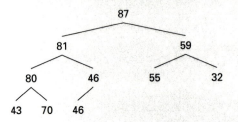

The items in positions 1 and 10 are swapped and ReHeap (1, 9) is executed, causing three parent–child swaps. The tree in positions 1 through 9 is now a heap, and the whole tree is:

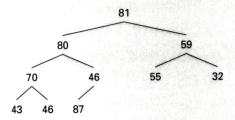

After swapping the items in positions 1 and 9 and reheaping 1 through 8, we get:

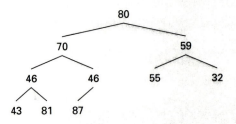

This swapping and reheaping process is repeated seven more times, and the resulting tree is:

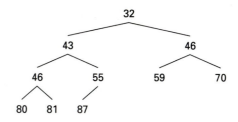

Verification.   A suitable loop assertion for the third For statement (for I :=
N downto 2 do...) is "The tree from positions 1 through $I - 1$ is a heap;
the items in positions I through N are sorted and greater than or equal
to the items in position 1 through $I - 1$." The correctness proof is left as
an exercise.

Analysis.   The analysis of HeapSort depends on the analyses of the heap
methods InsertLast, ReHeap, Swap, and Retrieve. We'll start with a worst-
case analysis of the time requirements because, surprisingly, this will give
us the average-case analysis as well!

> *WARNING: In the next few paragraphs, the mathematics gets a
> bit serious. If you don't feel up to it, skip directly to the
> paragraph starting with "Therefore, for HeapSort, ..."*

The first loop (inserting) is always executed exactly N times, as is the
fourth loop (retrieving), and both InsertLast and Retrieve take O(1) time.
Thus, the first and fourth loops each take O(N) time.

   To reheap a subtree rooted at position I, with no more than J items, the
number of iterations of the While loop (or recursive calls, in the recursive
version) in ReHeap is equal to the distance from I to its farthest descendant
leaf, namely Trunc $(\log_2 (J/I))$.

   The total number of iterations to make the tree a heap is thus:

$$\sum_{I=1}^{N\,\mathrm{div}\,2} \mathrm{Trunc}\,((\log_2(N/I))$$

Let $M = N$ **div** 2. The above sum is, approximately,

$$\sum_{I=1}^{M} \log_2 (N/I) = M \log_2 N - \sum_{I=1}^{M} \log_2 I$$

$$= M \log_2 N - \log_2 \prod_{I=1}^{M} I$$

$$\left(\prod_{I=1}^{M} I \text{ is the product of the first } M \text{ positive integers.}\right)$$

$$= M \log_2 N - \log_2 (M!).$$

By the logarithmic form of Stirling's approximation of factorials,

$$
\begin{aligned}
\log_2(M!) &\approx \log_2(M/e)^M \\
&= M \log_2 M - M \log_2 e \\
&\approx M \log_2 M - 1.5\ M.
\end{aligned}
$$

Thus,

$$
\begin{aligned}
M \log_2 N - \log_2(M!) &\approx M \log_2 N - [M \log_2 M - 1.5M] \\
&\approx M \log_2 N - M[\log_2 N - 1] + 1.5M \\
&= 2.5M \\
&= 1.25N
\end{aligned}
$$

We conclude that the time to complete the heaping process, in the worst case, is $O(N)$.

The total number of iterations to sort is

$$
\sum_{I=2}^{N} \text{Trunc}\ (\log_2(I - 1))
$$

This sum is, approximately,

$$
\begin{aligned}
\sum_{I=2}^{N} \log_2 I &= \log_2 \prod_{I=2}^{N} I \\
&= \log_2(N!) \\
&\approx N \log_2 N - 1.5N
\end{aligned}
$$

Thus, the time for the sorting phase is, in the worst case, $O(N \log N)$.

To summarize, for the four loop statements, the times in the worst case are $O(N)$, $O(N)$, $O(N \log N)$, and $O(N)$, respectively.

Therefore, for HeapSort, WorstTime is $O(N \log N)$. However, we noted earlier that the average time for any comparison-based sort is at least $O(N \log N)$. This implies that the (average) Time is also $O(N \log N)$. In fact, the sorting loop takes $O(N \log N)$ time in all cases, so BestTime is also $O(N \log N)$.

Space for a complete binary tree of size MaxListSize must also be allocated. Technically, this is an $O(1)$ requirement, so Space is $O(1)$.

7.   QuickSort

One of the most efficient (and, therefore, widely used) sorting subalgorithms is QuickSort, developed by C. A. R. Hoare (1962). Essentially, the QuickSort subalgorithm is a simple application of the principle of "divide and conquer." To "QuickSort" an array A, we first partition the array into a left subarray and a right subarray so that each item in the left subarray is less than or equal to each item in the right subarray. We then Quicksort the left and right subarrays, and we are done. Since this last statement is easily accomplished with two recursive calls to QuickSort, we will concentrate on the partitioning phase.

The partitioning begins by selecting an item in $A\,[1..N]$; the chosen item is referred to as the "pivot." For purposes of discussion, let us choose the middle item as the pivot. For example, if we started with the following in $A\,[1..14]$,

$$19 \quad 56 \quad 28 \quad 101 \quad 47 \quad 16 \quad 39 \quad 54 \quad 27 \quad 18 \quad 92 \quad 45 \quad 61 \quad 72$$

then 39 would be the pivot since it is in the middle position, that is, position $(1 + 14)$ **div** 2. We now want to move all the items that are less than 39 to the left-hand side of the array and move all the items that are greater than 39 to the right-hand side of the array. Items with a value of 39 may end up in either subarray, and the two subarrays need not have the same size.

To accomplish this partitioning, we introduce two counters: one of them starts at position 1 and works upward; the other starts at position 14 and works downward. The upcounter looks for items greater than or equal to 39 and the downcounter looks for items less than or equal to 39.

In this example, the upcounter is incremented once before it stops (at 56); then the downcounter is decremented four times before it stops (at 18). We have:

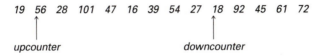

We now swap these two items and bump the two counters. This gives us:

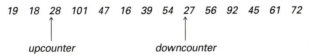

Upcounter is now incremented once and stops (at 101). Downcounter stops immediately (at 27). After swapping and bumping, we get:

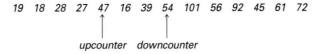

Upcounter stops immediately (at 47). Downcounter is decremented once and stops (at 39). After swapping and bumping, we get:

We are not through partitioning yet, because 16 has not yet been compared to the pivot. Upcounter is incremented once and stops (at 47). Downcounter stops immediately (at 16). Upcounter is now greater than

Downcounter and, since each item has been examined, no more swaps need to be made. We now have:

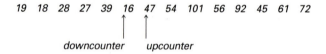

The left subarray goes from position 1 to 6 (= downcounter); the right subarray goes from position 7 (= upcounter) to 14. Each item in the left subarray is less than or equal to each item in the right subarray. We now apply this idea to each subarray.

In partitioning $A[1..6]$, the pivot is 28. Upcounter starts at position 1 and is incremented twice until it stops (at 28). Downcounter starts at position 6 and stops right away (at 16). After swapping and bumping, we get:

Upcounter is incremented once and stops (at 39). Downcounter is decremented once and stops (at 27). Since Upcounter is now greater than Downcounter, no more swaps can be made. We now have:

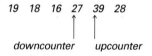

The two subarrays just created are $A[1..4]$ and $A[5..6]$. To Quicksort $A[1..4]$, we begin partitioning with 18 as the pivot. Upcounter starts at position 1 and stops right away (at 19). Downcounter starts at position 4 and is decremented once until it stops (at 16). After swapping and bumping, we get:

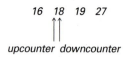

Upcounter stops immediately (at 18) and downcounter stops immediately (at 18). After swapping (needlessly) and bumping, we get:

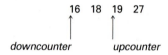

The left subarray consists of $A[1..1]$ and the right subarray consists of $A[3..4]$. Since $A[2]$ is already in its correct final position, we omit that item (which has the same value as the pivot) from either subarray. The left subarray, $A[1..1]$, is already (trivially) sorted. Quicksorting the right subarray, $A[3..4]$, is left as an exercise, as is the Quicksorting of the previous right subarrays, $A[5..6]$ and $A[7..14]$.

The following notes may clarify some of the details of Quicksorting.

1. The rationale for choosing the middle item as the pivot is this: If the array is already sorted, or nearly so, the middle item is the best choice. Otherwise, the middle item is as good a (blind) choice as any other.

2. Because we are using a contiguous design of the list, the retrieval of the middle item takes only $O(1)$ time, versus $O(N)$ time for a linked design.

3. In partitioning a subarray, each item, including the pivot itself, is compared to the pivot. Therefore, all possible swaps will be carried out.

4. No attempt is made to sort an empty subarray or a subarray consisting of a single item. Thus, to sort an array of size N, we must apply Quicksort approximately N times. Later in this chapter we will show how the number of calls to Quicksort can be drastically reduced.

The QuickSort subalgorithm is simply the shell for an embedded recursive subalgorithm with parameters for the first and last indexes in the subarray to be partitioned:

<u>QuickSort</u>

```
DoQuickSort (1, N)
```

Quicksorting the left and right subarrays is easily accomplished by calling DoQuickSort recursively twice. The subalgorithm DoQuickSort is:

<u>DoQuickSort (First, Last)</u>

```
if Last > First then
    Partition (First, Last, LeftLast, RightFirst)
    DoQuickSort (First, LeftLast).
    DoQuickSort (RightFirst, Last).
```

The Partition subalgorithm is as follows:

<u>Partition (First, Last, LeftLast, RightFirst)</u>

```
UpCounter    := First
DownCounter  := Last
Pivot        := A [(First + Last) div 2]

{ Make A[First..UpCounter-1] <= Pivot <=              }
{ A[DownCounter+1..Last]} and UpCounter > DownCounter. }
repeat
```

```
        { Make A [First..UpCounter-1] <= Pivot <= }
        { A[DownCounter+1..Last]: }
        while A [UpCounter] < Pivot do
            Increment (UpCounter)
        while A [DownCounter] > Pivot do
            Decrement (DownCounter)
        if UpCounter <= DownCounter then
            Swap A [UpCounter] with A [DownCounter] and bump
            counters
    until UpCounter > DownCounter
    LeftLast    := Downcounter
    RightFirst := UpCounter
```

Verification.   The verification of DoQuickSort and the repeat statement in Partition are left as exercises.

Analysis.   We stated earlier that approximately N partitions are required to sort an array of size N. When we partition a subarray into two parts, the number of iterations of the two While loops is approximately equal to the size of the subarray (since each item is compared to the pivot). Thus, the total number of iterations depends on the sizes of the subarrays that are partitioned.

We can view the effect of QuickSorting as creating a binary sort tree, whose root item is the pivot and whose left and right subtrees are the left and right subarrays (without the pivot). For example, Fig. 9.1. shows an example of the perfectly balanced binary sort tree induced when Quicksort is most efficient, that is, when each partition splits its subarray into two subarrays that have the same size. We would get such a tree if the items were originally in order or in reverse order.

Since each partition splits its (sub)array into two equal parts, the number of partitioning levels in the tree in Fig. 9.1 is equal to its height, Trunc $(\log_2 7)$, namely 2. The total number of iterations is approximately 14 (that is, N Trunc $(\log 2 N)$, where $N = 7$). For an array size of N, if we get equal size subarrays for each partition, the number of calls to Partition is approximately $\log_2 N$, and so the total number of iterations is, approximately, $N \log_2 N$. Therefore, BestTime (N) is $O(N \log N)$.

Figure 9.1

The binary sort tree created by repeated partitions, into equal sized subarrays, of an array with seven items.

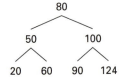

Figure 9.2

Worst case
partitioning: Each
partition produces a
subarray of size 1
(or 0).

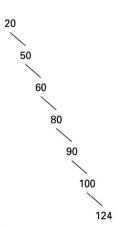

Contrast the tree shown in Fig. 9.1 with the tree shown in Fig. 9.2. The tree in Fig. 9.2 could be generated, for example, by Quicksorting the list:

    50 100 80 20 60 90 124

For an array of size N, the number of partitions in this worst case is $N - 1$, so the total number of iterations is approximately $N * (N - 1)/2$. Thus, WorstTime (N) is $O(N^2)$.

Incidentally, this worst-case behavior is not something that you are likely to run across every day. In Exercise 9.8 you are asked to develop an algorithm to produce the worst case. In this sense, QuickSort is far superior to TreeSort, which will yield $O(N^2)$ Time if the original list happens to be in order or in reverse order. Often, a list may be left in order from some previous operation.

Finally, we determine the order of the average (over all $N!$ initial arrangements of items in the list) case. The number of partitions is the average height of the binary sort tree created by partitioning. Since the average height of a binary sort tree is $O(\log N)$, we conclude that the total number of iterations is $O(N \log N)$.

The space requirements depend on the number of nested recursive calls to DoQuickSort. This, in turn, depends on the height of the binary sort tree created, so BestSpace and Space are $O(\log N)$, and WorstSpace is $O(N)$.

Quickening QuickSort

Because QuickSort is so widely used, it will be well worth our while to see if we can improve its efficiency. We propose two enhancements:

1. Do not QuickSort small subarrays. The machinery of partitioning a subarray of two or three items is more time-consuming than sorting

them directly. We will QuickSort a subarray only if its size is greater than some cutoff value, *C*. For example, with a cutoff of 3, we would replace:

```
if Last > First then
```

with:

```
if Last - First >= 3
```

DoQuickSort would then be applied only to subarrays of size 4 or more.

For example, suppose we partition the following list:

> 55 42 50 70 91 83 22 59

The left subarray would be:

> 55 42 50 59 22

and the right subarray would be:

> 83 91 70

This latter subarray would not be QuickSorted.

When the execution of the QuickSort-with-Cutoff subalgorithm has been completed, A $[1..N]$ will not be fully sorted, but will be "semisorted"; that is, A $[1..N]$ will consist of K segments for some positive integer K:

$$A\ [1..N_1],\ A\ [N_1 + 1..N_2],\ A\ [N_2 + 1..N_3],\ldots A\ [N_{K-1}..N]$$

For any *J* between 1 and $K - 1$, all of the items in segment *J* are less than or equal to all of the items in segment *J* + 1. The size of each segment is at most *C*, the cutoff.

To achieve these semisorted segments takes O(*N* log *N*) Time, because there are approximately $\log_2(N/C)$ levels of partitioning with approximately *N* iterations per level.

"But," you may exclaim, "we're still taking O(*N* log *N*) Time and we don't even get a sorted list? What's the point?" The point, as we will see when we look at run times, is that this version is quite a bit faster than the original version, and the time to finish sorting, O(*N*), is negligible.

To complete the sorting, we apply Improved InsertionSort to *A* $[1..N]$. Recall that the time for that subalgorithm is O(*N*) for a list that is sorted or nearly so. Specifically, since each semisorted segment has size less than or equal to *C*, the number of loop iterations executed by Improved InsertionSort in sorting such a segment is approximately $C^2/4$. There are at most *N* segments, so to sort *A* $[1..N]$ this way takes, at most, $N * C^2/4$ loop iterations, which is O(*N*) (recall that the cutoff *C* is a constant).

Thus, Time (N) for this improved version of QuickSort is still $O(N \log N)$, but as we will see in the next section, the actual run-time performance will be faster than for the original version.

2. Replace recursion with iteration in DoQuickSort. One way to accomplish this is to have a stack that holds pairs of indexes. The stack is initially empty. A Repeat loop continues until the stack is empty. During each iteration, A [First..Last] is partitioned. What happens next depends on the sizes of the two subarrays:

   a. If neither subarray is big enough to partition, the top pair of indexes is retrieved into Last and First and then popped.

   b. If only one subarray is big enough to partition, its first and last indexes are stored in First and Last.

   c. If both subarrays are big enough to be partitioned, one of them is chosen (for example, the larger one) and its indexes are stored in First and Last. The first and last indexes of the other one are pushed.

How much of an improvement in time does this change provide? No help in the order of the subalgorithm, which remains $O(N \log N)$ in the average case and $O(N^2)$ in the worst case. But what about the run time performance? As we will see in the next section, replacing recursion with iteration has virtually no effect on run time because most of the time in QuickSorting is spent in the inner loops of Partition.

VALIDATION AND RUN-TIME ANALYSIS OF SORTING SUBPROGRAMS

Each of the above sorting subalgorithms was converted into Turbo Pascal and validated with the help of a driver program.

The time to sort random lists of 2000 and 4000 integers was tested and the results are shown in Table 9.1.

Table 9.1 has several noteworthy features:

1. The run-time performance of BubbleSort is pitiful!

2. Each of the first four sorts takes $O(N^2)$ Time, so the run time nearly quadruples when N is doubled.

3. The improved version of InsertionSort is about 40% faster than the original version. This speedup illustrates an important principle: *If you want a dramatic improvement in the run-time efficiency of a program, your best hope is to fine-tune the innermost loop.*

Table 9.1 The time, in seconds, to sort contiguous lists of random integers by each of the sorting methods described above.

	N = 2000	N = 4000
SelectionSort	65.14	260.35
BubbleSort	114.08	457.14
InsertionSort	77.23	307.69
Improved InsertionSort	44.05	175.54
TreeSort	3.57	7.52
MergeSort	2.36	5.11
HeapSort	4.45	9.67
QuickSort	1.54	3.18
QuickSort with CutOff of 10	1.21	2.58
Iterative QuickSort with CutOff of 10	1.27	2.64

4. Each of the last six sorts listed takes $O(N \log N)$ Time, so the run time slightly more than doubles when N is doubled. Exercise 9.9 provides a tighter estimate of the change in run time.

5. QuickSort with a cutoff gives the fastest time. There is virtually no difference between the recursive and iterative versions. Finding the "best" cutoff is the goal of Laboratory Exercise 9.1.

QuickSort is wonderful on average, but what about its worst-case performance? We saw earlier that WorstTime for QuickSort is $O(N^2)$, as opposed to $O(N \log N)$ WorstTime for HeapSort and MergeSort. Table 9.2 translates these estimates into hard figures.

Table 9.2 The worst-case time, in seconds, to sort contiguous lists of integers by each of the sorting methods described above.

	N = 2000	N = 4000
SelectionSort	65.14	260.35
BubbleSort	163.29	653.17
InsertionSort	154.34	617.42
Improved InsertionSort	88.05	352.12
TreeSort	179.44	715.52
MergeSort	2.36	5.16
HeapSort	4.62	10.16
QuickSort	47.84	190.10
QuickSort with CutOff of 10	48.00	190.32
Iterative QuickSort with CutOff of 10	48.28	190.81

By comparing the results in Table 9.2 with those of Table 9.1, we confirm what we learned earlier about WorstTime for the sorting methods:

1. For SelectionSort, the worst-case performance is the same as the average-case (and best-case) performance, because the execution of the subprogram is independent of the arrangement of values.

2. For BubbleSort and the InsertionSorts, the time nearly doubles, from N $(N - 1)/4$ iterations to N $(N - 1)/2$ iterations. BubbleSort is still pitiful.

3. For MergeSort and HeapSort, the worst-case and average-case times are about the same, as we saw in the analyses of their subalgorithms.

4. For TreeSort and QuickSort, the worst-case times are $O(N^2)$, which are much worse than their average-case times. They are like the little girl

    who had a little curl
    Right in the middle of her forehead
    When she was good, she was very, very good
    And when she was bad, she was horrid.

Now that you have all the figures at your disposal, can you decide which is the best sort method? The answer depends on the application and the performance specifications. In a production environment, you might value QuickSort's average speed above all, even if that means a long wait in the worst case (which will happen once in a blue moon).

In some environments, however, such as national defense and life support systems, you may not have the luxury of tolerating a rare long wait ("Okay, so the patient died, but don't blame me or my program. Blame the weird arrangement of data that the program sorted!"). Furthermore, if the performance specifications say that the sort must be completed in fewer than 25 seconds, then you cannot allow worst-case time of more than 25 seconds, no matter how infrequently it occurs. In such cases, HeapSort and MergeSort work well, but both require more space than QuickSort.

Finally, consider this situation: You must have $O(N \log N)$ time, even in the worst case. Space is at a premium, and the list is not static, but will grow and shrink during execution. After each insertion or deletion, the sorted values are to be printed. Don't despair—AVL TreeSort will come to the rescue (See Programming Assignment 9.3).

To summarize, for every situation there is a best sort method, but there is no sort method that is best for every situation.

FILE SORTING

Sorting a file is a fairly common file operation. We now outline how this can be done efficiently. Suppose we want to sort a large file of items. We assume that the maximum array size allowed is $K = 10000$ **div** SizeOf (ItemType), so we cannot simply read the file into an array, QuickSort the array, and then write the array out onto the file. Quicksorting will play a major role on *pieces* of the file, but not on the entire file.

We start by reading in the file of items, in blocks of K items each. Each block is QuickSorted and stored, in an alternating fashion, on one of two temporary files: LeftTop and LeftBottom. Figure 9.3 illustrates the effect of this first stage in file sorting.

We then go through an alternating process that continues until all the items are sorted and in a single file. The temporary files used are LeftTop, LeftBottom, and RightBottom; ItemFile itself plays the role of RightTop. At each stage, we merge a top and bottom pair of files, with the resulting double-sized blocks stored alternately on the other top and bottom pair. Figure 9.4 illustrates the first merge pass.

If RightBottom is still empty after a left-to-right merge, then the sort is complete (and ItemFile holds the sorted numbers). Otherwise, a right-to-left merge is performed, after which we check to see if LeftBottom is still empty (in which case LeftTop is copied onto ItemFile and the sort is complete).

How much time will this take? Suppose that we have N/K blocks of size K. In the QuickSort phase, each of the N/K blocks takes, roughly, $K \log_2 K$ time, on average. In the Merge phase, each pass takes about N iterations, and there are about $\log_2(N/K)$ passes. The total Time is the sum of the Times for both phases, roughly:

$$(N/K) * K \log_2 K + N * \log_2(N/K) = N \log_2 K + N \log_2(N/K)$$
$$= N \log_2 K + N \log_2 N - N \log_2 K = N \log_2 N$$

Because the order of the average time is optimal, namely $O(N \log N)$, a sorting method such as this is often used for a system sort utility or to implement COBOL's SORT verb.

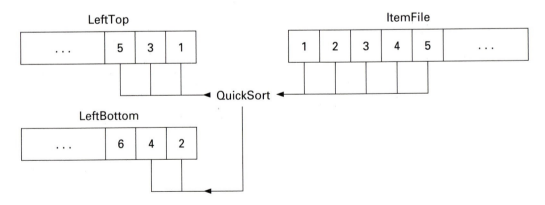

Figure 9.3   The first stage in file sorting: Each of the unsorted blocks in ItemFile is Quicksorted and stored in LeftTop or LeftBottom.

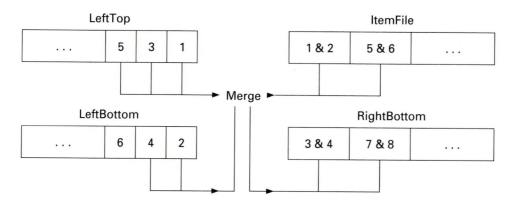

Figure 9.4 The first merge pass in file sorting. LeftTop and LeftBottom contain sorted blocks, and ItemFile and RightBottom contain double-sized sorted blocks.

SUMMARY

In this chapter we introduced a number of sort methods in the Orderable List ADT. The methods fall into two categories: those whose average time is $O(N^2)$, and those whose average time is $O(N \log N)$. SelectionSort, Bubble-Sort, and InsertionSort all take $O(N^2)$ time, on average. TreeSort, Merge-Sort, HeapSort, and QuickSort take only $O(N \log N)$ time, on average. In empirical studies, QuickSort has been the fastest of these in the average case, but its worst-case performance is $O(N^2)$. MergeSort and HeapSort take only $O(N \log N)$ time even in the worst case, so either of these is preferable to QuickSort in applications where $O(N^2)$ time is never acceptable.

With the help of the QuickSort method and a merge subalgorithm, arbitrarily large files can be sorted in $O(N \log N)$ time, on average.

EXERCISES

9.1 Trace the execution of each of the sort methods discussed in this chapter with the following list of values:

10 90 45 82 71 96 82 50 33 43 67

9.2 **a.** For each sort method, rearrange the list of values in Exercise 9.1 so that the minimum number of item comparisons would be required to sort the list.

b. For each sort method, rearrange the list of values in Exercise 9.1 so that the maximum number of item comparisons would be required to sort the list.

9.3 For which three sort methods do the BestTime and WorstTime have the same Big O estimate?

9.4 Throughout this chapter, we discussed only a contiguous design (and implementation) of various sort methods. Describe a situation in which a linked design (and, in particular, a dynamic implementation) would be more appropriate.

9.5 Show how QuickSort's Partition subalgorithm can be used by a subalgorithm to find the median[2] of a list of values in only O(N) Time.

> *HINT   Suppose we want to find the median of A [1..9999]. Of course, if we sort the list, the median would be in A [5000], but sorting would take O(N log N) Time. To get an idea of how to proceed, let's say that the first call to Partition yields a left sublist A [1..3039] and a right sublist A [3040..9999]. Since every item in the left sublist is less than or equal to every item in the right sublist, which sublist* must *contain the median? The other sublist can be ignored from then on, so the list is not completely sorted.*

9.6 Consider the following modification to QuickSort:
Instead of choosing A [(First + Last) **div** 2] as the pivot at the start of partitioning, choose as the pivot the median (see Footnote 2) of A [First], A [(First + Last) **div** 2], and A [Last]. For example, if those three values are:

　　30582 27 17025

then their median, 17025, would be chosen as the pivot.

Give an example of a list of values in which choosing the median would be an improvement over simply choosing A [(First + Last) **div** 2]. What is a drawback to this modification?

---

[2]The *median* of a list of values is the value that would be in the middle position if the list were sorted. For example, the median of:

　　100 32 77 85 95

is 85. If the list contains an even number of values, the median is the average of the two values that would be in the two middle positions if the list were sorted. For example, the median of:

　　100 32 77 85 95 80

is 82.5.

9.7 Complete the QuickSorting of the array given in the discussion on QuickSort in this chapter.

9.8 Develop an algorithm to obtain the worst case for QuickSorting the integers $1..N$.

*HINT   Put 1 in position N **div** 2 and put N in position N **div** 2 + 1.*

9.9 Assume, for simplicity, that MergeSort (or any other fast sort) takes $C * N * \log_2 N$ seconds to sort N random integers, where C is a constant. From the time given for $N = 2000$ in Table 9.1, calculate C. Then estimate how long it will take to MergeSort 10000 items.

9.10 Show that the average number of inner-loop iterations in Improved InsertionSort is:

$$\frac{N(N + 1)}{4} - \frac{N}{2}$$

HINT   First show that for K in [1..N], the average number of inner-loop iterations to insert the Kth item is $(K - 1)/2$.

9.11 Show that $O(\log (N!)) = O(N \log N)$.

HINT   By Stirling's Approximation of N!,

$$N! \approx \sqrt{2\pi N} * (N/e)^N * [1 + 1/12N + O(N^{-2})]$$

9.12 Verify DoQuickSort and the repeat statement in Partition.

9.13 Verify the SplitAndMerge subalgorithm.

9.14 Prove the correctness of the repeat statement in BubbleSort.

9.15 The implementations of the Orderable List ADT in this chapter used six units from previous chapters that implemented ADTs. What were those units?

LABORATORY EXERCISES

9.1 Find the best cutoff for QuickSort on your computer system.

9.2 Use Exercise 9.9 to estimate how long it will take to QuickSort 10000 random integers. Then test your estimate.

9.3 Make the modification to QuickSort suggested in Exercise 9.6. Do you think this will significantly improve QuickSort's run-time performance? Explain why or why not. Perform a run-time analysis on the resulting method. Were you right?

PROGRAMMING ASSIGNMENTS

9.1   Rewrite each of the above sorting subalgorithms for a linked design domain. Then convert each such subalgorithm into Turbo Pascal. Validate and analyze the resulting subprograms.

9.2   Design and implement a file sorting subalgorithm. Test the subprogram on a file of 25,000 random integers.

9.3   (If you implemented the AVL Tree data type in Chapter 8.) Develop an AVL TreeSort sorting method. Determine the average-case and worst-case times for sorting 2000 and 4000 integers.

Search Methods and the Table Data Type

CHAPTER 10

INTRODUCTION

In Chapter 9 we designed and implemented several sort methods. We now present a parallel study of search methods. We have already devoted some effort to search methods for lists, ordered lists, and binary search trees. We will start by summarizing this work as a prelude to the introduction of a new data type, the Table ADT. With an appropriate design, tables provide searches (as well as insertions and deletions) in O(1) Time. This remarkable performance is due to a special technique well suited to tables: hashing.

SEARCH METHODS

The general form of a search method is:

```
   ↑       ↑
   ↓
Search (Item, Found)
```

It is assumed that the calling instance consists of items. If there is an item in the instance that is equal to Item, then Item gets a copy of that item and

Found gets the value True. Otherwise, Item is unchanged and Found gets the value False.

Because the search may be successful or unsuccessful, the analysis of search subalgorithms must include both possibilities. For each search subalgorithm we estimate $Time_s N$, the average time (over all N items in the instance) of a successful search. We assume that each item in the instance is equally likely to be sought.

We also estimate $Time_u N$, the average time of an unsuccessful search. For an unsuccessful search, we assume that, on average, every possible failure is equally likely. For example, in an unsuccessful search of an ordered list of N items, the given item can occur in any one of $N + 1$ possible locations:

Before the first item in the instance;

Between the first and second items;

Between the second and third items;

. . .

Between the $(N - 1)$st and Nth items;

After the Nth item.

In analyzing the average-case performance of a Search subalgorithm for an ordered list, we assume that each of these events is equally likely.

For lists and ordered lists, the search method has a third parameter in addition to Item and Found:

```
Search (Item, Found, Position)
```

After a successful search, Position contains the position in the list of an item (there may be more than one) that equals Item. After an unsuccessful search of an ordered list, Position contains the position where Item belongs in the list.

For all successful searches, Item gets the value of an item in the instance that was found to equal Item. There are many situations where this can be valuable. For example, suppose that the items are employee objects and that two items are equal if they have the same value in the ID field. Such a field is called a **key**: the field (or fields) by which items are uniquely identified. In the instance Employees, to obtain the complete item for the employee whose ID is 24096, we could proceed as follows (if Employees is a list):

```
Employee.ID := 24096
Employees.Search (Employee, Found, Position)
```

If Employees is not a list, the Search message does not include a Position parameter:

```
Employees.Search (Employee, Found)
```

The three kinds of searches we have studied so far are sequential searches, binary searches, and binary search trees.

Sequential Search

In a sequential search, we access the instance's first item, second item, and so on, until either the item sought has been found or we are certain that item is not in the instance. Because the items must be accessed linearly, sequential searches are applied mostly to lists. For an ordered list, an unsuccessful search terminates once we have accessed an item that is Greater-Than the given item. With an unordered list, we must access all N items before we can conclude that the given item is not in the list.

For a successful sequential search of an unordered or ordered list, each item is equally likely to be sought, so the average number of loop iterations (or recursive calls) is approximately $N/2$. Thus, $\text{Time}_S(N)$ is $O(N)$.

For an unsuccessful search of an unordered list, all N items must be accessed, so $\text{Time}_U(N)$ is $O(N)$. For an unsuccessful search of an ordered list, the search stops as soon as an item is accessed that is GreaterThan the given Item. Because about half of the list items will be accessed, on average, $\text{Time}_U(N)$ is also $O(N)$.

Binary Search

The "binary search" technique was developed in conjunction with a contiguous design of the Ordered List ADT in Chapter 5. For the average-case analysis of a binary-search subalgorithm that stops when a match is found, there are N possibilities. If the item at index:

```
(N+1) div 2
```

is the sought item, only one loop iteration (or recursive call) is required. Two iterations are needed for the two items at indexes:

```
    (N+1) div 4 and
3 * (N+1) div 4.
```

Three iterations are needed for the four items at indexes:

```
    (N+1) div 8,
3 * (N+1) div 8,
5 * (N+1) div 8, and
7 * (N+1) div 8.
```

The average number of loop iterations (or recursive calls) in a successful search is approximately

$$\frac{1*1 + 2*2 + 4*3 + 8*4 + 16*5 + \ldots + \dfrac{N+1}{2} \log_2(N+1)}{N}$$

$$= \frac{N+1}{N} \log_2(N+1) - 1.$$

So $\text{Time}_S(N)$ is $O(\log N)$.

For an unsuccessful search, the execution of the loop statement (or recursive subalgorithm) continues until the item is discovered to be unequal to the middle item in a list of size 1. The number of loop iterations (or recursive calls) is, approximately, the number of times that N can be divided by two until $N = 1$, namely, Trunc ($\log_2 N$). We conclude that $Time_U(N)$ is also $O(\log N)$. Note that the average time for an unsuccessful search is about the same as the average time for a successful search.

Binary Search Tree

Binary search trees were introduced in Chapter 8 as specializations of binary trees. The time for a successful or unsuccessful search depends on the shape of the tree.

In the case of a perfectly balanced binary search tree, the analysis is the same as that of a binary search of a contiguous list, with the middle item in the list corresponding to the root item in the tree. But we can construct a perfectly balanced binary search tree of size N only if N is one less than a power of 2 (for example, if N is 31).

In general, for any positive integer N, the best case occurs when the tree is perfectly balanced, except (possibly) at the level farthest from the root. For example, if N is 10, a best-case binary search tree is:

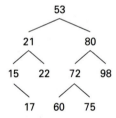

The height is Trunc ($\log_2 N$), so $BestTime_S(N)$ and $BestTime_U(N)$ are both $O(\log N)$.

In the worst case, the binary search tree is a chain and the search is sequential. $WorstTime_S(N)$ and $WorstTime_U(N)$ are both $O(N)$.

The average height of a binary search tree is $O(\log N)$, so $Time_S(N)$ and $Time_U(N)$ are $O(\log N)$.

THE TABLE DATA TYPE

In the preceding section on search methods, we defined the concept of a *key*, the collection of one or more fields by which an item is uniquely identified. The fact that no two distinct items can have the same key makes it possible for us to work with keys rather than entire items. The importance of keys increases as the ratio of item size to key size increases. For example, if the item size is 1000 bytes and the key size is 10 bytes, it is much more efficient to work with the keys rather than the entire items.

A table allows us to take advantage of the efficiency of keys over items. Given a collection of items, a **table** is a function that associates each key with its corresponding item. For example, suppose a student's ID is the key field in a student record that also contains name and GPA fields. We can set up the following table StudentTable, with commas to separate fields:

StudentTable (51597) = Raju Meyappan, 51597, 3.77
StudentTable (35183) = Vikram Bedi, 35183, 3.89
StudentTable (80019) = Colleen Dayton, 80019, 3.91

Here is an equivalent logical representation of that table:

| | StudentTable | |
Name	ID { key }	GPA
Raju Meyappan	51597	3.77
Vikram Bedi	35183	3.89
Colleen Dayton	80019	3.91

A table is a function—specifically, a set of ordered pairs of the form ⟨key, item⟩. Because a set is unordered, a table has no implicit ordering. For example, the following logical representation of the table is equivalent to those given earlier:

| | StudentTable | |
Name	ID { key }	GPA
Colleen Dayton	80019	3.91
Raju Meyappan	51597	3.77
Vikram Bedi	35183	3.89

Of course, if the keys are ordered, we can think of the table as being ordered according to the keys; but this ordering is in our minds, not in the table. Similarly, we can think of a table as an array, but a table is a logical construct, whereas an array is a design or implementation construct. At this point, we are better off if we abstract the *what* from the *how*.

Now that we have seen what a table is (and isn't), we turn our thoughts to what a table can and cannot do—that is, to the responsibilities of the Table ADT.

Responsibilities of the Table Data Type

What should the Table ADT provide to its users? Perhaps we should first mention what it doesn't provide: the association of an item with a position in the table. A table does not have a first item, next item, last item, root item, child, or parent. A user cannot retrieve an item based on the item's position in the table, or start a traversal at a given position.

Those prohibitions aside, the Table ADT allows a user to perform the usual operations:

To make an empty table;

To see if a table is empty;

To determine the size of the table;

To make a distinct copy of the table;

To traverse the table (although the order in which the items are accessed may appear to be random);

To search the table for an item;

To insert an item in the table;

To delete an item from the table.

These responsibilities are easily refined into methods, so we are ready to define the Table ADT.

Definition of the Table Data Type

In the Table ADT, the logical domain is the collection of all tables, so each instance is simply a table. We assume that a user of the Table ADT will supply:

An Item data type, with a KeyOf method that returns the item's key.

MaxTableSize (the maximum number of items allowed in the table).

Two key-related functions:

a. KeyNumber (Key), which returns a nonnegative integer corresponding to the key. We will soon see how we might represent a non-integer key with an integer. By using the KeyNumber function, the designer of the Table ADT need not worry about whether the keys themselves are numbers, strings, or even records.

b. EqualKeys (Key1, Key2), which returns True or False depending on whether Key1 and Key2 are equal.

As many Visit subalgorithms as desired, for use in traversals of the table.

There are eight methods in the table ADT:

1. `Initialize.`

   Postcondition: The table is empty.

   Note: An implicit precondition of every other method is that the calling instance is not undefined (that is, the calling instance has already called Initialize or has been the actual parameter in a call to CopyTo).

2. `IsEmpty.`

   Postcondition: True has been returned if the table is empty. Otherwise, False has been returned.

3. `Size.`

   Postcondition: The number of items in the table has been returned.

4. `Search (Item, Found).`

   Postcondition: If there is an item in the table with the same key as Item, that item has been copied into Item, and Found has the value True. Otherwise, Item is unchanged and Found has the value False.

5. `Insert (Item).`

   Precondition: The number of items in the table is less than MaxTable-Size. There is no item in the table with the same key as Item.

   Postcondition: Item has been inserted into the table; that is, the pair <Item.KeyOf, Item> has been added to the number of ordered pairs in the function.

6. `Delete (Item).`

   Precondition: There is an item in the table with the same key as Item.

   Postcondition: The item with the same key as Item has been deleted from the table.

7. `CopyTo (NewTable).`

   Postcondition: NewTable has a distinct copy of the table.

8. Traverse (Visit).

Postcondition: The table has been traversed; the action taken with
each item accessed during the traversal is given by the user-
supplied subalgorithm Visit.

*Note: A table, unlike a list or a binary tree, does not have an
implicit order, so Traverse does not specify which item will be
accessed first, second, and so on. Through the keys, the items
themselves may be ordered (either as scalars or by the item
methods LessThan, EqualTo, and GreaterThan). With the proper
user-supplied Visit subalgorithm, the items can be sorted and
then printed in order. See Exercise 10.3.*

Designs of the Table Data Type

In trying to design the Table ADT, you might ask, "Since a table is a function, why not use a function for the design?" Such a function would have to
be completely defined beforehand; there would be no facility for inserting
or deleting items into or from the table. In function parlance, there would
be no way to insert ordered pairs into or to delete them from the set of ordered pairs that defines the function.

Another possibility is to bring back a linked, multi-linked, or contiguous
design from a previous chapter. However, if the items are unordered, we
will need sequential searches, and these take O(N) Time. Even if the items
are ordered and we utilize that ordering, the best we can get is O(log N)
Time for searches. At this point, there is no reason to believe that an improvement is possible.

The rest of this chapter is devoted to showing how, through the miracle
of hashing, we can achieve table searches (and insertions and deletions) in
virtually O(1) Time. Once we have defined what hashing is and how it
works, the designs of the table methods will be relatively easy.

HASHING

As often happens in designing an ADT, the crucial decision in the design of
the Table ADT involves the design domain (the fields in the table object).
The first design domain we will study has two fields:

A: array [0..TableSize − 1]. Each component will be a record with an
item field and an IsOccupied field; the value of IsOccupied will be True
or False depending on whether one of the table's items is currently stored
in that component. For now, we let TableSize be MaxTableSize, so that
there can be, at most, MaxTableSize items in the array.

N: the number of items in the table.

We have the IsOccupied field in each component of *A* because, at any time, every component in an array contains something. When the table is initialized, each IsOccupied field is set to False. Later, when an actual item is stored at a component, the IsOccupied field at that component is set to True.

Let's start with a simple example and then get to something more realistic. Suppose that MaxTableSize is 1000 and each item consists of a Name field and a three-digit key field that holds an ID. After initialization, we have the table shown in Fig. 10.1.

At what index should we store the item with key 251? An obvious choice is index 251. The advantages are several:

1. The item can be directly posted to the array without accessing any other items.

2. Subsequent searches for the item require accessing only location 251.

3. The item can be deleted directly, without first accessing other items.

Figure 10.2 shows what the table might look like after three items, with keys 251, 118, and 335, have been inserted.

So far, this is no big deal. Now suppose that MaxTableSize is still 1000, but each item has a name field and a Social Security–Number field (the key field). To allow fast access, we can take the rightmost 3 digits of a social security number and store the item at the location whose index is that three-digit number. For example, the item with a key value of 214-30-3261 (the hyphens are shown for readability only) would be stored at location 261. Similarly, the item with a key value of 033-51-8000 would be stored at location 0. Figure 10.3 shows the resulting table, called a ***hash table,*** after these two insertions.

Figure 10.1

The design representation of an empty table.

	Name	ID	Is Occupied	N
0	?	?	False	0
1	?	?	False	
2	?	?	False	
⋮				
999	?	?	False	

Figure 10.2

The table of Fig. 10.1
after three items
have been inserted.

A

	Name	ID	Is Occupied		N
0	?	?	False		3
1	?	?	False		
2	?	?	False		
⋮					
118	Chu, Sung-chi	118	True		
⋮					
251	Schwar, James	251	True		
⋮					
335	Long, Douglas	335	True		
⋮					
999	?	?	False		

You might already have noticed a potential pitfall with this scheme: Two distinct keys might have the same rightmost three digits (for example, 214-30-3261 and 814-02-9261). Such colliding keys are called **synonyms.** We will deal with collisions shortly. For now we simply acknowledge that the possibility of collisions always exists when the size of the key space (the number of legal key values) is larger than the size of the address space (the number of locations available).

Hashing is the process of transforming a key into an address. The transformation involves some quickly computable operation on the key, together with a collision handler. Collision handling will be investigated in the next section; for now, we focus on the computable operation. For an integer key, the operation can be:

```
Key mod TableSize
```

that is, the remainder when the key is divided by the size of the table. In a table with a maximum size of 1000, the **mod** operation yields the rightmost three digits.

The rightmost three digits in Social Security numbers are distributed fairly evenly among the population. The probability that an individual num-

Figure 10.3

A hash table with two items. The key field in each item is the Social Security number.

A

	Name	ID	Is Occupied		N
0	Clemens, Roger	033-51-8000	True		2
1	?	?	False		
2	?	?	False		
⋮					
261	Chu, Sung-chi	214-30-3261	True		
⋮					
999	?	?	False		

ber chosen at random will have, say, 251 as the rightmost three digits is about one in 1000.

What if we had chosen for the index the leftmost three digits in the Social Security number? The leftmost three digits are based on the area of the country in which the individual registered for a Social Security card. If most of the people in the application are from the same area of the country, we could have a lot of collisions. As we will see later, hashing works best when the transformation minimizes the number of collisions.

The rightmost digits in a number do not always provide a good index either. For example, suppose that an application for a certain factory in a corporation uses the rightmost four digits of a key as the index into a 10000-item array. If the rightmost four digits contain the factory number, then *every* key will initially hash to the same index!

Another way to obtain an initial address from an integer key is to use the key as the seed for a call to a random-number generator. For example, if each key is a four-digit integer, we can set:

```
RandSeed := Key
Address  := Random (TableSize)
```

Address will get a (pseudo-) random value between 0 and TableSize − 1—just the range we want. As long as the function Random can be calculated quickly, this kind of initial hash works well.

Noninteger Keys?

A user of the Table ADT is required to supply a KeyNumber function that returns a nonnegative integer corresponding to an item's key. How can this be done if, for example, the keys themselves are strings? To obtain an integer in this case, the user can add up the ordinal values of the key's characters. For an extra degree of scattering, the partial totals are multiplied by three. The function KeyNumber returns the final total, called a ***hash total***.

For example, the hash total for "Top" is obtained as follows:

KeyCharacter	Ord (KeyCharacter)	HashTotal
		0
T	84	84 (= 0 * 3 + 84)
o	111	363 (= 84 * 3 + 111)
p	112	1201 (= 363 * 3 + 112)

Thus, the user function KeyNumber would have the following subalgorithm:

```
KeyNumber (Key)

HashTotal := 0
for I := 1 to Length (Key) do
    HashTotal := HashTotal * 3 + Ord (Key [I]) * 3
Return the value of HashTotal
```

Notice that if the Key were "Rup" the function KeyNumber would return the same value, 1201. So two different keys can have the same key number.

The term "hashing" suggests that we scramble up the key in some way; in other words, that we "make hash" out of the key. No matter how successfully we hash the keys, collisions may still occur, so we must deal with them as part of our hashing algorithm. We will investigate two kinds of collision handlers: open addressing and chaining.

Open Addressing

Open addressing is a collision handler that works as follows: When a collision occurs, the table is searched according to some strategy until an open address is found; the item is then stored at this address.

Perhaps the simplest collision handler is this: Keep adding 1 to the address until an available slot is found. Here is a preliminary version of the subalgorithm, which is used for searching and deleting as well as inserting

```
Hash (Key)

Address := KeyNumber (Key) mod TableSize
Probes  := 0
Done    := False
while (Probes < TableSize) and (not Done) do
    if not A [Address].IsOccupied then
        Done := True
```

```
        else
            if EqualKeys (Key, A [Address].Item.KeyOf) then
                Done := True
            else
                Address := (Address + 1) mod TableSize
                Add 1 to Probes
Return the value of Address
```

A *probe* is a table access (hence the identifier Probes). The reason that we keep track of the number of probes is that otherwise there would be an infinite loop if Hash were called as part of an unsuccessful search for an item in a full table. As the subalgorithm is designed, the loop would eventually terminate, but the address returned would be occupied by another item. The Search method can easily handle this situation.

Let's illustrate the effect of calling Hash with our earlier example of posting up to 1000 items with Social Security numbers as keys. Suppose the keys of the items to be posted are:

```
214-30-3261
033-51-8000
214-19-9528
819-02-9261
033-30-8262
215-09-1766
214-17-0261
```

The first three calls to Hash will return the addresses 261, 000, and 528, respectively, and those items will be posted at those locations. When 819-02-9261 is hashed, the address returned is 262 (A [261] is occupied by a different item), so the item with key 819-02-9261 is posted at A [262]. When 033-30-8262 is hashed, the address returned is 263, and the item is posted at that location. The last two items are posted at locations with indexes 766 and 264, respectively. The resulting table is shown in Fig. 10.4. The values in the name fields are irrelevant, so we omit them for simplicity.

Suppose we now delete the item whose key is 214-30-3261; the IsOccupied field at address 261 would be set to False. But what if we then search for the item whose key is 819-02-9261? Since its initial hash address, 261, is unoccupied, we would incorrectly conclude that there is no item in the table whose key is 819-02-9261.

To overcome this flaw, we will add another Boolean field, WasDeleted, to each component in the array A. Initially, each WasDeleted field gets the value False. This value is set to False during an insertion, and set to True during a deletion. Figure 10.5 shows the effect of deleting, from the table in Figure 10.4, the item whose key is 214-30-3261. A subsequent hash of 819-02-9261 would correctly return the address 262, so a search for the item with the key of 819-02-9261 would be successful.

Figure 10.4

A table generated by
hashing, with
modular arithmetic
and open addressing
(offset of 1).

		Name	A	ID	Is Occupied		N
0				033-51-8000	True		7
1				?	False		
2				?	False		
:							
261				214-30-3261	True		
262				819-02-9261	True		
263				033-30-8262	True		
264				214-17-0261	True		
:							
528				214-19-9528	True		
:							
766				215-09-1766	True		
:							
999				?	False		

Here is the corrected version of the Hash subalgorithm:

```
Hash (Key).

KeyNum       := KeyNumber (Key)
Address      := KeyNum mod TableSize
Probes       := 0
Done         := False
SpaceFound   := False
while (Probes < TableSize) and (not Done) do

   { Loop Assertion: For any k in 0..Probes - 1, if        }
   {                    A [Address + k] is occupied, then its }
   {                    item's key <> Key.  Otherwise, the item}
   {                    at that location had been deleted.    }
   if A [Address].IsOccupied
         and EqualKeys (Key, A [Address].Item.KeyOf) then
      Done := True
   else
      if not (A [Address].IsOccupied)
            and not (A [Address].WasDeleted) then
         Done := True;
         if SpaceFound then
            Address := SaveAddress
```

	Name	A	ID	Is Occupied	Was Deleted		N
0			033-51-8000	True	False		6
1			?	False	False		
2			?	False	False		
...							
261			214-30-3261	False	True		
262			819-02-9261	True	False		
263			033-30-8262	True	False		
264			214-17-0261	True	False		
...							
528			214-19-9528	True	False		
...							
766			215-09-1766	True	False		
...							
999			?	False	False		

Figure 10.5 The table from Figure 10.4, with a WasDeleted field in each component of A, after deleting the item whose key is 214-30-3261.

```
        else
            if not A [Address].IsOccupied
                    and A [Address].WasDeleted then
                SpaceFound   := True
                SaveAddress := Address
            Address := (Address + 1) mod TableSize
            Inc (Probes)
        if not Done and SpaceFound then
            Hash := SaveAddress
        else
            Hash := Address
```

Clustering

A good hashing algorithm should minimize the occurrence of collisions, but it cannot eliminate them if the key space is larger than the address space. Our hashing algorithm appeared to cause clustering at location 261 only because the given keys were rigged for that purpose to illustrate open addressing with an offset of 1. The rightmost three digits of a company's list of social security numbers will probably be uniformly distributed between 0 and 999.

As we noted earlier, if we had instead chosen the leftmost three digits for the initial hash address, we most likely would have had a lot of clustering (in our example, starting at index 214). This phenomenon is known as ***primary clustering***—the condition of having an excessive number of keys hashing to the same initial address.

However, the function Hash we are using does create ***secondary clustering***—the buildup of table entries along the path traced by synonyms from different collisions. For example, if we start with Fig. 10.4, a new key that hashes to 261, 262, 263, or 264 must travel to 265 to find an empty location. Any hashing method that entails secondary clustering is inefficient because it leads to sequential searches.

In the example shown in Fig. 10.4, could we have avoided secondary clustering if we had used an offset of 2? No, because the path for collisions at 261 would be 261, 263, 265, ...; the path for collisions at 263 would be 263, 265, ..., and so on. Clearly, any constant offset would still produce secondary clustering. In fact, some large constants would create an additional problem. For example, since 200 is a factor of 1000, an offset of 200 would make the path for synonyms have a maximum length of 5 (such as 261, 461, 661, 861, 61). Thus, if five synonyms had already been posted in the table, any additional synonyms would have no place to go.

Quotient Offsets

Secondary clustering can be overcome by using the quotient offset in open addressing. For a given key, the initial address is still the remainder when the key number is divided by the table size; the offset is the (integer) quotient of the key number and the table size. Since the quotient is independent of the remainder, two key numbers with the same remainder will most likely have different quotients and different offsets.

The function Hash is only slightly changed from before:

```
Hash (Key).

KeyNum       := KeyNumber (Key)
Address      := KeyNum mod TableSize
Offset       := KeyNum div TableSize
Probes       := 0
Done         := False
SpaceFound := False
if Offset mod TableSize = 0 then
   Offset := 1
while (Probes < TableSize) and (not Done) do

   { Loop Assertion: For any k in 0..Probes - 1, if      }
   {                     A [Address + k] is occupied, then its }
   {                     item's key <> Key.  Otherwise, the item}
   {                     at that location had been deleted.    }
```

```
if A [Address].IsOccupied
      and EqualKeys (Key, A [Address].Item.KeyOf) then
   Done := True
else
   if not (A [Address].IsOccupied)
         and not (A [Address].WasDeleted) then
      Done := True;
      if SpaceFound then
         Address := SaveAddress
   else
      if not A [Address].IsOccupied
            and A [Address].WasDeleted then
         SpaceFound  := True
         SaveAddress := Address
      Address := (Address + Offset) mod TableSize
      Inc (Probes)
if not Done and SpaceFound then
   Hash := SaveAddress
else
   Hash := Address
```

To avoid the possibility of infinite loops, Offset is set to 1 if the offset is a multiple of the table size. For example, if Key has a value of 157-00-0425, then:

```
KeyNum mod TableSize = 425    { the rightmost three digits }
KeyNum div TableSize = 157000 { the leftmost six digits }
```

If we used 157000 (instead of 1) as Offset and the location at index 425 were occupied by an item with a different key, the calculation

```
Address := (Address + Offset) mod TableSize
```

would give Address the value

```
(425 + 157000) mod 1000 = 157425 mod 1000 = 425
```

In other words, Address would be unchanged!

To illustrate the effect of open addressing with the quotient offset, suppose we want to post items with the following keys into an empty table (for later reference, the initial addresses and offsets are also shown):

Key	Initial Address	Offset
214-30-3261	261	214303
191-24-4261	261	191244
530-56-4261	261	530564

The first item is posted at index 261. For the second key, the While loop in Hash is executed twice. At the end of the first iteration, Address is given the value:

```
(Address + Offset) mod TableSize = (261 + 191244) mod 1000
                                 = 191505 mod 1000
                                 = 505
```

As a result, the item with a key of 191-24-4261 would be posted at index 505. For the third key, at the end of the first iteration of the While loop, Address is given the value:

```
(Address + Offset) mod TableSize = (261 + 530564) mod 1000
                                 = 530825 mod 1000
                                 = 825
```

The third item would then be posted at index 825.

With the quotient-offset collision handler, secondary clustering is avoided, since synonyms from different collisions (and even from the same collision) would not follow the same path. Whether primary clustering is minimized (it cannot be completely avoided) depends on the calculation of the initial address—specifically, on how well the initial addresses are scattered across the address space.

Choosing the Table Size

With quotient offsets, we saw that a problem arose when the offset was a multiple of the table size. We can also have trouble if the offset and table size have common factors. For a simple example, suppose that TableSize is 10 and each key is a two-digit integer. If the first two items have keys of 23 and 98, those items will be posted at indexes 3 and 8, respectively. If the next item has a key of 53, the function Hash will assign:

```
Address := KeyNum mod TableSize,  that is, 53 mod 10, which is 3
Offset  := KeyNum div TableSize,  that is, 53 div 10, which is 5
```

Since there is another item, 23, at index 3, a new value for Address is calculated:

```
Address := (Address + Offset) mod TableSize
         = (3 + 5) mod 10
         = 8 mod 10
         = 8
```

However, there is another item, 98, at index 8, so a new value for Address is calculated:

```
Address := (Address + Offset) mod TableSize
         = (8 + 5) mod 10
         = 13 mod 10
         = 3
```

However, this address has already been tried. The only addresses probed would be 3 and 8.

This problem can be avoided by making sure that the table size and the offset have no common factors (other than 1, of course). The easiest way to accomplish this for all offsets is to make the table size a prime number. A positive integer $p > 1$ is a ***prime number*** if p has no positive-integer factors other than 1 and p. For example, the first few prime numbers are 2, 3, 5, 7, 11, 13, 17, and 19.

By making the table size a prime number, we ensure that the table size and offset will have no common factors. The case where the offset is a multiple of the table size is taken care of in the Hash function. It can then be shown (see Exercise 10.6) that for any key number, the addresses calculated will cover the entire table if the While loop is executed TableSize times.

The rest of the correctness proof of the While statement is left as an exercise. The all-important analysis of the function Hash is postponed until later in this chapter.

Designing the Table Data Type with Open-Address Hashing

Now that we have settled on a design domain and chosen the Hash function, the designs of the table methods proceed smoothly:

1. `Initialize.`

```
for I := 0 to TableSize - 1 do
    A [I].IsOccupied := False
    A [I].WasDeleted := False
N := 0
```

↑

2. `IsEmpty.`

```
Return the value of (N = 0)
```

↑

3. `Size.`

```
Return the value of N
```

↓   ↑

4. `Search (Item, Found).`

```
ItemKey  := Item.KeyOf
Address  := Hash (ItemKey)
TableKey := A [Address].Item.KeyOf
if A [Address].IsOccupied then
        and EqualKeys (ItemKey, TableKey) then
    Item  := TableItem
    Found := True
else
    Found := False
```

Note: If the table is full and the search is unsuccessful, Found will get the value False, as expected.

5. Insert (Item).

```
Address                 := Hash (Item.KeyOf)
A [Address].Item        := Item
A [Address].IsOccupied  := True
A [Address].WasDeleted  := False
Add 1 to N
```

6. Delete (Item).

```
Address                 := Hash (Item.KeyOf)
A [Address].IsOccupied  := False
A [Address].WasDeleted  := True
Subtract 1 from N
```

7. CopyTo (NewTable).

```
NewTable.Initialize
for I := 0 to TableSize - 1 do
   if A [I].IsOccupied then
      NewTable.A [I] := A [I]
   else
      if A [I].WasDeleted then
         NewTable.A [I].WasDeleted := True
NewTable.N := N
```

8. Traverse (Visit).

```
for I := 0 to TableSize - 1 do
  if A [I].IsOccupied then
    Visit (A [I].Item)
```

An interesting feature of the CopyTo and Traverse designs is that the number of loop iterations depends not on N, but on TableSize. Amazingly, the number of loop iterations in the function Hash does not depend on N directly, but only on the ratio of N to TableSize. We establish this fact in the next section.

Analysis of Open-Address Hashing

We now estimate the average times for successful and unsuccessful searches in open-address hashing. We assume that both primary and secondary clustering are avoided and that, for any given item, each probe accesses an address not accessed in earlier probes for that item. In developing the formulas below, we represent TableSize by M. The functions Time_S and Time_U will both have N and M as arguments.

We will use the number of probes to estimate $\text{Time}_S(N, M)$ and $\text{Time}_U(N, M)$. The number of probes needed for an unsuccessful search of an item with $k \geq 0$ items already in the table is exactly the same as the number of probes needed to post the $(k + 1)$st item, and that is also the number of probes needed for a successful search of that $(k + 1)$st item. For any k such that $0 \leq k < M$, let $E(k, M)$ represent the expected number of probes needed to post the $(k + 1)$st item. Clearly,

$$E(0, M) = 1 \text{ for any } M \geq 1.$$

For any $k > 0$, $E(k, M) = 1$ if the $(k + 1)$st item initially hashes to an open address, and the probability of this is $(M - k)/M$. Otherwise, with probability k/M, the $(k + 1)$st item will initially hash to an occupied address, so the number of probes required is one plus the number of probes required in the rest of the table. However, the number of probes needed in the rest of the table is exactly the number of probes needed to post the kth item in a table of size $M - 1$ (namely, $E(k - 1, M - 1)$).

Writing this last paragraph as an equation, we get:

$$E(\text{k}, M) = \frac{M - k}{M} * 1 + \frac{k}{M}(1 + E(k - 1, M - 1)),$$

where $1 \leq k < M$.

This equation is called a "recurrence relation" because when we combine it with the initial condition (namely, $E(0, M) = 1$ for all $M \geq 1$), we get a recursive definition for the function E. Simplifying the recurrence relation, we get:

$$E(k, M) = 1 + \frac{k}{M} E(k - 1, M - 1), \quad \text{where } 1 \leq k < M.$$

In Appendix 1, we develop a closed form for this equation; that is, the calculation of the result requires neither loops (such as summations) nor recursive calls. The solution is:

$$E(k, M) = \frac{M + 1}{M + 1 - K}, \text{ for all } M \text{ and } k \text{ such that } 0 \leq k < M.$$

This conjecture can be proved by induction (on either k or M).

For a table of size M with N items, we define the **load factor** L to be $N/(M + 1)$. L is, approximately, the proportion of the table that has been filled in. Then,

$$\text{Time}_U(N, M) \approx E(N, M) = \frac{M + 1}{M + 1 - N} = \frac{1}{1 - N/(M + 1)} = \frac{1}{1 - L}$$

$Time_S(N, M)$ is, approximately, the average number of probes needed to post each of the N items into the table; that is,

$$Time_S(N, M) \approx \frac{E(0, M) + E(1, M) + \ldots + E(N - 1, M)}{N}$$

$$= \frac{1}{N}\left(\frac{M + 1}{M + 1} + \frac{M + 1}{M} + \frac{M + 1}{M - 1} + \ldots + \frac{M + 1}{M - N + 2}\right)$$

$$= \frac{M + 1}{N}\left(\frac{1}{M + 1} + \frac{1}{M} + \frac{1}{M - 1} + \ldots + \frac{1}{M - N + 2}\right)$$

As shown in Appendix 1, this last parenthesized expression is approximately equal to $\ln(M + 1) - \ln(M - N + 1)$. Thus,

$$Time_S(N, M) \approx \frac{M + 1}{N}[\ln(M + 1) - \ln(M - N + 1)]$$

$$= \frac{M + 1}{N}\ln\left(\frac{M + 1}{M - N + 1}\right)$$

$$= \frac{1}{L}\ln\left(\frac{1}{1 - L}\right).$$

We have shown, for open-address hashing,

$$Time_S(N, M) \approx \frac{1}{L}\ln\left(\frac{1}{1 - L}\right)$$

$$Time_U(N, M) \approx \frac{1}{1 - L}$$

The significance of these estimates is that the time for successful and unsuccessful searches depends only on the load factor. For example, if the load factor is $\frac{1}{2}$,

$$Time_S(N, M) \approx \frac{1}{L}\ln\left(\frac{1}{1 - L}\right) = 2\ln 2 \approx 1.39 \text{ statements.}$$

$$Time_U(N, M) \approx \frac{1}{1 - L} = 2 \text{ statements.}$$

These values hold for $N = 1000$ and $M = 1999$, as well as for $N = 5000$ and $M = 9999$. Since the time for successful and unsuccessful searches does not depend directly on N (only on the ratio of N to $M + 1$), we say loosely that open-address hashing is an O(1) search technique.

Chaining

Open addressing, with a quotient offset and prime table size, will resolve collisions. Another way to resolve collisions is to store in each location the list of all the items whose keys hash to that address. The design domain for chained hashing is:

> A: array [0..TableSize - 1] of ListType;
> N: 0..TableSize

Theoretically, the design of ListType could be contiguous, but the space requirements for each list would then be substantial. In practice, ListType is invariably linked, so the items in each list form a chain. That is where the name "chaining" comes from. As a user of the List ADT, the developer of the Table ADT cannot specify how the list should be designed or implemented, but the developer can choose the implementation of the List ADT that uses the (spacious) heap.

To see how chained hashing works, consider the problem of storing up to 1000 records with Social Security numbers as keys. The hash function will be Key **mod** 1000; with chaining, we need not assume that the table size is prime. Initially, each location would contain an empty list. For purposes of illustration, we will assume a linked design of ListType. Figure 10.6 shows what we would have after posting items with the following keys;

        214-30-3261
        033-51-8000
        214-19-9528
        819-02-9528
        819-02-9261
        033-30-8262
        215-09-1766
        214-17-0261

For chained hashing, the function Hash simply returns the address to which the key hashes. For example, if we use modular arithmetic as the basis for hashing, we would have:

```
Hash (Key)
Return the value of KeyNumber (Key) mod TableSize
```

The design of some of the table methods would also be simplified, but only because the real work is shunted off to the design of the List ADT. For example, the design of the Search method calls the Search method from the List ADT:

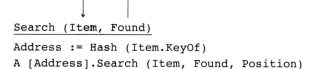

```
Search (Item, Found)
Address := Hash (Item.KeyOf)
A [Address].Search (Item, Found, Position)
```

Chaining is also useful for direct accessing of disk files. The list of items stored at a given file position is called a ***bucket.*** When a key hashes to a file position, the entire bucket is brought into main memory with only one cylinder access. Keeping cylinder accesses to a minimum is a primary goal of file processing because each cylinder access requires movement of the electro-mechanical arm on the disk.

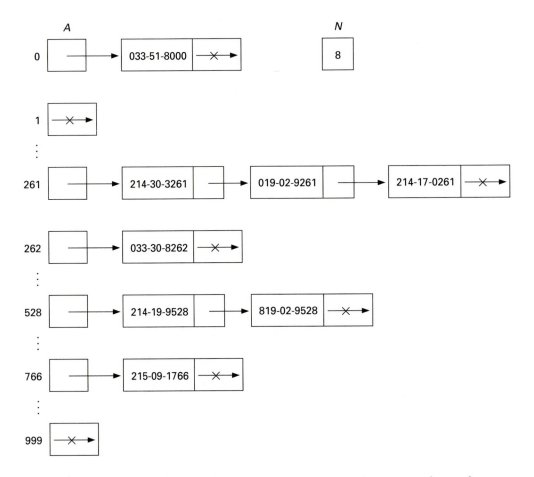

Figure 10.6   **A chained hash table to which eight items have been posted. Non-key fields are not shown.**

There are several advantages to chaining over open addressing. First, collisions are easily (but sequentially) handled. Secondary clustering has been avoided, since each address has its own linked list (whether or not primary clustering is avoided depends on the hash function). A third advantage of chaining over open addressing is that we can post more than TableSize items into the table.

Which hashing technique uses more space, open addressing or chaining? With open addressing, we must allocate enough space for the maximum number of items to be posted. With chaining (assuming linked lists), extra space must be allocated with each item for the address of the next item. Therefore, either technique may require more space than the other, depending on the size of the items to be posted and the actual number of items posted.

Suppose, for example, that each item takes up 20 words of computer memory, and the maximum number of items to be posted is 1000. Open addressing would require 20,000 words to be allocated; if only 500 items are actually posted, the wasted space will be 10,000 words. Chaining would initially allocate only 2000 words (assuming each address requires two words). If 500 items were posted, the words of memory used would be 2000 + 500 * 22 = 13,000. In this case, chaining would consume 35 percent less space than open addressing. On the other hand, if the item size is small and the actual number of items posted is close to the maximum, open address-ing can use as little as one-third of the space required for chaining.

Finally, there are some situations where chaining is inherently inappro-priate. For example, the first phase of a compiler, the *lexical analyzer*, groups the characters in a program into tokens. As we saw in Chapter 6, each token has a generic part (with the token's class) and a specific part. For identifiers, the specific part is an address in a table, called a *symbol table*, that contains information about the identifier, such as its type, size, initial value, and starting location in memory.

The tokens themselves, rather than the identifiers, are used in subse-quent phases of the compiler, so chaining is not feasible. Why? If each table contained a *list* of identifier records, there would be no way to determine, from a token such as:

```
[identifier, 283]
```

which identifier record at address 283 was being referred to.

Analysis of Chained Hashing

The analysis of chained hashing is far simpler than that of open-address hashing. We assume that primary clustering is avoided (we noted earlier that secondary clustering is automatically avoided with chained hashing). Just as in the analysis of open-address hashing, we let M = Tablesize and $L = N/(M + 1)$. Since primary clustering is avoided, the N items will be uni-formly distributed over M lists. A successful search will examine a list in which there will be the item sought, plus (on average) an additional $(N - 1)/M$ items. A successful sequential search of a list requires, on aver-age, (Size (List) + 1)/2 iterations (or recursive calls). Since Size (List) = $1 + (N - 1)/M$, we have:

$$\text{Time}_s(N, M) \approx \frac{\left(1 + \dfrac{N - 1}{M} + 1\right)}{2}$$

$$= 1 + \frac{1}{2}\left(\frac{N - 1}{M}\right)$$

$$\approx 1 + \frac{1}{2}(L) \text{ statements}$$

For an unsuccessful search with chained hashing, an entire list must be searched. Since each list contains, on average, N/M items,

$$\text{Time}_U(N, M) \approx N/M \approx L \text{ statements}$$

This is slightly less than the time for an average successful search, since an unsuccessful search of an empty list requires no loop iterations (or recursive calls).

Figure 10.7 summarizes the search-time estimates for open-address hashing as well as chained hashing. By "time," we mean the number of loop iterations. In each approximation, the time depends only on the load factor, not on the number of items already posted.

Finally, Fig. 10.8 estimates the times for successful and unsuccessful searches with various load factors.

Implementations of the Table Data Type

From Fig. 10.8, it is clear that chaining requires fewer loop iterations, on average, than open addressing. But the connection between loop iterations and run time is tenuous. To find out which technique is faster, we need to implement both designs. This was done straightforwardly.

For all implementations, the user is notified that "The KeyOf function is assumed to return an integer of up to nine digits, with the values of KeyOf (Item) **mod** MaxTableSize uniformly distributed over $0 .. \text{MaxTableSize} - 1$."

All three implementations (open addressing with offset of 1, open addressing with quotient offsets, and chaining) were validated with the help of a driver program similar to those used in earlier chapters.

To test the three implementations for successful searches, the following experiment was conducted: N different random integers, where $N = 1000$ or 2000, were inserted into a table of size 2003 and into positions 1 through N of a temporary array, Temp. We then randomly generated 1000 integers R in $1..N$. For each value of R, we calculated the time for a successful

Figure 10.7

A summary of the time estimates for successful and unsuccessful searches for both open-address hashing and chained hashing. $N =$ number of items posted; $M =$ table size; L, the load factor, $= N/(M + 1)$.

Open addressing:

$$\text{Time}_S(N, M) \approx \frac{1}{L} \ln\left(\frac{1}{1 - L}\right)$$

$$\text{Time}_U(N, M) \approx \frac{1}{1 - L}$$

Chaining:

$$\text{Time}_S(N, M) \approx 1 + \frac{1}{2}L$$

$$\text{Time}_U(N, M) \approx L$$

Figure 10.8

Search-time
(= number of loop
iterations) estimates
for various load
factors.

Load Factor	0.25	0.5	0.75	0.9	0.99
Open Addressing:					
Successful	1.15	1.39	1.85	2.56	4.65
Unsuccessful	1.33	2.00	4.00	10.00	100.00
Chaining:					
Successful	1.13	1.25	1.38	1.45	1.50
Unsuccessful	0.25	0.50	0.75	0.90	0.99

search of Temp $[R]$ in the table. The results of the experiment are shown in Table 10.1.

Table 10.1 tends to confirm our earlier impressions about the three collision handlers:

1. The offset-of-1 collision handler performs fairly well if the load factor is much less than 1.0 and poorly if the load factor is close to 1.0.

2. The quotient-offset collision handler performs fairly well if the load factor is much less than 1.0 and fairly well if the load factor is close to 1.0.

3. Chaining performs well for any load factor.

At this point, you might conclude that hashing makes the Table ADT superior to the other data types we have studied. Certainly the ability to make N retrievals, insertions, or deletions in $O(N)$ time is impressive. But suppose, for example, that after each insertion or deletion we want to print out all of the items in the instance in order. We cannot simply call:

```
Traverse (WriteOut)
```

because the traversal is not necessarily in order.

We could use a binary sort tree, as follows:

```
Tree.Initialize
Traverse (Tree.Insert)
Tree.TraverseInOrder (WriteOut)
```

but then *each* call to the second statement in this sequence would take $O(N \log N)$ Time. A better alternative is simply to use a binary sort tree

Table 10.1 *The time, in seconds, for 1000 successful searches of a table of size 2003 into which N items were posted by hashing.*

N	Offset of 1	Quotient Offset	Chaining
1000	1.16	2.03	0.99
2000	5.93	4.18	0.99

instead of a table. It will then take O(N log N) time to make N retrievals, insertions, or deletions, but the time to print out the items in order will be only O(N).

SUMMARY

A ***table*** is a function that associates a key with an item that contains that key. There is no notion of *position* in a table, so the Table ADT differs from the data types introduced in previous chapters in that there is no Retrieve method.

In considering how to design the Table ADT, we introduced ***hashing***, the process of transforming a key into a table address. A hashing algorithm must include the calculation of an initial address, together with a collision handler to deal with the possibility that two keys might hash to the same address. ***Primary clustering*** is the phenomenon that occurs if the initial transformation does not scatter the keys throughout the table.

Two widely used collision handlers are *open addressing* and *chaining*. With ***open addressing***, the table is represented as an array in which each component has an Item field and an IsOccupied field. The table is searched according to some strategy until an open address is found or it is discovered that the table is full.

A simple open-addressing strategy is to add an offset of 1 to the current address, but this leads to ***secondary clustering:*** the buildup of table entries along the path traced by synonyms from different collisions. Secondary clustering is avoided with the ***quotient-offset*** strategy, whereby:

```
InitialAddress := Key mod TableSize
Offset         := Key div TableSize
```

With ***chaining,*** the table is represented as an array of lists. Each list contains the items that hashed to that index in the array. Chaining automatically avoids secondary clustering.

For a table of N items, the ***load factor,*** L, is defined to be

$$\frac{N}{(\text{TableSize} + 1)}$$

The load factor is an approximation of what proportion of the table has been filled in. With both open addressing and chaining, if primary and secondary clustering are avoided, the time for successful and unsuccessful searches depends only on L. The same is true for insertions and deletions.

EXERCISES

10.1 a. Use the "Key **mod** TableSize" hash function with the offset-of-1 collision handler to post the following items into a table with indexes in 0..10:

23, 83, 56, 17

Note: 23 **mod** *11 = 1; 23* **div** *11 = 2*
        83 **mod** *11 = 6; 83* **div** *11 = 7*
        56 **mod** *11 = 1; 56* **div** *11 = 5*
        17 **mod** *11 = 6; 17* **div** *11 = 1*

b. Use the "Key **mod** TableSize" hash function with the Quotient Offset collision handler to post the items from part a into a table with indexes in 0..10.

c. Use the "Key **mod** TableSize" hash function with chaining to post the items from part a into a table with indexes in 0..10.

10.2 a. With the quotient-offset collision handler, hash the following strings into a table of size 101:

Top

A3

Roster

HINT See the discussion of hash totals.

b. How many probes would you expect to make in posting the 50th entry to that table? In posting the 100th entry?

10.3 As a *user* of the Table data type, develop a Sort subalgorithm.

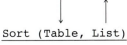

Sort (Table, List)

Postcondition: List is an ordered list that contains all of the items in Table.

HINT As a user, you cannot assume any design domain information (such as an array A), and there is no Retrieve method in the Table data type.

10.4 For each of the following subalgorithms, find the smallest functions g and h in the order hierarchy such that Time is $O(g)$ and Worst-Time is $O(h)$. The functions g and h may be the same for some subalgorithms.

a. Making a successful call (that is, the item was found) to the Search method in the linked design of the Ordered List data type.

    b. Making a successful call to the Search method in the contiguous design of the Ordered List data type.

    c. Making a successful call to the Search method in the multi-linked design of the Binary Search Tree data type.

    d. Making a successful call to the Search method in the quotient-offset design of Table data type (assume that primary and secondary clustering have been avoided and that N is less than the table size).

    e. Making a successful call to the Search method in the chained-hashing design Table data type (assume that primary clustering has been avoided and that N is less than the table size).

10.5 In each of the following situations, decide whether open addressing or chaining would be preferable:

    a. The number of items to be posted may exceed MaxTableSize.

    b. Space is important, the item size is large, and the actual number of items to be posted will be much less than MaxTableSize.

    c. Space is important, the item size is small, and the actual number of items to be posted will be only slightly less than MaxTableSize.

    d. Time is important, and the actual number of items to be posted will be only slightly less than MaxTableSize.

10.6 (This exercise assumes familiarity with modular algebra.) For the quotient-offset collision handler, assume that the table size is a prime number, p. Show that, for any values for Address and Offset, the following set has exactly p distinct elements:

$$\{ \ (\text{Address} + k*\text{Offset}) \ \textbf{mod} \ p; \ k = 0, 1, \ldots, p - 1 \}$$

10.7 Prove the correctness of the While statement in the function Hash for Quotient offsets.

LABORATORY EXERCISE

Rerun the experiment shown in Table 10.1 for different load factors and different table sizes.

The Graph Data Type

CHAPTER 11

INTRODUCTION

There are many situations in which we want to study the relationships between entities. For example, in a curriculum, the entities are courses, and the relationship is based on prerequisites. In airline travel, the entities are cities; two cities are related if there is a flight between them. It is visually appealing to describe such situations graphically, with points (called *vertices*) representing the entities, and lines (called *edges*) representing the relationships.

In this chapter we will define, design, and implement the abstract data type Graph. As always, our first task is to define what a graph is (to determine the values in the data type). We will spend some time on graph terminology (and there is quite a bit of it) before we get back on track by describing the responsibilities of the Graph ADT. These responsibilities are easily refined into methods. We then develop method subalgorithms corresponding to the design domains; the implementations are straightforward. The remainder of the chapter is devoted to special kinds of graphs—directed graphs, trees, and networks.

A **graph** consists of a collection of distinct items called **vertices** and a collection of vertex pairs called **edges**; in each edge the two vertices must be different. Here is an example of a graph:

Vertices: A, B, C, D, E
Edges: $\{A,B\}, \{A,C\}, \{B,D\}, \{C,D\}, \{C,E\}$

Figure 11.1

A visual
representation of a
graph.

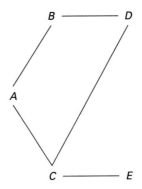

We use set notation for the edges to indicate that the vertex pairs in an
edge are unordered. For example, to say there is an edge from *A* to *B* is the
same as saying there is an edge from *B* to *A*. Figure 11.1 depicts this graph,
with each edge represented as a line connecting its vertex pair.

From the illustration in Fig. 11.1, we could obtain the original mathematical formulation of the graph as a collection of vertices and edges. Furthermore, Fig. 11.1 gives us a better grasp of the graph than the original
formulation. From now on, then, we will often use illustrations such as
Fig. 11.1 instead of the mathematical formulations.

Figure 11.2 contains several additional graphs. Notice that the number
of edges can be fewer than the number of vertices (Fig. 11.2a), equal to
the number of vertices (Fig. 11.2b), or greater than the number of vertices
(Fig. 11.2c).

Two vertices are **adjacent** if they form an edge. For example, in
Fig. 11.2(b), Charlotte and Atlanta are adjacent, but Atlanta and Raleigh are
not adjacent. Adjacent vertices are called **neighbors**.

A **path** is a list of vertices in which each successive pair is an edge. For
example, in Fig. 11.2(c),

A, B, E, H

Figure 11.2(a)

A graph with six
vertices and five
edges.

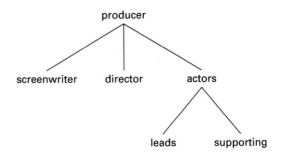

Figure 11.2(b)

A graph with eight vertices and eight edges.

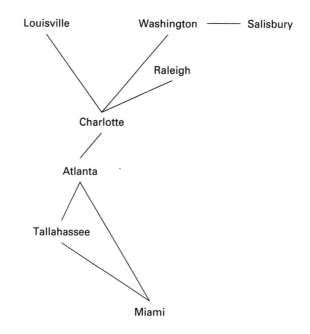

Figure 11.2(c)

A graph with eight vertices and eleven edges.

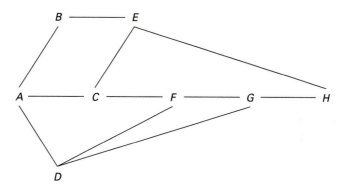

is a path from A to H because $\{A, B\}$, $\{B, E\}$ and $\{E, H\}$ are edges. Another path from A to H is:

> A, C, F, D, G, H

Let $V_1, V_2, \ldots, V_k$ be a path of k vertices, where $k > 1$. The vertices $V_2, V_3, \ldots, V_{k-1}$ are called **interior** vertices in the path. For example, in the path,

> A, C, F, D, G, H

$C, F, D,$ and G are interior vertices. For a path of k vertices, the **length** of the path is $k - 1$. In other words, the path length is the number of edges in the path. For example, in Fig. 11.2(c) the following path from *C* to *A* has a length of 3:

    C, F, D, A

There is, in fact, a shorter path from *C* to *A*, namely:

    C, A

In general, there may be no single shortest path between two vertices. For example, in Fig. 11.2(c),

    A, B, E

and

    A, C, E

are both shortest paths from *A* to *E*.

    A ***cycle*** is a path in which the first and last vertices are the same and there are no repeated edges. For example, in Fig. 11.2(b),

        Atlanta, Tallahassee, Miami, Atlanta

is a cycle. In Fig. 11.2c,

    B, E, C, A, B

is a cycle, as is:

    E, C, A, B, E

The graph in Fig. 11.2(a) is ***acyclic***; that is, it does not contain any cycles. In that graph,

        producer, director, producer

is *not* a cycle, since the edge {producer, director} is repeated—recall that an edge is an unordered pair.

    A graph *S* is ***subgraph*** of a graph *G* if every vertex in *S* is also a vertex in *G* and every edge in *S* is also an edge in *G*. For example, here is a subgraph of the graph in Fig. 11.2(c):

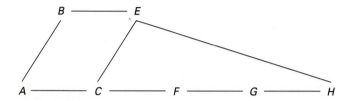

Every graph is a subgraph of itself.

    A graph is ***connected*** if there is a path between any two distinct vertices in the graph. Informally, a graph is connected if it is "all one piece."

For example, all of the graphs in Fig. 11.2 are connected. The following graph, with six vertices and five edges, is not connected:

A graph ***traversal*** is an algorithm that accesses each vertex in the graph exactly once. Graphs have less structure than either lists or binary trees, so graph traversals are not as well organized as list and binary tree traversals. For example, list traversals always start at the first (or last) item, and binary-tree traversals always start at the root. However, a graph does not have a distinct vertex, so a graph traversal can start at any vertex. Furthermore, with lists and binary trees, we always know which item to visit next, whereas if we want to visit a vertex's neighbors in a graph traversal, there is no forced choice as to which neighbor to visit first.

Later in this chapter we will study two widely used traversals: breadth-first traversal and depth-first traversal.

RESPONSIBILITIES OF THE GRAPH DATA TYPE

Now that we have defined the term *graph* and some of its associated terms, we can use these terms to help us determine the responsibilities of the Graph ADT to its users. As usual, we will frame the data type's responsibilities in terms of users' rights, since they are equivalent.

In view of what we have seen with other ADTs, a few of the users' rights are obvious:

To make the graph empty;

To see if the graph is empty;

To copy the graph to another graph.

What about the size of a graph? Since a graph consists of vertices and edges, we want both:

To determine the number of vertices;

To determine the number of edges.

Similarly, several of the other typical responsibilities will have a vertex version and an edge version:

To search for a vertex;

To search for an edge;

> To insert a vertex;
>
> To insert an edge;
>
> To delete a vertex (and its associated edges);
>
> To delete an edge.

For a given vertex, we also want:

> To find all of its neighbors;
>
> To find a shortest path to another vertex (if there *is* a path).

With ordered lists and binary search trees, we were not allowed to replace an item with another item, because this operation could destroy the ordering. Therefore, we could replace items only by deleting the old item and then inserting the new item. This strategy also worked for non-ordered data types, such as lists, stacks, and queues. For a graph, that approach would be very time-consuming because, when a vertex is deleted, all of the edges with that vertex must also be deleted. Therefore, we will want to be able:

> To replace a vertex with another vertex.

The remaining responsibilities apply to the graph as a whole:

> To traverse the graph;
>
> To determine if the graph is connected.

DEFINITION OF THE GRAPH DATA TYPE

The responsibilities of the preceding section are easily refined into method interfaces, so we can now define the Graph ADT.

We assume that a user of the Graph data type will supply MaxVertices and the data type VertexType, in which there is an operator that tests for equality of vertices. We need to be able to compare vertices for equality, because two vertices may be deemed equal even if they are not identical. For example, if each vertex's value consists of Employee ID and Salary fields, we can define EqualTo according to the Employee ID field only.

In the Graph ADT, the logical domain is simply the collection of all graphs. In other words, each value in the data type is a graph.

There are sixteen methods in the Graph ADT. The method interfaces are as follows:

1. `Initialize.`

   Postcondition: The graph is empty.

   Note: An implicit precondition of every other method is that the calling instance already has a value. An instance can get a value by being the calling instance in a call to Initialize or by being the actual parameter in a call to CopyTo.

↑

2. `IsEmpty.`

Postcondition: True is returned if the graph is empty. Otherwise, False is returned.

↑

3. `CopyTo (NewGraph).`

Postcondition: NewGraph contains a distinct copy of the graph; that is, subsequent modifications to the graph will not affect New-Graph, and vice versa.

↑

4. `NumberOfVertices.`

Postcondition: The number of vertices in the graph has been returned.

↑

5. `NumberOfEdges.`

Postcondition: The number of edges in the graph has been returned.

↕   ↑

6. `SearchForVertex (Vertex, Found).`

Postcondition: If the graph contains a vertex that is EqualTo Vertex, Found has the value True and Vertex contains a copy of that vertex in the graph. Otherwise, Found has the value False and Vertex is unchanged.

7. `SearchForEdge (Vertex1, Vertex2, Found).`

Postcondition: If there is a pair of vertices V_1, V_2 in the graph such that:

V_1 is EqualTo Vertex1;
V_2 is EqualTo Vertex2;
$\{V_1, V_2\}$ is an edge;

then Found has the value True and Vertex1 and Vertex2 contain copies of V_1 and V_2, respectively. Otherwise, Found has the value False, and Vertex1 and Vertex2 are unchanged.

Example: Suppose each vertex consists of a name, address, and Social Security number, with equality defined by Social Security numbers, and an edge between two vertices means the two people are related. We can call SearchForEdge even if all we have are two Social Security numbers. If the two people are related, we also get their names and addresses.

8. **`InsertVertex (Vertex).`**

Precondition: The number of vertices in the graph is less than MaxVertices; there is no vertex in the graph that is EqualTo Vertex.

Postcondition: The graph includes a copy of Vertex.

9. **`InsertEdge (Vertex1, Vertex2).`**

Precondition: The graph contains a pair of vertices V_1 and V_2 such that

V_1 is EqualTo Vertex1;
V_2 is EqualTo Vertex2;
$\{V_1, V_2\}$ is *not* an edge.

Postcondition: $\{V_1, V_2\}$ is an edge (V_1 and V_2 were described in the precondition).

10. **`DeleteVertex (Vertex).`**

Precondition: The graph contains a vertex V_1 that is EqualTo Vertex.

Postcondition: V_1 and all of the edges containing V_1 have been deleted from the graph.

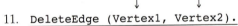

11. **`DeleteEdge (Vertex1, Vertex2).`**

Precondition: The graph contains a pair of vertices V_1 and V_2 such that

V_1 is EqualTo Vertex1;
V_2 is EqualTo Vertex2;
$\{V_1, V_2\}$ is an edge.

Postcondition: $\{V_1, V_2\}$ is not an edge in the graph.

12. **`FindNeighbors (Vertex, NeighborList).`**

Precondition: There is a vertex V in the graph that is EqualTo Vertex.

Postcondition: NeighborList contains the list of all neighbors of V.

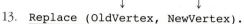

13. `Replace (OldVertex, NewVertex).`

   Precondition: OldVertex is EqualTo NewVertex; there is a vertex *V* in the graph such that *V* is EqualTo OldVertex.

   Postcondition: Each occurrence of *V* in the graph (including *V*'s occurrence in edges) has been replaced by a copy of NewVertex.

   Note: The precondition precludes the possibility that the graph might contain duplicate items after a call to Replace.

14. `Traverse (Visit).`

   Postcondition: A traversal of the graph has been performed. The action performed when each vertex was accessed is given by the subalgorithm Visit.

15. `IsConnected.`

   Postcondition: True has been returned if the graph is connected; otherwise, False has been returned.

16. `FindShortestPath (Vertex1, Vertex2, PathList).`

   Precondition: There are vertices V_1 and V_2 in the graph such that:

   V_1 is EqualTo Vertex1;
   V_2 is EqualTo Vertex2;
   V_1 is not EqualTo V_2.

   Postcondition: PathList contains a shortest path from V_1 to V_2. If there is no path from V_1 to V_2, PathList is empty (recall that a *path* is a list of vertices).

DESIGNS OF THE GRAPH DATA TYPE

When we develop a design for a data type, the crucial decision usually involves the design domain (the fields in the object). The Graph ADT is no exception. The fields we choose to represent the vertices and edges will strongly influence the design of the method subalgorithms.

Let's start with the vertices. We can store the vertices in a list, VertexList, whose maximum size is MaxVertices. Since we would be *using* the List ADT, we would not care at this point whether the list is linked or contiguous. All the list activity is handled through the appropriate list messages.

An ordered list or binary search tree is not a feasible option because, in general, the vertices will not be ordered. A hash table would allow O(1) time for associating a vertex with a table address. This advantage is especially appealing if the number of vertices is large. As we saw in Chapter 10, the efficiency of hashing is proportional to the wasted space. Therefore, whether a hash table is a good idea or not will depend, at least partly, on how much extra space we can afford. This, in turn, will depend on how the edges are represented.

What about the edges? We certainly do not want to represent each edge as a pair of vertices. For one thing, that might take up a lot of space—each vertex might contain a large number of fields. Also, having duplicate copies of each vertex would complicate the design of the Replace method: an occurrence of OldVertex in any edge would have to be replaced with NewVertex.

Since a vertex list or a vertex table associates a position with each vertex, an edge can be conveniently represented by a pair of positions. For example, suppose we assign vertex positions to vertices as shown in Fig. 11.3: Then the edge between Karen and Joan can be represented by positions 3 and 5.

Exactly how will we represent all the edges? Our main concern is to quickly determine, for a given pair of vertices, whether they are adjacent (that is, whether they form an edge). This consideration leads us to a construct called an *adjacency matrix*. An **adjacency matrix** is a two-dimensional, Boolean array in which each row and column subscript represents a vertex position; a True entry means that the corresponding vertices are adjacent, a False entry means they are not. For example, Fig. 11.4 shows an adjacency matrix for the graph in Fig. 11.3. We assume that MaxVertices is 7.

Figure 11.3

A graph and associated vertex positions.

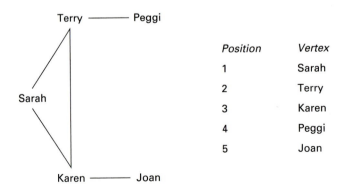

Position	Vertex
1	Sarah
2	Terry
3	Karen
4	Peggi
5	Joan

Figure 11.4

An adjacency matrix for the graph and vertex list in Fig. 11.3. **T** (boldfaced for visibility) stands for True and F for False.

	1	2	3	4	5	6	7
1	F	**T**	**T**	F	F	F	F
2	**T**	F	**T**	**T**	F	F	F
3	**T**	**T**	F	F	**T**	F	F
4	F	**T**	F	F	F	F	F
5	F	F	**T**	F	F	F	F
6	F	F	F	F	F	F	F
7	F	F	F	F	F	F	F

Because edges are unordered pairs, adjacency matrices are **symmetric**: the entry at row I and column J will always be the same as the entry at row J and column I. For example, in Fig. 11.4, the entry at row 2 and column 4 is the same as the entry at row 4 and column 2.

The beauty of an adjacency matrix is that, given two vertex positions, we can determine in O(1) time whether the corresponding vertices are adjacent. The storage requirements, however, are considerable. If MaxVertices is 200 (and some graphs are much larger), the adjacency matrix would consume 40,000 locations!

Another way to store edge information is with an **adjacency list**—an array in which each component is a list of positions. Specifically, assume that some vertex V is at position i in VertexList or VertexTable (a hash table). In AdjacencyList, the component at index i is the ordered list of all positions (from VertexList or VertexTable) of vertices that are adjacent to V. For example, Fig. 11.5 shows an adjacency list for the graph and vertex list in Fig. 11.3. We assume that MaxVertices is 7.

Let N be the number of vertices and E the number of edges. At most, E can be $O(N^2)$ (see Exercise 11.3). In that case the space required for an adjacency list will be about the same as the space for an adjacency matrix. But if E is of a smaller order, an adjacency list will take up less space than an adjacency matrix. This assumes that the component lists in the adjacency list are linked rather than contiguous. In a linked design, space is allocated according to the list size, whereas a contiguous design requires the maximum number of locations, MaxVertices.

What are the time implications of adjacency matrices versus adjacency lists? Recall that linked lists require $O(N)$ Time for insertions, deletions,

Figure 11.5

The adjacency list for the graph and vertex list in Fig. 11.3.

Index	AdjacencyList
1	2, 3
2	1, 3, 4
3	1, 2, 5
4	2
5	3
6	(empty)
7	(empty)

searches, and retrievals. Thus, an adjacency list fares poorly compared with the $O(1)$ time for accessing or modifying an entry in an adjacency matrix. In fairness to adjacency lists, we note that accessing *all* neighbors of a given vertex always takes $N - 1$ iterations in an adjacency matrix, but may take fewer iterations in an adjacency list. In fact, no iterations are needed if a list is empty, nor are any needed to make a list empty.

What we have is a classic time-space tradeoff. If the number of vertices is reasonably small (say, fewer than 100), the performance of an adjacency matrix makes it the compelling favorite. If the number of vertices is large, an adjacency list may be the only choice because the adjacency matrix may not fit in memory.

It might seem at this point that we have a welter of choices for storing vertex and edge information, but we can now simplify our decisions. For both adjacency matrices and adjacency lists, we work with vertex *positions* rather than with the vertices. This has a significant bearing on how the vertices themselves are stored.

For example, consider the FindNeighbors method. Using either an adjacency matrix or an adjacency list, we can easily obtain the list of neighboring-vertex positions, but we then need to retrieve the vertices corresponding to those positions. If the vertices were stored in a hash table, there would be no way (short of a traversal) to retrieve vertices from the table. Why? Because the ADT Table lacks a Retrieve method; the table addresses are for internal use only.

Therefore, the vertices should be stored in a vertex list. We indicated earlier that we didn't care whether the list was contiguous or linked, but this new emphasis on retrievals mandates that we choose the design with the better retrieval time. The contiguous design of the ADT List took only $O(1)$ time for retrievals, compared with $O(N)$ time for the linked design.

To summarize, the vertices will be stored in a (contiguous[1]) vertex list. The edge information can be stored in either an adjacency matrix or adjacency list; the former is time-efficient, the latter space-efficient. We now present a design of the Graph ADT based on a design domain of a vertex list and adjacency matrix. Later we will look at a design of the Graph ADT in which the design domain is a vertex list and an adjacency list.

A Design Based on a Vertex List and an Adjacency Matrix

In the following design of the Graph ADT, the vertices will be stored in a vertex list and the edge information in an adjacency matrix. VertexList will

---

[1] Technically, since we are mere users of the List ADT, we would be violating the Principle of Data Abstraction to specify whether the list is linked or contiguous. What we can and should specify is "the design in which Retrieve, Size, and inserting at the end of the list take $O(1)$ Time." This feature, not contiguity, is what we are interested in.

contain items of type VertexType (supplied by the user of the Graph ADT). AdjacencyMatrix will be a two-dimensional Boolean array with MaxVertices (supplied by the user) rows and MaxVertices columns. For any row i and column j, AdjacencyMatrix $[i, j]$ is True or False depending on whether or not the vertices in positions i and j of VertexList are adjacent.

The designs for the method subalgorithms are as follows:

1. `Initialize.`

    We must initialize VertexList. We need not initialize AdjacencyMatrix: Entries there are irrelevant until vertices have been inserted into the graph. The subalgorithm is:

    `Initialize.`

    `VertexList.Initialize`

    This subalgorithm requires only O(1) Time and Space.

2. `IsEmpty.`

    `Return the value of VertexList.IsEmpty`

3. `CopyTo (NewGraph).`

    We need to copy both VertexList and AdjacencyMatrix:

    ```
    VertexList.CopyTo (NewGraph.VertexList)
    N: = VertexList.Size
    for I := 1 to N do
      for J := 1 to N do
         NewGraph.AdjacencyMatrix[I,J] := AdjacencyMatrix[I,J]
    ```

    For copying a list, Time is $O(N)$. The assignment of AdjacencyMatrix takes $O(N^2)$ time. $O(N) + O(N^2) = O(N^2)$; thus, for the entire subalgorithm, Time is $O(N^2)$. Space is $O(1)$, since the space for NewGraph was allocated in the calling algorithm.

4. `NumberOfVertices.`

    `Return the value of VertexList.Size`

    Time and space are $O(1)$. Recall that we chose the design of the List ADT that took $O(1)$ time for the Size method.

5. `NumberOfEdges.`

    For each edge, there is a pair of indices I and J such that Adjacency-Matrix $[I, J]$ contains True. Since AdjacencyMatrix is symmetric, we need search only about half of the array (specifically, the entries below the diagonal where the columns and rows have equal value). We need not include that diagonal because an edge cannot go from a vertex to itself.

The subalgorithm is:

NumberOfEdges
TrueCount := 0
N := VertexList.Size
for I := 1 to N
    for J := 1 to I - 1 do
        if AdjacencyMatrix [I,J] then
            Add 1 to TrueCount

Time is $O(N^2)$ and Space is $O(1)$.

> *Note: If we had included in the design domain a variable to hold the number of edges, this subalgorithm could be replaced with a one-liner. However, the subalgorithms for InsertEdge, DeleteEdge, and DeleteVertex would then be responsible for maintaining the current value for the number of edges. It would be appropriate to have such a variable only if the developer of the Graph ADT decided that the NumberOfEdges method would be called frequently.*

6. SearchForVertex (Vertex, Found).

    VertexList.Search (Vertex, Found, Position)

Time is $O(N)$ and Space is $O(1)$. These orders were derived in Chapter 4.

7. SearchForEdge (Vertex1, Vertex2, Found).

We first search VertexList for vertices EqualTo Vertex1 and Vertex2. If both are found, we check to see if the corresponding entry in AdjacencyMatrix is True. The only precaution in the subalgorithm is that we must use temporary variables for Vertex1 and Vertex2, so that neither Vertex1 nor Vertex2 will be changed if they are EqualTo vertices in VertexList but do not form an edge.

The subalgorithm is:

SearchForEdge (Vertex1, Vertex2, Found)

```
V1 := Vertex1
V2 := Vertex2
VertexList.Search (V1, Found1, Pos1)
VertexList.Search (V2, Found2, Pos2)
if Found1 and Found2 and (AdjacencyMatrix [Pos1, Pos2]
then
    Found := True
    Vertex1 := V1
    Vertex2 := V2
else
    Found := False
```

Time is $O(N)$, due to the searching of VertexList. Space is $O(1)$.

8. <u>InsertVertex (Vertex).</u>

After adding Vertex to the end of VertexList, we initialize the appropriate row and column in AdjacencyMatrix to False. The subalgorithm is:

InsertVertex (Vertex)

```
N := VertexList.Size
VertexList.Insert (Vertex, N + 1)

{ Initialize row and column N + 1 of matrix to False: }
for K := 1 to N + 1 do
    AdjacencyMatrix [N + 1, K] := False
    AdjacencyMatrix [K, N + 1] := False
```

Time is $O(N)$ and Space is $O(1)$.

9. <u>InsertEdge (Vertex1, Vertex2).</u>

```
VertexList.Search (Vertex1, Found, Pos1)
VertexList.Search (Vertex2, Found, Pos2)
AdjacencyMatrix [Pos1, Pos2] := True
AdjacencyMatrix [Pos2, Pos1] := True
```

Time is $O(N)$, due to the search of VertexList. Space is $O(1)$.

10. <u>DeleteVertex (Vertex).</u>

Removing Vertex from VertexList is easy. We must also adjust all of the entries in AdjacencyMatrix at higher positions. For example, if we delete the vertex at position 4 in VertexList, then references to positions

5, 6, 7, and so on in AdjacencyMatrix should become references to positions 4, 5, 6, and so on.

The subalgorithm is:

DeleteVertex (Vertex)

```
with VertexList do
   ListSize := Size
   Search (Vertex, Found, Position)
   Delete (Position)

{ Delete row Position in AdjacencyMatrix: }
for I := Position + 1 to ListSize do
   for J := 1 to ListSize do
      AdjacencyMatrix [I-1, J] := AdjacencyMatrix [I, J]

{ Delete column Position in AdjacencyMatrix: }
for J := Position + 1 to ListSize do
   for I := 1 to ListSize do
      AdjacencyMatrix [I, J-1] := AdjacencyMatrix [I, J]
```

Time is $O(N^2)$ and Space is $O(1)$.

11. DeleteEdge (Vertex1, Vertex2).
```
VertexList.Search (Vertex1, Found, Pos1)
VertexList.Search (Vertex2, Found, Pos2)
AdjacencyMatrix [Pos1, Pos2] := False
AdjacencyMatrix [Pos2, Pos1] := False
```

Time is $O(N)$ and Space is $O(1)$.

12. FindNeighbors (Vertex, NeighborList).
```
NeighborList.Initialize
VertexList.Search (Vertex, Found, Position)
for J := 1 to VertexList.Size do
   if AdjacencyMatrix [Position, J] then
      VertexList.Retrieve (Neighbor, J)
      NeighborList.Insert (Neighbor, NeighborList.Size+1)
```

Time is $O(N)$ and Space is $O(1)$.

13. **Replace (OldVertex, NewVertex).**

with VertexList do
   Search (OldVertex, Found, Position)
   Delete (Position)
   Insert (NewVertex, Position)

Time is $O(N)$ and Space is $O(1)$.

14. **Traverse (Visit).**

A simple traversal subalgorithm is easy to come by:

for I := 1 to VertexList.Size do
   VertexList.Retrieve (Vertex, I)
   Visit (Vertex)

For this subalgorithm, Time is $O(N)$ and Space is $O(1)$.

Two other strategies, breadth-first traversal and depth-first traversal, are more widely used. These are especially important for specializations of graphs (i.e., trees and networks); also, a modification of the breadth-first traversal subalgorithm allows us to find the shortest path between two vertices in a graph. It is worth our while, then, to investigate these two traversals.

Breadth-First Traversal

A ***breadth-first traversal*** of a graph is similar to a breadth-first traversal of a binary tree: After visiting a vertex, we visit all vertices adjacent to that vertex, then all vertices adjacent to those vertices, and so on. A queue holds neighbors that have not yet been visited. A binary tree traversal always starts at the root, whereas a graph can start at any vertex. Furthermore, from a given vertex, we can visit any of its neighbors; we need not follow a left-right regimen, as we did for binary trees.

Another complication with traversing a graph is that we must avoid visiting the same vertex more than once. For example, suppose we have the following graph:

V———— W

If we start the traversal by visiting vertex V, we then visit the vertex adjacent to V, namely W; but we must make sure that we do not visit V again later, even though V is adjacent to W.

To avoid the trap of revisited vertices, we use a Boolean array Enqueued with MaxVertices components. We initialize each entry to False and then set an entry to True when the position is enqueued (prior to being visited).

Figure 11.6

A breadth-first
traversal of a graph.

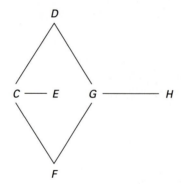

Vertices Visited in a
Breadth-First Traversal:

C, D, E, F, G, H

Figure 11.6 shows a graph and the vertices traversed in a breadth-first traversal of that graph according to the positions in VertexList. We assume that the vertices are assigned to VertexList alphabetically, so that vertex C is in position 1, vertex D in position 2, and so on.

Because the graph might not be connected, we must loop through all vertices to make sure each vertex is visited. Other than that, the subalgorithm is similar to the BreadthFirstTraversal subalgorithm for binary trees in Chapter 7. The complete subalgorithm is as follows:

```
Traverse (Visit)                        { Breadth-First }
VisitQueue.Initialize
N := VertexList.Size

{ Establish that no vertices have been visited: }
for I := 1 to N do
   Enqueued [I] := False

{ Visit each unvisited vertex: }
for I := 1 to N do
   if not Enqueued [I] then
      with VisitQueue do
         InsertTail (I)
         Enqueued [I] := True
         repeat

            { Delete head of queue and visit that vertex: }
            RetrieveHead (J)
            DeleteHead
            VertexList.Retrieve (Vertex, J)
            Visit (Vertex)

            { Enqueue each unenqueued neighbor of J: }
            for K := 1 to N do
```

```
            if AdjacencyMatrix [J, K] and not Enqueued [K]
            then
                InsertTail (K)
                Enqueued [K] := True
        until IsEmpty
```

Most of the subalgorithms in the rest of this chapter are based on breadth-first traversals, so it will be well worth your while to spend a few extra minutes studying this subalgorithm.

Example. Figure 11.7 shows a graph, the position of each vertex in VertexList, and the contents of VisitQueue at the start of each iteration of the repeat loop. During the breadth-first traversal subalgorithm described above, the vertices would be visited in almost-alphabetical order: *A, B, C, D, E, G, F. G* is visited before *F* because *G* is a neighbor of *B*, so *G* gets enqueued before *F*, which is a neighbor of *D*.

The postcondition of the outer (For) loop statement is simply:

The *I*th vertex has been visited.

Figure 11.7

The contents of VisitQueue during the execution of the breadth-first traversal of the given graph.

VisitQueue (at the start of each iteration of the repeat loop)

1

2, 3, 4

3, 4, 5, 7

4, 5, 7

5, 7, 6

7, 6

6

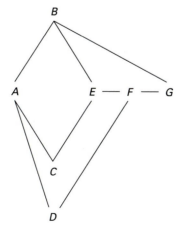

Vertex	Position
A	1
B	2
C	3
D	4
E	5
F	6
G	7

This follows immediately from the postcondition of the repeat statement:

> The Ith vertex and all vertices connected to it (by a path) have been visited.

This postcondition, in turn, follows from the easily established loop post-invariant:

> The position that had been at the head of the queue has been deleted from the queue; the corresponding vertex has been visited and its unenqueued neighbors' positions enqueued.

Since one vertex is visited during each iteration of the repeat loop, the total number of iterations is N. During each iteration there are N iterations of the inner For loop, so Time is $O(N^2)$.

The space requirements for Enqueued are only $O(1)$, since that array's size is the constant MaxVertices. What about VisitQueue? If the design domain for the Queue ADT is contiguous, then VisitQueue's size is the same as that of Enqueued, namely $O(1)$; but if the design domain is linked, then the space required for VisitQueue depends on the shape of the graph. For example, if the graph is linear:

A———————B———————C———————D   . . .

then VisitQueue's maximum size is 1. At the other extreme, vertex 1 could have $N - 1$ neighbors, so the space required would be $O(N)$.

Depth-First Traversal

A **depth-first traversal** of a graph is similar to a preorder traversal of a binary tree. First, to refresh your memory, Fig. 11.8 shows a binary tree and the order in which items would be visited in a preorder traversal.

A preorder traversal of a binary tree always starts with a leftward path from the root. Once the end of a path is reached, the algorithm *backtracks*

Figure 11.8

A binary tree and the order in which items would be visited during a preorder traversal.

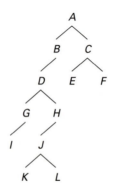

The order of visiting items in a preorder traversal:

A B D G I H J K L C E F

to an item that has an unvisited right child. Another leftward path is begun, starting with that right child.

A depth-first traversal of a graph proceeds similarly. After visiting a given vertex, we visit each unvisited vertex in a path that starts at the given vertex. We then back up to the most recently visited vertex that has an unvisited adjacent vertex. Another path is begun, starting with that unvisited vertex.

With a breadth-first traversal, we saved vertex positions in a queue so that the vertices were visited in the order in which they were saved. With a depth-first traversal, the next vertex to be visited is an unvisited neighbor of the *most recently visited* vertex, so the vertex positions will be *stacked* instead of queued.

Figure 11.9 shows a graph and the order in which vertices are visited in a depth-first traversal. We assume that the vertices are stored alphabetically in VertexList.

The following subalgorithm for a depth-first traversal is similar to the breadth-first version given earlier. There are two main differences. The Boolean array is Visited (instead of Stacked) because a vertex position is visited only once but is kept on the stack until all of its neighbors have been visited. Instead of stacking all unvisited neighbors of a vertex, we stack only the first one found.

Here is the subalgorithm:

```
                        ↓


Traverse (Visit)                    { Depth-First }
VisitStack.Initialize
N := VertexList.Size

{ Establish that no vertices have been visited: }
for I := 1 to N do
    Visited [I] := False

{ Visit each unvisited vertex: }
for I := 1 to N do
    if not Visited [I] then
        with VisitStack do
            Push (I)
            repeat

                { Visit the top unvisited vertex: }
                RetrieveTop (J)
                if not Visited [J] then
                    VertexList.Retrieve (Vertex, J)
                    Visit (Vertex)
                    Visited [J] := True
```

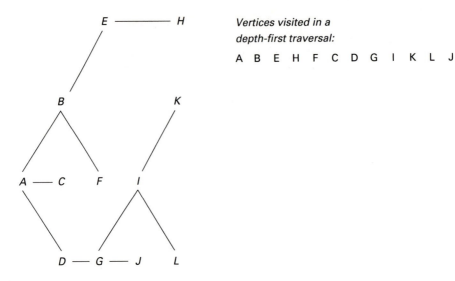

Vertices visited in a
depth-first traversal:

A B E H F C D G I K L J

Figure 11.9   A depth-first traversal of a graph.

```
{ Stack the first unvisited neighbor (of J) in
VertexList: }
Found := False
K     := 1
while (K <= N) and not Found do
    if AdjacencyMatrix [J, K] and not Visited [K]
    then
        Push (K)
        Found := True
    else
        Add 1 to K
if not Found then
    Pop
until IsEmpty
```

Figure 11.10 shows the effect of the execution of this subalgorithm on the graph in Fig. 11.9. The verification and analysis of this subalgorithm are similar to those of the breadth-first traversal subalgorithm.

We now resume the method designs.

15. **IsConnected.**

A graph is *connected* if, starting at any vertex, we can construct a path to any other vertex. We can test for connectivity by making a few minor modifications to the breadth-first traversal subalgorithm given earlier. (Changing the depth-first version would be similarly easy.)

If VertexList is not empty, we count how many vertices can be reached from vertex 1. Instead of looping through all unvisited vertices ("for

I: = 1 to N do"), we set *I* equal to 1 and Count equal to 0. After the execution of the repeat statement, we see if Count = *N*. If so, there is a path from vertex 1 to every other vertex, and the graph is connected. Note that vertex 1 is automatically included in the count.

The complete subalgorithm is

```
IsConnected
if VertexList.IsEmpty then
    Return the value True
else
    VisitQueue.Initialize
    N := VertexList.Size
    { Establish that no vertices have been visited: }
    for I := 1 to N do
        Enqueued [I] := False

    I       := 1
    Count := 0

    {Count how many vertices can be reached from vertex 1:}
    with VisitQueue do
        InsertTail (1)
        Enqueued [1] := True
        repeat
            RetrieveHead (J)
            DeleteHead
            Add 1 to Count
            for K := 1 to N do
                if AdjacencyMatrix [J,K] and not Enqueued [K]
                    then
                        InsertTail (K)
                        Enqueued [K] := True
        until IsEmpty
    Return the value of (Count = N)
```

Time is $O(N^2)$ for a connected graph. For a graph that is not connected, Time varies from $O(1)$ to $O(N^2)$, depending on the shape of the graph. The space requirements vary from $O(1)$ to $O(N)$, depending on the shape of the graph and on the design domain for the Queue ADT.

A simpler and cleverer (but slower) test for connectedness was devised by S. Warshall. Essentially, we "fill out" the original graph by connecting, with an edge, any pair of vertices for which there is a path. This expanded graph is called the ***transitive closure*** of the original graph. To determine whether the original graph is connected, we check to see if there is an edge between any two vertices in the transitive closure. Equivalently, and more easily, we check to see if

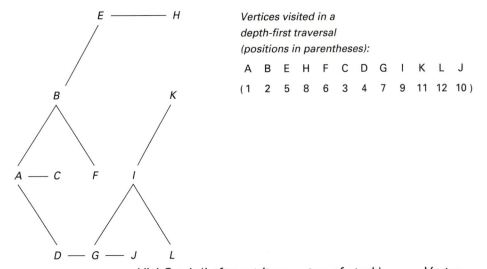

Vertices visited in a
depth-first traversal
(positions in parentheses):

A   B   E   H   F   C   D   G   I   K   L   J

(1   2   5   8   6   3   4   7   9   11 12 10)

VisitStack (Leftmost item = top of stack)	Vertex	Position
1	A	1
2 1	B	2
5 2 1	C	3
8 5 2 1	D	4
6 2 1	E	5
3 1	F	6
4 1	G	7
7 4 1	H	8
9 7 4 1	I	9
11 9 7 4 1	K	11
12 9 7 4 1	L	12
10 7 4 1	J	10

Figure 11.10   The effect of executing the depth-first traversal subalgorithm on the given graph. The item at the top of the stack is visited next.

there is an edge between the first vertex (in VertexList) and every other vertex. Specifically, we construct a Boolean matrix Closure [1 .. MaxVertices, 1 .. MaxVertices], which will be the adjacency matrix for the expanded graph. Initially, Closure gets a copy of AdjacencyMatrix. We then loop as I goes from 1 to N. For each pair of vertex positions J and K, if there are edges from J to I and from I to K in the expanded graph, we draw an edge between J and K. That is, we set Closure [J, K] equal to True provided Closure [J, I] and Closure [I, K] are True. Otherwise, Closure [J, K] is unchanged from before.

As a result, if we can construct a path with the vertex positions:

$$J, I, K$$

in the expanded graph, then Closure [J, K] will have the value True. In other words, we can replace every path of length 2 in the expanded graph with a path of length 1 (that is, an edge). However, any path of length 3, say,

$$u, v, x, y$$

contains a path of length 2,

$$u, v, x$$

which can be replaced with an edge u, x. Then the path of length 2,

$$u, x, y$$

can be replaced with an edge u, y. Thus, any path of length 3 can be replaced with an edge. Therefore, by induction on the length of the path, any path in the expanded graph can be replaced with an edge.

After we have constructed Closure, the graph is connected if the first N entries in row 1 of Closure are all Trues.

The subalgorithm is as follows:

```
IsConnected                              { Warshall's Algorithm }
Closure := AdjacencyMatrix
N := VertexList.Size
for I := 1 to N do
    for J := 1 to N do
        if Closure [J, I] then
            for K := 1 to N do
                if Closure [I, K] then
                    Closure [J, K] := True
Connected := True
for I := 1 to N do
    if Closure [1, I] = False then
        Connected := False
Return the value of Connected
```

Example. The following example illustrates the gradual development of the closure matrix. Suppose we start with the graph

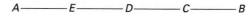

A————————E————————D————————C————————B

with vertex A in position 1 of VertexList, B in position 2, and so on. In the initial version of Closure, the entries marked T^0 in Fig. 11.11 would be True and every other entry would be False. After the first pass through the outermost For loop, with $I = 1$, the entries marked T^1 would be changed from False to True. The changes from False to True in the remaining passes are marked T^2, T^3, T^4, and T^5, respectively.

A value of True in the matrix Closure never reverts to False. Therefore, if there is a path between vertices x and y in the original graph, there will also be a path between x and y in the expanded graph, since Closure initially gets a copy of AdjacencyMatrix. Furthermore, the

Figure 11.11

The development of
the transitive closure
of a graph from
Warshall's algorithm.
T^0 represents an
entry of True in the
graph's adjacency
matrix. For $I =$
$1, 2, 3, 4, 5$: T^I
represents an entry
of True made during
the Ith pass through
the outermost
For loop.

Closure	1	2	3	4	5	Original Graph
1	T^5	T^5	T^5	T^5	T^0	
2	T^5	T^3	T^0	T^3	T^4	$A-E-D-C-B$
3	T^5	T^0	T^2	T^0	T^4	
4	T^5	T^3	T^0	T^3	T^0	(Vertex A in position 1, B in
5	T^0	T^4	T^4	T^0	T^1	position 2,...)

transitive closure allows us to shorten only the existing paths, so if
there is no path between x and y in the original graph, there will be no
path between x and y in the transitive closure.

For the outermost For statement, the postcondition is:

> For any pair of vertices x and y, there is a path between x
> and y in the original graph if and only if x and y form an
> edge in the transitive closure.

A suitable and easily verified post-invariant of that loop is:

> For any pair of vertex positions J and K, if $\{J, I\}$ and $\{I, K\}$
> are edges in the transitive closure, then $\{J, K\}$ is an edge in
> the transitive closure.

The postcondition then follows from the inductive proof alluded
to earlier.

Time is $O(N^3)$, since we have a triply nested loop. Space for Closure is
$O(1)$, since MaxVertices is constant.

16. `FindShortestPath (Vertex1, Vertex2, PathList).`

We will attempt to find a shortest path from Vertex1 to Vertex2 with
the help of a breadth-first traversal starting at Vertex1. The queue will
consist of ordered pairs in the form (First, Second), where the vertices
at positions First and Second (in VertexList) form an edge, and First
was encountered before Second in the breadth-first traversal. Path will
be an array of lists: For each vertex position P in VertexList, Path $[P]$
will contain the list of vertex positions in the shortest path from $P1$—
Vertex1's position—to P.

When a pair (First, Second) is dequeued, the shortest path from P1 to
First is already stored in Path [First]. So to get the shortest path from
P1 to Second, we copy Path [First] to Path [Second] and then tack Second onto the end of Path [Second]. We finish looping when either the
queue is empty or the path from P1 to P2 (Vertex2's position) has
been constructed.

If we did find the shortest path from position P1 to P2, we must construct the corresponding list of vertices, PathList. If there was no shortest path from P1 to P2, then PathList will be empty.

The subalgorithm is:

```
            ↓          ↓          ↑

FindShortestPath (Vertex1, Vertex2, PathList)
with VertexList do
   Search (Vertex1, Found, P1)
   Search (Vertex2, Found, P2)
   N := Size

{ Establish that no vertices have been enqueued: }
 for I := 1 to N do
    Enqueued [I] := False

P2PathFound := False
Path [P1].Initialize
Edge.First := P1
Edge.Second := P1
with VisitQueue do
   Initialize
   InsertTail (Edge)
   Enqueued [P1] := True
   repeat
      RetrieveHead (Edge)
      DeleteHead
      with Edge do

         { The path from 1 to Second is the path from }
         { 1 to First followed by Second:             }
         Path [First].CopyTo (Path [Second])
         Path [Second].Insert(Second,Path[Second].Size+1)
         if Second = P2 then
             P2PathFound := True
         else
             First := Second

             {Enqueue each unenqueued neighbor of First:}
             for K := 1 to N do
                if AdjacencyMatrix [First, K]
                      and (Enqueued [K] = False) then
                   Second := K
                   InsertTail (Edge)
                   Enqueued [K] := True
   until IsEmpty or P2PathFound
```

```
{ Construct the list of vertices in PathList from the }
{ list of vertex positions in Path [P2]:              }
PathList.Initialize
if P2PathFound then
    for I := 1 to Path [P2].Size do
        Path [P2].Retrieve (Position, I)
        VertexList.Retrieve (Vertex, Position)
        PathList.Insert (Vertex, I)
```

Example.   To illustrate the execution of this subalgorithm, suppose we want to find the shortest path from *A* to *I* in the following graph:

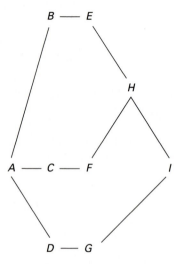

If vertex *A* is in position 1 in VertexList, vertex *B* in position 2, and so on, then the values for the Path array will be as follows:

```
Path [1]: 1            {Constructed when <1,1> dequeued}
Path [2]: 1,2          {Constructed when <1,2> dequeued}
Path [3]: 1,3          {Constructed when <1,3> dequeued}
Path [4]: 1,4          {Constructed when <1,4> dequeued}
Path [5]: 1,2,5        {Constructed when <2,5> dequeued}
Path [6]: 1,3,6        {Constructed when <3,6> dequeued}
Path [7]: 1,4,7        {Constructed when <4,7> dequeued}
Path [8]: 1,2,5,8      {Constructed when <5,8> dequeued}
Path [9]: 1,4,7,9      {Constructed when <7,9> dequeued}
```

A suitable post-invariant for the Repeat loop is:

> Either a shortest path from *P*1 to *P*2 has been found, or
>
> a.   the shortest path from *P*1 to Edge.First has been constructed;
>
> b.   every neighbor of Edge.First has been enqueued.

The Repeat statement will be executed, on average, about $N/2$ times (assuming that Vertex1 and Vertex2 have the same chance of being selected as any other pair of vertices). Within each iteration of the Repeat loop, there will be N iterations of the For loop (unless the path from $P1$ to $P2$ is found). Thus, Time is $O(N^2)$. Space is also $O(N^2)$ because Path consists of N lists, each of size $O(N)$.

Finding a shortest path between vertices is helpful in solving maze problems (see Programming Assignment 11.3).

This completes the design of the Graph ADT based on a vertex list and an adjacency matrix. In the next section, we consider a design that replaces the adjacency matrix with an adjacency list.

A Design Based on a Vertex List and an Adjacency List

In this section, we outline the design of the graph subalgorithms using a design domain of a vertex list and an adjacency list. Specifically, VertexList will be a list of vertices; the design of the List ADT should be such that the time for retrieving, calculating size, and inserting at the end of the list will be $O(1)$. AdjacencyList will be an array of MaxVertices components; AdjacencyList $[I]$ will contain the ordered list of positions of vertices that are adjacent to the vertex whose position is I.

Rather than plodding through all of the subalgorithm designs, we select the most difficult and leave the rest as exercises. Most of the computational work will be performed in the background by the methods in the List and OrderedList ADTs.

7. `SearchForEdge (Vertex1, Vertex2, Found).`

    If Vertex1 is found at Pos1 in VertexList, and Vertex2 is found at Pos2, then we search AdjacencyList [Pos1] for Pos2 to see if Vertex1 and Vertex2 form an edge. The temporary variables $V1$ and $V2$ ensure that neither Vertex1 nor Vertex2 will be altered unless they form an edge.

    The subalgorithm is:

```
SearchForEdge (Vertex1, Vertex2, Found)

V1 := Vertex1
V2 := Vertex2
VertexList.Search (V1, V1Found, Pos1)
VertexList.Search (V2, V2Found, Pos2)
if V1Found and V2Found then
    AdjacencyList [Pos1].Search (Pos2, Found, Position)
```

```
      if Found then
          Vertex1 := V1
          Vertex2 := V2
else
    Found := False
```

The search of VertexList takes O(N) time, on average, so Time is O(N) and Space is O(1).

↓

10. **DeleteVertex (Vertex).**

```
VertexList.Search (Vertex, Found, P)
for I := 1 to VertexList.Size do

    { Delete P from AdjacencyList [I]; }
    { decrement positions greater than P: }
    with AdjacencyList [I] do
        Search (P, Found, PPos)
        if Found then
            Delete (P)
        for J := PPos to Size do
            Retrieve (Item, J)
            Delete (Item)
            Item := Item - 1
            Insert (Item)

{ Close up the space for AdjacencyList [P]: }
for I := P + 1 to VertexList.Size do
        AdjacencyList [I-1] := AdjacencyList [I]

VertexList.Delete (P)
```

The analysis depends not only on N, the number of vertices, but also on E, the number of edges. In particular, the size of one of the lists in the array AdjacencyList is $O(E/N)$ on average, so each retrieval, deletion, and insertion within the inner For loop will take $O(E/N)$ time. However, the inner For loop is executed $O(E/N)$ times, as is the outer For loop, so Time is $O(E^3/N^3)$.

Recall that for the adjacency matrix representation of the previous section, the Time for DeleteVertex was $O(N^2)$. Which is faster? It depends on the relationship between the E and N. For example, if $E = 2N$, then the adjacency lists will have a size of 2, on average, so the adjacency list version will be faster. On the other hand, if $E = N^2/4$ (about half of the maximum possible number of edges), then the Time for the adjacency list version is $O(N^3)$; therefore, in this case the adjacency-matrix representation gives better results.

14. <u>Traverse (Visit)</u>.

We could take the easy way out by using the traversal subalgorithm from the preceding section that relied not on the adjacency matrix representation, but only on VertexList:

```
for I := 1 to VertexList.Size do
   VertexList.Retrieve (Vertex, I)
   Visit (Vertex)
```

However, we should not overlook the value of a breadth-first traversal in developing the IsConnected and FindShortestPath subalgorithms. Here, then, is a breadth-first traversal subalgorithm based on an adjacency list. It is only slightly different from the adjacency-matrix–based version in the preceding section.

```
Traverse (Visit)                          { Breadth-First }
VisitQueue.Initialize
N := VertexList.Size

{ Establish that no vertices have been visited: }
for I := 1 to N do
   Enqueued [I] := False

{ Visit each unvisited vertex: }
for I := 1 to N do
   if not Enqueued [I] then
      with VisitQueue do
         InsertTail (I)
         Enqueued [I] := True
         repeat

            {Delete queue's head and visit that vertex:}
            RetrieveHead (J)
            DeleteHead
            VertexList.Retrieve (Vertex, J)
            Visit (Vertex)

            { Enqueue each unenqueued neighbor of J:}
            AdjacencyList [J].Traverse (PutOnQueue)
         until Is Empty
```

The subalgorithm PutOnQueue is as follows:

```
PutOnQueue (Item)

if not Enqueued [Item] then
   VisitQueue.InsertTail (Item)
   Enqueued [Item] := True
```

Since one item is dequeued during each iteration of the Repeat loop, the total number of Repeat loop iterations is N. Traversing AdjacencyList [J] takes $O(E/N)$ Time, on average. The Visit subalgorithm, PutOnQueue, takes $O(1)$ time, so Time is $O(N * E/N) = O(E)$.

As was the case with the breadth-first subalgorithm in the preceding section, the space requirements (mainly for VertexQueue) range from $O(1)$ to $O(N)$, depending on the shape of the graph.

IMPLEMENTATIONS OF THE GRAPH DATA TYPE

The designs of the two preceding sections easily lead to implementations of the Graph ADT. In the first implementation, the object GraphType has two fields, VertexList and AdjacencyMatrix. Here are the highlights:

```
unit Graph1Manager;
{ This unit implements the Graph ADT with a vertex list and}
{ an adjacency matrix.                                      }
interface
uses
   Maxima, { declares MaxVertices (= MaxListSize) }
   ItemInList, { declares ItemType (= VertexType) }
   List3Manager, { implements the List ADT, with O(1) Time }
                 { for retrieving, calculating Size and    }
                 { inserting at end of list                }
   ...
   VertexInGraph; { declares VertexType }
type
   MatrixType = array [1..MaxVertices,1..MaxVertices] of
   boolean;
   GraphType = object
        VertexList     : ListType;
        AdjacencyMatrix: MatrixType;
        procedure Initialize;
        ...
        procedure FindShortestPath (Vertex1,
                                    Vertex2     :VertexType;
                                    var PathList: ListType);
     end; { GraphType }
implementation
...
end. { Graph1Manager }
```

To illustrate VertexInGraph, suppose that each vertex consists of a name and a salary, with Name as the key field. Then we could declare:

```
unit VertexInGraph;
{ This unit implements VertexType for the Graph ADT. }
interface
type
   ValueType = record
      Name  : string [30];
      Salary: real
   end; { ValueType }
   VertexType = object
      Value: ValueType;
      procedure SetValue (NewValue: ValueType)
      ...
      function EqualTo (Vertex: VertexType): boolean;
   end; { VertexType }
   ProcedureType = procedure (Vertex: VertexType);
implementation
...
function VertexType.EqualTo (Vertex: VertexType): boolean;
begin
   EqualTo := (Value.Name = Vertex.Value.Name)
end; { EqualTo }
end. { VertexGraph }
```

The unit ItemInList simply equates ItemType with VertexType:

```
unit ItemInList;
{This unit implements ItemType for the current application.}
interface
uses
   VertexInGraph;
type
   ItemType = VertexType;
implementation
end. { ItemInList }
```

The unit List3Manager would use the identifiers ItemType, EqualTo, and ProcedureType (for list traversals). The unit Graph1Manager would use the identifiers VertexType, EqualTo, and ProcedureType (for graph traversals). A program that used Graph1Manager would work with VertexType, SetValue, GetValue, EqualTo, and ProcedureType.

The unit Graph1Manager was validated with a driver program similar to the drivers of Chapters 4 through 10.

In the second implementation of the Graph ADT, the object GraphType has VertexList and AdjacencyList fields. Each component of the array AdjacencyList is a scalar, ordered list.

For SOList1Manager, the space for each adjacency list of size N is N nodes, versus MaxVertices nodes for the other ordered list implementations. Therefore, the use of SOList1Manager will save space in most cases. We say "in most cases" because each node occupies six bytes: two for the vertex position and four for the pointer to the next node. Thus, if N is greater than MaxVertices/3, we may actually consume *more* space; however, this space will come from the heap rather than from the data segment.

An outline of Graph2Manager is as follows:

```
unit Graph2Manager;
{ This unit implements the Graph ADT with a vertex list and}
{ an adjacency list.                                        }
interface
uses
   Maxima, { declares MaxVertices (= MaxListSize) }
   Item1InList, { declares ItemType (= VertexType) }
   Item2InList, { declares ItemType (= PositionType) }
   List3Manager, { implements the List ADT, with O(1) time }
                 { for retrieving, calculating Size and     }
                 { inserting at end of list                 }
   SOList1Manager; { implements the Ordered List ADT, with }
                   { scalar items                           }
type
   VertexListType    = List3Manager.ListType;
   PositionListType = SOList1Manager.ListType;
   ListArrayType     = array [1..MaxVertices] of
                         PositionListType;
   GraphType         = object
       VertexList    : VertexListType;
       AdjacencyList: ListArrayType;
       procedure Initialize;
       ...
       procedure FindShortestPath (Vertex1,
                                   Vertex2     : VertexType;
                                   var PathList: ListType);
   end; { GraphType }
implementation
...
end. { Graph2Manager }
```

The unit Graph2Manager was validated with GraphDriver, the same program used to validate Graph1Manager.

Analysis of Graph Implementations

It might seem, at first, that we can perform run-time analyses to compare the two graph implementations, just as we have compared implementations of other ADTs in earlier chapters. However, our usual benchmark (the time for random insertions) is inappropriate, because InsertVertex takes $O(N)$ Time with an adjacency matrix due to the initializing of an entire row and column to False. In the adjacency list implementation, only $O(1)$ Time is needed. There is no point in comparing the run times of methods whose Big O times are different.

How about comparing the run times for the two implementations of InsertEdge? Both versions take $O(N)$ Time, but this is due to the searches of VertexList:

```
VertexList.Search (Vertex1, Found, Pos1);
VertexList.Search (Vertex2, Found, Pos2);
```

The adjacency matrix version, then, takes $O(1)$ Time to insert two True entries into the matrix, whereas the adjacency list version takes $O(E/N)$ Time to insert Pos2 into AdjacencyList [Pos1] and to insert Pos1 into AdjacencyList [Pos2]. Therefore, the adjacency-list implementation will certainly take longer. The situation is similar for the DeleteEdge method.

Another possibility is to compare the DeleteVertex methods in the two implementations. However, we already know from the algorithm analyses that the adjacency matrix version takes $O(N^2)$ Time, versus $O(E^3/N^3)$ Time for the adjacency list version.

Despite these failed attempts at finding a method for comparing the run-time performance of the two implementations, we can make some distinctions. An adjacency matrix occupies MaxVertices bytes in the data segment[2]; therefore, if MaxVertices is large (say, more than 200), an adjacency list implementation may be the only feasible one. On the other hand, if MaxVertices is small but E is $O(N^2)$, the adjacency list version will be inferior for inserting an edge and vastly inferior for deleting a vertex.

SPECIALIZATIONS OF GRAPHS

In this section we introduce several specializations of graphs—trees, networks, and directed graphs. Along the way we will develop subalgorithms for some of the well-known methods in the data types of these specializations.

---

[2]Turbo Pascal allocates an entire byte (eight bits) for each Boolean value. We could save space by encoding eight Boolean values into an integer of type byte. For example, $37 = 00100101_2$ could represent FFTFFTFT, but the tradeoff would be the increased time for encoding and decoding.

Figure 11.12

A tree.

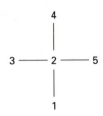

Trees

A ***tree*** is a connected, acyclic graph. For example, the graph in Fig. 11.2(a) is a tree. Figure 11.12 contains another tree.

Where is the root of the tree in Fig. 11.12? Actually, any of the vertices could be called the root. An ***oriented*** tree is one in which a vertex has been designated as the root. For example, suppose we designate vertex 5 as the root of the tree in Fig. 11.12. Figure 11.13 is a redrawing of Fig. 11.12 to correspond to this orientation, with the root in its conventional position at the top of the figure and adjacent vertices drawn below it.

Oriented trees allow us to study hierarchical relationships such as parent-child and supervisor-supervisee. Later in this chapter we will look at the kind of tree most useful in computer science: the directed tree.

Not every graph is a tree. For example, the graph in Fig. 11.14 is connected, but is not a tree because it contains a cycle: *CDBAC*.

For a small graph, we can easily determine whether or not it is a tree. What about the general case? Can we develop an IsATree operator for the Graph ADT? It turns out that there is a surprisingly simple subalgorithm based on the observation that the number of edges in a tree is the minimum number needed to preserve connectedness. How many edges is that? A tree with two vertices must have an edge. A tree with three vertices must have two edges. We conjecture that the number of edges in a tree is always one less than the number of vertices, and so we get the following subalgorithm.

Figure 11.13

An oriented tree whose root is 5.

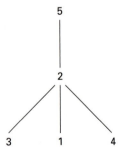

Figure 11.14

A graph that is not a tree: it contains a cycle (in fact, it contains four cycles).

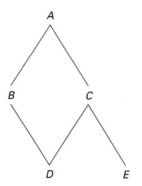

<u>IsATree (Graph)</u>

with Graph do
    Return the value of IsConnected
            and (NumberOfEdges = NumberOfVertices - 1)

And that's it! Ordinarily, we do not prove the correctness of a subalgorithm that has neither loops nor recursive calls, but here we should make an exception. We must show that the given function returns True when Graph is a tree and False when Graph is not a tree. We already know that every tree is connected, so we will prove that if Graph is connected, then Graph is a tree if and only if the number of edges is one less than the number of vertices. We will assume, then, that Graph is connected and prove both of the following:

> Claim 1. If Graph is a tree, then the number of edges is one less than the number of vertices;
> Claim 2. If the number of edges is one less than the number of vertices, then Graph is a tree.

Proof of Claim 1: The proof is by induction on the number of vertices. (a) *Base case.* If Graph is a tree with one vertex, then Graph clearly has no edges, so the claim is correct.
(b) *Inductive case.* Let N be any positive integer and assume that any tree with $K \leq N$ vertices has $K - 1$ edges. Let Graph be a tree with $N + 1$ vertices. We must show that Graph has N edges. Since Graph is acyclic, if we delete an edge from Graph, we obtain two trees: G_1 and G_2 with, say, N_1 and N_2 vertices, respectively. $N_1 \leq N$ and $N_2 \leq N$, and so, by the induction hypothesis, G_1 has $N_1 - 1$ edges, and G_2 has $N_2 - 1$ edges.

How does Graph compare with G_1 and G_2? Graph has the same number of vertices, and so,

$$N_1 + N_2 = N + 1$$

Furthermore, Graph has one more edge than G_1 and G_2, so the total number of edges in Graph is:

$$(N_1 - 1) + (N_2 - 1) + 1 = N_1 + N_2 - 1 = N$$

This completes the proof of Claim 1.

Proof of Claim 2:   Let N be any positive integer and let G_1 be any connected graph with N vertices and $N - 1$ edges. If G_1 has a cycle, remove one of the edges from the cycle to obtain a new connected graph G_2, with N vertices and $N - 2$ edges. Now do the same thing to G_2, if it contains a cycle, to obtain a new graph G_3 with N vertices and $N - 3$ edges. Continue this process until we obtain a connected, acyclic graph G_K with N vertices and $N - K$ edges.

Since G_K is connected and acyclic, it must be a tree; and so, by Claim 1, it must have $N - 1$ edges. Therefore, $K = 1$, and so the original graph G_1 had no cycles! In other words, any connected graph with N vertices and $N - 1$ edges is a tree. This completes the proof of Claim 2.

Given a connected graph G, we say that a tree T is a ***spanning tree*** of G if T is a subgraph of G that includes all of G's vertices. Figure 11.15 shows

Figure 11.15

A connected graph
(top) and one of its
spanning trees
(bottom).

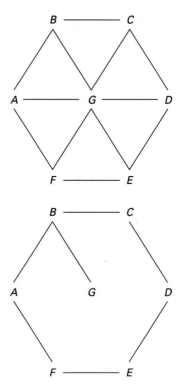

a connected graph and one of its spanning trees. Can you find another spanning tree?

We can construct a spanning tree from a connected graph with the help of a breadth-first traversal similar to the one we used in finding the shortest path between two vertices. The queue consists of ordered pairs of vertices that will be added to the tree. A Boolean array IsOnTree [1..MaxVertices] will allow us to easily determine if a vertex is already on the tree.

For the sake of simplicity, the following subalgorithm works with vertex positions from VertexList rather than with the vertices themselves. For the sake of abstraction, we will not specify whether an adjacency matrix or adjacency list is being used.

```
ConstructSpanningTree (Graph, Tree)

Start with an empty Tree and an empty queue.
if the graph consists of a single vertex then
    Insert vertex 1 into Tree { and we are done }
else
    for I := 1 to Graph.Size do
        IsOnTree [I] := False
    Find the first edge { I, J }.
    Insert vertices I and J, and edge {I, J} into Tree.
    for any vertex K distinct from J, if {I, K} forms an
    edge,
        Enqueue the ordered pair (I, K).
    for any vertex K distinct from I, if {J, K} forms an
    edge,
        Enqueue the ordered pair (J, K).
    Loop until Tree has as many vertices as Graph:
        Dequeue the ordered pair (X, Y).
        if not IsOnTree [Y] then
            Insert vertex Y and edge {X, Y} into Tree.
            IsOnTree [Y] := True
            for any vertex Z
                if not IsOnTree [Z]
                    and {Y, Z} forms an edge in the graph then
                        Enqueue the ordered pair (Y, Z)
```

For example, if the vertex positions are assigned alphabetically to the graph at the top of Fig. 11.15 (*A* in position 1, *B* in position 2, . . .), then edge {*A, B*} would be chosen first, and the following ordered pairs would be enqueued:

> (*A, B*)
> (*A, F*)
> (*A, G*)

(B, C)
(B, G)
(F, E)
(G, D)

The resulting spanning tree is:

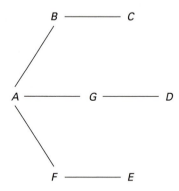

Notice that by the time (B, G) was dequeued, G had previously been added to the tree, so the edge $\{B, G\}$ was not added to the tree.

Any spanning tree for a graph contains the minimum number of edges that the graph needs to remain connected. In this context, we can think of a graph as a communications structure, such as a mail system or a telephone system. The vertices would represent locations and the edges would represent communication links between the locations at each end of an edge. A spanning tree for such a graph can be thought of as the smallest number of links that still permit communication between any two locations.

Now suppose that each link has an associated cost. Can we find a spanning tree that minimizes the total cost of the links? To answer this question, we must first define a new kind of graph, the network, in which each edge has an associated value.

Networks

A **_network_** is a graph in which each edge has associated with it a nonnegative number, called the **_weight_** of the edge. Figure 11.16 shows a network in which each edge's weight represents the cost of a one-way plane ticket between the two vertices (representing cities). Figure 11.17 shows a network with the same vertices as in Fig. 11.16, but with the weights representing the distances between the cities.

Since a network is a graph, a network can have a spanning tree (in fact, several spanning trees). Figures 11.18 and 11.19 show two different spanning trees for the network in Fig. 11.17.

Figure 11.16

A network of cities.
Each edge's weight is
the cost in dollars of
a one-way plane
ticket between
the cities.

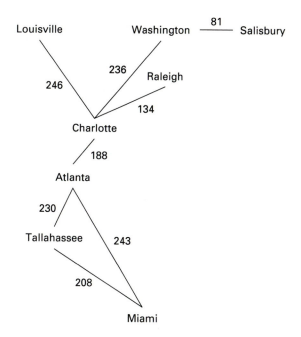

Now suppose that your company has branch offices in all of these cities. You want to construct a spanning tree, but you want to keep the total distance as low as possible. In other words, you want a spanning tree for the network of Fig. 11.17 that minimizes the total edge weights. Such a tree is called a **minimal spanning tree**.

Figure 11.17

Another network of
cities. Each edge's
weight is the
distance in miles
between the cities.

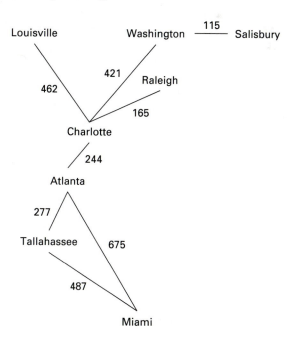

Figure 11.18

A spanning tree for
the network in
Fig. 11.17.

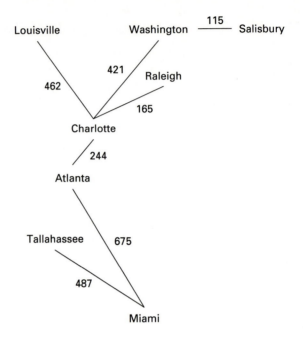

Figure 11.19

Another spanning
tree for the network
in Fig. 11.17.

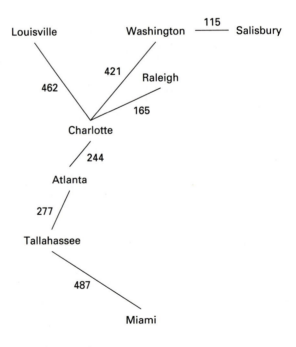

A network may have several minimal spanning trees. For example, the network,

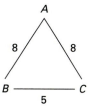

has two minimal spanning trees, namely:

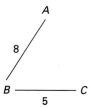

and

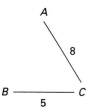

J. B. Kruskal (see Kruskal, 1956) developed an algorithm for constructing a minimal spanning tree for a connected graph. The essence of the algorithm was given in the preceding section to construct a spanning tree. How do we have to modify that algorithm to construct, not just a spanning tree, but a minimal spanning tree? To start with, the first edge we want to put in the tree is the one with the smallest weight. The only other change to the spanning tree algorithm is that the queue will be a priority queue, with the lowest weight having highest priority. That way, the edge we dequeue will have the *lowest* weight of all the edges on the priority queue.

The beauty of Kruskal's algorithm is that its "greedy" approach works: At each stage we add to the tree the edge on the queue whose weight is smallest (unless this would produce a cycle), and we end up with a spanning tree whose total edge weight is smallest.

The subalgorithm, as a method in the Network ADT, is:

ConstructMinimalSpanningTree (Tree)   { Kruskal's Algorithm }

Start with an empty Tree and an empty priority queue.

```
if the graph consists of a single vertex then
   Insert vertex 1 into Tree { and we are done }
else
   for I := 1 to Graph.Size do
      IsOnTree [I] := False
   Find the edge {I, J} with lowest weight in the network.
   Insert vertices I and J, and edge {I, J} into Tree.
   for any vertex K distinct from J, if {I, K} forms an
   edge,
      Enqueue the ordered pair (I, K).
   for any vertex K distinct from I, if {J, K} forms an
   edge,
      Enqueue the ordered pair (J, K).
   Loop until Tree has as many vertices as the network:
      Dequeue the ordered pair (X, Y).
      if not IsOnTree [Y] then
         Insert vertex Y and edge {X, Y} into Tree.
         IsOnTree [Y] := True
         for any vertex Z
            if not IsOnTree [Z]
               and {Y, Z} forms an edge in the network then
               Enqueue the ordered pair (Y, Z)
```

Let's see how Kruskal's algorithm works. Suppose we start with the following network:

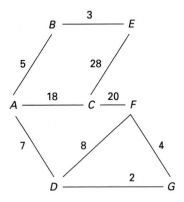

The edge with lowest weight is $\{D, G\}$, so the tree becomes:

D———2———G

All pairs of the form (D, X) or (G, X), where $\{D, X\}$ or $\{G, X\}$ is an edge, are enqueued. The priority queue is now:

```
(G, F)    { weight = 4 }
(D, A)    { 7 }
(D, F)    { 8 }
```

(G, F) is dequeued and added to the tree:

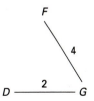

(F, C) is now enqueued, so the priority queue is:

```
(D, A)    { weight = 7 }
(D, F)    { 8 }
(F, C)    { 20 }
```

(D, A) is dequeued and added to the tree:

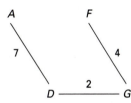

After (A, B) and (A, C) are enqueued, the priority queue is:

```
(A, B)    { weight = 5 }
(D, F)    { 8 }
(A, C)    { 18 }
(F, C)    { 20 }
```

(A, B) is dequeued and added to the tree:

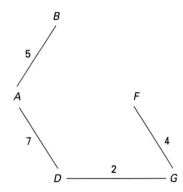

(B, E) is enqueued:

```
(B, E)    { weight = 3 }
(D, F)    { 8 }
(A, C)    { 18 }
(F, C)    { 20 }
```

Now (B, E) is dequeued and added to the tree:

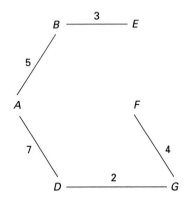

(E, C) is enqueued:

```
(D, F)    { weight = 8 }
(A, C)    { 18 }
(F, C)    { 20 }
(E, C)    { 28 }
```

(D, F) is dequeued, but nothing is added to the tree, since F is already in the tree. (A, C) is then dequeued and added to the tree. The resulting tree is a minimal spanning tree:

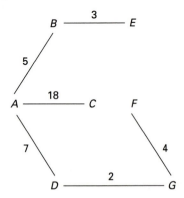

Notice that when we finished, the priority queue was not empty, but those remaining items could not affect the composition of the minimal spanning tree.

A ***greedy algorithm*** is one in which the optimal choice is made at each stage. In Kruskal's algorithm, the priority queue guarantees that each edge added to the tree has the lowest weight of all edges on that queue. Kruskal's algorithm is, therefore, a greedy algorithm. What we have not yet shown is that greed is successful in this case.

To prove the correctness of Kruskal's algorithm, we need to verify the loop's postcondition:

> Tree is a minimal spanning tree for the network.

The postcondition follows from the invariance of the loop assertion:

> Tree is a minimal spanning tree for that part of the original network consisting of those vertices in Tree and all the edges joining them in the original network.

Prior to the first iteration of the loop, Tree has only two vertices and one edge, and there is only one edge joining those vertices in the original network. Therefore, the loop assertion is true prior to the first iteration.

Now, suppose that the loop assertion is true prior to some loop iteration. We must show that the assertion is also true after that iteration. During that iteration, a pair (X, Y) is dequeued. If Y is already in Tree, then Tree is unchanged, and the assertion is true after the iteration. If Y is not already in Tree, then vertex Y and edge $\{X, Y\}$ are inserted in Tree. Clearly, Tree is still a spanning tree, so all we need to show is that Tree is still a *minimal* spanning tree.

If Tree is no longer minimal, there must be a vertex V in Tree such that the edge $\{V, Y\}$ has lower weight than the edge $\{X, Y\}$. Pictorially,

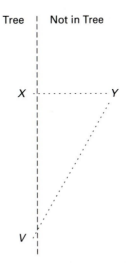

Note that since V was already in Tree, the pair (V, Y) must have been enqueued earlier.

However, $\{V, Y\}$ could not have a lower weight than $\{X, Y\}$, because (X, Y) was dequeued, not (V, Y). Therefore, Tree, with vertex Y and edge $\{X, Y\}$ inserted, must still be minimal. This completes the proof of correctness for Kruskal's algorithm.

Design Domains for the Network ADT

The algorithm we have just discussed did not make any assumptions about a specific design domain in the Network ADT; so, before we leave this section, let's discuss what would be needed.

The design domain for ADT Network would include the same VertexList that we had for design domains of the Graph ADT. However, an adjacency matrix or adjacency list indicates only where the edges are, not their weights. To store this additional information, we use either a weight matrix or a weight list. A weight matrix has MaxVertices rows and columns, just like an adjacency matrix, but the entries are different. At row I and column J,

WeightMatrix $[I, J]$ = 0, if $I = J$ (there is no *cost* in
 getting to a vertex if you are
 already there);
 the weight of edge $\{I, J\}$, if $\{I, J\}$ forms an
 edge;
 MaxWeightPlus, otherwise.

MaxWeightPlus is a user-supplied value greater than any weight.

For example, Fig. 11.20 shows a network and its weight matrix; MaxWeightPlus is 100 and vertex positions are assigned alphabetically (A in position 1, and so on).

A weight list is similar to an adjacency list, except that the weights are included. Figure 11.21 shows the weight list for the network in Fig. 11.20. In Fig. 11.21, WeightList [1] contains three items, since vertex 1 (namely, A) is adjacent to three vertices:

vertex 2—the weight of edge $\{1, 2\}$ is 8;

vertex 3—the weight of edge $\{1, 3\}$ is 2;

vertex 4—the weight of edge $\{1, 4\}$ is 6.

Shortest Paths in a Network

Kruskal's algorithm enables us to find a minimal spanning tree in a connected network. An extension of the algorithm, Dijkstra's algorithm, finds the shortest path between any two vertices. In a connected network, a path between two vertices is *shortest* if the total weight of all edges in the path is minimal. Dijkstra's algorithm does even more than find the shortest path between any pair of vertices; for any given vertex, it finds the shortest path to all other vertices. The given vertex becomes the root in a shortest path

Figure 11.20

A network and its
weight matrix.

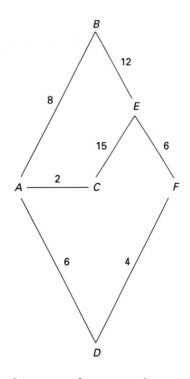

	1	2	3	4	5	6
1	0	8	2	6	100	100
2	8	0	100	100	12	100
3	2	100	0	100	15	100
4	6	100	100	0	100	4
5	100	12	15	100	0	6
6	100	100	100	4	6	0

tree. A ***shortest path tree*** is one that contains the shortest path (of all
paths in the network) from the root to each nonroot vertex. Figure 11.22
has a network and the shortest path tree with vertex *A* at the root.

Figure 11.22 illustrates that the shortest path in the network sense is different from the shortest path in the graph sense. For example, the path:

   A, B, D

with only two edges is the shortest path, graph-wise, between *A* and *D*.
However,

   A, C, B, D

is the shortest path, network-wise, because the total edge weight of 27 is
less than the total edge weight of any other path between *A* and *D*.

Figure 11.21

A weight list for the
network in
Fig. 11.20. In each
box, the first value
is the position (in
VertexList) of an
adjacent vertex. The
second is the weight
of the edge.

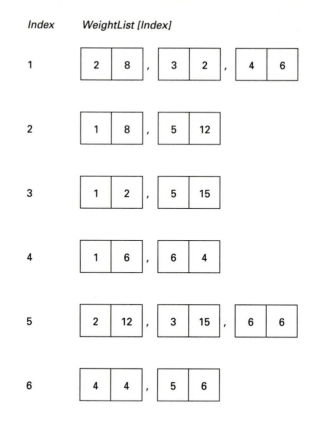

Figure 11.22

A network and the
shortest path tree
from *A*.

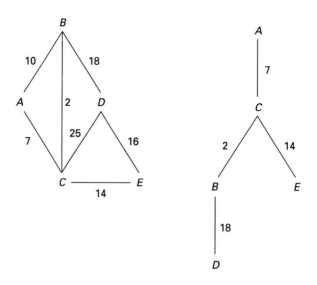

Figure 11.23

A network with a
minimal spanning
tree and a shortest
path tree from
vertex *A*.

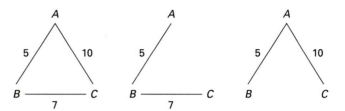

There is one other point worth making before we look at Dijkstra's algorithm. A minimal spanning tree is not necessarily the same as a shortest path tree. For example, Fig. 11.23 shows a network with a minimal spanning tree and a shortest path tree rooted at vertex *A*.

For another example, the shortest path tree from *A* for the network in Fig. 11.22 is not the minimal spanning tree for that network. Can you construct that network's minimal spanning tree?

We now develop Dijkstra's algorithm for a shortest path tree. As we did with Kruskal's algorithm, we will work with the vertex positions from VertexList rather than with the vertices themselves. For simplicity, we assume that vertex 1 is the root vertex from which we want to construct the shortest path tree.

Like Kruskal's algorithm, Dijkstra's is a greedy algorithm; and, like Kruskal's algorithm, the items on the priority queue are ordered pairs of vertices. The main difference between the two algorithms is that in Dijkstra's algorithm, priorities are based on total path weights rather than individual edge weights.

Specifically, suppose that (I, J) and (K, L) are two pairs on the priority queue. The pair (I, J) has *higher* priority than the pair (K, L) if the total weight of the (currently shortest) path from 1 to J is *less than* the total weight of the (currently shortest) path from 1 to L.

To simplify the task of finding these total weights, we will maintain an array TotalWeight [1..MaxVertices]: For each value of J between 1 and N,

TotalWeight [J] = the total weight of the currently
shortest path from 1 to J

When the execution of the algorithm has ended, this array will have the correct final values for all indices.

Dijkstra's algorithm, in the Network ADT, is as follows:

FindShortestPathTree (Tree)   { Dijkstra's Algorithm }

Start with an empty Tree, an empty priority queue and the
arrays TotalWeight and IsOnTree as follows: for each value
of I in [1..N],

```
                        0, if I = 1;
        Total Weight [I] = the weight of edge {1, I}, if {1, I} is
                            an edge;
                        MaxPathPlus, otherwise.³
        IsOnTree [I] = False
Insert vertex 1 in Tree and set IsOnTree [1] to True.
For each vertex I adjacent to vertex 1,
        Enqueue (1, I)
Loop until Tree has as many vertices as the network
        Dequeue the ordered pair (J, K)
        if not IsOnTree [K] then
            Insert vertex K and edge {J, K} in Tree
            For any vertex L,
                If not IsOnTree [L] and {K, L} forms an edge then
                    if the sum of TotalWeight [K] and the Weight of
                    edge {K, L} is less than TotalWeight [L] then
                        Replace TotalWeight [L] with that sum.
                    Enqueue (K, L)
```

Example.   Let's use Dijkstra's algorithm to find the shortest path tree from vertex 1 (namely A) for the following network:

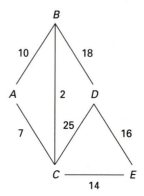

The initial total weights and the correspondence between vertices and vertex positions are as follows (MaxPathPlus = 1000):

Vertex	A	B	C	D	E
Vertex Position	1	2	3	4	5
TotalWeight	0	10	7	1000	1000

---

³MaxPathPlus is a user-supplied constant greater than the total weight of any cycle-free path. Paths with cycles can have infinitely large total weights.

Prior to the first loop iteration, the vertex at position 1 is inserted in Tree, and the pairs (1, 2) and (1, 3) are enqueued:

Tree A	Priority Queue: (J, K)	Total Weight [K]
	(1, 3)	7
	(1, 2)	10

The pair (1, 3) is dequeued because it has highest priority (TotalWeight [3] > TotalWeight [2]). That edge and the vertex at position 3 are added to the tree:

Vertex positions 2, 4, and 5 are not already in Tree and are adjacent to vertex 3, so their TotalWeights are updated. For example,

$$\text{TotalWeight } [2] := \min \{\text{TotalWeight } [2], \text{TotalWeight } [3] + \text{Weight } [2, 3]\}$$
$$= \min \{10, 7 + 2\}$$
$$= 9$$

The pairs (3, 2), (3, 4), and (3, 5) are enqueued.

Priority Queue: (J, K)	Total Weight [K]
(3, 2)	9
(1, 2)	10
(3, 5)	21
(3, 4)	32

Notice that when the pair (1,2) was enqueued earlier, the value 10 was associated with that pair because TotalWeight [2] was 10 at that time. The value 10 is still associated with that pair even though the value of TotalWeight [2] is later changed to 9.

During the next iteration, (3, 2) is dequeued and Tree is updated accordingly:

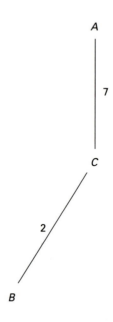

TotalWeight [4] is updated because:

$$\text{TotalWeight } [2] + \text{Weight } [2, 4] < \text{TotalWeight } [4]$$

$$(9 + 18 < 32)$$

The values in TotalWeight are now as follows:

Vertex	A	B	C	D	E
Vertex Position	1	2	3	4	5
TotalWeight	0	9	7	27	21

At the end of this iteration, the pair (2, 4) is enqueued, and the priority queue is as follows:

Priority Queue: (J, K)	TotalWeight [K]
(1, 2)	10
(3, 5)	21
(2, 4)	27
(3, 4)	32

During the next iteration, (1, 2) is dequeued, but nothing happens because vertex 2 (namely, B) is already in Tree.

During the next iteration, (3, 5) is dequeued and Tree is updated:

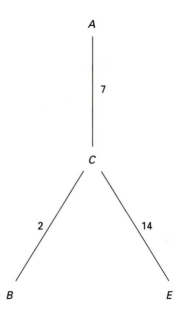

Vertex 4 (namely, D) is adjacent to vertex 5 (namely, E), but:

TotalWeight [4] $\leq$ TotalWeight [5] + weight of edge {5, 4}

(27 $\leq$ 21 + 16)

Therefore, no total weight is updated, and nothing is enqueued.

During the final iteration, (2, 4) is dequeued, and the tree is updated for the last time:

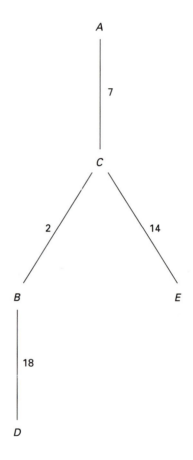

The correctness proof for Dijkstra's algorithm is similar to that for Kruskal's algorithm. The postcondition for the loop statement is:

Tree is a shortest path tree for the network.

The postcondition follows from the invariance of the following loop assertion:

Tree is a shortest path tree for that part of the original network consisting of all the vertices in Tree and all the edges that connect those vertices in the original network.

We now prove that this assertion is a loop invariant. This assertion is true prior to the first iteration, since Tree consists of only one vertex.

Suppose the assertion is true prior to some iteration. To show that the assertion is true after that iteration, we will assume that the assertion is false after that iteration and reach a contradiction. During that iteration, the pair (J, K) is dequeued. Since the assertion was true prior to the iteration, the path in Tree from 1 to J must be a shortest path in the network. If the assertion is false after that iteration, then (J, K) and K must have been added to Tree during that iteration, and the path in Tree from 1 to K must *not* be a shortest path in the network. Therefore, there must be a shorter path P from 1 to K in the network.

At the start of the iteration, vertex 1 was in Tree and vertex K was not in Tree, so there must be a pair of vertices, i_1 and i_2, such that:

1. $\{1, i_2\}$ forms an edge in P;

2. the path from 1 to i_1 was in Tree (unless $i_1 = 1$) at the start of the iteration;

3. i_2 was not in Tree at the start of the iteration.

Figure 11.24 illustrates the relationship among the vertices at the start of the iteration in which K is inserted in Tree.

Figure 11.24

The relationship among some vertices just before K and (J, K) are inserted in Tree. The path P (with dotted lines) goes from vertex 1 to vertex K through the edge $\{i_1, i_2\}$.

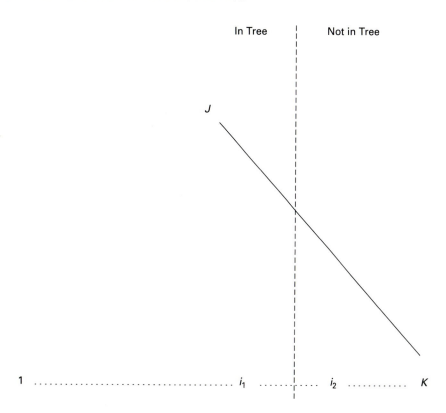

Since i_1 was inserted in Tree earlier, the pair (i_1, i_2) would have been enqueued at that time. However, the value of TotalWeight $[i_2]$ at that time must have been less than the total weight for all of P, which in turn was less than the value of TotalWeight $[K]$ when (J, K) was dequeued. (i_1, i_2) would then have had higher priority than (J, K), so (i_1, i_2) would then have been dequeued instead of (J, K) during the iteration in which (J, K) was dequeued.

This contradiction implies that if the loop assertion is true prior to some iteration, it will also be true after that iteration, and so it will be true prior to the next iteration. We conclude that the loop assertion is true before and after each iteration (that is, the loop assertion is a loop invariant).

We now estimate the time requirements for Dijkstra's algorithm. The While loop is executed approximately N times. During each iteration, a pair (J, K) is dequeued from the priority queue and the neighbors of K are enqueued (unless they are already in the tree).

The total number of pairs on the queue over all iterations is approximately E, so the average queue size is about E/N. Assuming that the priority queue uses a heap for its design domain, the time to dequeue is $O[\log(E/N)]$—see Chapter 8.

If a weight matrix is used for storing the edges and their weights, the time to investigate (to see whether to enqueue) the neighbors of vertex K is N iterations. Therefore, the total time for the While loop is approximately:

$$N * [O(\log(E/N)) + N]$$

In short, Time is $O(N_2)$ if a weight matrix is used.

If a weight list is used instead of a weight matrix, the time to investigate all of vertex K's neighbors is only $2E/N$ iterations, on average (there are N lists, and each edge appears twice). Thus, the total time is approximately:

$$N * [O(\log(E/N)) + 2E/N]$$

In other words, Time is $O(E)$ if a weight list is used.

In a connected network, the value of E can range from $N - 1$ to $N * (N - 1)/2$, and the latter is $O(N^2)$. In other words, a weight list will often provide better (and never provide worse) Time than a weight matrix.

With a heap-based design of the priority queue, we must allocate space for all possible edges, namely, MaxVertices^2. So Space for Dijkstra's algorithm is $O(1)$.

Directed Graphs

We have not yet concerned ourselves with the direction of edges. If we could go from vertex V to vertex W, we assumed that we could also go from vertex W to vertex V. In many situations this assumption may be unrealistic. For example, if the edges represent streets, the street connecting point V to point W may be one-way, so there would not be an edge connecting W to V.

Even if one can travel in either direction on an edge, the weight for going in one direction may be different from the weight going in the other direction. For example, suppose the weights represent the time for a plane flight between two cities; due to the prevailing westerly winds, the time to fly from New York to Los Angeles is greater than the time to fly from Los Angeles to New York.

These deficiencies are overcome with directed graphs. A ***directed graph*** is a collection of vertices together with a collection of ordered pairs of vertices called ***arcs***. Pictorially, arcs are represented by arrows, with the arrow's direction going from the first vertex in the ordered pair to the second vertex. For example, Fig. 11.25 contains a directed graph.

In Fig. 11.25, the arrow from A to B represents the ordered pair of vertices (A, B). There is no arrow from B to A, and so (B, A) is not an arc in the directed graph.

A path in a directed graph must follow the direction of the arrows. Formally, a ***directed path*** in a directed graph is a list of $K > 1$ vertices $V_1, V_2, \ldots, V_K$ such that $(V_1, V_2), (V_2, V_3), \ldots, (V_{K-1}, V_K)$ are arcs in the directed graph. For example, in Fig. 11.25,

$$B, D, E, F$$

is a directed path from B to F because (B, D), (D, E), and (E, F) are arcs in the graph. However,

$$B, D, F$$

is not a directed path because there is no arc from D to F.

Figure 11.25

A directed graph.

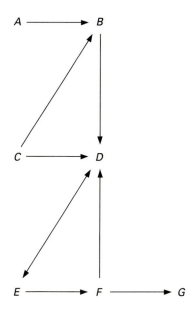

Connectedness for directed graphs corresponds to the intuitive meaning of "all one piece;" a directed graph is connected if the underlying graph (ignoring the direction of arrows) is connected. Formally, a directed graph is **connected** if, for any two distinct vertices x and y in the graph, there is a list of K vertices $V_1, V_2, \ldots, V_K$ such that $x = V_1$, $y = V_K$, and for each value of i between 1 and $K - 1$, either (V_i, V_{i+1}) is an arc, or (V_{i+1}, V_i) is an arc.

The directed graph in Fig. 11.23 is connected. For example, for the vertices A and C, we can construct the following sequence of vertices:

   A, B, C

(A, B) is an arc and (C, B) is an arc. Note that there is no directed path from A to C, nor is there a directed path from C to A. Here is an example of a directed graph that is not connected:

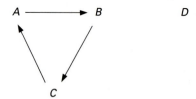

In most applications, the directed graphs will be connected; so we assume, for the remainder of the section, that each directed graph we consider is connected.

A somewhat stricter notion is "strongly connected." A directed graph is **strongly connected** if there is a directed path between any pair of vertices. For example, the following graph is strongly connected:

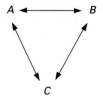

The graph in Fig. 11.24 is not strongly connected; for example, there is no directed path from G to A.

Most of the terms from the preceding sections can be extended to directed graphs. For example, a *cycle* in a directed graph is a directed path from a vertex to itself. In Fig. 11.25,

   E, D, E

is a cycle. Another cycle in that directed graph is:

   F, D, E, F

Figure 11.26

A directed network.

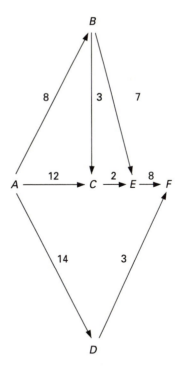

Figure 11.26

A directed network.

A ***directed network*** is a network in which each arc has an associated nonnnegative number, called the *weight* of the arc. Figure 11.26 contains a directed network.

A ***directed tree*** is a directed graph in which one vertex, the *root*, has no arcs coming into it, and every other vertex has exactly one arc coming into it. Each vertex can have any number of arcs coming out of it. For example, Fig. 11.27 shows a directed tree (we use lines rather than arrows because the direction is always top-down).

Figure 11.27

A directed tree.

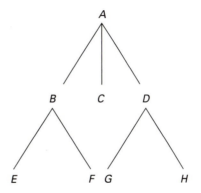

Figure 11.28

An ordered directed tree.

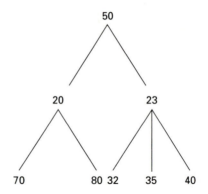

For any vertices *V* and *W* in a directed tree, if there is an arc from *V* to *W*, we say that W is a *child* of V, and that *V* is the *parent* of W. For example, in Fig. 11.27, *B* is a child of *A* and *D* is the parent of *G*. Vertices with the same parent are called *siblings*. For example, in Fig. 11.27, *B*, *C*, and *D* are siblings.

An ***ordered directed tree*** is one in which each parent's children are ordered. For example, if the vertices are numbers and the ordering is based on increasing order, Fig. 11.28 contains an ordered directed tree.

The main idea behind an ordered directed tree is that the following two trees are the same when viewed merely as directed trees, but different when viewed as ordered directed trees:

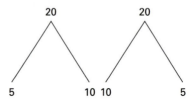

A recursion tree is a good example of an ordered directed tree. The ordering in a recursion tree is chronological: The action specified by the leftmost sibling is performed first, and so on.

Binary trees, the focus of Chapters 7 and 8, can be defined as specializations of ordered directed trees. A ***binary tree*** is an ordered directed tree in which each parent has at most two children, and each child is identified as being a *left* child or a *right* child. We need the last part of this definition to distinguish between:

and

A has a left child in the former binary tree and a right child in the latter. As ordered directed trees, the two trees are the same.

Another important example of an ordered directed tree is a parse tree, constructed by a compiler as it determines the syntactic structure of a program. Assume that we have defined the syntax of a language using BNF notation (see Chapter 2). A **_parse tree_** is an ordered directed tree in which each parent represents the left-hand side of a BNF definition and each child, in turn, represents the symbols on the right-hand side for one alternative in the definition. For example, we can define the structure of very simple expressions as follows:

```
<expression> ::= <term> | <expression> + <term>
<term> ::= <factor> | <term> * <factor>
<factor> ::= <identifier> | ( <expression> )
```

where ⟨identifier⟩ was defined in BNF in Chapter 2 as a letter or underscore followed by zero or more letters, underscores, or digits.

Here is a parse tree for *A* + *B* (the subtrees rooted at ⟨identifier⟩ are abbreviated):

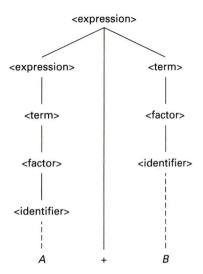

The parse tree for $C * A + D$ is slightly more complicated:

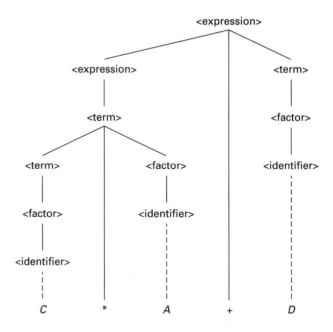

Compare that parse tree with the parse tree for $C + A * D$:

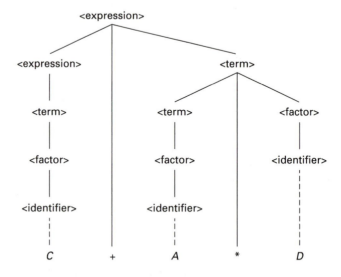

In a parse tree, operators farther from the root will be evaluated before those that are closer to the root. In both of the preceding parse trees, the multiplication will be performed before the addition, as you would expect. Furthermore, additions will be performed from left to right, as will multiplications. For example, the parse tree for $A * B * C$ indicates that the multiplication of A and B will be performed first because it is farther from the root than the second multiplication:

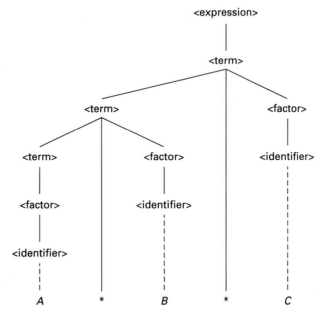

Note that we cannot redraw the parse tree to indicate that the multiplication of B and C should take place first:

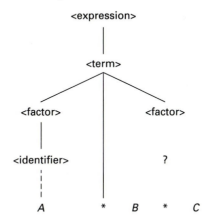

There is no way to obtain $B * C$ from ⟨factor⟩. The only way to force $B * C$ to be evaluated first is to rewrite the expression, either as:

$$B * C * A$$

or as:

$$A * (B * C)$$

SUMMARY

A *graph* is a collection of items called *vertices*, together with a collection of unordered pairs of distinct vertices, called *edges*. In the Graph ADT, users can insert, delete, retrieve, or replace a vertex, and insert or delete an edge. Two other operators allow a user to find the shortest path (that is, the path with fewest edges) between two vertices and to traverse the entire graph.

We studied two design domains. In the first, the vertices are stored in a list, VertexList. Edge information is stored in a Boolean matrix, Adjacency-Matrix, where the entry at row I and column J is True if there is an edge connecting the vertices at positions I and J in VertexList. The second design domain also uses VertexList, but edge information is stored in an array of lists, AdjacencyList. AdjacencyList $[I]$ contains the list of all vertex positions (from VertexList) of vertices that are adjacent to the vertex in position I in VertexList. The analysis of the method subalgorithms indicates that an Ad-jacencyList is more efficient than an AdjacencyMatrix, for both Time and Space, if the number of edges is less than $O(N^2)$, where N is the number of vertices. In some situations, such as Warshall's algorithm for testing whether a graph is connected, an adjacency matrix is virtually indispensable.

A *tree* is a connected, acyclic graph. The number of edges in a tree is always one fewer than the number of vertices. Given any connected graph, it is possible to construct a *spanning tree*, a tree that contains all of the graph's vertices. A *network* is a graph in which each edge has an associated *weight*, a nonnegative number that may represent the time, cost, or distance between two vertices. Kruskal's algorithm enables us to construct a *minimal spanning tree* for a network (that is, a spanning tree for which the total of the edge weights is minimal).

In a network, a *shortest path* between two vertices is one whose total weight is minimal. Dijkstra's algorithm, an extension of Kruskal's, constructs a shortest path tree rooted at a given vertex. A *shortest path tree* in a network is a spanning tree for which the path from the root to any other vertex is a shortest path.

A *directed graph* is a collection of items called *vertices*, together with a collection of ordered pairs of vertices called *arcs*. Of special interest are *ordered directed trees* (such as recursion trees, binary trees, and parse trees) in which the children of each parent are ordered.

EXERCISES

11.1 **a.** Draw a picture of the following graph:

> Vertices: *A, B, C, D, E*
> Edges: {*A, B*}, {*C, D*}, {*D, A*}, {*B, D*}, {*B, E*}

b. Is the graph a tree? If not, find all cycles.

11.2   Define, as a collection of vertices and edges, each of the following
graphs:

a.

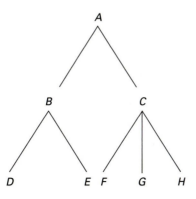

b.

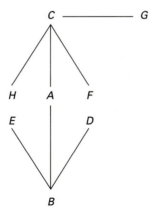

11.3   **a.** Draw a graph that has four vertices and as many edges as possible. How many edges does the graph have?
b. Draw a graph that has five vertices and as many edges as possible. How many edges does the graph have?
c. What is the maximum number of edges for a graph with N vertices?
d. Prove the claim you made in part c.

HINT   *Use induction on N.*

11.4   Give an example of an acyclic graph that is not a tree.

11.5   Suppose we have the following graph:

   a.   Insert vertices into VertexList alphabetically.
   b.   Trace the execution of the breadth-first traversal subalgorithm for the IsConnected method in the Graph ADT.
   c.   Trace the execution of Warshall's algorithm for the IsConnected method.
   d.   Trace the execution of the subalgorithm for the FindShortestPath method to try to find the shortest path from *A* to *E*. How would the trace be different if you wanted to find the shortest path from *E* to *A*?

11.6   Trace the execution of the subalgorithm for the FindShortestPath method in the Graph ADT to try to find the shortest path from *A* to *F* in the following graph:

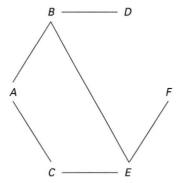

Assume that the vertices are stored alphabetically in VertexList.

11.7   As a *user* of the Graph ADT, develop subalgorithms for each of the following operators:

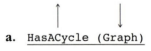

   a.   `HasACycle (Graph)`

Postcondition: True has been returned if Graph has a cycle. Otherwise, False has been returned.

b. `IsIsolated (Graph, Vertex)`

Precondition: Vertex is a vertex in Graph.

Postcondition: True has been returned if Vertex has no neighbors. Otherwise, False has been returned.

c. `IsASubGraph (Graph, SubGraph)`

Postcondition: True has been returned if SubGraph is a subgraph of Graph. Otherwise, False has been returned.

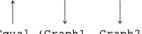

d. `Equal (Graph1, Graph2)`

Postcondition: True has been returned if Graph1 is the same graph as Graph2.

H I N T   *See part (c).*

11.8   Develop a subalgorithm based on a depth-first traversal for the Is-Connected method in the Graph ADT.

11.9   For the network given below, find a minimal spanning tree and a shortest-path tree rooted at *A*:

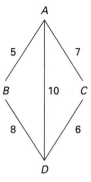

11.10   For the network given below, assume that vertices are stored alphabetically in VertexList.

a.   Trace the execution of Kruskal's algorithm to find a minimal spanning tree.

b. Trace the execution of Dijkstra's algorithm to find a shortest path tree rooted at *A*.

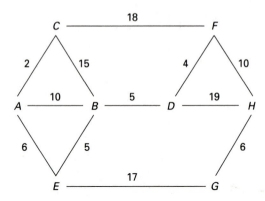

11.11 Kruskal's algorithm and Dijkstra's algorithm are both ***greedy***: the locally optimal choice is always made. In both cases, greed succeeds in the sense that the locally optimal choices lead to the globally optimal solution. Do all greedy algorithms succeed for all inputs? In this exercise we explore coin-changing algorithms. In one situation, the greedy algorithm succeeds for all inputs. In the other situation, the greedy algorithm succeeds for some inputs and fails for some inputs.

Suppose you want to provide change for any amount under a dollar using as few coins as possible. Since fewest is best, the greedy (that is, locally optimal) choice at each step is the coin with largest value whose addition will not surpass the original amount. Here are the steps in a greedy algorithm:

```
Coin [1] := 25
Coin [2] := 10
Coin [3] := 5
Coin [4] := 1
Read in Amount
for I := 1 to 4 do
   Loop as long as Coin [I] <= Amount
      Write out Coin [I]
      Amount := Amount - Coin [I]
```

For example, suppose the Amount read in is 62. The output will be:

> 25
> 25
> 10
> 1
> 1

Five coins is the minimal number of coins needed to make 62 cents from quarters, nickels, dimes, and pennies.

a. Show that the given algorithm is optimal for any Amount between 0 and 99 cents, inclusive.

b. Give an example to show that a greedy algorithm is not optimal for all inputs if nickels are not available, that is, if we have:

```
Coin [1] := 25
Coin [2] := 10
Coin [3] := 1
Read in Amount
for I := 1 to 3 do
    ...
```

then the algorithm will not be optimal for some inputs.

11.12 Modify Dijkstra's algorithm to find, not a shortest path tree, but merely a shortest path between two vertices.

11.13 Modify Dijkstra's algorithm to find all shortest paths in a network. In other words, the algorithm should find a shortest path from V to W for all distinct pairs of vertices V and W in the network. A total of $N * (N - 1)/2$ paths will be produced.

11.14 **(Floyd's Algorithm)** Modify Warshall's algorithm to find all shortest paths in a network.

HINT Suppose that the matrix Total holds the total weight of the current path between two vertices.

```
    ...
for I := 1 to N do
   for J := 1 to N do
      for K := 1 to N do
         { Is there a path from J to K that runs }
         { through I and is shorter than the      }
         { current shortest path from J to K?     }
         if Total [J, I] + Total [I, K] < Total [J, K]
         then
               Total[J, K] := Total[J, I] + Total[I, K]
               Path [J, K] := I { I is on the shortest
                                  path from J to K. }
    ...
```

11.15 The *Traveling Salesperson Problem* can be stated as follows: Given a network in which there is an edge between any two vertices, find a cycle that includes all of the vertices and whose edges have the smallest total weight of all cycles that include all vertices. For example, consider the following network:

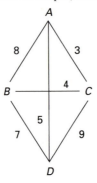

The cycle,

$$C, B, D, A, C$$

has a total weight of:

$$4 + 7 + 5 + 3 = 19$$

and this value is minimal. Of course, any other cycle with those same edges will also be minimal. For example,

$$A, D, B, C, A$$

The phrase "traveling salesperson" refers to the interpretation of the network in which the vertices represent cities and the weights represent distances between cities. The cycle with minimal total weight is the shortest path that includes all of the cities and returns to the starting point.

a. Solve the Traveling Salesperson Problem for the following network:

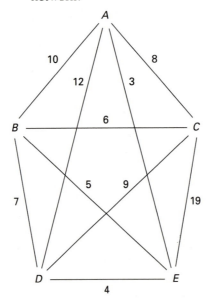

b. Develop an algorithm to solve the Traveling Salesperson Problem.

HINT   One strategy is to use brute force; that is, to calculate the total weights for all possible cycles and then pick a cycle whose total weight is minimal. To obtain all cycles, we can start at any vertex. There are $N - 1$ possibilities for the second vertex in a cycle. For each of those $N - 1$ vertices, there are $N - 2$ possible vertices that can be chosen as the third vertex, and so on.

The total number of cycles investigated will be

$$(N - 1) * (N - 2) * \ldots * 3 * 2 * 1 = (N - 1)!$$

Such an algorithm will have Time that is at least $O(N!)$, which is approximately $O(N^N)$.

c. (Win fame and fortune!) Develop an algorithm to solve the Traveling Salesperson Problem that takes only $O(N^K)$ Time for some positive integer K.

11.16 Modify Dijkstra's algorithm so that it finds the shortest path in a directed network.

11.17 From the BNF definition of ⟨expression⟩ given earlier in this chapter, develop parse trees for each of the following:

a. First + Second * Third
b. (W + X) * (Y + Z)
c. A + B + C * D * E

11.18 The following sequence of Backus-Naur Form definitions allows exponentiation, represented by ^, within an expression:

```
<expression> ::= <term> | <expression> + <term>
<term>       ::= <factor> | <term> * <factor>
<factor>     ::= <primary> | <primary> ^ <factor>
<primary>    ::= <identifier> | ( <expression> )
```

Develop parse trees for each of the following expressions:

a. $A \char`\^ B * C$
b. $A * B \char`\^ C$
c. $A * B \char`\^ C \char`\^ D * E$
d. $(A * B) \char`\^ C \char`\^ (D * E)$

11.19 According to the definitions in Exercise 11.18,

a. Which operator (+, *, or ^) has the highest precedence?
b. Are exponentiations to be evaluated from left to right or from right to left? Rewrite the definition of ⟨primary⟩ to change the order in which exponentiations are to be evaluated.

**LABORATORY
EXERCISE**

11.1 For each of the following methods in the Graph ADT, conjecture whether the AdjacencyMatrix or AdjacencyList implementation would be faster in a graph with $2N$ edges:

    a. InsertVertex
    b. InsertEdge
    c. DeleteVertex
    d. DeleteEdge

Conduct experiments to reject or not reject your conjectures. For simplicity, assume $N = 20$ and the vertices are the integers $1..20$. Randomly generate the graphs.

**PROGRAMMING
ASSIGNMENTS**

11.1 For the Network ADT, determine its responsibilities to users, and then define, design, and implement the data type.

11.2 For the Directed Graph ADT, determine its responsibilities, and then define, design, and implement the data type.

11.3 A *maze* is a matrix of Xs and blanks. On the outside rows and columns there are two blanks labelled *Entrance* and *Exit*. A maze cannot contain a square of blanks, such as the following grid:

```
XXXX
X  X
X  X
XXXX
```

Here is a simple maze:

```
Entrance

    |
    |
    |
    |
    |
    |
    |
    X XXXXX
    X XXXXX
    X     X
    X XX XX
    X  X XX
    X XX XX
    X           ————Exit
    X XXXXX
    X     X
    X XX XX
    XXXXXXX
```

We can convert such a maze into a graph as follows:

1. The entrance and exit blanks become vertices.

2. A blank becomes a vertex if three of that blank's horizontal and vertical neighbors are blanks. For example, in the following 3×3 grid, the blank in the center becomes a vertex:

```
X X
X
X X
```

Such vertices represent junctions in the maze.

3. A blank becomes a (dead end) vertex if exactly one of that blank's horizontal or vertical neighbors is a blank. For example, in the following 4×4 grid, the blank in the next-to-bottom row becomes a vertex:

```
X XX
X XX
X XX
XXXX
```

4. Each remaining sequence of one or more consecutive (horizontal or vertical) blanks becomes an edge. For example, in the following 4×8 grid, the blanks in rows 4, 5, and 6 become an edge.

```
XX X
XX X
   X
XX X
XX X
XX X
XX
XX X
```

5. Also, if any two adjacent blanks become vertices, an edge is constructed to join them. For example, in the following 4×5 grid, an edge is constructed to join the vertices from positions (3, 3) and (4, 3):

```
XX X
XX X
   X
XX
XX X
```

Here is one graph for the maze given earlier:

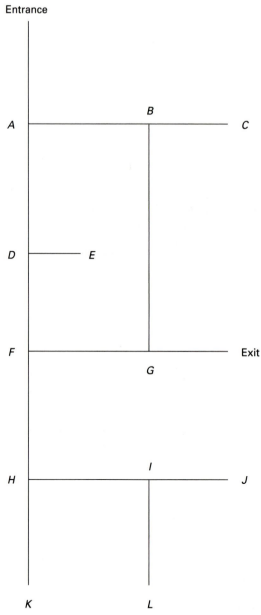

Solving the original maze is now nothing more than finding a path from Entrance to Exit. We can do even better with the help of the FindShortestPath method in the Graph ADT. For example, an optimal solution to the maze, in terms of the generated graph, is:

Entrance, *A*, *B*, *G*, Exit

Design and implement a program to read in and solve a maze.

Turbo Vision

Thomas C. McMillan

CHAPTER 12

INTRODUCTION

When designing a program, we usually concentrate on what the program is supposed to do and give little attention to how, from the perspective of the user, the program will be used. If you have a difficult problem to solve, it is natural to concentrate on the solution rather than the way the solution will be packaged. The packaging is important, however, because a program that does the right thing but is difficult to use is of little or no value. In this chapter, we will concentrate on the user interface of a program. It is the user interface that gives the user of your program access to its computational resources. We begin with a brief discussion of the user interface. This will be followed by an example that illustrates Turbo Vision, a collection of tools that aids in designing and implementing a good user interface.

A GOOD USER INTERFACE

A good user interface should facilitate the natural flow of information between the user and the program. When the user supplies data to the program, the dialog between user and program should be easy, leaving the user confident that he or she has done the right thing. When the program presents data to the user, it should be clear and understandable. This requires more than just a list of numbers. Values displayed by a program should include labels and should be formatted for clarity. If the user makes a mistake, the program should display meaningful error messages so that recovery is quick and easy. Finally, the user, not the program, should be in control. For example, suppose the user has entered data to be processed and then discovers an error in one of the values. If the program simply processes the data as entered without giving the user a chance to correct the erroneous entry, then it is the program that is in control. The user is forced to wait for and see the results of a useless computation. A good user interface puts the user in control of the program's computational resources and facilitates the two-way flow of information between the user and those resources.

Another characteristic of a good program is robustness. The **robustness** of a program is a measure of its ability to recover from erroneous input. Robustness is an important characteristic. Imagine the frustration you would feel if, after entering hundreds of lines of code but before you were able to save them to a disk file, the editor "crashed" because you used some sequence of keystrokes that the editor's designer had not anticipated. A robust program is protected from abnormal termination.

Suppose, for example, that a program requires a nonzero value to be entered for the real variable Coefficient, and that entering a value of zero for this variable will lead to an eventual crash of the program as a result of attempted division by zero. The following lines of code do not protect the program from this possibility. (Assume Prompt is an appropriately defined constant.)

```
Write(Prompt);
ReadLn(Coefficient)
```

The program is not robust because there is no attempt to recover from an error that will lead to an abnormal termination. A better approach is represented in the following attempt:

```
Write(Prompt);
ReadLn(Coefficient);
While Coefficient = 0 do
   begin
      WriteLn(ErrorMessage);
      Write(Prompt);
      ReadLn(coefficient)
   end
```

This code at least attempts to recover from an input error, and is therefore more robust than the first example. There are still problems, however. Suppose, for example, that the user enters the value for Coefficient and uses the letter "O" where zero should be used. ReadLn will not be able to process the user's input and the program will terminate abnormally. This illustrates a problem with using Read and ReadLn to read numeric data. Our attempt at trapping errors improves the program's robustness, but there is still room for improvement. In this chapter and in the exercises we will discuss tools for improving the robustness of a program.

We will use an example to illustrate some of the Turbo Pascal tools that can be used to design a good user interface. These tools are mainly a hierarchy of objects collectively referred to as "Turbo Vision." These objects and their methods can be used to place menus and windows on the screen and to establish a connection between user responses (typed responses and mouse clicks) and actions performed by the program.

EXAMPLE PROGRAM SPECIFICATIONS

Suppose we need a program that will aid in making financial projections. The program will make projections of three different kinds:

1. The value of an account after a given number of periods if a constant amount is deposited into the account each period.
2. The value of an account if deposits of varying size are made to the account each period.
3. The amount that must be deposited into an account each period to reach a specified goal after a given number of periods.

To make the program more general, the length of a period (e.g., month, quarter, year) is not specified. The interest rate is always for a period (not necessarily an annual rate) and the interest is compounded periodically.

The user specifies which type of projection he or she wants by calling up a "dialog box" from a menu and selecting the desired projection with a mouse click (or using the appropriate keystrokes if a mouse is not available). Another dialog box can be used to set the initial conditions that are common to all of the projections (the initial deposit and the periodic interest rate). For the first projection, another dialog box is used to obtain the amount of each deposit and the number of periods from the user. For the second projection, the value of each deposit is obtained from the user as the final value of the account is accumulated. For the third projection, a separate dialog box is used to obtain the desired goal and the number of periods from the user.

When the program is started, all of the parameters (projection, initial deposit, periodic deposit, interest rate, number of periods, and goal) are given default values. These defaults are displayed in the dialog boxes, and as new values are entered by the user or calculated, they become the new defaults. The dialog boxes for selecting a projection and for setting parameters are called up by selecting the corresponding command from an "Operation" menu.

Another Operation menu item the user can select is "Do Projection." When this command is selected (with a mouse click or a function key), the program performs the currently selected projection with the current values of the appropriate parameters. These values may be user-entered values, default values, or values resulting from previous projection calculations. The results of the projection are displayed in a dialog box. Finally, the user can select a command from the "System" menu for exiting the program.

The design of this program reflects an attempt to keep the user in control. The user can visit and revisit the dialog boxes in any order. The flow of events is controlled by the user from the keyboard and mouse. This style of programming is called "event-driven programming." Turbo Vision provides the objects and methods for "hooking" these events to the specific actions they're related to in the program.

TURBO VISION OBJECTS

Figure 12.1 gives a portion of the Turbo Vision hierarchy. TView is an object for controlling the screen. As is apparent from Fig. 12.1, TView has many specialized descendant types. It is generally these more specialized types that will be instantiated. As you might expect, objects inherit some methods from their ancestors and add some methods appropriate for their particular type. When you define a descendant object, you may inherit some methods, override others, and define new methods. We will see examples.

Figure 12.1

Turbo Vision
Hierarchy

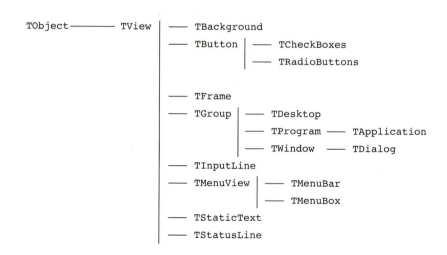

Associated with each of the "T" objects in Fig. 12.1 is a corresponding "P" object. For example, PDialog is of type ^TDialog. These pointer types are necessary because dialog boxes are specified by linking various views together and associating them with their owner. Pointers are used to construct these linked structures.

The best way to get a feel for the capabilities of Turbo Vision is to look at it in use.

FinancialPlanner: Implementation

The Math. The actual computational requirements of our program are easily handled. If regular (one per period) deposits of size M are made to an account, then the value of the account after n periods is:

$$b_n = (1 + r)^n b_o + \frac{M((1 + r)^n - 1)}{r}$$

where n is the number of periods, b_o is the initial deposit, and r is the periodic interest rate. The algorithm for determining the final balance is implemented in procedure DoRegularProjection:

```
procedure DoRegularProjection(InitialDeposit,
                              PeriodicDeposit,
                              InterestRate:real;
                              NumberOfPeriods:integer;
                              var FinalValue:real);
var
   S,
   Rate:real;
begin
   Rate := InterestRate/100.0; {Convert percentage rate to
                                decimal fraction.}
   S := Power(1+Rate,NumberOfPeriods);
   FinalValue := S*InitialDeposit + PeriodicDeposit * ((S -
                 1)/Rate);
   FinalValue := Round(FinalValue*100.0)/100.0
end; {DoRegularProjection}
```

Notice that InterestRate is first converted to a decimal fraction. Power is a function that implements the needed exponentiation. The last line in the procedure rounds the result to the nearest penny.

To find a formula for the monthly deposit required to reach a certain goal, G, replace b_n with G in the preceding formula and solve for M:

$$M = \frac{(G - (1 + r)^n b_o)r}{(1 + r)^n - 1}$$

This calculation is performed by the procedure DoDetermineProjection:

```
procedure DoDetermineProjection(InitialDeposit:real;
                                var PeriodicDeposit:real;
                                InterestRate:real;
                                NumberOfPeriods:integer;
                                var FinalValue:real);
var
   S,
   Rate:real;
begin
   Rate := InterestRate/100.0; {Convert percentage rate to
                                decimal fraction.}
   S := Power(1+Rate,NumberOfPeriods);
   PeriodicDeposit := (FinalValue - S*InitialDeposit)*Rate/
                      (S-1);
   PeriodicDeposit := Round(PeriodicDeposit*100.0)/100.0;
   DoRegularProjection(InitialDeposit,PeriodicDeposit,
                       InterestRate,NumberOfPeriods,
                       FinalValue)
end; {DoDetermineProjection}
```

Once DoDetermineProjection determines the required periodic deposit, it calls DoRegularProjection to determine what the final value actually is. Of course, this should be equal to the desired goal, but it won't be exactly equal because the results are calculated only to the nearest penny.

The other style of projection, in which the size of the periodic deposits vary, is performed by procedure DoVariableProjection:

```
procedure DoVariableProjection(InitialDeposit:real;
                               var AverageDeposit:real;
                               InterestRate:real;
                               var NumberOfPeriods:integer;
                               var FinalValue:real);
var
   Rate,
   TotalDeposits,
   Amt         :real;
   Done        :boolean;
begin
   Rate := InterestRate/100.0;
   TotalDeposits := 0;
   NumberOfPeriods := 0;
   Amt := AverageDeposit;
   FinalValue := InitialDeposit;
   repeat
      NumberOfPeriods := NumberOfPeriods +1;
      GetADeposit(Amt,NumberOfPeriods,Done);
```

```
        TotalDeposits := TotalDeposits + Amt;
        FinalValue := FinalValue*(1+rate) + Amt
    until Done;
    FinalValue := Round(FinalValue*100.00)/100.00;
    AverageDeposit := TotalDeposits/NumberOfPeriods
end; {DoVariableProjection}
```

This procedure repeatedly obtains the value of the next deposit from the
user and uses that information to update the value of the account. It then
reports the value of the account, the average size of a deposit, and the
number of periods. This procedure includes a call to procedure GetADeposit. GetADeposit uses a dialog box to obtain the size of a deposit from
the user. GetADeposit uses NumberOfPeriods as part of the prompt for the
user. By selecting a special button within the dialog box, the user can indicate that this is the last deposit. In this case, GetADeposit sets Done to
True. We will return to the implementation of GetADeposit after we have
covered some of the details of dialog boxes. Incidentally, when GetADeposit starts executing, it uses the value that comes in through the parameter Amt as a default value in the dialog box.

Handling Events

To prepare for handling events, we declare some constants that will be
used to identify commands.

```
const
    cmParameters            = 100; { Command to set general
                                     parameters. }
    cmProjectionType        = 101; { Command to determine
                                      projection. }
    cmProjectionParameters  = 102; { Command to set specific
                                     parameters. }
    cmDoProjection          = 103; { Command to do a
                                     projection. }
    RegularPeriodicDeposit   = 0; { Radio Button commands for
                                    selecting which
                                    projection to do. }
    VariablePeriodicDeposit = 1;
    DeterminePeriodicDeposit = 2;
```

The "cm" constants are named according to Turbo Pascal conventions for
naming commands. The only thing that is important to note right now is
that the values of these constants do not conflict with values reserved by
Turbo Pascal. These commands will be invoked by user responses (such as
a mouse click) within a menu. The other constants declared here correspond to the types of projections that the program can perform. These are
not commands, but represent the values that can be returned from the dialog box used to select the projection the user wants to perform.

We now define an object that will be used to intercept events caused by user input and will cause the appropriate actions to take place. This object is called Banker, a descendant of TApplication:

```
type
   Banker = object(TApplication)
      ProjectionType : Word;
      InitialDeposit,
      PeriodicDeposit,
      Goal,
      FinalValue,
      InterestRate : real;
      NumberOfPeriods : integer;
      procedure HandleEvent(var Event: TEvent); virtual;
      procedure InitializeDefaults;
      procedure InitMenuBar; virtual;
      procedure InitStatusLine; virtual;
      procedure SetInitialParameters;
      procedure SelectProjectionType;
      procedure SetProjectionParameters;
      procedure DoProjection
   end;
```

Notice that Banker will override TApplication's methods HandleEvent, Init-MenuBar, and InitStatusLine (which are really inherited from TProgram). This is where we tailor the screen-handling capabilities of the object to our particular needs. The data fields in the type Banker are the parameters needed by the various projections.

The action is managed by Banker.HandleEvent, whose declaration is:

```
procedure Banker.HandleEvent(var Event: TEvent);
begin
   TApplication.HandleEvent(Event);
   if Event.What = evCommand then
      begin
         case Event.Command of
            cmParameters           : SetInitialParameters;
            cmProjectionType       : SelectProjectionType;
            cmProjectionParameters: SetProjectionParameters;
            cmDoProjection         : DoProjection
         else
            Exit
               {case}
         end;
            ClearEvent(Event)
      end      {if}
end; {HandleEvent}
```

The first thing Banker.HandleEvent does is pass the Event to the HandleEvent method of its parent type (TApplication). This is because commands that are not being added should be executed exactly as they are defined in TApplication's HandleEvent. An example of such a command is cmQuit, the command for terminating execution of the program. If TApplication.HandleEvent handles the event, it sets Event's What field to the value evNothing, and no further processing takes place. In the next statement of Banker.HandleEvent, Event's What and Command fields are used to determine if the event is a command that is defined for the object Banker. If it is, the appropriate method (e.g., DoProjection) is called, and the event is cleared. If the event represents a command (or other event) that is not defined for the object Banker, then control returns from Banker.HandleEvent without further action and without clearing the event. The effect of ClearEvent is to set Event's What field to the value evNothing. This approach allows us to define descendant objects with new events and to keep or modify the events of ancestor objects. In this case, if we wanted to eliminate or change any of the events handled by Banker's parent type, TApplication, then we would put the code that implements the change *before* the call to TApplication.HandleEvent.

Banker.HandleEvent calls the appropriate method when it intercepts a command that is defined for this object, but where do the commands come from? They are generated by the user when he or she selects the action from a menu. Next, we will examine the methods for setting up the menus.

Menus and Status Lines

Before discussing the methods used for setting up menus, we must take care of a minor detail. The type TRect is an object type used for specifying a rectangle. An object of type TRect has two data fields, A and B, of type TPoint. The point A is the upper left hand corner of a rectangle on the screen; the point B is the lower right hand corner. Objects of type TPoint have two data fields representing the coordinates of a point. An object of type TRect has (among others) the method Assign. The call R.Assign (XA,YA,XB,YB) defines the rectangle. The coordinates of the corner points of a TRect are given in grid positions on the screen, with x coordinates increasing left to right and y coordinates increasing top to bottom. The lowest coordinate in each direction is 0. The grid positions define lines between the character positions on the screen:

	0	1	2	3	4	...
0						
	A	B	C	D		
1						
	U	V	V	X		
2						
	E	F	G	H		
3						
	K	L	M	N		
4						

The method Banker.InitMenuBar defines the format of the menu bar (which contains two submenus) and establishes a connection between menu selections and commands. Here is the declaration for Banker.InitMenuBar:

```
procedure Banker.InitMenuBar;
var R: TRect;
begin
   GetExtent(R);
   R.B.Y := R.A.Y + 1;
   MenuBar := New(PMenuBar, Init(R, NewMenu(
      NewSubMenu('~S~ystem', hcNoContext, NewMenu(
         NewItem('E~x~it', 'Alt-X', kbAltX, cmQuit,
         hcNoContext,  nil)),
      NewSubMenu('~O~peration', hcNoContext, NewMenu(
         NewItem('~I~nitial Conditions','F7',kbF7,
         cmParameters,hcNoContext,
      NewItem('~P~rojection Type', 'F2', kbF2,
            cmProjectionType, hcNoContext,
      NewItem('~S~et Projection Parameters', 'F6', kbF6,
            cmProjectionParameters, hcNoContext,
      NewItem('~D~o Projection', 'F5', kbF5,
            cmDoProjection, hcNoContext,
      nil))))),
   nil)) )));
end; {InitMenuBar}
```

In this method, GetExtent is a method inherited by Banker from TView. The coordinates of the rectangle that defines the current view are placed in *R* by the call to GetExtent. (Because initialization takes place before this method is called, the current view will be the entire screen.) The next line of the method defines the rectangle that covers the top row of the screen. The last statement of Banker.InitMenuBar assigns a value to the variable MenuBar, which is a global pointer variable supplied by the Turbo Vision system. Notice that the function form of New is being used: New(PMenuBar, Init(.....)) calls the constructor Init for the object type TMenuBar and returns a pointer to the resulting object. As a result of the assignment statement, this pointer is stored in MenuBar. Notice that Init uses the rectangle *R* to define the location of the menu bar.

The linked nature of views is evident from the structure of the calls to NewMenu, NewSubMenu, and NewItem, each of which are functions that return pointers to the corresponding objects. In particular, MenuBar has two submenus named "System" and "Operation." Here is how the menu bar appears at the top of the screen:

System Operation

The "S" and "O" are highlighted as a result of the '~S~' and '~O~' in the NewSubMenu calls. The tildes identify the "S" and "O" as "hot keys." This means that the Operation submenu, for example, can be opened by typing Alt-O. Of course, it can also be opened by clicking on the word "Operation" with the mouse.

Each of these submenus is associated with a menu that can be opened when the label is selected from the keyboard or with a mouse click. For example, when the Operation submenu is selected, the screen will look like this:

```
System Operation
```

Initial Conditions	F1
Projection Type	F2
Set Projection Parameters	F6
Do Projection	F5

Once the menu is open, one of the choices can be selected by using its highlighted letter (no Alt is necessary) or clicking on it with the mouse. Note that the call to NewItem binds a menu item to both a set of keystrokes for selecting the item and a command to be executed when the menu item is selected. For example, the menu item "DoProjection" in the Operation submenu can be selected by the function key F5 or, once the menu is open, by the letter "D." The selection of this menu item causes the event cmDo-Projection—which, as we have seen in the method Banker.HandleEvent, causes the execution of the method DoProjection to occur. Selection of the item "Exit" in the System submenu causes the event cmQuit, which is passed by Banker.HandleEvent to TApplication.HandleEvent, which processes cmQuit by terminating execution of the program.

The constants hcNoContext can be replaced at a later time if context-sensitive help is added to the program.

Summarizing, Banker.InitMenuBar binds menu items to both keystrokes for selecting the menu item and to command events. Banker.HandleEvent interprets the command events that result from menu selection.

Hot key commands can be defined and displayed in a status line across the bottom of the screen. Here is the method that sets up the status line:

```
procedure Banker.InitStatusLine;
var R: TRect;
begin
   GetExtent(R);
   R.A.Y := R.B.Y - 1;
   StatusLine := New(PStatusLine, Init(R,
```

```
     NewStatusDef(0, $FFFF,
        NewStatusKey('~Alt-X~ Exit', kbAltX, cmQuit,
        nil),
     nil)
   ))
end; {InitStatusLine}
```

StatusLine is a global variable supplied by the Turbo Vision system. The structure of a StatusLine is a linked list (similar to but simpler than a MenuBar). This method defines the following status line, in which "Alt-x" is bound to cmQuit:

Alt-X Exit

The 0 and $FFFF define a range of help contexts, which can be used if context-sensitive help is added to the program.

The menu bar and status line have menu items that are bound to command events. These command events are interpreted by Banker.HandleEvent by calls to methods that perform the desired task. Each of these methods must get additional information from the user or display the results of calculation to the user. This information transfer between program and user is accomplished through dialog boxes.

Dialog Boxes

A dialog box is an object, of type PDialog (= ^TDialog), that displays views of other types that can be used to present information to, or get information from, the user. Our first example is the dialog box that is used when the user selects "Projection Type" from the Operation submenu to select one of the three projections to perform. This dialog is accomplished using a view type called TRadioButtons—a set of buttons with the property that only one button can be down at any time (like the buttons on a car radio). The procedure SetUpProjectionTypeWindow defines (but does not draw) the dialog box for obtaining the projection type:

```
procedure SetUpProjectionTypeWindow(var Dialog:PDialog);
var ViewBuffer:PView;
   R:TRect;
begin
   R.Assign(20, 4, 59, 15);
   Dialog := New(PDialog, Init(R, 'Projection Type'));
   with Dialog^ do
     begin
        R.Assign(3, 3, 36, 6);
        ViewBuffer := New(PRadioButtons, Init(R,
           NewSItem ('~R~egular Periodic Deposit',
           NewSItem('~V~ariable Periodic Deposit',
```

```
                    NewSItem('~D~etermine Periodic Deposit',
                    nil)))
              ));
              Insert(ViewBuffer);
              R.Assign(10, 2, 26, 3);
              Insert(New(PLabel, Init(R, 'Projection Type',
              ViewBuffer)));
              R.Assign(8, 7, 18, 9);
              Insert(New(PButton, Init(R, '~O~k', cmOK,
              bfDefault)));
              R.Assign(21, 7, 31, 9);
              Insert(New(PButton, Init(R, 'Cancel', cmCancel,
              bfNormal)))
         end {with}
end; {SetUpProjectionTypeWindow}
```

The variable ViewBuffer is used in constructing the subviews to be inserted into the dialog box. ViewBuffer is of the generic type PView because the subviews may be of different types. The first two lines of the procedure set up an empty dialog box and define its position on the screen. Notice that the second parameter of the Init method is a string giving the title of the dialog box.

Within the with Dialog^ do statement, rectangle coordinates are relative to the upper left hand corner of the dialog box. The assignment statement ViewBuffer := ... causes a radio button menu to be constructed and a pointer to this menu to be stored in ViewBuffer. Items are linked onto a radio button menu, and the position of the radio button menu is defined in a manner similar to the way it is done for menu bars. Insert(ViewBuffer) is a call to a method that Dialog inherits from TGroup. It links the radio button just defined into the list of subviews for the dialog box.

The next two lines illustrate why we need the ViewBuffer variable. We could have inserted the radio button menu into the dialog box without using ViewBuffer just by calling Insert with the call to New as its parameter: Insert(New(...)). However, we need the pointer to the radio button menu because the next two lines insert a label (of type Plabel) into the dialog box and establish a link between the label and the radio button menu. The Init method for the label needs a pointer to the radio button menu in order to establish the connection. This makes it possible to select the radio button menu subview by clicking on the label.

The last two Inserts insert buttons into the dialog box. A button is a Turbo Vision view that is activated with a single mouse click (or by tabbing to the button and hitting the space bar). The parameters of the TButton.Init method are the position of the button, a label for the button, a command that is bound to the button, and a flag that affects the button's behavior. In this example, the button labelled "OK" is bound to the Turbo Vision command cmOK. The button flag bfDefault makes this button the default view of the dialog box. This means that the user can activate this button without first having to tab to it by hitting the space bar or the letter "O," which is highlighted on the label. The effect of activating a button is to close the dialog box and send the command bound to that button back to the calling procedure.

The dialog box is set up by the procedure SetUpProjectionTypeWindow. This action will occur when the method Banker.SelectProjectionType is executed. (As can be seen from the declarations of Banker.HandleEvent and Banker.InitMenuBar, Banker.SelectProjectionType is executed as a result of the user's clicking on "Projection Type" in the Operation submenu.) Here is the declaration for Banker.SelectProjectionType:

```
procedure Banker.SelectProjectionType;
var
    Dialog: PDialog;
    Command: Word;
begin
    SetUpProjectionTypeWindow(Dialog);
    Dialog^.SetData(ProjectionType);
    Command := DeskTop^.ExecView(Dialog);
    if Command <> cmCancel then
        Dialog^.GetData(ProjectionType);
    Dispose(Dialog, Done)
end; {SelectProjectionType}
```

The first line calls the procedure we just defined. That procedure sets up a dialog box that has only one subview with a data field, the radio button menu. The value of the radio button menu's data field indicates which button is pushed: 0 = first button, 1 = second button, 2 = third button. (Recall our const declarations.) The call to Dialog's SetData method initializes this data field to the current value of ProjectionType and causes the dialog box to be drawn:

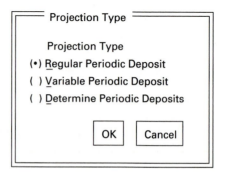

The user can make a selection by clicking on one of buttons of the radio button menu and then clicking on the "OK" button. Notice that the menu contains a default which can be selected by activating the "OK" button. In the method Banker.SelectProjection Type, the call to DeskTop^.ExecView causes execution to wait until the user closes the dialog box. The user closes the dialog box by clicking on either one of the buttons. When this happens, the command bound to that button is passed back to Banker.Select-ProjectionType and is stored in Command. At this point, if the command was not cmCancel, then the content of the radio button data field is stored in Banker's ProjectionType data field and the dialog box is disposed of with a call to its destructor, Done. The global variable DeskTop, provided by Turbo Vision, contains a pointer to this application's desktop environment (which contains the menu bar, status line, and work surface for displaying dialog boxes.) DeskTop is initialized before the application is run.

As another example, consider the dialog box that is used when the user selects the menu item "Initial Conditions" from the Operation menu. This dialog box is used to get initial values for the data fields InitialDeposit and InterestRate. Here is the declaration for the procedure that defines the Initial Conditions dialog box:

```
procedure SetUpInitialParameterWindow(var Dialog:PDialog);
var ViewBuffer:PView;
    R:TRect;
begin
   R.Assign(20, 4, 59, 15);
   Dialog := New(PDialog, Init(R, 'Initial Conditions'));
   with Dialog^ do
     begin
        R.Assign(19,3,36,4);
        ViewBuffer := New(PInputLine, Init(R,128));
        Insert(ViewBuffer);
        R.Assign(2,3,18,4);
        Insert(New(PLabel, Init(R, '~I~nitial Deposit',
             ViewBuffer)));
        R.Assign(19,5,36,6);
        ViewBuffer := New(PInputLine, Init(R,128));
        Insert(ViewBuffer);
        R.Assign(2,5,18,6);
        Insert(New(PLabel, Init(R, 'Interest ~R~ate ',
             ViewBuffer)));
        R.Assign(8, 7, 18, 9);
        Insert(New(PButton, Init(R, '~O~k', cmOK,
             bfNormal)));
        R.Assign(21, 7, 31, 9);
        Insert(New(PButton, Init(R, 'Cancel', cmCancel,
             bfNormal)))
     end {with}
end; {SetUpInitialParameterWindow}
```

In this procedure, Dialog is initialized in a manner similar to the preceding
example; pointers to new subviews of type TInputLine are then inserted
into the dialog box. A TInputLine view is used to return a string (in this
case, of length 128 at most) that is typed by the user. The label "Initial Deposit" is linked to the first TInputLine view, and the label "InterestRate" is
linked to the second TInputLine. Thus, selecting a label will activate the
corresponding TInputLine view. "OK" and "Cancel" buttons are inserted
into this view as before, except that "OK" is not a default button.

The method that uses this procedure is called when the user selects
the "Initial Conditions" menu item from the Operation menu. (See the
declarations of Banker.HandleEvent and Banker.InitMenuBar.) Here is that
method's declaration:

```
procedure Banker.SetInitialParameters;
{
   Get from the user values for the initial deposit and the
   interest rate.
}
const
   InitialDepositError =
'Error: The initial deposit must be >= $1000000 and <= $0.1;
   InterestRateError =
'Error: The interest rate must be >= 0% and <= 50%.';
type ParamType = record
        InitialDepositStr,
        InterestRateStr:LineType
     end;
var Dialog: PDialog;
   Command: Word;
   Params:ParamType;
   LocalInitialDeposit,
   LocalInterestRate:real;
   Code:integer;
   Notice: LineType;
begin
   SetUpInitialParameterWindow(Dialog);
   with Params do
      begin
         Str(InitialDeposit:1:2,InitialDepositStr);
         Str(InterestRate:1:3,InterestRateStr)
      end; {with Params do}
   Dialog^.SelectNext(False);
   Dialog^.SetData(Params);
   Command := DeskTop^.ExecView(Dialog);
if Command <> cmCancel then
```

```
begin
   Dialog^.GetData(Params);
   with Params do
      begin
         Val(InitialDepositStr,LocalInitialDeposit,Code);
         if (Code <> 0) or (LocalInitialDeposit < 0.00)
              or (LocalInitialDeposit > 1000000.00) then
            begin
               SendNotice (InitialDepositError);
               SetInitialParameters
            end { initial deposit error }
         else
         InitialDeposit := LocalInitialDeposit;
         Val(InterestRateStr,LocalInterestRate,Code);
         if (Code <> 0) or (LocalInterestRate <= 0.00)
              or (LocalInterestRate > 50.0) then
            begin
               SendNotice (InterestRateError);
               SetInitialParameters
            end { Interest rate error }
          else
          InterestRate := LocalInterestRate
       end {with Params do}
    end; {if Command <> cmCancel}
  Dispose(Dialog, Done)
end; {SetInitialParameters}
```

The first statement is a call to the procedure we just defined for setting up the dialog box Dialog. This Dialog box has two subviews with data fields (the two TInputLines). Each of the data fields is a string of characters of length 128. The record variable Params has two data fields that correspond to the data fields in the Dialog subviews. The data fields in Params are initialized by converting Banker's InitialDeposit and InterestRate fields to string values and storing the results in Params' data fields. This is done with a call to Turbo Pascal's Str procedure. The method call Dialog^.SetData-(Params) causes the string values in Params' data fields to be put into the data fields of Dialog's TInputLine subviews, and causes the dialog box to be displayed. Thus, when the dialog box is displayed, the user will see default choices that are equal to the current values of InitialDeposit and InterestRate.

As in the preceding example, the call to DeskTop^.ExecView causes the calling procedure to wait until the user closes the dialog box by clicking on one of the buttons. If the user does not close the dialog box using the Cancel button (if Command <> cmCancel ...), then the program changes the values of InitialDeposit and InterestRate to the values typed in by the user.

This is done by getting those values with a call to Dialog^.GetData and converting them back to numeric form using Turbo Pascal's Val procedure. The code within the with Params do statement accomplishes the conversion of the string values. The call to Val converts the string value of a variable (e.g., InitialDepositStr) to a numeric value. The result is stored in a local variable of the appropriate type (e.g., LocalInitialDeposit). If the conversion is successful, then the value of Code is zero. In this case, and if there are no additional errors, the value of the local variable is used to update the value of the appropriate data field in the object of type Banker.

If an error occurs, either in the conversion process or as a result of the value returned by Val (for example, if the user supplies a negative initial deposit), an error message is displayed for the user in a dialog box. After the user acknowledges the error, another call to SetInitialParameters gives the user the opportunity to correct the error. The procedure SendNotice draws a dialog box with the appropriate error message. Here is the declaration for SendNotice:

```
procedure SendNotice (Notice: LineType);
{
    This procedure is used to draw a dialog box for sending
    the error message Notice to the screen.
}
var
    Dialog: PDialog;
    R: TRect;
    C: Word;
begin
    R.Assign(2, 6, 79, 19);
    Dialog := New(PDialog, Init(R, 'Notice Dialog'));
    with Dialog^ do
        begin
            R.Assign(1, 2, 76, 3);
            Insert(New(PLabel, Init(R, Notice, nil)));
            R.Assign(15, 10, 25, 12);
            Insert(New(PButton, Init(R, '~O~K', cmOK,
                    bfDefault)));
        end; {with}
    C := DeskTop^.ExecView(Dialog);
    Dispose(Dialog, Done)
end; { SendNotice }
```

In the method Banker.SetInitialParameters, the method call Dialog^.SelectNext(False) is used to select a particular subview so that when the dialog box is opened, that subview is active and the user can start typing in that field without first having to select it (with the mouse or from the keyboard). If you think of Insert as inserting a subview at the front of a linked list (look at the code for SetUpInitialParameterWindow), then the Cancel button is at the head of the linked list of views, since it was the last subview inserted. We would use the method call Dialog^.SelectNext(True) if we wanted to preselect this view. The method call Dialog^.SelectNext(False) follows the (circularly) linked list in the other direction and selects the TInputLine subview corresponding to "Initial Deposit." Thus, when the dialog box is opened, it is ready to accept an initial deposit from the user.

The other dialog boxes used in this program are set up in a manner similar to the ones we have discussed so far, with minor variations. For example, the results of a projection are shown in a dialog box with TInputLine subviews for displaying the values of the parameters and the results of the projection. In this dialog box, the TInputLine subviews are only for displaying information. Since they cannot be used to accept typed input from the user, these subviews should not be selectable. (If the user cannot select the subviews, their values cannot be altered.) A subview can be made non-selectable when it is entered into the dialog box. Here is an example of such code:

```
R.Assign(21,7,37,8);
ViewBuffer := New(PInputLine, Init(R,128));
ViewBuffer^.Options := ViewBuffer^.Options and not
                       ofSelectable;
Insert(ViewBuffer);
R.Assign(2,7,20,8);
Insert(New(PStaticText, Init(R, 'Interest Rate')));
```

ViewBuffer^.Options is a bit-mapped word containing option flags. The assignment statement that alters the value of this word turns off the ofSelectable flag without changing the values of the other flags. The constant ofSelectable is provided by Turbo Vision. Notice in this example that the label is of type PStaticText rather than PLabel. Since the TInputLine is not selectable, there is no need to associate a label with it.

Another variation from the preceding examples is in the dialog box used for obtaining deposits from the user for the projection in which the size of the deposit can vary. Recall that this dialog box is drawn by procedure GetADeposit and requires an additional button to indicate that this is the last deposit. Here is the code used by the setup procedure to put this extra button in the dialog box:

```
Insert(New(PButton, Init(R, '~L~ast', cmYes, bfNormal)));
```

This binds the button to the command cmYes, which is a command provided by Turbo Vision that can be passed back to the calling procedure, GetADeposit, through a call to DeskTop^.ExecView. When GetADeposit receives this command, it interprets it by setting its Done parameter to True.

Some of the data obtained from the user through dialog boxes must be of type Integer, which leads us to yet another variation from the preceding examples. For example, the number of periods should be an integer value. The procedure Val does not indicate an error when a string variable contains a syntactically correct representation of a Real value. In those situations in which an Integer value is expected, a call to the function Real-Check gives a preliminary indication that a string represents a Real value. The call RealCheck(Strng) returns True if and only if Strng contains one or more of the characters present in a syntactically correct Real value: ".," "e," or "E." When an Integer value is needed, RealCheck can be used with Val to make sure that a string variable contains a syntactically correct representation of an Integer value. The declaration of RealCheck is left as an exercise.

Putting It All Together

After Banker and all its methods have been declared, it is relatively easy to run the system. Here is the main program:

```
var Adviser:Banker;
begin
    Adviser.Init;
    Adviser.InitializeDefaults;
    Adviser.Run;
    Adviser.Done
end.
```

The method call Adviser.Init initializes memory, video, and other system elements, and then calls the Init method which was inherited from TProgram. This inherited method initializes the DeskTop, MenuBar, and StatusLine variables that define the desktop environment in which the application will run. The method Adviser.Run actually executes a method inherited from TGroup. This method is responsible for intercepting events and sending them to the event handler method. It is essentially a loop that repeats processing until a terminating event occurs. The method Adviser.Done executes the destructor inherited from TProgram, and then cleans up the memory, video, and other system elements.

We have discussed an example that illustrates some of the event-driven program features available in Turbo Vision. We have given examples of menus and dialog boxes. A complete implementation of the financial planner program is left as an exercise. One possible implementation is given on the disk that accompanies the instructor's manual for this text.

SUMMARY

In this chapter we have examined the structure of a program with respect to its computational specifications and the quality of its user interface. We have considered a program as a computational "engine," insulated from the user by a layer of code that provides an effective user interface. The quality of the user interface is largely dependent on its ease of use and robustness, which is a measure of its ability to recover gracefully from erroneous input. In this chapter, we have illustrated the use of some of the Turbo Vision tools that can be used to construct a high-quality, event-driven user interface, and we have discussed techniques for detecting and handling erroneous input. By using the techniques discussed here, you should be able to "dress up" your programs with a sophisticated and robust user interface.

EXERCISES

12.1 Write the declaration for the function RealCheck described in the text.

12.2 Modify the process for handling errors so that when a dialog box is re-displayed after an error message, the subview in which the erroneous data were entered is automatically selected as the active subview. With this approach, the user can immediately correct the erroneous entry without first having to select the appropriate subview.

PROGRAMMING ASSIGNMENTS

12.1 In the program FinancialPlanner, as supplied on the disk, the Cancel button in the dialog box used by GetADeposit is not very useful; all it does is ignore information that the user entered in this dialog box. Either by modifying the effect of the Cancel button or by adding a new button to this dialog box, add the capability to backup a deposit. For example, if we are currently entering deposit 100, then pressing the backup button would back out the 99th deposit and allow us to reenter it. Pressing the backup button again would back out the 98th deposit and allow us to continue from that point. Continuing to press the backup key would take us back to the first deposit. Note that adding this capability has implications on how this particular projection is run.

12.2 In the program FinancialPlanner, add a new menu item, "Print," to the System submenu. Selection of this menu item will cause the results of the latest projection to be sent to the printer. If this menu item is selected before a projection has been run, an error message dialog box should be used to display a message to the user.

12.3 Add a mortgage analysis capability to FinancialPlanner. This facility should, at the minimum,

    a. determine the monthly payment as a function of the amount borrowed, the monthly interest rate, and the length of the loan;

      b. determine the amount that can be borrowed as a function of the monthly payment, the monthly interest rate, and the length of the loan; and

      c. print an amortization table.

12.4 Design and implement a checking account maintenance program. The program should be able to produce individual checks from input supplied by the user, and produce checks in batch from information contained in a file. The date on the checks should be supplied by the program. All other information should come from the user (or file). The user should be able to select a menu item that causes a summary of the activity from the current session to be printed. Of course, it's natural to include in this system a dialog box resembling a check.

12.5 Add a Turbo Vision user interface to one of your previous programming projects.

12.6 Use Turbo Vision to display a game board. For example, a chess board or a "go" board can be represented by a square view with an appropriate number of square subviews.

12.7 Use Turbo Vision to develop a user interface for a four-function calculator. The buttons on the calculator will be button subviews of a dialog box. Another subview will be the calculator display. As the user enters operands and performs operations (by clicking on buttons), the calculator display should be appropriately updated by your program. The calculator should have a "clear" button, a "clear entry" button, and an "off" button. When the user clicks the "off" button, the dialog box representing the calculator should close.

Mathematical Background

Mathematics is one of the outstanding accomplishments of the human mind. Its abstract models of real-life phenomena have fostered advances in every field of science and engineering. Most of computer science is based on mathematics, and this book is no exception. This appendix provides an introduction to the mathematical concepts referred to in the chapters. Exercises are given at the end of the appendix so that you can practice the skills while you are learning them.

Functions and Sequences

An amazing aspect of mathematics, first revealed by Whitehead and Russell (1910), is that only two basic concepts are required. Every other mathematical term can be built up from the primitives *set* and *element*. For example, an ordered pair $\langle a, b \rangle$ can be defined as a set with two elements:

$$\langle a, b \rangle = \{a, \{a, b\}\}$$

The element a is called the *first component* of the ordered pair, and b is called the *second component*.

Given two sets A and B, we can define a *function* f *from A to B*, written,

$$f: A \longrightarrow B$$

as a set of ordered pairs $\langle a, b \rangle$, where a is in A, b is in B, and each element in A is the first component of exactly one ordered pair in f. Thus, no two ordered pairs in a function have the same first element. The sets A and B are called the *domain* and *co-domain*, respectively.

For example,

$$f = \{ \langle -2, 4\rangle, \langle -1, 1\rangle, \langle 0, 0\rangle, \langle 1, 1\rangle, \langle 2, 4\rangle \}$$

defines the "square" function with domain $\{ -2, -1, 0, 1, 2 \}$ and co-domain $\{ 0, 1, 2, 4 \}$. No two ordered pairs in the function have the same first component, but two ordered pairs may have the same second component. For example, the pairs,

$$\langle -1, 1\rangle \text{ and } \langle 1, 1\rangle$$

have the same second component, namely 1.

If $\langle a, b\rangle$ is in f, we can write $f(a) = b$. This gives us a more familiar description of the above function: the function f is defined by:

$$f(i) = i^2, \text{ for } i \text{ in } -2..2.$$

A **_finite sequence_** t is a function such that for some positive integer k, called the _length_ of the sequence, the domain of t is the set $\{ 1, 2, \ldots, k \}$. For example, the following defines a finite sequence of length 6:

$t(1) =$ "Karen"
$t(2) =$ "Don"
$t(3) =$ "Mark"
$t(4) =$ "Sarah"
$t(5) =$ "Minnie"
$t(6) =$ "Spike"

Because the domain of each finite sequence starts at 1, the domain is often left implicit, and we write:

$t =$ "Karen", "Don", "Mark", "Sarah", "Minnie", "Spike"

Sums and Products

Mathematics entails a considerable amount of symbol manipulation. For this reason, brevity is an important consideration. An example of abbreviated notation can be found in the way that sums are represented. Instead of writing

$$x_1 + x_2 + x_3 + \ldots + x_n$$

we can write

$$\sum_{i=1}^{n} x_i$$

This expression is read as "the sum, as i goes from 1 to n, of x sub i." We say that i is the "count index." A count index corresponds to a loop-control variable in a For statement. For example, the following code will store in Sum the sum of components 1 through N in the array X:

```
Sum := 0.0;
for I := 1 to N do
   Sum := Sum + X[I]
```

Of course, there is nothing special about the letter *i*. We can write, for example,

$$\sum_{j=1}^{10} \frac{1}{j}$$

as shorthand for

$$1 + 1/2 + 1/3 + \ldots + 1/10.$$

Similarly, if $N \geq M$,

$$\sum_{k=M}^{N} (k2^{-k})$$

is shorthand for

$$M2^{-M} + (M + 1)2^{-(M+1)} + \ldots + N2^{-N}$$

Another abbreviation, less frequently seen than summation notation, is product notation. For example,

$$\prod_{k=1}^{5} A[k]$$

is shorthand for:

$$A[1] * A[2] * A[3] * A[4] * A[5].$$

Logarithms

John Napier, a Scottish baron and part-time mathematician, first described logarithms in a paper he published in 1614. From that time until the invention of computers, the principal value of logarithms was in number-crunching: they enabled multiplication (and division) of large numbers to be accomplished through mere addition (and subtraction).

Today, logarithms have only a few computational applications (for example, the Richter scale for measuring earthquakes), but they do provide a useful tool for analyzing algorithms, as you saw (or will see) in Chapters 3, 5, and 7 through 11.

We define logarithms in terms of exponents, just as subtraction can be defined in terms of addition, and division can be defined in terms of multiplication.

Given a real number $a > 1$, which is called the *base* of the logarithm, the **logarithm** of any real number $x > 0$, written

$$\log_a x$$

is defined to be that real number y such that:

$$a^y = x$$

For example, $\log_2 16 = 4$, because $2^4 = 16$. Similarly, $\log_{10} 100 = 2$, because $10^2 = 100$. What is $\log_2 64$? What is $\log_8 64$? Estimate $\log_{10} 64$.

The following relations can be proved from the definition of logarithm and the corresponding properties of exponents: For any real value $a > 1$ and for any positive real numbers x and y,

1. $\log_a 1 = 0$
2. $\log_a a = 1$
3. $\log_a (xy) = \log_a x + \log_a y$
4. $\log_a (x/y) = \log_a x - \log_a y$
5. $\log_a a^x = x$
6. $a^{\log_a x} = x$
7. $\log_a x^y = y \log_a x$

From these equations, we can obtain the formula for converting from one base to another. For any bases a and $b > 1$ and for any $x > 0$,

$$\log_b x = \log_b a^{\log_a x} \ (\text{ by property 6 })$$
$$= (\log_a x)\ (\log_b a) \ (\text{ by property 7 })$$

The base e (≈ 2.718) has special significance in calculus; for this reason logarithms with base e are called *natural logarithms* and are written with ln instead of $\log_e$. For example, for any $x_1, x_2 > 0$,

$$\int_{x_1}^{x_2} dx/x = \ln x_2 - \ln x_1$$

From this we obtain (see Fig. A1.1) the following crude approximation of:

$$\sum_{k=1}^{n} 1/k$$

for any positive integer n:

$$\sum_{k=1}^{n} 1/k \approx \int_{1}^{n} dx/x = \ln n - \ln 1 = \ln n.$$

To convert from natural logarithm to base 2 logarithm, we apply the base-conversion formula. For any $x > 0$,

$$\log_2 x = (\ln x)\ (\log_2 e)$$
$$\approx 1.44 \ln x.$$

Similarly, for any $x > 0$,

$$\ln x = (\log_2 x)\ (\ln 2)$$
$$\approx .69 \log_2 x.$$

Figure A1.1

Using rectangles of width 1 to approximate the area under the curve of the function f(x) = 1/x, for x between 1 and 5. For K = 1, 2, 3, 4, 5, the height of the Kth rectangle (starting on the left) is 1/K.

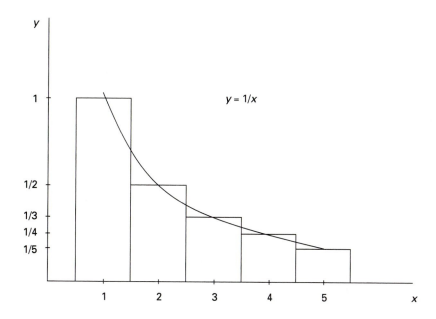

The function Ln is predefined in Pascal. Ln, together with its inverse Exp, enables us to perform exponentiation. For example, suppose we want to calculate X^Y where X and Y are of a real type and X > 0. We first rewrite X^Y mathematically:

$$X^Y = e^{\ln X^Y} \text{ (by Property 6, above)}$$
$$= e^{Y \ln X} \text{ (by Property 7)}$$

This last expression can be written in Pascal as

```
Exp (Y * Ln (X))
```

The restriction X > 0 is necessary because the argument to Ln must be positive.

Mathematical Induction

For many algorithms, verification involves proving a claim that can be stated in terms of integers. For example, to prove that a loop assertion is a loop invariant, we must show that the assertion is true before and after each iteration. (That is, we need to show that the assertion is true before and after the ith iteration for $i = 1, 2, \ldots$.)

Similarly, many of the claims in the analysis of algorithms can be stated as properties of integers. For example, for any positive integer n,

$$\sum_{i=1}^{n} i = n (n + 1)/2$$

In both situations, the claims can be proved by the Principle of Mathematical Induction.

Principle of Mathematical Induction.   Let $S_1, S_2, \ldots$ be a sequence of statements.
If

1. S_1 is true;
2. For any positive integer n, whenever S_n is true, S_{n+1} is true;

then

the statement S_n is true for any positive integer n.

To help you to understand why this principle makes sense, suppose that $S_1, S_2, \ldots$ is a sequence of statements for which 1. and 2. are true. By (1.), S_1 must be true. By (2.), since S_1 is true, S_2 must be true. Applying (2.) again, since S_2 is true, S_3 must be true. Continually applying (2.) from this point, we conclude that S_4 is true, then that S_5 is true, and so on. This indicates that the conclusion in the principle is reasonable.

To prove a claim by mathematical induction, we first state the claim in terms of a sequence of statements $S_1, S_2, \ldots$. We then show that S_1 is true—this is called the "base case." Finally, we need to prove (2.), the "inductive case." The outline of this proof is as follows: Let n be any positive integer and assume that S_n is true. To show that S_{n+1} is true, relate S_{n+1} back to S_n, which is assumed to be true. The remainder of the proof often utilizes arithmetic or algebra.

Example 1.   We will use the Principle of Mathematical Induction to prove the following:

Claim: For any positive integer n,

$$\sum_{i=1}^{n} i = \frac{n(n+1)}{2}$$

Proof: We start by stating the claim in terms of a sequence of statements. For $n = 1, 2, \ldots$, let S_n be the statement,

$$\sum_{i=1}^{n} i = \frac{n(n+1)}{2}$$

1. Base case.

$$\sum_{i=1}^{1} i = 1 = \frac{1(2)}{2}.$$

Therefore, S_1 is true.

2. Inductive case. Let n be any positive integer and assume that S_n is true. That is,

$$\sum_{i=1}^{n} i = \frac{n\,(n+1)}{2}.$$

We must show that S_{n+1} is true:

$$\sum_{i=1}^{n+1} i = \frac{(n+1)\,(n+2)}{2}.$$

We relate S_{n+1} back to S_n by making the following observation: The sum of the first $(n+1)$ integers is the sum of the first n integers plus $n+1$. That is,

$$\sum_{i=1}^{n+1} i = \sum_{i=1}^{n} i + (n+1)$$

$$= \frac{n\,(n+1)}{2} + (n+1) \quad \text{[because } S_n \text{ is assumed true]}$$

$$= \frac{n\,(n+1)}{2} + \frac{2\,(n+1)}{2}$$

$$= \frac{n\,(n+1) + 2\,(n+1)}{2}$$

$$= \frac{(n+2)\,(n+1)}{2}$$

$$= \frac{(n+1)\,(n+2)}{2}.$$

We conclude that S_{n+1} is true whenever S_n is true. Thus, by the Principle of Mathematical Induction, the statement S_n is true for any positive integer n.

End of Example 1.

Example 2.   In this example we illustrate how the Principle of Mathematical Induction can help in correctness proofs. Specifically, we will show that the loop assertion in the Binary Search subalgorithm is a loop invariant.

```
Search (Item, Found, Position)
Initialize First to 1, Last to N and Found to False
{ Find where Item is or belongs in the list: }
while (not Found) and (First <= Last) do
```

```
{ Loop assertion: For all I in [1..N]:              }
{              if I < First, A[I] is LessThan Item;   }
{              if I > Last, A[I] is GreaterThan Item. }
Middle := (First + Last) div 2
if A [Middle] is EqualTo Item then
    Item      := A [Middle]
    Found     := True
    Position  := Middle
else
    if A [Middle] is LessThan Item then
        First := Middle + 1
    else
        Last := Middle - 1
if not Found then
    Position := First
```

Note that the precondition of the While statement is:

```
First = 1; Last = N; Found = False.
```

For $K = 1, 2, \ldots,$ let S_k be the statement:

> The loop assertion is true prior to the kth iteration.

We now establish parts 1 and 2 of the Principle of Mathematical Induction:

1. The precondition ensures that, prior to the first iteration, First = 1 and Last = N, and so there are no values of I between 1 and N such that I < First or I > Last. Therefore, the loop assertion is true[1] prior to the first iteration; that is, S_1 is true.

2. Let k be any positive integer and assume that S_k is true (that is, assume that the loop assertion is true prior to the kth iteration). We need to show that S_{k+1} is true (that is, that the assertion is true prior to the $(k + 1)$st iteration). During the kth iteration, there are three possible cases:
    a. A [Middle] is EqualTo Item. Since this leaves First and Last unchanged, the loop assertion will be true after the kth iteration, and therefore before the $(k + 1)$st iteration.
    b. A [Middle] is LessThan Item. First is then assigned the value of Middle + 1, so we still have:

        > if I < First then A [I] is LessThan Item.

        Last is unchanged. Therefore, the loop assertion will be true after the kth iteration, and thus before the $(k + 1)$st iteration.

---

[1]In logic, a statement of the form "If P then Q" is defined to be true whenever P is false.

    c.   A [Middle] is GreaterThan Item. This is analogous to b., except that Last is used instead of First.

In each case, the assertion is true prior to the $(k + 1)$st iteration (that is, for any positive integer k, if S_k is true, then S_{k+1} is true).

Therefore, by the Principle of Mathematical Induction, the loop assertion is true prior to each iteration. During that proof we showed that for any positive integer k, if the assertion is true prior to the kth iteration, the assertion must also be true after the kth iteration. We conclude that the assertion is true before and after each iteration. In other words, the loop assertion is a loop invariant.

End of Example 2.

An important variant of the Principle of Mathematical Induction is the following:

Principle of Mathematical Induction (Strong Form).   Let $S_1, S_2, \ldots$ be a sequence of statements.
If

1. S_1 is true;
2.   For any positive integer n, whenever $S_1, S_2, \ldots, S_n$ are true, S_{n+1} is also true;

then

       the statement S_n is true for any positive integer n.

The difference between this version and the preceding version is in the inductive case. When we want to establish that S_{n+1} is true, we can now assume that $S_1, S_2, \ldots, S_n$ are true.

Before you go any further, try to convince yourself that this version of the principle is reasonable.

At first glance, you might think that the strong form is more powerful than the original version. In fact, they are equivalent. Let $S_1, S_2, \ldots$ be any sequence of statements. If each statement in the sequence can be shown to be true by either version of the Principle of Mathematical Induction, then each statement can also be shown to be true by the other version.

We now apply the strong form of the Principle of Mathematical Induction to obtain a simple but important result.

Example 3.   Show that for any positive integer N, the number of iterations of the following loop statement is Trunc $(\log_2 N)$:

```
while N > 1 do
   N := N div 2
```

For $N = 1, 2, \ldots$, let $T(N)$ be the number of loop iterations. For $N = 1, 2, \ldots$, let S_N be the statement:

```
T (N) = Trunc (log₂N)
```

1. Base case. When $N = 1$, the loop is not executed at all, and so $T(N) = 0 = \text{Trunc}(\log_2 N)$; that is, S_1 is true.

2. Inductive case. Let N be any positive integer and assume that $S_1, S_2, \ldots, S_N$ are all true. We must show that S_{N+1} is true. There are two cases to consider:

   a. $N + 1$ is even. The number of iterations after the first iteration is equal to $T((N + 1) \text{ div } 2)$. Therefore, we have:

$$
\begin{aligned}
T(N + 1) &= 1 + T((N + 1) \text{ div } 2) \\
&= 1 + T((N + 1)/2) \quad \text{(since } N + 1 \text{ is even)} \\
&= 1 + \text{Trunc}(\log_2((N + 1)/2)) \\
&\quad \text{(by the induction hypothesis)} \\
&= 1 + \text{Trunc}(\log_2(N + 1)) - 1 \\
&= \text{Trunc}(\log_2(N + 1))
\end{aligned}
$$

   Thus, S_{N+1} is true.

   b. $N + 1$ is odd. The number of iterations after the first iteration is equal to $T(N/2)$. Therefore, we have

$$
\begin{aligned}
T(N + 1) &= 1 + T(N/2) \\
&= 1 + \text{Trunc}(\log_2(N/2)) \\
&\quad \text{(by the induction hypothesis)} \\
&= 1 + \text{Trunc}(\log_2 N - \log_2 2) \\
&= 1 + \text{Trunc}(\log_2 N) - 1) \\
&= 1 + \text{Trunc}(\log_2 N) - 1 \\
&= \text{Trunc}(\log_2 N) \\
&= \text{Trunc}(\log_2(N + 1)) \\
&\quad \text{(since } \log_2(N + 1) \text{ cannot be an integer)}
\end{aligned}
$$

   Thus, S_{N+1} is true.

Therefore, by the strong form of the Principle of Mathematical Induction, S_N is true for any positive integer N.

Before we leave this example, we note that an almost identical proof shows that in the worst case for a binary search, the number of iterations is:

$$
\text{Trunc}(\log_2 N) + 1
$$

End of Example 3.

In the original and "strong" forms of the Principle of Mathematical Induction, the base case consists of a proof that S_1 is true. In some situations, we may need to start at some integer other than 1. For example, suppose we want to show that:

$$n! > 2^n$$

for any $n \geq 4$. (Notice that this statement is false for $n = 1, 2,$ and 3.) The sequence of statements is $S_4, S_5, \ldots$. For the base case, we must show that S_4 is true.

In still other situations, there may be several base cases. For example, suppose we want to show that:

Fib$(n) < 2^n$, for any positive integer n.

(The function Fib, defined in Chapter 2, calculates Fibonacci numbers.) The base cases are:

Fib$(1) < 2^1$ and Fib$(2) < 2^2$.

These observations lead us to another form of the Principle of Mathematical Induction.

Principle of Mathematical Induction (General Form): Let K_0 and K_1 be any integers such that $K_0 \leq K_1$, and let $S_{K_0}, S_{K_0+1}, \ldots$ be a sequence of statements.
If:

1. $S_{K_0}, S_{K_0+1}, \ldots, S_{K_1}$ are true;
2. For any integer $n \geq K_1$, if $S_{K_0}, S_{K_0+1}, \ldots, S_n$ are true, then S_{n+1} is true;

then the statement S_n is true for any integer $n \geq K_0$.

The general form extends the strong form by allowing the sequence of statements to start at any integer (K_0) and to have any number of base cases $(S_{K_0}, S_{K_0+1}, \ldots, S_{K_1})$. If $K_0 = K_1 = 1$, then the general form reduces to the strong form.

The next three examples use the general form of the Principle of Mathematical Induction to prove claims about Fibonacci numbers.

Example 4. Prove that the loop assertion in the iterative Fibonacci function is a loop post-invariant. For your convenience, here is the loop statement:

```
{ Precondition: N >= 3; Previous = 1; Current = 1 }
for I := 3 to N do
        { Loop assertion: Current holds the Ith Fibonacci }
        {                     number and Previous holds the   }
        {                     (I-1)st Fibonacci number.       }
```

```
  begin
     Temp       := Current;
     Current   := Current + Previous;
     Previous := Temp
  end; { for I := 3 to N }
{ Postcondition: Current holds Nth Fibonacci number. }
```

Proof: (By induction on I) Let N be any integer ≥ 3. For $I = 3, 4, \ldots, N$, let C_I hold the value of Current after $I - 2$ iterations of the loop and let P_I hold the value of Previous after $I - 2$ iterations of the loop. Finally, for $I = 3, 4, \ldots, N$, let S_I be the statement: C_I holds the Ith Fibonacci number and P_I holds the $(I - 1)$st Fibonacci number.

1. Base case. The precondition implies that Previous and Current hold the first and second Fibonacci numbers, respectively, prior to the first execution of the loop. Because the first iteration of the loop yields $C_3 = 2$ and $P_3 = 1$, the loop assertion is true when $I = 3$.

2. Inductive case. Let I be any integer ≥ 3 and assume that S_I is true. C_I then holds the Ith Fibonacci number and P_I holds the $(I - 1)$st Fibonacci number. By the action of the loop, $C_{I+1} = C_I + P_I$. Thus, by the induction hypothesis, C_{I+1} holds the sum of the Ith and $(I - 1)$st Fibonacci numbers; that is, C_{I+1} holds the $(I + 1)$st Fibonacci number. The loop also implies that $P_{I+1} = C_I$, which, by the induction hypothesis, holds the Ith Fibonacci number. Because C_{I+1} holds the $(I + 1)$st Fibonacci number and P_{I+1} holds the Ith Fibonacci number, S_{I+1} is true.

    Therefore, by the Principle of Mathematical Induction, S_I is true for all $I \geq 3$. Thus, after each iteration of the loop, Current holds the Ith Fibonacci number and Previous holds the $(I - 1)$st Fibonacci number. This establishes that the loop assertion is a loop post=invariant.

Example 5.   Show that:

$$\text{Fib}(n) < 2^n$$

for any positive integer n.

Proof: For $n = 1, 2, \ldots$, let S_n be the statement,

$$\text{Fib}(n) < 2^n.$$

In the terminology of the general form of the Principle of Mathematical Induction, $K_0 = 1$ because the sequence starts at 1; $K_1 = 2$ because there are two base cases.

1. $\text{Fib}(1) = 1 < 2 = 2^1$, so S_1 is true.

    $\text{Fib}(2) = 1 < 4 = 2^2$, so S_2 is true.

2. Let n be any integer ≥ 2 and assume that $S_1\ S_2, \ldots, S_n$ are true. We need to show that S_{n+1} is true (that is, that $\text{Fib}(n + 1) < 2^{n+1}$).

By the definition of Fibonacci numbers,

$$\text{Fib}(n + 1) = \text{Fib}(n) + \text{Fib}(n - 1), \text{ for } n \geq 2.$$

Since $S_1, S_2, \ldots, S_n$ are true, S_{n-1} and S_n must be true. Thus,

$$\text{Fib}(n - 1) < 2^{n-1}$$

and

$$\text{Fib}(n) < 2^n.$$

We then get:

$$\begin{aligned}
\text{Fib}(n + 1) &= \text{Fib}(n) + \text{Fib}(n - 1) \\
&< 2^n + 2^{n-1} \\
&< 2^n + 2^n \\
&= 2^{n+1}
\end{aligned}$$

Therefore, $\text{Fib}(n + 1)$ is true.

We conclude, by the general form of the Principle of Mathematical Induction, that:

$$\text{Fib}(n) < 2^n,$$

for any positive integer n.

End of Example 5.

You could now proceed, in a similar fashion, to develop the following lower bound for Fibonacci numbers:

$$\text{Fib}(n) > (6/5)^n, \text{ for } n \geq 3.$$

HINT   *Use the general form of the Principle of Mathematical Induction, with $K_0 = 3$ and $K_1 = 4$.*

Now that lower and upper bounds for Fibonacci numbers have been established, you might wonder if we can improve on those bounds. We will do even better; in the next example, we verify an exact, closed formula for the nth Fibonacci number. (A "closed" formula is one that is neither recursive nor iterative.)

Example 6.   Show that for any positive integer n,

$$\text{Fib}(n) = \frac{1}{\sqrt{5}}\left[\left(\frac{1 + \sqrt{5}}{2}\right)^n - \left(\frac{1 - \sqrt{5}}{2}\right)^n\right].$$

Before you look at the following proof, calculate a few values to convince yourself that the formula actually does provide the correct values.

Proof: For $n = 1, 2, \ldots$, let S_n be the statement:

$$\text{Fib}(n) = \frac{1}{\sqrt{5}}\left[\left(\frac{1 + \sqrt{5}}{2}\right)^n - \left(\frac{1 - \sqrt{5}}{2}\right)^n\right].$$

Let $x = \dfrac{1 + \sqrt{5}}{2}$ and $y = \dfrac{1 - \sqrt{5}}{2}$.

Note that:

$$x^2 = \left(\frac{1 + \sqrt{5}}{2}\right)^2 = \frac{1 + 2\sqrt{5} + 5}{4}$$

$$= \frac{3 + \sqrt{5}}{2} = x + 1.$$

Similarly, $y^2 = y + 1$.

We now proceed with the proof.

1. $\dfrac{1}{\sqrt{5}}\left[\left(\dfrac{1 + \sqrt{5}}{2} - \dfrac{1 - \sqrt{5}}{2}\right)\right] = 1,$

    Thus, S_1 is true. Also,

    $$\frac{1}{\sqrt{5}}\left[\left(\frac{1 + \sqrt{5}}{2}\right)^2 - \left(\frac{1 - \sqrt{5}}{2}\right)^2\right]$$
    $$= 1/\sqrt{5}\ [x^2 - y^2]$$
    $$= 1/\sqrt{5}\ [x + 1 - (y + 1)]$$
    $$= 1/\sqrt{5}\ [x - y]$$
    $$= \frac{1}{\sqrt{5}}\left(\frac{1 + \sqrt{5}}{2} - \frac{1 - \sqrt{5}}{2}\right)$$

    $= 1$, which equals, by definition, Fib(2), and so S_2 is also true.

2. Let n be any positive integer greater than 1 and assume that $S_1, S_2, \ldots,$ S_n are true. We need to show that S_{n+1} is true; that is,

    $$\text{Fib}(n + 1) = \frac{1}{\sqrt{5}}\left[\left(\frac{1 + \sqrt{5}}{2}\right)^{n+1} - \left(\frac{1 - \sqrt{5}}{2}\right)^{n+1}\right].$$

    By the definition of Fibonacci numbers,

    $$\text{Fib}(n + 1) = \text{Fib}(n) + \text{Fib}(n - 1)\ .$$

    Since S_n and S_{n-1} are true, we have (using x and y),

    $$\text{Fib}(n) = \frac{1}{\sqrt{5}}\ (x^n - y^n)$$

    and

    $$\text{Fib}(n - 1) = \frac{1}{\sqrt{5}}\ (x^{n-1} - y^{n-1}).$$

By the definition of Fibonacci numbers,

$$
\begin{aligned}
\text{Fib}(n + 1) &= \text{Fib}(n) + \text{Fib}(n - 1) \\
&= \frac{1}{\sqrt{5}}(x^n + x^{n-1} - y^n - y^{n-1}) \\
&= \frac{1}{\sqrt{5}}[(x + 1)x^{n-1} - (y + 1)y^{n-1}] \\
&= \frac{1}{\sqrt{5}}[x^2 x^{n-1} - y^2 y^n - 1] \\
&= \frac{1}{\sqrt{5}}(x^{n+1} - y^{n+1})
\end{aligned}
$$

Therefore, S_{n+1} is true.

We conclude, by the general form of the Principle of Mathematical Induction, that S_n is true for any positive integer n.

As a final note on this formula, we discuss its representation in Pascal. At first glance, it may seem we can simply convert the exponentiations into expressions that have Exp and Ln. For example,

```
var
   Sqrt5,
   X,
   Y      : real;
begin
   Sqrt5 := Sqrt (5);
   X     := (1 + Sqrt5)/2;
   Y     := (1 - Sqrt5)/2;
   Fib   := (1 / Sqrt5) * (Exp (N * Ln (X))-Exp (N * Ln(Y)))
```

However, this will yield a run-time error, because Y is negative. We avoid this error with the help of the following observation:

> Since N *is a positive integer, if* N *is odd,* Y^N *must be negative, and so* $-Y^N = Abs\ (Y^N)$. *If* N *is even,* Y^N *must be positive, and so* $-Y^N = -Abs\ (Y^N)$.

The function Fib can be written as follows:

```
type
   PosIntType = 1..MaxLongInt;
function Fib (N: PosIntType): PosIntType;
{ Calculate the Nth Fibonacci number directly. }
var
   Sqrt5,
   X,
   Y      : real;
```

```
begin
   Sqrt5 := Sqrt (5);
   X     := (1 + Sqrt5) / 2;
   Y     := (1 - Sqrt5) / 2;
   if Odd (N) then
      Fib := Round ((1 / Sqrt5) * (Exp (N * Ln (X))
              + Exp (N * Ln (Abs (Y)))))
   else
      Fib := Round ((1 / Sqrt5) * (Exp (N * Ln (X))
              - Exp (N * Ln (Abs (Y)))))
end; { Fib }
```

End of Example 6.

The next example establishes a result about nonempty binary trees: the number of leaves is at most half of the number of items in the tree plus one. The induction is on the height of the tree, so the base case is for a tree of height 0.

Example 7. Let T be a nonempty binary tree, with $L(T)$ leaves and $N(T)$ items. Then

$$L(T) \le \frac{N(T) + 1}{2}$$

Proof: For $k = 0, 1, 2, \ldots$, let S_k be the statement: For any nonempty binary tree T of height k,

$$L(T) \le \frac{N(T) + 1}{2}$$

1. If T has height 0, then $L(T) = N(T) = 1$; and so,

$$L(T) \le \frac{N(T) + 1}{2} \quad \left(\text{in fact, } L(T) = \frac{N(T) + 1}{2} \right)$$

    Therefore, S_0 is true.

2. Let k be any nonnegative integer and assume that $S_0, S_1, \ldots, S_k$ are true. We must show that S_{k+1} is true. Let T be a nonempty binary tree of height $k + 1$.

    Case 1. If Left(T) is empty, then Right(T) is a nonempty binary tree of height k; and so, by the induction hypothesis,

$$L(\text{Right}(T)) \le \frac{N(\text{Right}(T)) + 1}{2}$$

Thus,

$$L(T) = L(\text{Right}(T)) \le \frac{N(\text{Right}(T)) + 1}{2}$$

$$< \frac{N(T) + 1}{2}$$

That is, S_{k+1} is true in this case.

Case 2. Similarly, if Right(T) is empty,

$$L(T) \le \frac{N(T) + 1}{2}$$

Again, S_{k+1} is true.

Case 3. Finally, if neither Left(T) nor Right(T) is empty, then both satisfy the induction hypothesis, so:

$$L(\text{Left}(T)) \le \frac{N(\text{Left}(T)) + 1}{2}$$

and

$$L(\text{Right}(T)) \le \frac{N(\text{Right}(T)) + 1}{2}$$

However, each leaf in T is either in Left(T) or in Right(T). Since

$$L(T) = L(\text{Left}(T)) + L(\text{Right}(T))$$

we have:

$$L(T) \le \frac{N(\text{Left}(T)) + 1}{2} + \frac{N(\text{Right}(T)) + 1}{2}$$

$$= \frac{N(\text{Left}(T)) + N(\text{Right}(T)) + 1 + 1}{2}$$

Except for the root item of T, each item in T is either in Left(T) or in Right(T), and so:

$$N(T) = N(\text{Left}(T)) + N(\text{Right}(T)) + 1$$

Substituting, we get:

$$L(T) \le \frac{N(T) + 1}{2}$$

Once again, S_{k+1} is true.

Therefore, by the general form of the Principle of Mathematical Induction, S_k is true for any nonnegative integer k. This completes the proof of the claim.

End of Example 7.

Induction and Recursion

Induction and recursion are similar processes. Each has a number of base cases, and each has a general case that reduces to one or more simpler cases, which eventually reduce to the base case(s). However, the two processes flow in opposite directions. With recursion, we start with the general case and eventually reduce it to the base case; with induction, we start with the base case and use it to develop the general case.

The next example, referred to in the analysis of open−address hashing (Chapter 10), starts with a recursive definition and then conjectures a closed form. The proof of the correctness of the closed form is by induction.

Example 8.

Develop a closed form for the function E for any k and M such that $0 \leq k < M$:

$$E(0, M) = 1 \text{ for any } M \geq 1;$$

$$E(k, M) = 1 + \frac{k}{M} E(k - 1, M - 1), \quad \text{where } 1 \leq k < M.$$

First, we note that:

$$E(1, M) = 1 + \frac{1}{M} E(0, M - 1)$$

$$= 1 + \frac{1}{M} * 1$$

$$= \frac{M + 1}{M}$$

for all $M > 1$.
Similarly,

$$E(2, M) = 1 + \frac{2}{M} E(1, M - 1)$$

$$= 1 + \frac{2}{M} \frac{M}{M - 1}$$

$$= \frac{M + 1}{M - 1}$$

for all $M > 2$.

Furthermore,

$$E(3, M) = 1 + \frac{3}{M} E(2, M - 1)$$

$$= 1 + \frac{3}{M} \frac{M}{M - 2}$$

$$= \frac{M + 1}{M - 2}$$

for all $M > 3$.

Therefore, we conjecture that:

$$E(k, M) = \frac{M + 1}{M + 1 - k}$$

for all M and k such that $0 \le k < M$.

This conjecture can be proved by induction (on either k or M). For example, if the induction is on k, the sequence of statements S_k, for $k = 0, 1, 2, \ldots$, is:

$$E(k, M) = \frac{M + 1}{M + 1 - k}$$

for all M such that $M > k$.

End of Example 8.

EXERCISES

1. Use mathematical induction to show that, in the Towers of Hanoi game from Chapter 2, moving N disks from pole "A" to pole "B" requires a total of $2^N - 1$ moves for any positive integer N.

2. Use mathematical induction to show that for any positive integer n,

$$\sum_{i=1}^{n} af(i) = a \sum_{i=1}^{n} f(i)$$

where a is a constant and f is a function.

3. Use mathematical induction to show that for any positive integer n,

$$\sum_{i=1}^{n} (i * 2^{i-1}) = (n - 1) 2^n + 1$$

4. Let n_0 be the smallest positive integer such that:

$$\text{Fib}(n_0) > n_0^2$$

   a. Find n_0.

   b. Use mathematical induction to show that, for all $n \geq n_0$,

$$\text{Fib}(n) > n^2$$

5. Show that Fib is:

$$O\left(\left(\frac{1 + \sqrt{5}}{2}\right)^n\right).$$

   HINT   See the formula in Example 6 above. Note that Abs
   $\left(\dfrac{1 - \sqrt{5}}{2}\right) < 1,$ *and so* $\left(\dfrac{1 - \sqrt{5}}{2}\right)$ *becomes insignificant for*
   "large" n.

6. Show that

$$\sum_{i=0}^{n} 2^i = 2^{n+1} - 1$$

   for any nonnegative integer n.

A Pascal Programming Standard

Most of your programming efforts are aimed at the development of correct and efficient programs. However, the readability of your programs is also important, so this appendix proposes a standard for Turbo Pascal programs. You may well disagree with some of the conventions suggested here, and you (or your instructor or supervisor) may decide to modify or mollify them. The essential point is that a program is a medium of communication between humans, and a clear, consistent style will make it easier for you to communicate.

I. Variables and Constants

1. Each variable identifier that occurs in a subprogram should be local to that subprogram (that is, declared in the subprogram's heading or block). Exceptions may be made if the use of a nonlocal variable will have a substantial time or space effect on an application that is time or space-critical. In such cases, a warning comment should be given.

    a. If the variable may have its value changed in the statement part of the subprogram, and that new value will be needed back in the calling program, the variable should be declared as a variable formal parameter.

    b. If the variable gets its initial value from the calling program but does not send a different value back, the variable should be declared as a value formal parameter.

    c. If the variable does not get its initial value from the calling program and does not send its value back, the variable should be declared in the variable declaration part of the subprogram block. As suggested above, an exception may be made for large arrays, but be aware of the time–space tradeoff (see Laboratory Exercise 2.1 at the end of Chapter 2).

2. The data type of each variable should be given by a type identifier.

3. A loop-control variable should not be referenced outside of its **for** statement.

4. Constants in algorithms should be replaced by constant identifiers in the program. Exceptions should be made only when the constant conveys its own meaning, such as 0 as an initial value for a total or 1 to start a count.

5. In a block, the variable declarations should come *after* the subprogram declarations.

II. Program Formatting

1. Blank lines should be used to separate the **const**, **type**, **var**, **procedure**, and **function** declaration parts. In general, blank lines should be used wherever their use will improve readability.

2. In a declarations part, each identifier should be declared on a separate line, starting in column 4. In the constant declaration part and the type declaration part, the equal signs should line up. In the variable declaration part, the colons should line up to the right of the variable identifiers, and should be followed by the type identifiers. Use commas to separate variable identifiers of the same type.

    For example, we might declare:

```
const
    MaxSize = 100;
    Prompt  = 'Please enter your password';

type
    IndexType = 1..MaxSize;
    TableType = array [IndexType] of longint;

var
    I,
    J    : IndexType;
    Table: TableType;
```

3. In a subprogram heading, there should be one formal parameter per line, with the colons lined up as in the following example:

```
procedure ListType.Retrieve (var Item: ItemType;
                             Pos      : word);
```

4. For the statement that follows **if**, **else**, **while**, **for**, **repeat**, **case**, and **with**, the statement should start on the next line and be indented three spaces. For example,

```
if First = Last then
   Found := True
```

5. If a statement requires more than one line, the second line should be indented six spaces, and successive continuation lines should be aligned with the second line of the statement. For example, we might write

```
while (Line [I] in ['a'..'z', 'A'..'Z'])
      and (I <= Length (Line)) do
   I := I + 1;
```

6. Column alignment should be observed for each of the following pairs of reserved words:

begin and **end**
if and **else**
repeat and **until**
case and **end**

Indent by three spaces each line between the first and second reserved words in each pair. For example,

```
if A [Middle].EqualTo (Item) then
   begin
      Item     := A [Middle];
      Found    := True;
      Position := Middle
   end { match found }
```

7. Within the statement part of a block, comments that describe one or more statements should be immediately above and aligned with the statement or collection of statements they describe. There should be a blank line before such comments and a blank line after the collection of statements. In particular, loop invariants and loop post-invariants should be included with each nontrivial loop. For example,

```
while (J > 1) and (A [J - 1] > A [J]) do
   { Loop invariant:A [1..J-1] sorted; A [J..I] sorted}
   begin
      Swap (A [J], A [J - 1]);
      J := J - 1
   end { while }
```

8. The main **begin–end** block for programs and subprograms should line up with the corresponding heading. For example,

```
procedure ...
...
begin
...
end;
```

9. At least one space should be used in the following locations within Pascal text (this does not apply within comments and character strings):
   a. before and after :=, {, }, any relational operator, and any arithmetic operator
   b. before (
   c. after :

10. The statement part of a program or subprogram should take up at most two screens (about 50 lines). Exceptions should occur only rarely — for example, if there is a long case statement.

III.   *Program Documentation Guidelines*

1. Program Heading

   The beginning of each program should have a comment section in the following form and with the following information:

```
program Example;
{*****************************************************}
{                                                   }
{ Programmer   :                                    }
{ Date Written :                                    }
{                                                   }
{ Input        :                                    }
{ Output       :                                    }
{                                                   }
{ Files Read   :                                    }
{ Files Written:                                    }
{                                                   }
{ (A brief statement of the problem)                }
{                                                   }
{*****************************************************}
```

2. Subprogram Headings

   Include documentation of the following form:

```
procedure Sample ... ;
{ Precondition :                                    }
{ Postcondition:                                    }
```

```
{ Called By      : (The subprograms and main program   }
{                      that this subprogram is called by) }
{ Calls          : (The list of subprograms that this   }
{                      subprogram calls)                 }
```

3. Identifiers should be chosen to be self-documenting. Abbreviations, except where standard, should be avoided.

4. Comment the ending of each compound statement. Such comments should be quite brief, mnemonic, and *unique* within the subprogram or main program. For example,

    procedure Try (...);

    ...

    begin

    ...

       while not Done **do**

          begin

            ...

          end; { while not Done }

    ...

    end; { Try }

    Comment the **end** for case statements as well as record and object declarations.

5. Comment code to improve clarity. Comments should tell *what* is being done or *why* it is being done, not *how* it is being done. For example,

    ```
    { Adjust I to point to the end of the previous word: }
    I := I - 1
    ```

    is better than

    ```
    { Subtract 1 from I: }
    I := I - 1
    ```

6. Comments should be in good English. Grammar and spelling should be correct.

7. Abbreviations should rarely be used in comments, and then only those that would be found in a standard dictionary.

8. Reserved words should be in lowercase. Each word in an identifier should start with an uppercase letter. Exceptions are made for predeclared type identifiers, such as *integer*, *longint*, *boolean*, and *text*.

File Data Types

A *file* is an arbitrarily large, ordered collection of values from some type, known as the *component type* of the file. The size of a file in Turbo Pascal may exceed the size of main memory, so every file is stored on disk. As such, every file is non-volatile: its values are not lost after the execution of a program. Files can hold huge quantities of data for an indefinite period of time.

Here are examples of several file declarations:

```
type
    TimerFileType = file of integer;
    PayrollRecordType = record
        Name  : string [30];
        Salary: real
    end; { PayrollRecordType }
    PayrollFileType = file of PayrollRecordType;
var
    TimerFile     : TimerFileType;
    PayrollFile,
    NewPayrollFile: PayrollFileType;
```

For TimerFile, the component type is integer. For PayrollFile and for NewPayrollFile, the component type is PayrollRecordType.

For any file data type, Turbo Pascal provides a variety of operators in the form of predeclared procedures and functions. We now explore several of these operators. The format for each operator is as given in the Turbo Pascal Library Reference manual, which does not necessarily adhere to our conventions in Appendix 2.

The Assign operator associates a Turbo Pascal identifier with an external file (such as a named disk file). The syntax for Assign is as follows:

```
Assign (var F; Name : string);
```

For example,

```
Assign (TimerFile, 'a:TimeFile.dat')
```

where the variable TimerFile was declared earlier. Changes made to Timer-File within the program actually affect the disk file a:TimeFile.dat.

After the Assign operator is called, the file variable must be opened for input and output. The Reset operator opens an existing file for input. For example,

```
Reset (PayrollFile)
```

prepares PayrollFile to be read (that is, accessed), starting at the first component in the file. The Rewrite operator destroys the contents of the file (unless the file is already empty) and opens the file for output. For example,

```
Rewrite (NewPayrollFile)
```

makes NewPayrollFile an empty file onto which values can be written (that is, stored).

Each component in a file has an associated position: The first component is at position 0, the second component is at position 1, and so on. To read the component at the current file position, the operator Read is called. For example,

```
Read (PayrollFile, PayrollRecord)
```

accesses the current component from PayrollFile, stores a copy of that component in the variable PayrollRecord, and then advances to the next file position.

Similarly,

```
Write (NewPayrollFile, PayrollRecord)
```

stores a copy of PayrollRecord at the current file position in NewPayrollFile and then advances to the next file position.

After the last component of each file, there is a special character called an *end of file marker*. The predefined function Eof tests the end-of-file status of a file. For example,

```
Eof (PayrollFile)
```

returns the value True if the current file position is beyond the last component of the file. Otherwise, False is returned.

After a program has completed its processing of a file, the file must be closed so that its associated external file, from the Assign statement, can be completely updated. For example, the execution of:

```
Close (TimerFile)
```

causes the associated external file, a:TimeFile.dat, to be updated.

We now consider two important categories of files in Turbo Pascal: text files (also called *character* files or *human-readable* files) and typed files (also called *binary* files or *machine-readable* files).

The TextFile Data Type

Text files allow programs to accept input and produce output in human-readable form. The identifier *text* is predeclared in Pascal:

```
type
   text = file of char;
```

In a text file, the component type is char. Each text file is subdivided into lines, and each line ends with a special character called an *end-of-line* marker. Text files must be organized and accessed *sequentially*: Whenever a character is written out onto a text file, it becomes the last component in the file; text files are always read starting with the first character in the file, then the second character, and so on.

We can declare a variable to be of type text:

```
var
   SalaryFile: text;
```

Because of the sequential nature of text files, reading from and writing to the same text file cannot be interleaved. For example, if we have:

```
Rewrite (SalaryFile)
```

we can write onto SalaryFile; but before we can read from SalaryFile, we must first call

```
Reset (SalaryFile)
```

The Read operator, when applied to a text file, can be used to read in integers, reals, and strings, as well as single characters. Its format is as follows:

```
Read ( [var F: Text;] V1 [, V2, ..., VN] )
{ Note: Terms in square brackets are optional. }
```

For example, suppose we have:

```
var
   ScoreFile: text;
   Score    : longint;
begin
   Assign (ScoreFile, 'Scores.dat');
   Reset (ScoreFile);
   Read (ScoreFile, Score)
```

If ScoreFile starts with:

      48375 219253 ...

the digit characters "4," "8," "3," "7," and "5" are converted into the integer 48375 and stored in Score. In reading in a value for an integer or real variable from a text file, blanks and end-of-line markers are skipped over.

For an input variable of type string, the Read procedure reads in all characters up to, *but not including*, the next end-of-line marker. The resulting character string, truncated if its size is larger than the maximum length of the string variable, is stored in that string variable.

Similarly, the Write operator, when applied to a text file, allows integers, reals, strings, packed strings, boolean values, and single characters to be appended to a text file. The format of this procedure is as follows:

```
Write ( [var F: Text; ] P1 [, P2, ..., PN ])
```

Other than the optional file parameter, each parameter is of the following form:

```
OutExpr [: MinWidth [: DecPlaces]]
```

where

OutExpr is an expression of type integer, real, char, boolean, or string;

MinWidth and DecPlaces are expressions of type integer.

The value of each output expression is converted into an output string of, say, k characters and appended to the file, with zero or more leading blanks. For output expressions that are not of a real type, the spacing is determined as follows: If MinWidth is either not provided or has a value less than or equal to k, there are no leading blanks appended. Otherwise, MinWidth $- k$ leading blanks are appended before the k characters are appended. For example, if Score has a value of 198, and

```
Write (ScoreFile, Score: 5)
```

is executed, the five characters,

```
bb198
```

would be appended to ScoreFile ("b" represents a blank space).

What if the output expression has a real type? If either MinWidth or DecPlaces is not provided, the output string will be in floating-point format in 17 positions (at most). If both Minwidth and DecPlaces are provided, the output string will be in fixed-point format, with DecPlaces digits to the right of the decimal point. For example, if Salary has the value 427.3682, and

```
Write (SalaryFile, Salary: 8: 2)
```

is executed, eight characters would be appended to SalaryFile:

```
bb427.37
```

Note that MinWidth provides the total number of positions, not merely the number of positions to the left of the decimal point; and that the output expression is rounded to the DecPlaces position to the right of the decimal point.

In addition to the generic file operators listed in the preceding section, the following operators are available only for text files:

1. `Eoln [ (var F: Text) ].` This function returns the value True if either the character at the current file position is an end-of-line marker, or if Eof (*F*) returns True. Otherwise, the value returned is False.

2. `Readln.` The format of this procedure is as follows:

   `Readln [ ( [ var F: Text; ] V1 [ , V2, ..., VN ] ) ]`

   The Readln procedure operates as follows: Each variable (whose type may be integer, real, char, or string) has its value read in, just as in the Read procedure. The file position is then advanced to point to the first character in the next line of the file. If there is no next line, the file position is advanced beyond the last position in the file; thus, Eof (*F*) will return the value True if called.

3. `Writeln.` The format of this procedure is as follows:

   `Writeln [ ( [ var F: Text; ] P1 [ , P2, ..., PN ] ) ]`

   The output expressions (if any) are appended to the file just as in the Write procedure, and an end-of-line marker is appended to the file.

The Identifiers Input and Output

The identifiers *Input* and *Output* are predeclared in Pascal:

```
var
    Input,
    Output: text;
```

The identifier Input is associated with the operating system's standard input device, typically the keyboard, and Output is associated with the standard output device, typically the display screen. Both Input and Output are automatically opened prior to program execution, just as if the following statements were pre-executed:

```
Assign (Input,'');
Assign (Output,'');
Reset (Input);
Rewrite (Output);
```

Also, Input and Output are automatically closed at the end of a program's execution.

If a textfile variable is not specified in a call to Eof, Eoln, Read, or Readln, then Input is assumed. For example,

```
Read (Score)
```

is equivalent to:

```
Read (Input, Score)
```

Furthermore, if a textfile variable is not specified in a call to Eof, to Eoln, or to Readln with no output expressions, then even the parentheses are omitted. For example, if no parameters are supplied in a call to:

```
Readln
```

then that is equivalent to:

```
Readln (Input)
```

Similarly, if a textfile variable is not specified in a call to Write or Writeln, then Output is assumed. For example,

```
Writeln (Salary: 9: 2)
```

is equivalent to:

```
Writeln (Output, Salary: 9: 2)
```

Also, if no parameters are supplied in a call to:

```
Writeln
```

then that is equivalent to:

```
Writeln (Output)
```

Typed Files

Text files are in human-readable form, which makes it easy for us to create input and to understand output. But text files do have drawbacks. For example, suppose we have declared the following:

```
type
   EmployeeType = record
      Name        : string [30];
      ID,
      Dependents: integer;
      Salary    : real
   end; { EmployeeType }
var
   Employee: EmployeeType;
```

To read in an employee record from a text file, we would need to specify each field:

```
with Employee do
    Read (Name, ID, Dependents, Salary)
```

Furthermore, the values entered would be in character form (including digits), so the Read procedure would have to convert those characters into binary numbers before they could be stored in the ID, Dependents, and Salary fields. Also, text files must be processed sequentially.

All of these problems—the need to specify individual fields, the conversion of characters into binary numbers, and the restriction to sequential processing—are avoided with "typed files." In a typed file, also called a "binary file" or "machine-readable file," the component type need not be *char*. The component type of a typed file can be any type, except a file type or a type with file components. For example, using the above declaration for EmployeeType, one could declare:

```
type
    PersonnelType = file of EmployeeType;
var
    Personnel: PersonnelType;
    Employee : EmployeeType;
```

To read one component from Personnel and store the value of that record in Employee, we simply call:

```
Read (Personnel, Employee)
```

Similarly,

```
Write (Personnel, Employee)
```

stores a copy of Employee at the current file position in the file Personnel, and then advances to the next file position.

Within each component of Personnel, the values for ID, Salary, and Dependents are stored as binary numbers. There is no conversion to or from character format.

Typed files allow *direct*, as well as sequential, processing for both Read and Write. In direct processing, a component can be stored at, or retrieved from, any position in the file. To make this possible, the procedure Seek is used to change the current file position. For example, suppose we have read in the 100th component in Personnel. The current file position is 100. If we call:

```
Seek (Personnel, 30)
```

the current file position becomes 30. The next Read or Write[1] will either read from or write to the 30th component in Personnel.

---

[1]Reading and writing can be interleaved in a typed file.

The following program segment writes out the name of every 10th employee in Personnel (the predeclared function FileSize returns the number of components in a file, and FilePos returns the current file position):

```
Reset(Personnel);
for I:= 1 to FileSize (Personnel) div 10 do
   begin
      Seek (Personnel, FilePos (Personnel) + 9);
      Read (Personnel, Employee);
      Writeln (Employee.Name)
   end { for }
```

If Personnel has fewer than ten components, the loop is not executed at all. If Personnel has between 10 and 19 components, inclusive, the loop is executed once, and the 10th employee's name is written out. Similarly, if Personnel has between 20 and 29 components, the loop is executed twice, and the 10th and 20th employee names are output.

The String Data Type

The ability to manipulate strings is helpful in a variety of non-numeric applications, from text editing to compiler writing. The String data type is predeclared in Turbo Pascal, so we present that version rather than defining, designing, and implementing a String ADT. The format of each string operator is as given in the Turbo Pascal Library Reference manual.

To declare a string type, the reserved word **string** is used. For example,

```
type
    NameType = string [20];
var
    Name: NameType;
```

NameType is a type identifier for a string of up to 20 characters, and Name is a varible that can hold up to 20 characters. For example, suppose we have:

```
Readln (Name);
```

If the input contains:

```
Karen Tocci
```

then Name will contain the eleven characters 'Karen Tocci'. However, if the input contains:

```
Mike Tocci
```

then Name will contain only ten characters.

If we declare:

```
type
    MessageType = string;
```

then MessageType is a type identifier for a string of up to 255 characters, the maximum allowed in Turbo Pascal. The following is an equivalent declaration for MessageType:

type
```
    MessageType = string [255];
```

Turbo Pascal provides nine operators in the string data type. To illustrate the effect of applying each operator, the examples assume either of the declarations just given for MessageType and the following variable declaration:

```
var
    Message: MessageType;
```

String Operators

1. +

    Postcondition: The values of the operands are joined (concatenated), in order. The resulting string, truncated to 255 characters if necessary, is returned.

    For example, if Message has the value 'Character', then:

    ```
    Message := Message + ' is fate.'
    ```

    will give Message the value 'Character is fate.'

    Note: The beginning and ending quotes are not part of Message's value: They are delimiters that indicate where that value begins and ends.

2. Concat (S1 [, S2, ..., SN]: String)

    Postcondition: The values of the parameters are joined (concatenated), in order. The resulting string, truncated to 255 characters if necessary, is returned.

    For example, if Message has the value 'Character', then:

    ```
    Message := Concat (Message, ' is fate.')
    ```

    will give Message the value 'Character is fate'. Thus, Concat as applied to two strings has the same effect as +. Also, Concat ('ABC', 'DEF', 'GHIJK') returns the value 'ABCDEFGHIJK', which is the value returned from 'ABC' + 'DEF' + 'GHIJK'.

3. Insert (Source: String; **var** S: String; Index: Integer)

    Postcondition: Source has been inserted into *S*, starting at position Index. The resulting value has been truncated, if necessary, to the declared maximum length of the actual parameter corresponding to *S*.

    For example, if Message has the value 'Bet', then:

    ```
    Insert ('udg', Message, 2)
    ```

will give Message the value 'Budget'. For another example, if we have:

```
var
    S: string [10];
begin
    S := 'ABCDEFGH';
    Insert ('12345', S, 4)
```

then the value of *S* will be 'ABC12345DE'.

4. Delete (**var** S: String; Index: Integer; Count: Integer)

Postcondition: Count characters have been deleted from *S*, starting at position Index. If Index is greater than the length of *S*, no characters have been deleted. If Count is greater than the number of characters in *S* from position Index on, the remainder of *S*, from position Index on, has been deleted.

For example, if we first assign:

```
Message := 'Resist the silly urge to code.'
```

then Delete (Message, 12, 6) will give Message the value 'Resist the urge to code.'

5. Pos (Substr, S: String)

Postcondition: If Substr occurs within *S*, the value returned is the starting position, in *S*, of the first occurrence of Substr within *S*. Otherwise, the value returned is 0.

For example, if Message has the value:

```
'The snow is now on the ground'
```

then Pos ('now', Message) returns the value 6, Pos (' now', Message) returns the value 12, and Pos ('own', Message) returns the value 0, because 'own' is not a substring of Message.

6. Copy (S: String; Index: integer; Count: integer)

Postcondition: The value returned is the string of Count characters starting at position Index in *S*. If Index is greater than the length of *S*, an empty string has been returned. If Count is greater than the number of characters in *S* from position Index on, the remainder of *S*, from position Index on, has been returned.

For example, if Message has the value:

```
'bare ruined choirs'
```

then Copy (Message, 8, 2) returns 'in', Copy (Message, 40, 2) returns the empty string (because Message contains only 18 characters), and Copy (Message, 16, 5) returns 'irs' — the last three characters in Message.

7. `Length (S: String)`

Postcondition: The current length of the string *S* has been returned.
For example, if Message has the value:

`'This too shall pass away.'`

then Length (Message) returns the value 25.

8. `Val (S: String; `**`var`**` V; `**`var`**` Code: Integer)`

Precondition: The actual parameter corresponding to *V* is of an integer
or real type.

Postcondition: If the characters in *S* do not form a signed number that
can be assigned to *V*, then the position of the first incorrect character
has been stored in Code, and *V* is undefined. Otherwise, the numeric
representation of *S* has been stored in *V*, and Code has the value 0.

For example, suppose we have the following:

```
var
    VelocityString: string [20];
    Velocity       : real;
    ErrorPos       : integer;
begin
    Readln (VelocityString);
    Val (VelocityString, Velocity, ErrorPos);
    if ErrorPos = 0 then
        Writeln ('Velocity is legitimate.')
```

If the input contains:

```
234.56
```

then Velocity will get the value 234.56 and ErrorPos will get the value 0,
so the Writeln statement will be executed. But if the input contains:

```
23J.56
```

then Velocity will be undefined and ErrorPos will get the value 3, because 'J' is in the third position in VelocityString. In this case, the
Writeln statement will not be executed.

The procedure Val permits input editing of values that are supposed to
be (but might not be) numbers. In the preceding example, if we had
simply written:

```
begin
    Readln (Velocity);
```

then execution of the program would have halted if the input contained:

```
23J.56
```

9. Str (X [: Width [: Decimals]]; **var** S: String)

Postcondition: The string representation of the number *X* has been stored in *S*.

For example, if Velocity has the value 41.3259, then:

Str (Velocity: 6: 2, Message)

gives Message the value '41.33'.

Note: The effect of the Str procedure is the same as that of the Write procedure, except that Str stores the string representation in a string variable, whereas Write stores the string representation, character-by-character, into the given file, starting at the current file position.

String Manipulation Program

The following name-rearranging program illustrates how several of these string operators can be used in concert. For input such as "John Quincy Adams," the output would be:

```
Adams, John Q.
program Convert;
{ The input is a name in the form }
{                                           }
{     <first name> <middle name> <last name>  }
{                                           }
{ and the output is the name in the form    }
{                                           }
{ <last name>, <first name> <middle initial>. }
const
   MaxLength = 80; { maximum size of a full name }
   Blank     = ' ';
   Comma     = ',';
   Period    = '.';
type
   NameType   = string [MaxLength];
   LetterType = string [1];
var
   FullName,
   FirstName,
   MiddleLast,
   LastName,
   RevisedName  : NameType;
   MiddleInitial: LetterType;
   BlankPos1,
   BlankPos2,
   NameLength   : integer;
```

```
begin
   Readln (FullName);
   NameLength := Length (FullName);

   { Find the first name: }
   BlankPos1      := Pos (Blank, FullName);
   FirstName      := Copy (FullName, 1, BlankPos1 - 1);
   MiddleInitial := Copy (FullName, BlankPos1 + 1, 1);

   { Find the last name: }
   MiddleLast := Copy (FullName, BlankPos1 + 1,
                        NameLength - BlankPos1);
   BlankPos2  := BlankPos1 + Pos (Blank, MiddleLast);
   LastName   := Copy (FullName, BlankPos2 + 1,
                        NameLength - BlankPos2);

   RevisedName := LastName + Comma + Blank + FirstName
                  + Blank + MiddleInitial + Period;
   Writeln (RevisedName)
end. { Convert }
```

Implementation Details

A string is stored as an array of characters. The indexes go from 0 to the declared maximum length of the string. The character at index 0 is the one whose ordinal value is the current length of the string. For example, suppose we declare:

```
type
   NameType = string [20];
var
   Name: NameType;
```

Internally, Name is treated as an array with indexes going from 0 to 20. The first byte, Name [0], holds the ASCII character whose ordinal value is the current length of the string, and the next 20 bytes hold the characters in the string. For example, if we assign:

```
Name := 'Jose Canseco'
```

then,

```
Name [0] = '♀'; { note that Ord ('♀') = 12 }
Name [1] = 'J';
Name [2] = 'o';
Name [3] = 's';
...
Name [11] = 'c';
Name [12] = 'o';
```

The values in Name [13] through Name [20] are undefined. They may be leftover values from a previous assignment to Name, or values that happened to be in those locations at the start of execution of the program. Those characters would not, however, be treated as part of Name in assignment statements, output statements, or Boolean expressions (such as "if Name = OldName").

If the value of Name is later changed, Name [0] is automatically updated. For example, if we later set:

```
Name := 'Wade Boggs'
```

then the value stored in Name [0] will be the character whose ordinal value is 10. Of course, Name [1 .. 10] will also be changed.

Sometimes we need to use this array-of-characters implementation. Note that a string of length 1 is actually stored as an array of two characters, so a string of length 1 cannot be assigned to a variable of type char. What if we want to apply some character operator to the individual characters in a string? For example, suppose we want to write out the ordinal value of each character. The following would be illegal:

```
type
   NameType = string [20];
var
   Name  : NameType;
   Letter: char;
   I     : word;
begin
   Readln (Name);
   for I := 1 to Length (Name) do
      begin
         Letter := Copy (Name, I, 1); { illegal! }
         Writeln (Ord (Letter))
      end
```

We can easily avoid this difficulty by replacing the assignment to Letter with:

```
Letter := Name [I];
```

Since Name [I] is a character, it can be assigned to Letter.

EXERCISE

This exercise illustrates the danger of using the details of the array-of-characters implementation of a string. Here are two program fragments to generate 100 random, six-character strings and store them in an array. The first fragment uses only the string operators; the second uses the array of characters in the string implementation.

```
Randomize;
for I := 1 to 100 do
   begin
      RandString := '';
      for J := 1 to 6 do
         RandString := RandString + Chr (Random (256));
      RandArray [I] := RandString
   end { for }
Randomize;
for I := 1 to 100 do
   begin
      for J := 1 to 6 do
         RandString [J] := Chr (Random (256));
      RandArray [I] := RandString
   end { for }
```

This second fragment is incorrect. What is wrong with it?

More on Types

Denoting Types

In languages that allow type declarations, we can denote a variable's type by using either a named type or an anonymous type. In the following example, EmployeeType is a named type:

```
type
   EmployeeType = record
      Name  : string [30];
      Salary: real
   end; { EmployeeType }
var
   Employee: EmployeeType;
```

If the denotation uses anything other than a type identifier, the type of the variable is said to be ***anonymous***. For example, we can declare:

```
var
   Employee: record
      Name : string [30];
      Salary: real
   end; { Employee }
```

The relationship between pairs of types plays a key role in the rules for assignment statements and for parameter correspondence. In Turbo Pascal, two types are considered identical only if they are name-equivalent. T1 and T2 are ***name-equivalent*** types if either T1 and T2 are the same type identifier, or if T1 has been declared equal to a type that is name-equivalent to T2. For example, suppose we declare:

```
type
   A1 = array [1..5] of real;
   A2 = array [1..5] of real;
   A3 = A2;
```

In this case, A1 and the first anonymous type are name-equivalent. A2, A3, and the second anonymous type are name-equivalent to each other. However, A1 and A2 (as well as A1 and A3) are not name-equivalent. A1 and A2 are considered distinct types, even though they are **structurally equivalent** (that is, they denote the same collection of values).

A further illustration of name equivalence can be seen in the following example:

```
type
   R1 = real;
   R2 = real;
   R3 = R2;
```

R1 is name-equivalent to real, and R2 is name-equivalent to real. This makes R1 and R2 name-equivalent to each other. Since R3 is declared equal to R2, we conclude that R1, R2, R3, and real are all name-equivalent to each other.

Assignment Compatibility

A value of type T2 is said to be **assignment-compatible** with a variable of type T1 if the value can be assigned to the variable. Under what circumstances does assignment compatibility hold? As we will see shortly, assignment compatibility may not apply even if T1 and T2 are name-equivalent. On the other hand, sometimes assignment compatibility applies even when T1 and T2 are not structurally equivalent.

A value of type T2 is assignment-compatible with a variable of type T1 if any one of the following is true:[1]

1. T1 and T2 are name-equivalent, and neither is a file type or a structured type that contains a file-type component at any level of structuring.

    For example, suppose we declare:

```
type
   RecordType = record
      Name: string;
      Age : integer
```

---

[1] See your current Reference Guide for a complete list of assignment-compatibility rules.

```
   end; { RecordType }
   FileType = file of integer;
var
   A,
   B : RecordType;
   C,
   D : FileType;
```

The assignment statement

```
A := B
```

is legal, but

```
C := D
```

is illegal, because *C* and *D* are variables of a file type.

2. T1 and T2 are simple types, and the value from type T2 is in the range of values of the type T1.

   For example, suppose we have:

```
type
   Int1Type = 100..200;
   Int2Type = 150..225;
var
   A: Int1Type;
   B: Int2Type;
begin
   A := 173;
   B := A;
   B := 220;
   A := B;
```

   The assignment B := A is legal, because 173 is in the subrange 150..225. However, the assignment A := B is illegal, because 220 is not in the subrange 100..200. This illegality will not be detected at compile time, and will be detected at run time only if the "Range checking" option is "on." This option, in the Compiler submenu of the Options menu, directs the compiler to generate code that will detect out-of-range values and array index errors at run time.

3. T1 and T2 are string types.

   For example, suppose we have:

```
type
   S1Type = string [3];
   S2Type = string [5];
var
   S1: S1Type;
   S2: S2Type;
```

```
begin
    S1 := 'abc';
    S2 := S1;
    S2 := 'vwxyz';
    S1 := S2;
```

The assignment S2 := S1 is legal: S2 gets the value "abc". The assignment S1 := S2 is also legal: S1 gets the value "vwx".

4. T1 is a real type and T2 is an integer type (or a subrange of an integer type).

    Note that in this case, T1 and T2 cannot be structurally equivalent, because real and integer types contain different collections of values.

5. T1 and T2 are pointers to object types, and the object type pointed to by T1 is an ancestor of the object type pointed to by T2.

    For example, if AType is an ancestor of DType, and we declare:

```
type
    T1 = ^AType;
    T2 = ^DType;
var
    APtr: T1;
    DPtr: T2;
```

then the following assignment is legal:

```
APtr := DPtr
```

The significance of this rule will be seen in Appendix 6, when we study a property of objects called *polymorphyism*.

Compatibility of Actual and Formal Parameters

Procedures and functions are called subprograms because they have the same structure as a program. That is, each subprogram consists of a heading followed by a *block*—a declaration part followed by a statement part. A subprogram heading usually includes a formal parameter. The syntax diagram for a formal parameter list is as follows:

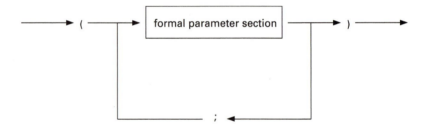

The syntax diagram for a formal parameter section is:

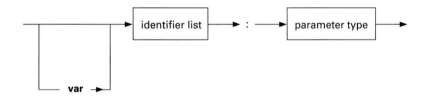

An identifier list is simply a list of identifiers (referred to as *formal parameters*) separated by commas. A parameter type in Turbo Pascal must be either a type identifier or **string**. For example, here is a procedure heading:

```
procedure FindASolution (Tree         : TreeType;
                     var Goal,
                         Head,
                         Tail         : ListType;
                         GoalState    : BoardType;
                         SolutionFound: boolean);
```

In this heading, there are four formal parameter sections and a total of six formal parameters. The formal parameters Goal, Head, and Tail are called *variable formal parameters* because their section begins with **var**. Tree, GoalState, and SolutionFound are *value formal parameters* because their sections do not begin with **var**.

It is important to note that **var** applies only to a formal parameter section, not to the rest of the formal parameter list. That is why GoalState and SolutionFound are value formal parameters, not variable formal parameters.

A procedure is activated through a procedure statement, a function through a function call. If the subprogram heading has formal parameters, the calling statement must have a matching list of actual parameters—expressions (usually variables) separated by commas. For example, a call to the procedure FindASolution might be as follows:

```
FindASolution (Tree, Goal, Head, Tail, GoalState,
               SolutionFound);
```

In this example, the actual parameters have the same names as the corresponding formal parameters. This is often done to make it easy to keep track of the variables, but it is not a requirement of Pascal. There is a strictly positional correspondence between the actual parameters in the procedure statement (or function call) and the formal parameters in the subprogram heading. The first actual parameter is matched with the first formal parameter, and so on.

Each variable formal parameter (one whose formal parameter section begins with **var**) represents the same variable as the corresponding actual parameter. The variable formal parameter's type must be name-equivalent to either the actual parameter's type *or an ancestor of the actual parameter's type*. The significance of the phrase "or an ancestor of the actual parameter's type" will be seen in Appendix 6, when we study virtual methods.

Each value formal parameter (one whose formal parameter section does not begin with **var**) must be assignment-compatible with its corresponding actual parameter, because a copy of the actual parameter is stored in the value formal parameter. Thus, by condition 1 in the preceding section, the type of a value formal parameter must not be a file type, nor a type with file components.

The following simple example may clarify the essential difference between value and variable formal parameters. The exercises at the end of this appendix explore some of the finer points of parameter passing.

```
program Sample;
var
   I,
   J : integer;
procedure Both (var I: integer;
                 J    : integer);
begin
   I := 2 * I;
   J := 2 * J
end; { Both }
begin
   I := 5;
   J := 5;
   Both (I, J);
   Writeln (I: 3, J: 3)
end. { Sample }
```

The output from this program is:

```
10   5
```

Finally, the result type of a function must be either the reserved word **string** or a type identifier for a simple, string, or pointer type. Other modern languages, such as Ada and Eiffel, allow any type to be used as the result type of a function.

Typed Constant

A **typed constant** is actually a variable whose type and initial value are provided in one declaration. Typed constants are convenient for declaring constant arrays and records. The syntax diagram for a typed constant is as follows:

For example, we can write

const
    Sum: real = 0.0;

For arrays and records, the syntax of the initial value depends on the type
of the constant:

1. If the type is an array, parentheses enclose the entire list of component
    values; each component value is separated from the next by a comma.
    For example, we can declare a constant array of headings:

    const
        Heading: **array** [1..5] **of string** [15] = ('Initialize ',
                    'IsEmpty ', 'Retrieve ', 'Insert ', 'Delete ');

    The execution of:

    Writeln (Heading [4])

    would produce output of:

    Insert

2. In a typed constant for a two-dimensional array, a pair of parentheses
    enclose each row's values. For example, we can declare:

    type
        ActionType   = (Push, Pop, Append, Done);
        TransTableType = **array** [1..2, 1..3] **of** ActionType;
    const
        TransTable: TransTableType = ((Append, Append, Push),
                                      (Pop,   Push,   Done));

    Notice that in Turbo Pascal, declarations can come in any order. It is
    not necessary that **const** declarations precede **type** declarations.

    The initial value of TransTable is shown in Fig. A5.1.

Figure A5.1

The typed constant
TransTable.

	Column 1	Column 2	Column 3
Row 1	Append	Append	Push
Row 2	Pop	Push	Done

3. For a record typed constant, each field identifier is followed by a colon and an initial value. Semicolons separate the component parts, and the entire list is enclosed in parentheses. For example, we can declare:

```
type
   FranchiseType = record
      City  : string [15];
      OnHand: word;
      Sales : real
   end;{ FranchiseType }
const
   Sample: FranchiseType = (City   : 'Hana';
                            OnHand: 100;
                            Sales : 400.00);
```

LABORATORY EXERCISES

For each of the following exercises, conjecture what the answer should be; then enter and run the corresponding program to confirm or reject your conjecture.

1.1 Given the following declarations, determine which seven of the following 12 assignment statements satisfy the assignment-compatibility rules. In each assignment statement, assume that the expression on the right-hand side of the ":=" has a value in its type (that is, assume that the expression is not undefined).

```
program Assignment;
{ Testing assignment-compatibility }
type
   R1 = record
      Field1: integer;
      Field2: real
   end;{ R1 }
   R2 = record
      Field1: integer;
      Field2: real
   end; { R2 }
   R3 = R2;
   A1 = array[1..10] of real;
   A2 = array[1..10] of real;
   F1 = file of integer;
   P1 = ^R1;
   P2 = ^R1;
```

```
var
  VR1: R1;
  VR2: R2;
  VR3: R3;
  VR4,
  VR5: record
         Field1: integer;
         Field2: real
       end; { VR4, VR5 }
  VA1: A1;
  VA2: A2;
  VF1,
  VF2: F1;
  VP1: P1;
  VP2,
  VP3: P2;
begin
  VR1 := VR2;
  VR2 := VR3;
  VR1.Field1 := 10.0;
  VR1.Field2 := 10;
  VA1 := VA2;
  VA1 [1] := VA2 [2];
  VF1 := VF2;
  VP1 := VP2;
  VP2 := VP3;
  VP1^ := VP2^;
  VP1^.Field1 := VR1.Field1
end. { Assignment }
```

1.2 Rewrite the following function heading as a procedure heading with an additional formal parameter for the median. The procedure identifier should be FindMedian.

```
type
  ArrayType = array[1..100] of real;
function Median (A: ArrayType;
                 N: integer): real;
```

1.3 Each of the following three headings contains an error. Can you find the errors?

```
a.  function LastName (FullName: string): string [20];
b.  procedure Sort (var A: array [1..500] of string;
                     N    : integer);
```

c. **type**
```
    FileType = file of real;
  procedure Copy (Source         : FileType;
                    var Destination: FileType;
```

1.4 Declare a typed constant for an array Frequency with indexes ranging from 1 to 10 and whose initial values are all zeros.

1.5 Declare two typed constants, Value1 and Value2, both of type Value-Type, where

```
type
   ValueType = record
      Weight,
      Cost    : real
   end; {ValueType}
```

For Value1, Weight is 10.6 and Cost is 50. For Value2, Weight is 15.0 and Cost is 27.

Polymorphism and Virtual Methods

The three distinguishing features of objects are encapsulation, inheritance, and polymorphism. The topics in Chapters 4 through 11 relied heavily on encapsulation and inheritance. The concept of polylmorphism is essential for advanced applications in object-oriented programming, such as the Turbo Vision material in Chapter 12.

Before we can define polymorphism and its associates, virtual methods, let's highlight one of the parameter-correspondence rules from Appendix 4:

> *A variable formal parameter's type must be name-equivalent to either the corresponding actual parameter's type or an ancestor of the actual parameter's type.*

For example, in Chapter 1, we declared an object type StudentType; later, we declared DormStudentType, a descendant of StudentType. Given those declarations, we can declare:

```
procedure Legal (var Student: StudentType);
begin
...
end; { Legal }

var
   Student1: StudentType;
   Student2: DormStudentType;
```

```
begin
   ...
   Legal (Student1);
   ...
   Legal (Student2);
   ...
end.
```

Both procedure statements are legitimate, because in each case the formal parameter's type is the same as, or an ancestor of, the actual parameter's type. Notice that the type of the actual parameter corresponding to Student can change from one call to the next. In other words, the type of Student's actual parameter cannot be known until run time.

This parameter-correspondence rule enables us to declare virtual methods. A ***virtual method*** is one that is associated with compiled code at run time. When the calling instance occurs in a procedure as a variable formal parameter V, the meaning of the method call depends on the type of the actual parameter corresponding to V. This type can be determined only at run time.

The following example (adapted from Meyer, 1989) may help you to see what this means and how it can be valuable.

An Example of a Virtual Method

Suppose we have declared an object PolygonType (a ***polygon*** is a closed plane figure bounded by straight lines). The only field is VertexList, which contains the list of vertices of the polygon. One of the methods is Area, which calculates (nontrivially) the area of the polygon. Area is a virtual method, indicated by the reserved word **virtual.** Some of the code is as follows:

```
unit PolygonManager;
{ This unit implements the polygon data type. }
interface
uses
   ListManager; { implements the list data type }
type
   PolygonType = object
      VertexList: ListType;
      constructor Initialize; { The meaning of this is
                                explained later.        }
      .
      .
      .
```

```
        function Area: real; virtual; { Area is a virtual
                                          method.           }
            .
            .
            .

    end; { PolygonType }
implementation
constructor PolygonType.Initialize;
{ This procedure makes the polygon empty. }
begin
    VertexList.Initialize
end; { Initialize }
.
.
.

function PolygonType.Area: real;
{ This function returns the area of the polygon. }
.
.
.

end; { Area }
.
.
.

end. { PolygonManager }
```

We also declare another object, RectangleType, a descendant of Polygon-Type. RectangleType could inherit its ancestor's way of calculating Area, but the area of a rectangle can be calculated much more easily: We simply multiply the first two sides (that is, the distances between the first two pairs of vertices).

Part of the code for RectangleType is included in the following:

```
unit RectangleManager;
{ This unit implements the rectangle data type. }
interface
uses
    ListManager,
    PolygonManager;
type
    RectangleType = object (PolygonType)
        .
        .
        .
```

```
        function Area: real; virtual;

            .

            .

            .

    end; { RectangleType }
implementation
    .

    .

    .

function RectangleType.Area: real;
{ Straightforward code for calculating the area of a
  rectangle.                                          }
    .

    .

    .

end; { Area }
    .

    .

    .

end. { RectangleManager }
```

Now, suppose that Figures is a program that works with both arbitrary polygons and rectangles. Part of the code for Figures is:

```
program Figures;
{ This program utilizes polygons in general and rectangles.}
uses
    PolygonManager,
    RectangleManager;
    .

    .

    .

procedure Compute (var V: PolygonType);
var
    CurrentArea: real;
begin
    .

    .

    .

    CurrentArea := V.Area;
    .

    .

    .

end; { Compute }
```

```
var
   PV: PolygonType;
   RV: RectangleType;
begin
   PV.Initialize;
   RV.Initialize;
   .

   .

   .
   Compute (PV);
   .

   .

   .
   Compute (RV);
   .

   .

   .
end. { Figures }
```

In the procedure Compute, when the actual parameter is *PV*, the call:

```
V.Area
```

calculates (nontrivially) the area of the polygon *PV*. But if the actual parameter to Compute is *RV*, then the call:

```
V.Area
```

calculates (trivially) the area of the rectangle *RV*.

The beauty of all this is the reusability of the procedure Compute. Compute can be called by instances of polygons and rectangles (even though Compute calls Area, which is a different method for a polygon than for a rectangle).

Polymorphism (from the Greek for "many shapes") is the ability of a variable to refer, at run time, to instances of different objects in an object hierarchy. In the preceding example, the formal parameter *V* is polymorphic because it can refer to either *PV* or *RV*.

Virtual methods and polymorphism are indispensable to each other. Without polymorphism, there would be no way to activate the different virtual methods. Without virtual methods, there would be nothing special for a polymorphic variable to activate.

How Virtual Methods Are Compiled and Executed

There is one aspect of the above example that is puzzling: How can the compiler determine the correct machine code corresponding to the method call V.Area? The answer is that the compiler can't determine whether the Area method for a polygon or for a rectangle is being referred to.

Thus, the link to the correct code (for the polygon Area or for the rectangle Area) cannot be made at compile time. Instead, the decision is deferred until run time, when the type of the actual parameter is available for any given call to Compute. However, the mechanism also has a compile time component, because it is only at compile time that executable code is generated.

Here is what happens. When an object has one or more virtual methods (indicated by the reserved word **virtual**), a Virtual Method Table (VMT) is created at compile time. This table contains, for each virtual method in the object, the address of the compiled code for that method. For example, suppose that PolygonType contained a virtual method for Perimeter as well as for Area. The Virtual Method Table for PolygonType would then look like this:

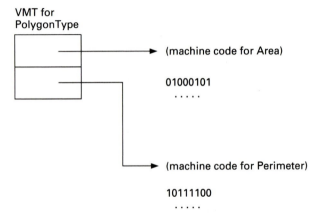

Similarly, the Virtual Method Table for RectangleType would have:

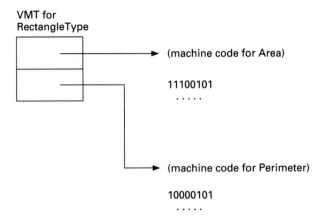

At run time, an instance must be initialized by calling one of its constructor methods before it can call any of its virtual methods. A constructor method has the reserved word **constructor** in place of **procedure** or **function.** When an instance calls a constructor, a link (in the form of a pointer) is established between that instance and the Virtual Method Table for the instance's object type. For example, the execution of:

```
PV.Initialize
```

makes VertexList empty, and also creates a link to the Virtual Method Table for PolygonType:

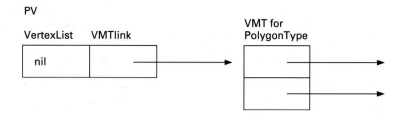

Similarly, the execution of:

```
RV.Initialize
```

creates a link to the Virtual Method Table for RectangleType:

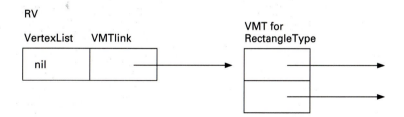

Within Compute, the execution of:

```
CurrentArea := V.Area;
```

will use the version of Area that is appropriate for the actual parameter corresponding to *V*.

The upshot of all this is that the program does as expected. The execution of:

```
Compute (PV);
```

calculates the area of the polygon *PV*, whereas the execution of:

```
Compute (RV);
```

calculates (the easy way) the area of the rectangle *RV*.

In this example, and in general, a descendant's virtual method should be an improvement over its ancestor's virtual method. For example, the descendant's virtual method might have a weaker precondition, a stronger postcondition, or be more efficient than its ancestor's method with the same name.

Here is one final bit of terminology related to virtual methods. As we saw above, the link between the identifier Area and the appropriate code (for a polygon's area or for a rectangle's area) is not made until run time. The process by which the linkage is made is called *late binding* or *dynamic binding*. This is in contrast to static binding (used for all methods except virtual methods), where the linkage is made at compile time.

Another Example of a Virtual Method

There is one other situation in Turbo Pascal in which polymorphic objects can combine with virtual methods. Let's start by recalling one of the compatibility rules from Appendix 5:

> *If T1 and T2 are pointers to objects, and T1's object is an ancestor of T2's object, then a value of type T2 can be assigned to a variable of type T1.*

For example, suppose we have the following:

```
program PolyVirt;
type
   AType = object                    { ancestor }
      constructor Initialize;
      procedure Print; virtual;
   end; { AType }
   DType = object (AType)        { descendant }
      procedure Print; virtual;
   end; { DType }
   APtrType = ^AType;
   DPtrType = ^DType;
constructor AType.Initialize;
begin
end; { Initialize }
procedure AType.Print;
begin
   Writeln ('A')
end; { AType.Print }
procedure DType.Print;
begin
   Writeln ('D')
end; { DType.Print }
```

```
var
   APtr: APtrType;
   DPtr: DPtrType;
   Code: integer;
begin
   APtr^.Initialize;
   DPtr^.Initialize;
   Readln (Code);
   if Code = 0 then
      APtr := DPtr;
   APtr^.Print
end. { PolyVirt }
```

If the value read in for Code is 0, what will be printed, "A" or "D"? At first glance, it might appear that "A" will be printed. After all, APtr is declared as a pointer to an instance of AType, whose Print method writes out "A". However, the assignment:

```
APtr := DPtr
```

makes APtr^ an instance of DType, whose Print method writes out "D". Therefore, the output from the above program will be "D", provided Code = 0.

In the preceding example, APtr^ is polymorphic; it can refer to either an instance of AType or an instance of DType, depending on the value of Code. Of course, the value of Code can only be known at run time, and that is the whole idea behind polymorphism.

The preceding examples should give you some idea of the whys and hows of virtual methods. Chapter 12 will allow you to see more examples of virtual methods, and (more importantly) to develop your own.

Answers to Selected Exercises

2.1 For any value of $N > 1$, the function call Fact (N) will not terminate because the simplest case, $N = 1$, will never be reached.

2.2
```
program Binary;
{ This program implements an iterative version of the}
{ WriteBinary procedure.                             }
const
   MaxBinSize = 1000;
   Prompt     = 'Enter the value of N: ';
type
   ArrayType = array [1..MaxBinSize] of integer;
procedure WriteBinary (N : integer);
var
   Bit: ArrayType;
   I  : integer;
begin
   I := 0;
   while N <> 0 do
      begin
         I := I + 1;
         Bit [I] := N mod 2;
         N := N div 2
      end; { while }
   for I := I downto 1 do
      Write (Bit [I])
```

```
end; { WriteBinary }
var
   N: integer;
begin
   Write (Prompt);
   Readln (N);
   Writebinary (N)
end. { Binary }
```

2.4
$$f(1) = 1$$
$$f(2) = 3$$
$$f(3) = 7$$
$$f(4) = 15$$
For $N > 1$, $f(N) = 2^N - 1$
$$= (2 * f(N - 1)) + 1$$

2.7

```
         Permute('ABC',1)
   /          |          \
Permute('ABC',2)  Permute('ABC',2)  Permute('BAC',2)
  /    \        /    \         /    \
P('ABC',3) P('ABC',3) P('ABC',3) P('ABC',3) P('BAC',3) P('BAC',3)
  |         |         |          |          |          |
ABC       ABC       ABC        ABC        BAC        BAC
```

2.11
```
program FindGCD;
const
   Prompt = 'Enter two positive integers: ';
function GCD (I,
              J: longint): longint;
begin
   if I mod J = 0 then
      GCD := J
   else
      GCD := GCD (J, I mod J)
end; { GCD }
var
   I,
   J: longint;
```

```
            begin
               Write (Prompt );
               Readln (I, J);
               Writeln (GCD (I, J))
            end. { FindGCD }

2.12  program TestPalindrome;
      const
          Prompt = 'Enter a string: ';
      function Palindrome (S: String): boolean;
      function Pal (S: string;
                         I,
                         J: integer): boolean;
      begin
         if (J <= I) then
            Pal:= True
         else
            Pal := (S[I] = S[J]) and Pal(S, I+1, J-1)
      end; { Pal }
      begin { Palindrome}
         Palindrome := Pal (S, 1, Length (S))
      end; { Palindrome }
      var
         S: string;
      begin
         Write (Prompt);
         Readln (S);
         if Palindrome (S) then
            Writeln ('This is a palindrome.')
         else
            Writeln ('This is not a palindrome.')
      end. { TestPalindrome }
```

Chapter 3

3.1 b.

Functional Specifications

1. The input for each employee consists of the employee number, the hours worked, and the pay rate.

2. For each hour worked over 40, an employee gets an overtime rate of 1.5 times the pay rate.

3. The gross pay is the regular pay (for up to 40 hours) plus the overtime pay.

4. The net pay is the gross pay minus the deductions.

5. The deductions, as percentages of gross pay, are:

   FICA (Federal Insurance Contribution Act): 6.65%

   state tax withheld: 7.5%

   federal tax withheld: 15%

6. Each line of input will contain an employee number, hours worked, and pay rate. The employee number should be an integer between 1000 and 9999, the hours worked an integer between 0 and 168, and the pay rate a real value between 3.50 and 30.00.

7. For incorrect input, the error messages are:

```
Error: Employee number should be between 1000 and 9999.
Error: Hours worked should be between 0 and 168.
Error: Pay rate should be between 3.50 and 30.00.
```

8. The program will be conversational. The prompt is:

```
Please enter an ID, hours worked, and pay rate:
```

9. The sentinels are -1, -1 and -1.00.

Sample Conversation 1 (the input is boldfaced)

```
Calculate net pay for each employee.
The sentinels are -1, -1, -1.0.
Please enter an ID, hours worked, and pay rate: 3042 45 5.50
   The net pay is $185.10.
Please enter an ID, hours worked, and pay rate: 2107 37 400
   Error: Pay rate should be between 3.50 and 30.00.
Please enter an ID, hours worked, and pay rate: 2107 37 4.00
   The net pay is $104.86.
Please enter an ID, hours worked, and pay rate: 2806 420 .350
   Error: Hours worked should be between 0 and 168.
   Error: Pay rate should be between 3.50 and 30.00.
Please enter an ID, hours worked, and pay rate: 2806 42 .350
   Error: Pay rate should be between 3.50 and 30.00.
Please enter an ID, hours worked, and pay rate: 2806 42 3.50
   The net pay is $106.63.
Please enter an ID, hours worked, and pay rate: 3001 39 3.80
   The net pay is $105.00.
Please enter an ID, hours worked, and pay rate: -1 -1 -1.00
```

Sample Conversation 2 (the input is boldfaced)

```
Calculate net pay for each employee.
The sentinels are -1, -1, -1.0.
```

```
Please enter an ID, hours worked, and pay rate: 3605 40 25.00
   The net pay is $708.50.
Please enter an ID, hours worked, and pay rate: -1 -1 0.00
   Error: Employee number should be between 1000 and 9999.
   Error: Hours worked should be between 0 and 168.
   Error: Pay rate should be between 3.50 and 30.00.
Please enter an ID, hours worked, and pay rate: -1 -1 -1.00
```

3.3   **a.** Precondition: `Position = 1; for some I in 1..N, A [I] = Item;`

           Loop invariant: `For all I in 1..N, if I < Position, A[I] <> Item.`

           Postcondition: `Position is the smallest integer in 1..N for which A [Position] = Item.`

  b. The outer For statement:

           Loop post-invariant: `A [1..I] sorted and <= A [I+1..N].`

           Postcondition: `A [1..N] sorted.`

           The inner For statement:

           Precondition: `Position = I.`

           Loop post-invariant: `A [Position] smallest of A [I..J].`

           Postcondition: `A [Position] smallest of A [I..N].`

3.6   **a.** For $I = 2$, there are $N - 2$ iterations of the inner loop.
           For $I = 3$, there are $N - 3$ iterations of the inner loop.

  b. $F(N) = N (N - 1)/2$

  c. N^2

3.7   **a.** $O(N \log N)$

  b. $O(N)$

  c. $O(N^2)$

  d. $O(N^2)$

  e. $O(N \log N)$

  f. $O(N)$

  g. $O(\log N)$

  h. $O(N)$

Chapter 4

4.1   **a.** `( The list is empty. )`

```
f
fi
efi
erfi
```

```
erfci
erfeci
rfeci
prfeci
perfeci
perfecit
perfect
```

b.
```
unit ItemInList;
{ This units implements the Itemtype for the the
list object. }
interface
type
    ItemType = char;
procedure WriteOut;
implementation
procedure WriteOut;
begin
    Write (Item);
end; { WriteOut }
end. { ItemInList }

unit Maxima;
{ This unit implements MaxListSize. }
interface
const
    MaxListSize = 100;
implementation
end. { Maxima }
```

c. & d.
```
program ListDriver;
    { This is a driver program for implementations
      of the List ADT. }
    uses
        ItemInList,
        Maxima,
        SList1Manager;
    var
        Letters : ListType;
    begin
        with Letters do
            begin
                Initialize;
                Insert ('f', 1);
                Insert ('i', 2);
                Insert ('e', 1);
                Insert ('r', 2);
```

```
                              Insert ('c', 4);
                              Insert ('e', 4);
                              Delete (1);
                              Insert ('p', 1);
                              Insert ('e', 2);
                              Insert ('t', 8);
                              Delete (7);
                              Traverse (WriteOut)
                         end { with }
                    end. { ListDriver }
```

4.2 unit ItemInList;

```
{ This unit implements the ItemType for the List
  object }
interface
type
   ValueType = record
      Name    : string[20];
      Address : string [30]
   end; { ValueType }
   EmployeeType = object
      Value : ValueType
   end; { EmployeeType }
   ItemType = EmployeeType;
   implementation
   end. { ItemInList }
```

4.5 Retrieve and Size

4.6
```
if (1 <= Position) and (Position <= 1 + Petition.Size)
  and (Petition.Size < MaxListSize) then
Petition.Insert (Name, Position)
```

4.8 **a.** <u>DeleteItem (Item, List)</u>

```
List.Search (Item, Found, Position)
List.Delete (Position)
```

b. <u>Merge (List1, List2)</u>

```
Position := List1.Size + 1
for I := 1 to List2.Size do
   List2.Retrieve (Item, I)
   List1,Insert (Item, Position)
   Position := Position + 1
```

4.9 O(N^2).

4.21 CopyTo (List, NewList)
```
TempList.Initialize
while not List.IsEmpty do
    List.Retrieve (Item, 1)
    List.Delete (1)
    TempList.Insert (1)
while not TempList.IsEmpty do
    Templist.Retrieve (Item, 1)
    TempList.Delete (1)
    NewList.Insert (1)
    List.Insert (1)
```

Size (List)
```
List.CopyTo (TempList).
Count := 0
with TempList do
    while not IsEmpty do
        Delete (1)
        Count := Count + 1
Size := Count
```

Search (List, Item, Found, Position)
```
Found    := False
Position := 1
with List do
    while not Found and (Position <= Size) do
        Retrieve (TempItem, Position)
        if Item EqualTo TempItem then
            Item  := TempItem
            Found := True
        else
            Add 1 to Position
```

Traverse (List, Visit)
```
for I := 1 to List.Size do
    List.Retrieve (Item, I)
    Visit (Item)
```

4.22 For the original linked design:

CopyTo: $O(N)$

Size: $O(N)$

Search: $O(N^2)$

Traverse: $O(N^2)$

↓ ↓

4.24 a. `TraverseBackwards (List, Visit)`

```
for I := List.Size downto 1 do
   List.Retrieve (Item, I)
   Visit (Item)
```

b. For the contiguous design, the loop is executed *N* times, and Retrieve takes $O(1)$ Time, so the overall Time is $O(N)$.

c. For the linked design, the loop is also executed $O(N)$ times; but Retrieve takes $O(N)$ time, so the overall Time is $O(N^2)$.

d. Contiguous

↓

`TraverseBackwards (Visit)`

```
for I := N downto 1 do
   Visit (A [I])
```

Chapter 5

5.1 a. `(the list is empty )`
```
dog
cow dog
cow dog pig
cow dog goat pig
cat cow dog goat pig
cat cow dog goat pig sheep
cat cow dog goat horse pig sheep
cat chicken cow dog goat horse pig sheep
```

5.4 Search, Retrieve, and Size.

5.5 a. `...`
```
if A [Middle] is LessThan Item then
   First := Middle + 1
else
   if A [Middle] is GreaterThan Item then
      Last := Middle - 1
```

```
else
    Item       := A [Middle]
    Found      := True
    Position := Middle
```

b. Time is still O(log *N*). Run-time speed will be improved by about 20 percent.

5.7   `Search (Item, Found, Position)`

Initialize First to 1, Last to N and Found to False
SearchItem (First, Last)

`SearchItem (First, Last)`

```
if First <= Last then
    Middle := (First + Last) div 2
    if A [Middle] EqualTo Item then
        Found      := True
        Position := Middle
        Item       := A [Item]
    else
        if A [Middle] LessThan Item the
            SearchItem (Middle + 1, Last)
        else
            SearchItem (First, Middle - 1 )
else
        Position := First
```

5.8   If the list is empty, Middle will get the value 0, so *A* [Middle] will be out of bounds.

5.9   `Search (Item, Found, Position)`

Initialize FirstHead to Head, First to 1, Last to N
    and Found to False.

{ Find where the item belongs in the list: }
while not Found and (First <= Last) do
    Middle := (First + Last) div 2

    { Get to the middle of the current list: }
    MiddleHead := FirstHead
    for I := First to Middle - 1 do
        MiddleHead := MiddleHead's Next

```
         if MiddleHead's Item is EqualTo Item then
             Item     := MiddleHead's Item
             Found    := True
             Position := Middle
         else
             if MiddleHead's Item is LessThan Item then
                 First     := Middle + 1
                 FirstHead := MiddleHead's Next
             else
                 Last := Middle
    if not Found then
         Position := First
```

b. If the While loop is executed just once, the number of iterations of the For loop is N div 2. If the While loop is executed just twice, the number of iterations of the For loop is (N div 2) + (N div 4). If the While loop is executed just three times, the number of iterations of the For loop is (N div 2) + (N div 4) + (N div 8). In general, the total number of iterations of the For loop will be at least N div 2 and at most $N - 1$, because ($N/2$) + ($N/4$) + ... is less than N. Therefore, Time is O(N), the same as for the original and improved linked designs. Run time, however, is faster than either of those implementations.

5.10 A dynamic contiguous implementation would be preferable if there were a lot of searches and retrievals (hence the need for a contiguous implementation), but the list would not fit into the Data Segment (hence the need for a dynamic implementation).

5.11 a. <u>DeleteFrom (List, Item)</u>

```
    with List do

         { Delete all items EqualTo Item: }
         Search (Item, Found, Position)
         while Found do
             Delete (Item)
             Search (Item, Found, Position)

         { Delete all items GreaterThan Item: }
         for I := Position to Size do
             Retrieve (Item, Position)
             Delete (Item)
```

Note: In the For loop, after the item at Position is deleted, its successor is then located at Position; so Position is used every time for retrieving.

5.13 For $K = 1, 2, 3$, let S_K be the statement:

$$\sum_{i=1}^{K} (i * 2^{i-1}) = (K - 1) * 2^K + 1$$

a. (base case) $K = 1$.

$$\sum_{i=1}^{1} (i * 2^{i-1}) = 1 * 2^0 = 1 = (1 - 1) * 2^1 + 1$$

Therefore, S_1 is true.

b. (inductive case) Let K be any positive integer and assume that S_K is true.

$$\sum_{i=1}^{K+1} (i * 2^{i-1}) = \sum_{i=1}^{K} (i * 2^{i-1}) + ((K + 1) * 2^{K+1-1})$$
$$= (K - 1) * 2^K + 1 + ((K + 1) * 2^K)$$
$$= [(K - 1) + (K + 1)] * 2^K + 1$$
$$= 2K * 2^K + 1$$
$$= K * 2^{K+1} + 1$$

That is, S_{K+1} is true.

Therefore, by the Principle of Mathematical Induction, S_K is true for any positive integer K.

Chapter 6

6.4
```
Print (Stack)
Stack.CopyTo (TempStack)
with TempStack do
    while not IsEmpty do
        RetrieveTop (Item)
        Write out Item
        Pop
```

6.6 **a.** $X\,Y\,Z * +$
b. $X\,Y + Z *$
c. $X\,Y - Z\,A\,B + * -$
d. $A\,B + C * D\,E\,F * G\,H\,/\,I + J - K * / + / L -$
e. $A\,B\,C\,D \char`\^ * E\,/ + F -$
f. $A\,B\,C\,D\,E\,F - \char`\^ * G\,/ +$

6.8 $5\ 2\ 30\ 10\ 5\ / - * +$

			5				
		10	10	2			
		30	30	30	28		
	2	2	2	2	2	56	
5	5	5	5	5	5	5	61

6.11   *D* will be deleted next from the queue.

6.12   The free list is an instance of the Stack ADT.

$$\downarrow$$

6.15   <u>Print (Queue)</u>

```
Queue.CopyTo (TempQueue)
with TempQueue do
    while not IsEmpty do
        RetrieveHead (Item)
        Write out Item
        DeleteHead
```

$$\downarrow$$

6.19   <u>Print (PQueue)</u>

```
PQueue.CopyTo (TempPQueue)
with TempPQueue do
    while not IsEmpty do
        RetrieveHighest (Item)
        Write out Item
        DeleteHighest
```

Chapter 7

7.1   **a.**   *A*
  b.   8
  c.   3
  d.   4
  e.   3
  f.   0
  g.   3
  h.   2
  i.   1
  j.   *D*
  k.   *C E H*
  l.   *D B A*
  m.   *C H E B F D G A*
  n.   *H E C F G D B A*
  o.   *A B C E H D F G*
  p.   *A B C D E F G H*

7.3   **a.**   5 Items

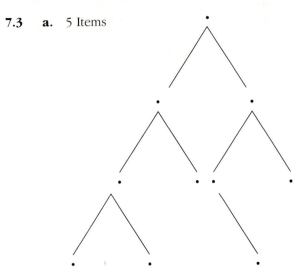

Note: The idea is to get a binary tree with the minimum height so that most of the items are leaves.

b.   One leaf. All we are doing here is maximizing the height of the tree.

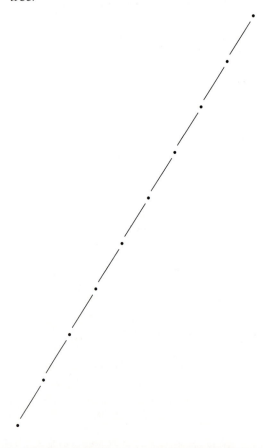

7.4   **a.**

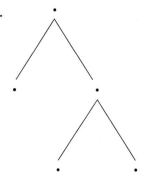

b.

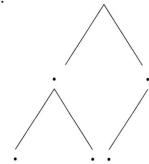

c.

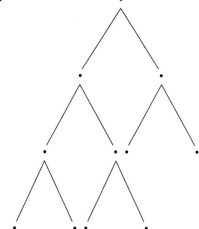

d.   9 leaves (see Theorem 7.1).
e.   366 leaves (see Theorem 7.1).
f.   Since $L(T) = (N(T) + 1) / 2$,
         $2L(T) = N(T) + 1$ (that is, $N(T) + 1$ is even).
g.   31 items (see Theorem 7.1).
h.   8191 items (see Theorem 7.1).
j.   32 leaves.

7.5   LeafCount (Tree)

```
if Tree.IsEmpty then
   Return 0
else
   Tree.RetrieveLeft (LeftTree)
   Tree.RetrieveRight (RightTree)
if LeftTree.IsEmpty and RightTree.IsEmpty then
   Return 1
else
   Return LeafCount (LeftTree) + LeafCount (RightTree)
```

7.10   TraversePostOrder (Visit)

```
if Root <> null then
   with Root's node do
      Left.TraversePostOrder (Visit)
      Right.TraversePostOrder (Visit)
      Visit (Item)
```

7.13   TraversePostOrder (Visit)

```
if N > 0 then
   PostOrderTraverse (1)
```

PostOrderTraverse (I)

```
if I <= N then
   PostOrderTraverse (2 * I)
   PostOrderTraverse (2 * I + 1)
   Visit (A [I])
```

Chapter 8

8.6   All of the rotations are single left rotations. The final AVL tree is as follows:

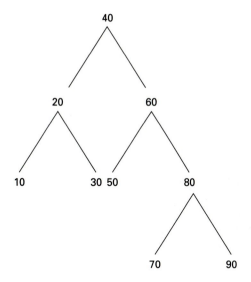

8.7 **a.**

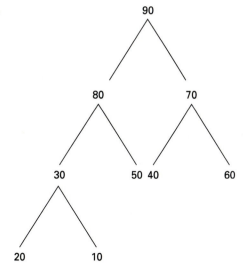

8.13 For h $= 0, 1, 2, \ldots$, let S_h be the statement:

Fib $(h + 3) - 1 \geq (3/2)^h$

    a. (base cases) h $= 0$ and h $= 1$.

Fib $(3) - 1 = 2 - 1 = 1 \geq (3/2)^0$

Therefore, S_0 is true.

$$\text{Fib } (4) - 1 = 3 - 1 = 2 \geq (3/2)^1$$

Therefore, S_1 is true.

b. (inductive case) Let h be any integer greater than 1 and assume that S_k is true for any k in $0..h - 1$. We must show that S_h is true.

$$\begin{aligned}
\text{Fib}(h + 3) - 1 &= \text{Fib } (h + 2) + \text{Fib } (h + 1) - 1 \\
&= \text{Fib } (h + 2) - 1 + \text{Fib } (h + 1) - 1 + 1 \\
&\geq (3/2)^{h-1} + (3/2)^{h-2} + 1 \\
&> (3/2)^{h-1} + (3/2)^{h-2} \\
&= (3/2)^{h-2} * (3/2 + 1) \\
&> (3/2)^{h-2} * (9/4) \\
&= (3/2)^{h-2} * (3/2)^2 \\
&= (3/2)^h
\end{aligned}$$

That is, S_h is true.

Therefore, by the Strong Form of the Principle of Mathematical Induction, S_h is true for h $= 0, 1, 2, \ldots$.

8.15

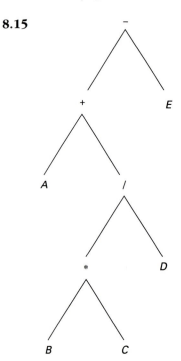

8.17 `BuildTree (Postfix)`

`Postfix.CopyTo (NewPostfix)`
`Build (Root, NewPostfix)`

For Build, start with the last item in the list New Postfix. If the item is an operator then build the right subtree and then the left subtree. The subalgorithm is:

`Build (Root, Postfix)`

`Last := Postfix.Size`
`if not Postfix.IsEmpty then`
`  Postfix.Retrieve (Item, Last)`
`  Postfix.Delete (Last)`
`  Allocate space for a new node pointed to by Root`
`  Copy Item into Root's Item fied, and initialize`
`    Root's Left and Right subtrees`
`  if Item.IsAnOperator then`
`      with Root's node do`
`        Build (Right.Root, Postfix)`
`        Build (Left.Root, Postfix)`

8.18
$$T(2000) \approx \frac{1.37\ (2000)\log_2 2000}{1000\ \log_2 1000} = 3.02 \text{ seconds.}$$

Chapter 9

9.2 **a.** Selection Sort: For this sort method, any arrangement of the items will produce the same number of item comparisons. Therefore, we can leave the list intact.

b. Bubble Sort:

Minimum: 10 33 43 45 50 67 71 82 82 90 97

Maximum: 97 90 82 82 71 67 59 45 43 33 10

c. Insertion Sort:

Minimum: 10 33 43 45 50 67 71 82 82 90 97

Maximum: 97 90 82 82 71 67 50 45 43 33 10

d. Tree Sort:

Minimum: 67 43 90 33 45 82 97 10 50 71 82

Maximum: 10 33 43 45 50 67 71 82 82 90 97

e. Merge Sort:

Minimum: 10 33 43 45 50 67 71 82 82 90 97

Maximum (for the top down, that is, recursive subalgorithm):
                    10 71 82 33 67 97 43 50 82 45 90

f. Heap Sort: For each arrangement of items, the number of comparisons is the same. (Incidentally, the difference between best and worst run times depends on the number of swaps, with fewest swaps if the items are in reverse order and most swaps if the items are in order.)

g. Quick Sort:

Minimum: 10 33 43 45 50 67 71 82 82 90 97

Maximum: 33 43 45 50 67 10 97 71 82 82 90

9.3   Selection Sort, Merge Sort, Heap Sort

9.4   Suppose we want to sort a list of 1000 items, where each item occupies 100 bytes. A contiguous design would require an array to hold 100,000 bytes—too large a structure for Turbo Pascal. Therefore, a linked design would be more appropriate. Since 100,000 bytes is too large for the Data Segment, a dynamic implementation would be needed.

9.5   **Case 1:** N is odd. The median would be at index $(N + 1)$ div 2 if the list were completely sorted. Therefore, after each call to Partition, ignore the subarray that does not include index $(N + 1)$ div 2. Eventually, the item that ends up at index $(N + 1)$ div 2 is the item that would have ended up there if we had completely sorted the list. In other words, the median will end up at index $(N + 1)$ div 2.

Case 2: N is even. The median is the average of the items that would be at indexes N div 2 and N div 2 + 1 if the list were completely sorted. Therefore, after each call to Partition, ignore the subarray that does not include either of those indexes. It may happen that after a call to Partition, the left subarray includes index N div 2 and the right subarray includes index N div 2 + 1. From that point on, there will be twice as many calls to Partition as in Case 1, because there will be two indexes sought. Therefore, Case 2 can take up to twice as long as Case 1, but the Time is still O(N).

9.9 $$T(10000) \approx \frac{2.36 \ (10000) \ \log_2 1}{2000 \ \log_2 2000} \approx 14.31 \text{ seconds.}$$

9.10   Suppose we need to insert the item in the list $A [1 \ldots K]$. Therefore, we assign to Temporary the value of $A [K]$. In the worst case (that is, if Temporary belongs in the first position), there will be $K - 1$ loop iterations. In the best case (that is, if Temporary is where it belongs), there will be no loop iterations. The average case will be the case when Temporary belongs in the middle of the list. In this case, there will be $(K - 1)/2$ iterations.

Overall, there are now $N - 1$ outer loop iterations, so if we add all the inner loop iterations at each outer loop iteration, we get the following sum:

$$1/2 + 1 + 3/2 + 2 + 5/2 + \ldots = \sum_{K=2}^{N} \frac{K - 1}{2}$$

$$= \frac{1}{2} \sum_{K=2}^{N} K - \frac{1}{2} \sum_{K=2}^{N} 1$$

$$= \frac{1}{2} \left[\frac{N(N + 1)}{2} - N + 1 - 1 \right]$$

$$= \frac{1}{2} \left[\frac{N(N + 1)}{2} - N + 1 - 1 \right]$$

$$= \frac{N}{4} (N + 1) - \frac{1}{2} N$$

Chapter 10

10.1 a.

Index	Contents
1	23
2	56
6	83
7	17

b.

Index	Contents
0	56
1	23
6	83
7	17

c.

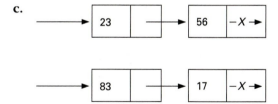

10.3   `Sort (Table, List)`

       `List.Initialize`

       `Table.Traverse (List.Insert)`

10.4   **a.**   Both Time and WorstTime are O(N).

        b.   Both Time and WorstTime are O(log N).

        c.   Time is O(log N); WorstTime is O(N).

        d.   Time is O(1); WorstTime is O(N). (With very bad luck, the off-set locations may be occupied.)

        e.   Both Time and WorstTime are O(1).

Chapter 11

11.1   **a.**

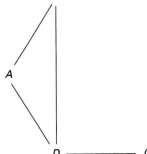

        b.   The graph is not a tree. The cycles are:

           A, B, D, A

           A, D, B, A

           B, D, A, B

           B, A, D, B

           D, A, B, D

           D, B, A, D

11.2   **a.**   Vertices = A, B, C, D, E, F, G, H

           Edges = $\{A, B\}, \{A, C\}, \{B, D\}, \{B, E\}, \{C, F\}, \{C, G\}, \{C, H\}$

        b.   This tree has the same vertices and edges as the tree in part a.

11.3   **d.**   For $N = 0, 1, \ldots$, let S_N be the statement:

           A graph with N vertices can have, at most, $N (N - 1)/2$ edges.

1. (base case) $N = 0$. A graph with no vertices has no edges. Since $0 * (-1)/2 = 0$, S_0 is true.

2. (inductive case) Let N be any non-negative integer and assume that S_N is true. We must show that S_{N+1} is true. Suppose that G is a graph with $N + 1$ vertices and as many edges as possible. Let V be any vertex in G. Since G has as many edges as possible, for every other vertex in G, there must be an edge between that vertex and V (that is, there must be N edges to V). If we delete V and all of its edges, we will have a graph G' with N vertices and, by induction hypothesis, $N (N - 1)/2$ edges. Therefore, the total number of edges in G is:

$$N (N - 1)/2 + N,$$

which is equal to

$$(N + 1) * N/2.$$

Therefore, S_{N+1} is true.

By the Principle of Mathematical Induction, S_N is true for every non-negative integer N (that is, a graph with N vertices can have, at most, $N (N - 1)/2$ edges).

11.4 A B

$\uparrow$ $\downarrow$

11.7 **a.** <u>HasACycle (Graph)</u>

```
with Graph do
    if IsConnected then
        if NumberOfEdges > NumberOfVertices-1 then
            Return True
        else
            Return False
    else
        CycleFound := False
        Traverse (ConstructAndTest)
        Return the value of CycleFound
```

$\downarrow$

<u>ConstructAndTest (Vertex)</u>

```
{ Construct SubG, the largest connected subgraph }
{ of Graph that contains Vertex: }
SubG.Initialize
SubG.InsertVertex (Vertex)
AddToSubG (Vertex)
```

The subalgorithm AddToSubG inserts in SubG all vertices in Graph connected to *V*. The subalgorithm is:

```
AddToSubG (V)

if not CycleFound then
    Graph.FindNeighbors (V, NeighborList)
    for I := 1 to NeighborList.Size do
        NeighborList.Retrieve (W, I)
        SubG.SearchForVertex (W, Found)
        if not Found then
            SubG.InsertVertex (W)
            SubG.InsertEdge (V, W)
            AddToSubG (W)
        else
            {If vertex W is already in SubG, but edge}
            {{V, W} is not, then Graph has a cycle! }
            SubG.SearchForEdge (V, W, Found)
            if not Found then
                CycleFound := True
```

b. `IsIsolated (Graph, Vertex)`

```
Graph.FindNeighbors (Vertex, NeighborList)
Return the value of NeighborList.IsEmpty
```

c. `IsASubGraph (Graph, SubGraph)`

The basic idea is to traverse SubGraph: If for any vertex *V* in SubGraph, *V* is not in Graph, or some neighbor of *V* in Sub-Graph is not a neighbor of *V* in Graph, then SubGraph is not a subgraph of Graph.

The subalgorithm is:

```
IsASubGraph (Graph, SubGraph)

StillOK := True
SubGraph.Traverse (CheckGraph)
Return the value of StillOK
```

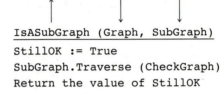

```
CheckGraph (Vertex)

Graph.SearchForVertex (Vertex, Found)
```

```
          if not Found then
             StillOK := False
          else
             SubGraph.FindNeighbors (Vertex, SubGraphList)
             Graph.FindNeighbors (Vertex, GraphList)
             I := 1
             while StillOK and (I <= SubGraphList.Size) do
                SubGraphList.Retrieve (W, I)
                GraphList.Search (W, Found)
                if not Found then
                   StillOK := False
```

    ↑   ↓   ↓

d. <u>Equal (Graph1, Graph2)</u>

    Return the value of IsASubGraph (Graph1, Graph2)
                          and IsASubGraph (Graph2, Graph1)

11.9   Minimal spanning tree:

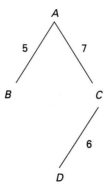

Shortest path tree rooted at *A*:

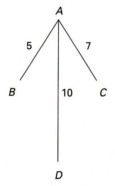

11.11 b. To make change for 30 cents with a greedy algorithm requires six coins (one quarter and five pennies). The minimum number of coins to make change for 30 cents is three (three dimes).

11.15 a. *A, E, D, B, C, A*

11.17 b.

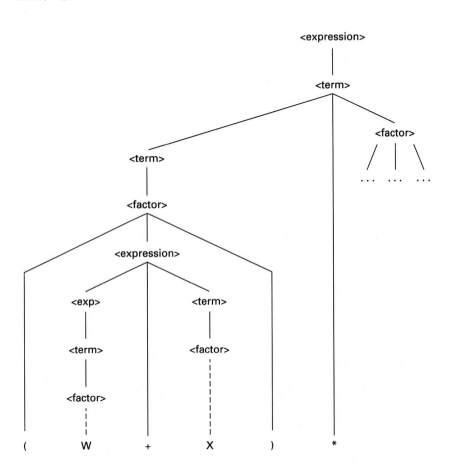

11.19 a. Exponentiation (^) has the highest precedence.
      b. Exponentiations are evaluated from right-to-left:

```
<factor> ::= <primary> | <factor> ^ <primary>
```

Bibliography

ACM/IEEE-CS Joint Curriculum Task Force. *Computing Curricula 1991.* New York: Association for Computing Machinery, 1991.

Adel'son-Vel'skii, G M. and Landis, E M. "An Algorithm for the Organization of Information." *Soviet Mathematics,* vol. 3, 1962, p. 1259.

Aho, A V., Hopcroft, J E., and Ullman, J D. *Data Structures and Algorithms.* Reading, MA: Addison-Wesley, 1983.

Bentley, J L. "How to Sort." *Communications of the ACM,* April 1984, vol. 27, no. 4, p. 287.

Bentley, J L. "Writing Correct Programs." *Communications of the ACM,* December 1983, vol. 26, no. 12, p. 1040.

Boehm, B. *Software Engineering Economics.* Englewood Cliffs, NJ: Prentice-Hall, 1981.

Booch, G. *Software Engineering with Ada.* Menlo Park, CA: Benjamin/Cummings, 1987.

Christofides, N. *Graph Theory, An Algorithmic Approach.* London: Academic Press, 1975.

Coad, P. and Yourdon, E. *Object-Oriented Analysis.* Englewood Cliffs, NJ: Yourdon Press, 1990.

Collins, W. "Estimating Execution Times: A Laboratory Exercise for CS2." *Proceedings of the Twenty-Second SIGCSE Technical Symposium,* vol. 23, no. 1, March 1991, p. 358.

Collins, W. *Intermediate Pascal Programming.* New York: McGraw-Hill, 1986.

Collins, W. "The Trouble with For-Loop Invariants." *Proceedings of the Nineteenth SIGCSE Technical Symposium,* vol. 20, no. 1, February 1988, p. 1.

Collins, W. and McMillan, T. "Implementing Abstract Data Types in Turbo Pascal." *Proceedings of the Twenty-First SIGCSE Technical Symposium,* vol. 22, no. 1, February 1990, p. 134.

Cox, B J. *Object Oriented Programming: An Evolutionary Approach.* Reading, MA: Addison-Wesley, 1986.

Dale, N. "If You Were Lost on a Desert Island, What One ADT Would You Like to Have with You?" *Proceedings of the Twenty-First SIGCSE Technical Symposium,* vol. 22, no. 1, February 1990, p. 139.

Dale, N. and Lilly, S C. *Pascal Plus Data Structures, Algorithms, and Advanced Programming.* (3rd ed.). Lexington, MA: D. C. Heath, 1991.

Decker, R. *Data Structures.* Englewood Cliffs, NJ: Prentice Hall, 1989.

Dijkstra, E W. *A Discipline of Programming.* Englewood Cliffs, NJ: Prentice-Hall, 1976.

Glezzi, C. and Jazayeri, M. *Programming Language Concepts* (2nd ed.). New York: John Wiley & Sons, 1982.

Gries, D. *Science of Programming.* New York: Springer-Verlag, 1981.

Helman, P. and Veroff, R. *Intermediate Problem Solving and Data Structures.* Menlo Park, CA: Benjamin/Cummings, 1986.

Henderson-Sellers, B. and Edwards, J M. "The Object-Oriented Systems Life Cycle." *Communications of the ACM,* September 1990, vol. 33, no. 9, p. 142.

Hoare, C A R. "Quicksort." *Computer Journal,* April 1962, vol. 5, no. 4, p. 10.

Hogg, R V. and Tanis, E A. *Probability and Statistical Inference* (2nd ed.). New York: Macmillan 1983.

Khosraviyani, F. "Using Binary Search on a Linked List," SIGCSE Bulletin, vol. 22, no. 3, September 1990, p. 7.

Knuth, D E. *The Art of Computer Programming,* Vol. 1: "Fundamental Algorithms" (2nd ed.). Reading, MA: Addison-Wesley, 1973.

Knuth, D E. *The Art of Computer Programming,* Vol. 2: "Seminumerical Algorithms" (2nd ed.). Reading, MA: Addison-Wesley, 1973.

Knuth, D E, *The Art of Computer Programming,* Vol. 3: "Sorting and Searching." Reading, MA: Addison-Wesley, 1973.

Korfhage, R R. *Discrete Computational Structures.* New York: Academic Press, 1974.

Korson, T. and McGregor, J D. "Understanding Object-Oriented: A Unifying Paradigm." *Communications of the ACM,* September 1990, vol. 33, no. 9, p. 40.

Kruse, R L. *Data Structures and Program Design.* Englewood Cliffs, NJ: Prentice-Hall, 1987.

Lewis, T G. and Smith, M Z. *Applying Data Structures* (2nd ed.), Boston: Houghton Mifflin, 1982.

MacLennan, B J. *Principles of Programming Languages.* New York: Holt, Rinehart & Winston, 1987.

McMillan, T. and Collins, W. "A Recurrence Relation in Uniform Hashing." *Proceedings of the Seventeenth Annual Computer Science Conference,* February 1989, p. 410.

Meyer, B. "Lessons from the Design of the Eiffel Libraries." *Communications of the ACM,* September 1990, vol. 33, no. 9, p. 68.

Meyer, B. *Object-Oriented Software Construction.* London: Prentice-Hall International, 1988.

Mynatt, B T. *Software Engineering with Student Project Guidance.* Englewood Cliffs, NJ: Prentice Hall, 1990.

Roberts, S. *Thinking Recursively.* New York: John Wiley & Sons, 1986.

Sedgewick, R. "The Analysis of Quicksort Programs." *Acta Informatica,* vol. 7, 1977, p. 327.

Sedgewick, R. "Implementing Quicksort Programs." *Communications of the ACM,* October 1978, vol. 21, no. 10, p. 847.

Sedgewick, R. "Quicksort" (Ph.D. thesis). *Stanford Computer Science Report,* STAN-CS-75-492, Stanford University, 1975.

Shiflet, A B. *Elementary Data Structures with Pascal.* St. Paul, MN: West, 1990.

Singleton, R C. "An Efficient Algorithm for Sorting with Minimal Storage: Algorithm 347." *Communications of the ACM,* March 1969, vol. 12, no. 3, p. 185.

Sommerville, I. *Software Engineering* (3rd ed.) Reading, MA: Addison-Wesley, 1989.

Stubbs, D F. and Webre, N W. *Data Structures with Abstract Data Types and Pascal,* (2nd ed.). Pacific Grove, CA: Brooks/Cole, 1989.

Tremblay, J P. and Sorenson, P G. *An Introduction to Data Structures with Applications.* New York: McGraw-Hill, 1976.

Turbo Pascal 6.0 Programmer's Guide. Scotts Valley, CA: Borland International, 1990.

Turbo Pascal 6.0 Run-Time Library. Scotts Valley, CA: Borland International, 1990.

Turbo Pascal 6.0 Turbo Vision Guide. Scotts Valley, CA: Borland International, 1990.

Turbo Pascal 6.0 User's Guide. Scotts Valley, CA: Borland International, 1990.

Whitehead, A N. and Russell, B. *Principia Mathematica* (3 volumes). Cambridge, 1910–1913.

Wiest, J D. and Levy, F K. *A Management Guide to PERT/CPM* (2nd ed.). Englewood Cliffs, NJ: Prentice-Hall, 1977.

Wirth, N. *Algorithms + Data Structures = Programs.* Englewood Cliffs, NJ: Prentice-Hall, 1976.

Index